Lecture Notes in Computer Science　　　　9617

Commenced Publication in 1973
Founding and Former Series Editors:
Gerhard Goos, Juris Hartmanis, and Jan van Leeuwen

Editorial Board

David Hutchison
　Lancaster University, Lancaster, UK
Takeo Kanade
　Carnegie Mellon University, Pittsburgh, PA, USA
Josef Kittler
　University of Surrey, Guildford, UK
Jon M. Kleinberg
　Cornell University, Ithaca, NY, USA
Friedemann Mattern
　ETH Zurich, Zurich, Switzerland
John C. Mitchell
　Stanford University, Stanford, CA, USA
Moni Naor
　Weizmann Institute of Science, Rehovot, Israel
C. Pandu Rangan
　Indian Institute of Technology, Madras, India
Bernhard Steffen
　TU Dortmund University, Dortmund, Germany
Demetri Terzopoulos
　University of California, Los Angeles, CA, USA
Doug Tygar
　University of California, Berkeley, CA, USA
Gerhard Weikum
　Max Planck Institute for Informatics, Saarbrücken, Germany

More information about this series at http://www.springer.com/series/7409

Richard Kronland-Martinet · Mitsuko Aramaki
Sølvi Ystad (Eds.)

Music, Mind, and Embodiment

11th International Symposium, CMMR 2015
Plymouth, UK, June 16–19, 2015
Revised Selected Papers

Editors
Richard Kronland-Martinet
CNRS - LMA
Marseille Cedex 20
France

Sølvi Ystad
CNRS - LMA
Marseille
France

Mitsuko Aramaki
CNRS - LMA
Marseille
France

ISSN 0302-9743 ISSN 1611-3349 (electronic)
Lecture Notes in Computer Science
ISBN 978-3-319-46281-3 ISBN 978-3-319-46282-0 (eBook)
DOI 10.1007/978-3-319-46282-0

Library of Congress Control Number: 2016951652

LNCS Sublibrary: SL3 – Information Systems and Applications, incl. Internet/Web, and HCI

© Springer International Publishing Switzerland 2016, corrected publication 2018
This work is subject to copyright. All rights are reserved by the Publisher, whether the whole or part of the material is concerned, specifically the rights of translation, reprinting, reuse of illustrations, recitation, broadcasting, reproduction on microfilms or in any other physical way, and transmission or information storage and retrieval, electronic adaptation, computer software, or by similar or dissimilar methodology now known or hereafter developed.
The use of general descriptive names, registered names, trademarks, service marks, etc. in this publication does not imply, even in the absence of a specific statement, that such names are exempt from the relevant protective laws and regulations and therefore free for general use.
The publisher, the authors and the editors are safe to assume that the advice and information in this book are believed to be true and accurate at the date of publication. Neither the publisher nor the authors or the editors give a warranty, express or implied, with respect to the material contained herein or for any errors or omissions that may have been made.

Printed on acid-free paper

This Springer imprint is published by Springer Nature
The registered company is Springer International Publishing AG Switzerland

Preface

The 11th International Symposium on Computer Music Multidisciplinary Research, CMMR2015 "Music, Mind and Embodiment" (http://cmr.soc.plymouth.ac.uk/cmmr2015/), was held in Plymouth during June 16–19, 2015, and was hosted by the Interdisciplinary Centre for Computer Music Research (ICCMR) in their newly built Performance Arts Centre, The House. The conference theme, "Music, Mind and Embodiment," reflected the highly interdisciplinary research interests of this center, which span from musicology and composition to biomedical applications of music and development of new music technologies.

This 11th CMMR event, which was co-organized by the ICCMR and the LMA-CNRS (France), hosted delegates from Europe, Asia, Australia, and America over four days. The scientific program covered a total of ten oral sessions, three poster sessions, and four installations that included traditional topics of previous CMMR events and specific topics related to the theme of the conference and the specific research interests of ICCMR. Three keynote speakers were invited to the conference: Hugues Vinet (Director of Research and Development, IRCAM), David Rosenboom (Professor of Music and Dean of the School of Music at California Institute of the Arts), and Eduardo Miranda (Professor of Computer Music and Director of ICCMR). The symposium also included two satellite workshops, one on music neurotechnology and another on motion and music. In addition, a series of 3 concerts were held in the evenings after the scientific sessions.

The CMMR symposium was initiated in 2003 and has been organized in various cities in Europe and Asia. Although the CMMR acronym has remained unchanged since the first symposium, its meaning changed slightly from "Computer Music Modelling and Retrieval" to "Computer Music Multidisciplinary Research" in 2012 owing to the strong expansion of topics that were present in CMMR 2012, covering computer science, social science, and humanities. The CMMR 2015 proceedings volume is the 11th book published by Springer in the *Lecture Notes in Computer Sciences* series (LNCS 2771, LNCS 3310, LNCS 3902, LNCS 4969, LNCS 5493, LNCS 5954, LNCS 6684, LNCS 7172, LNCS 7900, LNCS 8905). This year's volume contains a total of 30 peer-reviewed and revised articles centered around the conference theme "Music, Mind and Embodiment." It is divided into six sections devoted to various sound and technology issues with a particular emphasis on performance, music generation, composition, analysis, and information retrieval (Chapters 2 to 5), as well as relations between sound, motion, and gestures (Chapter 1) and human perception and culture (Chapter 6).

We would like to thank all the participants of CMMR2015 who contributed to make this 11th symposium a memorable happening. We would also like to thank the Program Committee members for their indispensable paper reports and the Music Committee for selecting the music contributions. We are very grateful to the local Organizing Committee at the ICCMR, who took care of all the practical issues and insured a smooth and efficient coordination between attendees, speakers, audiences, and musicians in both the scientific and artistic program. Finally, we would like to thank Springer for accepting to publish the CMMR 2015 proceedings in their LNCS series.

June 2016

Richard Kronland-Martinet
Mitsuko Aramaki
Sølvi Ystad

Organization

The 11th International Symposium on Computer Music Multidisciplinary Research CMMR 2015 "Music, Mind and Embodiment" was co-organized by the Interdisciplinary Centre for Computer Music Research (ICCMR), Plymouth, UK, and the Laboratoire de Mécanique et d'Acoustique, Marseille, France.

Symposium Chair

Eduardo R. Miranda   ICCMR, Plymouth University, UK

Paper, Program, and Proceedings Chairs

Richard Kronland-Martinet   CNRS-LMA, France
Mitsuko Aramaki   CNRS-LMA, France
Sølvi Ystad   CNRS-LMA, France
Joel Eaton   ICCMR, Plymouth University, UK

Local Organizing Committee

Eduardo R. Miranda   ICCMR, Plymouth University, UK
Joel Eaton   ICCMR, Plymouth University, UK
Duncan Williams   ICCMR, Plymouth University, UK
Federico Visi   ICCMR, Plymouth University, UK
Jared Drayton   ICCMR, Plymouth University, UK
Ed Braund   ICCMR, Plymouth University, UK
Aurélien Antoine   ICCMR, Plymouth University, UK
Michael McLoughlin   ICCMR, Plymouth University, UK
Nuria Bonet Filella   ICCMR, Plymouth University, UK

Program Committee

Richard Kronland-Martinet   CNRS-LMA, France
Mitsuko Aramaki   CNRS-LMA, France
Sølvi Ystad   CNRS-LMA, France
Eduardo R. Miranda   ICCMR, Plymouth University, UK
Joel Eaton   ICCMR, Plymouth University, UK
Duncan Williams   ICCMR, Plymouth University, UK

Paper Committee

Mitsuko Aramaki   CNRS-LMA, France
Federico Avanzini   University of Padova, Italy
Mathieu Barthet   Queen Mary University of London, UK

Frédéric Bevilacqua	IRCAM, France
Stefan Bilbao	University of Edinburgh, UK
Tim Blackwell	Goldsmith, UK
Andrew Brown	Grith University, Australia
Jamie Bullock	Birmingham Conservatoire, UK
John Ashley Burgoyne	University of Amsterdam, The Netherlands
Marcelo Caetano	INESC Porto, Portugal
Emilios Cambouroupoulos	Aristotle University of Thessaloniki, Greece
Amilcar Cardoso	University of Coimbra, Portugal
John Dack	Middlesex University, UK
Olivier Derrien	Toulon-Var University and CNRS-LMA, France
Arne Eigenfeldt	Simon Fraser University, Canada
Simon Emmerson	De Montfort University, UK
Georg Essl	University of Michigan, USA
Bruno Giordano	University of Glasgow, UK
Rolf Inge Gødoy	University of Oslo, Norway
Brian Gygi	National Biomedical Unit for Hearing Research, UK
Fernando Iazzetta	USP, Brazil
Kristffer Jensen	Aalborg University, Denmark
Alexander Jensenius	University of Oslo, Norway
Luis Jure	University of Montevideo, Uruguay
Timour Klouche	National Institute for Music Research, Germany
Richard Kronland-Martinet	CNRS-LMA, France
Darius Kucinskas	Kaunas University of Technology, Lithuania
Thor Magnusson	University of Sussex, UK
Sylvain Marchand	University of Brest, France
Jean-Arthur Micoulaud-Franchi	University of Bordeaux, France
Peter Nelson	University of Edinburgh, UK
Mark Plumbley	University of Surrey, UK
Marcelo Queiroz	University of São Paulo, Brazil
Matthew Rodger	Queen's University Belfast, UK
Emery Schubert	University of New South Wales, Australia
Diemo Schwarz	IRCAM, France
Anna Troisi	Bournemouth University, UK
Marcelo Wanderley	CIRMMT, Canada
Ian Whalley	University of Waikato, New Zealand
Sølvi Ystad	CNRS-LMA, France

Additional Reviewers

Darryl Cameron
Song Hui Chon
Simon Conan
Maximos Kaliakatsos-Papakostas
Mindaugas Kavaliauskas
Sven-Amin Lembke
Marcella Mandanici
Nicola Orio
Gaëtan Parseihian
Charalampos Saitis
Bertrand Scherrer
Etienne Thoret
Yinan Tsao
Doug Van Nort
Olivier Warusfel
Asterios Zacharakis

Contents

Sound, Motion and Gesture

Comparing the Timing of Movement Events for Air-Drumming Gestures.... 3
   Luke Dahl

Assessing the Influence of Constraints on Cellists' Postural Displacements
and Musical Expressivity... 22
   *Jocelyn Rozé, Mitsuko Aramaki, Richard Kronland-Martinet,
Thierry Voinier, Christophe Bourdin, Delphine Chadefaux,
Marvin Dufrenne, and Sølvi Ystad*

Musical Meter, Rhythm and the Moving Body: Designing Methods
for the Analysis of Unconstrained Body Movements 42
   *Luiz Naveda, Isabel C. Martínez, Javier Dameson,
Alejandro Pereira Ghiena, Romina Herrera,
and Manuel Alejandro Ordás*

Evaluating Input Devices for Dance Research...................... 58
   Mari Romarheim Haugen and Kristian Nymoen

Estimation of Guitar Fingering and Plucking Controls Based on Multimodal
Analysis of Motion, Audio and Musical Score 71
   Alfonso Perez-Carrillo, Josep-Lluis Arcos, and Marcelo Wanderley

Analysis of Mimed Violin Performance Movements of Neophytes: Patterns,
Periodicities, Commonalities and Individualities 88
   *Federico Visi, Esther Coorevits, Rodrigo Schramm,
and Eduardo R. Miranda*

Digital Musical Instruments, Embodiment and Performance

Skill Development and Stabilisation of Expertise for Electronic
Music Performance... 111
   Jan C. Schacher and Patrick Neff

The Hybrid Brain Computer Music Interface - Integrating Brainwave
Detection Methods for Extended Control in Musical Performance Systems... 132
   Joel Eaton and Eduardo R. Miranda

Feeling Sound: Exploring a Haptic-Audio Relationship 146
   Joanne Armitage and Kia Ng

BOEUF: A Unified Framework for Modeling and Designing
Digital Orchestras... 153
  Florent Berthaut and Luke Dahl

Decomposing a Composition: On the Multi-layered Analysis of Expressive
Music Performance 167
  *Esther Coorevits, Dirk Moelants, Stefan Östersjö, David Gorton,
  and Marc Leman*

3CMS: An Interactive Decision System for Live Performance 190
  *Rodrigo Schramm, Helena de Souza Nunes, Leonardo de Assis Nunes,
  Federico Visi, and Eduardo R. Miranda*

Composition Tools

A Viewpoint Approach to Symbolic Music Transformation 213
  Louis Bigo and Darrell Conklin

Balancing Audio: Towards a Cognitive Structure of Sound Interaction
in Music Production 228
  Mads Walther-Hansen

Conchord: An Application for Generating Musical Harmony by Navigating
in the Tonal Interval Space....................................... 243
  *Gilberto Bernardes, Diogo Cocharro, Carlos Guedes,
  and Matthew E.P. Davies*

Musical Variation and Improvisation Based on Multi-resolution
Representations... 261
  Johan Loeckx

Music with Unconventional Computing: Granular Synthesis
with the Biological Computing Substrate *Physarum Polycephalum* 271
  Edward Braund and Eduardo R. Miranda

Data Mining, Music Information Retrieval and Artificial Intelligence

Evaluation and Prediction of Harmonic Complexity Across 76 Years
of Billboard 100 Hits... 283
  Kristoffer Jensen and David G. Hebert

Information Rate for Fast Time-Domain Instrument Classification.......... 297
  Jordan Ubbens and David Gerhard

Escaping from the Abyss of Manual Annotation: New Methodology
of Building Polyphonic Datasets for Automatic Music Transcription 309
  Li Su and Yi-Hsuan Yang

The Clustering of Expressive Timing Within a Phrase in Classical Piano
Performances by Gaussian Mixture Models 322
   Shengchen Li, Dawn A.A. Black, and Mark D. Plumbley

Modeling Affective Responses to Music Using Audio Signal Analysis
and Physiology. 346
   Konstantinos Trochidis and Simon Lui

A New Look at Musical Expectancy: The Veridical Versus the General
in the Mental Organization of Music. 358
   Emery Schubert and Marcus Pearce

Music Analysis, Music Generation and Emotion

Emotional Experiences of Ascending Melodic Lines 373
   Hans T. Zeiner-Henriksen

σGTTM III: Learning-Based Time-Span Tree Generator Based on PCFG. . . . 387
   Masatoshi Hamanaka, Keiji Hirata, and Satoshi Tojo

BioComputer Music: Generating Musical Responses with *Physarum
polycephalum*-Based Memristors. 405
   Edward Braund and Eduardo R. Miranda

'Understood at Last'?: A Memetic Analysis of Beethoven's 'Bloody Fist' . . . 420
   Steven Jan

Music and Dementia: Two Case-Studies 438
   Alexis Kirke, Belinda Dixon, and Eduardo R. Miranda

Strictly Rhythm: Exploring the Effects of Identical Regions and Meter
Induction in Rhythmic Similarity Perception. 449
   Daniel Gómez-Marín, Sergi Jordà, and Perfecto Herrera

Cross-Cultural Comparisons of Unconstrained Body Responses
to Argentinian and Afro-Brazilian Music 464
   *Luiz Naveda, Isabel C. Martínez, Javier Dameson,
   Alejandro Pereira Ghiena, Romina Herrera,
   and Manuel Alejandro Ordás*

Correction to: Music, Mind, and Embodiment. E1
   Richard Kronland-Martinet, Mitsuko Aramaki, and Sølvi Ystad

Author Index 483

Sound, Motion and Gesture

Comparing the Timing of Movement Events for Air-Drumming Gestures

Luke Dahl(✉)

Department of Music, University of Virginia, Charlottesville, USA
lukedahl@virginia.edu

Abstract. New air-instruments allow us to control sound by moving our bodies in space without manipulating a physical object. However when we want to trigger a discrete sound at a precise time, for example by making a drumming gesture, the timing feels wrong. This work aims to understand what aspects of a performer's movement correspond to their subjective sense of when the sound should occur. A study of air-drumming gestures was conducted, and the timing of eight movement events based on movements of the hand, wrist, elbow joint, and wrist joint are examined. In general, it is found that movement events based on peaks in acceleration are better because they occur earlier and have less noise than do events based on changes of direction.

Keywords: Gesture · Musical gesture · Air-instruments · Air-drumming · New interfaces for musical expression

1 Introduction

We evolved to touch and manipulate physical objects. Our ancestors survived by using their hands and bodies to acquire food and resources and to modify their environment. They created tools that fit in hand and amplified their power, precision, and reach, and these tools were used not only for practical purposes but also for the creation of culture and art.

Traditional musical instruments are tools we manipulate with our bodies and hands in order to transform bodily energy into delightful sounds: we strike a drum, pluck a string, draw a bow across a string, or blow into a flute. Even today most of our new instruments require the musician's touch: we press a key, push a slider, turn a knob. However, our physical connection with our instruments is becoming tenuous. When we drag a mouse or swipe across a touchscreen we touch a physical object, but we don't feel the moment our pointer contacts a virtual button or plucks a virtual string.

Some new instruments, beginning with the Theremin, require no contact with the instrument itself, allowing us to control sound by making gestures "in the air". The recent affordability of motion sensing technologies such as inertial sensors and depth cameras, has led to a proliferation of experimental "air-instruments" which enable a performer to create music by moving their body in free space. We still move our bodies, yet touch is missing.

How does the lack of touch affect the way we perform these new air-instruments? Some instruments, such as the Theremin, provide continuous sonic feedback as the performer moves their body in space. These do not seem to suffer in their ability to afford expressive musical performance, as is evidenced by the history of virtuosic Theremin performers. However, instruments which allow the performer to trigger a sonic event – for example by making a sudden movement of the hand in the air – do seem to suffer from the lack of tactile feedback. These instruments often feel unpredictable, sometimes triggering sound at the wrong time, and other times failing to trigger a sound at all. This makes performing complex rhythmic material challenging, to say the least.

The goal of the research described in this paper is to better understand the gestures that performers make with these air-instruments, so that we can design instruments which are more accurate and responsive, thus enabling better musical experiences for both performer and listener.

1.1 The Challenges of Designing Air-Instruments

I define *instrumental air-gestures* as purposeful movements of a performer's body in free space which are used to control an immediately responsive sound-generating instrument. These can be divided into *continuous air gestures*, in which some aspect of movement (e.g. the height of the hand) is continuously mapped to some sonic variable (e.g. filter cutoff frequency), and *discrete air-gestures*, which are meant to trigger a sonic event (e.g. a note onset) at a precise time.

In my experience designing air-instruments [4], and from observing performances of other air-instruments, it is difficult to design an instrument that senses discrete air-gestures in a way that allows for precise rhythmic performance. From the performer's perspective the timing often feels wrong. To design such instruments we must create an algorithm that uses movement data to decide when to trigger a sonic event. It seems that most instrument designers do this based on some heuristic, and the poor performance of these instruments suggests that we are choosing the wrong heuristic.

A Subjective Movement Event. The work in this paper is based on the assumption that when a performer makes a discrete air-gesture, such as striking a non-existent drum, they do *something* with their body to create an *internal sensation of a moment in time*, and they intend the resulting sound, a sonic event, to occur at the same time as this internally sensed movement event. I call this embodied sensation the *subjective movement event*. If instrument designers understood which aspects of the performer's movement correspond to the subjective movement event we could design our instruments to detect it.

1.2 Studying Discrete Air-Gestures

With the goal of better understanding discrete air-gestures and the accompanying subjective movement event, I conducted a study in which musicians were recorded performing air-drumming gestures in time to the sound of a simple drum rhythm. Their movements were analyzed to detect a number of *movement events*, which are hypothetical candidates for the subjective movement event. By looking at the timing of these movement events with respect to the sonic events to which they are intended to correspond, we can begin to understand the enacted and embodied sense of discrete moments in gestures. In [3] I presented the details of this study and an analysis of movement events based on tracking the position of the hand and wrist in space. This paper summarizes that work and extends it to include an analysis of movement events based on the changing angles of the elbow and wrist joints.

1.3 Related Work

There is a large body of research describing new digital musical instruments which enable gestural control of sound generating processes. Much of this work is concerned with strategies for mapping from gestural data to sound parameters (see [15] for a summary, and [14] for a recent example).

Godøy et al. discuss the mimetic instrumental performance-like gestures that people often make when listening to music [6]. They conducted a study of "air piano" performance, and analysed the degree of correspondence between listeners' gestures and the gestures of the pianist who performed the music.

Previous work related to discrete air-gestures includes descriptions of performance systems which enable discrete air-gestures [4,7,8,11], studies of discrete musical air-gestures [2,10], a study of snare drumming movements [5], and studies of conducting gestures [9,13]. These employ a variety of techniques for detecting the end of a striking gesture or the beat of a conducting gesture, or for triggering sounds from the movement of the performer's hand or of the tip of a drumstick or baton. These techniques can be grouped into the following categories:

- Detecting when the position passes through some spatial threshold [10,11].
- Detecting extrema in position, such as vertical minima [2,13].
- Detecting when the velocity surpasses some threshold [4,7].
- Detecting positive extrema (i.e. peaks) in the magnitude acceleration [9,13].
- Detecting when the acceleration surpasses some threshold [8].
- Detecting when the third derivative of position (a.k.a. *jerk*) surpasses some threshold [5].

Interestingly, all of these track external spatial variables or their derivatives, and none employ tracking the movement of the performer's joint angles.

Sensorimotor Synchronization. Gesturing in time to music is form of *sensorimotor synchronization*, which has been the topic of research for decades [1,12]. One of the primary findings is that when tapping in time to an audible beat (usually a metronome click), most people tap before the beat by up to 100 msec. This shows that when a performer intends a movement event to correspond to a sonic event, they may not occur at the same time, *even though to the performer they seem to*. This suggests that the subjective movement event (the event we hope to detect) may not coincide with, and is likely to precede, the sonic event it is meant to trigger.

2   A Study of Air-Drumming Gestures

The goal of this research is to understand discrete air-gestures and their timing with respect to the intended sound, so that we can design better air-instruments. However, it is difficult to study this situation directly. If we record a musician performing an air-instrument which generates sound, the resulting sound may not occur at the time the performer intended. But we, as instrument designers, want to know at what time they intended the sound to occur. I address this chicken-and-egg problem by substituting a proxy activity – performing drumming gestures in time to a pre-recorded sound (which I call *mimetic air-drumming*) – for the activity we wish to understand – performing drumming gestures in order to trigger sounds (or *productive air-drumming*).

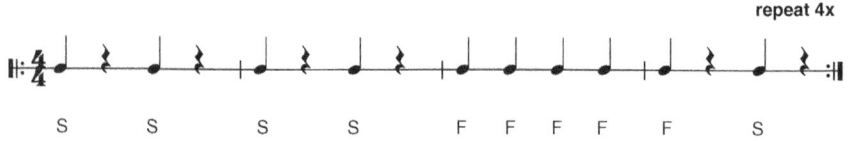

Fig. 1. The stimulus rhythm, played at 100 BPM. Slow notes are labeled 'S' and fast notes 'F'

The study participants heard a recording of a drum playing the rhythm shown in Fig. 1, which has an equal number of "slow" and "fast" notes. Participants were instructed to gesture *as if they were performing* these sounds by striking an imaginary drum somewhere in front of them. The movements of each participant's right hand, wrist, elbow, and shoulder were recorded with a motion capture system. The drum rhythms were also recorded into the motion capture system in order to facilitate precise comparison of the timing of the movement and the sound.

The participants were 5 women and 5 men, all of whom had experience playing a musical instrument and were able to read notated music. The median age was 23 years, and the median length of musical experience was 16 years. Further details on the data recording and participants can be found in [3].

2.1   Detecting Movement Events

In this paper I examine eight externally-detectable *movement events*, which are hypothetical candidates for the subjective movement event. These are based on the movement of the performer's hand and wrist in space, and on the changing angles of the performer's elbow and wrist joints. These movement events can be divided into *change-of-direction events* – moments when the body part or joint angle suddenly changes direction – and *acceleration peak events*, which are moments of sudden deceleration of the body part or joint angle. The movement events and techniques for detecting them will now be described in detail.

Hand and Wrist Hits. The *hand hit* is the moment at the end of the striking gesture when the performer's hand suddenly changes direction. If they were striking a physical drum, the hit would correspond to the moment when the hand (or drumstick) contacts the head of the drum, imparts energy to the instrument, thus initiating the sound, and rebounds in the opposite direction.

For a gesture in free space where no physical contact occurs, how do we detect the end of the strike? If the movement were in a single dimension (e.g. up and down) we could simply detect extrema (i.e. the moment of minimum height). Since the virtual drum's location and orientation were not precisely specified, participants' movements were not restricted to any particular plane or direction. So I define the hand hit as the moment at the end of a striking gesture where the hand suddenly changes direction.

An algorithm for detecting sudden changes of direction was presented in [3]. In brief, the motion capture system tracks the location of a reflective marker on the back of the participant's right hand, and from this the 3-D velocity of the hand is calculated. This velocity vector is passed through two low-pass filters. One filter has a time constant of 100 msec, and the other has a time constant of 5 msec. The outputs of these filters can be thought of as slow and fast estimates of the hand's velocity vector. When the hand changes direction quickly the angle between these vectors briefly increases as the slow estimate lags behind the fast estimate. Hits are detected as peaks in the rate of change of this angle (see Fig. 2).

If the angle between the performer's forearm and hand is not held still (i.e. the wrist joint is allowed to move), the performer's hand and wrist may change direction at different times. The same hit detection algorithm is applied to the movement of the wrist, where the wrist is defined as the point half-way between markers on the distal condyles of the radius and ulna. The resulting events, or *wrist hits*, are moments when the wrist suddenly changes direction at the end of a drumming gesture.

Acceleration Peaks of the Hand and Wrist. Upon examining the movement data I discovered that large peaks in the magnitude acceleration of the hand often occur close to the onset of the associated audio event. (In fact these peaks are decelerations as the participant sharply halts the movement of the hand.) For an unimpeded movement, an acceleration is the result of a muscular force, and so an acceleration peak is a good candidate for the subjective movement event. An algorithm for detecting these *hand acceleration peaks* is described in [3], and a result is shown in Fig. 3. The same algorithm is applied to the location of the wrist to detect *wrist acceleration peaks*.

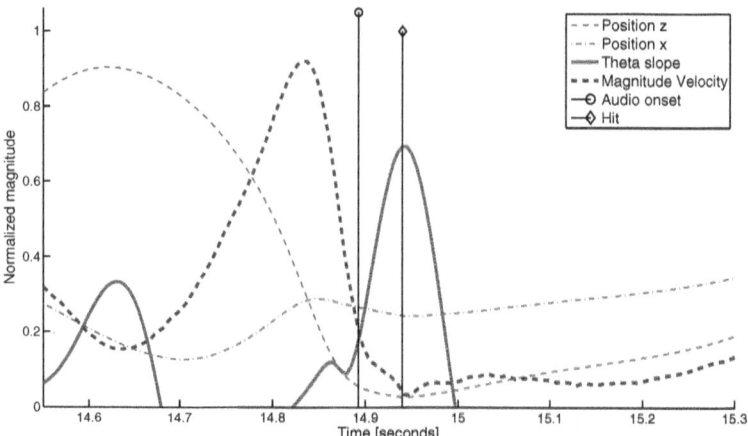

Fig. 2. Detecting the *hand hit* for an air-drumming gesture. Fast and slow estimates of the hand's velocity vector are calculated. The angle between these estimates is Theta. Hits are detected as peaks in the rate of change (Theta slope) of this angle. In this case the hit corresponds to a minima in magnitude velocity, and falls near to extrema in both the vertical (z) and forward (x) directions. We can see that this hit occurs after the onset of its associated audio event.

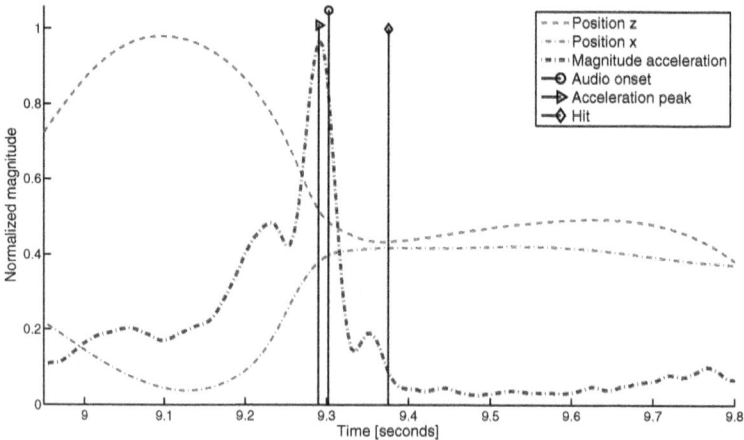

Fig. 3. Detecting the *hand acceleration peak* for a strike gesture. This acceleration peak occurs before the associated audio onset, and almost 100 msec before the hand hit.

Calculating Joint Angles. The remaining four movement events are based on the angle of the performer's elbow and wrist joints. To calculate the elbow angle, a line segment representing the upper arm is defined as passing from a marker on the top of the right shoulder to a point half-way between markers on the lateral and medial condyles of the elbow joint. A line segment representing the lower arm (or forearm) is defined as passing from the elbow to the wrist (as defined above). The elbow angle is calculated as the angle between the upper and lower arm segments. An angle of π radians represents a fully extended elbow joint.

Unlike the elbow, the wrist is a complex joint. Its movements can be defined in two dimensions. In flexion/extension the hand moves in the direction of the palm (flexion) or the back of the hand (extension). In ulnar/radial deviation the hand moves in the direction of the little finger (ulna) or thumb (radius). I observed that for air-drumming gestures the ulnar/radial deviation has a small range, its measurements are noisy, and it tends to correlate with flexion/extension. Thus I used only the flexion/extension angle of the wrist. Two line segments are used to define the wrist angle: the lower arm segment described above, and a segment representing the hand which passes from the wrist to a marker on the back of the hand at the base of the third finger. I find a plane whose normal passes from the ulnar side of the wrist to the radial side of the wrist. The lower arm and hand segments are projected onto this plane, and the wrist angle is taken as the angle between these two projections.

Peaks of the Elbow and Wrist Joint Angles. In an air-drumming gesture with a downward strike, the elbow joint is extending as the hand falls. I define the moment near the end of the strike when the elbow angle changes direction, from extending to flexing, as the *elbow angle peak*. Similarly, for most participants the wrist joint angle also changes direction, from flexion to extension, near the end of the strike. The moment this occurs is defined as the *wrist angle peak*.

Since the changing position of the hand and wrist take place in three-dimensional space, detecting changes-of-direction was not simple. However, the angular movements of the elbow and wrist joints are, as I've defined them, one-dimensional. Therefore, detecting the moment the joint changes direction is straight-forward, and is equivalent to finding peaks in the joint angle. To do so, I find all negatively-sloped zero-crossings in the angular velocity (these correspond to positive peaks in angle), and then discard those for which the joint angle is below a threshold. This ensures that only peaks near the end of the strike are detected. Figure 4 shows some examples.

Acceleration Peaks of the Elbow and Wrist Joint Angles. The sudden changes in the angular velocity of the elbow and wrist joints at the end of the striking gesture are the result of torques applied to the joints. These torques are either the result of muscular effort, or they are due to the mechanical constraints of the joint itself. Figure 4 shows that both the wrist and elbow joints experience sharp negative peaks in angular acceleration before the corresponding joint angle peak. These are detected in a manner similar to that used for detecting angular peaks. First I locate positively-sloped zero-crossings in the angular jerk (the third derivative of joint angle), and then remove those for which the acceleration does not surpass a threshold. These events are then labelled as *elbow angle acceleration peaks*, and *wrist angle acceleration peaks*.

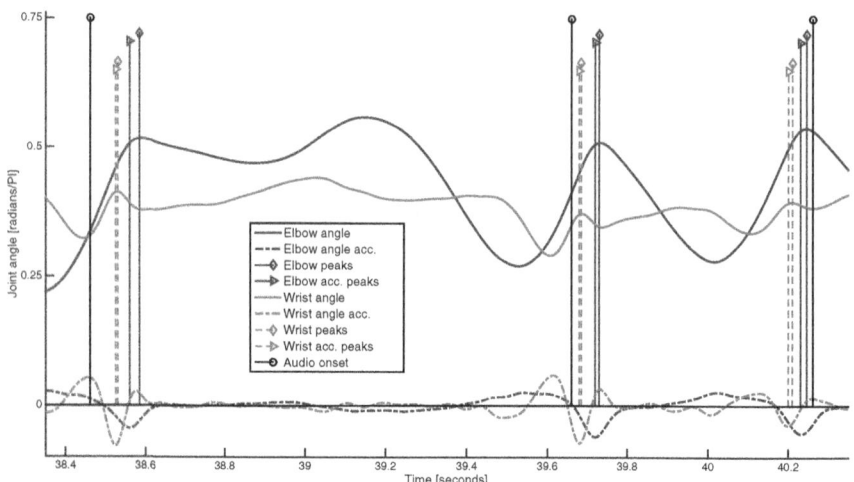

Fig. 4. Detecting joint angle peaks and angular acceleration peaks of the elbow and wrist joints for a single participant. Elbow and wrist angle peaks occur at positive extrema of the respective joint angle, and acceleration peaks occur at negative extrema of the joint's angular acceleration. One slow note and two fast notes are shown.

2.2 Summary of Movement Events

We now have eight movement events, summarized in Table 1, which can be categorized with respect to three dimensions:

1. *Position vs. joint angle*: Four events are based on tracking the position of parts of the body, and four are based on the angles of joints.
2. *Body part*: Two events are based on the hand, two on the wrist, two on the elbow joint, and two on the wrist joint.
3. *Direction change vs. acceleration peak*: Four events detect changes of direction (in either position or joint angle), and four detect peaks in positional or angular acceleration.

Table 1. The movement events analyzed in this paper.

	Change-of-direction	Peak in acceleration
Position	Hand hits	Hand acceleration peaks
	Wrist hits	Wrist acceleration peaks
Joint angle	Elbow angle peaks	Elbow angle acceleration peaks
	Wrist angle peaks	Wrist angle acceleration peaks

3 Analysis and Results

We are interested in understanding the subjective movement event, that is, the internal sensation that the air-drummer enacts in their movement, and which they intend to correspond to the resulting sound. Each movement event functions as a hypothetical candidate for this subjective movement event. In order to evaluate a movement event we examine its timing with respect to the sonic event (i.e. the drum sound) to which it is meant to correspond. This analysis proceeds as follows: for each trial the audio recording is analyzed to detect the onset time of each note (see [3] for implementation details). This functions as the "ground truth" of when the performer intended the sound to occur. Each audio onset is then paired with the movement events, one of each type of movement event, which occurred closest to it in time.

For each movement event time the associated audio onset time is subtracted to get the time offset (or asynchrony) between the audio event and the movement event. A negative offset indicates that the movement event preceded the audio event, and a positive offset means the movement event came after. All subsequent analysis is performed on these offset times.

3.1 Calculating Timing Statistics

For each participant, the data from each trial were aggregated and then split into the slow note and fast note conditions. This results in 40 events for each condition (5 events per rhythm × 4 repetitions of the rhythm × 2 trials). In order to reject bad data due to detection errors or participant mistakes, events whose offset is greater than half the time between notes (600 msec for slow notes, 300 msec for fast notes) were removed. And events which lay more than two standard deviations from the mean for each condition and participant were rejected as outliers.

For the following results we want to know whether the mean or standard deviation offset times differ between various conditions. For a given condition and movement event, the mean tells us by how much the event tends to precede or lag behind the audio onset, and the standard deviation can be considered a measure of the "noise" in the event detection or in the movement itself. To infer whether two conditions differ in the population, we compute the mean (or standard deviation) of each participant's offset times for the conditions we wish to compare. We then conduct a two-sided paired-sample t-test of the ten participants' means (or standard deviations) for the two conditions. For example, to compare whether the standard deviation of hand hit times is different between slow notes and fast notes, I calculate the standard deviation of each participant's slow hits, then the standard deviations of each participant's fast hits. With these ten sample standard deviations for each condition I conduct a t-test with nine degrees of freedom.

3.2 Analysis of Mean Offsets

We can begin to evaluate these eight movement events by looking at the mean offset time between the movement event and the sonic event to which it corresponds. Real-time systems require us to detect the event before the sound is meant to occur. Do some movement events occur earlier or later than others? Do some occur before the audio onset? The rhythm which the participants gestured in time to has notes at two different metric levels. Does the timing of these movement events change with note speed? The answers to these questions can begin to tell us which movement events are most useful, and may suggest which are better candidates for the subjective movement event.

Comparing Change-of-Direction Events and Acceleration Peak Events. Figure 5 shows box plots of the mean offset times for all movement events and both note speeds. Examination shows that for each pair of movement events the acceleration peak event comes before the change-of-direction event. This appears to be true for both slow notes and fast notes, but the differences seem smaller for fast notes.

A repeated measures two-way analysis of variance (ANOVA) was conducted on all offset means. The two within-subjects factors were movement event, with 7 degrees of freedom, and note speed with one degree of freedom. There were significant effects of both movement event ($F = 14.599, p = 3.9e - 11$) and

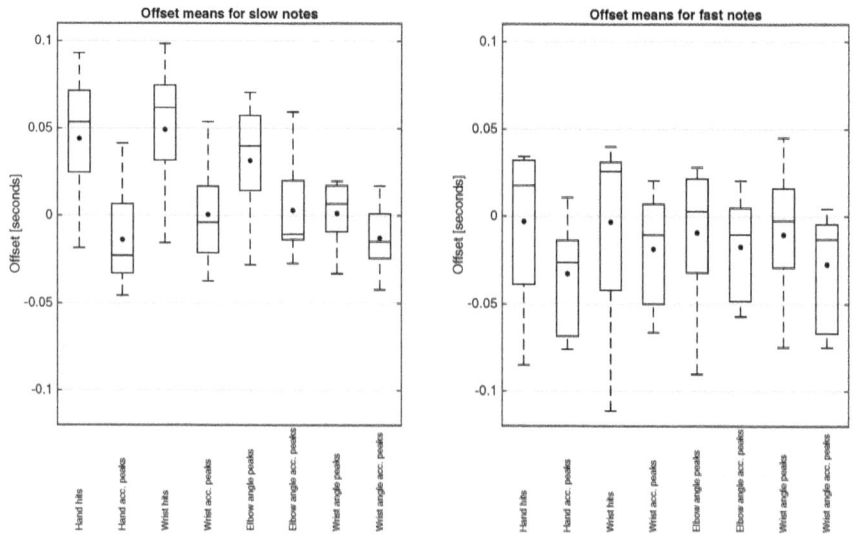

Fig. 5. Box plots of the mean offset times for all participants for each movement event. For each event, the line marks the median, the dot marks the mean, the edges of the box are the 25th and 75th percentiles, and the whiskers extend to the most extreme data. Negative times indicate the movement event came before the audio onset.

note speed ($F = 8.426, p = 0.0175$). There was also a significant interaction between movement event and note speed ($F = 13.188, p = 2.5e - 10$). Post hoc comparisons were conducted between the four change of direction events and their associated acceleration peak events for both slow and fast notes using paired samples t-tests. Results are shown in Table 2.

Table 2. The results of t-tests comparing the offset means for each change-of-direction event (hits and peaks) and the acceleration peak event for the related body location or joint angle. The 95 % confidence interval is in milliseconds.

Body location	Result	T(9)	P	95 % CI
Slow notes				
Hand position	Acceleration peaks precede hits	4.884	0.0009	31 to 85
Wrist position	Acceleration peaks precede hits	4.1889	0.0023	22.4 to 75
Elbow joint angle	Acceleration peaks precede peaks	3.3777	0.0082	9.5 to 47.9
Wrist joint angle	Acceleration peaks precede peaks	3.1416	0.0119	4 to 24.3
Fast notes				
Hand position	Acceleration peaks precede hits	4.5294	0.0014	15 to 44.8
Wrist position	No difference found		n.s	
Elbow joint angle	No difference found		n.s	
Wrist joint angle	Acceleration peaks precede peaks	2.5824	0.0119	2.1 to 31.8

If we apply the conservative Bonferroni correction to these eight results, in which case only p-values less than 0.00625 would be considered significant, we find that the joint angle results do not pass significance. Nevertheless, the trend which we observed is, for the most part, true: acceleration peak events precede their associated change of direction event, and the difference is less pronounced for fast notes and for joint angle events.

Comparing Fast and Slow Notes. Figure 5 shows that fast notes appear to occur earlier than slow notes for all movement events. This difference appears to be smaller for events based on acceleration peaks than it is for the change-of-direction events. To test these observations the mean offsets of slow and fast notes for all eight events were compared and the results shown in Table 3.

In general we find that the timing of change-of-direction events changes significantly between slow and fast notes, with fast notes occurring earlier than slow notes, whereas the timing of acceleration peak events does not differ with note speed. The exception to this rule is the wrist angle. Like the other acceleration peak features, wrist angle acceleration peaks are not found to differ with note speed. Unlike the other change-of-direction events, wrist angle peaks are not found to be different between fast and slow notes. These results are visualized in Fig. 6.

Table 3. The results of t-tests comparing the offset time of fast notes with that of slow notes for each movement event. The 95% confidence interval is in milliseconds.

Movement event	Result	T(9)	P	95% CI
Hand hits	Fast notes are earlier than slow	4.1889	0.0023	22.4 to 75
Hand acc. peaks	No difference found		n.s.	
Wrist hits	Fast notes are earlier than slow	5.2030	$5.6e - 04$	9.5 to 47.9
Wrist acc. peaks	No difference found		n.s.	
Elbow angle peaks	Fast notes are earlier than slow	4.1615	0.0024	18.7 to 63.1
Elbow angle acc. peaks	No difference found		n.s.	
Wrist angle peaks	No difference found		n.s.	
Wrist angle acc. peaks	No difference found		n.s.	

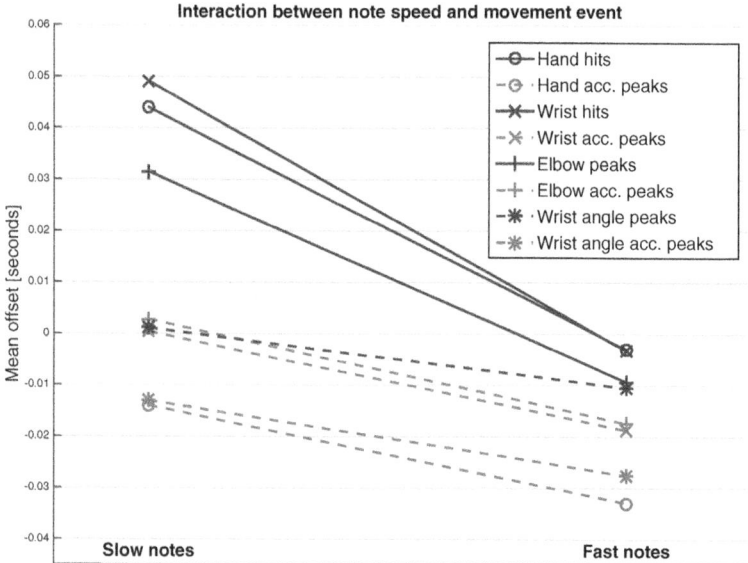

Fig. 6. Comparing fast and slow notes for all movement events. Solid lines are significant differences, and dashed are not significant. Dark lines are change-of-direction events, and light lines are acceleration peak events.

Linked Movement Events. Table 4 contains the the means across the population of both the mean offsets and the offset standard deviations. Figure 6 visualizes the same data for mean offsets. Upon inspection these yield the following observations.

The acceleration peaks of the hand, and the angular acceleration peaks of the wrist joint occur earliest, and appear to be nearly identical for both slow notes and fast notes. T-tests comparing these events find no significant difference for either note speed. The movement of the hand is the result of rotations in the

Table 4. The means of all offset means and of all offset standard deviations for each movement event. All times are in milliseconds.

Movement event	Offset mean		Offset standard deviation	
	Slow notes	Fast notes	Slow notes	Fast notes
Hand hits	43.0	−3.03	35.94	33.97
Hand acceleration peaks	−13.92	−32.9	31.34	25.69
Wrist hits	49.14	−3.29	40.86	32.33
Wrist acceleration peaks	0.45	−18.7	32.26	28.06
Elbow angle peaks	31.54	−9.35	36.95	29.05
Elbow angle acceleration peaks	2.84	−17.4	29.68	24.82
Wrist angle peaks	1.14	−10.53	38.86	34.28
Wrist angle acceleration peaks	−12.99	−27.48	35.46	32.44

shoulder, elbow, and wrist joints, and possibly to a small degree, movements of the trunk. This finding suggests that the last joint in the chain, the wrist, contributes most to the acceleration of the hand.

The movement of the wrist location is primarily a result of the elbow angle, and to a lesser degree the shoulder and trunk movements. Since it is earlier in the kinematic chain, the wrist location is not affected by movements in the wrist joint. Thus, it is not surprising to see that the timing appears to be nearly identical for the acceleration peaks of the wrist location and those of the elbow joint angle. This is true for both slow and fast notes. T-tests find no significant differences between these two movement events at either note speed.

3.3 Analysis of Noise

There are two possible sources of variability in the timing of movement events. One is due to people's inability to execute their movements with precise timing. The other is the noise or inaccuracy in the algorithms for detecting the movement events. Events which can be performed and detected more reliably will be more successful at generating the sound at the time intended by the performer. The question then is, do some movement events have less noise than others?

Figure 7 shows box plots of the standard deviations for each movement event for both slow and fast notes. We notice that for each pair of movement events, the mean standard deviation for the acceleration peak event appears to be lower than that for the associated change-of-direction event. A repeated measures two-way ANOVA on the measured standard deviations finds a significant effect for movement event ($F = 3.541, p = 0.0029$), but none for note speed. Table 5 shows the results of post hoc t-tests comparing the change-of-direction and acceleration peak events.

If we apply Bonferroni correction, only the first two results would be significant. While it is not a strong result, it does seem that acceleration peaks events

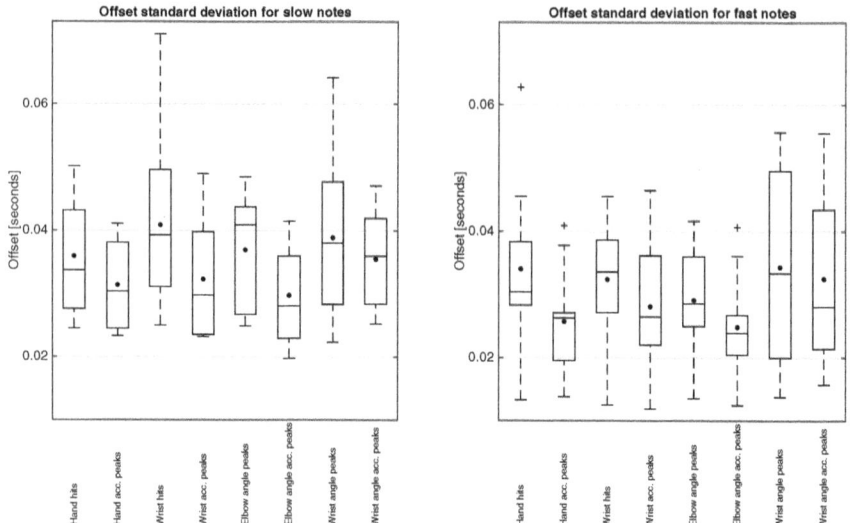

Fig. 7. Box plots for each movement event of the offset time standard deviation for all performers.

Table 5. The results of t-tests comparing the standard deviations of each change-of-direction (c.o.d.) event and its related acceleration peak event. The 95 % confidence interval is in milliseconds.

Movement event	Result	T(9)	P	95 % CI
Slow notes				
Hand position	Acc. peaks have lower noise than c.o.d.	4.5366	0.0014	1.4 to 7.8
Wrist position	Acc. peaks have lower noise than c.o.d.	3.8552	0.0039	3.6 to 13.7
Elbow joint angle	Acc. peaks have lower noise than c.o.d.	2.8488	0.0191	1.5 to 13
Wrist joint angle	No difference found		n.s.	
Fast notes				
Hand position	Acc. peaks have lower noise than c.o.d.	2.4022	0.0398	0.5 to 16.1
Wrist position	Acc. peaks have lower noise than c.o.d.	2.5487	0.0313	0.5 to 8.1
Elbow joint angle	Acc. peaks have lower noise than c.o.d.	2.7508	0.0224	0.8 to 7.7
Wrist joint angle	No difference found		n.s.	

have less noise than change-of-direction events. And the difference is more prominent for slow notes than for fast. As was found to be the case with offset means, the wrist angle events are different: the standard deviations of wrist angle peaks and wrist angle acceleration peaks were not found to differ for either note speed. For both slow and fast notes, the two events with the lowest mean standard deviations are hand acceleration peaks and elbow angle acceleration peaks.

4 Discussion

By summarizing the results presented above we begin to understand more about discrete air-gestures, their timing, qualities, and which are likely to be most useful in implementing real-time air-instruments.

4.1 Acceleration Peaks vs. Change of Direction

If a digital instrument builder wants to design a system to trigger sounds with air-drumming gestures which movement event should they use? There are a number of reasons why events based on acceleration peak are better.

Acceleration Peaks Occur Earlier. A real-time air-instrument needs to predict when an audio event should be triggered before it occurs, ideally early enough to account for any latencies in the system. The acceleration peaks for hand location, wrist location, and elbow angle occur before the change-of-direction event for the same body part. On average the acceleration peaks of the hand location occur earlier than any other movement event (14 msec before the audio onset for slow notes and 33 msec before for fast notes), with wrist angle acceleration peaks only slightly later (13 msec before the audio onset for slow notes and 27 msec for fast notes). These events occur early enough that they may be successfully implemented on some current real-time systems.

Finding that acceleration peaks tend to occur before the audio onset reminds us of the sensorimotor synchronization research which shows that people tapping in time to a metronome tend to tap before the beat. This lends support to the hypothesis that the subjective movement event is an acceleration peak.

Acceleration Peaks Have Less Noise. For hand location, wrist location, and elbow angle, the acceleration peak events had less timing variability than their associated change-of-direction events. Hand acceleration peaks and elbow angle acceleration peaks had the lowest noise.

This finding may seem surprising at first. The time at which the body part changes direction is a result of the accelerations applied to it. Shouldn't the change-of-direction and acceleration peak events have similar noise characteristics? The difference may simply be a result of the physics: acceleration is integrated twice to give position, so small differences in acceleration result in larger differences in position. Furthermore, we detect only the time of the peak acceleration and do not measure the shape of the acceleration over time. Two movements with identical peak acceleration time could have different acceleration curves, leading to different change of direction times. Regardless of the reason, the fact that acceleration peaks have less noise makes them better suited for triggering sounds from discrete air-gestures.

Acceleration Peaks Change Less with Note Speed. The task which study participants performed required them to make air-drumming gestures at two repetition speeds. An ideal movement event for triggering sounds from discrete air-gestures would have the same timing regardless of the tempo or speed of repetition. Using a movement feature which does vary with speed would require the system to infer before a gesture occurs what metric level the note is intended to occur on. This is not simple, to say the least.

We saw that for hand location, wrist location, and elbow angle, the timing of the change-of-direction event changed significantly between fast and slow notes, with slow notes occurring much later. However, for acceleration peak events no significant differences were found between fast and slow notes.

Best Movement Event Overall. Hand acceleration peaks occur earlier than any other event and have the second lowest noise. And, as we saw, acceleration peaks vary less with note speed. Given these results, from a practical standpoint hand acceleration peaks seem to be the best overall choice for triggering sounds from discrete air-gestures in a real-time system.

If the causality constraints were reduced, for example in a non-realtime system, or in a system where hardware input and output latencies were very low, elbow angle acceleration peaks might also be a good choice. They have the least noise of all the events, and the only events which occur closer to zero offset are the wrist peaks and wrist acceleration peaks.

4.2 How the Wrist Joint is Different

The wrist joint seems to behave differently than the elbow joint. For the elbow joint, the timing of peaks changes with note repetition speed, but the timing of acceleration peaks do not. For the wrist joint, neither the peaks nor the acceleration peaks change with note speed (see Fig. 6). This may indicate that when we air-drum we treat the elbow and wrist joints differently. One possible difference is that the movement in the elbow joint may be primarily intentionally directed, whereas the movement in the wrist may be more passive. That is, perhaps we extend our elbow joint by activating the triceps, and then we decelerate that extension through a sudden deliberate activation of the biceps. However, for the wrist joint, the muscles of the forearm may be used to maintain a constant force on the wrist joint. When the elbow angle is decelerated the wrist is pulled back, but the hand is carried forward by its inertia, causing the wrist angle to change. This movement in the wrist is eventually impeded, either by the muscular tension on the joint or by the joint reaching the limits of its range of motion, causing the wrist to suddenly decelerate and change direction.

We might call this the "flinging hypothesis", because the hand is passively flung by the active elbow joint. That the elbow angle acceleration peaks have the least noise somewhat supports this hypothesis. If the timing of sudden decelerations of the elbow joint is what the performer is controlling for, it seems plausible that these would have the least variability.

Other findings from this study do not support the flinging hypothesis. In Fig. 4 we see that for this participant, the wrist angle peaks before the elbow angle does, and the acceleration peaks in the wrist angle also occur before acceleration peaks in the elbow angle. Table 4 confirms that this is also true on average across the population. It is interesting to note that the peaks in the acceleration profiles of the wrist joint seem to be sharper than those of the elbow joint (again see Fig. 4).

4.3 External and Internal Perspectives on Movement

The hand hit and wrist hit movement events are based on the changing location of the hand and wrist in space. The location of these body parts can be observed by an external viewer, and they are easy to track with camera-based technologies such as marker-based motion capture systems. Such measurements are made with respect to an origin and coordinate system that is external to the body.

We can think of joint angles as externally viewable aspects of quantities which are referenced to a body-centric frame. A movement in my elbow joint feels the same to me regardless of which direction I am facing (as long as I am upright with respect to gravity). This makes joint angles, in a sense, more "internal", or closer to my subjective experience of myself than are body part locations.

Even more internal is the sense of muscular effort I experience as I apply forces to my joints in order to move my body about in space. An initial assumption in this research is that when we make a discrete air-gesture, we do something with our body to create on internal sense of a moment in time. The forces we generate on our own bodies, which result in accelerations on joints and body parts, can be very close to our subjective experience of movement. This may be especially true in the case of discrete air-gestures, for which the movement is deliberately sudden, and for which there is no external contact or referent. (The experience may be entirely different for the case of hammering, where our sense of both our body and the hammer, the hammer being ready-to-hand, disappears as our awareness focuses on the task.) For this reason, I find peaks in acceleration to be likely candidates for this internal sense of a moment in time. The findings from this study regarding acceleration peaks support this view.

4.4 Conclusions

This work examined the timing of eight movement events for triggering sounds from air-drumming gestures, and shows that events based on detecting sharp accelerations in the movement perform better than events based on detecting changes of direction at the end of a gesture. This suggests that the subjective movement event – the thing we do with our bodies to create a sense of a discrete moment, and to which we intend the sound to correspond – is likely to be a sense of acceleration, such as that generated by a sudden muscular effort.

Because of this research, we no longer have to rely on heuristics or intuition when designing algorithms to detect when to trigger a sound from a discrete air-gesture. We can use the findings described above to inform our design, and this will hopefully result in more responsive and rhythmically accurate air-instruments. Further work implementing and evaluating real-time air-instruments will help to validate and refine these findings.

These results are useful not only for non-tactile air-instruments but for any movement-controlled musical instrument, such as traditional instruments augmented with inertial sensors. They may also be helpful in improving the timing and user experience of any gesture controlled systems, such as those used in video games or home entertainment systems.

Acknowledgments. This research was performed as part of my PhD thesis at CCRMA, Stanford University.

References

1. Aschersleben, G.: Temporal control of movements in sensorimotor synchronization. Brain Cogn. **48**(1), 66–79 (2002)
2. Collicutt, M., Casciato, C., Wanderley, M.M.: From real to virtual: a comparison of input devices for percussion tasks. In: Proceedings of NIME, pp. 4–6 (2009)
3. Dahl, L.: Studying the timing of discrete musical air gestures. Comput. Music J. **39**(2), 47–66 (2015)
4. Dahl, L., Wang, G.: SoundBounce: physical metaphors in designing mobile music performance. In: Proceedings of the 2010 Conference on New Interfaces for Musical Expression, Sydney, Australia, pp. 178–181 (2010)
5. Dahl, S.: Playing the accent-comparing striking velocity and timing in an ostinato rhythm performed by four drummers. Acta Acustica United Acustica **90**(4), 762–776 (2004)
6. Godøy, R.I., Haga, E., Jensenius, A.R.: Playing "air instruments": mimicry of sound-producing gestures by novices and experts. In: Gibet, S., Courty, N., Kamp, J.-F. (eds.) GW 2005. LNCS (LNAI), vol. 3881, pp. 256–267. Springer, Heidelberg (2006)
7. Havel, C., Desainte-Catherine, M.: Modeling an air percussion for composition and performance. In: Proceedings of the 2004 Conference on New Interfaces for Musical Expression, pp. 31–34. National University of Singapore (2004)
8. Kanke, H., Takegawa, Y., Terada, T., Tsukamoto, M.: Airstic drum: a drumstick for integration of real and virtual drums. In: Nijholt, A., Romão, T., Reidsma, D. (eds.) ACE 2012. LNCS, vol. 7624, pp. 57–69. Springer, Heidelberg (2012)
9. Luck, G., Toiviainen, P.: Ensemble musicians' synchronization with conductors' gestures: an automated feature-extraction analysis. Music Percept. **24**(2), 189–200 (2006)
10. Mäki-Patola, T.: User interface comparison for virtual drums. In: Proceedings of the 2005 Conference on New Interfaces for Musical Expression, pp. 144–147. National University of Singapore (2005)
11. Mathews, M.V.: Three dimensional baton and gesture sensor, US Patent 4,980,519, 25 December 1990
12. Repp, B.H.: Sensorimotor synchronization: a review of the tapping literature. Psychon. Bull. Rev. **12**(6), 969–992 (2005)
13. Sarasúa, Á., Guaus, E.: Beat tracking from conducting gestural data: a multi-subject study. In: Proceedings of the 2014 International Workshop on Movement and Computing, p. 118. ACM (2014)

14. Visi, F., Schramm, R., Miranda, E.: Gesture in performance with traditional musical instruments and electronics: use of embodied music cognition and multimodal motion capture to design gestural mapping strategies. In: Proceedings of the 2014 International Workshop on Movement and Computing, p. 100. ACM (2014)
15. Wanderley, M.M., Depalle, P.: Gestural control of sound synthesis. Proc. IEEE **92**(4), 632–644 (2004)

Assessing the Influence of Constraints on Cellists' Postural Displacements and Musical Expressivity

Jocelyn Rozé[1]([✉]), Mitsuko Aramaki[1], Richard Kronland-Martinet[1], Thierry Voinier[1], Christophe Bourdin[2], Delphine Chadefaux[2], Marvin Dufrenne[2], and Sølvi Ystad[1]

[1] LMA (Laboratoire de Mécanique et d'Acoustique), CNRS, UPR 7051, Aix-Marseille Université, Centrale Marseille, 13009 Marseille, France
roze@lma.cnrs-mrs.fr
[2] ISM (Institut des Sciences du Mouvement), CNRS, UMR 7287, Aix Marseille Université, 13288 Marseille, France

Abstract. This article presents the preliminary results from an experiment investigating the influence of cellists' ancillary gestures on their musical expressivity. Seven professional cellists were asked to play a score while their movements were recorded by a force platform (on which they were seated) and a 3D motion capture system for joint kinematics. Specific torso and head contributions to their global postural displacements were analyzed through the use of 4 playing conditions: (a) a *normal* condition without any constraints, (b) a *mentally static* condition where the cellists were asked to keep their posture as static as possible, (c) a *physically semi-constrained* condition where the cellists' torso was attached to the back of a chair by a safety race harness, and (d) a *physically fully constrained* condition where the cellists wore a neck collar in addition to the race harness to limit their head movements. We here investigate the influence of these constraints on global postural features computed from the force platform data, and on fundamental acoustical features linked to musical expressivity for one cellist. The first results reveal that the cellists' immobilization conditions give rise to different postural adaptation strategies depending on the torso-head coupling, and alter significantly the expressive intentions through changes in spectro-temporal features and rhythmical variations of the produced sounds.

Keywords: Cellist · Music · Ancillary/postural gestures · Force platform · Acoustical features · Performance

1 Introduction

1.1 Background

The expressive play of a musician is intrinsically connected to his or her gestures. These connections have been thoroughly investigated through the embodied music cognition approach [12]. While continuously interacting with the instrument, the player's body encodes sensorymotor information that induces a spontaneous reenaction of musical gestures from the perceived audio. This information determines the player's motor process as a function of the instrument's ergonomy, the musical structure and interpretative choices [17]. Some studies directly investigated connections from score structure to interpretation through a note by note analysis [2,6]. Others explored the musician's body as a mediator of expressive sensitivities according to two gestural levels [3]: The effective or instrumental gestures, which are directly at the origin of the produced sound, and the ancillary or accompanist gestures, that are not directly responsible for the sound production, but that might ease the performer-instrument interaction. The musical significance of such ancillary gestures has been investigated in the case of the clarinet [8,18], the piano [15], the harp [4], and the violin [16]. Results from these studies showed that ancillary movements play an important role in the musicians' expressive intentions, by supporting the phrasing, and facilitating technical gestures. The previous findings also highlighted that the influence of ancillary gestures on a given expressive audio feature varies according to the instrument.

1.2 Motivation

In line with previous research, we're interested in better understanding the significance of ancillary gestures for professional cellists, in particular their postural displacements, and their influence on the musical expressivity. Some studies examined the influence of physical parameters of the cello bow on spectral features [1,5]. Others extracted coordination patterns of joint movements in the cellists' bowing arm to characterize musicality [19], or attempted to identify trends of cellists' motor process through expressive timing and dynamic audio features [9]. However, to our knowledge, no studies have so far investigated in depth the relationship between cellists' postural displacements and their musical expressivity. An insight in this exciting field can be obtained from experimental concepts described in *The Alexander Technique* adapted to the cello [7]. In fact, F.M. Alexander demonstrated that a specific orientation of the cellists' head, neck, and upper back enables optimal body coordination. What would happen to the produced sound if we perturb this perfect body coordination described by Alexander? To answer some of these questions, we decided to constrain the cellists' natural postural adjustments and observe the effects on expressivity.

2 Aims and Hypothesis

This paper presents preliminary results of a large experiment aiming at investigating the influence of professional cellists' postural displacements on their musical expressivity. A multi-modal environment combining a force platform, motion-capture, and audio recordings was used. Cellists were asked to play a score as expressively as possible in 4 types of postural conditions, and according to *legato* or *detached* playing modes with two different tempi *(slow/fast)*. We here explore the influence of such immobilization conditions on a global postural measure and on acoustic descriptors relevant for musical expressivity. Moreover, results described in this paper will only focus on variations depending on the playing mode and not on the tempo. We predicted that modifications induced by immobilization constraints on the cellist's postural coordination, and particularly the torso-head connection, would be explicitly revealed by the selected postural and acoustical descriptors, with substantial differences according to the playing mode.

3 Experiment

3.1 Participants

Seven professional cellists (4 males, 3 females) were invited to participate in the experiment. All the participants had received professional music training, some of them hold a position at the Opera of Marseille and all are renown cello teachers. They all gave written consent and were payed for the participation. In this paper, we present the global tendencies for all the cellists.

3.2 Scores

Design. The choice of an adequate score as support of investigation for ancillary gestures, required some thoughts. Selections from the standard cello repertoire are colored by emotional connotations, which can result in very different natural bowing and fingering strategies, according to the chosen interpretation. This is a problem with respect to our objectives. Actually we're looking for adaptive postural strategies, as function of the musical structure, and not of a particular expressive intent. This implies the use of a sufficiently annotated score material, adaptable to different bow strokes and tempi, and not too loaded with affective emotional content, to achieve a common base for decoding and comparing cellists' ancillary gestures. Consequently, we designed a specific expressive score, combining short study fragments of cello suite excerpts from the Bach repertoire in which the bowing strokes and fingering positions are imposed. The score is composed of 6 parts, each related to specific difficulties of cello playing. In this paper we focus on part four that corresponds to fast syncope shifts of the left hand (Fig. 1).

Qualitative Factors. Our experiment explored cellists' postural displacements according to qualitative factors of playing modes and global tempi. The *detached* playing mode is characterized by the fact that each bow stroke produces a single note, while *legato* mode is obtained when several notes are played by the same bow stroke. To take into account the playing modes, we designed 2 versions of the same score with different lengths of note ties. In the present study we focus on the slow tempo.

a) Mode Detached

b) Mode Legato

Fig. 1. Part 4 of the score: fast syncope shifts of the left hand. Two versions of this score part correspond to the two playing modes: *(a)* **Detached** playing mode, *(b)* **Legato** playing mode

3.3 Apparatus

The investigation of the cellists' postural strategies in different playing conditions was made possible by several experimental devices.

Force Platform. The cellists were seated with their instrument on a force platform AMTI (model SGA34CE), a dynamometrical plate capturing the forces and moments applied on its surface. Collected at a frame rate of 250 Hz, these data allowed us to compute the COP (Center Of Pressure) projection for the system {cellist-instrument} on the platform. Several useful descriptors could be computed from the trajectories described by the COP, taken as a global postural measure.

Mocap System. To get finer details on postural adjustments and segmental coordination of performers, a 3D tracking motion capture system (VICON) was used. This system consisted in a network of 8 high-speed infrared cameras distributed around the performer, and acquiring kinematic data at a frame rate of 125 Hz. These recordings will not be discussed in this article.

Audio and Video Recordings. Audio data were recorded at a 44.1 kHz sampling rate via a MOTU interface (Ultralite MIC3) by a microphone DPA 4096 placed under the cello bridge. The full performance was recorded by a standard digital video camera to disambiguate Mocap data when needed. As for the mocap, video recordings won't be discussed here.

3.4 Protocol

Constraints and Materials. The experimental procedure was divided in 4 sessions corresponding to 4 different postural playing conditions (Fig. 2):

1. **N:** *Normal Condition.* Cellists were asked to play naturally as in a performance context.
2. **SM:** *Static Mental Condition.* Cellists were asked to be as immobile as possible while playing.
3. **SC:** *Static Chest Condition.* Cellists were asked to play in a physically semi-constrained situation, with the torso attached to the back of their chair by a 5-point safety race harness that did not constrain their shoulder movements.
4. **SCH:** *Static Chest and Head Condition.* Cellists were asked to play in a physically fully constrained situation, with the torso attached as in the SC condition and a neck collar adjusted to limit their head movements.

In all the conditions the cellists were asked to play as expressively as possible. As the material weight varied according to the condition, the force platform was re-calibrated between each postural session.

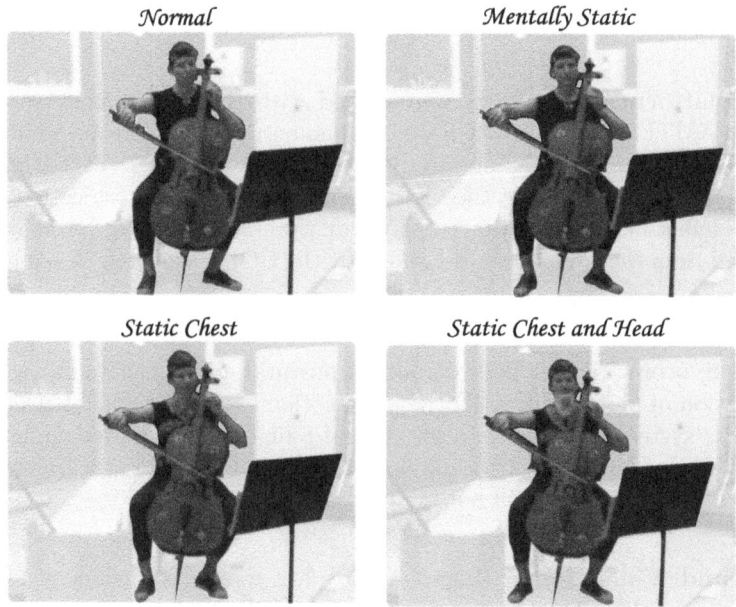

Fig. 2. The 4 postural conditions of experiment: *(TopLeft)* Normal Condition (**N**, *(TopRight)* Static Mental Condition (**SM**, *(BottomLeft)* Static Chest Condition (**SC**, *(BottomRight)* Static Chest and Head Condition (**SCH**

Design. For each postural session, the experimental design included 2 playing modes (legato/detached) × 2 tempi (slow/fast) × 3 repetitions within-subjects, resulting in 12 takes by session and by subject. The 4 experimental sessions were carried out in a different order for each cellist, to avoid order effects. In the same way, the order of execution for playing modes, tempi, and repetition modalities within each session were randomized. Hence, the chronological order achievement of the 12 session takes was different for each subject. This design yielded a total of 12 takes × 4 sessions = 48 trials by cellist.

Procedure. The musicians received the score before the experiment, to familiarize with bow strokes and fingerings printed in the 2 score versions. Upon arrival, each cellist was informed about the procedure and signed a consent form. The musicians were asked to play as expressively as possible whatever the postural condition. At the beginning of each recording session, the musicians were equipped according to the material required by the postural condition. For each take, the playing mode and tempo was given. A clap was used as mean for synchronizing all the signals collected from the platform, the motion capture, the audio and video devices. Once the clap emitted, an operator indicated the global tempo to the musician through 4 metronome beats. The cellist then started to play on the 5th beat (without the metronome). Each postural session was separated by a short break. At the end of each session, the musicians were invited to answer a short questionnaire. This enabled a better understanding of the potential discomfort experienced during the postural instructions and how the musicians felt that the constraint influenced the movements and the sound. The entire experiment lasted for approximately 4 h for each cellist.

4 Descriptors

4.1 Postural Descriptors

Method. The COP displacements of the system {cellist-instrument} on the force platform stand for its postural oscillations as a function of time. A common method for postural analysis consists in estimating the ellipse encompassing 95 % of the COP data points on the trial duration. We estimated 3 relevant descriptors from the geometrical features of this COP confidence ellipse to characterize the global postural behavior of the subject: Area, Principal orientation and Flatness. To measure the general tendencies of the COP displacements, these postural descriptors were computed on the complete duration of the score, i.e. not only on part four.

COP Ellipse Area. The area of the ellipse is an estimation of the total surface covered by 95 % of the COP displacements.

COP Ellipse Orientation. The two main ellipse orientations are computed by a principal component regression on the COP centered data. This process results in a pair of orthogonal components standing for the 2 trigonometrical angles of the semi-major and semi-minor axes. The first component (the angle of the semi-major axis) characterizes the main direction of the postural displacement.

COP Ellipse Flatness. The flatness of the ellipse was computed from its eccentricity, a measure obtained from the ratio between its semi-major and semi-minor axes, which provide information on how circular the ellipse is. The eccentricity e is given by:

$$e = \sqrt{1 - \frac{b^2}{a^2}} \qquad (1)$$

with a, b respectively the semi-major and the semi-minor axes.

- If $e \simeq 0$, the ellipse is quasi-circular
- If $e \simeq 1$, the ellipse approaches a straight line

The combination of the main orientation and eccentricity of the ellipse revealed the antero-posterior *(forward/backward)* or medio-lateral *(left/right)* tendency of postural displacements. The COP descriptors were computed on a full score sequence (Fig. 3).

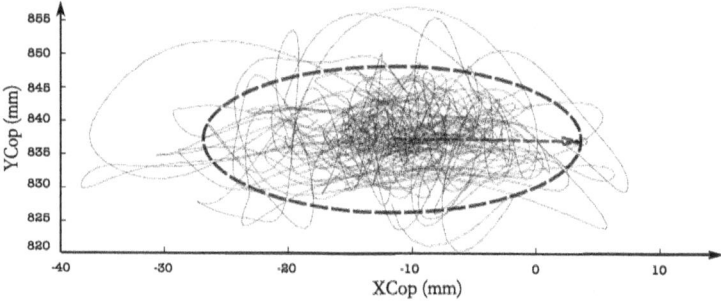

Fig. 3. Example of **Confidence ellipse** estimated from COP displacements of the system {cellist-instrument} on the force platform. The sequence is a player's trial in the *StaticChest* postural condition

4.2 Audio Descriptors

Method. The choice and design of the audio descriptors were chosen according to different zoom levels of the score part, i.e. at note level on specific notes or at beat level including a set of consecutive notes. To compute the descriptors, we first extracted the chosen note or note sequence from the audio recordings using the Praat software. Then, we adapted an audio pitch tracking algorithm from the Matlab MIR toolbox [11], in order to segment each note in the sequence. Within this process, each audio signal is divided into frames overlapped by a factor compatible with the frame rate of the mocap system, i.e. 8 ms *(1/125 Hz)*. Within this process, each audio signal was divided into frames overlapped by a factor compatible with the frame rate of the mocap system, i.e. 8 ms *(1/125 Hz)*. The pitch could then be estimated for each frame by computing the autocorrelation function of the signal spectrum and thus isolating the fundamental frequency.

Temporal and spectral descriptors were computed for each note of the sequence, on the basis of the information provided by the pitch segmentation process. The temporal descriptors were derived from the note transitions and temporal envelopes of the signal. The spectral descriptors were computed from the frequency contents at the frame level, before being averaged for all the frames encompassing each note.

Temporal Descriptors

Local Tempo Deviations. A common way to assess the finesse in phrasing consists in computing the metric or local tempo variations of each note. The computation of these variations was based on the IOI (Inter-onset interval) deviations of each note according to their theoretical durations. An IOI stands for the duration between each onset of two consecutive notes. Since there was no silence between the notes of our sequences, we roughly assimilated the IOI of a given note to its total duration. For each note n, the descriptor of IOI deviation $IOIdev$ was computed as the difference in frames between the theoretical and real durations of the note:

$$IOI_{dev}(n) = IOI_t(n) - IOI_r(n) \qquad (2)$$

with $IOI_t(n)$, $IOI_r(n)$ denoting respectively theoretical and real IOIs of the note n.

Attack Slope. The classical descriptor Attack Time could have been adopted as a temporal descriptor for each note, but the Attack Slope (ATS) was preferred in the present case to overcome energy differences within a musical note sequence. For a single note n, the descriptor ATS represents the temporal increase or average slope of the energy during the attack phase [13]:

$$ATS(n) = \frac{PeakValue(n)}{AT(n)} \qquad (3)$$

where AT is the Attack Time, i.e. the time it takes for the temporal envelope to deploy from 10 % to 90 % of its maximal value $PeakValue$.

Spectral Descriptors

Relative Brightness. By attentively listening to the sound recordings, we noticed certain timbre differences between postural conditions, perceived as spectral enrichments or impoverishments, that contributed to more or less metallic colorations of the sound. Hereby, we searched for an estimate of the proportion of high-frequency partials within the notes by the spectral centroid, an estimation of the barycenter of the spectral energy distribution, correlated to the perceived *brightness*. Nevertheless, this well-known descriptor is pitch-dependent and is therefore not adapted to characterize the *brightness* within a note sequence of different pitches. For this reason, we designed a relative *brightness* descriptor based on the Tristimulus criterion [14], which displays the energy distribution of harmonics in three frequency bands determined by the amount of spectral energy inside each band relatively to the total energy of harmonics. The first band contains the fundamental frequency, the second one the medium partials (2, 3, 4) and the last one higher order partials (5 and more). If a note n is composed of L frames, the tristimulus of this note constitutes three spectral coordinates, corresponding to spectral barycenters of each band:

$$TR_1(n) = \frac{1}{L}\sum_{l=1}^{L-1} TR_1(l) = \frac{1}{L}\sum_{l=1}^{L-1} \frac{A_1(l)}{\sum_{h=1}^{H} A_h(l)} \qquad (0 \leq l \leq L-1) \qquad (4)$$

$$TR_2(n) = \frac{1}{L}\sum_{l=1}^{L-1} TR_2(l) = \frac{1}{L}\sum_{l=1}^{L-1} \frac{\sum_{h=2}^{4} A_h(l)}{\sum_{h=1}^{H} A_h(l)} \qquad (0 \leq l \leq L-1) \qquad (5)$$

$$TR_3(n) = \frac{1}{L}\sum_{l=1}^{L-1} TR_3(l) = \frac{1}{L}\sum_{l=1}^{L-1} \frac{\sum_{h=5}^{H} A_h(l)}{\sum_{h=1}^{H} A_h(l)} \qquad (0 \leq l \leq L-1) \qquad (6)$$

where $A_h(l)$ is the amplitude of the hth harmonic in frame l, and H denotes the total number of harmonics taken into consideration.

From this descriptor, we designed the Tristimulus ratio (TRIratio), a more compact descriptor focusing on the spectral transfer between low and high frequencies that is independent of the note pitch and is given by the formula:

$$TRIratio(n) = \frac{TR_3(n)}{TR_1(n) + TR_2(n)} \qquad (7)$$

Hence, relative energy transfers towards higher partials induce an increase in the TRIratio, resulting in sounds that are perceived as more *harsh*, metallic and brilliant.

Spectral Richness. The previous TRIratio descriptor informs us about the relative localization of spectral energy within a note. However, it doesnt necessarily provide a suitable characterization of how the spectral energy is deployed around its barycenter and how this contributes to the coloring of the sound. This information might be obtained with the Harmonic Spectral Spread descriptor (HSS), which increases when the spectral bandwidth increases, resulting in a spectrally richer sound. At the frame level, the HSS is defined as the power-weighted RMS deviation from the Harmonic Spectral Centroid (HSC), i.e. the amplitude-weighted mean of the harmonic peaks [10]:

$$HSS(n) = \frac{1}{L}\sum_{l=1}^{L-1} HSS(l) = \frac{1}{L}\sum_{l=1}^{L-1} \frac{1}{HSC(l)}\sqrt{\frac{\sum_{h=1}^{H}[(f_h(l) - HSC(l))^2 A_h(l)^2]}{\sum_{h=1}^{H} A_h(l)^2}} \qquad (8)$$

where $f_h(l)$ and $A_h(l)$ are respectively the frequency and the amplitude of the hth harmonic in frame l.

5 Influence of Constraints on the Postural Displacements

We here discuss the influence of the experimental conditions on the postural features of the COP ellipse across all seven cellists.

5.1 Method

For each of the 4 postural conditions, we computed the geometrical features of a COP confidence ellipse, obtained by averaging the 3 COP ellipses corresponding to the repetitions of a given playing mode (*legato/detached* at slow tempo). This yielded a set of 4 postural conditions × 2 playing modes = 8 averaged data of ellipse descriptors for each cellist. In particular, we here focused on the area descriptor of the mean postural ellipse, as it turned out to present the most interesting variations across postural conditions and playing modes. For this ellipse area descriptor, the final data set was thus composed of 7 cellists × 8 posture/mode combinations.

To assess the influence across all cellists of the factors *postural conditions* and *playing modes* on the mean ellipse area descriptor, we performed two-way repeated measures ANOVAs and post-hoc pair-wise comparisons with Least Significant Difference (LSD) procedure.

5.2 Results

Analysis by two-way repeated measures ANOVAs first revealed an effect of the playing mode, $F(1,6) = 5.87, p = .051$. Indeed, the mean COP ellipse area was significantly greater for *detached* mode ($27\,\text{cm}^2$) than for *legato* mode ($19\,\text{cm}^2$). The effect of the postural condition was marginally significant, $F(3,18) = 2.84, p = .066$. Pair-wise post-hoc comparisons revealed that the COP ellipse areas of the *Static Mental* condition were significantly lower in average (SM = $13\,\text{cm}^2$) than those of the physically constrained conditions (SC = $27\,\text{cm}^2$, SCH = $28\,\text{cm}^2$ with $p < .05^*$), and marginally lower than the *Normal* condition (N = $24\,\text{cm}^2$ with $p = .074$). Furthermore, the analysis didn't reveal any effects of interactions between the two factors.

In order to increase the precision of these results, we carried out two separate one-way repeated measures ANOVAs with the postural condition as a factor, for each playing mode across the cellists. Regarding the *detached* mode, no significant differences emerged between the mean postural COP ellipse areas (N = $27\,\text{cm}^2$, SM = $15\,\text{cm}^2$, SC = $33\,\text{cm}^2$, SCH = $32\,\text{cm}^2$ with $p = .13$). However, regarding the *legato* playing mode, the effect of the postural condition was significant, $F(3,18) = 3.65, p < .05^*$. Associated pair-wise post-hoc comparisons reinforced the results obtained from two-way repeated measures ANOVAs. Indeed, the mean COP ellipse areas of the *Static Mental* condition were significantly lower (SM = $13\,\text{cm}^2$) than the other postural conditions (N = $22\,\text{cm}^2$, SC = $21\,\text{cm}^2$ with $p < .05^*$, and SCH = $24\,\text{cm}^2$ with $p < .05^{**}$).

5.3 Discussion

The first result of the two-way ANOVA suggested a global impact of the playing mode on the surface encompassing the cellist's postural oscillations. Figure 4 depicts more finely this impact for each of the four postural conditions across all cellists. It can be observed that the mean COP areas in the normal situation remained relatively stable between the two playing modes. Thus, most of the cellists didn't really need to adapt their corporeal displacements to the playing mode while playing normally. By contrast, the three constrained situations caused a global decrease of mean COP areas from the *detached* to the *legato*

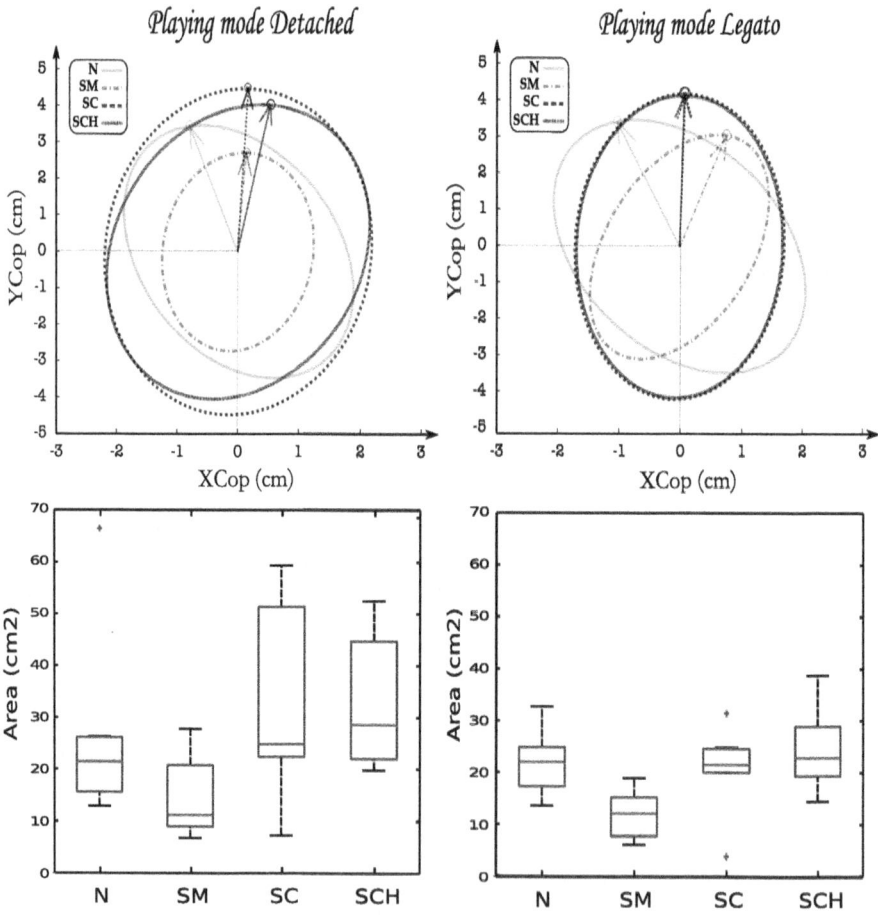

Fig. 4. *(Up)* COP ellipses averaged across the repetitions of the 7 cellists in each postural condition. *(Bottom)* Corresponding statistics of ellipse areas for each postural condition. The central lines are the medians, the edges of the boxes are the 25th and 75th percentiles. Mean COP ellipses and area statistics are given for the two playing modes: *(Left)* Detached mode and *(Right)* Legato mode

playing mode. This observation would suggest that on the whole, the cellists had to struggle more with the postural constraints while playing *detached*. This might seem a little bit counterintuitive at first sight, since we could expect that the musicians corporeally move more in the constrained condition when performing large bowing movements (*legato* than when they perform small ones (*detached*. However, the higher frequency of small bowing strokes might explain this difference, since within this context, the cellists might have produced a greater motor effort to make sure they succeeded each bowing transition. The broader postural displacements observed for physical immobilizations in the *detached* playing mode, might hereby reflect the cellists' effort to complete the numerous small downbow/upbow movements.

The second result suggested by the two-way ANOVA and reinforced by the 2 one-way ANOVAs, indicate that for the constraint of mental immobilization, the cellists more easily managed to reduce their postural oscillations while playing *legato* than when playing *detached*. This can actually be observed in Fig. 4. Nevertheless, in spite of their efforts, cellists couldn't completely inhibit their displacements whatever the playing mode. An incompressible postural quantity of movement always subsisted, which complies with studies on clarinetists' ancillary gestures [18]. Furthermore, in the *legato* mode, the mean COP ellipse area of the fully-constrained conditions coincides with the normal one. Consequently, these latter analyses confirm that the cellists felt more comfortable when dealing with the constraint in the *legato* than in the *detached* playing mode. From here, we could infer and discuss interesting aspects of the connection between a cellist and his/her instrument. Indeed, within a natural postural situation, this connection works as a kind of dynamical resistance. But forcing a cellist to perform with the back stuck to the chair or with an additional neck collar, breaks some elements of the musician-instrument interaction. Previous postural analyses revealed that such a situation created a discomfort felt by the musicians especially while playing in a *detached* way. Thus we can suppose that the cellists need to use more chest and head movements to produce small bowing strokes than for larger ones encompassing several notes. This observation reveals an interesting motor pattern characterizing the cellists, since a *detached* playing mode seems to involve more visible postural compensation strategies, whereas those mobilized by the *legato* process would rely on finer corporeal synergies.

The geometrical features of COP ellipses averaged across all cellists (Fig. 4) suggest other aspects relative to the influence of postural constraints. Indeed, in the normal situation, the major part of the cellists' postural displacements comprises a lateral and left-oriented component. This orientation roughly coincides with the direction in which the score has been placed. From the figure, it can be noticed that the constrained situations seem to imply an anteroposterior reorientation of the postural displacements with a slight increase of the ellipse's flatness, whatever the playing mode. This tendency is observed graphically, even though one-way repeated measures ANOVAs carried out on the features of the ellipse orientation and the flatness didn't yield to significant differences between the postural conditions. Finally, we can notice an interesting effect of the playing modes in the behavior of the two mean postural ellipses corresponding to physically-constrained situations. Indeed, they seem to coincide in the *legato* playing mode, which suggests that the head movements do not seem to improve the postural compensation within this context. By contrast, they differ in the *detached* playing mode, which may signify a more complex repartition of the roles played by the chest and the head for ensuring the postural regulation within this context. Hereby, geometrical features of the COP ellipse reinforced the previous assumptions regarding the cellists' motor patterns adapted to a given playing mode.

6 Influence of Constraints on the Musical Expressivity

We here discuss the influence of the experimental conditions on the audio features relevant for the musical expressivity across all seven cellists.

6.1 Method

For each cellist and postural condition, we computed acoustic descriptors on each note of part four for a given playing mode (*legato/detached* at slow tempo). Since the cellists performed 3 repetitions in each condition, averaged data across repetitions were considered. This yielded a set of 4 postural conditions × 2 playing modes = 8 averaged data of acoustic descriptors for each cellist. This process was achieved at a single note level and at a beat level comprising a set of four notes corresponding to the strong beat of the first musical bar of part 4 of the score (Fig. 5).

a) **Mode Detached**

b) **Mode Legato**

Fig. 5. The notes selected for analyzing the influence of postural constraints on the musical expressivity: Two occurrences of E3 (circles) and a group of four consecutive notes (squares). These notes are extracted from the two playing modes : *(a)* **Detached** playing mode, *(b)* **Legato** playing mode

For each one of these contexts, we assessed the influence across all cellists for the factors *postural conditions* and *playing modes* on the mean acoustic descriptors, by carrying out two-way repeated measures ANOVAs and post-hoc pair-wise comparisons with the Honest Significant Difference (Tukey's HSD) procedure when possible.

6.2 Influence on One Note

The note selected for the analysis was the E3 highlighted by circles in (Fig. 5). This note occurs twice in part four, and corresponds to the first note of the strong beat within each musical bar. This note was frequently degraded across all the musicians, sounding more *harsh* and metallic in the fully-constrained postural condition, which suggests that this movement execution was hard to accomplish, even for professional cellists.

Analysis. We analyzed spectral and temporal feature evolutions for this note according to the playing mode and postural conditions, by performing a two-way repeated measures ANOVA on the averaged descriptors ATS and TRIratio (Sect. 4). This gave rise to 14 repetitions, corresponding to the 2 occurrences of E3, for each of the 7 cellists. In the end, we provided the ANOVA with a data set composed of 14 repetitions × 8 posture/mode combinations, for each averaged acoustic descriptor.

Results. The two-way repeated measures ANOVA carried out on the ATS descriptor, revealed significant effects of the postural condition, $F(3,39) = 3.39, p = .027^*$, and the playing mode, $F(1,13) = 9.73, p = .008^{**}$. Pair-wise post-hoc comparisons revealed that the Attack Slope was significantly lower in average for the fully-constrained postural condition than in the normal situation, whatever the playing mode (SCH = 0.245 and N = 0.3 with $p < .05^*$).

The two-way repeated measures ANOVA carried out on the TRIratio descriptor, revealed significant effects of the postural condition, $F(3,39) = 4.31, p = .010^*$, and the playing mode, $F(1,13) = 5.22, p = .039^*$. Pair-wise post-hoc comparisons revealed that the Tristimulus ratio was significantly higher in average for the fully-constrained postural condition than in the normal situation, whatever the playing mode (SCH = 0.33 and N = 0.27 with $p < .05^{**}$).

Discussion. The influence of the factors *postural condition* and *playing mode* on the sound descriptors can be observed Fig. 6. Interestingly, the figure reveals inverse effects of the postural condition on the temporal and spectral features of the note. Indeed, the TRIratio descriptor increases with the postural constraint whatever the playing mode, whereas the opposite effect is observed for the ATS descriptor. Furthermore, the results of ANOVA analyses revealed the statistical significance of these tendencies across all the cellists between the extreme postural conditions (normal and fully-constrained) for the two descriptors. Consequently, in the context of the note E3, the sound features are in average degraded with the postural constraint: Deprived of their postural freedom of movement, most cellists produce a shift in spectral energy towards higher frequencies (increase of the TRIratio), which results in a more metallic and *harsh* sound and apply a smoother attack (decrease of the ATS).

Note that for the *legato* playing mode, a stronger decrease of ATS and a stronger increase of the TRIratio can be observed than in the *detached* mode. This might be due to the large bowing movements used in the *legato* mode and the transition between E3 and the three following notes, that necessitates a quicker pulling of the bow on the E3 than in the *detached* mode. An interesting cross-effect of the factors also seems to emerge from Fig. 6. Indeed, for the fully constrained postural condition, the difference between the average descriptor values in the two playing modes decreases compared to the normal situation. This observation might reflect a global tendency of the constraint to limit the technical and expressive possibilities independently of the playing mode: Once immobilized, it becomes more difficult for most cellists to conserve the precise gestures needed to produce the required attack slope and the spectral features for any playing mode.

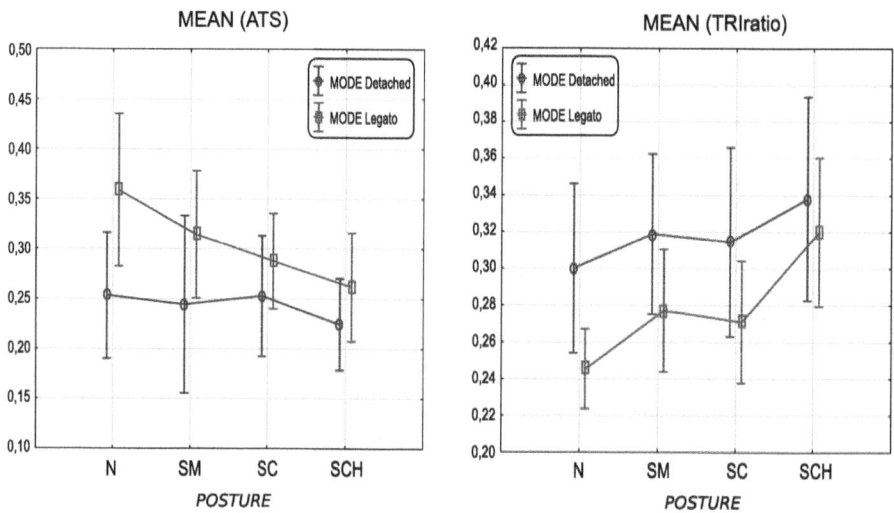

Fig. 6. Influence of the factors *postural condition* and *playing mode* on spectro-temporal acoustic descriptors analyzed for the note E3, and averaged across all the cellists: *(Left)* Temporal Attack Slope (ATS), *(Right)* Tristimulus ratio (TRIratio). The vertical bars represent confidence intervals at 95%

6.3 Analysis of Four Consecutive Notes

A group of four consecutive notes was extracted from the examined score part. These notes compose the strong beat of the first musical bar (Fig. 5). The rhythm is based on two patterns of dotted sixteenth note followed by a thirty-second note. This musical passage turned out to be particularly difficult to play in a correct way by most cellists when posturally constrained. For all the musicians, we frequently noticed a disorganization of the natural rhythm, as well as a certain decrease of tone colors in the sequence.

Analysis. We analyzed the evolution of rhythmic and spectral features for this sequence of four notes according to the playing mode and the postural conditions, by performing a two-way repeated measures ANOVA on averaged descriptors IOIdev and HSS. This gave rise to 7 repetitions, one for each cellist. In the end, we provided the ANOVA with a data set composed of 7 repetitions × 8 posture/mode combinations, for each acoustic descriptor.

Results. The two-way repeated measures ANOVA performed on the mean values of the IOIdev and the HSS descriptors over the four notes didn't reveal any significant effect of the factors. By contrast, when applied to their standard deviation over the four notes, the obtained results became interesting.

The two-way ANOVA carried out on the standard deviation of IOIdev descriptor, revealed a significant effect of the playing mode, $F(1,6) = 18.28, p = .005**$, but not of the postural condition, $F(3,18) = 2.47, p = .094$. The two-way ANOVA carried out on the standard deviation of IOIdev descriptor, revealed a significant effect of the playing mode, $F(1,6) = 18.28, p = .005**$, but not of the postural condition, $F(3,18) = 2.47, p = .094$. However, when processing two separate one-way repeated measures ANOVAs with postural condition as a factor for each playing mode, the effect of the postural condition was significant, $F(3,18) = 4.86, p = .011*$ in the *detached* playing mode. Further pair-wise post-hoc comparisons revealed that mean standard deviations of the IOIdev descriptor were significantly lower in the normal postural condition than in the fully-constrained one (N = 16 frames, SCH≈20 frames with $p < .05**$).

The two-way repeated measures ANOVA carried out on the standard deviation of the HSS descriptor, revealed significant effects of the postural condition, $F(3,18) = 4.56, p = .015*$, but not of the playing mode, $F(1,6) = 3.25, p = .12$. Pair-wise post-hoc comparisons showed that standard deviations of the HSS descriptor were significantly lower in average in the fully-constrained postural condition than in the normal condition, whatever the playing mode (N = 0.045 and N = 0.035 with $p < .05*$).

Discussion. The influence of the factors *postural condition* and *playing mode* on the standard deviation of rhythmical fluctuations can be observed in the left part of Fig. 7. Metrical deviations are known to be important for the musician's expressivity. In the normal playing situation, the cellists used certain timing variations to communicate their expressive interpretation of the musical structure along the four consecutive notes. The results of the ANOVA analyses revealed that in average, the cellists tended to produce more rhythmical fluctuations between the notes while being posturally fully-constrained (approximately 4 frames more (32 ms) around the mean of their IOI deviations), than in

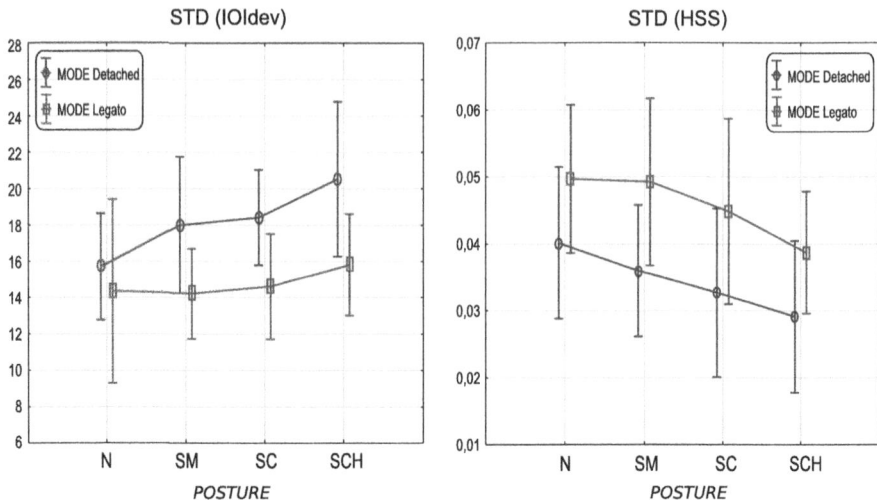

Fig. 7. Influence of the factors *postural condition* and *playing mode* on the standard deviation of rhythmical and spectral acoustic descriptors analyzed for four consecutive notes, and averaged across all the cellists: *(Left)* Inter-onset interval deviations (IOIdev), *(Right)* Harmonic Spectral Spread (HSS). The vertical bars represent confidence intervals at 95 %

the normal playing condition. It turned out to be primarily true and statistically significant for the *detached* playing mode across all the cellists. Interestingly, this result matches with a perceptual sensation of more disorganized and fragmented phrasing, as if the cellists had to struggle more with the rhythmic management when constrained. Consequently, the fully-constrained condition - and hereby the torso-head connection - might play a significant role to ensure phrasing fluidity, namely the coherency in the organization of rhythmical structural units. This deduction complies with the assumptions from the previous section, which suggested a more complex postural regulation mechanism between the chest and the head in the task of *detached* playing mode. The limitation of these natural motor pattern adjustments among cellists seems to affect the harmonious balance of their metric deviations.

The influence of the factors *postural condition* and *playing mode* on the standard deviation of spectral richness can be observed in the right part of Fig. 7. Like the IOI deviations, the timbre modulations play an important role in the expressivity of a musical performance. When freely playing, most cellists conferred an identity or a special color to each note of the sequence, which contributed to their expressivity. This feature isn't obvious to capture in a signal, because the relative amount of low or high frequencies doesn't explain alone why a tone is more colored and alive. For example, a note that sounds more *harsh* and metallic contains more energy in the high frequencies, but nevertheless does not have the ideal round color expected from a cello tone. This explains why the relative *brightness* (TRIratio) descriptor is unsuitable to capture the musical color variations. By contrast, the perceptual sensation of spectral richness within a note appears more clearly encoded in its spectral bandwidth (HSS), i.e. the spread of spectral energy distribution, since more partials are involved around the barycenter. In fact, the results of the ANOVA analyses on the HSS deviations revealed that in average, the cellists tended to significantly reduce the range of their spectral spread variations between the notes while being posturally fully-constrained, and whatever the playing mode. Besides, the *detached* mode globally presented lower spectral spread variations than the *legato* mode, which may indicate an increased difficulty in controlling the timbre color variations in a context of small bowing strokes than in the case of large ones encompassing several notes. Consequently, the torso-head connection might play a significant role to ensure the expressive modulations of timbral colors. Limiting these natural motor pattern adjustments seems to cause dull timbral colors, i.e. an impression of a more uniform musical interpretation, without life and relief.

7 Conclusions

In this paper, we investigated the influence of constraints on the postural displacements and the musical expressivity of 7 experimented cellists. The main effects of these constraints appeared on a specific part of the score, corresponding to rhythmical difficulties conceived as fast syncope shifts of the left hand. The global postural displacements were estimated through the geometrical features of a confidence ellipse encompassing the cellist's COP (Center Of Pressure) oscillations. The musical expressivity was assessed through spectro-temporal descriptors at a note level, and deviations of rhythmical and spectral descriptors at a chunk level of four consecutive notes.

The constraints caused different effects on the cellists' global postural displacements, according to the considered playing mode, *detached* and *legato*. Indeed, the musicians clearly felt more discomfort in the *detached* than in the *legato* playing mode. This tendency could be revealed by comparing their specific reactions to the three types of constraints between the playing modes. First, regarding the mentally static condition, they had in average increased difficulty to perform the task in the *detached* mode, since their mean COP areas were significantly lower than for the normal condition in the *legato* playing mode only. Then, regarding the two physically constrained conditions, they seemed in average struggling more in the *detached* mode, since their mean COP areas considerably increased, while remaining relatively stable in the *legato* mode and close to the values of the normal condition. In a nutshell, the cellists seemed to adopt more postural compensation strategies when playing *detached* than *legato*, to achieve the same tasks while constrained. Hereby, the chest and head coupling seems to be a more critical component of the cellist's posture while performing small bowing strokes on each note (*detached* mode) than larger ones encompassing several notes (*legato* mode).

The effects of the postural constraints were also clearly audible on given sound features for most cellists. Indeed, the musical expressivity declined considerably in average along the three postural constraints, with more or less sharp effects according to the playing modes. This is a tendency which could be revealed at different chunk levels of the score part. Regarding the note level, the first tone of the strong beat within each musical bar was frequently perceived as poor and deteriorated with less matter and a more metallic aspect for the fully-constrained situation. We demonstrated that this acoustic degradation corresponded to a dual spectro-temporal transformation, i.e. a decrease in attack slope of the note (ATS), combined with an increase in spectral energy in its upper partials (TRI-ratio). These results remained roughly valid for any playing mode across all the cellists. Moreover, we noticed a loss in the cellists' expressiveness between the playing modes in the fully-constrained situation, since the mean descriptor values ATS and TRIratio globally varied less between the playing modes than in the normal condition. Further investigations should enable to characterize this acoustic transformation more precisely by perceptual validations of the loss in sound quality perceived in this situation and currently qualified as *harshness* for bowing instruments. It would also be interesting to explore how this *harshness* phenomenon might correlate with its associated gestural features, like bowing velocity and pressure profiles, and postural descriptors.

Finally, we could highlight an influence of the postural constraints on the sound features extracted from a chunk of 4 notes. In particular, the fully-constrained condition caused a decrease of musical expressivity in the sequence, with more or less sharp effects according to the playing modes. This tendency was revealed as affecting the natural variations of rhythme and timbre color along the sequence. Regarding the rhythmic variations, the cellists unveiled in average increased difficulty to ensure fluidity and coherency of the phrasing in the fully constrained condition. Indeed, the standard deviation of the 4 successive varying note durations (IOIdev) turned out to be significantly higher in the *detached* mode for this constraint than in the normal condition. Within this context, most of the cellists couldn't prevent themselves from being disorganized and fragmenting the phrasing, a tendency that was coherent with the increase in area of their postural oscillations. Further investigations should thus enable to relate rhythmic deviations and postural features like the chest-head coupling. Regarding the variations of timbre color, the fully constrained condition reduced the timbre variations among cellists. Indeed, the standard deviation of the spectral spreads (HSS) of 4 successive notes turned out to be significantly lower in the constrained condition inducing a loss in timbre changes and color, whatever the playing mode. In addition, since the *detached* mode globally presented lower spectral spread variations than the *legato* mode, further investigations might reveal links between the loss in tone colors and the alteration of the cellists postural features like the chest-head coupling. In a nutshell, the cellists postural movements related to the chest-head coupling might be required to ensure coherent rhythmic deviations and timbre modulations.

Acknowledgements. This work is partly supported by the French National Research Agency and is part of the Sonimove project (ANR-14-CE24-0018).

References

1. Askenfelt, A., Guettler, K.: Bows and timbre-myth or reality. In: Proceedings of the International Symposium of Musical Acoustics, Perugia (2001)
2. Barthet, M., Kronland-Martinet, R., Ystad, S.: Improving musical expressiveness by time-varying brightness shaping. In: Kronland-Martinet, R., Ystad, S., Jensen, K. (eds.) CMMR 2007. LNCS, vol. 4969, pp. 313–336. Springer, Heidelberg (2008)
3. Cadoz, C., Wanderley, M.: Gesture-music. In: Wanderley, M., Battier, M. (eds.) Trends in Gestural Control of Music. IRCAM - Centre Pompidou, Paris (2000)
4. Chadefaux, D., Lecarrou, J.L., Wanderley, M.M., Fabre, B., Daudet, L.: Gestural strategies in the harp performance. Acta Acustica United Acustica **99**(6), 986–996 (2013)
5. Chudy, M., Carrillo, A.P., Dixon, S.: On the relation between gesture, tone production and perception in classical cello performance. In: Proceedings of Meetings on Acoustics, vol. 19, p. 035017. Acoustical Society of America (2013)
6. De Poli, G., Roda, A., Vidolin, A.: Note-by-note analysis of the influence of expressive intentions and musical structure in violin performance. J. New Music Res. **27**(3), 293–321 (1998)
7. DeAlcantera, P.: The alexander technique: a practical lesson. http://pedrodealcantara.com/practical-lesson/
8. Desmet, F., Nijs, L., Demey, M., Lesaffre, M., Martens, J.P., Leman, M.: Assessing a clarinet player's performer gestures in relation to locally intended musical targets. J. New Music Res. **41**(1), 31–48 (2012)
9. Hong, J.L.: Investigating expressive timing and dynamics in recorded cello performances. Psychol. Music **31**(3), 340–352 (2003)
10. Kim, H.G., Moreau, N., Sikora, T.: MPEG-7 Audio and Beyond: Audio Content Indexing and Retrieval. Wiley, Hoboken (2006)
11. Lartillot, O., Toiviainen, P.: A matlab toolbox for musical feature extraction from audio. In: Proceedings of the International Conference on Digital Audio Effects, pp. 237–244 (2007)
12. Leman, M.: Embodied Music Cognition and Mediation Technology. MIT Press, Cambridge (2008)
13. Peeters, G.: A large set of audio features for sound description (similarity and classification) in the cuidado project. Technical report, IRCAM (2004)
14. Pollard, H.F., Jansson, E.V.: A tristimulus method for the specification of musical timbre. Acta Acustica United Acustica **51**(3), 162–171 (1982)
15. Thompson, M.R., Luck, G.: Exploring relationships between pianists' body movements, their expressive intentions, and structural elements of the music. Musicae Sci. **16**(1), 19–40 (2012)
16. Visi, F., Coorevits, E., Miranda, E., Leman, M.: Effects of Different Bow Stroke Styles on Body Movements of a Viola Player: An Exploratory Study. Michigan Publishing, University of Michigan Library, Ann Arbor (2014)
17. Wanderley, M.M.: Quantitative analysis of non-obvious performer gestures. In: Wachsmuth, I., Sowa, T. (eds.) GW 2001. LNCS (LNAI), vol. 2298, pp. 241–253. Springer, Heidelberg (2002)
18. Wanderley, M.M., Vines, B.W., Middleton, N., McKay, C., Hatch, W.: The musical significance of clarinetists' ancillary gestures: an exploration of the field. J. New Music Res. **34**(1), 97–113 (2005)
19. Winold, H., Thelen, E.: Coordination and control in the bow arm movements of highly skilled cellists. Ecol. Psychol. **6**(1), 1–31 (1994)

Musical Meter, Rhythm and the Moving Body: Designing Methods for the Analysis of Unconstrained Body Movements

Luiz Naveda[1(✉)], Isabel C. Martínez[2], Javier Dameson[2],
Alejandro Pereira Ghiena[2], Romina Herrera[2],
and Manuel Alejandro Ordás[2]

[1] School of Music - State University of Minas Gerais, Belo Horizonte, Brazil
luiznaveda@gmail.com
[2] Laboratorio para el Estudio de la Experiencia Musical, Facultad de Bellas Artes, Universidad Nacional de La Plata, La Plata, Buenos Aires, Argentina
isabelmartinez@fba.unlp.edu.ar

Abstract. The process of retrieving meaningful information from rhythm responses to music imposes several methodological challenges. For one side, the indivisible connection between body actions and the musical action confines the musical phenomenon in a closed action-perception cycle. For another side, the attempts to examine internalized rhythm descriptions require a sort of action and body movements are the natural medium for musical actions. In this study, we propose strategies for the analysis of movement responses that are capable of retrieving emergent rhythmic and metrical structures encoded in free movements, which are less constrained by experimental designs and less dependent on methodological assumptions. The first technique processes zero-crossing events across velocity patterns in order to retrieve the changes of directions across metric levels. The second technique uses local accumulation of instantaneous velocity in order to describe the profiles of metric engagement abstracted from the morphology of the movement trajectories. The techniques help to trace comparisons and build new representations of embodied metrical structures. The paper discusses the possibilities and new perspectives using case studies of free spontaneous movement responses to Argentinian chacarera and Afro-Brazilian samba music.

Keywords: Movement analysis · Rhythm · Meter · Embodiment

1 Introduction

The musical theory the supports the study of musical meter and rhythm has been generally successful in predicting and explaining a relevant part of musical experiences, specially in the context of Western music. The algorithmic implementation of its basic principles have supported a number of technological developments for music, including technologies for music information retrieval, applications for music performance, media discovery and even new music styles (e.g.: electronic music). The relevance of this set of knowledge manifests inside every dance club, musical hall or concert where real people feel and move their bodies in ways that are similar to what is predicted in the theories of musical meter.

Although modern approaches to the study of musical rhythm and meter seem to inherit the formalism from the sciences, an important part of theory of musical meter has been based on "rules of preference", pre-defined in referential texts (such as [1], discussed in [2]). These set of principles, though effective in many cases, are assumed to govern metrical and rhythmical structures in music. However, there is no widespread consensus on how they emerge in the cognition and the causal relationships that lead to the performance or perception of metrical categories [3]. Recent evidences indicate that rhythm and meter models emerge from symmetrical structures, hierarchies and structures [4–6] and that we are able to perceive and elaborate on them [7–9] from early age [10, 11] to adulthood. However, it is also known that the actual structures of musical rhythms, from which tempo and meter categories emerge, are extremely variable and complex [10]. Such a level of dissociation between what are the actual rhythm events being performed and the model of metrical structure may explain, for instance, why attempts to define a musical beat frequently involve references to body movements [12], such as movement of the foot or hands. Whether periodic body movements result from metaphors and schemes of rhythm parsed in the auditory system or emerge from the interdependence between music cognition and the human motor system, it is a problem that still needs to be better approached from a pool of different disciplines. The problem is that we still approach a diversity of musical cultures and phenomena with the same set of general rules designed to comply to a very specific cultural domain.

The excessive dependency of the studies on musical meter and rhythm on evidences collected from "tapping" experiments[1] seems to be part of the same problem. Although most of the musical activities in culture are accompanied by spontaneous body movement or dance, empirical approaches opted to rely on a narrowed version of the bodily movement, that is explicitly controlled and mostly absent from the musical or choreographic context itself (e.g.: someone being oriented to tap the finger on a table, on the beat). The reduction of bodily rhythmic behavior into to a set of repetitive tasks realized or collected from a single body action may represent a dangerous bias towards a superficial assessment of the cognitive aspects of rhythm. Such dependency and the lack of interaction with ethnomusicological reports corrupt the generalization of findings and reproduce a mind-body dichotomy that is inconsistent with the actual understanding of human cognition: the body as a channel to the musical mind versus the the body as an integral part of the musical mind. Does musical rhythm and meter are really limited by the sound medium? Can we really proceed in the development of musical theory by only looking to music as sound or scores?

1.1 Hidden Assumptions in Modeling Rhythm

Part of the problems reported here may be a result of a tacit understanding of the musical knowledge as a knowledge about the musical sound. The multimodal, embodied nature

---

[1] In the methodological perspective of "tapping" experiments we include not only hand tapping but other simple isochronous time event tasks such clicking or speaking on the beat.

of the musical knowledge imposes methodological challenges to the organization of the information from sound and other sources, such as body movement and image. Even the connection between body actions and the musical action itself seems inaccessible: It confines the musical phenomenon in a closed action-perception cycle in which the subjects' responses to music are realized by means of actions, but actions are mediated by body movements hardwired to mechanisms of perception. Additionally, body movements in response to music may not be easily recorded, detected or even perceived by the subjects. Not enough, the specificity of subjects' cultural background, their cultural habits and the environment drastically interfere in the motivation or obstruction of movements. In summary, accessing musical understanding through accurate categories of perception remains a problematic issue for music researchers in the field.

Prior the emergence of the theories of embodiment [13, 14] and enaction [15, 16], the separation between musical mind, auditory and motor domains would not be considered a problem. The human cognition was interpreted according to action-perception and mind-body perspectives and the musical knowledge was mostly considered as knowledge of the mind. Most of the tapping literature or the general theories of rhythm and meter were assembled from results that partly reflected mind-body dualisms in the experimental design. Tapping would be considered a channel to mental models and mental models would fulfill the necessary representations of meter or rhythm, without the need of accessing other body responses. Until recently, even the motor theories used to approach human movement were organized according to a generalized motor program theory [17], which generally conceives the human movement action as a result of a mental planning and evaluation (further questioned by dynamic system approaches, as described in [18]). In some extent, the complex rhythm engagement of the body would represent a challenging task without actual possibilities of movement capture. Although it is comprehensible that experimental designs were forced to comply with a set of assumptions that simplify measurements, we still reproduce methods that shape results according pre-defined methodologies imported from sciences almost without adaptation. Examples of the such assumptions include:

1. **Assumptions of metrical and pulse isochrony** - The assumption that subjects recognize periodicities of metrical levels as a sequence of evenly spaced metrical accents in time.
2. **Assumptions of tapping efficiency** - The assumption that inter-onset-intervals collected from tapping represent a reliable account of rhythmical and metrical structure, and would efficiently reflect rhythm engagement.
3. **Assumptions of hand preference** - The assumption that hands, wrist or fingers are efficient mediators of the rhythm responses and that other body parts would not add further information.
4. **Assumptions of unimodal experience** - The assumption that rhythm engagement is expressed and perceived as a single channel of events distributed in time.
5. **Assumptions of homogeneity of variances and independence** – the widespread application of statistic central measures to rhythm observations covertly imply the assumption that measurements that deviate from the mean come from random disturbances (**homogeneity of variances**) and that measurements are not related to each other (**independence**).

Although the concatenation of assumptions and limitations should have a direct impact on the generalization of findings, most of the literature rarely acknowledge the impacts of such constrains (see [19] for a discussion on the topic). More precisely, assumptions generally indicate a choice for a specific experimental design build for testing hypotheses, which should be ideally supported by previous exploratory evidence. The choice for an experimental design strongly based on control of the variables, limitation of the universe and isolation of sources of bias, often reflects an epistemological view where the quest for numerical evidence takes over the quest for better representations of the complexity of real-world phenomena. By ignoring such level of complexity, a great part of the validity of the experiment is decreased, which impacts on subsequent applications.

1.2 Definition of the Problem

Less control in the experimental design results in more analytical complexity but more external validity [19]. Due to the constraints of traditional statistical analyses, the limitations and assumptions discussed above strongly influence the definition of the subject's tasks. The shift to a different method for capturing and analyzing data demands a set of methods that are able to capture events produced by unconstrained bodily actions. A move to an exploratory study of rhythm would require a less restrictive task control and methods that detect underlying rhythm structures that are not explicitly instructed in the task procedures. How free and spontaneous movement responses to musical rhythm could contribute to the understanding of rhythm mechanisms? How to uncover rhythm events or metrical descriptors in unconstrained movement responses to music?

In this study, we discuss two strategies that aim at identifying metrical accents and rhythm structures in free movement responses to music. The strategies are designed to describe and evaluate the occurrence of kinematic events in the morphology and dynamics of "free" movement trajectories in the 3D space. The events are organized according a representation of metrical structure imposed by the music stimuli. Our main motivation is to provide alternatives to the typical methods applied to rhythm analysis using less restrictive experimental setups.

In the next section, we provide a brief overview of previous approaches in the field of study. In the following sections, we describe the mechanisms of two methods, which are illustrated by case studies.

2 Previous Work

The vast majority of the empirical approaches to musical movement prioritize task control in the design of experiments. Therefore, the literature on methods to analyze spontaneous or free movement responses to musical rhythm tends to be very limited. Researchers opt to invest time and resources in a predictable analytical process by shaping the tasks to an experimental design that isolates bias and complexity, including isolating creative and artistic complexity as a form of bias. However, few exceptions thrive to cope with the complexity of design and analysis in the attempt to approximate the experimental approaches to real-world phenomena.

For example, Toiviainen and colleagues [20] approached the problem of spontaneous full body movements to music by means of a selection of numerical methods. PCA was used to detect movement primitives in spontaneous movement across body parts and subjects. The analysis of mechanical energy and kinematic periodicity revealed associations of metrical levels to specific body parts and the tendency to reflect tactum levels in the vertical axis. Zentner and Eerola [21] studied rhythmic behavior in preverbal infants in a context where infants could not easily reproduce tasks, and spontaneous responses would be more reliable. They found that human infants spontaneously display "rhythmical patterns with a regular beat, and isochronous drumbeats", which was not expected for this age. Styns and colleagues [22] analyzed walking movements while listening to music. Although walking movements differ from spontaneous movements, the relevant spontaneous response to music may still be present in the data. The study suggests that real musical stimuli (in contrast to synthetic or metronomic pulse) induce more walking activity and a number of indications of a resonance effects (which takes into account the typical 2 Hz frequency often reported for walking cycles). Demos and colleagues [23] studied spontaneous coordination of movements with music and a partner. The study shows a preference for social coordination even when musical stimulus is present.

The majority of empirical studies that access rhythm responses seems to rely on discrete actions that are explicitly instructed and generally involve a movement action applied to a surface (e.g.: a sensor), such as hand tapping or percussion. The inter-onset-interval (IOI) of the successive actions provides a measurement of the period of repetition, used to realize comparisons and processing. An extensive tapping literature gives support this type of approach (see [24] for a review), which seems to be the most straightforward way to describe rhythm and metrical structure. Other attempts to uncover periodicity in spontaneous movement use linear methods based on autocorrelation such as the ones found in [20, 21] or non-linear methods such as Periodicity Transforms [25] as applied in [26], for the analysis of traditional popular dances.

So far, the literature is unclear about specific methods that cope with the unpredictable trends in spontaneous responses to music. Measures of periodicity or frequency (e.g.: autocorrelation, FFT) may not reflect the nature of metrical engagement (c.f. subjects do not rely or are not able to analyze sinusoidal frequency components of their actions). The discrete detection of movement events and inter-onset times still provide the best descriptor for rhythm events. Continuous features such as the estimation of physical forces applied to the limbs may also contribute to describe metrical engagement. Velocity, as a component that follows the dynamics of mechanical energy, may provide a clue of the forces applied to spontaneous movements, as used in [20, 21].

3 Methodology

Spontaneous movement patterns impose extrinsic and intrinsic problems for the interpretation and analysis. The extrinsic characteristics of movement recordings registered in 3D Cartesian space do not provide a clear indication of what could be considered a rhythm accent in the movement trajectories. The dynamics of motion descriptors (displacement, velocity, acceleration) overlap each other in several levels of information and possible events that do not provide a clear indication of what could be considered a rhythm accent. Simple detection of changes in the trajectories results in meaningfulness data because trajectories are infected by the interaction between the coordinate system of the motion capture and the subject's movement. Unintentional changes in movement profiles might interfere in the results by inserting false-positives in places and orientations imposed by coordinate systems of motion capture devices. In short, simple detection of changes in movement profiles oriented in the motion captures coordinate system will result in unreliable data.

The intrinsic characteristics of movement profiles are even less clear. We cannot access intentionality of movement actions: one cannot assume that a change in velocity or direction is deliberate, intentional or if it reflects a reaction to a stimuli or a musical metaphor translated into movement. In the context of unconstrained movement and spontaneous movements, the lack of detailed instructions imposes a considerable level of uncertainty and variability to the performance. Variability spreads not only across events in time but also influences the positioning, directionality and variations of the performance. Challenges in this context involve the interpretation of variability and isolation of sources of bias. The use of extensive recording and strategies to improve multiple repetitions of the task (e.g.: single subject analysis in [27]) which provide higher sampling necessary to uncover tendencies in the data.

In this study we present two features that contribute to representation of metrical properties in the context of less restrictive tasks in response to music: **Level of accumulative velocity (LAV)** and **Density of directional changes** (DDC). The methods take as the starting point the trajectory of points or rigid bodies in the time domain, registered in the 3D Cartesian representation space by means of a motion capture system (mocap). In what follows, we specify the elements behind the algorithms.

3.1 Feature 1 – Level of Accumulative Velocity (LAV)

The subjective notion of "effort" applied to human movement seems to be an important component in the associations between body movement and music. The main theories of dance such as the Laban theory and analysis [28] involve references to effort and weight. In the context of spontaneous responses to music, the choice for the representations motion descriptor fulfills the demand for a continuous feature that expresses the subjective effort deployed by the subject.

The mechanical concept of physical "work" would be the best candidate to express subjective effort but the actual procedures to calculate it can be misleading due to biomechanical constraints [29]. The mechanical energy and its components – kinetic and potential energy – might be also good candidates because their variation relates to the concept of mechanical work. However, the calculation of mechanical energy from 3D trajectories involves a number of impractical assumptions and parameterizations (such as the measurement of the mass of body parts). A practical solution is to rely on the simple relationship between the kinetic energy and the dynamics of the instantaneous velocity. More specifically, kinetic energy (*K*) is calculated by the following formula, where *m* stands for mass and *v for* velocity.

$$K = \frac{1}{2}mv^2 \qquad (1)$$

In order to provide a metrical account of the velocity in the spontaneous movement to music, we opted to organize the profile of accumulative velocities across the structure of the musical meter, annotated in the stimuli. In short, we visualize velocity according to "metrical segments", which provides a repetitive representation of classes of the musical meter imposed by the stimuli. Metrical segments are time sequences annotated using the models of meter used in the annotation. For example, if the model conveys only beats (tactus), the metrical segments will provide a window of 1 beat around the time point of every beat. Figure 1 displays the schematic view of the process. First the time points of the metrical elements are selected. They provide a temporal window (±1/2 of the metrical segment) in which the analysis will take place. Second, all values of instantaneous velocity inside the temporal window are accumulated and registered. The process extends until the end of the movement segment.

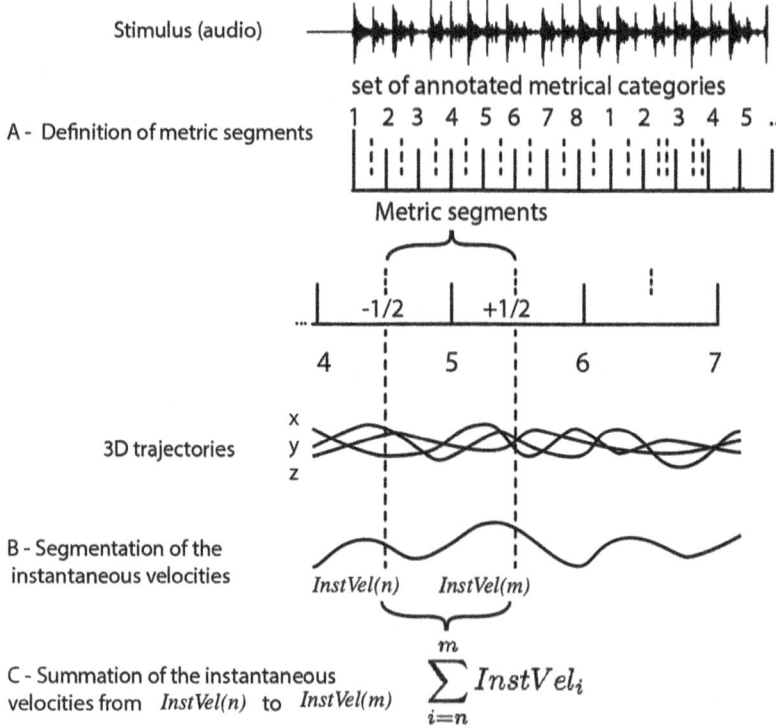

Fig. 1. Process of calculation of the velocity weightings for each metrical level.

The accumulation of the velocity patterns across the metrical positions in the stimuli generates a distribution formed by all measurements of accumulation of velocities in the metric levels. However, these levels do not directly reflect the effort but the dynamics of the energy accumulated at the positions of metric levels. Higher velocity patterns indicate that the limbs are moving across trajectories and not necessary inducing the sensation of physical effort. Lower velocity accumulation may indicate that the limbs are in rest in the referred metric positions or in process of deceleration (which would produce substantial effort). The occurrences of changes in velocity patterns may (high-to-low or low-to-high) are better indications of the deployment of physical effort.

3.2 Feature 2 - Density of Directional Changes (DDC)

Differently from traditionally controlled tasks (such as tapping), free spontaneous movement responses to music exhibit a great diversity of trajectory shapes, changes of orientation and changes of direction. Sharp changes of the direction of the trajectory in orthogonal directions (axes) might be the only cue to access deliberate musical metrical accents in the shape of movement trajectories. However, the coordinate system imposed by motion capture devices is not natural and does not provide a reliable and comprehensive root system of directional components used by the subject. For example, the orientation of axes defined in the calibration of the mocap system may not be aligned to the axes of the movement trajectories of the hand, which may be changed spontaneously by the subject to any direction. Approaching the variation of the orientation of the limbs with thresholds does not seem an elegant solution because it would involve the definition of constants (thresholds) that are not described in the literature. Our solution to uncover meaningful directional changes involves four steps (illustrated in Fig. 2):

(A) First, we reconstruct the orientation system by means of a linear transformation processed with Principal Component Analysis (PCA) applied to the whole trajectories of one point. It practically results in the linear transformation of the three-dimensional vectors into components that best explain the variance in the trajectories.
(B) After the PCA process, the changes of direction in each component are detected by detecting the zero-crossings in the first order time derivative (cf. velocity).
(C) The estimation of time positions between the time points of the zero crossings and the beginning of metrical structure (8 beat in the figure) allows the representation of a histogram of changes of direction across metric levels.
(D) The histogram represents the density estimation of directional changes at each metrical element.

The word density was chosen not only to reflect the construction of an estimate (a density estimation) but also to acknowledge the possibility of different, non temporal annotation categories, including qualitative or quantitative annotations in space (otherwise, in our particular case, the probability would be better defined as a frequency).

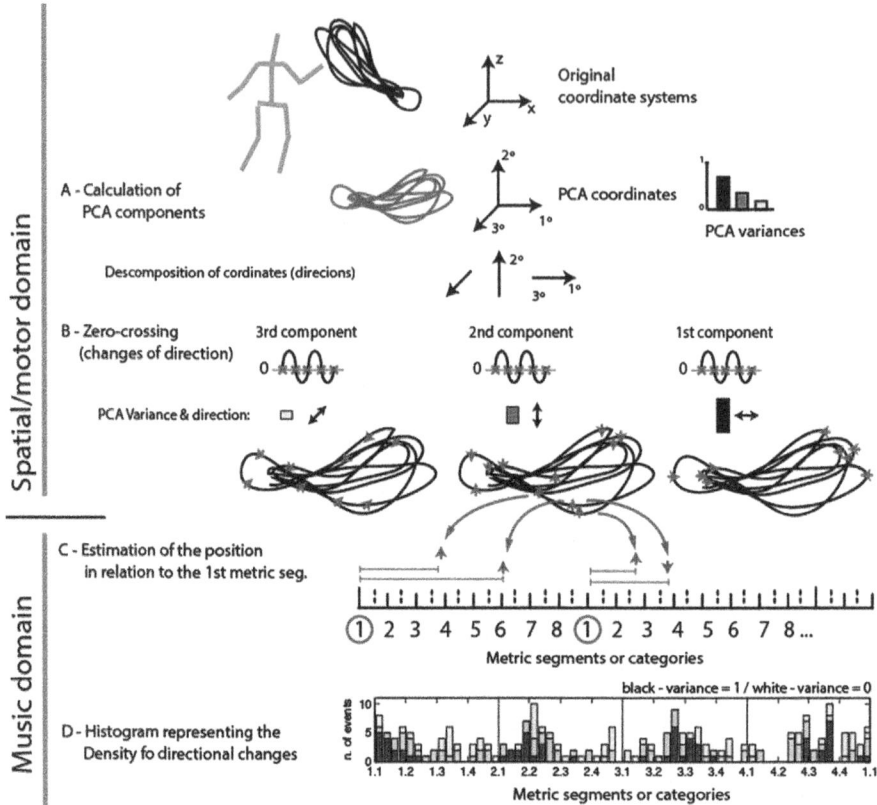

Fig. 2. Schematic process of the processing stages for the feature detection.

Note that the detection of directional changes is applied to all three PCA components, which reflects the transformation of 3D trajectory vectors. They represent orthogonal changes of directions in respect to the coordinate system that best represents the variance of the data. In other words, the method collects changes of directions organized across orthogonal axes (or directions) that best represent the morphology of the movement sequence as expressed by the shape of the trajectories.

However, the variances of the trajectories are not necessarily equal. For example, the concentration of the PCA variances in only one component indicates that the movement profiles are organized as a "line". Variances equally distributed in two components indicate a "planar" morphology, while equally distributed variances across the 3 components indicate "spherical" explorations of the space. The different variances also imply that directional changes in the first component (higher variance), for example, denote changes in a component that is more important, visible and variable than the others. Figure 5 shows the density of directional changes for the left-hand of a subject and its respective trajectories in the 3D Cartesian space. The variances indicate a large prevalence of the first component, reflecting the line-like shape of the movements.

3.3 Complementary Nature of the Features

The features proposed here provide two complementary descriptions of the metrical and rhythmic characteristics of spontaneous free movements, apart from kinematic and dynamic summaries describing the structure of the trajectories. The **Level of accumulative velocity** helps to evaluate the effort deployed across the metrical structure. Its profile and variability across metric levels indicates when the subject engages into energetic profiles of movement and how they vary in relation to the cycles of metric levels. The **Density of directional changes** complements the image of metrical engagement by indicating the density of discrete events in the metrical structure. Density of events and continuous energy profiles provide information to compare kinematic and kinetic cues, respectively. The following section shows the application of the methods to a small set of case studies.

4 Case Studies

The case studies demonstrate the use of the proposed methods by means of examples of spontaneous free movement responses to music. The recordings involve the tracking of movements synchronized with musical stimuli. For illustrative purposes, only 2 subjects were used to illustrate the methods. The procedures and details are briefly described below.

4.1 Procedures

The motion capture recordings were realized with an Optitrack system (Natural Point) composed of 8 infrared cameras and 14 infrared markers placed at the torso, head, left and right hands of the subjects. The musical stimuli were composed of three clicks (used to synchronize motion capture recordings) followed by excerpts of samba (Brazil) and chacarera (Argentina) rhythm patterns. The subjects were trained musicians and dancers.

The recordings involved two main parts: In the first part the subjects were asked to test free movement strategies in relation to the music. In the second part the subject was instructed to chose one movement strategy and repeat it for 60 s. The recordings were realized in Brazil and Argentina using the same setup. Argentinians and Brazilians participated in the experiment. All the subjects declared their consent and filled in questionnaires about their experience. Further details of each subject will be described in the analyses.

4.2 Case Study – Level of Accumulative Velocity

Figure 3 shows the distributions of levels of accumulative velocity across the categories of metric model, which are modeled as a 4 beats × 4 sixteenth-note levels (16 metrical elements). For the music style samba, used for stimulus, this model represents 2 musical bars (2/4). The data involves 12 repetitions collected from the recordings. Note that the box-plot graphs are not used to infer statistical significance (such as ANOVA) but to demonstrate the distributions and variance of the data.

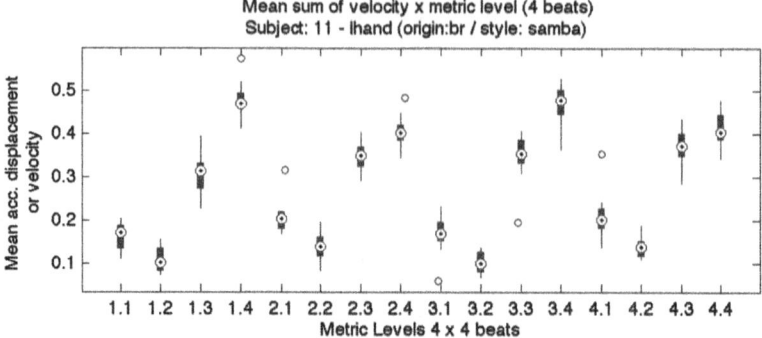

Fig. 3. Levels of accumulated velocity for a Brazilian subject, left hand. Stimulus: samba music (N = 12).

The example shown in Fig. 3 illustrates how velocity patterns across metrical levels reveal more than simply metrical periodicity. The subject exhibit peaks of velocity at every 4th 16th-note and seems to stop abruptly at every beat (following and subsequent release). This periodic beat pattern also seems to be accompanied by a marginal variation of peak velocity every 2 beats. The results show the contrast between symmetry of the models of meter and the embodiment of metrical structures. As seen here, a typical beat periodicity unfolds in the form of asymmetries that may reflect individual, non-generalizable specific ontology of meter for this style.

Figure 4 shows the second example reproducing the same type of graphical representation, in this case for an Argentinian subject. The stimulus was a typical chacarera sequence. Chacarera style involves a percussion set often accompanied by other instruments. It is rooted in a 12/8 bar, displayed in the graph.

The first characteristic revealed in the graph is the variability encoded in the distributions for this subject. Variability represents two possibilities: the lack of clear relationships between velocity patterns and metrical structure or hidden relationships inside the distributions. The interdependence between the samples is acknowledged by

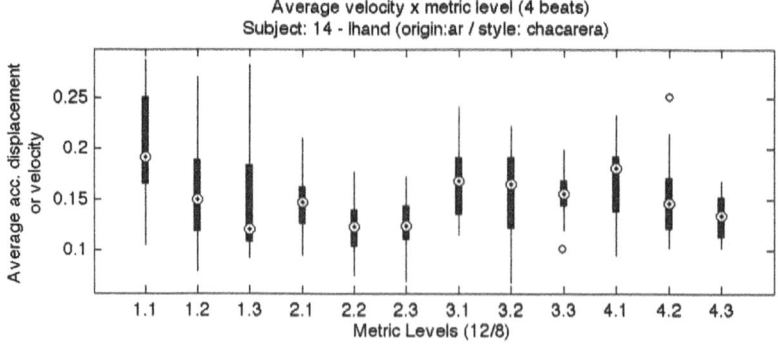

Fig. 4. Levels of accumulated velocity for an Argentinian subject, left hand. Stimulus: chacarera music (N = 12).

exposing variability and tendency to normality at each metric level. The metrical engagement implies relationships that may induce a change or repetition of patterns across the repetition of metric cycles. This relationship – a metrical relationship – encodes interdependencies across distant metrical segments as much as interdependencies across subsequent segments.

Other interesting explanations may illustrate how complex the analysis of subjective engagement to musical meter can be. The standard deviation from 1.1 to 1.3 indicates that the first three 8th-notes may configure a metrical "region" without clear metrical engagement, pattern or metrical characteristics. After the first half beat the velocity pattern stabilizes into a less variable sequence, slightly stressing the 3rd beat. In this case, metrical engagement may be rendered not in terms of position or velocity formulas but in terms of more flexible or more constant velocity patterns. Another characteristic is that the changes of velocities seem to be less abrupt than the example in Fig. 3.

4.3 Case Study - Density of Directional Changes (DDC)

Figure 5a and b illustrate the results of the calculation of Density of directional changes. Figure 5a shows the trajectories placed in relation to their original orientation.

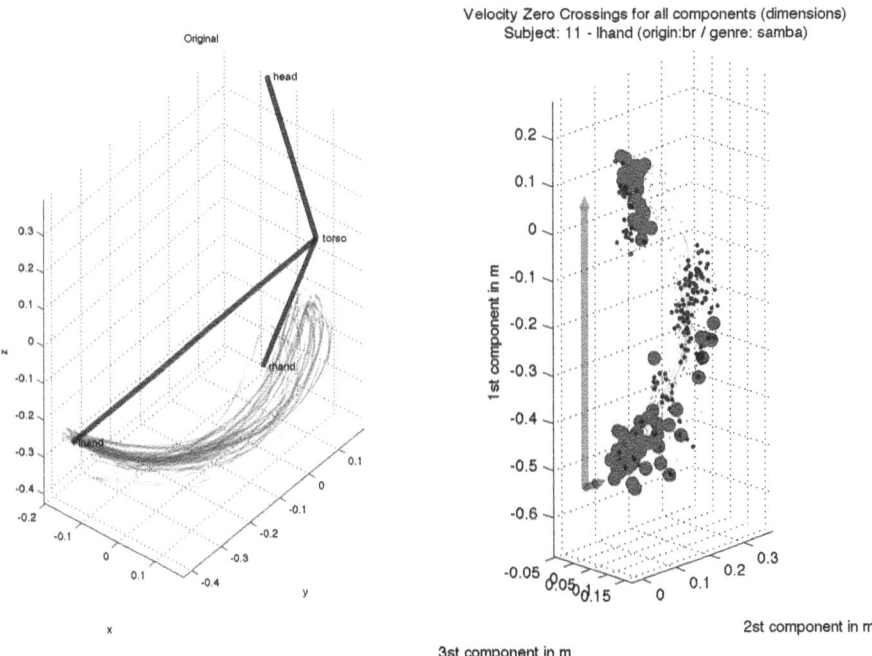

Fig. 5. (a) Representation in the 3-dimensional space showing the trajectories before the PCA analysis and the stick figure representation connection between head, torso and hands. 5(b) Representation in the 3-dimensional space showing the trajectories and events of change of direction in the coordinates after the PCA transformation. The size of the markers indicates the magnitude of the variance related to each component. The size of the arrows is proportional to the variances: 1st component = 0.9, 2nd component = 0.08, 3rd component 0.007.

After the PCA processing, in Fig. 5b, the components act like a rotation of the original coordinates, which places the principal component (higher variance) in the vertical dimension. Figure 5b also shows the metrical events – changes of direction – calculated using zero-crossing processing. As seen in the figure, the strong concentration of the variances in the first component (variance = 0.9) reflects the "line-like" shape that characterizes this example. As such, changes of direction in the principal component are stronger and are likely to indicate more significant and intentional metric accents.

Figure 6 shows the histograms of directional changes for each component (graphs 1 to 3), across the categories of metrical levels, global histogram (graph 4) and its respective variances. The variance of each component must be taken into account for the proper interpretation of the histograms. The third graph shows that the principal component accounts for 90 % of the variance. This component is responsible for the axis that shapes the trajectories in a kind of "line". Regardless the shape of the trajectories, the histogram of events in the 3rd graph indicates the affirmation of beat levels. The density of events close to the beat indicates that changes of direction are always situated around beat or slightly delayed. Although metrical isochrony and

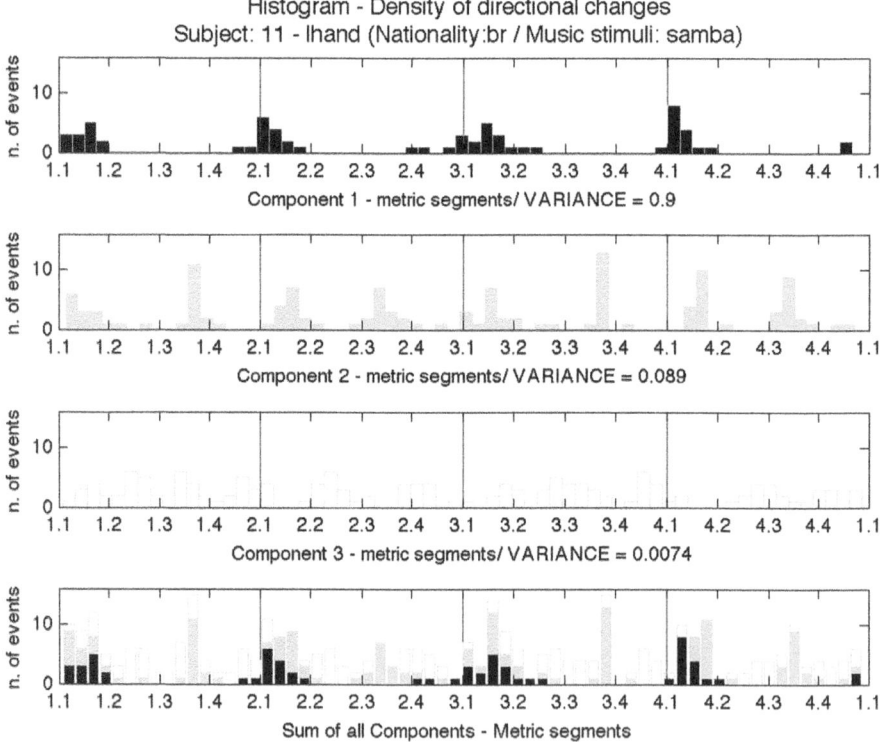

Fig. 6. Histograms displaying the density of events or changes of direction for each component (graphs 1 to 3) and global histogram showing the sum of the three histograms (graph 4). The histogram comprises 64 bins, which represents, for the actual stimuli, a metrical definition of 1/16 beat segment (4/64).

symmetry are important characteristics discussed in the theory of musical meter, the signalization of the beat level (tactus) and the temporal precision is not symmetrical and flexible. Perhaps controlled experimental tasks (e.g.: follow the beat) induces temporal precision, while the spontaneity of unconstrained movements reflects a more diverse perspective of metric engagement. The interpretation of the global histogram must be realized with caution, because events resulted from components with lower variances have the same unitary contribution of the components with higher variance.

5 General Discussion

The proposals in this study aim at developing alternative methods that provide meaningful descriptors of the rhythm encoded in unconstrained movement responses to music. As discussed in the introduction, traditional methods used to access rhythmic engagement in the literature were developed to comply with strict experimental control of variables. Our attempt is to discuss and propose alternatives to exploratory research that precedes the development and the test of hypothesis in the field. The two features presented here may help to pursue proper elements to build better controlled experiments and to grasp the qualities of rhythm engagement across a larger variety of contexts.

The change of experimental perspective in this study demands new forms of analyses that are able to collect meaningful information without limiting the emergent properties of the phenomena of rhythm. Emergent properties of musical movements may include a number of characteristic blocked by previous assumptions in highly controlled experiments, such as variability in timing, multi-level metrical engagement, uncertainty and variability as a signalization of metrical cycles among others, already discussed in the introduction.

It has been widely reported that the human motor system is characterized by variability [30] and that variability performs important functions that help the motor adaptation to contexts and motor efficiency. The dynamic system hypothesis [17], for example, sees the variability in the motor domain as a key to promote fast adaptation to unpredictable demands of the contexts. Such perspective sheds light to the typical musical or choreographical tasks that musicians and dancers are subjected to in a number of real-world musical tasks. Variability in dance and music may provide the necessary adaptations to cope with the performance, improvisation and group playing. Variability, as an artistic value can also be responsible to trigger creative solutions, as often noticed musicians working with improvisation forms.

The kind of features presented here present some advantages for the analysis and experimental design related to rhythm analysis:

(1) The analysis does not depend on discrete marker positions: subjects are free to realize movements according to the limitation of the capturing method.

(2) Rhythm movements are not significantly changed by task procedure.

(3) Tasks do not depend on instructions that shape the attentional focus of the subject. Ex: Subjects are not required to follow a perceived beat.

(4) Results can be easily accumulated across repetitions in time and subjects.

(5) Temporal and kinematic variability can be described and incorporated into the results and modeling.

However, a different perspective of assumptions also impacts on the summaries or statistical procedures involved in the analysis of datasets. The lack of control of some variables implies that most of the results cannot be interpreted using traditional statistics. Data visualization techniques, clustering, machine learning approaches may improve the reporting of results in large data-sets. Simple replication of experiments as suggested in [19] or Single subject analysis [27] could offer solution to the modeling of data using robust statistical methods.

The case studies presented in this work show that the features proposed provide a richer representation of the phenomena as continuous, spatial or musical representation. The characteristics of data indicate tendencies across measurements that reveal idiosyncratic perspectives of metrical engagement. The results show relevant individual characteristics that may contribute to a micro-analytical perspective of meter in the form of individual representation of metrical images.

Future work may be realized in several aspects of the techniques. Large datasets of movement recordings can be analyzed in the search for richer models of metrical engagement. The calculation of features can be improved to adapt weighting options, normalization and statistical description of the datasets. Features can also be implemented for real-time processing for interactive systems. Novel graphical visualizations may help to uncover hidden patterns in large datasets.

Acknowledgements. The author Luiz Naveda gratefully acknowledges FAPEMIG (Research Support Foundation of Minas Gerais) for the financial support (projects CHE - APQ-02689-15 and CHE - BIP-00223-16).

References

1. Lerdahl, F., Jackendoff, R., Jackendoff, R.S.: A Generative Theory of Tonal Music. MIT Press, Cambridge (1996)
2. Naveda, L., Leman, M.: Hypotheses on the choreographic roots of the musical meter: a case study on Afro-Brazilian dance and music. In: X Encuentro de Ciencias Cognitivas de la Música. SACCoM-Sociedad Argentina para las Ciencias Cognitivas de la Música (2011)
3. Naveda, L., Leman, M.: Hypotheses on the choreographic roots of the musical meter: a case study on Afro-Brazilian dance and music. In: X Encuentro de Ciencias Cognitivas de la Música. SACCoM-Sociedad Argentina para las Ciencias Cognitivas de la Música (2011)
4. London, J.: Hearing in Time: Psychological Aspects of Musical Meter. Oxford University Press, Oxford (2004)
5. Fitch, W.T., Rosenfeld, A.J.: Perception and production of syncopated rhythms. Music Percept. **25**, 43–58 (2007)
6. Palmer, C., Krumhansl, C.L.: Mental representations for musical meter. J. Exp. Psychol. Hum. Percept. Perform. **16**, 728 (1990)
7. Fitch, W.T.: Rhythmic cognition in humans and animals: distinguishing meter and pulse perception. Front. Syst. Neurosci. **7**, 1–16 (2013)
8. Phillips-Silver, J., Trainor, L.J.: Hearing what the body feels: auditory encoding of rhythmic movement. Cognition **105**, 533–546 (2007)
9. Temperley, D.: The Cognition of Basic Musical Structures. MIT Press, Cambridge (2004)

10. Hannon, E.E., Johnson, S.P.: Infants use meter to categorize rhythms and melodies: implications for musical structure learning. Cogn. Psychol. **50**, 354–377 (2005)
11. Phillips-Silver, J., Trainor, L.J.: Feeling the beat: movement influences infant rhythm perception. Science **308**, 1430 (2005)
12. London, J.: Hearing in Time: Psychological Aspects of Musical Meter. Oxford University Press, USA (2004)
13. Varela, F.J., Thompson, E., Rosch, E.: The Embodied Mind: Cognitive Science and Human Experience. MIT Press, Cambridge (1991)
14. Leman, M.: Embodied Music Cognition and Mediation Technology. MIT Press, Cambridge (2007)
15. Bruner, J.: Processes of Cognitive Growth: Infancy. Clark University Press, Worcester (1968)
16. Gibson, J.J.: The Ecological Approach to Visual Perception. Houghton Mifflin, Boston (1979)
17. Summers, J.J., Anson, J.G.: Current status of the motor program: revisited. Hum. Mov. Sci. **28**, 566–577 (2009)
18. Stergiou, N., Yu, Y., Kyvelidou, A.: A perspective on human movement variability with applications in infancy motor development. Kinesiol. Rev. **2**, 93–102 (2013)
19. Freedman, D.A.: Statistical Models and Causal Inference: a Dialogue with the Social Sciences. Cambridge University Press, Cambridge (2010)
20. Toiviainen, P., Luck, G., Thompson, M.R.: Embodied meter: hierarchical eigenmodes in music-induced movement. Music Percept. **28**, 59–70 (2010)
21. Zentner, M., Eerola, T.: Rhythmic engagement with music in infancy. Proc. Natl. Acad. Sci. **107**, 5768–5773 (2010)
22. Styns, F., van Noorden, L., Moelants, D., Leman, M.: Walking on music. Hum. Mov. Sci. **26**, 769–785 (2007)
23. Demos, A.P., Chaffin, R., Begosh, K.T., Daniels, J.R., Marsh, K.L.: Rocking to the beat: effects of music and partner's movements on spontaneous interpersonal coordination. J. Exp. Psychol. Gen. **141**, 49 (2012)
24. Repp, B.H.: Sensorimotor synchronization: a review of the tapping literature. Psychon. Bull. Rev. **12**, 969–992 (2005)
25. Sethares, W.A., Staley, T.W.: Periodicity transforms. IEEE Trans. Sig. Process. **47**, 2953–2964 (1999)
26. Leman, M., Naveda, L.: Basic gestures as spatiotemporal reference frames for repetitive dance/music patterns in samba and charleston. Music Percept. **28**, 71–91 (2010)
27. Stergiou, N.: Innovative Analyses of Human Movement. Human Kinetics Publishers, Champaign (2004)
28. Laban, R., Lawrence, F.C.: Effort. Macdonald and Evans, London (1947)
29. Nigg, B.M., MacIntosh, B.R., Mester, J.: Biomechanics and Biology of Movement. Human Kinetics, Champaign (2000)
30. Harbourne, R.T., Stergiou, N.: Movement variability and the use of nonlinear tools: principles to guide physical therapist practice. Phys. Ther. **89**, 267–282 (2009)

Evaluating Input Devices for Dance Research

Mari Romarheim Haugen[(✉)] and Kristian Nymoen

Department of Musicology, University of Oslo, Oslo, Norway
{m.r.haugen,kristian.nymoen}@imv.uio.no

Abstract. Recording music-related motions in ecologically valid situations can be challenging. We investigate the performance of three devices providing 3D acceleration data, namely Axivity AX3, iPhone 4s and a Wii controller tracking rhythmic motions. The devices are benchmarked against an infrared motion capture system, tested on both simple and complex music-related body motions, and evaluations are presented of the data quality and suitability for tracking music-related motions in real-world situations. The various systems represent different trade-offs with respect to data quality, user interface and physical attributes.

Keywords: Music and motion · Dance · Samba · Motion capture · Motion analysis · Qualisys · AX3 · iPhone · Wii

1 Introduction

A wide range of motion capture technologies enables measurements of music-related body motions. Infrared motion capture systems provide high precision position data and have successfully been used in a number of studies on music-related motions. However, these systems also have some limitations. If a marker gets occluded or moved outside the capture space, it will disappear from the recording, something that can restrict both the area for the performance, and also the number of people that can be captured simultaneously. In addition, the ecological validity of the experiment may be challenged by the visible reflective markers and the controlled environment required by the motion capture system. Previous studies suggest that using professional performers [9] or modifying the motion capture lab [13] can balance the influence of the artificial environment. Nevertheless, being able to record music-related motion in real-world situations, like a performing musician in a concert or a crowd dancing in a parade, is often desirable.

Several studies on music-related motion have used inertial sensors rather than optical systems. These are potentially less obtrusive and more affordable, thus possibly a better solution for studies where ecological validity is of importance. A popular choice among music researchers has been to use the Nintendo Wii controller [1,3,15]. Smartphones contain inertial sensors and have been deemed adequate for capturing the acceleration and orientation for certain types of motion [11]. Although smartphones have not been as popular as the Wii as recording device in studies on bodily motion, they have already been used extensively in musical interaction [14]. Besides the multi-purpose Wii and smartphones, other accelerometer-based sensing devices exist which are more dedicated to research purposes. The Axivity AX3 is one such device which has proven useful in recognizing everyday movement patterns [7]. It is clearly an advantage that these systems enable motion capture recordings outside a lab, but how do they perform in tracking of rhythmic motions in dance and other types of music-related motion? Our aim in this paper is to evaluate a selection of such devices with respect to the quality of the data they provided, but also their suitability for studies of music-related body motions in *real-world* situations.

2 Devices

The performances of three systems were evaluated in this study: The Axivity AX3, Apple iPhone and the Nintendo Wii controller. The AX3 is a logging device, meaning that data is recorded to the internal memory on the device without options for streaming the data to an external recording device. The iPhone and the Wii controller, on the other hand, both allow streaming of data. All systems provide three-dimensional acceleration data.

The dimensions of the Axivity AX3[1] device used in this study is $39 \times 36 \times 12.5$ mm, with a mass of 19 g (Fig. 1). The device has a built-in memory of 512 MB to store the acceleration data and is charged and controlled over a USB connection to a computer. All control of the device is done using the PC software OM GUI v1.10 whilst being connected via USB. The recording starts immediately when the device is disconnected. The AX3 provides accelerometer data (including gravity) measured in Gs. The system was set to track at 100 Hz.

An iPhone 4s, running iOS version 7.1.1 with dimensions $58.6 \times 115.2 \times 9.3$ mm and with a mass of 138 grams (Fig. 1) was used. The iPhone data was sent via the application GyrOSC[2] and recorded by a Max patch running on a MacBook Pro via Wi-Fi. The userAcceleration data (in Gs) is an estimate of the acceleration without gravity performed by the *CMDeviceMotion* class in Apple's API. The frame rate of the system was 40 Hz.

We also used a Nintendo Wii controller with dimensions $36.2 \times 180 \times 30.8$ mm and with a mass of 159 g (Fig. 1). Accelerometer data from the Wii controller was received by OSCulator[3] running on a MacBook Pro via Bluetooth and recorded using the software WiiDataCapture 2.1 [2]. The software imported the data to a text file containing time information and three-dimensional accelerometer data represented by numbers between 0 and 170 tracked at 100 Hz.

For reference, high-precision position data was recorded using an optical motion capture system from Qualisys[4]. The system tracked the motion of a reflective marker (diameter 16 mm) at a frame rate of 100 Hz (Fig. 1). Data was

---

[1] http://axivity.com.
[2] https://itunes.apple.com/us/app/gyrosc/id418751595?mt=8.
[3] http://www.osculator.net.
[4] http://qualisys.com.

Fig. 1. The devices used in this study: Nintendo Wii controller, iPhone 4s and Axivity AX3, and also the reflective marker used in the Qualisys recording.

recorded into Qualisys Track Manager (QTM) 3.7. The position data from Qualisys is measured in millimetres (mm).

3 Experiment

A total of four recordings were carried out in the fourMs motion capture lab at the University of Oslo[5]. In order to record the same motions simultaneously in all devices, the AX3, iPhone, and Wii were strapped together and a reflective marker was attached. The basic noise level in the sensors was tested in the first recording with all devices lying stationary on the floor (Fig. 2 (left)). The second and third recording were designed to test how accurately the data from each of the devices reflected simple and complex motion patterns, respectively, to pre-recorded music. The music used in this study was a samba groove played on a traditional Brazilian hand drum called *pandeiro*. Samba music was chosen because of its systematic microtiming features and also because it has a corresponding dance involving complex body motion. This enables investigations of music-related motions of different complexities. The playback of the music was synchronized with the Qualisys recording. In the second recording simple motion resembling shaker motion was performed, holding the device in one hand (Fig. 2 (middle left)). In the third recording the devices tracked complex hip motions in samba dancing, with the devices attached on a dancer's hip (Fig. 2 (middle right)). In both recordings eight metronome clicks at 105 BPM were added to the audio track both before and after the samba groove. In the shaker recording impulsive motions, performed with the hand holding the devices, were carried out in synchrony with the metronome, and in the samba dance recording the person wearing the devices jumped in time with the metronome, creating acceleration peaks in all the data streams simultaneously. In both cases the resulting peaks in the data streams from all the devices were used as a common reference points when aligning the data. These synchronization motions were initially intended

---

[5] http://www.uio.no/english/research/groups/fourms/about/labs/.

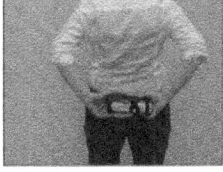

Fig. 2. Four recordings were carried out. (1) the devices lying stationary on the floor; (2) performing shaker motion to pre-recorded music while holding the devices in one hand; (3) dancing samba to pre-recorded music with the devices attatched to the dancer's hip; (4) a shaker recording using only an AX3 device and audio recording.

for aligning purposes only, however, they also proved to be a useful object of analysis. Such impulsive motions are indeed a type of music-related motion [5] and they provide yet another perspective on the differences between the recording devices.

In the first three recordings the acceleration data from the input devices was to be benchmarked and aligned with a Qualisys recording that in the shaker and samba recordings was synchronized with the playback sound. Since we additionally were interested in investigating how input devices could be used in real-world situations, a fourth recording was carried out in order to test whether data from an input device could be synchronized with sound data without using an optical infrared system like Qualisys. The AX3 was chosen for this task due to its size and light-weight properties. Additionally, the AX3 does not require network access or connection to external hardware during the recording, something that can be useful in many situations. The AX3 tracked shaker motions performed to a samba groove and the sound was recorded using Logic Pro X software running on a Macintosh computer. The AX3 was attached to a wood block that was hit against another wood block in the beginning and in the end of the recording (Fig. 2 (right)). The resulting simultaneous spikes in the audio recording and the acceleration recording were used as common reference points when aligning the data streams.

4 Data Processing

The devices used in this study provide data in different units, and also differ in how they stream and store data. Consequently, some data processing was executed before the data could be analyzed.

4.1 Post-Processing

Since the AX3 is a logging device, the data has to be downloaded from the device via USB and processed in the OM Gui software. We discovered a divergence between the specified sampling frequency of the AX3 and the actual sampling frequency. To investigate this two AX3 devices, both set to track at 100 Hz, were used. Neither of the two devices did sample at the specified rate. The average frame rates of the two AX3 devices were found to be closer to 103 Hz and 95 Hz, respectively. By exporting the AX3 data with time tags, that is, seconds relative to start instead of sample numbers, a more precise frame rate could be calculated. For this reason, AX3 data should be exported with time tags, rather than trusting the specified sampling rate.

The Qualisys position data was differentiated in order to compare it to the accelerometer-based devices. We applied a second order derivation with a Savitzky-Golay FIR smoothing filter (filter length of 5 frames). Alignment of individual axes of all devices is difficult, so our analysis in the following sections is based on the vector magnitude of the 3D acceleration data.

4.2 Aligning the Motion Data

The recorded data was imported into matlab. We implemented an automated process for aligning the data from the different devices. The data streams from the first three recordings were cropped and aligned to match the optical motion capture system. Each data stream was up-sampled to the frame rate of the Qualisys data using linear interpolation. Subsequently, cross-correlation was applied to calculate the time lag between the Qualisys data and each of the other data streams.

5 Analysis and Results

The data was analyzed using the MoCap Toolbox [2] and custom made matlab scripts. The following sections present analysis and results from the four recordings: the noise estimation based on the recording of the devices lying still on the floor (Sect. 5.1), impulsive motions to metronome and shaker motions to samba music (Sect. 5.2), jumps to metronome and hip motions in samba dance to samba music (Sect. 5.3), and a recording using only one accelerometer and sound recording (Sect. 5.4).

5.1 Noise

The noise level in the devices was calculated as the standard deviations (SD) of the acceleration vector magnitude based on a 140 s long recording where the devices were lying stationary on the floor. In the beginning and in the end of the recording five impulsive motions were executed for alignment purposes. The recordings were subsequently cropped to the 140 s where the devices were lying still.

Since the AX3 and the iPhone provide data in gravity units, the acceleration data from QTM, measured in mm/s^2, was also converted to Gs. The unit of the Wii-recording is unknown, hence, in order to compare the noise level in the

Wii with the other devices every data stream was normalized by the root-meansquare (RMS) values of the synchronization motions in the beginning and in the end of the recording. However, on closer look, it seems that the iPhone data does not show the highest peaks in the synchronization motion. Although not specified in the app used for acquiring iPhone data, various online discussion fora state that the iPhone acceleration data is limited to ± 2 G, which would explain why the iPhone data does not reflect the highest acceleration peaks. As a consequence of the limited range of the iPhone accelerometer the noise level of the iPhone is higher when normalized. Hence, the noise calculations based on both the raw data and the normalized data had to be included in the evaluation of the noise levels in the different devices.

The noise levels of the systems are displayed in Table 1. The first column displays the data as it is received directly from each system, with the exception of the QTM data which has been differentiated and converted to G unit. The second column shows the noise level normalized by the RMS value of the five synchronization motions. The results in Table 1 show quite low noise levels in Qualisys, iPhone and AX3. The data obtained from the Wii seems to be noisier than the data from the other systems. The jagged lines for the Wii in Fig. 3 shows that the bit depth of the data stream is lower than for the other devices (a range of less than 256 and resolution of 1 suggests 8 bits). This is possibly the reason why the Wii data is much noisier.

Table 1. Noise in absolute acceleration data for 140 s of the stationary recording. The columns show the standard deviations (SD) of the raw acceleration data, and data normalized by the RMS of the synchronization motions. Values are in 10^{-3} unit.

	Raw data	Normalized (RMS)
QTM*	0.80	0.92
AX3	2.64	1.88
iPhone	2.57	2.89
Wii	117.36	4.72

*QTM raw values converted to unit G. A 5 frame savitzky-golay filter was used in the acceleration calculation, complicating comparisons between QTM and the other devices.

5.2 Impulsive Motions to Metronome and Shaker Motions to Samba Music

The second recording was done to investigate how well the devices track impulsive and simple shaker motions. All the devices were held in one hand while performing shaker motions in accordance with the music (Fig. 2 (middle)). Impulsive synchronization motions were executed in the beginning and in the end of the recording. Since the unit of the Wii-recording is unknown, every data stream

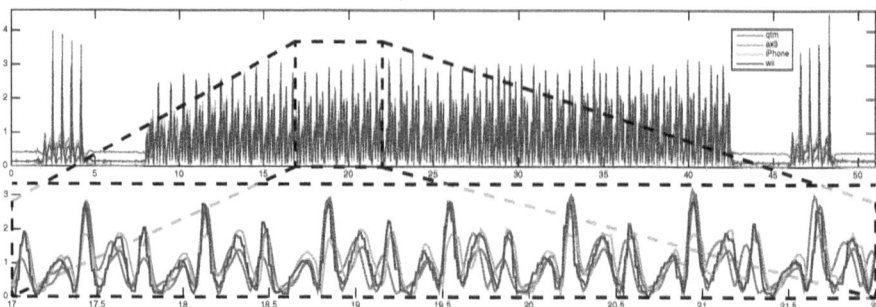

Fig. 3. Visual comparison between data from the different devices in the shaker recording (after RMS normalisation).

was normalized by the root-mean-square (RMS) value of the entire recording. Figure 3 shows the entire shaker recording (top), and a five-second excerpt (bottom). All devices follow the general tendencies recorded by the Qualisys system in this recording. The low bit depth of the Wii indicated by the jagged purple line was compensated for by applying a Butterworth smoothing filter.

When tracking the synchronization motion, the data streams from QTM, AX3 and Wii all showed clear spikes that seem to be in accordance with the metronome (Fig. 4). The data stream from the iPhone also showed acceleration peaks, however, limited by the range of the accelerometer as previously discussed.

Next, we investigated the correspondence between the shaker motion and a samba groove. A comparison between the acceleration plots and the plotted audio waveform reveals that there are four acceleration peaks in each beat, which indicates that the recorded shaker motion may correspond with the 16th-note level in the music (Fig. 5). According to previous research it has been suggested that the 4th 16th-note in a beat plays a significant role in samba groove being both longer in duration [4,6,10] and also more accentuated than the others [4]. A qualitative evaluation of the fluctuation in acceleration amplitude in the shaker motion showed that both QTM, AX3 and Wii indicated a higher acceleration

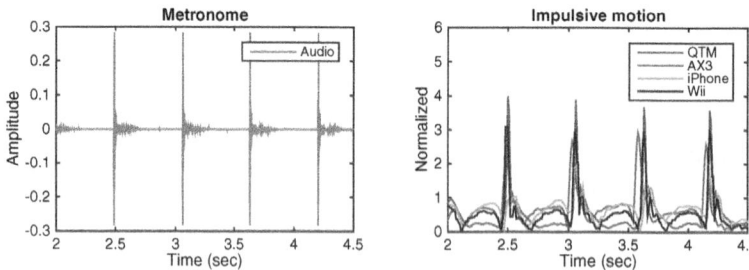

Fig. 4. The correspondence between metronome (left) and the impulsive motion holding the devices in one hand (right).

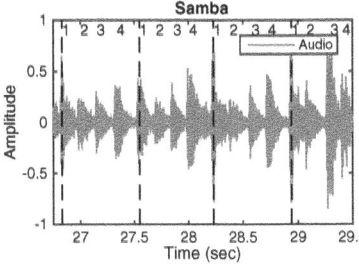 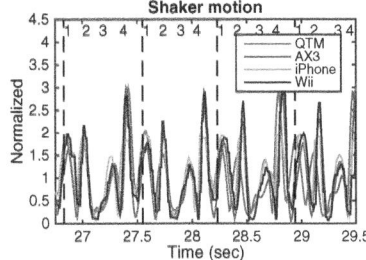

Fig. 5. The correspondence between samba music (left) and shaker motion (right) in two measures. The beat positions are indicated by dashed lines and 16th-note positions represented as numbers between 1–4. The shaker motion seems to correspond with the 16th-note level.

peak at the 4th peak in each measure than the others. The acceleration peaks in the iPhone data stream, on the other hand, showed approximately the same strength, something that supports the previous suggestion that the iPhone is unable to pick up the highest acceleration peaks (see Noise Sect. 5.1).

In order to investigate how accurately the acceleration peaks reflect the duration pattern on the 16th-note level we calculated the 16th-note duration in the music and the duration between corresponding acceleration peaks in the shaker motion in a total of four measures. Since all the 16th-notes were present in the sound as sudden increase in energy, their temporal position could be identified using the onset detection function in the MIRtoolbox for matlab [8]. The 16th-note durations were subsequently calculated by measuring the time from the onset of one 16th-note to the next. The temporal position of the acceleration peaks were estimated using a custom made matlab function picking peaks in a graph based on directional changes. The duration pattern based on the motion data was calculated by measuring the time of one peak to the next. Our audio analysis revealed a *medium — medium — medium — long* duration pattern on 16th-note level. However, our motion analysis showed that the person performing the shaker motions seemed to perform a motion duration pattern deviating from the audio 16th-note duration pattern. The QTM data showed that the shaker motion in this recording follows a *medium — long — short — medium* duration pattern. This duration pattern was also recognized by the AX3 and Wii. The iPhone data, on the other hand, showed a *medium — medium — long — medium* pattern. The low clipping threshold on the iPhone accelerometer data makes the peak times more difficult to detect. This may be the reason for the deviating duration pattern in the iPhone data.

5.3 Jumps to Metronome and Hip Motions in Samba Dance

A more complicated task than tracking shaker motion is the recording of hip motions in samba dance. In the third recording the devices were strapped onto

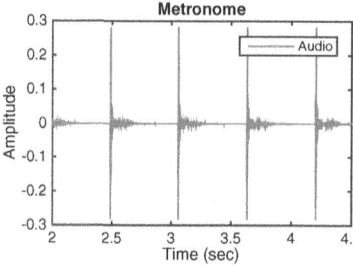 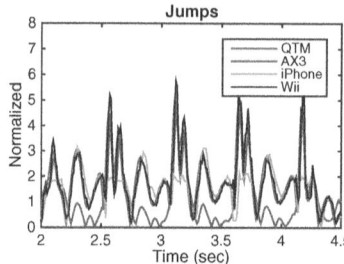

Fig. 6. The correspondence between metronome (left) and jumps (right). In addition to the peaks related to the temporal points when the dancer's feet meet the floor after the jump, preparation motions before the jump and bouncing motions after the jump is tracked.

the dancer's hip. Before and after the samba groove the dancer jumped in synchrony with the metronome.

The acceleration peaks caused by the synchronization jumping was recognizable in the QTM, AX3 and Wii, however, followed by a second lower peak. This is probably due to flexible knees allowing the body to bounce after the jump. In addition, jump preparation motions are recognized ahead of the peaks. Again, the iPhone was unable to pick up the highest acceleration peaks. A visualization of the metronome and the corresponding jumps is presented in Fig. 6.

The hip motion in samba dance are complex and involves a number of rapid direction changes. The motion pattern is periodic, however, a rhythm pattern is not easily detected by looking at the acceleration plots. In the recording of the simple shaker motion to samba music, the motion curves from AX3 and Wii were very similar to the QTM curve (see Fig. 5). In the hip recordings, on the other hand, the resemblance between the QTM data and the data from the other devices is less clear. A qualitative evaluation of the fluctuation in acceleration amplitude do however indicate a slight increase in acceleration around the 2nd and 4th 16-note in all devices. A visualization of the samba music and the corresponding dance is presented in Fig. 7.

5.4 Sound and Motion Recording

In the recordings presented above, the data from the portable devices were synchronized using cross-correlation against data from a state-of-the-art motion capture system. However, our motivation for testing the smaller devices in the first place is the use of such equipment outside a lab. In research on music and motion it is important to be able to do synchronized recordings of sound and motion. Accordingly, we did a recording where the AX3 tracked shaker motions performed to a samba groove and simultaneous audio recording using Logic Pro.

As described earlier the AX3 was attached to a wood block that was hit against another wood block creating simultaneous spikes in the beginning and end of both the sound and acceleration recordings (see Experiment Sect. 3).

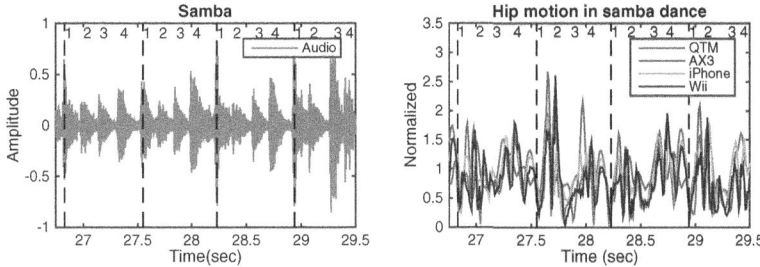

Fig. 7. The correspondence between samba music (left) and hip motion in samba dance (right) in two measures. The beat positions are indicated by dashed lines and 16th-note positions represented as numbers between 1–4.

The data streams were aligned by first transforming the audio recording into an envelope representation. Exerpts containing the synchronization motion and sound were extracted from both the sound and motion recording and cross-correlation was used to determine the time difference between the two.

Plots of the aligned sound and motion data is displayed in Fig. 8. The automated synchronization process appears to have aligned the two data streams satisfactorily. This suggests that recordings of music-related motion can be carried out in real-world situations using only an AX3 device and a sound recorder, as long as synchronization actions are carried out in the beginning and in the end of the experiment.

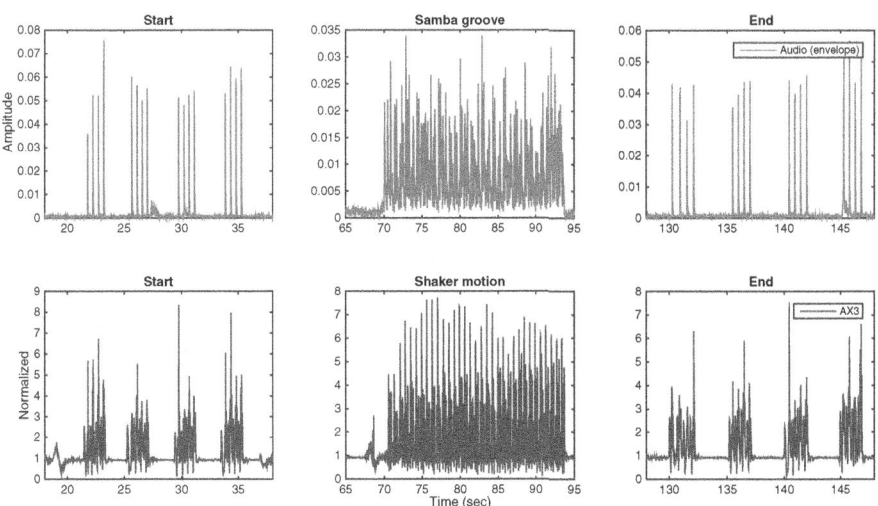

Fig. 8. Plot showing the audio envelope from a sound recording and data from the AX3 recording. The sections that are containing the synchronized peaks and spikes at the beginning (left) and in the end (right), and also the samba groove with corresponding shaker motion (middle) are extracted.

6 Discussion

In this paper we have evaluated the performance of three input devices, namely AX3, iPhone and Wii, tracking music-related motions featured by different qualities. The devices were benchmarked against an optical infrared motion capture system from Qualisys.

In order to compare data streams residual analysis or correlation might be suggested. However, with residual analysis, the effects of minor clock drift in each system would be drastic, even if the magnitude of the acceleration measurement is precise. Correlation analysis is also problematic due to autocorrelation [12]. For this reason, initial comparison between the data streams was done by visual inspection of the data streams from each device to the same recording.

Synchronization of all the devices was possible using the data obtained from the tracking of impulsive motions and jumps to a metronome in the beginning and in the end of each recording. In the jump recording the acceleration peaks was surrounded by multiple peaks caused by jump preparation motions and flexible knees after the landing. The participant in this study was instructed to land the jump in synchrony with the metronome. Jumping in synchrony with a metronome could, however, have a number of different interpretations. So in recordings where a device is to be attached onto a person, it would be better to perform synchronization actions similar to our impulsive hand motion before the sensor is attached to the person to ensure unambiguous acceleration spikes.

In the recording of impulsive hand motion and jump, the AX3 and the Wii both showed clear acceleration spikes. The iPhone data did also show acceleration spikes, however, not as clear as the others. This is probably because the iPhone data did not fully reflect the magnitude of the acceleration due to limited range of the accelerometer. This means that if motions resulting in high acceleration values are to be recorded and analyzed, an iPhone should not be used.

In the analysis of the simple shaker motion to samba music, we found that all the devices seemed to capture the general tendency. In order to investigate the precision of the acceleration peaks we calculated the inter onset intervals (IOIs) between the peaks. The motion analysis based on the QTM data revealed a *medium — long — short — medium* duration pattern on 16th-note level, a duration pattern that was recognized by AX3 and Wii as well. Again, the precision of the peaks in the data stream from the iPhone was low, resulting in a diverging duration pattern. This suggests that data obtained from AX3 and Wii can be used for detecting rhythmical patterns in simple motion based on acceleration peaks, while the data obtained from iPhone is too imprecise.

When tracking complex hip motions in samba dance, none of the data streams seemed to follow the QTM recording accurately. The hip motions in samba dance is featured by consecutive rapid directional changes, something that seem to be a challenge for the input devices. The data may not be precise enough to capture complex motion with rapid acceleration fluctuations. The iPhone may also be restrained by its low frequency rate (40 Hz). A qualitative examination of the fluctuation in acceleration amplitude does however indicate a slight increase in acceleration around the corresponding 2nd and the 4th 16-note in the music.

We also tested whether data from an input device could be aligned with a audio recording without using an optical infrared system. We found that data from AX3 could be aligned with the audio recording alone, understood that impulsive sound-producing actions, producing unambiguous spikes in the acceleration data and peaks in the sound recording simultaneously is carried out both in the beginning and in the end of each recording. This opens for a lot of possibilities since this suggests that music-related motions can be captured in ecologically valid environments using only an audio recorder and an input device.

In dance research, and also when recording body motions in musical performances, the size and the weight of the sensors being used must be considered. Because the AX3 is so small it can easily be attached to a participant's body, or even be carried in a pocket, without interfering with the music performance or experience. The built in memory chip also allows for long recordings. However, a disadvantage is the divergence in sample rate between devices. This can however be sidestepped by exporting the AX3 data with time tags instead of sample numbers.

7 Conclusion

Recording music-related motions in an ecologically valid environment can be challenging. Although optical infrared motion capture systems are unrivaled when it comes to data quality, there are some challenges regarding marker occlusion, limited capture space and ecological validity. In this study we have evaluated the performance of three sensing systems, namely AX3, iPhone and Wii and compared it to an infrared motion capture system from Qualisys. None of the systems could provide as precise data as an optical infrared motion capture system, however, the data obtained from AX3 and Wii was proven to be useful for analyzing rhythmical structures in music-related motions. In addition, the small and light-weight feature of the AX3 device makes it preferable in many situations. The various systems evaluated in this study represent different trade offs with respect to data quality, user interface and physical attributes.

References

1. Amelynck, D., Grachten, M., Van Noorden, L., Leman, M.: Toward e-motion-based music retrieval a study of affective gesture recognition. IEEE Trans. Affect. Comput. **3**(2), 250–259 (2012)
2. Burger, B., Toiviainen, P.: MoCap Toolbox – a matlab toolbox for computational analysis of movement data. In: Bresin, R. (ed.) Proceedings of 10th Sound and Music Computing Conference (SMC), pp. 172–178 (2013)
3. De Bruyn, L., Leman, M., Moelants, D., Demey, M.: Does social interaction activate music listeners? In: Ystad, S., Kronland-Martinet, R., Jensen, K. (eds.) CMMR 2008. LNCS, vol. 5493, pp. 93–106. Springer, Heidelberg (2009)

4. Gerischer, C.: O suingue baiano: rhythmic feeling and microrhythmic phenomena in Brazilian percussion. Ethnomusicology **50**(1), 99–119 (2006)
5. Godøy, R.I.: Gestural-sonorous objects: embodied extensions of Schaeffer's conceptual apparatus. Org. Sound **11**(02), 149–157 (2006)
6. Gouyon, F.: Microtiming in Samba de Roda – preliminary experiments with polyphonic audio. In: SBCM 2007 Proceedings, pp. 197–203 (2007)
7. Khan, A.M.: Recognizing physical activities using the axivity device. In: The 5th International Conference on eHealth, Telemedicine, and Social Medicine (2013)
8. Lartillot, O., Toiviainen, P.: A matlab toolbox for musical feature extraction from audio. In: International Conference on Digital Audio Effects (2007)
9. Naveda, L., Leman, M.: Sonification of Samba dance using periodic pattern analysis. In: 4th International Conference on Digital Arts, ARTECH 2008, pp. 16–26 (2008)
10. Naveda, L., Leman, M.: A cross-modal heuristic for periodic pattern analysis of Samba music and dance. J. New Music Res. **38**(3), 255–283 (2009)
11. Nymoen, K., Volsund, A., Skogstad, S.A., Jensenius, A.R., Torresen, J.: Comparing motion data from an iPod touch to an optical infrared marker-based motion capture system. In: Proceedings of International Conference on New Interfaces for Musical Expression, pp. 88–91 (2012)
12. Schubert, E.: Correlation analysis of continuous emotional response to music: correcting for the effects of serial correlation. Musicae Scientiae **5**(1 Suppl.), 213–236 (2002)
13. Van Dyck, E., Moelants, D., Demey, M., Deweppe, A., Coussement, P., Leman, M.: The impact of the bass drum on human dance movement. Music Percept.: Interdiscip. J. **30**(4), 349–359 (2013)
14. Wang, G.: Designing Smule's Ocarina: the iPhone's magic flute. In: Proceedings of International Conference on New Interfaces for Musical Expression, Pittsburgh, PA, pp. 303–307 (2009)
15. Witek, M.: '... and I feel good!': the relationship between body-movement, pleasure and groove in music. Ph.D. thesis, University of Oxford (2013)

Estimation of Guitar Fingering and Plucking Controls Based on Multimodal Analysis of Motion, Audio and Musical Score

Alfonso Perez-Carrillo[1,3](✉), Josep-Lluis Arcos[2], and Marcelo Wanderley[3]

[1] IDMIL, McGill University, Montreal, Canada
alfonso.perez@upf.edu
http://www.dtic.upf.edu/~aperez/
[2] IIIA-CSIC, Barcelona, Spain
[3] Music Technology Group, Universitat Pompeu Fabra, Barcelona, Spain

Abstract. This work presents a method for the extraction of instrumental controls during guitar performances. The method is based on the analysis of multimodal data consisting of a combination of motion capture, audio analysis and musical score. High speed video cameras based on marker identification are used to track the position of finger bones and articulations and audio is recorded with a transducer measuring vibration on the guitar body. The extracted parameters are divided into left hand controls, i.e. fingering (which string and fret is pressed with a left hand finger) and right hand controls, i.e. the plucked string, the plucking finger and the characteristics of the pluck (position, velocity and angles with respect to the string). Controls are estimated based on probability functions of low level features, namely, the plucking instants (i.e. note onsets), the pitch and the distances of the fingers (both hands) to strings and frets. Note onsets are detected via audio analysis, the pitch is extracted from the score and distances are computed from 3D Euclidean Geometry. Results show that by combination of multimodal information, it is possible to estimate such a comprehensive set of control features, with special high performance for the fingering and plucked string estimation. Regarding the plucking finger and the pluck characteristics, their accuracy gets lower but improvements are foreseen including a hand model and the use of high-speed cameras for calibration and evaluation.

Keywords: Guitar · Instrumental control · Motion capture · Audio analysis

1 Introduction

The acquisition of musical gestures and particularly of instrumental controls from a musical performance is a field of increasing interest with applications in acoustics [24], music pedagogy [27], automatic music generation [9,13,19], augmented performances [2,28] or performance transcription [29] among others. On the classical guitar, a performer can produce very distinct sounds and adjust the timbre by the way the strings are plucked and pressed [23]. A comprehensive study of guitar controls is described by Scherrer [21]. In that study, the principles of guitar playing in terms of controls are classified into left-hand (fingering) and right-hand (plucking). Fingering determines the pitch, as well as a set of more complex gestures such as vibrato, slurs, glissandi or damping. The main parameters during the plucking process are (a) the plucked string (b) the excitation with nail or flesh, (c) the plucking position, (d) the plucking velocity, (e) the displacement of the string during the pressure stage and (f) the angles of the pluck during the preparation and release stages.

Controlled measurement of every parameter is very difficult especially in a performance context. Reported methods in the literature generally focus on the estimation of a single parameter or a reduced set of them and methods are many times very intrusive. In this work we are able to extract a comprehensive set of control parameters from real performances by means of a multimodal combination of motion capture, sound analysis and information from a musical score. The extracted instrumental controls are the plucking instants (i.e. note onsets), the fingering (which bones of the left hand fingers are pressing which strings and frets), the plucked string, the plucking finger, the plucking position on the string and the plucking velocity and angles at the release stage.

Motion capture, based on high speed video cameras that detect the position of reflective markers, is used for tracking the position of the fingers and guitar strings. One problem inherent with optical motion capture is that of occlusion. Most motion capture involves the entire human body, which implies large body movements and the occurrence of occlusion is far less than that of small hand movements. Furthermore, it is the right hand of the guitarist that is extremely difficult to capture. In this work, motion capture is reinforced with audio analysis and the indications in the musical score.

Audio is recorded by means of a transducer measuring vibration on the guitar body and analyzed in order to detect the note onsets [20]. There exist many different onset detection algorithms and they perform particularly well with the guitar due to the impulsive characteristics of string plucking (a comparison of different methods for guitar onset detection is reported in [20]). Additionally, the fact that audio is measured as vibration of the guitar plate, makes onset detection even more accurate compared to a signal captured with a microphone, as the measured signal is not affected by room acoustics or sound radiation. Conversely to onset detection, pitch estimation algorithms such as [5] are not adapted to the guitar as note sustains are absent and note releases are very large making notes overlap in time. In order to have a robust estimation of the pitch, we use the note pitch information from the musical score as a ground truth, after an alignment to the audio signal.

The procedure for the parameter estimation proposed in this work is shown in Fig. 1. The algorithm starts with (1) the estimation of the plucking instants and the pitch by onset analysis of the audio signal followed by (2) an alignment to the score. At each plucking instant (3) the distances from the fingers to the strings are computed and (4) the possible combination of fret and string is estimated from the pitch. By means of a probability function based on distances, the (5) most likely plucked string and (6) and the most likely plucking finger are estimated. Finally, from the selected string and finger the rest of the parameters (i.e. the plucking position, velocity and angles) are computed based on Euclidean geometry.

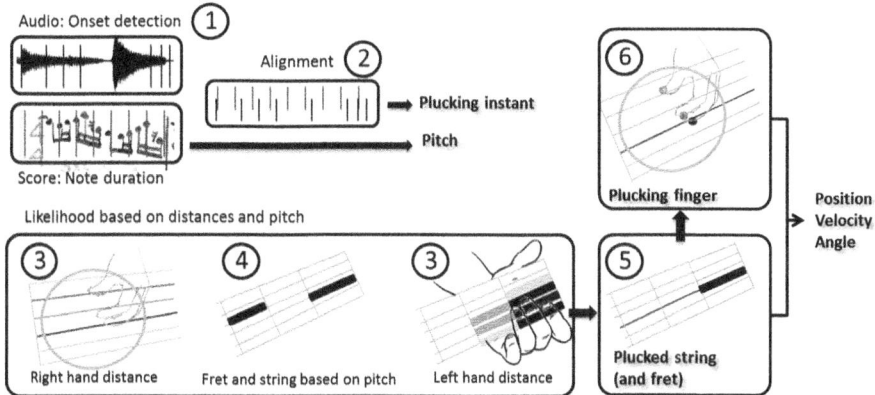

Fig. 1. Procedure for parameter estimation. It starts with (1) the estimation of the plucking instants by onset analysis of the audio signal and (2) pitch extraction by alignment of the score note onsets to the audio onsets. At each estimated plucking instant, (3) distances from fingers to the strings are computed. Given the pitch and the distances (4) a likelihood function is built in order to obtain (5) the most likely plucked string and fret and (6) the plucking finger. From the selected string and finger positions, the plucking position, velocity and angle are computed based on Euclidean geometry.

2 Literature Review

The acquisition of control parameters from musical performances is generally carried out either directly by measuring with sensors or indirectly by off-line analysis of an audio signal [17, 28]. In the case of the indirect acquisition, different methods allow for the extraction of the plucking position and fingering based on frequency-domain analysis techniques [25, 26] and time-domain approaches [16]. Reboursiere et al. [20] are able to detect left and right hand techniques (i.e. discriminating between left and right hand attacks and detection of right-hand palm-damping and harmonics) from audio analysis. Abesser et al. [1] propose an algorithm that detects plucking parameters and expression styles for bass guitar playing. Scherrer et al. [22] are able to estimate more complex features such as the plucking angle of release (AOR) by sound analysis informed with physical properties of the guitar.

The use of sensors allows to extract more parameters with higher accuracy and with the potential of acquisition in real time. The main reported techniques that provide a 3D representation of a live performance are based on mechanical, inertial, electro-magnetic or optical systems. Mechanical systems imply wearing a mechanical exoskeleton [6] that is very intrusive during performance. Inertial systems, most of them based on gyroscopes that measure rotational rates, have the disadvantage of being intrusive and of providing relative movement and not absolute position. Such systems have been used to track the movements of violin players [12]. Electro-magnetic field (*EMF*) technology used for instance to measure violin bowing controls [14,18] is very accurate but generally intrusive and may have interferences with metallic objects and external magnetic fields. Finally, optical systems are widely used as they are generally low-intrusive and allow for highly accurate measurements. Burns et al. [3] studied how to capture the left-hand fingerings of a guitarist in real-time using low-cost video cameras. Their prototype system, using fret and string detection to track fingertips, was able to successfully identify chords and a series of notes. This was accomplished without the use of markers on the hands. Two acknowledged drawbacks of the system are that it can only capture finger movement on the first five frets of the guitar due to the choice of camera, and there is no way to address finger occlusion. Although preliminary, it was a first step to a possible real-time video automatic transcriber. Norton et al. [15] uses motion capture based on cameras detecting reflective markers, similar to the system employed for this research, to measure classical guitar performances. Heijink [11] researched the complexity of left-hand classical guitar movements using an active optical motion capture system with four infrared light emitting diodes placed on the fingernails of the left hand, one on the left wrist, one each on the right index and middle fingers and three on the body of the guitar. Chadefaux et al. [4] used high speed video cameras to manually extract features during plucking of harp strings.

Other types of measuring techniques can also be found, including methods based on capacitive sensing [10] to capture left-hand fingering and indirect acquisition from audio [16,22,25,26]. The selection of a measuring system is largely determined by the objectives of the research. In this work the main objective is to measure hand controls from real performances with high accuracy and no (or very low) intrusiveness, which determined the choice for a high speed camera system that captures the position of small and ultra-light reflective markers as in [15].

3 Multimodal Data Acquisition

A multimodal database of guitar performances was recorded in order to test and evaluate the algorithms. The database is composed of ten musical fragments with an average duration of around one minute, performed by two different guitarists. The database contains the audio, 3D motion data, information from the musical score (note onset, note offset, pitch and the ground truth for the parameters plucked string, plucking finger, fret and left-hand fingering). Audio and Motion streams were recorded in different computers synchronized by means of a world clock generator that controls the sampling instants of the capturing devices and sends a SMPTE signal of 25 Hz that is saved as timestamps with the data. Audio to motion alignment consists of simply aligning the SMPTE timestamps.

3.1 Audio Recording

Audio is recorded with a contact microphone that captures the vibration of the guitar body. The captured signal is better adapted for audio analysis than that of a microphone as it is not affected by room acoustics or sound radiation. The audio stream is segmented into notes by means of onset detection based on the complex domain algorithm [7]. Conversely to pitch detection, onset detection in guitar playing is very accurate as notes are plucked, which implies a high energy peak at note onsets [20].

3.2 Musical Score

The musical score provides the nominal pitch, onsets and offsets of the notes, which are aligned with the ones detected in the audio. Figure 2 shows an example using wavesurfer software[1] of an audio segmentation showing three *label* tracks

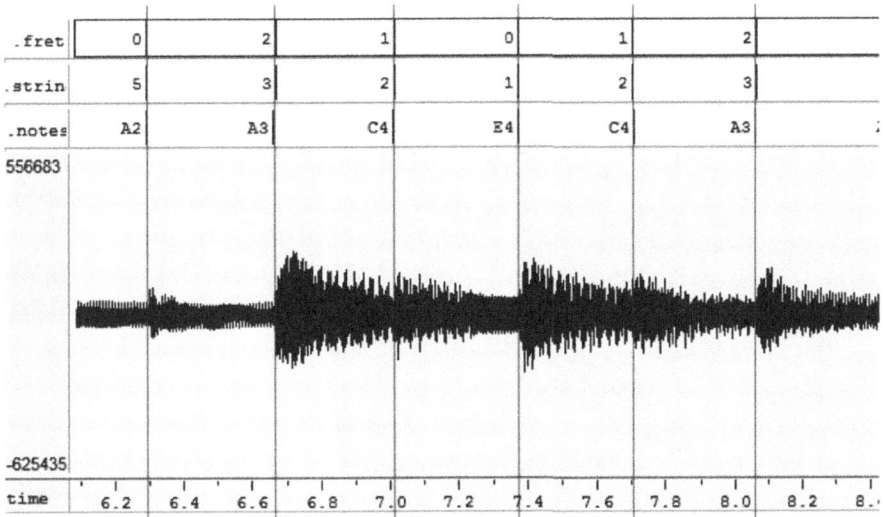

Fig. 2. Visualization with *wavesurfer* software of a fragment of a performed score showing the waveform segmented into notes together with three *label* tracks with the ground truth from the musical score information (the fret, the string and the note pitch). The segmentation is obtained after the onset detection and alignment of the score to the detected onsets.

[1] http://sourceforge.net/projects/wavesurfer/.

that indicate the score onsets and pitch (track *.notes*) along with the ground truth for the string (track *.string*) and the fret (track *.fret*) to be played.

3.3 Motion Capture

Motion capture is used to track the position of finger bones and articulations as well as the guitar strings. The capture is optical by means of *Qualysis*[2] high speed video cameras that detect the position of reflective markers. The main problem with such optical MoCap systems is marker occlusion. Each marker needs to be identified by at least three cameras placed at different angles and planes in order to correctly determine its 3D coordinates. In order to achieve a correct identification of the markers, it is necessary a careful placement of the cameras, the use of models for the hands and the guitar, and if necessary, the manual cleaning of the data, i.e. assigning the appropriate labels to incorrectly identified and non-identified markers.

3.4 Hand Tracking

The motion of the fingers is followed by attaching a marker at each finger articulation as shown in Fig. 3. Left-hand fingering estimation is very accurate as marker occlusion is low. Conversely, the right hand of the guitarist is extremely difficult to capture as it implies small hand movements and it gets especially complicated on the markers attached to the fingernails due to the particular way of

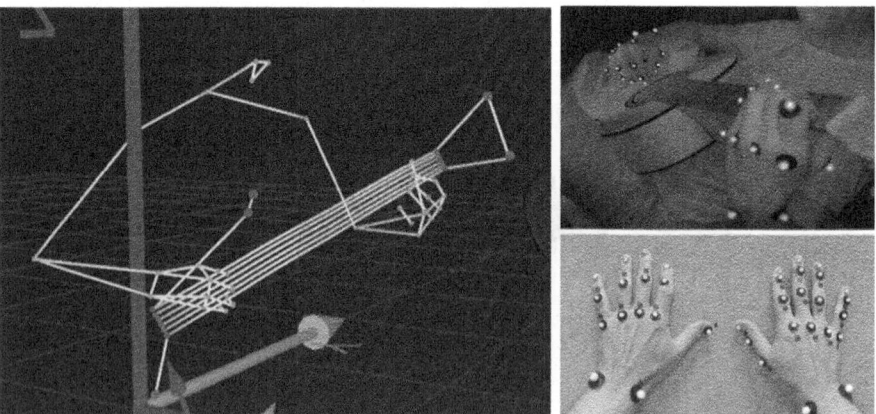

Fig. 3. To the left, a 3D visualization of the motion capture. Blue dots are the guitar auxiliary markers, which are used for the capture of the string positions, red dots represent the virtual markers on the strings ends, and green markers are the joints in the body of the performer. At the top-right, one of the capture frames with a camera. At the bottom-right, the position of the markers in the hands (Color figure online).

---

[2] http://www.qualisys.com/.

playing the guitar (when plucking, the nails face the guitar body). The *Qualisys* software includes algorithms for the definition of skeleton models that are trained with recordings of the hands moving smoothly and allow for the automatic identification and reconstruction of lost markers from skeleton objects. Proceeding this way, we achieve a higher rate of correctly recognized marker trajectories.

3.5 String Coordinates

The position of the strings is determined by the definition of a guitar Rigid Body (RB). A RB is a six degrees-of-freedom (6DOF) rigid structure defined by the position of a set of markers and associated with a local system of coordinates (SoC) with a corresponding 3D position and orientation with respect to the global SoC. The position of the markers is constant relative to the local SoC and their global coordinates can be obtained by a simple rotation and translation from the local to the global SoC. The guitar RB is built by placing markers at each string-end as well as *reference* markers attached to the guitar body. The markers at the string-ends can not remain attached during a performance as it would be very intrusive, so they are defined as virtual markers. Virtual markers are only used for calibration to define the SoC structure. During the actual tracking, virtual markers are reconstructed from the reference markers.

Special care has to be taken when attaching the reference markers to the guitar body as the plates are reflective to light, causing interferences with the markers. In order to avoid these unwanted reflections, the markers are placed on the edge of the guitar body and outside the guitar plates by means of antennas (prolongations attached to the body). Five reference markers were used and they were placed as shown in Fig. 3 (blue markers). The tracking of the position of the strings following this procedure achieves a nearly 100 % of correctly reconstructed frames.

4 Low Level Parameter Computation

The estimation of plucking and fingering features is based on the extraction of low level parameters, namely, the plucking instant t_0, the fundamental frequency (or pitch) f_0 and the finger distances (both hands) to the strings.

4.1 Plucking Instant t_0 and Fundamental Frequency f_0

The plucking instants are determined from the audio by means of a note onset detection algorithm [7] followed by an alignment and match to the note start times in the musical score.

Detected onsets (o^A) are aligned and matched with note starts in the score (o^S) in order to have a robust estimation that discards false detected onsets and allows to restore non detected ones. Once the score is aligned with the audio, we can extract the note pitch f_0 directly from the score.

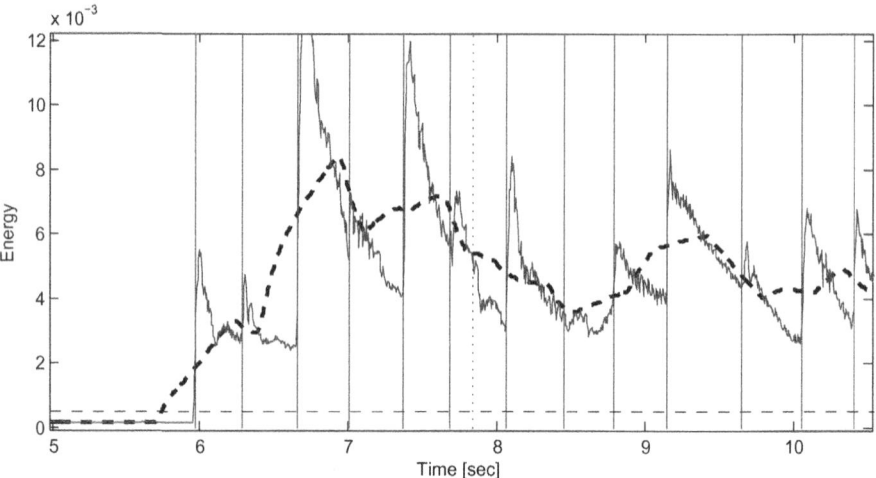

Fig. 4. Score to audio alignment. Energy in the audio is represented as continuous line in blue and the smoothed energy envelope is depicted with a thick dashed line. The hearing threshold is the straight dashed line close to zero and the aligned onsets are the vertical red lines. The boundaries of the recording are found inside the smoothed energy envelope and over the hearing threshold (Color figure online).

The alignment is performed in two steps. First, a window indicating the approximate start and the end of the performance in the recording must be found and then, we proceed to the alignment inside the window. The first step is necessary because audio recordings start and finish with a silence of undetermined duration and the window allows to discard false o^A due to noises outside the actual performance.

The boundaries of the performance are found by computing a smoothed audio energy envelope using a time-sliding window of length 100 frames (24 ms at a sample rate of 42100 Hz) and by defining a minimum hearing threshold (h_θ) as shown in Fig. 4. The procedure results in an envelope with high values of energy around the real performance. The threshold is used to determine the start and end of the window. The beginning of the performance will be at the first o^A that lays inside the window and the last note onset is at the last o^A inside the window. Once the boundaries of the performance are determined, the total score duration is stretched to fit the actual performance duration.

The second step consists of matching o^S (from the stretched score) to o^A. For this we define an algorithm that for each o_i^S looks for its closest o_j^A. If the found o_j^A is closest to o_i^S than to o_{i+1}^S, both o_i^S and o_j^A are matched together and the new time is updated in the stretched score (o_i^S is set equal to o_j^A and distances in the score are delayed or advanced o_i^S-o_j^A). If no match is found for o_i^S we consider that we have detected a missing onset:

```
for i=2:length(oS) {
    j=findClosest(oS(i), oA)
    if(i==finClosest (oA(j), [oS(i),oS(i+1)]))
        match(i,j)
}
function match(i,j) {
    diff=oS(i)-oA(j)
    oS(i).time=oA(j).time
    for k=i:length(oS(i))
        oS(k).time=oS(k).time+diff
}
```

4.2 Finger Distance to the Strings

Distance from the markers in the fingers to the strings is computed as the average distance in a small window around the note onsets. A distance of zero would indicate that a finger is in contact with the string, but in practice, there is an offset in the distance as markers are placed on the back of the hand and this offset has not been calibrated. However, the method does not need to know the exact distances as it is based on the probability of being in contact with a string.

Left Hand. The left-hand presses the strings at specific frets, determining this way the unique pitch that can be played at each string. A string can be pressed not only with the finger tips but with any part of the finger and the pressing position (and therefore the pitch) is discretized by the position of the frets. For this reason, both fingers and strings are represented as segments. A finger-segment is determined by two consecutive markers in the same hand and a fret-segment is defined as the string segment between two consecutive frets.

The coordinates of the finger-segments are obtained directly from the measured left-hand marker positions and the position of the string-segments are to be found along the string lines at distances from the nut x_N and the bridge x_B given by,

$$x_N(j) = \frac{x_B(j-1)}{k} + x_N(j-1),$$
$$x_B(j-1) = x_S - x_N(j-1),$$
(1)

where x_S is the string length, $k = 17.817$ is a known constant that relates distances among frets and $j = 1..24$ is the fret number.

At each plucking instant (determined by the note onsets) we compute the distances from fret-segments to any of the finger-segments and we define the left hand distances function $d_L(s, f, b)$, where s is the string, f the fret-segment and b the finger-segment or bone. Distances are computed as the shortest Euclidean distance between two line segments [8]. Additionally we define,

$$d_L(s, f) = \min_b d_L(s, f, b),$$
$$d_L(s) = \min_f d_L(s, f).$$
(2)

Right Hand. In a similar way to the left hand, we define the right hand distances function $d_R(s, fg)$, being fg the finger, as the distances from the fingernails to the strings, so distances are computed as the shortest distance between a point (finger nail) and a line (string) [8]. Additionally we define,

$$d_R(s) = \min_f d_R(s, fg). \tag{3}$$

4.3 Likelihood Functions

Control parameters are estimated based on likelihood functions obtained from the previously described low level features. Let $L_P(s, f|pitch)$ be the likelihood of pressing a fret f and plucking a string s given the *pitch*. As the confidence of the pitch is very high (it is the ground truth determined from the score) we can use a binary function to discard impossible combinations of *frets* and *strings*. Its value is set to one at the combinations where the *pitch* can be produced and zero otherwise. This function restricts the possible *frets* to at most one per *string*, so we can also define $L_P(s|pitch) = L_P(s, f|pitch)$.

To determine the likelihood that a finger is touching a string, we define a function θ that maps the distances d_L and d_R ($\in \mathbb{R}$) to likelihood ($\in \mathbb{R} \in [0..1]$). The range of distances of interest (where the finger could be considered to be in contact with the string or very close) is from a few millimeters below the string (negative distance) to around 1 cm above. We therefore need an asymptotic function that tends to 0 for large values of the distance and tends to 1 for small (positive and negative) distances. For distances around 0.5 cm, for which it is not clear if the finger is in contact with the string, the likelihood should be around 0.5. The function is defined as $\theta(d) = \arctan(d * 10)/\pi + 1/2$, where d is the distance, and therefore,

$$\begin{aligned} L_L &= \theta(d_L), \\ L_R &= \theta(d_R). \end{aligned} \tag{4}$$

In addition, we need to define the likelihood of playing an open string (i.e. not stopping the string with the left hand fingers, $f = 0$). It is computed as $L_L(s, 0) = 1 - \sum_f L_L(s, f)$, that is, one minus the sum of likelihoods of being pressing the other frets in the same string.

5 Control Parameter Estimation

From the low level features we estimate in a first step the plucked string, the fret, the left-hand segment pressing that string at that fret and the plucking finger. In a second step, the plucking position, the plucking velocity and the plucking angles are computed using the coordinates of the string and plucking finger.

5.1 Plucked String (*String*)

It is the most likely string to be plucked at a note onset. The likelihood that a string is being played (L_S) is determined as a function of the pitch and the distances to the strings of the left and right hand fingers, d_L and d_R.

$$string = \max_s(L_S(s))$$
$$L_S(s) = L_P(s) \times L_L(s) \times L_R(s), \qquad (5)$$

5.2 Plucking Finger (*Finger*)

Once we know the plucked *string* (string with maximum L_S), it is straightforward to obtain the right-hand *finger* that plucks the *string*. It is the closest finger to the *string*, that is, the finger that maximizes the likelihood function L_R given the string:

$$finger = \max_{s=s_i} \theta(d_R(s, fg)). \qquad (6)$$

5.3 Fingering (*Fret* and *Bone*)

Ir refers to the position of left-hand fingers on the strings. Once the *string*, and the left hand finger distances have been estimated we can define the *fret* and *bone* as

$$fret = \max_{s=s_i} \theta(d_L(s, f))$$
$$bone = \max_{s=s_i, j=j_j} \theta(d_L(s, f, b)). \qquad (7)$$

5.4 Plucking Position (*C*)

The plucking position, velocity and angle are computed from the *string* and *finger* based on Euclidean Geometry as shown in Fig. 5. Be A and B the plucking *string* ends, and P the position of the plucking *finger*, the plucking position is the point of contact of the *string* and *finger*. Due to the position of the markers on the back of the hand, this may not be zero, so we define the point C as the point in the string that is closest to P. This point computed as the projection of the point P on the string,

$$C = AB \cdot AP * \widehat{AB}. \qquad (8)$$

Given the parametric definition of a line in 3D, we can define the point C as

$$C = A + tAB, 0 < t < 1, t \in \mathbb{R}. \qquad (9)$$

From Eqs. 8 and 9 we derive the value of $t = (AB \cdot AP)/|AB|^2$ for the point C. The plucking distance to the bridge (i.e. plucking position) is just the length of the segment $|AC|$, which corresponds to the value of the dot product $AB \cdot AP$.

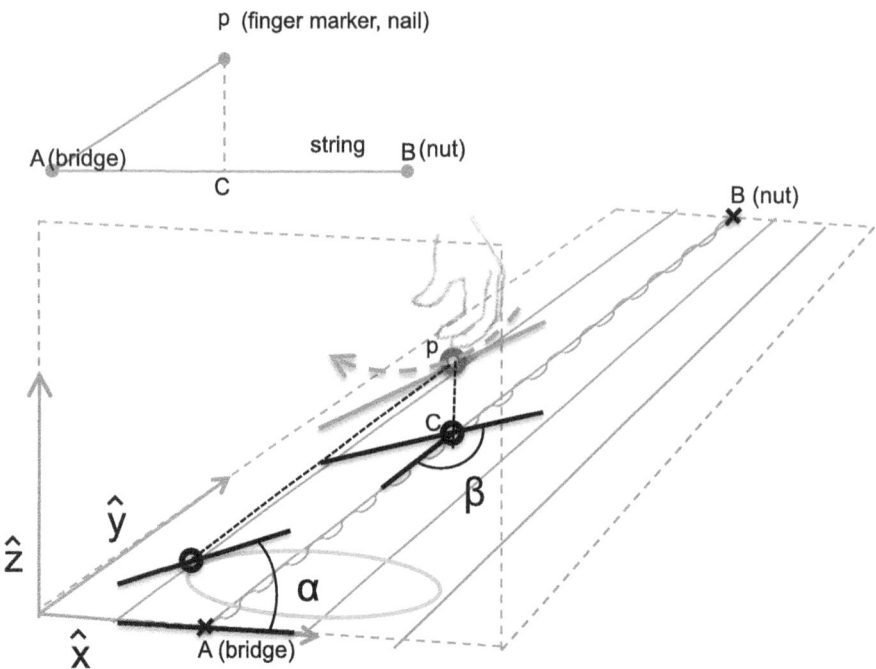

Fig. 5. Computation of plucking position, velocity and angles based on Euclidean Geometry.

5.5 Plucking Velocity (*v*)

The velocity is computed as the derivative of the marker trajectory at the plucking instant.

5.6 Plucking Angles (α and β)

Two angles are estimated as shown in Fig. 5. The angle α is the angle between the projection of the tangent of the finger trajectory at the plucking instant on the plane xz and the axis x. The second angle β is the angle between the projection of the tangent on the plane xy and the axis y. In order to simplify geometric computations, all points (string-end positions and finger trajectory around the plucking instant) are expressed relative to the local axis of coordinates (xyz), where the vector $\hat{x}$ is the unitary vector in the direction from the beginning of the sixth string to the beginning of the first string, vector $\hat{y}$ is the unitary vector in the direction of the playing string towards the frets, and $\hat{z}$ is obtained as the cross product $\hat{z} = \hat{x} \times \hat{y}$.

Any point P in global coordinates can be expressed in local coordinates P' by rotation (R) and traslation (T):

$$P' = (P - T) * R^{-1}, \tag{10}$$

where the traslation is given by the coordinates of the vector that connects the origin of coordinates from the global to the local system and the rotation is expressed as an Euler rotation matrix[3], which is computed from the rotation angles of the local coordinate axis with respect to the global axis. By using local coordinates, the computation of the projection of the finger trajectory $F(t)$ on the planes xy and xz (i.e. $F_{xy}(t)$ and $F_{xz}(t)$) becomes straight forward as they merely correspond to the coordinates of the axis. The tangents to the projected trajectories at the plucking instant have a slope equal to the derivative of the projected trajectories at that point, and this slope is also the tangent of the angles, so that:

$$\alpha = \arctan \frac{dF_{xy}(t)}{dt}, \ t = t_0$$
$$\beta = \arctan \frac{dF_{xz}(t)}{dt}, \ t = t_0. \tag{11}$$

6 Results

The performance of the presented method depends on a correct onset detection and marker identification. We can assume a very high rate of onset detection that is further improved by the alignment to the score (see Sect. 4) and marker identification rates are specified in Table 1, expressed as percentage of correctly identified markers relative to all frames as well as to the plucking instants. Identification of string markers achieves a rate of nearly 100 % but finger markers results are very variable depending on the marker.

Table 1. Percentage of correct marker identification taking all frames into account (*all frames*) and only frames at plucking instants (*at plucks*). The three joints in the left hand follow an order from closer to the palm towards the fingernail.

Marker	% all frames	% at plucks
String-ends	99	100
Left-index (3 joints)	99, 99, 83	100, 100, 87
Left-mid (3 joints)	99, 99, 60	100, 99, 58
Left-ring (3 joints)	100, 99, 77	100, 100, 71
Left-small (3 joints)	99, 99, 30	100, 100, 21
Right-thumb (nail)	99	100
Right-index (nail)	79	76
Right-mid (nail)	82	75
Right-ring (nail)	70	64
All 4 right hand markers	50	41

---

[3] http://mathworld.wolfram.com/EulerAngles.html.

6.1 Left Hand

Left hand markers have a higher rate of correct identification as, in general, they are always visible to the cameras. Additionally, fingering (i.e. left hand) is highly reinforced with the pitch, which largely determines the *string* and the *fret*, so even if a marker is lost, the closest finger is 100 % correctly estimated.

6.2 Right Hand

Regarding the right hand, only one marker per finger is considered, which is the one placed on the fingernail. It is especially these markers during the note onsets that are difficult to track due to occlusions. An average of 75 % of the markers are correctly identified but only around 41 % of the note onsets have all four markers (the four nails) and only 64 % of the plucks with the ring-finger are detected.

Two improvements have been added to the tracking of the right hand. First, markers are searched within a small window around the plucking instants, which allows to increase the chances that the plucking instant frame has every marker. For instance, in Table 2 we can see the difference of correctly estimated *plucking fingers* using a window of 3 frames (46 %) and a window of 21 frames (58 %). Second, marker trajectories are interpolated in order to fill missing gaps. Different types of interpolation were compared. If the marker trajectory gaps are small the type of interpolation does not affect the estimation but if the gap is big, the selection of the interpolating algorithm becomes very important. The best performing interpolation is a *piecewise cubic hermite spline* achieving rates for string and fret estimation of 100 % and around 75 % for the right and left fingers. In Table 2 we can find a summary of the results with different windows and interpolation algorithms.

Table 2. Percentage of correctly estimated plucking *finger* using different window sizes w (which allows to look for missing markers in frames around a plucking instant) and different marker interpolation algorithms: no interpolation (*no interp.*), cubic splines (*spline*), cubic smoothing splines (*csaps*), nearest neighbor (*nearest*), linear and piecewise cubic hermite polynomial (*pchip*).

	% plucking finger
no interp., $w = 3$	46
no Interp., $w = 21$	58
spline, $w = 3$	64
csaps, $w = 3$	64
nearest, $w = 3$	73
linear, $w = 3$	75
pchip, $w = 3$	78

6.3 Position, Velocity and Angles

The error of the characteristics of the pluck (position, velocity and angles) is estimated by using notes where the plucking fingernail markers are correctly identified. For these notes, plucking parameters are computed and their values compared to an estimation of the same pluck, but with missing marker position information. The trajectory of the marker is removed at a window of 10 frames around the note onset and a new trajectory is estimated through *pchip* interpolation. Such an evaluation results in a Correlation Coefficient of 0.83 for the plucking position, 0.75 for the velocity and 0.73 and 0.72 for the plucking angles α and β respectively.

7 Conclusion

In this study we showed a method for the extraction of a comprehensive set of control parameters from guitar performances based on hand-motion capture and supported by audio analysis and information on the score. The extraction of control parameters will allow for future research on the interaction between the guitar and the player, the relationship between gestures and sound and the analysis of different playing techniques to mention a few fields.

Results show that by combination of multimodal information, it is possible to estimate such a comprehensive set of control features, with special high performance for the fingering and plucked string estimation. The two most relevant contributions of the method are (1) the combination of multimodal data. Solely based on motion capture it would be very complicated to detect the correct onsets or plucking instants. Additionally, the availability of the ground truth pitch highly reinforces the detection of string, fingering and fret; (2) interpolation of marker trajectories and the use of a plucking window makes marker identification more robust and boosts the estimation rates.

Several improvements are foreseen for the future. (1) Develop an algorithm for pitch extraction from audio adapted to the guitar to avoid the use of a musical score; (2) build a 3D flexible object model of the hand and a hand motion grammar in order to restrict the possible positions of the flexible object and be able to reconstruct missing markers from the position and angles of the identified joints; (3) Use of a finger-tip model in order to calibrate the position of the real nail and flesh with respect to the marker; (4) The use of high speed video cameras to calibrate and evaluate data from the motion capture and deepen the analysis of the plucking process (start, contact and release) as done in [4].

Acknowledgments. A. Perez-Carrillo was supported by a Beatriu de Pinos grant 2010 BP-A 00209 by the Catalan Research Agency (AGAUR) and J. Ll. Arcos was supported by ICT -2011-8-318770 and 2009-SGR-1434 projects.

References

1. Abesser, G.S.J., Lukashevich, H.: Feature-based extraction of plucking and expression styles of the electric bass. In: Proceedings of the ICCASP Conference, Kyoto, Japan (2012)
2. Bevilacqua, F., Schnell, N., Rasamimanana, N., Zamborlin, B., Guédy, F.: Online gesture analysis and control of audio processing. In: Solis, J., Ng, K. (eds.) Musical Robots and Interactive Multimodal Systems. Springer Tracts in Advanced Robotics, vol. 74, pp. 127–142. Springer, Heidelberg (2011). doi:10.1007/978-3-642-22291-78
3. Burns, A.M., Wanderley, M.M.: Visual methods for the retrieval of guitarist fingering. In: Proceedings of NIME, pp. 196–199. IRCAM, Paris (2006). http://dl.acm.org/citation.cfm?id=1142215.1142263
4. Chadefaux, D., Carrou, J.L.L., Fabre, B., Daudet, L.: Experimentally based description of harp plucking. J. Acoust. Soc. Am. **131**(1), 844–855 (2012). http://link.aip.org/link/?JAS/131/844/1
5. de Cheveigné, A., Kawahara, H.: YIN, a fundamental frequency estimator for speech and music. J. Acoust. Soc. Am. **111**(4), 1917–1930 (2002). http://link.aip.org/link/?JAS/111/1917/1
6. Collins, N., Kiefer, C., Patoli, Z., White, M.: Musical exoskeletons: experiments with a motion capture suit. In: New Interfaces for Musical Expression, Sydney, Australia (2010)
7. Duxbury, C., Bello, J.P., Davies, M., Sandler, M.: Complex domain onset detection for musical signals. In: Proceedings of the DAFx. Queen Mary University, London (2003)
8. Eberly, D.H.: 3D Game Engine Design: A Practical Approach to Real-time Computer Graphics. Morgan Kaufmann Publishers Inc., San Francisco (2000)
9. Erkut, C., Välimäki, V., Karjalainen, M., Laurson, M.: Extraction of physical and expressive parameters for model-based sound synthesis of the classical guitar. In: Audio Engineering Society Convention 108, February 2000. http://www.aes.org/e-lib/browse.cfm?elib=9224
10. Guaus, E., Arcos, J.L.: Analyzing left hand fingering in guitar playing. In: Proceedings of the SMC. Universitat Pompeu Fabra, Barcelona, July 2010
11. Heijink, H., Meulenbroek, R.: On the complexity of classical guitar playing: functional adaptations to task constraints. J. Motor Behav. **34**(4), 339–351 (2002)
12. Linden, J.V.D., Schoonderwaldt, E., Bird, J.: Towards a real-time system for teaching novices correct violin bowing technique. In: IEEE International Workshop on Haptic Audio visual Environments and Games, pp. 81–86, November 2009
13. Maestre, E., Blaauw, M., Bonada, J., Guaus, E., Pérez, A.: Statistical modeling of bowing control applied to sound synthesis. IEEE Trans. Audio Speech Lang. Process. Special Issue on Virtual Analog Audio Effects and Musical Instruments (2010)
14. Maestre, E., Bonada, J., Blaauw, M., Pérez, A., Guaus, E.: Acquisition of violin instrumental gestures using a commercial EMF device. In: International Computer Music Conference, Copenhagen, Denmark (2007)
15. Norton, J.: Motion capture to build a foundation for a computer-controlled instrument by study of classical guitar performance. Ph.D. thesis, Department of Music, Stanford University (2008)

16. Penttinen, H., Välimäki, V.: A time-domain approach to estimating the plucking point of guitar tones obtained with an under-saddle pickup. Appl. Acoust. **65**(12), 1207–1220 (2004). http://www.sciencedirect.com/science/article/pii/S0003682X04001057
17. Pérez-Carrillo, A., Wanderley, M.: Indirect acquisition of violin instrumental controls from audio signal with hidden markov models. IEEE/ACM Trans. Audio Speech Lang. Process. **23**(5), 932–940 (2015)
18. Pérez-Carrillo, A.: Enhancing spectral synthesis techniques with performance gestures using the violin as a case study. Ph.D. thesis, Universitat Pompeu Fabra, Barcelona, Spain (2009). www.mtg.upf.edu/static/media/Perez-Alfonso-PhD-2009.pdf
19. Pérez-Carrillo, A., Bonada, J., Maestre, E., Guaus, E., Blaauw, M.: Performance control driven violin timbre model based on neural networks. IEEE Trans. Audio Speech Lang. Process. **20**(3), 1007–1021 (2012)
20. Reboursière, L., Lähdeoja, O., Drugman, T., Dupont, S., Picard-Limpens, C., Riche, N.: Left and right-hand guitar playing techniques detection. In: NIME. University of Michigan, Ann Arbor, 21–23 May 2012
21. Scherrer, B.: Physically-informed indirect acquisition of instrumental gestures on the classical guitar: extracting the angle of release. Ph.D. thesis, McGill University, Montréal, QC (2013)
22. Scherrer, B., Depalle, P.: Extracting the angle of release from guitar tones: preliminary results. In: Proceedings of Acoustics, Nantes, France (2012)
23. Schneider, J.: The Contemporary Guitar, New Instrumentation, vol. 5. University of California Press, Berkeley (1985)
24. Schoonderwaldt, E., Guettler, K., Askenfelt, A.: An empirical investigation of bow-force limits in the Schelleng diagram. AAA **94**(4), 604–622 (2008)
25. Traube, C., Depalle, P.: Deriving the plucking point location along a guitar string from a least-square estimation of a comb filter delay. In: IEEE Canadian Conference on Electrical and Computer Engineering, vol. 3, pp. 2001–2004, May 2003
26. Traube, C., Smith, J.O.: Estimating the plucking point on a guitar string. In: Proceedings of COST-G6 Conference on Digital Audio Effects, Verona, Italy (2000). http://profs.sci.univr.it/dafx/DAFx-final-papers.html
27. Visentin, P., Shan, G., Wasiak, E.B.: Informing music teaching and learning using movement analysis technology. Int. J. Music Educ. **26**(1), 73–87 (2008). http://ijm.sagepub.com/content/26/1/73.abstract
28. Wanderley, M.M., Depalle, P.: Gestural control of sound synthesis. In: Proceedings of the IEEE, pp. 632–644 (2004)
29. Zhang, B., Wang, Y.: Automatic music transcription using audio-visual fusion for violin practice in home environment. Technical report, TRA7/09, Shool of Computing, National University of Singapore (2009)

Analysis of Mimed Violin Performance Movements of Neophytes
Patterns, Periodicities, Commonalities and Individualities

Federico Visi[1(✉)], Esther Coorevits[2], Rodrigo Schramm[3], and Eduardo R. Miranda[1]

[1] Interdisciplinary Centre for Computer Music Research (ICCMR),
Plymouth University, Plymouth, EU, UK
{federico.visi,eduardo.miranda}@plymouth.ac.uk
[2] IPEM – Institute for Psychoacoustics and Electronic Music,
Ghent University, Ghent, EU, Belgium
esther.coorevits@ugent.be
[3] Universidade Federal do Rio Grande do Sul, Porto Alegre, Brazil
rodrigos@caef.ufrgs.br

Abstract. Body movement and embodied knowledge play an important part in how we express and understand music. The gestures of a musician playing an instrument are part of a shared knowledge that contributes to musical expressivity by building expectations and influencing perception. In this study, we investigate the extent in which the movement vocabulary of violin performance is part of the embodied knowledge of individuals with no experience in playing the instrument. We asked people who cannot play the violin to mime a performance along an audio excerpt recorded by an expert. They do so by using a silent violin, specifically modified to be more accessible to neophytes. Preliminary motion data analyses suggest that, despite the individuality of each performance, there is a certain consistency among participants in terms of overall rhythmic resonance with the music and movement in response to melodic phrasing. Individualities and commonalities are then analysed using Functional Principal Component Analysis.

Keywords: Movement · Gesture · Body motion · Motion capture · Violin · Musical instrument · Performance · Motion analysis · Periodic quantity of motion

1 Introduction

The study of embodiment, body movement and gestures in music has recently become an established field of study. Several theoretical accounts have been put forward through the years [17–19,21], often accompanied by empirical analysis of body movements of people performing, listening or dancing to music.

As pointed out in [27], musical instruments have a *a repertoire of sound-producing gestures* that contribute to build the *ecological knowledge* associated to that instrument. Hence, this shared knowledge affects one's musical experience, by creating expectations and guiding musical understanding. In fact, by adopting an ecological approach, musical perception is seen as an active experience influenced by a highly-structured environment rather than a passive, disembodied phenomenon. From this perspective *"exposure to the environment shape perceptual capacities of an individual"* and *"perception and actions are inextricably bound together"* [9].

The goal of the present study is to empirically explore the shared knowledge of the gestural repertoire of a well-known musical instrument among people that have no previous experience in playing that particular instrument. This is done by analysing the motion data gathered during an experiment where neophytes are asked to mime a violin performance. The analysis focuses on several body parts and movement features, in relation to the music and in comparison to the actual performance of an experienced violinist.

This experiment draws its motivation from the assumption that the musician encodes gestures in sound and the listener can decode particular aspects of them through corporeal imitation. As Leman notes, the listener is capable of grasping music as intended moving form and perception and understanding of musical expressiveness is based on corporeal resonance behaviour: *"Obviously the movements of the listener are not [...] the same as the movements of the player. What is more or less the same [...] is the motor system that encodes and decodes sonic forms."* [21]. Therefore, a more detailed analysis of the extent of the gestural vocabulary of an instrument also among non-experts can contribute to the understanding of musical perception and expression.

A relevant aspect of the design of this experiment is the use of an actual violin, specifically modified to not emit any sound when bowed and to be more accessible to people that have never used one before. Previous studies have analysed so-called "air performances" of experts and beginners mimicking the use of various instruments [11,16]. Here, the choice of using an actual instrument is motivated by the adoption of an ecological approach, assuming that the relationship with the object (indeed part of the aforementioned environment [9]) and its affordances [13,14] may have a significant impact on the movements of the subjects. In addition, experience using tools has also been the subject of embodied music cognition research [22] and the concept of affordance has seen renewed interest in multidisciplinary music research [1,24].

The analysis of the motion data gathered during the experiment focuses prevalently on intermediate and high-level movement descriptors. This is motivated by ecological perceptual theories suggesting that, when processing information, people seem to be aware of high-level features more directly than lower-level features [9]. Therefore, we expect high-level movement features to be more readily identified and shared by the participants. Moreover, body movement and entrainment in response to music are complex and dynamic phenomenons.

Therefore, movement analysis should try to address complex patterns from multidimensional motion data, rather than single values that capture a particular feature of a movement segment. Amelynck et al. [2] proposed a new method that avoids this segmentation and takes into account the complete movement dynamics. They analysed the spontaneous bodily responses of people to a musical stimulus and tried to model expressiveness in terms of commonalities and individualities using Functional Principal Component Analysis (FPCA) [26].

2 The Experiment: Materials and Methods

2.1 Participants

A total of thirteen participants took part in the study. This includes twelve neophytes (7 male, 5 female, average age: 33.4, SD of age: 9.8) and one experienced violinist (male, aged 23), who performed and recorded the stimuli for the experiment. All participants gave their informed consent and were free to take breaks or abandon the experiment at any point. Ethical approval was granted by the Arts and Humanities Research Ethics Sub-committee at the Faculty of Arts and Humanities, Plymouth University. Participants were also asked to fill out a brief anonymous questionnaire with basic personal data and information about their musical background.

2.2 Stimuli

Participants were asked to mime a violin performance using the modified violin along 5 randomly-ordered musical stimuli, which consisted of brief solo violin excerpts recorded by the experienced violinist. Stimuli were between 8.5 and 34 s long and were chosen to cover a variety of different styles and instrumental techniques.

List of Stimuli

- Antonio Vivaldi *"Violin Concerto in A minor, Op 3, No 6, RV 356"* (1711)
- Kaija Saariaho, *"Nocturne for solo violin"* (1994)
- Camille Saint-Sans *"Le Carnaval des Animaux - 10. Volière"* (1886)
- Niccolò Paganini *"Caprice No. 1 'The Arpeggio' in E major: Andante"* (1819)
- Sergei Prokofiev *"Five Melodies for Violin and Piano, Op. 35bis"* (1925)

This study focuses on the data collected using the first and second stimuli. The first stimulus consists of bars 1–12 of the first movement (Allegro) of Vivaldi's Violin Concerto in A minor (Fig. 1), whereas the second one includes bars 45–48 of the Nocturne for solo violin by Kaija Saariaho (Fig. 2).

Fig. 1. Excerpt of the violin part of Vivaldi's Violin Concerto in a minor. The audio recording of the first twelve bars was used as stimulus for the experiment.

Fig. 2. Excerpt of Saariaho's Nocturne for solo violin. The audio recording of bars 45–48 was used as stimulus for the experiment.

2.3 Apparatus

The multimodal recordings were carried out at the Interdisciplinary Centre for Computer Music Research (ICCMR), Plymouth University, United Kingdom and at fourMs - Music, Mind, Motion, Machines, University of Oslo, Norway. In Plymouth, participants' movements were recorded using a six-camera marker-based optical motion capture system (Natural Point Optitrack Flex 3[1]) tracking at a frame rate of 100 Hz. A total of 33 reflective markers were attached to each participant and to the instrument and were located as follow[2]: LF head, RF head, LB head, RB head, L shoulder, R shoulder, spine (T5), LF hip, RF hip, LB hip, RB hip, L elbow, R elbow, L wrist (radius), L wrist (ulna), R wrist (radius), R wrist (ulna), L knee, R knee, L ankle, R ankle, L heel, R heel, L toe, R toe, R scapula[3], violin scroll, violin L upper bout, violin R upper bout, violin L lower bout, violin R lower bout, bow tip, bow frog (see Fig. 3).

---

[1] http://www.optitrack.com.
[2] L = Left; R = Right; F = Front; B = Back. A similar configuration can be found in [5].
[3] Used to obtain an asymmetrical marker set, useful for marker identification and tracking. Not used for analysis.

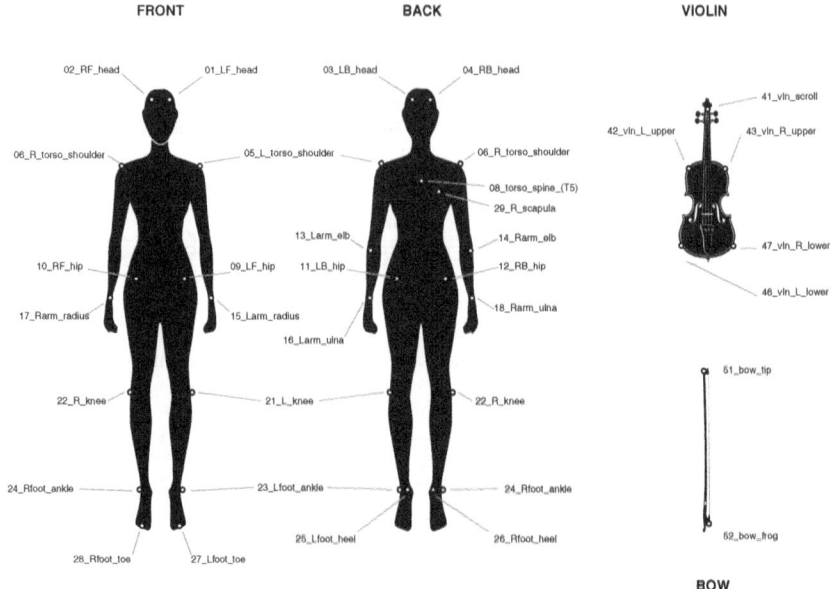

Fig. 3. Marker locations and labels.

In Plymouth, an additional marker located on the sternum of the participants was used. However, the data associated to that marker was eventually discarded as it contained too many dropouts due to the frequent occlusion caused by the right arm during bowing movements. That marker was therefore not used in the subsequent recording sessions in Oslo. The stimuli were played back through a pair of Genelec 8020C loudspeakers using a DAW[4]. The audio interface also generated the SMPTE signal used for synchronising audio, video and motion capture sources. The audio in the room was recorded by a pair of condenser microphones placed in a XY stereo configuration as well as by a video camera used to film the sessions.

In Oslo, the performances were recorded using a nine-camera marker-based optical motion capture system (Qualisys Oqus 300[5]) using the same frame rate (100 Hz) and marker configuration (except for the sternum marker) used in Plymouth. The feed from a digital video camera was recorded within the Qualisys Track Manager software alongside the motion tracking data. The stimuli were played back using the same model of loudspeakers and the same DAW software while recording and playback of the various sources was synchronised using a custom Max[6] patch.

---

[4] http://www.reaper.fm.
[5] http://www.qualisys.com.
[6] https://cycling74.com.

The participants were asked to simulate the performance using a modified violin designed specifically for the experiment. This violin was fitted with a support system that allowed the instrument to be safely strapped to the shoulder of the participant. This was done in order to allow the participants – which in most cases never had held a violin before – to move with more confidence without being afraid to drop the instrument. Two thin metal plates soldered to a metal strip that follows the profile of the bridge were mounted on the violin body above the strings (see Fig. 4). This add-on had a dual purpose—it helped novices to quickly overcome the initial difficulties of holding the bow in a correct standard playing position and it prevented contact between the strings and the bow hair, hence making the violin silent.

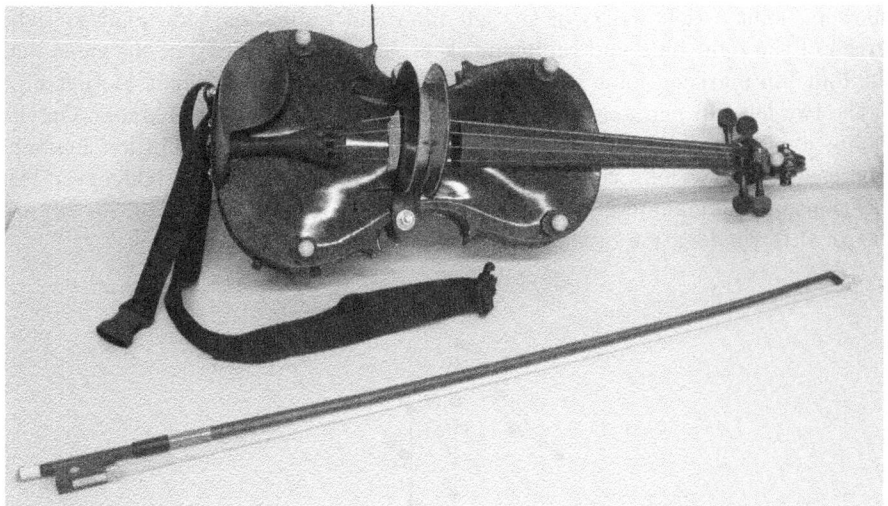

Fig. 4. The modified violin used for the experiment.

2.4 Procedure

The expert violinist was recorded first. He performed all the selected excerpts, which provided both the audio stimuli for the neophytes and video and motion data to use as a benchmark for the analysis of the participant's movements.

Each neophyte was recorded individually. For each stimulus, the participant was asked to first listen to the audio once in order to familiarise with the music and then use the modified violin to mime a performance along the played back audio twice. Audio, video and motion data were recorded during each trial.

3 Analysis of Periodicity and Phrasing Using Mocapgrams and Periodic Quantity of Motion

3.1 Movement Data Preprocessing

The motion data was first preprocessed, labeled and exported to C3D files using Optitrack Motive and Qualisys Track Manager. The C3D files were then loaded in MATLAB using Motion Capture (MoCap) Toolbox [6]. The 33 markers described above were then transformed into a set of 23 secondary markers, which in the MoCap Toolbox framework are referred to as 'joints' [5,6]. The locations of these joints is represented in Fig. 5. Seven joints are obtained by calculating the centroid of two or more markers: joint 1 (head) is the midpoint of the four head markers; joint 2 (manubrium) is the midpoint of the shoulder markers, joint 5 (left wrist) of the left ulna and radius markers, joint 8 (right wrist) of the right ulna and radius markers, joint 9 (mid torso) of the spine and the four hip markers, joint 10 (root) of the four hip markers, joint 11 (left hip) of the two left hip markers, joint 15 (right hip) of the right hip markers. On the violin, joint 20 (violin left bout) is the midpoint of the two violin left markers whereas joint 21 (violin right bout) is the midpoint of the two right ones. The locations of the remaining joints (3, 4, 6, 7, 12, 13, 14, 16, 17, 18, 19, 23, 22) are identical to the location of the respective markers (see Fig. 5).

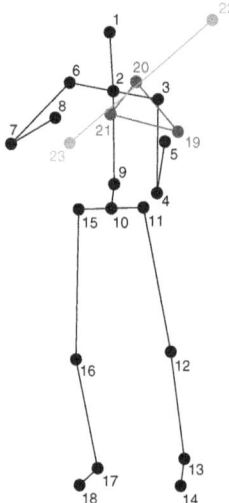

Fig. 5. Joints configuration: 1 = head; 2 = manubrium; 3 = left shoulder; 4 = left elbow; 5 = left wrist; 6 = right shoulder; 7 = right elbow; 8 = right wrist; 9 = mid torso; 10 = root; 11 = left hip; 12 = left knee; 13 = left ankle; 14 = right toe; 15 = right hip; 16 = right knee; 17 = right ankle; 18 = right toe; 19 = violin scroll; 20 = violin left bout; 21 = violin right bout; 22 = bow tip; 23 = bow frog.

3.2 Comparative Movement Data Analysis Using Full Mocapgrams

By plotting Mocapgrams [20] (a graph in which position coordinates of each marker are normalised and projected onto an RGB colorspace) it was possible to do a preliminary analysis and observe recurring patterns and periodicities in the motion data. Figure 6 shows full Mocapgrams for the performances of the expert violinist and of one of the neophytes (top left and top right graphs respectively) on Vivaldi's Violin Concerto excerpt (henceforth 'first stimulus'). Regular colour patterns in the horizontal rows corresponding to each marker suggest periodicity in certain parts of the body and the instrument. As an example, the thinnest pattern can be observed in the right elbow and wrist joints (labeled '7_R_elbow_J' and '8_R_wrist_J' respectively), which is consistent with the pattern visible in the bow markers ('22_bow_tip_J' and '23_bow_frog_J'). This shows, expectably, a certain coherence in the movement of the bow and the arm that holds it, as well as high frequency periodicity caused by the repetitive bowing movements. Similarly, it is straightforward to notice that the left toe of the expert ('14_L_toe_J') changes position only three times throughout the whole take.

For the purpose of this study, Mocapgrams are useful not only to observe general periodicity in the movement of certain parts of the body during the performance. By providing an overall view of all the motion data, they also allow to locate movements that affect the whole body, which are visualised by vertical stripes that go across all the marker rows. In the first stimulus, the most evident perturbation in the motion data of the expert can be clearly seen between sec. 23 and 25. The waveform aligned to the graphs shows that this general shift coincides with the peak the melody reaches at the beginning of bar 9, before concluding the phrase on the minim at the end of the same bar. A similar, albeit slightly delayed[7], general perturbation in the motion data can be observed in the neophyte around sec. 25. This is consistent with the data of the other participants. Figure 7 shows the magnitude of the mean velocities of the upper body joints (labelled 1 to 8 in Fig. 5) of all the neophytes. Right hand and elbow are plotted separately, since they are involved in the main instrumental movement and therefore show the highest magnitudes. As it can be seen in the graph of the first stimulus, the mean velocities of all joints drop near sec. 25, and so do he values of the standard deviation. This confirms what observed above for the expert and one of the neophytes and suggests a general tendency to parse evident melodic phrases with overt body movements. As it can be noticed from the full Mocapgrams, this phenomenon occurs repeatedly during the neophyte's performance and the same trend is visible in the data of the other participants. This is consistent with findings in previous studies on air-performance showing that beginners tend to move more than experts [16].

The second stimulus used is an excerpt from Kaija Saariaho's Nocturne for solo violin (Fig. 2). Compared to the first stimulus, the pulse of the piece is less steady and distinct. Each bar begins with a left hand pizzicato ('+' sign in the

---

[7] The delay is plausibly due to the fact that the neophytes follow the audio recorded during the expert's performance, therefore their movements slightly lag behind the ones of the expert.

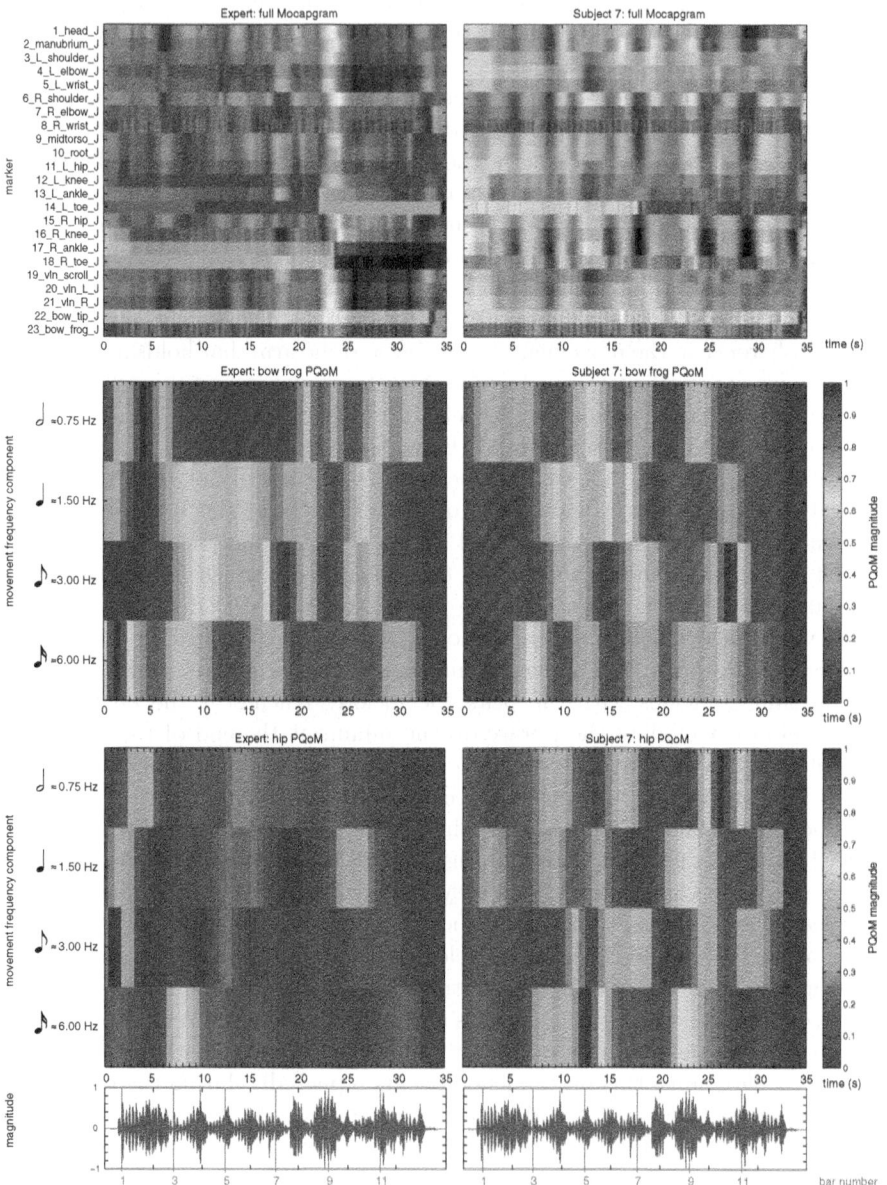

Fig. 6. First stimulus (Vivaldi, score in Fig. 1). Full Mocapgrams and Periodic Quantity of Motion (PQoM) estimates of the bow frog and hip markers for the expert violinist (left) and one of the neophytes (subject 7, right) aligned to the waveform of the audio.

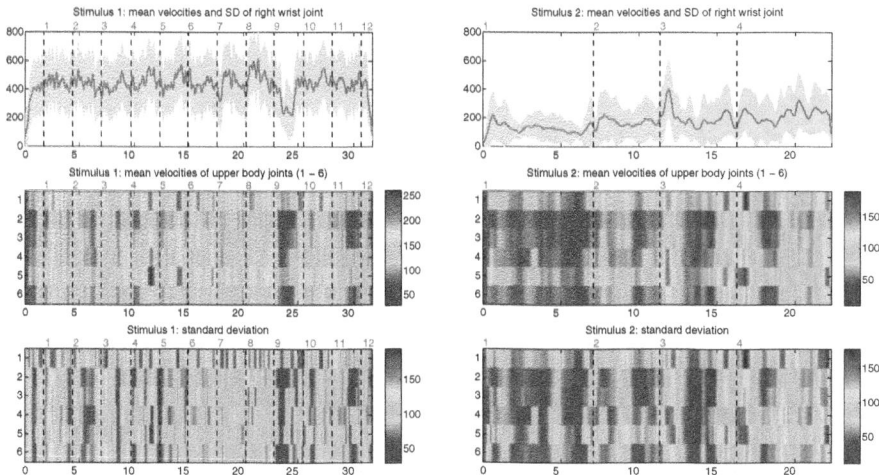

Fig. 7. Mean velocities of right wrist and upper body joints (labelled 1 to 6, see Fig. 5 for the location). The graphs on the left show the values for the first stimulus (Vivaldi, Fig. 1) while those on the right show the values for the second stimulus (Saariaho, Fig. 2). The red numbers and the vertical dashed lines indicate the bar number and downbeat location. Velocity is expressed in mm/sec and time in seconds. (Color figure online)

score) and continues with a glissando (or with two extra-metric groupings in the case of bar 48), which then leads to a tremolo. The downbeat of each bar is clearly punctuated by the pizzicato while the intermediate beats are more indistinct. In the mean velocities for the second stimulus depicted in Fig. 7 we can in fact notice sharper peaks and valleys around the bar lines. Those are the points were the tremolo reaches its peak leading to the onset of the pizzicato gesture. The individual Mocapgrams of the data (shown in Fig. 8 for the expert and one of the neophytes) also show general perturbations around those key points, especially around the downbeat of bar 3 and 4. Overall, there is ostensibly a clear intention among all the participants to interpret the musical gesture of the pizzicato with a sharp movement. Even though the location and extent of the movement may differ from subject to subject, those musical events are consistently mapped to similar gestural reactions.

3.3 Analysis of Movement Periodicity Using Periodic Quantity of Motion

Another useful descriptor used for analysing movement periodicity is Periodic Quantity of Motion (PQoM). First introduced in [28], this index gives an estimate of the resonance of the movement periodicity with different rhythmic subdivisions in the music. Inspired by the widely known Quantity of Motion (QoM) [7,8], PQoM is a motion descriptor useful to observe how movement

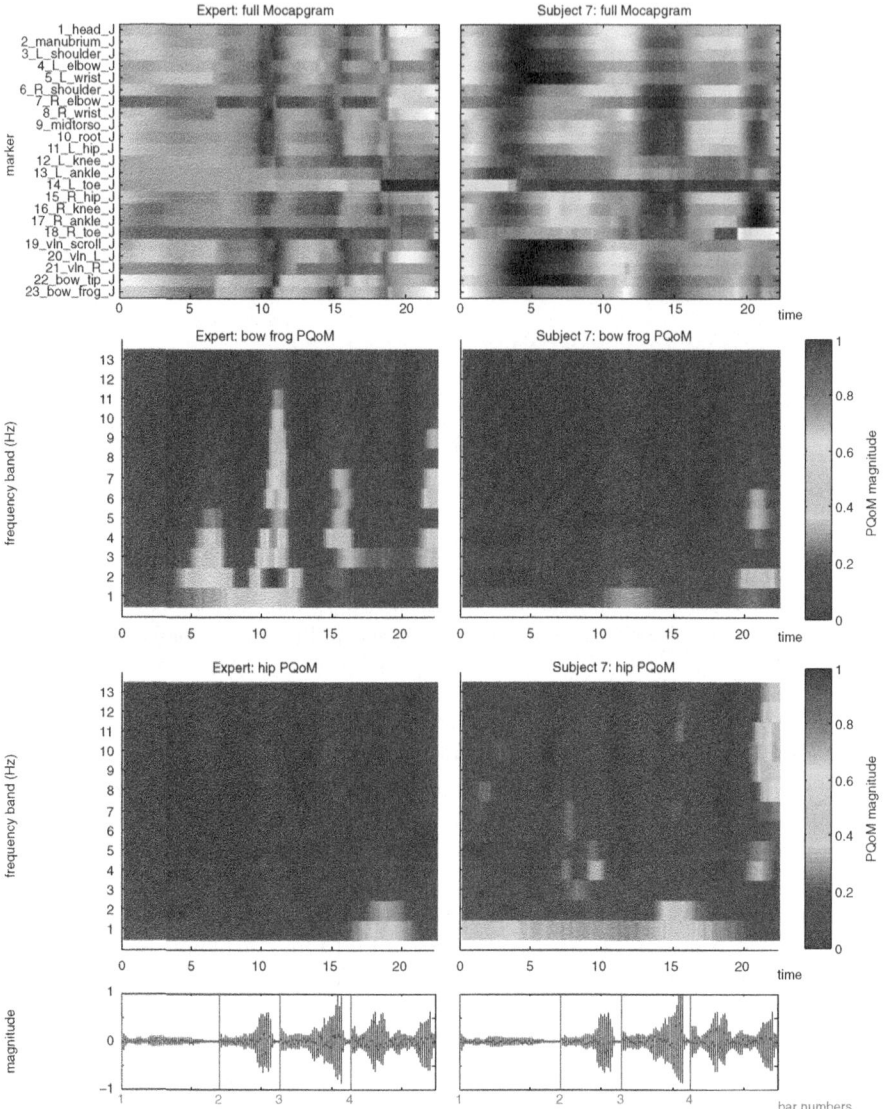

Fig. 8. Second stimulus (Saariaho, score in Fig. 2). Full Mocapgrams and Periodic Quantity of Motion (PQoM) estimates of the bow frog and hip markers for the expert violinist (left) and one of the neophytes (subject 7, right) aligned to the waveform of the audio.

relates to rhythmic aspects of the music. PQoM is calculated by subdividing the magnitude vector of the 3D motion data into frequency components by using filter banks. The frequencies of the filters correspond to multiples and subdivisions of the musical rhythm of the piece. In the case of the first stimulus (Fig. 1), a frequency of 1.5 Hz corresponds approximately to a steady crotchet beat, while

0.75 Hz correspond to a minim beat, 3 Hz to a quaver beat and 6 Hz to a semiquaver beat. The PQoM at a certain rhythmic subdivision is the magnitude of the corresponding frequency component in the movement normalised between 0 and 1. PQoM was estimated for four components until the end of the audio stimulus (sec. 33). By using PQoM, it is possible to relate the motion periodicities initially observed in the Mocapgrams to the actual rhythmic features of the musical stimulus. In Fig. 6, PQoM graphs of the bow frog marker and one of the hip markers are aligned to the Mocapgrams. These two markers were chosen as the former is a good indicator of the main instrumental gesture (bowing), while the latter traces ancillary movements occurring in the lower half of the body during the performance. As shown in a previous study [27], movements in this area in some cases do not resonate evenly with the instrumental movements in the upper body. This is noticeable here as well after a first glance at the PQoM graphs in Fig. 6. Expectably, the bow frog PQoM of the expert is generally higher. However, expert and neophyte seem to follow similar patterns throughout their performances, with PQoM peaking around sec. 4 and 25 in the 0.75 Hz component, between sec. 6 and 16 in the 1.5 Hz component and at sec. 26 in the 3 Hz one. However, the two hip PQoM graphs look very different from each other, sharing only a relative peak in the 1.5 Hz component around the minim that closes the phrase in bar 9. In fact, the neophyte's hip PQoM graph shows that entrainment is remarkably more frequent and intense in that area than in the expert's. Moreover, by aligning PQoM graphs with Mocapgrams, it is possible to add further details to previous observations. In correspondence with the end of the phrase described previously (bar 9, sec. 23–25), there is a sudden shift of the PQoM index from a peak in the minim beat frequency to a peak in the quaver beat frequency after sec. 25. This salient turning point in the melody is therefore consistently reflected in the movement of both subjects, denoting a shared, embodied knowledge of the expressive qualities of the music, which they express through their instrumental gestures regardless of their expertise with the instrument.

As noted also in the previous section, compared to the first stimulus the second stimulus (Fig. 2) lacks of the steady and evident *allegro* pulse. The excerpt used has a much slower pace with expressive variations (the tempo indication reads *Sempre espressivo, calmo* (♩ = c.54)). This is evident when looking at the red bar lines plotted on the waveforms in Fig. 8, which denote bars of slightly different durations. Therefore, we estimated the PQoM for several different frequency bands (from 1 Hz to 13 Hz with a step of 1 Hz). The results show, expectably, an overall less pronounced movement periodicity compared to the first stimulus. However, there are notable peaks in the PQoM of the expert's bow frog, especially in the 2 Hz and 4 Hz frequency bands. This peaks occur right before the downbeat of each bar, in correspondence of the tremolo notes that lead to the pizzicato notes. Notice the alignment of these peaks of periodicity with the vertical stripes denoting movement across the whole body in the expert's Mocapgram at sec. 10 and 15. This peaks in PQoM values are ostensibly due to the faster, repetitive bow strokes necessary to perform the tremolos.

A peak of periodicity, although weaker, can be observer also in the neophyte's bow frog marker, towards the end of bars 2 and 4 (approximately between sec. 10 and 12 and after sec. 20). Similarly to the previous stimulus, the bow frog PQoM of the expert is generally higher. However, there are relative peaks around the same areas, in correspondence with the tremolos.

The expert's hip marker shows much weaker periodicity. Apart from some barely noticeable peaks near in the areas leading to the downbeats of each bar (which may denote some modest resonance with the periodicity of the bow frog during the tremolo gestures), the PQoM values slightly increase in the low frequency bands in bar 4. On the other hand, the PQoM values of the neophyte's hip marker are noticeably higher throughout, confirming the tendency observed on the first stimulus. There is, again, more entrainment in the ancillary movements of the neophyte. This supports the assumptions made in Sect. 3.2 and is yet again consistent with the findings of previous studies [16].

3.4 Results

The preliminary comparative analysis of the motion data of the first stimulus suggests that high-level, structural features of the music are expressed through instrumental movements in similar ways by the subjects, regardless of their ability to play violin. In particular, the turning point of the melodic phrase at bar 9 seems to be something that is *'felt'* by the subjects also in a strongly embodied way, as it impacts the movement of the whole body and the periodicity of the instrumental movements, which shifts sharply from a frequency to the other. In addition to that, after the minim that closes the phrase there is a peak in the 3 Hz PQoM of the expert and an even higher one in the neophyte. This may suggest that the suspension created by a longer note ending a phrase creates a stronger expectation for the following melodic part, with which the neophyte engages also through ancillary movements, as shown by the hip PQoM graph. In fact, all the neophytes seem to have a more pronounced full-body periodicity. This can be hypothesised by simply looking at the vertical stripes in the Mocapgrams. However, PQoM gives a much more precise estimate of the periodicity in relation to the musical rhythm. Nearly all the neophytes seem to have a generally higher resonance with the periodicity of the music at the hip compared to the expert, whose PQoM is instead higher at the bow frog. This can be observed in both stimuli, and may lead to hypothesise that neophytes tend to follow the pulse and the features of the music with ancillary movements also to compensate for the lack of expressivity of their silent instrument. Doing so, they express the musical content of the stimulus using their full bodies.

Compatibly, the data of the second stimulus (even though musically very different from the first one) also suggest the major structural features of the musical excerpt are expressed through instrumental movements in similar ways. The second stimulus shows expectably less entrainment due to its slower and more implicit rhythmic features. However, the bar subdivision delineated by the rising tremolos and the pizzicatos are clearly expressed by the neophytes through instrumental and body movements.

4 Analysis of Individualities and Commonalities

Our interaction with music engages the whole body, but not all body parts show the same behaviour [4,27]. In this analysis, we focus on the movements of the head and the right wrist. In fact, previous research has shown that string players communicate expressive qualities of the music through head movements [10,15]. In addition, we also address the movements made by the right wrist, a body part that is directly involved in sound-producing gestures, as the bow is moved by the right hand.

In this analysis, the performances of all the 12 neophytes are taken in consideration. The first derivative (velocity) was calculated from the motion data of each subject using a Savitsky-Golay smoothing filter with a regression window of 7 frames [6] and the resulting signals were set equal to the norm of the derivatives. Secondly, the speed envelope was calculated using a moving average filter of 100 frames in case of the Vivaldi and 150 frames in case of the Saariaho to make sure the beat of the music (1.5 Hz for the Vivaldi, 0.7 Hz for the Saariaho) was covered by the window and at the same time avoid losing too much nuances in the movement. We then compared the speed of the body movements, as this feature is closely related to kinetic energy [12]. To check if the data was normally distributed, a Weibull function was fitted to the distribution of the speed values across subjects at all moments in time. The mean speed signal of both head and wrist at each timestamp over participants was approximately normally distributed, corresponding to a shape parameter of the fitted Weibull distribution between 2.7 and 3.2 for both pieces.

4.1 Modelling Head and Wrist Movements

The method for the analysis of expressiveness proposed by Amelynck et al. [2] is based on Functional Principal Component Analysis (FPCA). FPCA allows to describe a signal as the sum of an average signal $\bar{f}(t)$ with a linear combination of a set of eigenfunctions $\xi_k(t)$ (commonality). Each subject can then be represented by one score (α_i) per eigenfunction (individuality):

$$f_i(t) = \bar{f}(t) + \sum_{k=1}^{K} \alpha_{ik} \, \xi_k(t) \,. \tag{1}$$

This way, the dimensionality of the problem is reduced and as much variance as possible is covered by only a small set of eigenfunctions. According to this method, the set of eigenfunctions should explain at least 70 % of the variance. For our modelling, a correlation matrix based on the speed envelope of all subjects over time $C(t1, t2)$ is used as an input. An additional assumption for using FPCA is that there is a relationship between values in C that are only few samples apart. Therefore, the data is decomposed in a set of Cubic B-spline basis functions. To determine a reliable number of basis functions, the Mean Squared Error between model and signal was calculated. For both the head and wrist, and in both stimuli, the number of basis functions could be set to 60.

A set of eigenfunctions could then be calculated by means of FPCA, using a least square algorithm. As the human body show complex behaviour, Varamix rotation of the functional principal component axes was applied to calculate a basis of eigenfunctions that most economically represent each individual by a linear combination of only a few basis functions. FPCA was performed using Ramsay's FDA toolbox for MATLAB. His approach [26] was followed throughout the procedure.

4.2 Results

To cover more than 70 % of the variability of the head in the performance of the Vivaldi excerpt, we need up to three eigenfunctions that account for 40 %, 28 % and 19 % respectively, totalling 87 % of the variability (Fig. 9). An equal amount of eigenfunctions is needed for the wrist as 84 % of the variability is covered with 40 %, 15 % and 29 %. This means that, with only three eigenfunctions, we can model more than 80 % of the commonalities in the head and wrist movements of the neophytes miming a violin performance following the musical stimulus. The individuality of each subject was obtained by calculating the Functional Principal Component Score for the three eigenvalues. The individual performance can hence be modelled by three values indicating a positive or negative score for each eigenfunction. As few individualities were required for the model, this suggests that music was embodied in similar ways among the subjects (Fig. 9).

For the head, the first eigenfunction has a positive deviation from the group's mean for almost the entire stimulus. This means that subjects with a positive factor on this function will perform with higher speed than the average, nearly throughout the whole recording. In more detail, this eigenfunction reveals something about the periodic movement and phase of the head. Subjects scoring low on this eigenfunction will have low velocity in the beginning of the bar, and higher velocity in the middle (bars 1, 3, 4, 7, 9, 10, 11, 12), while subjects scoring high will have their velocity peak in the beginning of each bar. In the middle of bar 7, this is reversed and bar 8 and 9 have an opposite velocity profile. Note that this is the moment where the repeated note sequences end and new musical material starts. In the beginning of bar 6, the eigenfunction values are close to the mean. The second eigenfunction has a major positive deviation from the mean in bar 5, 6 and 7, the second half of bar 8 and bar 9, and the last two bars. This is complementary to the first eigenfunction. The third eigenfunction has a major negative deviation, especially in the first 4 bars and bar 8.

The first eigenfunction of the right wrist has a major positive deviation in bars 2–3, 6–7 and 10–12 and the second eigenfunction accounts for a positive offset in bars 1 and 8 in particular. Again, the third eigenfunction has a negative deviation from the group's mean, especially covering the variability in bars 3–6, and 8–10. Figure 10 shows the individualities for the head and wrist, clustered using k-means clustering. The number of clusters was set to 5 for the head and 4 for the wrist, after considering the optimal number with k-fold cross validation. These three variables are the principal component scores, or weights for the eigenscores, which represent the performance of the individual subject.

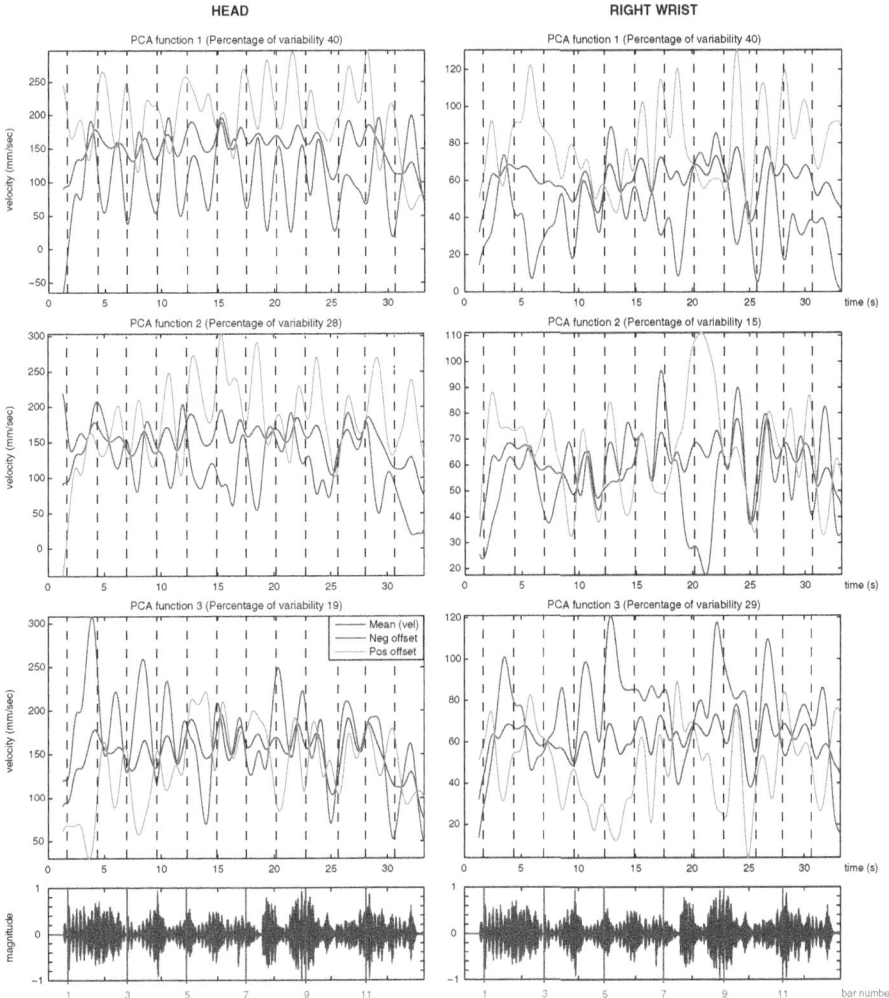

Fig. 9. First stimulus (Vivaldi, score in Fig. 1). Eigenfunctions for the speed envelope of head and right wrist movements after Varamix rotation. The green line indicates a positive offset from the group's mean, the red line a negative offset. (Color figure online)

Some intervals of coherence (i.e. time intervals of equal signs) could be derived from these results. When an eigenfunction has multiple intervals of coherence it can be considered consistent. For the head, the first eigenfunction shows this behaviour from the middle of bar 4 until the end of bar 5, as well as from bar 7 until the end of bar 10. The second eigenfunction covers this for bars 5–7, 9, 11 and 12. The third eigenfunction does not show long intervals of equal signs, except for the first bar. Coherence for the right wrist movement is found in

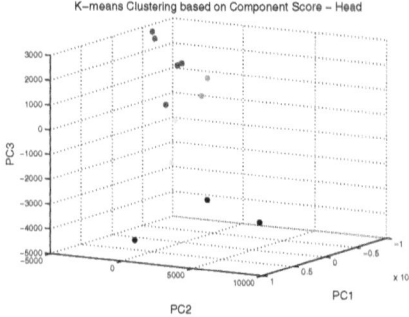
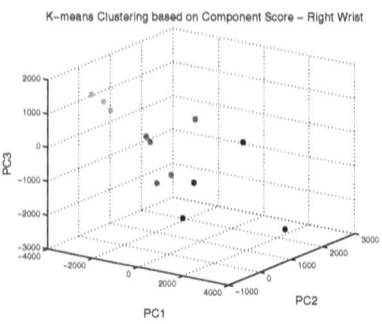

Fig. 10. First stimulus (Vivaldi, score in Fig. 1). Individualities for head and right wrist movements, clustered using k-means clustering.

the first eigenfunction from bars 2–4, the middle of bar 57 and bars 11–12. The second eigenfunction reveals coherence in the first bar and from the middle of bar 7 until the end of bar 8. From bar 3 until the beginning of bar 7 and bars 8–10 are coherent in the third eigenfunction. Thus, each eigenfunction dominates specific time intervals in the musical structure and they are mostly complementary to each other. The third eigenfunction of the wrist, for example, nicely reflects the repeated notes in the music (bar 37) and the new musical material introduced in bar 8–9 and 10. A similar effect can be seen in the second eigenfunction of the head. The last two bars of the musical stimulus (11–12) are also represented in two eigenfunctions (the second eigenfunction of the head and the first of the wrist).

For the second stimulus, two eigenfunctions are sufficient to explain 70 % of the variability of the head, and with three eigenfunctions, even 88 % of the variability is covered. For the wrist, three eigenfunctions (47 %, 18 % and 21 % resp.) are sufficient as well. Again, this means that we can model the behaviour of the neophytes with a limited number of eigenfunctions, pointing at similar embodied behaviour (Fig. 11).

The first two eigenfunctions considered in the head are very consistent, with the first eigenfunction showing increasing positive and decreasing negative offsets towards the end of the excerpt. The second interval shows very distinct intervals of coherence that correspond to the intervals of the bar. Participants with a positive eigenvalue for this function in general will have a lower velocity within each bar and an increase in velocity towards the next bar, while the participants with a negative eigenvalue show opposite behaviour. The points of convergence at the bar transitions show that the second eigenfunction mostly accounts for individual behaviour within each bar.

The third eigenfunction reveals different timing behaviour of the participants, with a negative offset meaning an earlier peak than a positive offset. This was validated using cross-correlation with the maximal correlation at -0.296 s, showing an interesting parallel with the typical reaction time of people in tapping tasks, which generally lies between 200–300 ms [3]. It could be that the

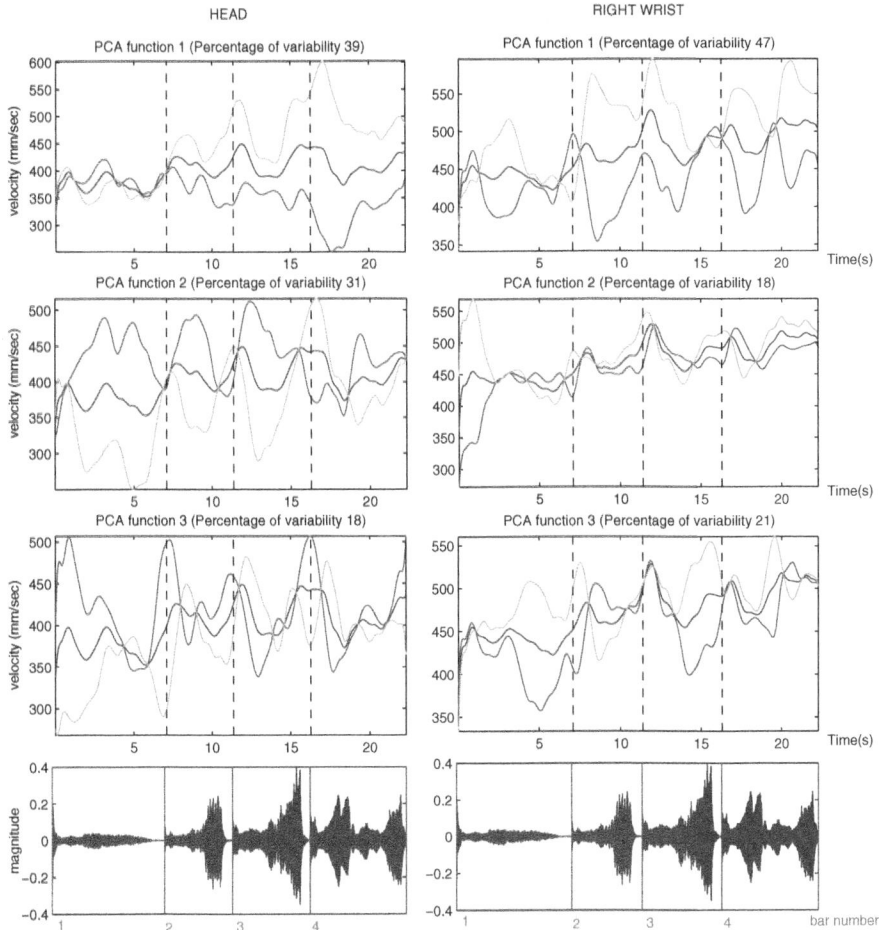

Fig. 11. Second stimulus (Saariaho, score in Fig. 2). Eigenfunctions for the speed envelope of head and right wrist movements after Varamix rotation. The green line indicates a positive offset from the group's mean, the red line a negative offset. (Color figure online)

difference between participants in how well they predict what will happen in the stimulus, is expressed with this eigenfunction.

The first eigenfunction of the wrist movement in the Saariaho excerpt shows a general positive offset. Moreover, it can be clearly observed that the difference in musical material in the fourth bar is reflected in the movement of the wrist: there is a point of convergence in the middle of the fourth bar, while this does not appear in the other three bars where pitch changes appear mostly in the beginning of the bar. The second and third eigenfunction of the wrist are very complementary in the case of the Saariaho piece, where the second eigenfunction accounts for the variability in the beginning of the first bar and the transitions between bar 2–3 and 3–4 and the last part of the fourth bar, while the third eigenfunction accounts for the variability in the middle of these bars. This last eigenfunction is very similar to the second eigenfunction of the head, but less pronounced though.

In general, it could be observed that the head is a body part that shows very clear intervals of coherence that match well with the timing structure of the piece (whole phrase, bars and reaction time of participants).

5 Conclusion and Future Work

Even though low-level features of movement appear to vary considerably in some of the subjects, there is a certain degree of consistency among participants, especially in response to melodic, rhythmic, and timbral features of the music. This suggests a shared knowledge of a vocabulary of instrumental movements, which is then combined with the idiosyncrasies of each subject. The analysis of commonalities and individualities confirms this, and other studies [23] support the idea that musical structure is communicated also through body movements, and idiosyncrasies contribute to express musical meaning.

Further work will go towards studying the response of the subjects also to the other musical stimuli recorded during the experiment. Each stimulus differs substantially from the other, providing material for analysis of movement in response to other musical features.

New approaches to movement analysis are in continuous development and there is an increasing need for tools that can aid the retrieval of meaningful features in complex, multidimensional motion data. Therefore, other approaches – like Topological Gesture Analysis (TGA) [25] – will be tested and possibly employed along with the methods we presented here. New techniques for motion data analysis could get inspired by concepts suggested by theories of music perception and cognition, therefore making the analysis more akin to how humans perceive and move to music. This is indeed a challenging task since retrieving meaningful, articulated information from motion data requires complex algorithms and technologies.

The PQoM algorithm will also be refined and improved for real-time implementation. This will be useful both for online analysis and interactive music performance (which was initially explored in [28]).

Motion data analysis has provided great detail for understanding the role of body movement in musical expression and cognition. However, it is felt that integrating quantitative data analysis with qualitative analysis and practice-based research may broaden the scope of the research, allowing to test the assumptions made through the analysis in musical contexts, outside of the sterile environment of the laboratory.

Acknowledgements. The authors would like to thank Alexander Refsum Jensenius and all the members of the *fourMs - Music, Mind, Motion, Machines* research group at the University of Oslo, Norway, for their hospitality and knowledgeable support. Special thanks to all the participants of the study and to Pierre-Emmanuel Largeron for his valuable input.

This study was partially realised under the FWO-project "Foundations of expressive timing control in music".

References

1. Altavilla, A., Caramiaux, B., Tanaka, A.: Towards gestural sonic affordances. In: Yeo, W., Lee, K., Sigman, A., H., J., Wakefield, G. (eds.) Proceedings of the International Conference on New Interfaces for Musical Expression, pp. 61–64. Graduate School of Culture Technology, KAIST, Daejeon, Republic of Korea (2013). http://nime2013.kaist.ac.kr/
2. Amelynck, D., Maes, P.J., Martens, J.P., Leman, M.: Expressive body movement responses to music are coherent, consistent, and low dimensional. IEEE Trans. Cybern. **44**(12), 2288–2301 (2014). http://www.ncbi.nlm.nih.gov/pubmed/25415938
3. Bååth, R.: Estimating the distribution of sensorimotor synchronization data: a Bayesian hierarchical modeling approach. Behav. Res. Methods, 1–12 (2015). http://dx.doi.org/10.3758/s13428-015-0591-2
4. Burger, B., Thompson, M.R., Luck, G., Saarikallio, S., Toiviainen, P.: Influences of rhythm-and timbre-related musical features on characteristics of music-induced movement. Front. Psychol. **4**, 183 (2013). http://www.pubmedcentral.nih.gov/articlerender.fcgi?artid=3624091&tool=pmcentrez&rendertype=abstract
5. Burger, B., Thompson, M.R., Luck, G., Saarikallio, S.H., Toiviainen, P.: Hunting for the beat in the body: on period and phase locking in music-induced movement. Front. Hum. Neurosci. **8**, 1–16 (2014). http://www.frontiersin.org/Human_Neuroscience/10.3389/fnhum.2014.00903/abstract
6. Burger, B., Toiviainen, P.: MoCap toolbox-a matlab toolbox for computational analysis of movement data. In: Proceedings of the Sound and Music Computing, pp. 172–178 (2013). https://jyx.jyu.fi/dspace/handle/123456789/42837
7. Camurri, A., Mazzarino, B., Volpe, G.: Analysis of expressive gesture: the EyesWeb expressive gesture processing library. In: Camurri, A., Volpe, G. (eds.) GW 2003. LNCS (LNAI), vol. 2915, pp. 460–467. Springer, Heidelberg (2004)
8. Camurri, A., Volpe, G.: Multimodal analysis of expressive gesture in music performance. In: Solis, J., Ng, K. (eds.) Musical Robots and Interactive Multimodal Systems. STAR, vol. 74, pp. 47–66. Springer, Heidelberg (2011)
9. Clarke, E.F.: Ways of Listening: An Ecological Approach to the Perception of Musical Meaning. Oxford University Press, New York (2005)
10. Coorevits, E., Moelants, D., Maes, P.J., Leman, M.: Studying the effect of tempo on music performance: a multimodal approach. In: 9th Conference on Interdisciplinary Musicology, CIM 2014, Berlin (2014)
11. Dahl, L.: Triggering sounds from discrete air gestures: what movement feature has the best timing? In: Caramiaux, B., Tahiroglu, K., Fiebrink, R., Tanaka, A. (eds.) Proceedings of the International Conference on New Interfaces for Musical Expression, pp. 201–206. Goldsmiths, University of London, London (2014). http://www.nime.org/proceedings/2014/nime2014_514.pdf
12. Dempster, W.T., Gaughran, G.R.L.: Properties of body segments based on size and weight. Am. J. Anat. **120**(1), 33–54 (1967). doi:10.1002/aja.1001200104

13. Gibson, E.J.: Where is the information for affordances? Ecol. Psychol. **12**(1), 53–56 (2000)
14. Gibson, J.J.: The theory of affordances. In: Perceiving, Acting, and Knowing, vol. Perceiving, pp. 127–142 (332) (1977)
15. Glowinski, D., Dardard, F., Gnecco, G., Piana, S., Camurri, A.: Expressive non-verbal interaction in a string quartet: an analysis through head movements. J. Multimodal User Interfaces **9**(1), 55–68 (2014). http://link.springer.com/10.1007/s12193-014-0154-3
16. Godøy, R.I., Haga, E., Jensenius, A.R.: Playing "air instruments": mimicry of sound-producing gestures by novices and experts. In: Gibet, S., Courty, N., Kamp, J.-F. (eds.) GW 2005. LNCS (LNAI), vol. 3881, pp. 256–267. Springer, Heidelberg (2006)
17. Godøy, R.I., Leman, M. (eds.): Musical Gestures: Sound, Movement, and Meaning. Routledge, Abingdon (2010)
18. Gritten, A.: Resonant listening. Perform. Res. **15**(3), 115–122 (2010). http://www.tandfonline.com/doi/abs/10.1080/13528165.2010.527221
19. Gritten, A., King, E. (eds.): Music and Gesture. Ashgate, Farnham (2006)
20. Jensenius, A.R., Skogstad, S.A., Nymoen, K., Tørresen, J., Høvin, M.E.: Reduced displays of multidimensional motion capture data sets of musical performance. In: Proceedings of ESCOM 2009: 7th Triennial Conference of the European Society for the Cognitive Sciences of Music (2009)
21. Leman, M.: Embodied Music Cognition and Mediation Technology. MIT Press, Cambridge (2008)
22. Leman, M., Lesaffre, M., Nijs, L., Deweppe, A.: User-oriented studies in embodied music cognition research. Musicae Sci. **14**(2), 203–223 (2010). http://msx.sagepub.com/content/14/2_suppl/203.abstract
23. MacRitchie, J., Buck, B., Bailey, N.J.: Inferring musical structure through bodily gestures. Musicae Sci. **17**(1), 86–108 (2013). http://msx.sagepub.com/lookup/doi/10.1177/1029864912467632
24. Menin, D., Schiavio, A.: Rethinking musical affordances. Avant **III**(2), 201–215 (2012)
25. Naveda, L., Leman, M.: The spatiotemporal representation of dance and music gestures using topological gesture analysis (TGA). Music Percept. **28**(1), 93–111 (2010)
26. Ramsay, J.O.: Functional Data Analysis. Wiley, Hoboken (2006)
27. Visi, F., Coorevits, E., Miranda, E., Leman, M.: Effects of different bow stroke styles on body movements of a viola player: an exploratory study. In: Proceedings of the Joint ICMC–SMC–2014 Conference, Athens, Greece (2014)
28. Visi, F., Schramm, R., Miranda, E.: Gesture in performance with traditional musical instruments and electronics: use of embodied music cognition and multimodal motion capture to design gestural mapping strategies. In: Proceedings of the 2014 International Workshop on Movement and Computing, MOCO 2014. ACM, Paris (2014). http://dl.acm.org/citation.cfm?id=2618013

Digital Musical Instruments, Embodiment and Performance

Skill Development and Stabilisation of Expertise for Electronic Music Performance

Jan C. Schacher[1,2(✉)] and Patrick Neff[1,3]

[1] Institute for Computer Music and Sound Technology,
Zurich University of the Arts, Zürich, Switzerland
jan.schacher@zhdk.ch, patrick.neff@uzh.ch
[2] Royal Conservatoire, AP Hogeschool, Antwerp, Belgium
[3] Department of Psychology, University of Zurich, Zürich, Switzerland

Abstract. Skill development, the stabilisation of expertise through practise, and processes of bodily as well as neural sharing in the context of gesture-based electronic music performance are the topic of this article. The key questions centre around the affective, embodied but also neurological aspects of these processes. The types of awareness on a corporeal level and the neural processes that occur within the musician and the listener-viewer are investigated, since in music performance the perceptions of musician and audience depend on shared embodiment and cognitive processes. The aim is to show that 'enactive', embodied concepts merely provide a different perspective of the same complex matter than what the cognitive neurosciences propose. A concrete musical piece is used as an example that shows a gestural practice using sensor-based instruments and digital sound processing in order to expose the critical relationships between musician, instrument, technology and the audience. The insights arising from blending the two complementary perspectives in this context can be productive both for artistic practice as well as systematic research in music.

Keywords: Cognitive sciences · Electronic music · Embodiment · Expertise · Neural plasticity · Performance · Shared perception · Skill development · Stabilisation

1 Introduction

In this article we look at how the perceptions of musician and audience shift depending on shared processes of embodiment and how they stabilise through practise. This is particularly the case in unusual music performance styles involving technical body sensing, extended instruments and digital sound generation. Its co-performative basis in body-perception can be traced to evolutionary, cultural, and social assets that transcend the mere music making situation. Here, these issues are approached by looking at the characteristics of embodied, situated cognition, at intentionality and agency, and the affordances in handling and recognising non-standard musical instrumental actions. A particular emphasis is given to the question how stabilisation processes operate in rehearsal and performance situations both for performers and audience. The underlying question is how we use the concept of gesture and corporeality to understand affective, embodied but also formal and structural aspects of music performance and perception. The foundation for this inquiry is provided by the 'enactive' [55] and embodied perspective, that can stem both from an experiential and performative perspective related to psychological philosophy and from an empirical, formalised approach represented by the cognitive neurosciences. This particular perspective, which is integral to the considerations in this article, is therefore based on the 'materialistic' conjuncture of body and mind rather than on the separation proposed by Cartesian dualism.

In order to ground this reflection in musical practice, the development process over time and the performance of the gestural electronic work entitled 'new islands' provides a concrete example. This contextualisation should make evident the situation both musicians and audience engage in with regard to non-traditional performance practices. With the aid of this use-case we also hope to show some principles that need to be paid attention to in the composition, development and design of musical performance that involve body-sensing, novel, extended, or abstracted instruments.

2 Background

Musical processes are manifested as chains of musical actions by performers and as a flow of perceptions on a multitude of levels to the listener-viewer, i.e., the person who partakes in a music performance. We believe that this type of music listening never occurs with the auditory sense alone but always includes the – sometimes inner – eye and above all the corporeal kinaesthetic sense. The way the senses combine to form a field of perception is a complex matter, which goes beyond the scope of this article.

The shared physical presence during a performance of music, in fact of any music 'consumption', is embedded in the flow of time. Contrary to other art forms, in music our being in time [20] becomes central. "Things take time" to unfold, in particular in the sensory medium of sound, but also in the embodied state and "environmental situatedness" of the musical performance. "We experience a kind of empathy for the performer, an awareness of physicality and an understanding of the effort required to create music. ... In improvisational music, this embodied empathy extends to an awareness of the performers coincident physical and mental exertion, of their in-the-moment (i.e., in-time) process of creative activity and interactivity" [22]. The nature of these processes is one of dynamic flows, not only of time, but of elements constituted of bodily actions that produce distinct sound impressions. Within musical perception the processes we are affected by, perceive and act out are produced by dynamic chains of sound-objects as well as action/sound pairs or multimodal 'gestural sonorous objects' [19]. These elements form "segregated streams and objects that lead, via the subjective sensing of the subject's body motion, to impressions of movement, gesture, tensions, and release of tension" [29]. As musicians perform, they construct a temporal, unfolding stream of movement dynamics which the listener-viewer re-enacts and co-performs through kinaesthetic, corporeal resonances and higher order dynamic sensing that is more akin to *moving* oneself than to *sounding* within oneself. The effect of a performance is that it is *indeed* the body which constitutes music perception on both the embodied, corporeal level as well as in the social sphere: "Music exists at the intersection of organised sounds with our sensorimotor apparatus, our bodies, our brains, our cultural values and practices, music-historical conventions, our prior experiences, and a host of other social and cultural factors. Consequently, musical motion is really experienced by us, albeit via our imaginative structuring of sounds" [24, p. 255]. These processes generate an "aware[ness] of a sense of mutual embodiment. This sense brings about the presupposition of shared time between the listener and the performer" [22]. However, the affective impact of the performance, i.e. the effectiveness of the music, within this 'shared time', is not immediately given but arises as the performance unfolds.

Considering this, how does the musician establish a shared process of temporal, corporeal, movement-and-sound shaping, when neither the tools or instruments, nor the idiom and style conform to a sufficient degree with culturally established norms? Being able to negotiate the flux and the instability of the performance moment demands that the musician prepare and train, which is hard enough with traditional instruments and musical styles, and presents particular challenges when the task includes exploring gestural instruments and abstract sound processes. The musical actions that constitute 'the music' might be prescribed by a 'score' or other instructions, or might be indeterminate, yet culturally or stylistically informed, for example through a shared improvisational practice. With non-traditional instruments and sound processes, learning as well as performing depend to a large degree on the models and methods used, since music is fundamentally shaped by the tools, the desired aesthetic outcome and the context within which it is enacted. This wider context is summarised by the term 'musicking' [54], that comprises the cultural, inter-personal and individual aspects which make up the joint social activity of music making.[1] Our focus will be on the 'enactive' and neuroscientific fields to further the understanding of those processes that occur within the practising and performing musician as well as the partaking listener-viewer.

---

[1] "This is how I have defined it. It is quite simple. *To music is to take part, in any capacity, in a musical performance.* That means not only to perform but also to listen, to provide material for performance (what we call composing), to prepare for a performance (what we call practising or rehearsing), or to take part in any activity that can affect the nature of that style of human encounter which is a musical performance." [54, p. 12, original italics].

3 Enactive, Embodied, and Situated Cognition in Music Performance

Let us look at the body and how perceiving and performing relate to musical actions. This is particularly important in the relationship with musical instruments, which represent the single most mediating factor in terms of corporeality for a musician.[2] Before we turn our attention to the instrument, the body's role and potential needs to be clarified. It is a truism that a musical live-performance involves physical presence of the musician. What is less obvious is that awareness of bodily states plays a central role in constituting the relational or affective power of such a performance. Picture the different degrees of physical presence between the schoolchild and the virtuoso musician, both possibly playing an identical piece. The different attitude here are not only informed by social status, identity formation and age difference, and they are not only a matter of self-confidence and developmental maturity. The difference between novice and expert lies in the amount of training, the depth of integrating and imprinting of the many levels of musical and perceptual activities that are necessary to perform music fluently and with ease. In training, the musician experiences over and over, during practising and rehearsal, the actions that produce a desired sound. The repetitive nature of practising coordinated movements of instrumental play fulfils the function of establishing body-schemata, "integral kinaesthetic structures" [31] (quoted in [53]), dynamic patterns, or so-called 'kinetic melodies'. However, the thus obtained "knowledgeability is not simply a know-*how*, a lesser of form of knowledge that is 'merely physical.' Kinetic melodies are saturated in cognitive and affective acuities that both anchor invariants and color and individualize the manner in which any particular melody [pattern] is run off" [53, p. 256]. Through the practising process the embodied 'know-how' becomes pre-reflective and can later, in the right environment and circumstances, be triggered as a unit without the necessity to individually deal with the actions that constitute it.

A classic example for such a pattern is the skill of running down the stairs. Your body is capable of automatically chaining a highly complex sequence of falling, catching your step and adapting to the steps in a rhythmical pattern. But if you do look at your feet, you will stumble and fall, which hints at a vulnerability of imprinted low-level motor schemata to conscious, intentional interaction.

The body accumulates knowledge of movements, dynamics and forces, and in the case of a traditional musical instruments links it to the perception, the adaptation, and the control of sound-qualities, thus dealing with movement-sound conjunctions rather than with movement and sound separately. This embodied knowledge encompasses the full range of the body's motion and audition control. It is completely interdependent with the environmental situation, within which it was learned or acquired. Music performance in concert provides one

---

[2] The obvious exception could be the singers, of course. But even here, the 'voice' and its techniques are considered as instruments in a more independent manner [34], than dancers consider the body.

such situation that brings the concept of embodied cognition into sharper focus, which Varela and colleagues have stated in more general terms: "By ... *embodied* we mean to highlight two points: ... cognition depends upon the kinds of experience that come from having a body with various sensorimotor capacities, ... these individual sensorimotor capacities are themselves embedded in a more encompassing biological, psychological, and cultural context. By ... *action* we mean to emphasize ... that sensory and motor processes, perception and action, are fundamentally inseparable in lived cognition. ... the enactive approach consists of two points: (1) perception consists in perceptually guided actions and (2) cognitive structures emerge from recurrent sensorimotor patterns that enable action to be perceptually guided" [55, p. 173].

3.1 Affordances and the Role of the Instrument

What does the instrument offer to the musician in parallel or in addition to the production of sound? 'Affordances' are what Gibson [18] defined as the ecological potential, as that which an object or environment is offering in terms of actions or resources. He derives the concept from 'Gestalt' psychology's terms of valence, invitation and demand, but he emphasises ecological embedding. "An affordance points two ways, to the environment and to the observer. ... this is only to reemphasize that exteroception is accompanied by proprioception – that to perceive the world is to coperceive oneself. ... The awareness of the world and of one's complementary relations to the world are not separable" [18, p. 141]. More recent research ties valence and arousal to the constitution of emotions and memory [25], and *indeed* within the ecological perspective these dimensions play a role as well.

To understand the scope of these *objective* affordances [38] that are clear in traditional instruments, but need to be deduced or extrapolated in Digital Musical Instruments, we also have to add the concept of *perceptual* affordances that arise, when entering into contact with the instrument. These perceptions form a multimodal field that encompasses the traditional five senses and arise when attentional awareness is guided towards the instrument in any of the sensory modes. Perceptual affordances represent also the potential for perceptions that arise out of the *interaction* with the instrument. The awareness that originates *within* the player represents a separate type of perceptual affordance, which does not exist independently of cognitive or pre-cognitive processes of the performer. It is based on a kind of sensing that is active within the body, such as kinaesthetic, vestibular and equilibrium sensing and belong to the pre-reflective, pre-cognitive levels of our perceptual system. For the musician the awareness of the instrument happens through an *object* perception.

Even though the instrument might only be peripherally perceived, while the focus lies for example on the sound or the music, nevertheless this "object perception involves an experience that is *directed at* the object. The relation at stake here is ... an intentional relation" [15, p. 56]. When the musician shifts the attention from sound to sound production, the intentional focus moves from an outer perception of sound as a goal to an object perception of the instrument. In both types of attention the instrument is peripherally present and the awareness can at any time be moved onto this object. "Attention can be directed either proprioceptively or exteroceptively, and it can be ... viewed as an alteration of the balance between focal and peripheral awareness. ... Even when the attention is fixed firmly on the ... dimension of tactile awareness, the exteroception dimension remains ... in background awareness" [1, p. 139]. The instrument, the musical content or even the body may move to the periphery of the perceptual field or obtain focal attention as a 'perceptual object'. In contrast, we perceive our bodies through an inner sense called proprioception and the kinaesthetic sense. We may become consciously aware of our body as an object, but "it is also possible that proprioceptive awareness can function as a non-perceptual or non-observational self-awareness ... and as such might be regarded as a more immediate and more reliable form of awareness than object perception" [15, p. 54].

A musician's training aims at imprinting instrumental dimensions, as well as the sound-producing and -controlling actions and adaptations into an extended body-image and a number of body-schemata. The image can be extended through habituation as shown by Merleau-Ponty in his example of the woman with the feather in her hat [33, p. 165], and the schemata will be executed pre-reflectively during performance. The intentional, object-related actions that are part of playing the instrument build upon this prenoetic knowledge without the necessity of making the body experientially visible. "To be proprioceptively aware of one's body does not involve making one's body an object of perception [...] Proprioceptive-kinesthetic awareness is usually a pre-reflective (non-observational) awareness that allows the body to remain experientially transparent" [16, p. 73]. Since the musician, through instrumental training, has achieved a fusion between body and instrument in the domain of the body-schema, the perception will be observational and begins to constitute a body-image. This "body-image consists of a system of perceptions, attitudes, and beliefs pertaining to one's own body" [16, p. 24]. By understanding the interrelationship between the somatic and physiological layers of perception and the cognitive processes deployed to interpret and act on them, an essential part of the communicative aspects of corporeal actions come to the foreground.

3.2 Corporeal Awareness, Agency and Intentionality

Apart from this body-object relationship there exist also various types of awareness *within* the body. On the lowest level operate the neurological and physiological mechanisms of proprioception and the somatic, kinaesthetic sense [3]. At this level, a large number of bodily signals are present and form a system that permits an automatic control of posture, locomotion, and physical actions adapted to specific tasks [16]. Somatic and proprioceptive awareness can take both a reflective and a pre-reflective form, a distinction that is important for the argument in the context of the performing electronic musician. If "the first element of broad self-consciousness that somatic proprioception provides is an awareness of the limits of the body" [1, p. 149], then for the instrumentalist the physical contact with the instrument provides a pre-reflective self-awareness that is informed by the instrument, constitutes an element of the sense of agency, and generates a clear context for the bodily awareness [17]. At the next level a fully focused attention on the body may exist. Once the musician, through instrumental training, has achieved a fusion between body and instrument in the domain of the body-schema, the perception becomes observational and constitutes a body-image. Beyond that level the body is only indirectly involved, since the musician needs to deal with musical awareness. The auditive attention of the perception guides expressive aspects of the performance through a different feedback loop than the somatic ones: "the body-image retreats into the background in order to enable the concentration on the sonic-expressive shaping of the entire piece of music" [26, p. 111; authors' translation]. With habituation this awareness on musical elements can sink to the level of pre-reflective, somatic proprioception and close the loop between metaphorical [27] musical awareness and sensory-motor integration in the body.

In a complementary view on the body, Legrand proposes four corporeal states: the *invisible body* is the body that is absent from experience, the *opaque body* is the object of an observational body experience; the *transparent body* is experienced only 'as one looks through it to the world' and the *performative body* is based directly on a pre-reflective experience of the body [28]. The latter two modes manage well to represent the situation of the performing musician and anchor the performance experience *at the same time*. The continuous adaptation occurs through the *performative body*, in the first person perspective; the observational awareness and attention is framed by the *transparent body*. Through the corporeal state of the performative body and in an explicit awareness mode the concept of 'performativity' implies that the sense of agency becomes an indispensable element that is constitutive of the experience: "This performative awareness that I have of my body is tied to my embodied capabilities for movement and action. ... my knowledge of what I can do ... is *in my body*, not in a reflective or intellectual attitude" [16, p. 74].

The sense of agency, that is "of oneself as the agent of action" or the fact "that when I'm aware of my actions and experience them as mine, I thereby experience myself: an experience of myself as agent." [32, p. 50] are constituting the self-awareness, which is necessary to perceive and maintain a musical performance. Intentions and bodily, as well as instrumental control represent the core cognitive aspects of musical actions, in particular on devices and processes that can potentially produce sound without any input or explicit intention from the performer. Neurologically speaking, the bidirectional afferent and efferent streams of information are continuously compared and integrated in the lower regions of the brain and produce a regulatory feedback that forms part of our awareness of actions. "To the extent that consciousness enters into the ongoing production of action, and contributes to the production of further action, *even if significant aspects of this production take place non-consciously*, our actions are intentional" [16, p. 238].

4 Musical Performance and Cognitive Neuroscience

Let us now move from the sense of agency, the body's senses and states to the processes they set in action or are based on within the brain. Musical perception and performance have been a subject in neuroscience for almost two decades and are recognised as "one of the most complex and demanding cognitive challenges that the human mind can undertake" [57]. Insights gained from specific brain functioning in these practices also lead to advanced models of general brain functioning organised in distributed, overlapping networks, and further the understanding of neuroplasticity [56]. This is particularly relevant since musical performance integrates perception, attention, cognition, and intentional movement in real-time on all used modalities. In turn, this activates the brain in a highly-specific manner that enables heightened experience and cognitive functioning. Musical expertise serves as a model of general expertise gain and intermodal transfer contributing to the understanding of how these integrated brain states lead to enhanced perception and performance as well as to their sustainability [23].

In the following we discuss in what way these principles apply to actual musical performance. We look at the question how expertise and stabilisation emerge on the time scale of the individual's entire life span, the individual's situative, i.e., musical skill acquisition, and we also look at these processes within the time span of an artistic development process (for example of a new piece). In addition, the communication and interpersonal domain is taken into account. Based on evolutionary processes and the neurobiology behind music, gesture and motion as well as the individual trajectories of the artist's lifespan pave the way to a (neuro-) phenomenological perspective of the artistic process.

Taken together, translational principles of expertise, stability and training originating from the neurosciences may contribute to the development of optimised artistic strategies, interfaces and supportive tools. Besides that, the reinspiration of basic as well as artistic research by posing new or differently situated questions and delivering new paradigms may also contribute to research outcomes.

4.1 Evolving Motion

The emergence of modern man is tightly linked to a cultural (r)evolution that produced language, music, arts, and eventually complex social systems. Respective changes in brain morphology and functioning move along these evolutionary lines [11]. Motion, always intimately tied to perception, is a common principle of these emerging cultural traits, since the integration of perception, the volitional initiation and sequencing of concrete actions is key in each of these cultural domains. In general it is assumed that the human evolution, which surpassed our primate ancestors', most prominently manifests itself in those brain regions responsible for planning and sequencing, but also for integrating stimuli with higher cognitive systems [43]. The main brain regions contributing to these skills are found in the frontal areas of the neocortex. Through a functioning mirror/echo neuron system, which is partly located in theses areas, we are capable of following the movement of others [44], or in the sense of 'enaction' [55] literally embody the perceived actions at the neural level. Interestingly enough, the activated neural systems are also involved in action planning, sequencing, and initiation, which leads to a neurological 'mirroring' of action that may be lacking its bodily execution. By extension these systems comprise brain regions relevant to language (e.g., an area traditionally known as 'Broca's Area') that link motion with semantic, communicative or even abstract context [43]. In further support of this perspective, recent neuroscientific studies provide evidence that hard-wired connections between motor cortices, visual, auditory, and language regions exist and are prone to neuroplasticity triggered by training [56]. When put into context, this evolutionary trajectory provides insights into the status quo of poly-modal, or with respect to motion, a unified modality of general brain functioning. This framework provides the neurobiological foundations that facilitate the integration, processing and acquisition of 'motion' sequences in any domain and specifically in the context of music performance and perception.

4.2 Lifespan Expertise

Recent neuroscience starts to focus on models of neuroplasticity across the entire life span of a person [39]. Despite this paradigm shift towards a more plastic perspective on brain development, there are critical phases in each individual's development trajectory, during which learning and performance in certain domains are more effective and sustainable. A multitude of studies confirm the useful tradition of early musical training in educational systems as the young brain is capable of profiting most from such trainings [56].

According to the *last in–first out* hypothesis of neural development [46], the (pre)frontal cortex plays a central role as it matures in late childhood and is subject to atrophy later in adulthood. This leaves the middle adulthood as the phase with the most 'mature' frontal cortex; here the optimisations of expertise and related executive functions converge as the individual profits from expertise acquired during childhood. Within or after the teenage years neural or synaptic 'pruning' occurs naturally and 'limits' the neural learning and dynamic networking capacities. Nonetheless, there is considerable inter-individual variability in the transition as the process can be prolonged through specific behaviour and slowed down or individually modified. This neuroplastic 'good news' is thus transferable to ageing, because brain structure and function can be stabilised, conserved or even improved into old age with respective training [56].

A parallel expression of these developmental trajectories with a focus on cognition can be seen in the model of '*fluid*' and '*crystallised*' intelligence [6]. This model theorises that how expertise can be generated in a 'fluid' phase early in life, is probably related to the aforementioned neural underpinnings. This may then serve as a foundation to 'crystallised' expertise later in life. The transition is gradual and occurs individually, and marks the shift from a roaming, all-absorbing young mind to an 'all-knowing' adult mind. Most relevant in the context of this article, 'fluid' intelligence primarily makes use of *enhanced learning*, i.e. sensory and memory functions, whereas 'crystalline' intelligence primarily applies *accumulated experience and advanced reasoning*. These insights can be related to the earlier sections that showed how embodiment [55], perceptual modes [28] and kinaesthetic melodies [31] function.

4.3 The Musician's State of the Brain

Let us leave the background of ontogenetic development to focus on actual brain and cognitive functions in 'practised' expertise in the context of musical performance. This context poses one of the most complex sensorimotor challenges to the brain [57]. It requires the integration of sensory (mostly auditory, visual and kinaesthetic) inputs with motor outputs in real-time. It is therefore not surprising that extensive training and a fully acquired expertise are for the performer to execute his skills with ease and to allow her to perform creatively beyond strictly learned schemata. Before going into these neural and cognitive mechanisms, let us examine the specific 'states of the brain' of a highly skilled musician. For a comprehensive review of this topic the reader is referred to [57].

Compared to non-musicians or musical laypeople, on a coarse neuroanatomical level, musicians usually exhibit: 1. A larger and denser corpus callosum connecting the two brain hemispheres, which is developed during the critical phase of juvenile training increasing interhemispheric connectivity and communication [51]. 2. A larger auditory cortex as well as a specific inter-hemispheric asymmetry. 3. A larger and more dense motor cortex, especially in somatotopic representation of the respective extremities (e.g., areas representing fingers in piano players). 4. Changes in the cerebellum (responsible for motor control, integration and simulation). 5. Increased hard-wired connections between auditory and (pre-) motor areas via fibre bundles (e.g., arcuate fasciculus) [56].

Traditionally the hemispheric division of the brain was seen as separating two systems. The left hemisphere seemed to favour acting more analytically in short temporal durations and was responsible for language and motor control, whereas the right hemisphere preferred emotions as well as longer temporal arcs and is responsible for spatial representation and attentional processes. Besides the asymmetry of the auditory cortex hemispheric preferences were also shown in language [40] as well as general motor control [52]. In its strictness, the view on this separation has become outdated, since it was shown that lateralisation is highly task-dependent and that it varies within a task over both stimulus or motor-action sequences. Still, the increased size of the corpus callosum found in musicians enables an enhanced inter-hemispheric communication. It allows rapid integration and contextualisation of emotional and analytic content, which in turn can lead to eased creativity (e.g., improvisation in musical performance). The enlarged auditory, kinaesthetic as well as motor areas are comparable to peripheral muscle training: The larger or thicker the cortex is at the respective place, the better usually the performance. Taken together, extensive training followed by expertise, reflected in their neuroplastic correlates, represents the underlying cause for the differences between experts and non-experts.

In the light of evolutionary and developmental processes, as well as current knowledge about the 'state of the brain', the heightened interconnectedness between temporal regions (auditory perception and probably also auditory memory), parietal regions (object integration, spatial aspects), and frontal regions (motor sequencing, language) – e.g. via the arcuate fasciculus – points to the fact that auditive musical perception and motor-controlled musical performance are *indivisible*. Some of these regions (i.e., mainly the frontal and parietal areas) are part of the mirror/echo neuron system, which expands the frame of reference to include perceptive and communication aspects (see Sect. 4.5). Related to these neurological differences, musicians furthermore exhibit exceptional executive functions such as attention, working memory, emotional control, planning and reasoning, over and beyond the normal lifespan [23]. Finally, the enhanced polymodal connectivity within the brain renders the musician capable of more efficiently coding and retrieving memories: They are capable of storing memories in connection with multiple modes, which allows them to more rapidly and successfully retrieve information from their memory systems.

Due to their fundamental connections and functions, as well as to the co-evolution and -development, the described neural systems ease the way to domain-specific and possibly -general learning, skills and expertise in contrast to more pronounced domain-specific learning in other activities. Moreover it becomes conceivable that performing is superior to 'passive' listening to music – be it in the specific brain regions or the entire brain. Even compared to other expertise demands in sports or visual arts, musical performance seems to be exceptionally 'demanding' as it activates more modalities and cognitive efforts. Gestural control, expression and dance within enriched acoustical and visual environments, non-traditional musical performance may provide highly relevant use-cases that push this neurocognitive envelope further.

4.4 Movement Expertise

How is (movement-) expertise achieved and how does it affect brain functioning and related cognitive and motor performance? Surprisingly, there seems to be a discernible trend towards less activation within less modalities the further the training process of an expertise evolves [4,8]. Part of this observation shows an additional trend towards more stability and more invariability, which could be partly explained by the specific tuning and wiring on the level of single neurons, thus minimising (neural) noise production and susceptibility. Linked to that the brain favours extensive expertise in one domain, which is in turn rewarded through dopamine-mediated learning and reward feedback loops. Even if the thresholds of expertise acquisition vary inter-individually, there is concise agreement that cross-domain multitasking, particularly task-switching is generally neither effective nor rewarding for this purpose [37]. Beyond that, general psychological enhancers like emotion and motivation support, on a neurophysiological level, the learning through reinforcing loops of the limbic system in the brain.

The transitions through the phases of expertise acquisition are gradual and described as occurring mostly step-wise, as laid out in an exemplary manner by Debarnot and colleagues [8]: In a first phase, the sequential motor control is acquired and rehearsed by applying the whole sensorimotor loop of the brain. The mirror/echo neurons are then possibly supporting and the kinaesthetic, visual and acoustic modalities are certainly helping along if the situation demands it. This phase is fundamental and crucial and can only be eased through the acquisition of extensive prior expertise (i.e., in adulthood or after very long training). A 'motor-memory' is built up in subcortical regions and gradually decoupled from cortical – thus 'conscious' – control and guidance, in what Gallagher [16] calls the establishment of body schemata or Sheets-Johnstone [53] calls kinaesthetic memory (see Sect. 3.2).

The next step is the goal-oriented mental simulation of the movement, i.e. 'motor imagery' that permits the individual to 'imagine' a movement without actually executing corporeal motion. Throughout these processes, reduced but more specific goal-oriented neural activity is introduced (see for example golf practice [4]); at this point the 'expert' usually has achieved a sufficient skill set. This can be observed in expert sportsmen as well as musicians in their ability to silently rehearse and prepare a performance.

Transcending this level is the decoupled and abstract level of 'meditation', where no prior motor rehearsal or training is necessary. This can be regarded as an example of transfer between domains, and as a meta-level of conceptual understanding and integration, as the performer becomes capable of 'pure' mental movement and unconstrained, freely flowing creative actions.

This state can be considered as mastery or complete 'top-down' control mediated through goal-oriented activity of the frontal cortex. In the case of golfing expertise, with differential motor, attentional as well as goal-oriented spatial demands, the activity of the experts on a neural level gets reduced to a mere representation of the goal while the body nearly automatically follows with executing an pre-established motor schema [4]. The identification of goals and goal-points within the action-perception loop is an essential part of our anticipatory perception, necessary to initiate an action. A recent study postulates that any projected movement in the immediate future activates motor-memory in the same way than the activation patterns of the actual movement [21].

4.5 Movement and Gesture Communication

After describing relevant processes of expertise and stability gain in a musical (and other artistic) performance within an individual person, let us expand the frame to the inter-individual domain. Mirror/echo neurons with their respective automated imitation processes are deemed key in these reasonings [43, 44]. While the actual mirror/echo neurons are highly disputed as the *gate* of movement or emotional imitation (e.g., [10]), the activated (pre-) motor cortices as a result of observant 'imitation' are indisputable [13, 43, 44]. It was shown that these specialised neural assemblies are not only activated during observation of goal and object-directed hand movements, the *same* sites get activated while observing communicative or expressive hand gestures [35], and body referring manual actions [30]. This implies an automatism of gestural communicative coding by the individual, which is based on the underlying principle of motion (-imitation). In a follow-up experiment, it was shown that when comparing the perception of social hand gestures with facial expressions, the activation pattern differed [36]: The condition of facial expression recognition and imitation activated the frontal part, whereas recognition of hand gestures showed larger activation in the posterior regions. This goes in line with the observation and intuition about the perception of gestures and general expression in a musical performance: Facial expression seems not to be necessarily linked to gestures in the rest of the body and tends to convey emotional content more directly.

Besides the automatic perception and integration of basic motion, semantics and emotions, the respective brain mechanisms seem to extend to the aspect of intention [5,12,14] or even identification [9]. Perspective taking, recognition of intentions and to a certain extent empathy [2], are usually subsumed under the term 'theory of mind' [12]. Following the continuum from mere motion perception to more complex semantic, emotional and finally social interactions, all these studies show the involvement of *emotional* basal, limbic systems (e.g., amygdala) as well as cortico-limbic transition zones (medial prefrontal cortex) that link to higher cognitive functions. In the context of music performance, Gallagher [13] showed differential cortical activation when comparing instrumental and expressive gestures: The perception of expressive gestures by a listener-viewer activated her brain regions that are associated with the 'social brain' while instrumental gestures activated preferably left-lateralised areas that are associated with language and (motion-) imitation.

In summary, there are no specific theories or studies available yet, that investigate these 'mirrored' perceptions and actions, when it comes to their evolution and stabilisation over time. This makes it impossible to infer mechanisms that would be involved in action or perception – in general and particularly in specific musical performance such as our use-case(s) – only from evolutionary, developmental or momentary neuroscientific data, since longitudinal or time-variant research is still missing. In the same way that research is missing concerning larger temporal scopes, the different positions possible in a musical performance situation have not sufficiently been investigated either: They cover the perspectives of performer and listener-viewer, and within these points-of-view differences between lay-person and experts.

The problem of diverging concepts, methodologies, and data becomes imminent [47]. The limits and future challenges of a research-approach covering these aspects are summarised by Decety and Chaminade in the following manner: "... the mechanisms involved in intersubjectivity cannot be reduced to this common mapping, neither at the neurophysiological level nor at the cognitive level. This system is interwoven with self-consciousness, as well as with the phenomenological experience of agency. Thus one highly relevant issue, both in neuropsychology but also from an evolutionary perspective, concerns how the self-versus-other distinction operates within these shared representations and which neural mechanisms are engaged in integrating and discriminating the representations activated by the self and those that are activated by external agents" [9]. The shared neural representation model highlights the self-other distinction, by making evident the importance of consciousness of self, of the experience of the proper and external agencies, and ultimately emphasises the inter-subjective and intertwining nature of music performance.

5 Performance Practice of Gestural Electronic Music

In almost all musical situations, as we've shown above (see Sect. 3.2), the combination of the body's action and perception potential and the instrumental affordances provide the driving force. This is particularly the case in a technological music practice, such as sensor-based electronic music, where instrumental actions cease to be exclusively perceptually guided, that is, not exclusively given by the physics of the instrument's acoustics, and where cognitive structures emerge that are informed less by *perceptually guided* actions than by *conceptually structured* perceptions. These mental processes are common in the playing of notated music, but the manner in which gesture, sound-production and musical structure are interdependent becomes more specific in electronic music performance and with digital musical instruments.

5.1 Empty Handed Play

The practice of performing with empty hands and physically with sensor-instruments has a history in the field of electronic music. Musicians such as Michel Waiszfisz, Laetita Sonami, Atau Tanaka have been exploring this practice for decades. A convincing performer of this type of gestural music was Michel Waisvisz[3], in particular because the integration of his instrument on a body-image level was clearly discernible. The mixture between instrumental control and physical movement, combined with direct treatment of vocal sounds, generated an expressive performance style that in our opinion appealed on the physical, corporeal as well as on the musical level.

A work from our own practice shall serve as a springboard to elucidate the connections established in the two preceding sections. The piece *'new islands'* was premiered in 2011 and has been in ongoing development since, with one or two performances per year.[4] The guiding principle for this composition is the exploration of sensor-based, gestural actions with empty-handed gestures, controlled with the aid of sensor-gloves and cameras, or with a symbolic sensor-instrument that restitutes the object character of an instrument without providing actual sound generation [48]. The current version of the piece concentrates on

---

[3] Videos can be found online (URL accessed 05/2015):
http://steim.org/2009/10/remembering-mw/.
https://www.youtube.com/watch?v=U1L-mVGqug4.

[4] For a collection of videos documenting the evolution of this piece please see: http://www.jasch.ch/island.html (URL accessed 01/2016).

Fig. 1. Video-still from the performance by Jan Schacher of 'new islands' at Darmstadt, Club 603qm, on 25 July 2012.

performing with a pair of sensor-gloves and a wireless headset microphone. The piece can be regarded as a composition insofar as the real-time sound-processing is highly structured and stable, but it could arguably also be regarded as a hybrid instrument encompassing the gloves, and their mapping to the digital sound processing. Currently there are no prerecorded materials, all the sounds used in the piece are captured in real-time through the microphone during the performance itself. The structure of the actions, the intended performance energy and the resulting forms are (re-) created every time, and have evolved on some levels, while in order respects have remained stable (Fig. 1).

The evolution of the piece and the way it 'feels' to the musician during performance provides a relevant connection to both the 'enactive' and the neuroscientific perspectives. The insights and reflections gained about the corporeal states inform on a fundamental level how the piece gets structured. These difference become visible when watching documentation video of several of the performances spanning four years. The reduction of instrumental elements and the developing clarity of the gestural actions across this process on the one hand, and the increasing ease and expertise of execution in each performance are direct consequences of a stable musical framework, within which experiences accumulate, and therefore an increasing focus from performance to performance can be noted. The reflections about corporeal presence and its affective power also leads the performer to a concentration on a movement repertoire and sound-language that emphasises the immediacy of decision-making during performance. In order to leverage the skills and expertise of the performer and at the same time leave enough space for an exploratory attitude, key aspects or principles of the 'composition' such as the stability of mapping [50], keeping manageable the size of the mental map of sound-processes, and an independence from visual representation need to be respected. This simultaneous fixing and opening of the compositional framework reflects the acquisition of skills and expertise on a corporeal, an experiential and a purely technical and even instrumental level, as well as the sharpening of the aesthetic, performative or musical intent.

Through these artistic development processes the four temporal frames of expertise and experiential stabilisation we established earlier can be observed. The experience over time by the musician of how the mental map of the piece evolves and the attitude in the playing of this piece changes indicates that a settling or crystallisation process has occurred. This long term solidification happens to a lesser degree for the audience as well: throughout the performance, the principles, actions and the ways the sounds and actions are correlated are first perceived, then learned, and then fully recognised. The analogous process within the duration of a single performance is based on cultural and social assets [42], but also on fundamental corporeal inter-subjective identifications [41] and is necessary to produce affective impact [45]. For the performer, thanks to the stable elements in the composition his or her body remembers how it *feels* to gesture with these sound processes. For the performer, the sensor-mapping and the mental map necessary to navigate the 'instrument' or 'piece' appear to have become imprinted – at least to some extent – and the corporeal impulses for certain gestures or movements during the performance start to resemble those that occur on a traditional instrument. For the listener-viewer who has witnessed *several* of these performances, the noticeable difference in the quality of performance – even if not specifically identifiable – indicates a similar settling; the situation becomes familiar and the expected actions and sounds fall within a known field of possibilities. This familiarity comes from the stable and recurring parts of the 'composition' and the unchanged stage situation that remains the same frontal setting for each performance. The familiarity is only be relativised when the character of the piece changes from one performance to another, due to evolving artistic concepts used for the 'narrative' aspects of the work. Thus the effect of this stabilisation also influences the perceptual integration of elements for the audience.

One of the listener-viewers who witnessed the first as well as the most recent performance of the piece provides this personal account of the experience: "I was able to let go and dwell in the web of linguistic, emotional, philosophical and perspective-changing 'synaesthesia' of the piece. The grains of sound were grains of discovery - within the stretched phrase all possibilities seemed to be conveyed but not accessible to the conscious mind. It gave me all the time I needed to discover and visit that island."

6 In Conclusion

This reflection on processes in the music performing and perceiving body is supported by insights from the partial overlap with two neighbouring fields of psychological philosophy and cognitive neuroscience.

The *primacy of movement* is a foundation of our individual development and corporeality, it underpins all human activities and in particular musical performance and perception. In order to understand the complex layering of our embodied, situated and cognitive performance, we propose to consider the dynamics of flow [7], and the continuous exposure and adaptation as the *key element* which enable skill stabilisation and the formation of expertise. The issue we approach here is how to transfer between, or how to stabilise within the domains, the multiple and intertwined modalities and the skills involved in music performance in particular, and in any complex corporeal activity in general. The resonances and imitation systems detailed in the mirror neuron theories find their equivalence in the complementarity of the performer-listener pair, where many of the mental and corporeal processes and cognitive mechanisms occur in mirrored constellations.

Having reviewed the mechanisms of expertise gain, we must re-emphasise the influence of emotions and motivation for the performer. The intrinsic motivation through joy and fun arise from recognition by an audience but also from mastering the challenges of the performance situation. From a neurological point of view, these intrinsic psychological enhancers are not directly involved in the processes described above, but rather boost the individual's performances and experiences. Intrinsic motivations are determining aspects for reinforcing learning and gain in expertise by providing arousal (basal and reactive), valence (personal and salient) and emotions [25]. The additional effects provided by these psychological factors are not merely key to improving the expertise development processes, the added value is also to be found in the personal fulfilment and success of the performance.

The embodied awareness and neural activity in the musician and the listener-viewer are interdependent states and processes, which we could also represented through the borrowed *metaphor* of the '*fluid*' and the '*crystalline*' [6]. In all the temporal frames we looked at, i.e., the life-long development span, the individual's formative training phase, the artistic development process for a single work, and the time-span of a single performance, we can observe recurring patterns that oscillate between these two polarities. The same states reached during performance, as well as within the process of musical training, are contributing factors to the stabilisation of skills and expertise. They seem to be present in all three of the expertise building modes: when activating 'motor-memory', when generating 'motor imagination' and even in states of free 'meditation' [8]. Finally, as an essential effect of the stabilisation of skills through increased expertise, they are freeing up the performer by providing sub-personal and cognitive resources that may be mobilised in order to better explore and shape the dynamic flow of a musical performance.

With this article we attempt to bridge the gap between cognitive neuroscience and psychological philosophy from the vantage point of the musician, particularly from a reflective position that draws on these neighbouring fields. The neuroscientific point of view – even if apparently only dealing with the brain – complements the embodied, 'enactive' perspective. From this standpoint it seems that the two fields merely represent *two perspectives of the same complex matter* that span across embodied awareness, neurological processes and beyond. Cognitive sciences have moved away from computational models of cognition and have begun to embrace the fact that there is no separation between brain and body, and that cognition involves the entire corporeal sphere. What phenomenology and psychological philosophy have established is now shown by the cognitive neurosciences: in perception and cognition brain and body fuse, and this unity extends to the ecological perspective.

At this point the challenge of developing methodologies about how to approach these questions becomes evident. In order to verify and ground the theories exposed here, systematic, cross-disciplinary procedures need to be developed to produce concrete insights based on acquired data rather than interpretations. Future studies could explore this particular perspective from both empirical, quantitative as well as qualitative perspectives. In experimental studies and setups the respective hypotheses could be tested in parallel with available mobile EEG and other bio-sensors, applied to both the performer and audience at the same time. This would also mean carrying out mixed methods research [49], by doing qualitative and quantitative performance movement analysis with canonical contemporary music pieces as well as newly developed pieces, obtaining data by motion-capture, collecting subjective observant data, developing software tools that leverage machine-learning techniques for cross-domain correlations, and investigating the semantic and terminological implications of composing, performing and perceiving gesture-based music.

Music performance provides a rich terrain within which to explore these connections. By exposing the musician and the audience to atypical and creative re-combinations in the gestural performance of electronic sound, the junctions, ruptures and fusions inherent to this field are revealed even more clearly.

Acknowledgments. This investigation originates from the 'Motion Gesture Music' project at the Institute for Computer Music and Sound Technology of the Zurich University of the Arts, and is funded by the Swiss National Science Foundation Grant No. 100016_149345.

References

1. Bermúdez, J.L.: The Paradox of Self-Consciousness. The MIT Press, Cambridge (2000)
2. Berrol, C.F.: Neuroscience meets dance/movement therapy: mirror neurons, the therapeutic process and empathy. Arts Psychother. **33**(4), 302–315 (2006)
3. Berthoz, A.: Le Sens du Mouvement. Odile Jacob, Paris (1997)
4. Bezzola, L., Mérillat, S., Jäncke, L.: The effect of leisure activity golf practice on motor imagery: an fMRI study in middle adulthood. Front. Hum. Neurosci. **6**, 1–9 (2012). Article 67
5. Blakemore, S.J., Decety, J.: From the perception of action to the understanding of intention. Nat. Rev. Neurosci. **2**(8), 561–567 (2001). http://dx.doi.org/10.1038/35086023

6. Cattell, R.B.: Theory of fluid and crystallized intelligence: a critical experiment. J. Educ. Psychol. **54**(1), 1–22 (1963)
7. Csikszentmihalyi, M.: Flow: The Psychology of Optimal Experience. Harper and Row, New York (1990)
8. Debarnot, U., Sperduti, M., Di Rienzo, F., Guillot, A.: Experts bodies, experts minds: how physical and mental training shape the brain. Front. Hum. Neurosci. **8**, 1–17 (2014)
9. Decety, J., Chaminade, T.: When the self represents the other: a new cognitive neuroscience view on psychological identification. Conscious. Cogn. **12**(4), 577–596 (2003)
10. Enticott, P.G., Kennedy, H.A., Bradshaw, J.L., Rinehart, N.J., Fitzgerald, P.B.: Understanding mirror neurons: evidence for enhanced corticospinal excitability during the observation of transitive but not intransitive hand gestures. Neuropsychologia **48**(9), 2675–2680 (2010)
11. Fitch, W.T.: The Evolution of Language. Cambridge University Press, Cambridge (2010)
12. Gallagher, H.L., Frith, C.D.: Functional imaging of 'Theory of Mind'. Trends Cogn. Sci. **7**(2), 77–83 (2003)
13. Gallagher, H.L., Frith, C.D.: Dissociable neural pathways for the perception and recognition of expressive and instrumental gestures. Neuropsychologia **42**(13), 1725–1736 (2004)
14. Gallagher, H.L., Jack, A.I., Roepstorff, A., Frith, C.D.: Imaging the intentional stance in a competitive game. NeuroImage **16**(3), 814–821 (2002)
15. Gallagher, S.: Bodily self-awareness and object perception. Theoria et Historia Scientiarum **VII**(1), 53–68 (2003)
16. Gallagher, S.: How the Body Shapes the Mind. Clarendon Press, Oxford (2005)
17. Gallagher, S., MarcelMarcel, A.J.: The self in contextualized action. J. Conscious. Stud. **6**(4), 4–30 (1999)
18. Gibson, J.J.: The Ecological Approach to Visual Perception. Lawrence Erlbaum, Hillsdale (1986)
19. Godøy, R.I.: Gestural-Sonorous objects: embodied extensions of Schaeffer's conceptual apparatus. Org. Sound **11**(2), 149–157 (2006)
20. Held, K.: Husserl's phenomenology of the life-world. In: Welton, D. (ed.) The New Husserl: A Critical Reader. Indiana University Press, Bloomington (2003)
21. Howard, I.S., Wolpert, D.M., Franklin, D.W.: The value of the follow-through derives from motor learning depending on future actions. Curr. Biol. **25**(3), 397–401 (2015)
22. Iyer, V.: Improvisation, temporality and embodied experience. J. Conscious. Stud. **11**(3–4), 159–173 (2004)
23. Jäncke, L.: Music making and the aging brain. Zeitschrift für Neuropsychologie **24**(2), 113–121 (2013). http://dx.doi.org/10.1024/1016-264X/a000095
24. Johnson, M.: The Meaning of the Body, Aesthetics of Human Understanding. The University of Chicago Press, Chicago (2007)
25. Kensinger, E.A.: Remembering emotional experiences: the contribution of valence and arousal. Rev. Neurosci. **15**(4), 241–252 (2004)
26. Kim, J.H.: Embodiment musikalischer Praxis und Medialität des Musikinstrumentes - unter besonderer Berücksichtigung digitaler interaktiver Musikperformances. In: Harenberg, M., Weissberg, D. (eds.) Klang (ohne) Körper, Spuren und Potenziale des Körpers in der elektronischen Musik, pp. 105–118. Transcript, Bielefeld (2010)

27. Lakoff, G., Johnson, M.: Metaphors We Live By. University Of Chicago Press, Chicago (1980)
28. Legrand, D.: Pre-reflective self-consciousness: on being bodily in the world. Janus Head **9**(2), 493–519 (2007)
29. Leman, M., Camurri, A.: Understanding musical expressiveness using interactive multimedia platforms. Musicae Sci. **10**(1 suppl), 209–233 (2006)
30. Lotze, M., Heymans, U., Birbaumer, N., Veit, R., Erb, M., Flor, H., Halsband, U.: Differential cerebral activation during observation of expressive gestures and motor acts. Neuropsychologia **44**(10), 1787–1795 (2006)
31. Luria, A.R.: The Working Brain. Penguin Books, Harmondsworth (1973)
32. Marcel, A.: The Sense of Agency: Awareness and Ownership of Action. In: Roessler, J., Eilan, N. (eds.) Agency and Self-Awareness, pp. 48–93. Oxford University Press, Oxford (2003)
33. Merleau-Ponty, M.: Phenomenology of Perception. Gallimard, Paris (1945). 2007, paperback edn
34. Michel-Dansac, D.: In a Personal communication, March 2014
35. Montgomery, K.J., Isenberg, N., Haxby, J.V.: Communicative hand gestures and object-directed hand movements activated the mirror neuron system. Soc. Cogn. Affect. Neurosci. **2**(2), 114–122 (2007)
36. Montgomery, K.J., Haxby, J.V.: Mirror neuron system differentially activated by facial expressions and social hand gestures: a functional magnetic resonance imaging study. J. Cogn. Neurosci. **20**(10), 1866–1877 (2008). http://dx.doi.org/10.1162/jocn.2008.20127
37. Ophir, E., Nass, C., Wagner, A.D.: Cognitive control in media multitaskers. Proc. Natl. Acad. Sci. **106**(37), 15583–15587 (2009)
38. Paine, G.: Towards unified design guidelines for new interfaces for musical expression. Organised Sound **14**(2), 142–155 (2009)
39. Pascual-Leone, A., Amedi, A., Fregni, F., Merabet, L.B.: The plastic human brain cortex. Annu. Rev. Neurosci. **28**(1), 377–401 (2005). http://dx.doi.org/10.1146/annurev.neuro.27.070203.144216
40. Poeppel, D.: The analysis of speech in different temporal integration windows: cerebral lateralization as 'asymmetric sampling in time'. Nat. Speech Percept. **41**(1), 245–255 (2003). http://www.sciencedirect.com/science/article/pii/S0167639302001073
41. Proust, J.: Perceiving intentions. In: Roessler, J., Eilan, N. (eds.) Agency and Self-awareness: Issues in Philosophy and Psychology, pp. 296–320. Oxford University Press, Oxford (2003)
42. Rancière, J.: The emancipated spectator. Art Forum XLV(7), March 2007
43. Rizzolatti, G., Arbib, M.A.: Language within our grasp. Trends Neurosci. **21**(5), 188–194 (1998)
44. Rizzolatti, G., Fogassi, L., Gallese, V.: Neurophysiological mechanisms underlying the understanding and imitation of action. Nat. Rev. Neurosci. **2**(9), 661–670 (2001). http://dx.doi.org/10.1038/35090060
45. Russell, J.A.: A circumplex model of affect. J. Pers. Soc. Psychol. **39**(6), 1161–1178 (1980)
46. Salat, D.H., Buckner, R.L., Snyder, A.Z., Greve, D.N., Desikan, S.R., Busa, E., Morris, J.C., Dale, A.M., Fischl, B.: Thinning of the cerebral cortex in aging. Cereb. Cortex **14**(7), 721–730 (2004)
47. Sawyer, K.: The cognitive neuroscience of creativity: a critical review. Creat. Res. J. **23**(2), 137–154 (2011)

48. Schacher, J.C.: The quarterstaff, a gestural sensor instrument. In: Proceedings of the Conference on New Interfaces for Musical Expression (NIME 2013), Daejeon & Seoul, Korea Republic (2013)
49. Schacher, J.C., Järveläinen, H., Strinning, C., Neff, P.: Movement perception in music performance - a mixed methods investigation. In: Proceedings of the International Conference on Sound and Music Computing, SMC 2015, Maynooth, Ireland (2015)
50. Schacher, J.C., Kocher, P., Bisig, D.: The map and the flock - emergence in mapping with swarm algorithms. Comput. Music J. **38**(3), 49–63 (2014)
51. Schlaug, G., Jäncke, L., Huang, Y., Staiger, J.F., Steinmetz, H.: Increased corpus callosum size in musicians. Neuropsychol. Dev. Stud. Corpus Callosum **33**(8), 1047–1055 (1995). http://www.sciencedirect.com/science/article/pii/0028393295000455
52. Serrien, D.J., Ivry, R.B., Swinnen, S.P.: Dynamics of hemispheric specialization and integration in the context of motor control. Nat. Rev. Neurosci. **7**(2), 160–166 (2006). http://dx.doi.org/10.1038/nrn1849
53. Sheets-Johnstone, M.: Kinesthetic memory. In: Sheets-Johnstone, M. (ed.) The Corporeal Turn: An Interdisciplinary Reader, pp. 253–277. Imprint Academic, London (2009)
54. Small, C.: Musicking – the meanings of performing and listening. A lecture. Music Educ. Res. **1**(1), 9–22 (1999)
55. Varela, F.J., Thompson, E.T., Rosch, E.: The Embodied Mind: Cognitive Science and Human Experience. The MIT Press, Cambridge (1991)
56. Wan, C.Y., Schlaug, G.: Music making as a tool for promoting brain plasticity across the life span. Neurosci. **16**(5), 566–577 (2010)
57. Zatorre, R.J., Chen, J.L., Penhune, V.B.: When the brain plays music: auditory-motor interactions in music perception and production. Nat. Rev. Neurosci. **8**(7), 547–558 (2007)

The Hybrid Brain Computer Music Interface - Integrating Brainwave Detection Methods for Extended Control in Musical Performance Systems

Joel Eaton[✉] and Eduardo R. Miranda

Interdisciplinary Centre for Computer Music Research, Plymouth University, Plymouth, UK
joel.eaton@postgrad.plymouth.ac.uk

Abstract. In the pursuit of creative interfaces for music making brain-computer interfacing (BCI) control methods offer limited usability especially in terms of providing simultaneous yet independent input controls. This article outlines the development of the hybrid brain-computer music interface (BCMI) and presents the work undertaken towards the design, implementation, and combined BCI control methods employed. Two active (steady state visually evoked potential (SSVEP) and motor imagery (MI)) and one passive (affective response) control methods are integrated in a new BCMI system, which can be applied to a range of music-making activities. This paper also briefly outlines the design of bespoke, customisable and modular SSVEP stimuli and feedback units. As a demonstration of the hybrid-BCMI, the performance piece A Stark Mind illustrates how such a system is in for live performance. The piece uses the brainwave control methods to generate and control a visual score for an ensemble of musicians to perform.

Keywords: Neuro-technology · Brain music · Brainwave control · Live performance · Brain-computer music interfacing

1 Introduction

Research spanning the last fifty or so years has seen a variety of approaches to applying brainwaves to music. Pioneers in the field include Alvin Lucier, Richard Teitelbaum and David Rosenboom, whose work since the 1960's fuse brainwaves and other bio-signals with experimental performances. During the early period of this creative era, brainwave detection techniques used in live performance was commonly the approximation of specific brainwave frequency bands with activity strongly associated with mental states, such as relaxation or mediation. In particular, systems that amplified alpha band (8–13 Hz) activity were popular during this time. This method is synonymous with bio-feedback, whereby the amplitude of these signals could be voluntarily controlled and then used to modify sound synthesis and amplification systems.

Electroencephalography (EEG) is the measure of electrical activity in the brain using electrodes placed across the scalp. EEG is currently the most viable, non-intrusive, and practical means of detecting brainwaves, and is a useful method of interfacing brain signals with external systems.

Brain-computer interfacing (BCI) offers a non-physical interface for explicit communication between a user and machine. Control over brainwaves has the potential to be mapped to systems for communication, expression, and for controlling creative applications. Recent advances in the field have led to brain-computer music interfaces (BCMIs) that can offer medical insights [2], provide benefits to patients with motor disabilities [3], and even provide a platform for combined brainwave control from multiple users [4]. We are interested in exploring the creative possibilities of such technologies for users of all abilities. And the recent advances in neuro-technologies have paved the way for BCMI to provide useful and creative solutions towards inclusive music making and control in live performance.

The system presented in this article builds on previous BCMIs to offer multiple EEG control methods, with many-to-many mappings; where users can control multiple commands simultaneously. On the whole, previous BCMIs adopt only one method of brainwave control, which is either passive or active. Passive control is determined by subconscious mental states of the user, where control is implicit. From a user perspective, using passive control is difficult for predicting musical outcomes, but offers an interesting perspective for mapping mental states to musical features. Active control provides a user with explicit choice based selection using cognitive tasks, and helps provide an objective measure of control suitable for the role of direct music making. Using one method of active control equates to either one-to-one or one-to-many musical mappings. With one method of active control, only one input channel can be controlled at a time, although it can be mapped to either one or multiple outputs. This limitation is the motivation for combining methods of control, to add additional dimensions of control to provide many-to-many mappings, with independent control over multiple input channels simultaneously.

In general, acoustic and digital music interfaces provide control over multiple parameters simultaneously. For example, the piano is rarely played by pressing one key at a time, or with just one finger. Instead, varieties of note selections, key-press timings, and key pressure are combined and overlapped to build chords and create complexity. The primary aim of this research is to find ways to implement more complex forms of user control for BCMI. Previous BCMIs have addressed the issue of control simplicity by creating musical complexity through complex mapping strategies, for example adding elements of randomness, generative processes or stochastic variables [5]. Instead, by focusing BCMI design towards expanding both the number and nature of input controls, the aim is to provide increased musical complexity and expression. However, increasing the complexity of control places greater demands on a user, and issues surrounding user experience must be taken into account, such as the enjoyment of playing, and the level of difficulty required for accomplished playing.

Many contemporary digital musical interfaces, particularly physical controllers, offer of a range of input control types. For example, controllers such as the Ableton Push[1] device offer a range of gestural-led controls based on combinations of rotary encoders, faders, buttons, as well as mobile devices with touchscreen controls. Such controllers provide three major features; different forms of control that are often

---

[1] https://www.ableton.com/en/push/.

directly related to gesture, simultaneous control over different inputs, and customisable mapping platforms where a user can design their own mapping strategies to suit a preferred style of composition or performance.

The hybrid-BCMI also offers these three elements of functionality. The system uses three different forms of user control, gives simultaneous control over different features, and has a framework for designing customised mappings. User control is derived from three BCI methods using EEG, known as steady-state visual evoked potentials (SSVEP), motor imagery (MI) through event-related de-synchronisation (ERD) of sensorimotor rhythms, and affective measures, which are closely linked to emotional indicators. The hybrid-BCMI is also designed for live concert performance with both minimal setup and portability in mind. To achieve this the hybrid-BCMI uses a minimal number of electrodes for EEG, whilst successfully providing a high level of accurate control. A single laptop computer performs EEG processing, classification, feature extraction, mapping, and dynamic musical score generation. Additionally, customisable and modular hardware SSVEP stimuli units are presented. These units are used in the performance of *A Stark Mind*, an audio-visual performance piece designed to demonstrate the capabilities of the hybrid-BCMI, and used as the example of hybrid-BCMI in discussions throughout this article.

2 Active Control

An active BCMI allows a user to exert musical control by making explicit selections from multiple choices. Active control methods fall into two categories, those that require external stimuli to generate specific brainwave patterns and those that rely on approximating brainwave patterns associated with mental tasks. BCMIs in the first category rely on event-based stimuli, where the system detects a change in brainwave activity in response to, commonly, a visual or audio event. Systems in the second category detect differences in brainwave patterns between conflicting mental tasks. For example, differences in brainwave patterns between a user imagining body movement and imagining remaining still, known as motor imagery. The use of auditory stimuli is not particularly well suited for music making due to the obvious issue of distraction when being attentive to stimuli that is not related to the music being generated. Because of this, active control methods through attending to visual stimulus or undertaking imaginative tasks are more suitable. One particular issue that occurs when using external stimuli for active control is that brainwave response is time-locked to the presentation of stimuli. For example, a BCI P300 spelling device, used for sequencing letters for communication, rapidly presents the letters of the alphabet in a quasi-random sequence [6]. The system monitors for a specific brainwave response, found when the user eventually sees the letter they have been waiting for. Here, the response is time-locked to the arrival of the anticipated element of the sequence, the expectant letter, and provides an obstacle for a user to be able to make a choice at any given time. The SSVEP technique is a more appropriate control method that uses visual stimulus, as it presents choices that are always available to a user. A user can make selections at a time suitable to them, without having to wait for a specific stimulus to be presented, as with the P300 method. Furthermore, a recent comparative study indicated that SSVEP offered greater accuracy, with a faster response time in comparison to MI and P300 [7].

Combining control techniques that require visual stimuli offers limitations with regards the ability of a user to direct visual attention towards to places or events at once. SSVEP and MI present a suitable pairing of active control methods as the action of visual gazing can be separate to imagining motor tasks, but occur at the same.

2.1 SSVEP

SSVEP control elicits an increase in the amplitude of a brainwave frequency, known as an event-related potential (ERP), when a user gazes at an icon that flickers ON/OFF at the same frequency. If a user is subjected to repeated alternating of an icon or pattern at short intervals, a positive amplitude response is detected via electrodes placed across the visual cortex. Before the amplitude of the brainwave has had time to return back to its unexcited state the rapid introduction of the next flashing onset elicits another response. This fast repetition of flickering induces a steady-state response where the brainwave amplitude rises and falls in real-time relative to the user's attention towards an icon. When multiple icons are presented, flickering at different frequencies, a user can make choices through gazing at different icons. When the waves of brainwave frequencies are monitored individually, amplitude rises associated with icon gazing are detected by a classification system, and can be used as a control switch. Furthermore, prolonged gazing and concentration can also control the strength of amplitude. Therefore, two consecutive elements of control can be used to map SSVEP choices to musical parameters. First, the icon selection detected when the amplitude breaches a threshold, and second the level of control through the subsequent control of the amplitude level.

SSVEP is detectable across frequencies between approximately 3.5–75 Hz across the visual cortex [6], with BCIs commonly adopting stimuli in the lower part of this range due to the efficiency of rendering icons that flicker at such high rates. The hybrid BCMI uses 8 SSVEP channels with icons that flicker at 7 Hz, 7.5 Hz, 8 Hz, 9 Hz, 10 Hz, 11 Hz, 12 Hz, and 12.5 Hz. A threshold classification system determines the minimum amplitude, $_a min$, value for determining positive selections, and the amplitude range monitored for amplitude control, $_a min$ - $_a max$. SSVEP response is monitored using one electrode channel at position Oz, from the international 10–20 electrode positioning system, located at the rear of the scalp. A reference electrode is located at position Cz, on the top of the scalp, and a ground electrode is placed at the AFz position, on the forehead.

2.2 Motor Imagery

MI detects differences in brainwave patterns between opposing mental tasks of mobility. MI can be measured by the detection of event-related desynchronisation (ERD) of sensorimotor rhythms, which relies on a user either imagining a distinct motor related task or relaxing, without any conflicting stimuli. The role of detecting distinctions in imaginations offers a less obtrusive approach to generating control than icon gazing, which can cause tiredness and discomfort, especially when undertaken for long periods of time.

For the hybrid-BCMI, musical parameters assigned to MI are controlled using either the thought of squeezing or relaxing the right hand. To obtain a measure of kinaesthetic motor imagery strength ERD is detected by extracting the alpha band-power over the left motor cortex, which is contralateral to the right hand. This is measured at electrode positions F3, T3, C3, Cz, and P3. By inverting the signal, performing kinaesthetic motor imagery of the right hand creates an ERD, with a decrease in alpha band power. Subsequently, a relaxing thought does the opposite and increases alpha band power [8]. In the hybrid-BCMI this two-state control is performed at the same time as SSVEP gazing, as an extended control function. Here, MI acts as a switch that can be used to alter an SSVEP selection, in one of two ways.

3 Passive Control Through Affective Measures

Music psychology typically documents three types of emotional responses to music: mood, affect, and emotion [9]. Russell's circumplex model of affect [10] provides a way of parameterising emotional responses to musical stimuli in two dimensions: valence (positivity) and arousal (energy or activation). Musical mood classification is a growing field in the realm of musical information retrieval, with one KTH study acknowledging a set of real-time musical performance rules whereby musical features can be mapped directly to differences in arousal and valence [11].

In the hybrid BCMI levels of arousal and valence are measured over the prefrontal cortex, at electrode positions AF3 and AF4, an area that plays a significant role in emotion handling. Arousal is derived from the ratio between alpha and beta activity and valence is determined by symmetry across the left and right hemispheres, in the method proposed by Ramirez and Vamvakousis [12]. Strong alpha activity is known to indicate a relaxed state of mind, and this combined with increased activity in the beta band can indicate an alertness in mental activity, arousal [13]. The balance of activation levels across the left and right hemispheres indicates a difference between a motivated approach or a more negative, withdrawn type of mental state, which is directly related to valence [14]. Band-power filters are used to capture activity across alpha and beta (16–24 Hz) bands. In the hybrid-BCMI affective values are averaged across windows between 10–30 s, and synchronised with a global clock that coordinates the audio-visual performance.

A previous study reported on successfully inducing affective states in response to musical stimuli with known emotional features [15] using this method. The hybrid-BCMI explores the artistic possibilities mapping changes in affective measures to music. Changes of arousal and valence are mapped to opposing musical parameters of widely accepted affective associations. For example, the link between arousal and tempo is well documented [16]. Increases in tempo have been found to induce an increase in arousal. In the hybrid-BCMI, increases in arousal are mapped to a decrease in tempo, in an attempt to regulate the affective state of the user during performance. Further opposing mappings are discussed in Sect. 7.2. Passive Control Mappings.

4 Hybrid BCMI Control

The success of the hybrid-BCMI can be measured against the performance of each control method and their integration within a usable and coherent platform suitable for musical control. In early 2015 a pilot study was conducted by the authors, to investigate the accuracy of the SSVEP method, using custom made stimuli units. The study measured SSVEP response times and accuracy over eleven subjects using the same single electrode channel technique described here with a single trial classifier to determine the value of $_a min$. The results showed a mean accuracy across all subjects of 96.4 % when choosing between four SSVEP channels. Response time was measured across eight SSVEP channels, with results showing a mean response time of 3.986 s, over the best performing four channels. A faster mean response time of 2.62 s for one user with previous experience was also recorded. The study showed yielded similar results to comparable studies using similar EEG equipment [17].

In the development of the hybrid-BCMI we devised a pilot system that demonstrates the combination of SSVEP control across 8 channels, alongside simultaneous affective measures. Here, both inputs were mapped to simultaneously control a step sequencer and the timbral qualities of synthesised drum voices [18]. In this example, the system allowed both techniques to be used without the brain activity generated from one technique interfering with the other. This is because the signals for each technique are generated from different locations across the scalp. SSVEP is detected at the rear, whilst affective responses are measured across the prefrontal area. In the updated hybrid-BCMI presented here we add a third control technique, MI. To validate the use of both SSVEP and MI, in 2010 Pfurtscheller et al. developed a hybrid-BCI that successfully combined these two methods to reinforce choice over two options. Here, greater accuracy was provided when a user gazed at a flashing SSVEP icon and imagined left hand motor imagery, by combining positive classification of both techniques [19]. Instead of reinforcing a selection our hybrid-BCMI takes the measure of MI as an extended control option during positive SSVEP detection. For example, gazing at 6 Hz and conducting a relaxing motor thought produces a different output to gazing at 6 Hz and performing positive kinaesthetic motor imagery. This system also improves on previous hybrid-BCIs by adding this two-state option during SSVEP detection across eight SSVEP channels.

5 System Design

Measuring EEG for BCI control in real-time presents issues of noise and interference from external sources that affect data classification. These are especially prominent in uncontrolled environments away from the laboratory, such as musical performance settings. Electrical interference from line-noise, lighting systems, or static electricity from sources such as the hair of a user can combine with an inherently poor signal-to-noise ratio from amplifying such small signals (microvolts) and artefacts caused by muscle movement. Noise picked up by EEG electrodes can result in the BCMI detecting control commands generated by noise instead of a user. As a result, this can reduce the feeling of control and frustrate a user. To reduce these issues, EEG signals are pre-processed to remove mains noise and BCMI equipment is isolated on-stage. Additionally, a user is grounded using an earth cable connected to a common ground point, and is also provided with instructions regarding equipment operation and movement (Fig. 1).

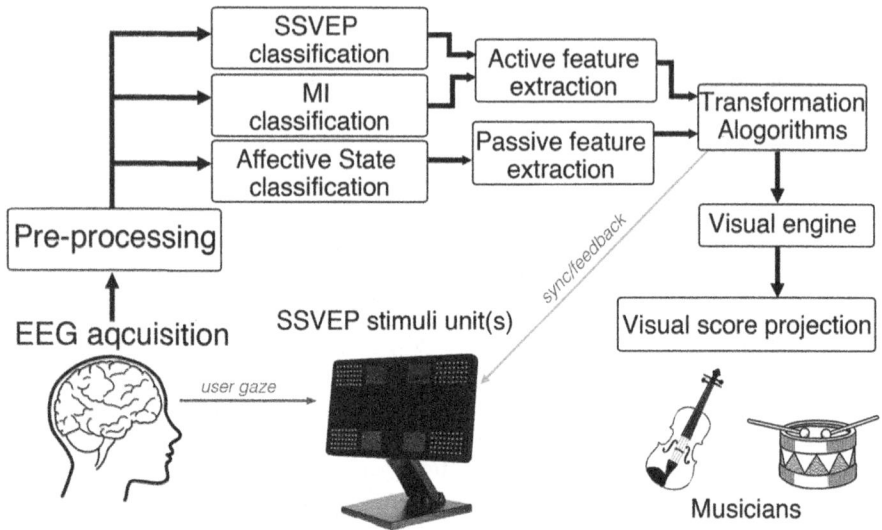

Fig. 1. The hybrid-BCMI connectivity and signal flow for *A Stark Mind*. All functions illustrated by text boxes are performed by a laptop PC. To provide eight channels of SSVEP stimuli two four-channel SSVEP stimuli units are required.

Overview of the Hybrid BCMI System

The hybrid-BCMI system is constructed of the following hardware and software components:

EEG Measuring. A g.tec[2] gamma brain cap is fitted with g.tec Sahara dry electrodes connected to a g.tec Sahara amplifier. The signal is digitised by a g.MOBIlab+ unit and sent wirelessly, using Bluetooth, to the laptop PC.

Pre-processing. The digitised signal is received in Matlab Simulink[3] and pre-processed to reduce line-noise and to extrapolate data from electrode groups and pairings.

Control Classification. EEG data is processed in real-time against three classifiers, one for each control method, in parallel. A four minute training period is undertaken before performance, to train each classifier. For parameter extraction, band-power in each channel is extracted by applying a 5th order band-pass filter across each target frequency with a bandwidth of 0.5 Hz. Each sample is squared and averaged over

---

[2] http://www.gtec.at/.

[3] http://uk.mathworks.com/products/simulink/.

consecutive samples with a window length of 128 samples. The system has the ability to store threshold values for individual users and environments and allow for on-the-fly adjustment.

Feature Extraction. Positive features detected across SSVEP, MI and affective measurements are passed to the transformation algorithm software via a custom Simulink *s*-function to transfer data using the Open Sound Control (OSC) data format using the User Data Program (UDP) data transfer protocol.

Transformation Algorithms. Feature data received in Pure Data[4] is sent to mapping rules that generate control commands for the visual score. Commands are quantised in synchronisation with the performance global clock. The clock is used to determine the current mapping rules to apply to control values, as mapping rules can change at specific times, or relative to previous control selections during performance. Feature data is scaled to fit the ranges of the parameters in the visual-rendering platform. Feature data is repackaged as a control signal from Pure Data to the visual platform, again using OSC. Control information is also sent via OSC to update the displays of the external SSVEP stimuli units for providing visual user feedback.

Live Visual Score Rendering. The graphic score is generated in the Resolume[5] software platform. The platform maps control commands from Pure Data and projects the resulting video output on-stage for the musicians to read, and for the audience to see.

External SSVEP Stimuli Units. Two external SSVEP units are used, providing for eight SSVEP channels. The units provide flickering SSVEP icons and display images next to each icon to show the user the mapping between each icon and graphical score control.

6 The Customisable SSVEP Stimuli Unit

External SSVEP stimuli units have been designed and manufactured based on a need to separate visual stimuli from a computer and monitor, due to the accuracy needed in rendering high-speed flickering frequencies for SSVEP detection. Flickering rates on computer monitors are determined by the divisors of the screen refresh rates. In general, accurate graphics rendering of this kind becomes less efficient on a computer when other tasks require processing power, such as processing EEG signals, mapping data and rendering the graphic score. The units are based on an open-source Arduino[6] microcontroller board, and each unit contains four RGB LED arrays for flickering icons. Each unit also contains four 2.2 inch TFT screens that display images relating to the mappings for each icon. The units also contain a wireless shield for receiving control signals across a wireless local area network. The units can be customised to provide different flickering frequencies to suit differences across individual user amplitude responses, which can vary. The images or symbols shown on the TFT

---

[4] http://puredata.info/.
[5] http://resolume.com/.
[6] http://www.arduino.cc/.

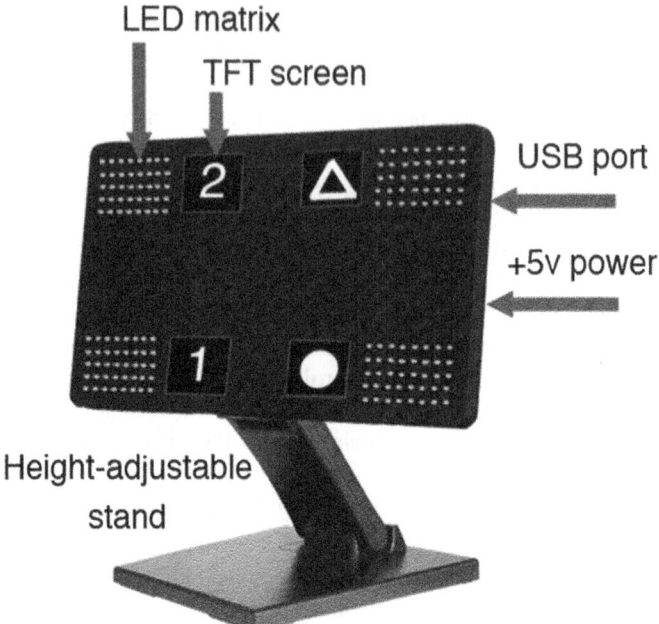

Fig. 2. The SSVEP stimuli unit. Units feature 4 × LED arrays, 4 × TFT screens and a WIFI shield. Units are modular and be combined to provide more SSVEP channels, in multiples of four.

screens to communicate the mappings can also be modified. Figure 2 illustrates the layout and connectivity of a unit, and shows the TFT screens displaying generic symbols that can relate to musical parameters. Either a WIFI or a USB connection allows for synchronisation to the host laptop during performance. For example, new images can be loaded on the TFT screens at specific times to reflect changes in mappings. The units are designed to be modular, where units can be used together to provide additional SSVEP channels, in multiples of four. For *A Stark Mind* two units are used providing 8 SSVEP channels, with the extended MI control.

7 A Stark Mind

A Stark Mind is a live audio-visual performance piece, approximately twelve minutes long. The piece demonstrates one application of the hybrid-BCMI as a real-time music controller for a live performance. The piece also attempts to reduce the effects of one of the barriers created when performing with a BCMI, which is the lack of visual stimulation for an audience. This is in large part due to the nature of BCI control, where a user has to remain motionless to avoid interference generated from movement. This issue is addressed through the visualisation of the user's brainwave control through the projection of a dynamic, graphic score to the audience. Translating the act of BCMI user intent, i.e. drawing a certain pattern or affecting a particular shape attempts to create a bridge between the audience and the BCMI 'performer', which is often missing in live performances involving BCMIs. Furthermore, the graphic score is presented in an abstract and colourful matter. The audience requires no prior musical knowledge to access the music control, which should be evident through the correlation of the musician's interpretation of the graphic score. The beginning of the performance starts with a very simple musical interpretation of very simple visual patterns, to draw the audience into the relationship between visuals and sound. The aim is for this to form a basis on which the link between brainwave control and music, via the graphic score, can then explored in more experimental and abstract directions.

A Stark Mind is designed for two string instruments and percussion, performed surrounding the BCMI performer on-stage. All of the performers are positioned away from the audience, facing the back of the stage and the projected score. The patterns that make up the graphic score patterns are abstract in nature but have associated musical characterises and performance rules, developed through workshop sessions with musicians. This approach to the composition allows the performers to be involved in the composition process and for each performance to be different, as they are tailored to the styles of different musicians. Figure 3 below shows an example snapshot of the score. The dominant circular pattern rotates to represent a moving rhythm for the percussion. The three moving squares on the left hand side signify a three-note violin arpeggio that is played relative to the speed at which it moves.

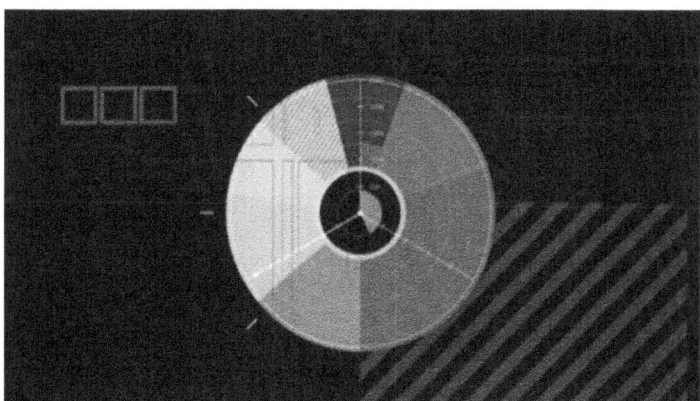

Fig. 3. Screenshot of Sect. 2 of the graphical score. Initial composition rules developed during workshop sessions result in a more democratic compositional process and add elements of musical freedom during performance.

The performance comprises three sections, each with associated score patterns that are triggered and controlled. As mentioned, the first section is designed to introduce the concept of the visual score to the audience. Here, the playing of each instrument is initiated by the introduction of three corresponding visual patterns. Manipulations to patterns, in all sections the piece, are the cue for variations to the musical motifs associated with each pattern. The second section combines different score patterns that are all synchronised to a visual pulse defined by the global clock, to generate a rhythmic cue. The third section features a call-and-response type of interplay between the violin and the viola. This is controlled by alternating the on-screen focus of the associative visual pattern for each instrument. Here, the speed of each part, the correlation between each instrument's part, and the range of overlapping are key cues provided by the score.

7.1 Active Control Mappings

One SSVEP stimuli unit provides four controls for selection of visual patterns and effects synchronised with a global clock. The second unit provides four channels for controlling visual effects parameters such as the intensity or depth, or the opacity against the non-effected pattern. The first unit acts as the macro arrangement controller, whereas the second unit provides the interface for applying and controlling visual, and subsequent, musical effects. The four macro control channels triggers the playback of patterns, and their removal from the score. The MI selector provides the additional choice of assigning score patterns to either the pre-assigned string instruments, or the percussion, for added musical variety.

MI detection is based on approximating alpha band-power in the run up to initial positive SSVEP detection. An experienced user with a mean response time of 2.6 s is instructed to focus on relaxation or squeezing their right hand as they make an SSVEP selection. Once positive SSVEP is detected at time $t = 0$ alpha band-power related to MI is collected from $t - 3\ s$ until $t + 3\ s$ providing a window of 6 s to measure against a baseline defined during the calibration stage. This 3 s delay for detecting MI changes is factored into synchronisation patterns for macro controls and acts as an extension to controls over visual effects.

7.2 Passive Control Mappings

Affective response is monitored throughout the performance of *A Stark Mind*. Measures of arousal and valence are averaged across windows of between 10–30 s, as indicators of the mood of the BCMI performer. Changes detected in mood between windows are mapped to two primary parameters, playback speed and contrast. Affective measures only contribute affect patterns at the beginning of a window. This is because continuous changes to the score would be difficult for the musicians to follow. For example, continuously varying the speed of pattern playback to affect tempo from fast to slow to fast to faster and slow on, is difficult for musicians to adapt to and be uncomfortable to listen to for sustained periods. In this example, an increase in arousal during window w, with tempo $t0$, gets mapped to a decreased tempo, $t - 1$, for window $w + 1$. At the beginning of window $w + 1$, the new tempo mapping will become a target tempo, shown as the score playback speed. Window $w + 1$ will begin with a tempo of $t0$ which will then linearly scale to a value of $t - 1$ by the end of window $w + 1$. Mappings with this smoothing effect allow for changes that, although subtle, do not have a detrimental effect on the musicians following the score. Therefore, when arousal lowers the score pattern speed and resulting tempo increase in an attempt to increase user arousal and reinforce mental activation. Arousal is also reflected in the ranges of the visual effect parameters that are controlled by SSVEP and MI. Positive arousal changes are mapped to trigger smaller effect ranges and negative arousal changes are mapped to select wider ranges. Examples of parameter ranges include brightness exposure of a score pattern or the level of distortion.

Changes in valence are mapped to the visual contrast, again in an inverted manner. Positive valence is mapped to low image contrast whereas negative valance is mapped to higher image contrast. For both arousal and valence, rules within the transformation algorithm are applied to move baseline corrections at key stages in the performance to reduce repetitive settings. Both arousal and valence mappings, although indicative of arousal and valence in terms of descriptors, are selected for their artistic functionality within the piece and instead of inducing affect-matching responses within the system they attempt to induce opposing levels, within the constraints of the mapping ranges.

8 Observations and Discussion

Performing with the BCMI for *A Stark Mind* requires a high level of concentration across a range of modes including the control methods, the visual projections and the subsequent music. To provide some respite so that the performer does not need to be actively engaged at all times, score patterns are looped during playback, allowing the user to rest when needed, and to take time for musical contemplation before engaging in active control again. Ultimately, the BCMI performer determines the level of engagement, and this is reflected in the levels of intensity and the dynamics of the score and music. This freedom of control, deciding when to rest and when to exert control, yet always still being in control is an important element of the user experience, as the user is not bound by external time constraints.

During performance it was observed that SSVEP control provided greater accuracy than MI control. As a result future MI control is less suitable for more important musical commands, such as those governing musical structure and arrangement, where failure is more likely to frustrate a user. It was also observed that the use of affective response provides an interesting means of musifying additional brainwave activity, as it provides an unpredictable element of controlled surprise that can also affect decision-making for active control.

9 Conclusions

This article presents a hybrid-BCMI that provides three methods of simultaneous control, SSVEP, motor imagery and affective states. EEG is demonstrated to be a reliable and useful method for measuring bio-signals for musical control outside of laboratory settings and lends itself suitable for users of all physical abilities.

As an artistic application of real-time compositional arrangement this system demonstrates a useful application of a hybrid-BCMI through the piece *A Stark Mind*.

The hybrid-BCMI showcases the potential of mapping multiple brainwave control signals to audio-visual parameters for real-time acoustic performance.

A custom-made SSVEP stimuli unit is presented, one that provides a high level of accuracy in detecting SSVEP across a single electrode channel. The hybrid BCMI demonstrates how more than one unit can be combined in a modular fashion to increase combined SSVEP and MI channels, with eight channels using two units providing reliable control.

From a technical perspective an initial study corroborates the success of SSVEP and the ability of the system to detect affective states in EEG with respect to musical stimuli. However, we acknowledge that a confirmatory study of the accuracy of control methods when combined would be useful.

The use of emotional measures via affective states as a source of musical control provides a novel approach to user engagement in BCMIs and presents a useful method for combining passive with active control methods in a hybrid-BCMI. We anticipate a focal point of future research to be the investigation of affective states in response to music performance towards exploring the affective relationships across multi-user hybrid-BCMIs that allow for more complexity in musical control as well as providing channels of active and passive communication between multiple users.

Acknowledgments. The authors gratefully acknowledge the support of a doctoral scholarship awarded by Plymouth University.

References

1. Biofeedback and the Arts: Results of Early Experiments: Aesthetic Research Center, Vancouver, British Columbia, p. 162 (1976)
2. de Campo, A., et al.: New sonification tools for EEG data screening and monitoring. In: 13th International Conference on Auditory Display, Montreal, Canada (2007)
3. Miranda, E.R., et al.: Brain-computer music interfacing (BCMI): from basic research to the real world of special needs. Music Med. **3**(3), 134–140 (2011)
4. Nijholt, A.: Competing and collaborating brains: multi-brain computer interfacing. In: Hassanien, A.E., Azar, A.T. (eds.) Brain-Computer Interfaces, vol. 74, pp. 313–335. Springer, Heidelberg (2015)
5. Eaton, J., Miranda, E.: BCMI systems for musical performance. In: 10th International Symposium on Computer Music Multidisciplinary Research (CMMR): Sound, Music and Motion, Marseille, France (2013)
6. Beverina, F., et al.: User adaptive BCIs: SSVEP and P300 based interfaces. PsychNol. J. **1**(4), 331–354 (2003)
7. Guger, C., Edlinger, G., Krausz, G.: Hardware/software components and applications of BCIs. In: Fazel-Rezai, R. (ed.) Recent Advances in Brain-Computer Interface Systems, pp. 1–24. InTech, Rjeka (2011)
8. Daly, I., et al.: Investigating music tempo as a feedback mechanism for closed-loop BCI control. Brain-Comput. Interfaces **1**(3–4), 158–169 (2014)
9. Russell, J.A., Barrett, L.F.: Core affect, prototypical emotional episodes, and other things called emotion: dissecting the elephant. J. Pers. Soc. Psychol. **76**(5), 805–819 (1999)
10. Russell, J.A.: A circumplex model of affect. J. Pers. Soc. Psychol. **39**(6), 1161–1178 (1980)

11. Friberg, A., Breson, R., Sundberg, J.: Overview of the KTH rule system for musical performance. Adv. Cogn. Psychol. **2**(2–3), 145–161 (2006)
12. Ramirez, R., Vamvakousis, Z.: Detecting emotion from EEG signals using the emotive Epoc device. In: Zanzotto, F.M., Tsumoto, S., Taatgen, N., Yao, Y. (eds.) BI 2012. LNCS, vol. 7670, pp. 175–184. Springer, Heidelberg (2012)
13. Schmidt, L.A., Trainor, L.J.: Frontal brain electrical activity (EEG) distinguishes valence and intensity of musical emotions. Cogn. Emot. **15**(4), 13 (2001)
14. Aftanas, L.I., Golocheikine, S.A.: High-resolution EEG investigation of meditation. Neurosci. Lett. **310**(1), 4 (2001)
15. Eaton, J., Williams, D., Miranda, E.: Affective jukebox: a confirmatory study of EEG emotional correlates in response to musical stimuli. In: 11th Sound and Music Conference, 14th International Computer Music Conference Joint ICMC and SMC 2014, University of Athens, Greece (2014)
16. Lamont, A., Eerola, T.: Music and emotion: themes and development. Musicae Sci. **15**(2), 139–145 (2011)
17. Liu, Y., et al.: Implementation of SSVEP based BCI with emotiv EPOC. In: Virtual Environments Human-Computer Interfaces and Measurement Systems (VECIMS). IEEE (2012)
18. Eaton, J., Miranda, E.: Expanding on brain control: a real-time hybrid BCMI for drum machine combining active (SSVEP) and passive (affective response) brainwave control. In: 9th Conference on Interdisciplinary Musicology – CIM14, Berlin, Germany (2014)
19. Pfurtscheller, G., et al.: The hybrid BCI. Front. Neurosci. **4**, 30 (2010)

Feeling Sound: Exploring a Haptic-Audio Relationship

Joanne Armitage[✉] and Kia Ng

School of Music and School of Computing, ICSRiM - University of Leeds,
Leeds LS2 9JT, UK
haptics@icsrim.org.uk, haptics@icsrim.leeds.ac.uk

Abstract. Sound propagates through space as a series of vibrations; the physical attributes of this motion excite and engage listeners. For example, when standing close to a loudspeaker, you can feel the propagation of waveforms through the speaker cone; this is particularly prominent at low frequencies. Instrumentalists feel parallel, physical sensations as their instrument produces sound. This project explores haptic and vibrotactile stimulation as an additional sensory modality, or channel of communication through which musical information can be enhanced. This paper describes the background, and design and development of a haptic interface for the purpose of audio-haptic performances in the context of the installation entitled, "*Enclosed*".

Keywords: Haptics · Composition · Multimodal · Correlation · Vibrotactile

1 Introduction

This project explores the application of haptics in the listening experience to bring *feeling* and somatic embodiment by augmenting, reflecting and subverting sonic parameters. At this time the project is looking at the relationship between audio and haptic parameters, specifically by relating the loudness of sound to vibration amplitude, investigating how haptic and auditory onsets interact, and of relevance to this paper in regard to the installation *enclosed*, it explores sound and tactile directionality. *Enclosed* forms part of a wider project exploring the auditory-tactile relationship as a compositional mechanism. As our bodies naturally engage with and decipher their surroundings using combinations of the senses, this work seeks to explore sensory integration as a way to immerse the sensory system.

It has been suggested by Barrett [2] that acousmatic listening can be impaired by 'spatial tangibility' – an inability for the listeners to absorb themself into the spatial form of the composition. The author suggests that works including visual elements avoid this by providing a distraction, or 'shifted perceptual focus' from the unnatural sound-space phenomena enshrouding their environment.

The immediacy of our listening sensation is well known, as is the immediacy of our sense of touch when there is a cutaneous interaction with the skins surface [9]. Whilst both our touch and hearing hold a high-acuity to spatiality [10], environmental factors such and noise and known illusions such as sound emanating on the vertical plane can impair our directional perception of sound.

This paper describes the design and development of a haptic interface for audio-tactile composition-installation and provides insight as to how it is applied in the installation enclosed.

2 Related Works

Of interest to this project are the physical aspects of sound, particularly the physical sensation and somatic stimulation of sound imparted on listeners. The somatic nature of live musical experiences is inherent in the physicality of sound waves produced by instruments and loudspeakers. When considering the relationship between sound and touch, Glennie [5] states: *"Hearing is basically a specialised form of touch"*. Whilst the *tactility* of the ear facilitates the listener's perception of an ensemble's sound, the physical sensations of these waveforms are imparted on both the body as a whole, and objects in the performance environment.

Whether the multimedia nature of performance detracts or distracts from musical experience or not is debatable, however, the author pertains to a Deleuzian listening that suggests *"art should lead the subject to an experience of multi-sensoriality"* [3]. For many composers, the advent of audio-visual technologies (real-time and fixed) has augmented their practice, allowing a greater control of multi-sensory listening experiences. No longer are composers limited to defining the auditory parameters of musical works.

Several artists have explored haptic installation art, in combination with audio stimuli. Dewey-Hagborg's [4] work *Buried Sound 2: Haptic Resonance*, uses sound to produce vibration, exploring it in its physical form, as an instrument of the somatic. The work employs an analogous audio-haptic relationship where a speaker is placed directly under the floorboards of a gallery space. Inspired by the deaf experience of sound as 'pure-vibration', the work seeks to transform sonic material by augmenting its inherent tactility on the body. Similarly, Salick [8] uses vibrations to invite participants to *Feel a Bit Like Beethoven*, using a wooden sculpture integrated with speakers. 'Feelers' place their hands over the installation, which allows them to explore the tactility of Beethoven's oeuvre, akin to the composer's deteriorated hearing.

Hayes' [7], *Skin Music* utilises a haptic-augmented chaise longue to vibrate the body, enhancing sounds natural, yet unconscious affect of the body. Sound is transmitted through motors in the chair to the body via its wooden struts. The work seeks to allow people with sensory impairments to experience sound in alternative ways. Motors are placed on the arms of the chair for the 'feeler' to hold on to, and also at the back of the head and the lower back. This work employs a synchronous musical accompaniment.

Organ Organ, a work by Eric Gunther [6] is another example of music for the body, employing a mouldable 12-channel vibrotactile surface that produces low-frequency vibrations together with a 2-min electronic music composition. The artist briefly describes his process; *"Spatial ideas led to musical phrases while rhythms and melodies motivated phrases of choreography on the space of the body"*.

These works present an interesting and diverse range of practice, and although lacking in written documentation, they clearly present as focussed explorations of the body as a sound-absorbing, vibration-reactive artefact. This idea runs through notions of the audio-haptic relationship, with a consideration of the listener/feeler's body as the instrument or vessel.

A difficulty with haptic-based art practice is that it requires a certain immediacy and bodily presence within a particular space. Installations such as these require bespoke hardware/software, often at considerable expense, and with limited instruction, difficult to replicate. A challenge for haptics hardware designers is producing cost efficient, reproducible and modular interfaces for these purposes. Another option for haptic-curious artists is to employ vibrations in smartphones, via applications and websites. Although such devices are common, their vibrational control is limited.

3 An Audio-Tactile Device

Hardware has been designed to physically translate and render triggers into haptic feedback; parameters controlled on this interface are Pulse-width-modulation, which translates to vibration intensity, vibration duration and location. This consists of a two-dimensional array of actuators, a microcontroller and drivers. The design process has involved the development of two circuit designs, the first interfaces an array of 16 Eccentric rotating mass (ERM) actuators with a TLC5940 driver that has 16 outputs; this allows Pulse width modulation (PWM) control and individual onset and duration triggering of each motor. This design has been successfully prototyped and tested (see Fig. 1).

Fig. 1. Prototype 1 – ERM motors and TLC5940 driver

A second, more advanced design is currently being finalised using the Texas Instruments DVR2605 haptic driver. These drivers come with pre-loaded waveforms and are compatible with both ERM and Linear resonant actuator (LRA). The individual PWM signals and extra controls available allow many different configurations, and increased flexibility. At the present stage a grid of 16 (4 × 4) vibrating motors has been implemented. The grid format allows a multi-channel delay that can also provide a range of established sensory illusions to the skin (see Fig. 2).

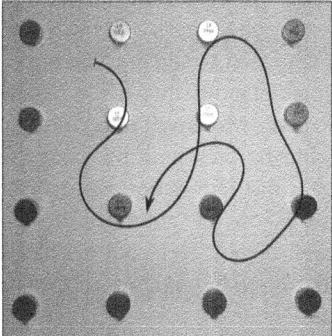

Fig. 2. Haptic gestural path through VAM

A recent study found that in terms of latency Precision Microdrive's 308-102 ERM performed best with an average latency of ∼25 ms with the least amount of jitter. Combined with their relatively high vibration normalised vibration amplitude of 5.5 G. Prior to this, LRA motors (see Fig. 3) were considered due to their greater reliability and longevity, however, their latency and jitter were greater than that of the ERM type. Although LRAs, with no external moving parts present lower levels of vibratory noise, it was found that the louder ERMs did not occlude audio, particularly when used alongside headphones.

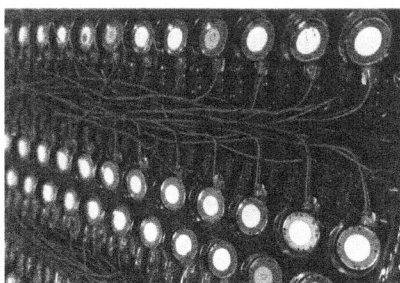 

Fig. 3. LRA actuators, one compared to a five pence piece

4 *Enclosed:* A Haptic-Audio Installation

This work explores the relationship between sound, space and the body through real-time haptic rendering of spatial sound data. Although as part of this project has been exploring haptic as an instrument in its own right, this work considers it as a guide, to establish a greater feeling of connect between auditory spatial data via synchronous somatic stimulation. Using simple concepts, such as relating single auditory and tactile parameters, allows us to explore the integration of information and investigate effective combinations of the different sensory domains in an artistic context.

Compositional material and sound elements do not occur simultaneously. It was initially considered that it would be generative, with binaural processing controllable by the listener. A generative approach would create a more varied output, but with that comes a certain degree of unpredictability thus it was decided that a pre-recorded audio element would be most effective. Moreover it became apparent that more effective transitions and directions could be presented by using 'pre-composed' material. An attractive feature of this setup is that it does not require user interaction with the laptop screen, allowing them to focus on the audio-tactile experience. Listeners will be encouraged to close their eyes if they feel comfortable. Furthermore, this approach allows motor latency to be more reliably integrated into the multimodal data stream.

In this installation we approach the relationship between spatial-temporal change in the auditory and somatic domains using binaural techniques and the aforementioned interface (see Fig. 4). Clearly, there are complexities to this approach and for this reason we have limited this investigation to representations of sound movement to the horizontal plane by controlling azimuth values. A Pure Data (PD) patch has been designed using the ~earplug library [6] to spatialise audio files in real-time, allowing the sound's spatial qualities to be manipulated by the listener.

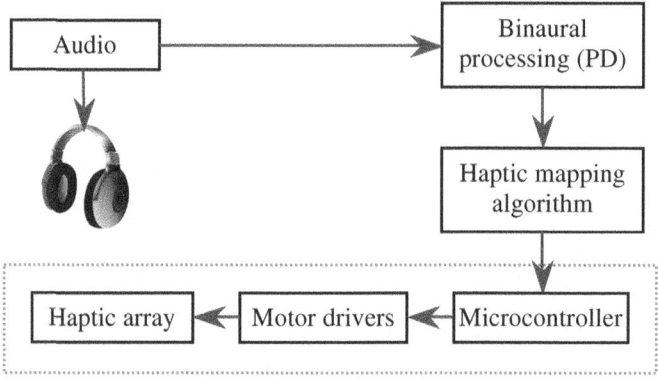

Fig. 4. Overall installation block diagram

The sound element is to played back using headphones. The binaural processing and amplitude data from PD are sent to a haptic mapping algorithm for processing. When the mapping algorithm receives the binaural values, the current prototype projects them onto a 2D plane to control the actuator array. Loudness is then mapped to vibration amplitude by altering PWM values of motor triggers. The haptic mapping algorithm employs the previously mentioned haptic illusion techniques to 'draw' the movement of the sound on to the haptic array, with a view to heightening the listener-feeler's awareness of sound-space and the body.

After experiencing the installation, participants will have the option of completing a short questionnaire, which will inform future developments and refinements.

5 Conclusions and Further Work

Whilst spatial audio techniques allow listeners a more immersive environment, at times they can become perceived as somewhat intangible. This paper has proposed a haptic interface that can work in the context of auditory-tactile installations. At the CMMR conference, this device has been implemented in an installation, *enclosed* as a tactile guide. We hope to find that conference delegates feel a greater physical connect whilst listening to the auditory element. It has also reviewed installations employing similar techniques, and briefly considered how haptic artwork can become more prevalent through accessibility of devices.

Several related multimodal works have been created for this system, which are being showcased over the next few months. First, a collaboration with Copenhagen based composer and percussionist Greta Eacott. She will be performing a haptic multimedia composition *ON/OFF* for solo concert bass drum and electronics at the Rytmisk Musikkonservatorium, Copenhagen as part of a week long haptic, percussion and code workshop. This piece uses a simple idea of haptic-fying beats on the drumhead to draw the listener towards an enhanced somatic awareness. A piezo sensor is placed on the skin of the drum to detect when it is struck; this onset is then rendered on the haptic interface.

'Unheard' sounds [1] will be premiered as part of V&A Digital Futures exhibition at the EVA (Electronic Visualisation and the Arts) London 2015 conference (http://www.eva-london.org/) hosted by the British Computer Society – the Chartered Institute for IT, London. The work explores the relationship between the auditory and somatic sensory systems by highlighting aspects of sound, such as masked noises, beats and other interplay that appear less apparent in an audio mix. Visitors experience a new dimension of musical expressivity, feeling parallel sensations of sound on their body.

Further work is planned using the haptic interface in this project, including exploring its application in real-time with instrumental ensembles and the synchronisation challenges that presents. Long-term, the project hopes to further and refine a haptic language for compositional practice and to work with a broader range of composers.

References

1. Armitage, J., Ng, K.: 'Unheard' sounds. In: Electronic Visualisation and the Arts (EVA), British Computer Society, London, UK (2015)
2. Barrett, N.: Ambisonics and acousmatic space: a composer's framework for investigating spatial ontology. In: Electroacoustic Music Studios Conference (2010)
3. Bidima, J.G.: Music and the socio-historical real: rhythm, series and critique in Deleuze and O. Revault d'Allonnes. In: Buchanan, I., Swiboda, M. (eds.) Deleuze and Music. Edinburgh University Press, Edinburgh (2004). (Transl.: J. Griffiths)

4. Dewey-Hagborg, H.: Buried Sound 2: Haptic Resonance (2011). http://www.deweyhagborg.com/hapticResonance/
5. Glennie, E.: Hearing Essay (1993). https://www.evelyn.co.uk/hearing-essay/
6. Gunther, E.: Organ, Organ (2007). http://www.ericgunther.info/projects/system.html
7. Hayes, L.: Skin Music (2012). http://laurensarahhayes.tumblr.com/tagged/skin_music/chrono
8. Natio Salkic, O.: Feel a Bit Like Beethoven (2009). http://www.oliversalkic.com/FEEL-A-BIT-LIKE-BEETHOVEN
9. Patterson, M.: The Senses of Touch: Haptics, Affects and Technology. Berg, Oxford (2007)
10. van Erp, J.B.F.: Guidelines for the use of vibro-tactile displays in human computer interaction. In: Eurohaptics, Edinburgh, UK (2002)

BOEUF: A Unified Framework for Modeling and Designing Digital Orchestras

Florent Berthaut[1(✉)] and Luke Dahl[2]

[1] CNRS, Centrale Lille, UMR 9189 - CRIStAL, University of Lille,
F-59000 Lille, France
florent@hitmuri.net
[2] University of Virginia, Charlottesville, USA
lukedahl@virginia.edu

Abstract. Orchestras of Digital Musical Instruments (DMIs) enable new musical collaboration possibilities, extending those of acoustic and electric orchestras. However the creation and development of these orchestras remain constrained. In fact, each new musical collaboration system or orchestra piece relies on a fixed number of musicians, a fixed set of instruments (often only one), and a fixed subset of possible modes of collaboration.

In this paper, we describe a unified framework that enables the design of Digital Orchestras with potentially different DMIs and an expandable set of collaboration modes. It relies on research done on analysis and classification of traditional and digital orchestras, on research in Collaborative Virtual Environments, and on interviews of musicians and composers. The BOEUF framework consists of a classification of modes of collaboration and a set of components for modelling digital orchestras. Integrating this framework into DMIs will enable advanced musical collaboration modes to be used in any digital orchestra, including spontaneous jam sessions.

Keywords: Boeuf · Orchestra · Collaboration · Framework · Digital musical instrument · Digital orchestra · DMI · NIME · Collaborative music

1 Introduction

Orchestras of Digital Musical Instruments (DMIs) began to appear at the end of the 1970s, with the League of Automatic Composers and later The Hub [8]. With the subsequent generalisation of hardware platforms, music software and communication protocols such orchestras have become more common. A Digital Orchestra (DO) can be composed of a single multi-user DMI [12]; a homogeneous collection of identical DMIs, such as in most laptop [24] and mobile phone [18] orchestras; or a set of DMIs of different types. In turn, DMIs may rely on various hardware interaction devices, audio and visual feedback modalities, software architectures and sound synthesis techniques.

Digital orchestras enable new modes of collaboration that were not possible in ensembles of acoustic or electric instruments. For example, musicians can share audio or control streams, thus processing the output of one instrument in another instrument. They may exchange building blocks, such as note sequences or sound material. Or a musician might even allow their instrument to be controlled by another musician. Finally, collaboration modes present in traditional ensembles, such as non-verbal communication for coordinating musical cohesion or variation [21], can be augmented in DOs.

However, the design and implementation of digital orchestras remains complex, especially when they include diverse musical instruments. In fact, most existing orchestras rely on frameworks that are specific to a software or hardware platform or even to a single instrument. These can be in the form of a set of Max/MSP patches that connect together, a fixed set of hardware interconnections (e.g. MIDI cables), and so on. Even if standard communication protocols such as MIDI or Open Sound Control (OSC) are used, each orchestra manages communication between instruments in a specific way (e.g. namespaces, ports, channels), thus prohibiting new instruments from easily joining. Therefore, orchestras of mixed instruments are more complex to organise, and, as in the case of spontaneous jam sessions, advanced collaboration modes may be completely inaccessible. Finally, collaboration modes are mostly reimplemented with every new orchestra or piece, often only as a limited subset of all collaboration possibilities.

These practises impede the development of new ensembles and the creation of music that uses the new modes of collaboration that DMIs enable. Therefore the computer music community would benefit from a framework that is simple enough to be integrated into any instrument, that takes into account existing modes of collaboration, and that can be expanded by adding new ones. Such a framework would facilitate the creation of orchestras and encourage exploration of new collaboration modes. The contributions presented in this paper are twofold:

(1) We present a classification of musical *modes of collaboration*. These modes were developed after conducting a literature review of research on DOs and Collaborative Virtual Environments (CVE), and interviews and discussions with composers and musicians in DOs at the SCRIME at University of Bordeaux, and at CCRMA at Stanford University. This classification, described in Sect. 2.1, allows for the practical analysis of musical collaboration and can be extended to include novel collaboration modes.
(2) We then provide a set of *components* that constitute a model of a digital orchestra. These components, described in Sect. 2.2, allow for the design of orchestras that can access any of the modes of collaboration in our classification, as demonstrated in Sect. 2.3.

The modes of collaboration and components form the conceptual basis of the BOEUF framework. The implementation and integration of such a framework into existing DMIs, which we discuss in Sect. 3, will enable advanced musical collaboration in DOs with any set of instruments, even in the context of improvised sessions.

Related work

A number of frameworks exist for describing orchestras of DMIs and collaborative instruments. Jordà [11] classifies multi-user instruments according to the number of users and whether this can be variable, the flexibility of roles, and whether users can influence others' musical output. Blaine and Fels [4] describe collaborative interfaces according to their use (focus), properties of the instrument (location, media, physical interface, musical range, level of physicality, and pathway to expert performance), and the structure of interactions between players (scalability, player interaction, directed interaction.) Hattwick and Wanderley [9] create a space of collaborative musical systems, with dimensions of texture, equality of roles, centralisation of information, the role of physical location, whether interactions are time synchronous, and whether sound production depends on more than one performer. Our framework is intended to span this space, with the exception that ours is intended to enable only synchronous (realtime) interactions. Weinberg [25] provides a historical overview of interconnected musical networks. Weinberg's examples, as well as his descriptions of intra-player interdependencies were influential on our development of the BOEUF framework.

Several protocols and software tools have been created to deal with the sharing of musical data for both single instruments and within networked orchestras. For example, Jamoma [20] and libMapper [14] both give access to the structure and parameters of networked DMIs, sometimes with features for watching and grabbing parameters. An interesting example is the Digital Orchestra Toolbox [15] which simplifies the collaborative creation and mapping of DMIs. Most of these tools in turn rely on the Open Sound Control protocol for network communication. However, while they provide all the generic sharing and mapping features required for networked musical control, these tools do not specifically cover the modes of collaboration used in DOs, and thus fail to provide a common basis for creating orchestras of mixed DMIs.

2 The BOEUF Framework

The conceptual part of the BOEUF[1] framework consists of a set of components that allow for designing any digital orchestra, and enables a set of collaboration modes, which are organised into three categories. Our framework draws on research done on CVEs. A Collaborative Virtual Environment is defined in [22] as a "computer-based, distributed, virtual space or set of places. In such places, people can meet and interact with others, with agents or with virtual objects". The challenges of CVEs are very similar to those of DOs. As with orchestras, users in CVEs need to perceive each other and to communicate within the virtual environment in order to cooperate for specific tasks. In CVEs as in DOs, this perception is often impaired by the digital mediation. However, unlike research on musical collaboration, CVE research has gone further than merely classifying

---

[1] For *BOEUF OrchEstras Unification Framework*, *boeuf* meaning *jam session* in French.

collaborative applications. Practical implementation-oriented models have been proposed [10,26], as have frameworks that aim at helping developers build CVEs [19]. Adapting CVE frameworks and models to the musical domain provides us with insights that inform our own practical collaboration framework.

2.1 Modes of Collaboration

From the existing work presented above and our interviews, we extract three categories of modes of collaboration between musicians: *Cooperation*, *Communication* and *Organisation*. We consider modes that are digitally mediated, as well as those that are not usually mediated, e.g. non-verbal communication.

We now describe these modes and present examples from a selection of orchestras, multi-user instruments, and pieces. Figure 1 shows the use of these modes in each piece.

Sound Bounce [6] is a piece for the Stanford Mobile Phone Orchestra [18]. Anahata and Les Complémentaires are both electro-acoustic trios at the SCRIME. Couacs [3] is a multi-user instrument in the form a 3D first person shooter video game. The Reactable [12] is a multi-user instrument based on a tabletop tangible user interface. LOLC [13] is an orchestra that relies on

Orchestras	Cooperation			Communication			Organisation	
	Independent	Complementary	Concurrent	Awareness	Indication	Exchange	Nomination	Grouping	Selection
Sound Bounce	X	X		X		X	X		X
Anahata	X	X		X		X			X
Les complémentaires	X	X		X		X	X		X
Couacs	X		X	X					X
Reactable	X	X	X	X		X	X		X
LOLC	X			X	X	X			X
The Hub	X	X							X
Intellectual Improperty	X			X	X		X	X	X
JamiOki	X			X	X				X
Cobra	X	X		X	X		X	X	X

Fig. 1. Modes of collaboration in various orchestras, pieces, and multi-user instruments

live-coding and instant messaging. The Hub [8] is one of the first digital orchestras. *Intellectual Improperty* is a piece for the Stanford Laptop Orchestra [24]. JamiOki [23] is a system for playing game pieces, providing instructions to each musician and getting feedback from them. *Cobra* is a game piece with various collaboration modes.

Cooperation modes describe the coordination of musicians' actions with respect to their instruments. We define three subcategories that correspond to different possible interconnections between musicians and their instruments. These subcategories are inspired by the CVE cooperation framework described in [16]. Cooperation modes can therefore be: **Independent** when each musician controls their own instrument or modules. **Complementary** when two or more musicians can affect the same musical output but at different levels of the audio synthesis graph, i.e. each musician controls a different sound parameter. **Concurrent** when musicians can affect the same musical output at the same level, i.e. when multiple musicians modify the same musical parameter on a single instrument.

Independent modes of cooperation exist whenever two musicians play at the same time. The cooperation in this case consists of the coordination of gestures as each musician performs their own instrument. Complementary modes of cooperation are used in many orchestras. Our interviews with musicians from Les Complémentaires and Anahata revealed that they were both using a non-mediated complementary mode of cooperation, by spreading one sound over several musicians, one playing the attack, another the sustained part and another the end of the sound. Similarly, with the Reactable, complementary cooperation occurs when two musicians manipulate different tangibles on the same audio path. Finally, concurrent modes of cooperation are less common as they imply either conflicts or games between musicians. In *Couacs* [3] for example, musicians control avatars in a musical video game and can override the parameters of other musicians by shooting at them. Concurrency handling strategies must be applied, as discussed for example in [7], such as always performing the newest action, averaging between actions of different musicians, using a physical model with different weights, or grabbing a parameter for exclusive use.

Communication modes do not directly impact the production of sound, but rather influence the actions of the musicians, in particular those who are involved in one of the cooperation modes. In most orchestras, communication modes are non-mediated and enable musical cohesion or variation [21]. However DOs often lack visibility [5], making it difficult for performers to see or understand the state of others' activities. This issue is amplified in the case of networked orchestras when musicians are not physically collocated. These difficulties can be addressed by integrating communication modes into the framework. In the field of CVE, similar communication problems have led to the use of concepts such as Embodiment [2], i.e. using avatars to represent users, CoPresence i.e. the feeling users have of being together in the virtual environment, and Awareness, i.e. the understanding of other users' actions [1]. This concept of awareness has also been discussed for the case of DOs in [7]. Modes of communication are divided into three subcategories. **Awareness** includes all non-intentional communication, such as making musicians' activities visible to each other for the purpose of enabling synchronisation, cohesion or variations. **Indications** are intentional communicative acts such as demonstrating gestures and intentions or sending commands. **Exchange** corresponds to transfers of musical data between musicians.

An example of awareness in Couacs [3] is the use of avatars that provide information on the musical output each player is generating. Awareness is especially important in mixed instruments orchestras, when it is not clear how each musician contributes to the musical output. One example of indication is the system of text messages sent by the conductor to instrumentists in the piece *Intellectual Improperty*. They are also used in Jamioki, to guide musicians through musical games or improvised pieces. An example of exchange can be found in *Sound Bounce* where musicians use ball-throwing gestures to pass a sound process from one player to another.

Organisation modes do not have any effect on the music produced but rather impact the communication and cooperation modes. We define three organisation modes: **Nomination** consists in defining the roles of musicians within the orchestra. **Grouping** consists in defining a hierarchy of groups of instruments. **Selection** is the act of choosing a single instrument or a group in the context of cooperation or communication, e.g. selecting which musician to send an indication to.

A common example of nomination is the role of a conductor. In most orchestras, this role is fixed and the conductor has a specific interface, such as in *Intellectual Improperty*. However, roles can also be dynamically changed as described in [11]. For example, a musician from Les Complémentaires explained how they use the role of soloist to give priority to one musician at certain moments of a performance. An example of grouping is found in *Intellectual Improperty*, where the conductor can group musicians. With the selection mode, he then chooses which group he sends a message to.

2.2 Orchestra Components

In order to design orchestras that enable the collaboration modes described above, our framework includes a generic model of a digital orchestra with a set of components: Session, Group, Instrument, Module, Parameter, Output, Meter, and Message.

A **session** represents an instance of a DO. It contains the instruments and the network of possible interactions between instruments.

A **group** is a set of instruments or groups. The parameters common to all instruments in a group can be grabbed and set simultaneously. Similarly, messages sent to a group are sent to all members. For example in a poly-instrument orchestra, a group can be all the musicians with the same instrument. A default group of all instruments is always defined, thereby giving access to parameters that are common to all instruments in the session e.g. tempo or scale.

An **instrument** represents a bounded set of music-generating processes (i.e. modules) and a user interface. It has parameters, outputs, meters and it can receive and send messages. We presume that each musician in the orchestra is in control of at least one instrument. Thus, in our modeling an instrument often acts as a proxy for the musician.

A **module** is a software component that produces musical data, of audio or control type. It is composed of several parameters and outputs. Modules have a type, possibly from a common set of types (each with a predefined number of parameters and data). This way a module can be copied by another instrument if this instrument handles modules of the same type. For example, a module of type LowPassFilter might have *Cutoff Frequency* and Q as parameters, whereas a module of type *MidiPattern* will hold an array of MIDI events. Many instruments have an internal structure that is more complex than a simple chain of modules. They may have complex audio graphs with many hierarchical levels or feedback. However, from the perspective of user interaction these can usually be flattened to a set of modules and associated parameters.

A **parameter** is an attribute of a module or instrument that influences its musical production. Parameters can be of various types such as MIDI events, float or integer values, input audio streams, and so on. Parameters can be:

- *Retrieved*: the current value of the parameter is returned once.
- *Watched*: the value of the parameter is sent every time it changes, until it is not watched anymore.
- *Indicated*: a new value is proposed for the parameter but not set.
- *Set*: the parameter is set to a new value.
- *Grabbed*: the parameter can only be set by the instrument that grabbed it.

These actions are always accessible to the instrument that owns the parameter, but authorisation might be needed for other instruments to access a parameter. Concurrent access can be managed in different ways, the simplest being by grabbing a parameter so that only one instrument can access it.

An **output** is a musical attribute that is produced by a module or instrument. Outputs can be of the same types as parameters. Outputs can be retrieved and watched by another instrument without requiring authorisation.

A **meter** is a component of an instrument that is not used in the actual sound production, but rather gives an indication on the activity of the instrument, e.g. spectrum or loudness.

A **message** is a text, image, or video sent from one instrument to another instrument or group. Messages can be standard (e.g. Start, Stop, Fade Out), defined per session instruments, or dynamically created.

2.3 Modelling Digital Orchestras with BOEUF

The BOEUF framework allows for the analysis and design of digital orchestras with respect to the collaboration modes described in Sect. 2.1, using the set of components defined in Sect. 2.2.

In this section we discuss how one can implement each mode of collaboration using the components. Where applicable, we will illustrate the process by referring to three examples: *Sound Bounce*, *Couacs* and *Intellectual Improperty*. We do not claim that these examples were designed with our framework in mind. Rather, we show how they could be implemented using the BOEUF components. This amounts to a form of analysis. A graphical representation of these analyses can be seen in Fig. 2.

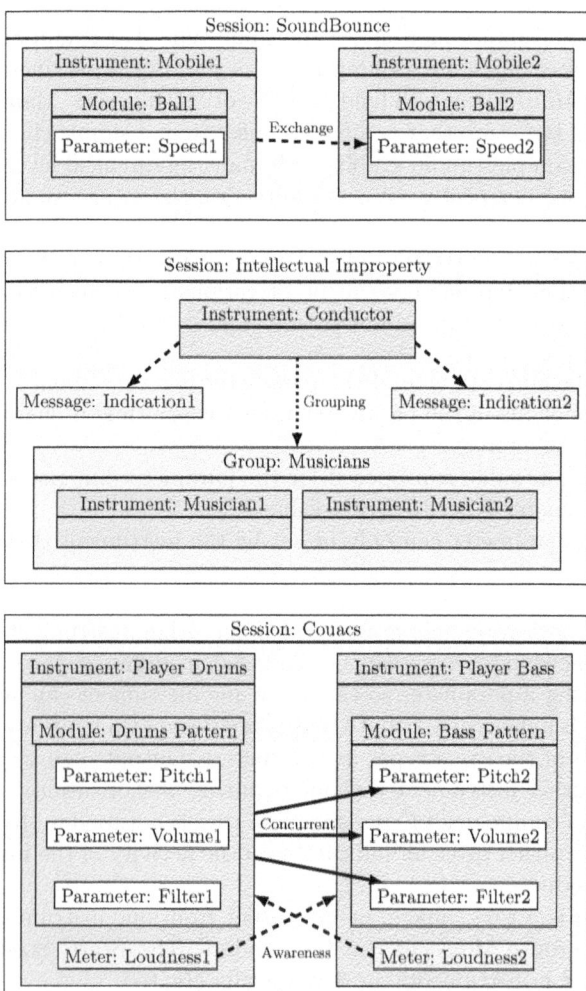

Fig. 2. Designing orchestras using our framework. Dashed lines are used for Communication, solid lines for Cooperation, and dotted lines for Organisation. From top to bottom: Sound Bounce, Intellectual Improperty, Couacs

Cooperation modes are handled by the access each instrument has to the parameters and outputs of other instruments. Independent cooperation is achieved simply by having each instrument belong to the same session.

Complementary cooperation is achieved when one musician, through his or her instrument, has permission to grab or set a parameter on another musician's instrument, and that parameter is not currently under control by the owner of that instrument. Another way to achieve complementary cooperation would be for one instrument to retrieve or watch the output of another musician's module or instrument, and process that output.

Concurrent cooperation occurs when two musicians (through their instruments) have access to set the same parameter on an instrument. Different strategies of concurrency handling can be defined by each instrument for each parameter. In Couacs concurrent cooperation involves one player (instrument) setting all the parameters of the module of another player at once by shooting this player.

Communication modes are implemented through various components. The most basic form of awareness is achieved when musicians can hear the musical output of each others' instruments. The possibility for awareness is enhanced when one musician (through their instrument) can watch a parameter, output, or meter on another musician's instrument. In Couacs the size of each player's avatar is scaled according to the current loudness of their instrument, allowing the musicians to perceive who is playing what. This can be achieved in our framework by adding a loudness meter to each instrument, and having each instrument watch the meters of the other instruments. The details of the GUI (e.g. in Couacs, avatars that change size) are not specified in BOEUF.

Indication can take the form of messages or commands from one instrument to another. This can be as simple as one instrument indicating a new value for a parameter on another's instrument. (It is up to the implementation to decide how to display this indication on the receiver's GUI.) In *Intellectual Improperty*, indication takes place when the conductor sends messages with instructions to various groups of musicians. Communicating by indication may also take place when a musician demonstrates a musical gesture, for example when they want other musicians to imitate them. This form of indication is enabled when various means of awareness are implemented, and can be achieved in a number of ways. For example, if some musicians are watching a parameter on the indicator's instrument, they may notice how this parameter changes when the indicator performs a demonstrative sound.

Exchange can be performed by copying modules or sets of parameters. For example, in *Sound Bounce*, when one player throws a soundball to another player, the values of all parameters in the thrower's Ball module are copied into the parameters of the receiver's Ball module.

Organisation modes are mostly implemented through the group and instrument components. Nomination of the conductor in *Intellectual Improperty* corresponds to the defining of a group containing only the conductor. The conductor can also define groups (grouping) to which they add (nomination) musicians (by proxy of their instruments).

An example of selection can be found in *Sound Bounce*, when a player aims their phone at another player to whom they wish to throw their soundball. In our framework, the player's instrument selects another instrument from a group in order to perform an exchange.

3 Discussion

We have described the BOEUF framework, which consists of the modes of collaboration that digital orchestras should have available to them, and a set of components which model digital orchestras and enable these modes. In this section we anticipate challenges that may arise when integrating our framework into new and existing DMIs. First we discuss issues related to implementation, and secondly we look at aspects related to interfaces for accessing BOEUF's features.

3.1 Integration

In order to ensure portability, the low-level layer of the BOEUF implementation should rely on a commonly used network protocol such as Open Sound Control. Depending on the type of DMI, we envisage four levels of integration of BOEUF, each with progressively greater functionality.

Hardware Box: In the case of black-box instruments (i.e. hardware synthesisers and instruments with fixed software structure), BOEUF integration would require a dedicated hardware device. This device would connect to the instrument via MIDI, audio and OSC input and output ports. The device would in turn connect to the BOEUF session via a network connection. It would provide a limited set of modes of collaboration with a limited number of instruments. This limitation depends on the number of ports, controls and displays available on the device.

Software Plugin/Standalone: In the case of DMIs implemented as non-reprogrammable software components, a BOEUF software plugin or standalone application can be connected to the virtual audio and control ports of the DMI. The BOEUF software would in turn connect to the BOEUF session. Compared to a BOEUF hardware device, the software application can enable more modes of collaboration. In particular, thanks to the software's graphical interface, awareness and indication modes of communication, as well as cooperation and organisation modes with a flexible number of other instruments, are now possible.

Open Sound Control Namespace: In the case of an instrument with programmable input and output layers, a BOEUF session can be accessed directly via Open Sound Control messages following the BOEUF protocol. The input layer must parse incoming messages, send them to the appropriate components of the instrument, and perform any required actions (e.g. set, grab, or retrieve the value of a parameter). The output layer must emit messages to other instruments, for example when the value of a watched parameter is changed, or when the user wants to send a message to another instrument or group of instruments. This integration would resemble that of the Jamoma framework in Max/MSP.

Software Library: Finally, in the case of open-source software instruments, a BOEUF software library can be integrated into the source code of the instrument. This library would manage the network connection to the session internally. The instrument must register its components with the BOEUF library and implement callback functions that provide access to its components.

3.2 Interfaces

The new modes of collaboration enabled by digital orchestras and described in our framework generate new streams of information that a musician must apprehend and respond to, and they create new opportunities for action. These lead to two challenges in the development of a DMI interface that would give access to these collaboration modes.

The first concerns the visualisation of information available through the BOEUF framework. In order to enable all modes of collaboration, an interface should provide ways of displaying information from various components in the framework, such as meters for awareness, messages for indication, modules for exchange modes, and so on. However, we also want to preserve non-mediated modes of collaboration such as the non-verbal communication the occurs between musicians who can see each other. If a DMI interface disrupts the perception a musician has of the other musicians in the orchestra, it might degrade rather than enhance the collaboration. For instance, meters can increase awareness of what each musician is playing, but only if they are easily associated with their respective musicians and their gestures.

The second challenge relates to the new actions that are made available in the modes of collaboration and through the components of BOEUF. Controls for these actions might be provided on a dedicated interface, such as a control surface or touchscreen. Or, in the case of setting a parameter on another instrument, the parameter under control might be temporarily mapped to sensors on the musician's own instrument. In the case of instruments with a graphical interface, representations of the components can be integrated as part of the interface of the instrument. However, these controls should not interfere with the interface of the instrument itself, for example by reducing the number of available sensors or possibilities for musical expression possibilities, or by disrupting the musician's perception.

One way to achieve these objectives might be through the use of Augmented Reality displays, such as those described in [17]. Semi-transparent mirrors and displays are combined to visually augment a physical space. The augmentations are only seen when looking at that space through the mirrors, either from only one or from both sides of them. This would allow for:

- Co-located visualisation of parameters, meters and messages with the physical musicians and instruments, e.g. displaying meters and messages overlapping musicians.

- Access to parameters of other instruments by overlapping a 3D representation of them with the physical interface.
- Individual views of the components depending on the role of the musician, so that a conductor can for example see the separation of musicians in groups of instruments.

When designing interfaces that increase the musicians' access to information, we must also consider how the interface affects the ability of the audience to perceive and understand the musicians' actions. This visibility is important in that it allows the audience to perceive the risk inherent in the situation, and thus know that they are co-participants in a valid musical performance [5].

To that extent, audience members can be given access to the BOEUF interface. Information from the BOEUF framework would be added to the usual perception of musicians' performance, and would help spectators understand both the interactions between musicians and the contribution of each musician to the music produced by the orchestra.

4 Conclusion

In this paper we introduced BOEUF, a framework for modeling, designing, building, and managing orchestras of DMIs. It consists of a classification of possible collaboration modes, and of a set of components that can be used to implement them. We demonstrated how BOEUF can be used for modelling and designing orchestras with three examples: a piece for mobile phone orchestra, a multi-user instrument, and a piece for laptop orchestra.

Our next steps are: to investigate the integration of the BOEUF framework into DMIs, following the guidelines described in Sect. 3; to design novel interfaces for accessing BOEUF, possibly using Augmented Reality displays as proposed in Sect. 3; to study the impact of BOEUF on musicians' collaboration in the context of spontaneous orchestras or jam sessions; and to use our framework for in-depth investigations into issues such as concurrent access to musical parameters, indication of musical gestures through parameters, and visualisation of musical activity with meters.

We believe that this research is essential in that it will empower the community to more easily explore new musical collaboration possibilities.

Acknowledgments. This project was partially funded through the Marie Curie FP7 framework (Grant Agreement PIEF-GA-2012-330770).

References

1. Benford, S., Bowers, J., Fahlén, L.E., Greenhalgh, C.: Managing mutual awareness in collaborative virtual environments. In: Proceedings of VRST, pp. 223–236 (1994)
2. Benford, S., Bowers, J., Fahlén, L.E., Greenhalgh, C., Snowdon, D.: User embodiment in collaborative virtual environments. In: Proceedings of CHI 1995, New York, NY, USA, pp. 242–249 (1995)

3. Berthaut, F., Katayose, H., Wakama, H., Totani, N., Sato, Y.: First person shooters as collaborative multiprocess instruments. In: Proceedings of NIME 2011, Oslo, Norway, pp. 44–47 (2011)
4. Blaine, T., Fels, S.: Contexts of collaborative musical experiences. In: Proceedings of 2003 Conference on New Interfaces for Musical Expression, NIME 2003, pp. 129–134. National University of Singapore, Singapore (2003). http://dl.acm.org/citation.cfm?id=1085714.1085745
5. Dahl, L.: Wicked problems and design considerations in composing for laptop orchestra. In: Proceedings of NIME 2012 (2012)
6. Dahl, L., Wang, G.: Sound bounce: physical metaphors in designing mobile music performance. In: Proceedings of NIME 2010, Sydney, Australia (2010)
7. Fencott, R., Bryan-Kinns, N.: Hey Man, you're invading my Personal Space! Privacy and awareness in collaborative music. In: Proceedings of NIME 2010, pp. 198–203 (2010). http://www.educ.dab.uts.edu.au/nime/PROCEEDINGS/papers/Paper%20J1-J5/P198_Fencott.pdf
8. Gresham-Lancaster, S.: The aesthetics and history of the hub: the effects of changing technology on network computer music. Leonardo Music J. **8**, 39–44 (1998)
9. Hattwick, I., Wanderley, M.M.: A dimension space for evaluating collaborative musical performance systems (2012)
10. Hindmarsh, J., Fraser, M., Heath, C., Benford, S., Greenhalgh, C.: Object-focused interaction in collaborative virtual environments. ACM Trans. Comput.-Hum. Interact. **7**(4), 477–509 (2000). http://doi.acm.org/10.1145/365058.365088
11. Jordà, S.: Multi-user instruments: models, examples and promises. In: Proceedings of NIME 2005, Singapore, pp. 23–26 (2005). http://dl.acm.org/citation.cfm?id=1085939.1085948
12. Jordà, S., Kaltenbrunner, M., Geiger, G., Bencina, R.: The reactable*. In: Proceedings of International Computer Music Conference (2005)
13. Lee, S.W., Freeman, J., Colella, A., Yao, S., Van Troyer, A.: Collaborative musical improvisation in a laptop ensemble with LOLC. In: Proceedings of 8th ACM Conference on Creativity and Cognition, C&C 2011, pp. 361–362. ACM, New York (2011). http://doi.acm.org/10.1145/2069618.2069696
14. Malloch, J., Sinclair, S., Wanderley, M.M.: Libmapper: (a library for connecting things). In: CHI 2013 Extended Abstracts on Human Factors in Computing Systems, pp. 3087–3090. ACM (2013)
15. Malloch, J., Sinclair, S., Wanderley, M.M.: A network-based framework for collaborative development and performance of digital musical instruments. In: Kronland-Martinet, R., Ystad, S., Jensen, K. (eds.) CMMR 2007. LNCS, vol. 4969, pp. 401–425. Springer, Heidelberg (2008). http://dx.doi.org/10.1007/978-3-540-85035-9_28
16. Margery, D., Arnaldi, B., Plouzeau, N.: A general framework for cooperative manipulation in virtual environments. In: Gervautz, M., Schmalstieg, D., Hildebrand, A. (eds.) Virtual Environments 1999. Eurographics, pp. 169–178. Springer, Vienna (1999)
17. Martinez Plasencia, D., Berthaut, F., Karnik, A., Subramanian, S.: Through the combining glass. In: Proceedings of 27th Annual ACM Symposium on User Interface Software and Technology, UIST 2014, pp. 341–350. ACM, New York (2014). http://doi.acm.org/10.1145/2642918.2647351
18. Oh, J., Herrera, J., Bryan, N.J., Dahl, L., Wang, G.: Evolving the mobile phone orchestra. In: Proceedings of NIME 2010, Sydney, Australia (2010)

19. Pinho, M.S., Bowman, D.A., Freitas, C.M.: Cooperative object manipulation inimmersive virtual environments: framework and techniques. In: Proceedings of ACM Symposium on Virtual Reality Software and Technology, VRST 2002, pp. 171–178. ACM, New York (2002). http://doi.acm.org/10.1145/585740.585769
20. Place, T., Lossius, T.: Jamoma: a modular standard for structuring patches in max. In: Proceedings of International Computer Music Conference, pp. 143–146 (2006)
21. Seddon, F., Biasutti, M.: A comparison of modes of communication between members of a string quartet and a jazz sextet. Psychol. Music **37**(4), 395–415 (2009). http://pom.sagepub.com/content/37/4/395.abstract
22. Snowdon, D.N., Munro, A.J.: Collaborative Virtual Environments: Digital Places and Spaces for Interaction. Springer-Verlag New York, Inc., Secaucus (2001)
23. Vigoda, B., Merrill, D.: JamiOki-PureJoy: a game engine and instrument for electronically-mediated musical improvisation. In: Proceedings of 7th International Conference on New Interfaces for Musical Expression, NIME 2007, pp. 321–326. ACM, New York (2007). http://doi.acm.org/10.1145/1279740.1279810
24. Wang, G., Bryan, N:, Oh, J., Hamilton, R.: Stanford laptop orchestra (slork). In: Proceedings of International Computer Music Conference, pp. 505–508 (2009)
25. Weinberg, G.: Interconnected musical networks: toward a theoretical framework. Comput. Music J. **29**(2), 23–39 (2005). http://dx.doi.org/10.1162/0148926054094350
26. Wolff, R., Roberts, D.J., Steed, A., Otto, O.: A review of telecollaboration technologies with respect to closely coupled collaboration. Int. J. Comput. Appl. Technol. **29**(1), 11–26 (2007). http://dx.doi.org/10.1504/IJCAT.2007.014056

Decomposing a Composition: On the Multi-layered Analysis of Expressive Music Performance

Esther Coorevits[1(✉)], Dirk Moelants[1], Stefan Östersjö[2], David Gorton[3], and Marc Leman[1]

[1] IPEM, Department of Musicology, Ghent University, Ghent, Belgium
esther.coorevits@ugent.be
[2] Orpheus Institute, Ghent, Belgium
[3] Royal Academy of Music, University of London, London, UK

Abstract. In our engagement with music, not only the physical experience of sound is important. Also the interplay between body movements, musical gestures and the cognitive processes of performers and listeners is part of our experience. Yet, this multimodal aspect is not always fully considered when analyzing music performance. In this paper, we want to establish a framework for a multi-layered analysis of music performance, building on data retrieved from quantitative and qualitative procedures and involving the perspectives of composer, performer and musicologist. The performance of a classical guitarist was analyzed in detail, using both a 'bottom-up' approach (audio-analysis and motion-capture) and a 'top-down' perspective (annotations from video-footage, perceived phrasing and the composer's, performer's and researcher's perspective). These different analytical layers were compared and evaluated, which pointed out that multiple perspectives can reinforce each other in understanding musical intentions and can help detecting mismatches between qualitative and quantitative data. The analytical framework developed could be an important step in the coupling of performer's intentions with the expressive enactment of a musical score.

Keywords: Music performance · Gesture · Multimodal analysis · Embodied music cognition

1 Introduction

Music performance is often described as a multimodal experience, both for the performer and the audience [1]. From an ecological point of view [2], our engagement with music, as listener or performer, is a process of perceiving what is happening around us and trying to understand, and adapt to, what is going on [3]. In other words, we are involved in sense-giving activities that take place in a multimodal environment. Auditory stimuli form an important part of that environment, but human perception engages all senses, and involves next to sound also vision, smell, touch, taste, sense of movement, emotion, bodily sensations and so on.

Consequently, music as a phenomenon is more than a physical experience of sound waves in the air. According to the Embodied Music Cognition theory [4], we perceive music by means of our body, which acts as a mediator between the external environment and our subjective sensations and experiences. Interaction with the environment, for example, would typically comprise inverse and forward prediction components [5], meaning that we can predict the subjective sensations we will perceive from certain actions in the physical world (forward modeling) but also that we will associate our immediate, personal sensations with a certain action (inverse modeling). Thus, action and perception prediction models are linked with sensorimotor and body-related articulations, resulting in what is called an action-oriented ontology [4] or the coupling of actions with their consequent outcome or goal. This repertoire of goal-directed actions or gestures can be considered as a collection of movements made to achieve a particular goal, linked with the experiences and sensations resulting from such actions.

The repertoire of gestures provides a basis for the enactment of music, both in music performance and in music listening. The coupling of actions and perceived sensations forms a mechanism that guides our understanding of music, which makes these gestures a vehicle for the construction of musical meaning. Musical gestures are inherent to music performance, and skilled musicians will be able to convey musical expression by means of their body movements [6–8]. High-skilled performers can encode their musical intentions or goals into 'moving sonic forms', which involves both mental processing and corporeal control over a musical instrument [4]. These musical intentions can be related to an overall stylistic target (general style of the piece) as well as intended expressive sensitivities at a local structural level [6, 9]. According to Godøy [10], these locally intended targets will guide the performer's grouping or co-articulating of smaller movements into gestures. As such, these local targets can be understood as a reference frame, which guides the musician's construction and shaping of a musical piece. In that sense, the musician is part of the creative process and establishes a relationship between notation, action and sound [11].

Given this framework, music performance can be seen as constructed out of different layers of significance and can therefore be described from different levels. Low-level or bottom-up descriptors such as physical characteristics of sound (i.e. timing, intensity,...) and movement (Quantity of Motion, kinematics,...) and high-level features (emotions, subjective experiences, verbal descriptions) accessed from a top-down approach, are both related with the musical material (score) [12–14]. All these different layers are connected in a sense to musical expression [15].

In this study, we want to access and explore the different levels of expressiveness in a performance and try to establish a relationship between these layers of analysis. By deconstructing a musical performance in different layers, the complexity of music as a multimodal experience can be reduced without losing the richness of impressions inherent in such an experience. The purpose was to develop a methodology that can provide a framework for further in-depth analysis of other performances in the future that takes into account the interplay between the different modalities inherent to music and the different actors involved, being the composer, performer and musicologist. This way, an attempt could be made to access expressiveness in music from the performer and observer's perspective [4].

2 Methods

2.1 Music

In this study, we consider a performance of "Austerity Measures I", a piece by the British composer David Gorton for ten-string guitar (Fig. 1). The piece consists of 64 bars of music, which can be divided in 5 sections in which different types of material are used. The first part (bars 1–15) consists of relatively isolated chords using harmonics on the guitar; the second part (bars 16–30) continues to use harmonics, but now presented as series of single notes mostly with large pitch intervals. The third part (bars 31–49) consists of a series of ascending melodies with 5–12 elements, played in a more 'lyrical' legato style. The fourth part (bars 50–58) is a series of 10-note arpeggio patterns and the fifth part (bars 59–64) is a kind of coda, stylistically reflective of part 3, but containing just one ascending pattern with gradually decreasing dynamics. However, it may be argued that this sequence of scored material is not 'the work' but rather material which is activated in performance according to rules that instruct the performer to 'decompose' the scored material.

Fig. 1. First 17 bars from the score of "Austerity Measures I".

During performance, the score should be repeated three or four times. When playing through four times, the performer labels each bar with the numbers 1, 2, 3 or 4, with a roughly equal distribution and frequently changing the order of the numbers throughout the piece. Only the first and the last bar have a fixed label, which is 4. In the first round, the piece should be played as it is written, but for the second run-through, all bars labeled 1 should be replaced with rests. On the third time, all the bars labeled 1 and 2 should be replaced with rests, and on the fourth time, all the bars labeled 1, 2, and 3 should be replaced with rests, leaving the performer only those bars labeled 4 to play. In other words: during the performance, the piece is constructed by deconstructing it. When playing through three times, the process is similar, using the numbers 1 to 3 instead of 1 to 4.

The instructions for the piece establish a rudimentary economic system, which governs the allocation of musical resources to the guitar player. While, through the numbering of the bars, the performer has control over which materials are cut, and at what stage in the piece they are cut, the implications of the cuts are difficult to envisage from the patterns of the numbers, and are only fully realised through the literal 'playing-out' of the system. When Austerity Measures I is created live on stage, the performer is forced to re-evaluate the surviving materials within their new contexts with each play-through and therefore, the expressive outcome in terms of timing, performance dynamics and bodily gestures are emergent from the immediate context. Phrases that span several bars become broken and fractured, requiring new phrasing and shapes to be sought by the performer. Musical material that was originally separate and distant, become adjacent gestures, connected by silence. Increasingly lengthy silences encroach upon the flow of the surviving materials, requiring preparation and framing. The tempo of the piece is flexible in order to leave space for the performer to phrase and shape the music to his expressive intentions. The loss of material during the piece forces the performer to rethink the musical material and adjust its musical ideas and goals, but the process should not be understood as automatic. The choice of which bars to keep and which ones to leave out influences the performer's priorities and structural notions of how to shape the music. Hence, the local musical targets that serve as a reference frame change, which will affect the musician's construction and shaping of the performance.

2.2 Procedure

Concert and rehearsal performances of both the four and three times run-through of the piece by the Swedish guitarist Stefan Östersjö were recorded at the Orpheus institute in Ghent, during the Orpheus Research festival on 1–3 October 2014. The four-times rehearsal and concert performance were recorded on the first day, in a concert auditorium and with a seated audience in the concert performance, while the three times rehearsal and concert were recorded in the central hall of the institute with a standing audience in the concert performance. The set-up of the recordings had to be flexible in order to move it to different locations and without interfering too much with the natural setting of the concert (the communication between musician and audience) to ensure ecological validity. This has important consequences for the technology used.

For both the rehearsal and concert performance of the two versions of the piece, audio, video and movement recordings were made. A contact microphone was used to record a dry guitar signal for analytical purposes, while a condenser microphone recorded the guitar sound with the ambience of the room. Two types of movement data were extracted from the performance: 4 sensors attached under the surface on which the guitar player was seated measured the executed pressure and displacement of weight. Active infrared markers were attached to the head, shoulders and right wrist and registered with two Wii-motes placed in front of the performer.

The amount of infrared markers that could be registered was limited to 4, so the body parts had to be chosen deliberately and in agreement with the performer. All data streams were synchronized using *Max/MSP/Jitter* [16] and *OSCulator* [17] and both the pressure sensors and the Wii-mote data were sampled at 100 Hz. In addition, the complete performance was recorded on video with a sample rate of 50 Hz.

3 Analysis

In this paper we mainly want to establish a suited methodology, therefore only the first concert performance (4 run-throughs) was taken into consideration. The main goal of the analysis was to extract expressive details to detect consistent and changing performance strategies. First, we give the details of the separate layers of analysis, followed by the method to combine these approaches.

3.1 Timing

Onset-Time Bars. The time structure of the piece was analyzed at the level of the bar. It is the main structural unit in the piece, as the units that are removed and replaced with silences are always bars. The start of each performed bar was manually annotated using *praat* [18], a program that gives an analysis of dynamics and pitch together with the sound wave and a spectrogram of the sound. This analysis gives us a precise view on how the global time structure evolves through the successive run-throughs of the piece. The analysis at the bar level forms the basis for an analysis at larger structural levels, such as the different run-throughs and the five sections mentioned in Sect. 2.1.

Perceived Phrasing. Perceived phrasing across the performances was reached through a process of negotiation between composer, performer and musicologists. By listening together to the recordings, the participants discussed and agreed upon a combined understanding of the shaping and phrasing of materials. While material within an individual bar was always considered an independent unit, the negotiation identified the perceived joining together of bars into phrases, and the perceived combination of these phrases into super-phrases. A new score was then compiled, which replaces with rests those bars that Stefan cut out in each run-through, and annotates the agreed phrasing structure using dashed slurs for the phrases, and dotted slurs for the super-phrases.

3.2 Video Analysis

To analyze the video recordings, a method consisting of several steps was applied building on a basic procedure referred to as 'stimulated recall'[1] [19]. The goal was to detect expressive movements in the performance that were not immediately related to technical (or sound-producing [20]) gestures. Performer, composer and two musicologists first watched the video of the performance together, using the software *Hyper Research* (HR) [21]. At any moment one of them marked an event they perceived as

---

[1] 'Stimulated recall' is the overarching term for introspective research procedures through which cognitive processes can be investigated by inviting subjects to recall their thinking during an event when prompted by a video sequence. Benjamin Bloom is considered the first to use the term in 1953, which he described as a method for retrieving memories: "The basic idea underlying the method of stimulated recall is that a subject may be enabled to relive an original situation with vividness and accuracy if he is presented with a large number of cues or stimuli which occurred during the original situation" [18].

'expressive', the video was stopped. To give the event a name (code), the four persons involved in the analysis negotiated about the meaning of this event, based on how they personally perceived it. If consensus was reached, the code was added to the video and annotated in HR. During this first phase not only some basic codes were introduced, but more important, a common frame of reference was agreed between the participants, which was crucial for the next stage.

In this next stage, the persons involved in the analysis watched the performance alone and coded the videos individually in order to obtain a rich list of codes, involving the different viewpoints of composer, performer and researcher. In a second session of common coding, the code lists from the individual coding were discussed. Overlaps of codes were deleted, meaning that different code names for the same expressive event were set equal (e.g., 'accentuating head movement' and 'head beats' were renamed as 'nodding'). Also, some specific codes were assigned to a more general code, like 'worried' and 'angry' which were assigned to 'facial expression'. In the end, a list of 18 codes for which the four parties agreed on the meaning was fixed and used for the second part of the video analysis. Here, the performer and one of the musicologists individually annotated the four recordings in HR using the new code list. Each time an expressive event occurred that matched a code in the list, this code was added to the video.

This resulted in two parallel annotations, which were discussed in a final common session. Here, all coded events for which in the end no consensus was reached were deleted from the annotations. The final result of the video analysis was one annotated file per recording, containing a list of 18 different codes, which were applied to all expressive events in the video where the four parties found an agreement on. The different steps of common and individual coding, involving the composer, performer and external observers, ensured that the result was a reliable annotation of a performance in terms of high-level descriptors.

3.3 Movement Data

Wii-Data. From the infrared markers, relative X- and Y-coordinates shoulders and right wrist could be extracted. Due to light conditions in the concert hall, the data from the head markers could not be used. X- and Y-coordinates were normalized to values from −1 to +1. From this signal, kinematic variables (velocity & acceleration) were calculated and the resulting data was smoothed using a first order Savitzky-Golay filter as outlined in the MoCap Toolbox [22].

Pressure Sensors. For each sample, the Cartesian coordinates of the point of gravity of the performer were derived from the 4 pressure sensors (1) (Fig. 2). For this point, polar coordinates (vector length & angle) were calculated and the result was smoothed using a local weighted regression filter with a polynomial order of 2 (Loess-filtering)[2].

---

[2] The filtering and smoothing process was based on the methods used in [12], where noise-measurements are used to obtain the most reliable smoothing result.

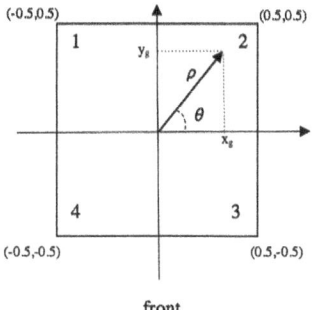

Fig. 2. Representation of the surface with pressure sensors (*1 2 3 4*). Let *W* be the sum of w_1, w_2, w_3, w_4 (the fractional weights of each sensor). The position of the point of gravity of the 4 sensors is then defined as in (1). The (x_g, y_g) coordinates are then converted to polar coordinates (θ, ρ). ρ is the length of the vector and is a measure of the intensity of movement.

$$x_g = -(w_1 + w_4)/W + 0.5 = (w_2 + w_3)/W - 0.5 \tag{1}$$

$$y_g = -(w_3 + w_4)/W + 0.5 = (w_1 + w_2)/W - 0.5$$

From these polar coordinates, the movement of the point of gravity was derived (norm of the vector), resulting in a measure for Quantity of Motion (QoM).

3.4 Multi-modal Analysis

Figure 3 gives an overview of the different layers of analysis. In order to align the different layers, the musical score was used as an overarching framework. A global evolution of timing, movement data and detected gestures throughout the run-throughs

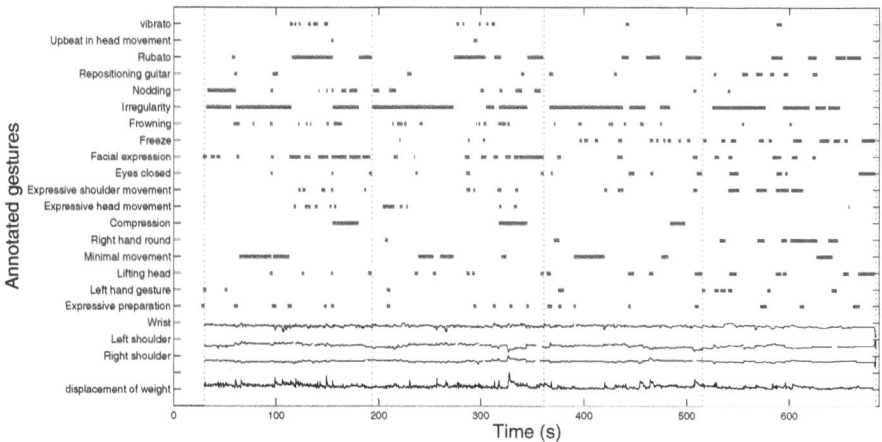

Fig. 3. Overview of the different layers of analysis over the full performance: movement data (*wrist, left & right shoulder, displacement of weight*) and annotated gestures (blue lines). (Color figure online)

of the piece was used as a guideline to detect general performance strategies. The next step was to compare the different sections within the score over each run-through and in the end, to use the annotated gestures from the video as a reference point for analyzing the movement data.

Bottom-up Approach. The timing analysis and processing of the movement data are considered as bottom-up strategies to analyze the musical performance. The data provides 'objective' measurements of expressiveness in the performance as no semantic interpretation of the data is given.

The timing of bars, sections and run-throughs give us an objective representation of the temporal structure of the performance. It allows us to see how the timing deviates from a strictly isochronic rendering of the score and how the process of compression influences the timing over the different run-throughs. Based on the annotations of sections and bars, the mean QoM was calculated within these different fragments by summing the QoM at each timing instance (as calculated in Sect. 3.3) and dividing it by the total duration of the fragment. The velocity derived from the positional data of the Wii gives an indication of the kinetic energy of the measured body parts ($E_k = 1/2\ mv^2$, following Dempster's human body model [23]). In order to detect specific performance cues, mean velocity and acceleration over the annotated sections, phrases and bars were calculated in a similar way as the QoM.

Top-down Approach. The perceived phrasing and the list of annotated gestures from the video-analysis containing start, end and duration of each gesture, offers a top-down approach, as these are "subjective descriptors" of the performance.

The % of time and number of appearances of annotated gestures in the different run-throughs were compared using a chi-square test. The chi-square test tells us whether or not a distribution is equal between categories. This comparison allows us to detect where changing the musical material alters performance gestures and which gestures are used consistently. A gesture was considered 'consistent' when appearing at least in 3 of the 4 run-throughs. Also, the correlation of gesture-occurrence was tested as follows: the amount of time gesture (y) appeared during gesture (x), divided by the total time of gesture (x) (2)

$$T(g(x) = g(y))/T(g(x)) \qquad (2)$$

In order to align this top-down approach with the results form the bottom-up analysis, the occurrence of the annotated performance gestures were also considered per bar. It is worth noting that the occurrence and duration of these gestures were not limited to the framework of the musical bar, but it allows an easy comparison between the different layers. When a gesture occurred over several bars, all the bars were judged as containing that particular gesture.

In a visual representation, the perceived phrasing could be compared with the annotated gestures in the score, and the timing structure as extracted from the onset-analysis. In the end, the performance targets that were detected using these different approaches were compared and evaluated. In the next section, this process will be explained in more detail.

4 Results

4.1 Bottom-up Analysis

Section-Level. The timing analysis based on the durations of the bars gives us insight in the evolution of the performance through the 4 run-throughs. As each run-through means that a number of bars are replaced by silence, we see that the average distance between the start of two successive bars increases gradually (2.55–3.23–4.40–8.52 s). This process is illustrated in detail in Fig. 4.

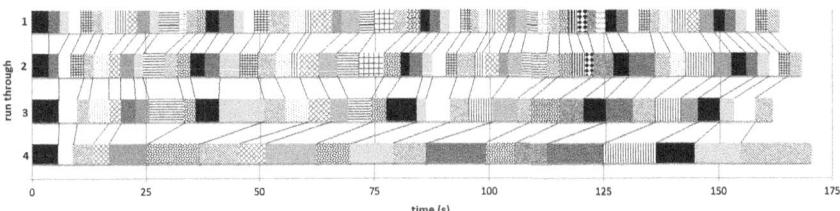

Fig. 4. Illustration of the deletion process in the performance of "Austerity Measures". Each cell represents the duration from the start of a bar to the beginning of the next bar, the black cells indicate the first bar of a section. The four horizontal layers represent the four run-throughs, the black lines in between them show which bars are deleted and how the time-scale is contracted or extended.

This figure also shows that the evolution of the timing is not strictly linear: sometimes the sum of the bars is shorter, while in other cases the duration increases. We can now look at this at a higher structural level and compare the length of the five main sections (Fig. 5). The comparison shows that there is a clear change between the second and the third run-through only in the second section, which clearly becomes shorter. The only other striking difference is the lengthening of the final part in the last run-through. Obviously, this is related to the length of the final bar, which is extended to convey the end of the piece.

When comparing the shaping of musical time in the five sections of each run-through with the mean QoM of each section, a striking similarity can be observed (Fig. 5). A similar relationship between the several sections is maintained in both the QoM and timing within the 4 run-throughs. In the first and second run-through, QoM and duration raise in the second section, to lower again in the third section. In the first run-through, both duration and QoM lower again, while in the second run-through, QoM rises to its highest point. Towards the last section, QoM and duration lower in both the first and second run-through. For the third run-through, the QoM reaches it lowest point in the second section and increases again towards the last section. This is in contrast with the shaping of time, as the duration seems to lower from the third section towards the end of the third run-through. In the last run-through, QoM and duration perfectly seems to mirror each other, similar to the first run-through.

176 E. Coorevits et al.

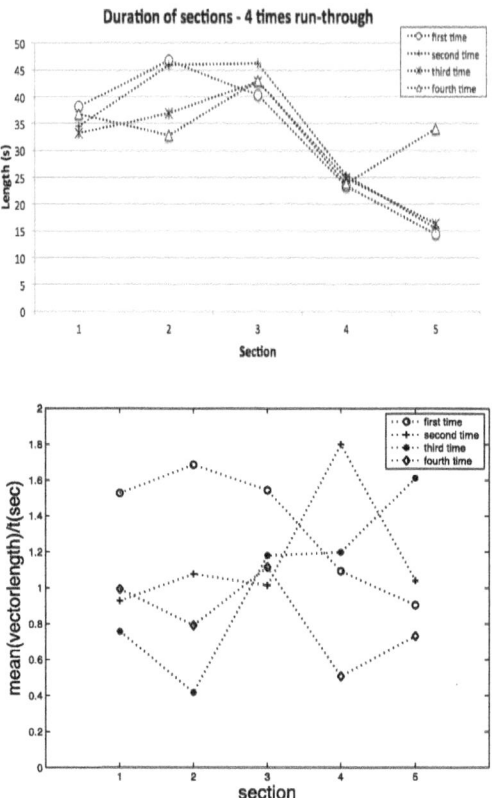

Fig. 5. Total duration (top) and QoM (bottom) for each of the five sections in the performance. The four lines represent the four run-throughs.

Bar-Level. Looking into more detail, the QoM within the bar was considered (Fig. 6). This gives a better view on the musical material that is 'lost' over the different run-throughs. Based on consistency and change in QoM, possible musical targets can be detected: In each of the four run-throughs, peaks in QoM can be seen at bars 26 and 30–33 and a general downwards trend in the last part of the third section (ca. bars 42–51). In bar 59, QoM is also generally low. On the other hand, we see a change in the movement through the decomposition process. In bars 15–16 and 27–28 for example, the increase of movement observed in the first two run-throughs is lost in the third and fourth repeat. The first part of the second section (bars 17–25) seems to be the most stable region for all the four run-throughs. In general, the second run-through mirrors the first repeat, as the third and fourth run-through seem to be more similar. The first repeat is the most active one and the third one the least.

To detect the amount of energy during the performance, we studied velocity and acceleration of shoulders and wrist, as additional information to the QoM. Looking at the shoulders (Fig. 7), bar 15 shows a decrease in energy, which is also found in bars 22, 40, 50 and 59. Energy peaks are present in bars 26 and 45–46, except for the last

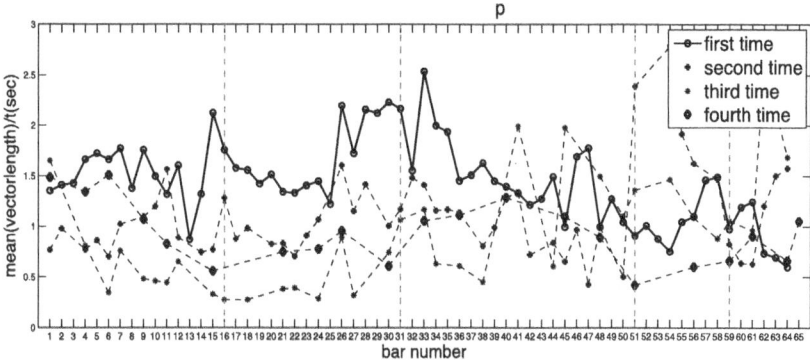

Fig. 6. QoM per bar for each run-through. The vertical dashed lines indicate the five sections.

run-through. Some points of increase and decrease in energy are shifted in the later run-throughs because some musical material is lost. This is the most clear in bars 32–33, where the peak is shifted from bar 32 to 33 in the last 2 repeats, as bar 32 is omitted. A similar shift is visible in bar 28 in the right shoulder. The acceleration profile of the shoulders closely follows the velocity curve. The wrist shows a somewhat different energy profile, as the largest energy peak occurs at bar 28 for the first two repeats, but two consistent peaks also occur at bars 26 and 58, except for the last run-through. Bar 27 on its turn is marked by a decrease in energy. A larger zone of low energy is situated here around bars 17–24, which can be found in the velocity profile of the left shoulder as well. Also, the acceleration of the wrist shows a new possible target: bar 51 shows decreased acceleration in all 4 repeats.

4.2 Top-Down Analysis

The results of the χ^2-tests on the annotated gestures are summarized in Table 1. The distribution of the frequency (number of occurrences) of the gestures 'freeze', 'nodding' and 'facial expression' was significantly different over the 4 run-throughs at a 99 % confidence level, while the distribution of 'right hand gesture', 'expressive head movement', 'frowning' and 'vibrato' were significantly different at a 95 % cl. When we consider the duration (% time of occurrence) of each gesture, all gestures included in Table 1 show significant changes, except for 'vibrato'. Interestingly, the direction of the distribution is not equal for all gestures. When we go back to Fig. 3, we can see that more 'freezes' appear towards the third and fourth repeat, while much more 'facial expression' and 'nodding' can be observed during the first two run-throughs. 'Right hand gestures' are most frequent in the last repeat, while 'expressive head movement', 'frowning' and 'vibrato' are mostly present in the beginning of the performance.

When looking at the level of the bar, some gestures appear to be consistently linked with particular bars. In each run-through, a 'left-hand gesture' occurs in bar 9. The guitar player used vibrato in three of the four run-throughs at bars 33 & 34, and bar 36 is aligned with an expressive shoulder movement (Fig. 8a). Similarly, 'lifting of the

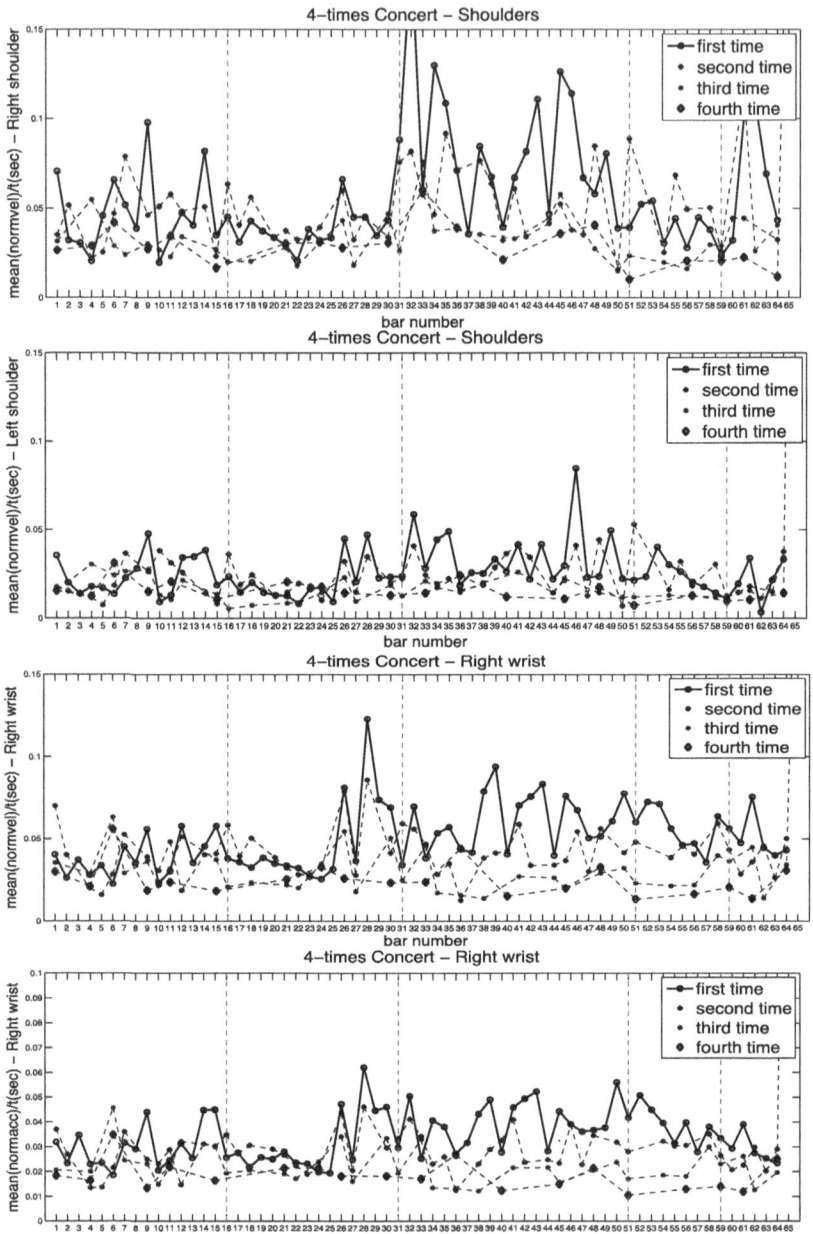

Fig. 7. Velocity profiles of left and right shoulder (top) and velocity and acceleration profiles of the right wrist (bottom) per bar for each run-through. The five sections in the score are indicated by the vertical dashed lines.

Table 1. χ^2-tests of the distribution of gestures during the 4-times concert performance.

Type of gesture	% Time of occurrence	Number of occurrences
Left hand gesture	$\chi^2(3) = 15.56, p < 0.01$	$\chi^2(3) = 6$, n.s.
Lifting head	$\chi^2(3) = 12.47, p < 0.01$	$\chi^2(3) = 0$, n.s.
Minimal movement	$\chi^2(3) = 10.00, p < 0.05$	$\chi^2(3) = 1$, n.s.
Right hand round	$\chi^2(3) = 74.68, p < 0.001$	$\chi^2(3) = 8.43, p < 0.05$
Compression	$\chi^2(3) = 16.18, p < 0.01$	$\chi^2(3) = 3.8$, n.s.
Expressive head movement	$\chi^2(3) = 19.43, p < 0.001$	$\chi^2(3) = 8.67, p < 0.05$
Expressive shoulder movement	$\chi^2(3) = 22.78, p < 0.001$	$\chi^2(3) = 0.65$, n.s.
Eyes closed	$\chi^2(3) = 15.52, p < 0.01$	$\chi^2(3) = 1.84$, n.s.
Facial expression	$\chi^2(3) = 31.07, p < 0.001$	$\chi^2(3) = 12.74, p < 0.01$
Freeze	$\chi^2(3) = 56.39, p < 0.001$	$\chi^2(3) = 19.71, p < 0.001$
Frowning	$\chi^2(3) = 10.14, p < 0.05$	$\chi^2(3) = 9.06, p < 0.05$
Irregularity	$\chi^2(3) = 24.30, p < 0.001$	$\chi^2(3) = 0.50$, n.s.
Nodding	$\chi^2(3) = 41.78, p < 0.001$	$\chi^2(3) = 14.73, p < 0.01$
Repositioning guitar	$\chi^2(3) = 13.93, p < 0.01$	$\chi^2(3) = 4.00$, n.s.
Vibrato	$\chi^2(3) = 7.58$, n.s.	$\chi^2(3) = 9.27, p < 0.05$

head' was observed for each run-through in bars 36 and 64 (Fig. 8b). In the last bar, the guitarist always closes his eyes, which we also see in bar 36, except for the first run-through (Fig. 8c). 'Frowning' occurred consistently in bar 40, while 'facial expression' could be detected but once in bar 33. In the end, three times 'minimal movement' could be observed in the transition between the third and fourth section (bars 50–51 - Fig. 8d).

Also, the occurrence of some gestures seems to be interrelated. Table 2 shows the co-occurrence of gestures in terms of duration in %, from which we can detect clusters of gestures. 'Eyes closed', 'lifting of the head', 'expressive shoulder movement' and 'freeze' seem to co-occur often, as well as 'left- and right-hand gestures' with 'freeze'. Obviously, some gestures can't occur together, as they are executed by the same body part, like 'vibrato' and 'left-hand gesture'. More striking is the 0-overlap between 'eyes closed' and 'expressive head movement', between 'nodding' and 'right-hand gestures' and between 'frowning' and 'left-hand gesture'. This can be partly explained by the difference in distribution over the several run-throughs: 'nodding' occurs most in the first two run-throughs while 'right-hand gesture' is mostly present in the last run-through.

4.3 Targets in Musical Expression

Comparison of Different Layers. The last step in detecting (changing) musical targets in the performance was to compare the different layers of analysis and connect

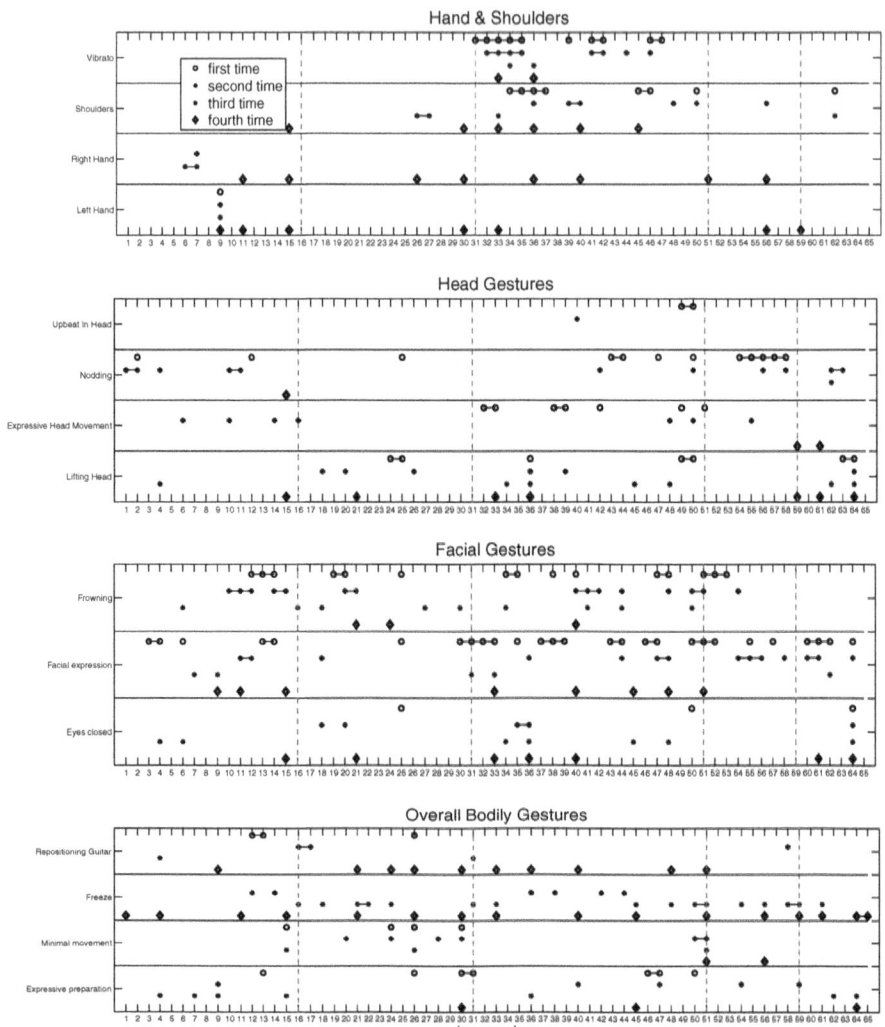

Fig. 8. Distribution of annotated gestures per bar for each run-through. The five sections in the score are indicated by the vertical dashed lines.

them with the musical material (score) and perceived phrasing. Considering the distribution of the annotated gestures throughout the piece, the distribution of the different gestures reflects the changing musical material. The more material is lost, the more the gestures used in the first run-through are absent or replaced by other gestures.

Table 3 gives an overview of possible targets detected in QoM, velocity and acceleration data and the gestural analysis at the level of the bar. When we look at the targets that were detected consistently throughout the performance in several layers of analysis, bars 26–27, 30–33, 40, 50–51 and 58–59 stand out. Three of these targets mark the transitions between sections in the score (bars 30–33, 50–51 and 58–59), bars

Table 2. Co-occurrence of gestures. Numbers are the % of time *gesture y* (column) occurs when *gesture x* (row) is present. Gray shading indicates that gestures don't occur together, black shading shows gestures that have an overlap of more than 30 %.

	LH gesture	Lifting head	Minimal movement	RH gesture	Expr. head movement	Expr. shoulder movement	Eyes closed	Facial expression	Freeze	Frowning	Nodding	Vibrato
Expr. preparation	10.01	21.86	10.40	15.08	4.66	24.35	12.52	31.18	7.78	5.77	10.80	9.00
LH gesture	100	6.97	2.12	30.39	9.08	9.98	6.97	35.80	30.63	0.00	14.55	0.00
Lifting head	3.22	100	2.71	4.33	0.82	38.32	67.05	24.46	31.01	3.12	5.99	6.94
Minimal movement	0.61	1.70	100	3.82	0.00	0.28	0.44	1.38	16.42	10.58	1.61	0.00
RH gesture	18.75	5.79	8.12	100	4.16	38.81	3.96	17.64	35.81	4.35	0.00	0.44
Expr. head movement	10.39	2.04	0.00	7.72	100	12.50	0.00	38.44	1.15	28.74	24.45	17.97
Expr. shoulder movement	4.69	31.95	0.45	29.56	5.13	100	27.50	47.75	29.38	5.27	12.59	9.89
Eyes closed	4.25	90.49	0.93	3.92	0.00	35.70	100	29.63	34.73	2.63	6.04	9.08
Facial expression	8.11	12.01	1.08	6.48	7.61	23.02	11.01	100	7.72	14.38	28.17	11.01
Freeze	12.57	27.58	23.24	23.82	0.41	25.66	23.36	13.99	100	5.31	1.22	0.00
Frowning	0.00	3.74	20.13	3.89	13.87	6.19	2.38	35.03	7.14	100	13.67	7.70
Nodding	6.81	6.07	2.60	0.00	10.00	12.53	4.63	58.14	1.39	11.59	100	1.58
Vibrato	0.00	16.59	0.00	0.79	17.33	23.23	16.43	53.63	0.00	15.40	3.74	100

Table 3. Musical targets detected at the bar-level for the different layers of analysis. Gray shading indicates the bars where a possible target could be detected in more than one layer of analysis

Bar	QoM	Vel/Acc	Gesture
9			LH gesture
15-16	+ (1st, 2nd)	- shoulders	
17-25	STABLE	STABLE	
22-24		- shoulders & wrist	
26	+	+ shoulders & wrist	
27	-	- wrist	
28	+ (1st, 2nd)	+ Right shoulder & wrist (1st, 2nd)	
30-33	+	+ shoulders	Vibrato & Facial expression (b 33)
36			Shoulder & lifting head & eyes closed
40		- shoulders	Frowning
45-46		+ shoulders	
42-51	GENERAL DECREASE		
50-51	-	- shoulders (b 50) & wrist (b51)	Minimal movement
58-59	-	+ wrist (58) & - shoulders(b59)	
64			Lifting head & eyes closed

26–27 form a point of transition in section two, where the movement restart after a long note at a lower dynamic level, and bar 40 marks a new ascending melodic line halfway the third section. On the other hand, some bars are only marked in specific run-throughs, for example bars 15–16 and 28. Bar 28 was left out in the third and fourth run-through, but bar 15 is played in all four run-throughs and bar 16 is left out only in the last repetition. This last point marks the end of the first section and the beginning of the second one. Surprisingly, we see a decrease of energy in the shoulder movement here, and an increase in QoM during the first and second run-through. Not all body parts thus behave in a similar way, an observation also made in bars 58–59 for wrist and shoulder. If we look at the bars that are left out in the third and fourth run-through, it becomes clear that bars 15 and 16 are isolated from their initial context. This blurs the transition between the first two sections, and could explain why they are not as clearly marked as in the first two repetitions.

As opposed to musical targets detected in several layers of analysis, some moments in the score are just marked firmly in one layer. Bars 36 and 64 for example are emphasized by a series of expressive gestures (shoulder, lifting head & eyes closed, the ones that formed a 'movement cluster' in Table 2). Bar 64 is the last bar of the score, which is an obvious musical target. Bar 36, just as bar 40, marks a transition to a new ascending melodic gesture within Sect. 3. In the QoM, larger structures can be detected in bars 17–25 & 42–51. The latter are characterized by a general decrease in movement, while the first section has a stable QoM. Wrist and left shoulder also seem to be stable in velocity during this section.

The perceived phrasing, at last, could be linked both with the onset timing of the bars, the annotated gestures and the movement data. Figure 9a gives a representation of bar 31–49, the section with the ascending arpeggios. Each cell represents the duration from the start of a bar to the beginning of the next, with the numbers indicating which bar each cell represents. The four horizontal layers represent the four run-throughs, and the vertical and diagonal black lines between them show the relative repositioning of the surviving bars. The curved lines on top of the cells represent the agreed phrasing structure. Thus, in the first run through, we found bars 31–46 to be shaped into 7 units that can be perceived also as two super phrases, each super phrase ending with a longer phrase (three bars instead of two).

The gradual process of cuts is reflected in the shaping of the music in the following run-throughs. In the second round, the music between bars 31 and 46 is again divided into 7 smaller units, shaped somewhat differently due to bars 37 and 43 being cut out. In principle, the lower level structure looks similar, but the perceived higher structure is divided into different super-phrases. Here, the duration of the last bars in the sub-phrases (=bars 32, 34, 36, 39, 41, 46, 48) are longer ($M = 3.25$ s) compared to the others ($M = 2.58$ s). In the third round, the number of bars lost is more radical and the music of bars 31–45 is now shaped into three units spanning across a number of empty bars, again with the last bar of each phrase being longer (except for bar 36). In the fourth round, the music has in a sense gone full circle and again consists of only two long phrases: one that stretches from bar 30 (before the section we are discussing here) up until bar 40, and one starting in bar 45 and stretching again outside of the section, now ending in bar 48, and with a super-phrase stretching far into the next section of broken chords, ending at bar 56. The changing musical structure of the piece cause different emerging timing and phrasing patterns, and in this final run-through, we see how the previously defined limits of the different sections break down, with materials from the different sections becoming joined together within the new phrase structure.

Figure 9b combines the timing and phrasing information from the previous image with some of the more commonly appearing qualitative codes for this section. Some movement

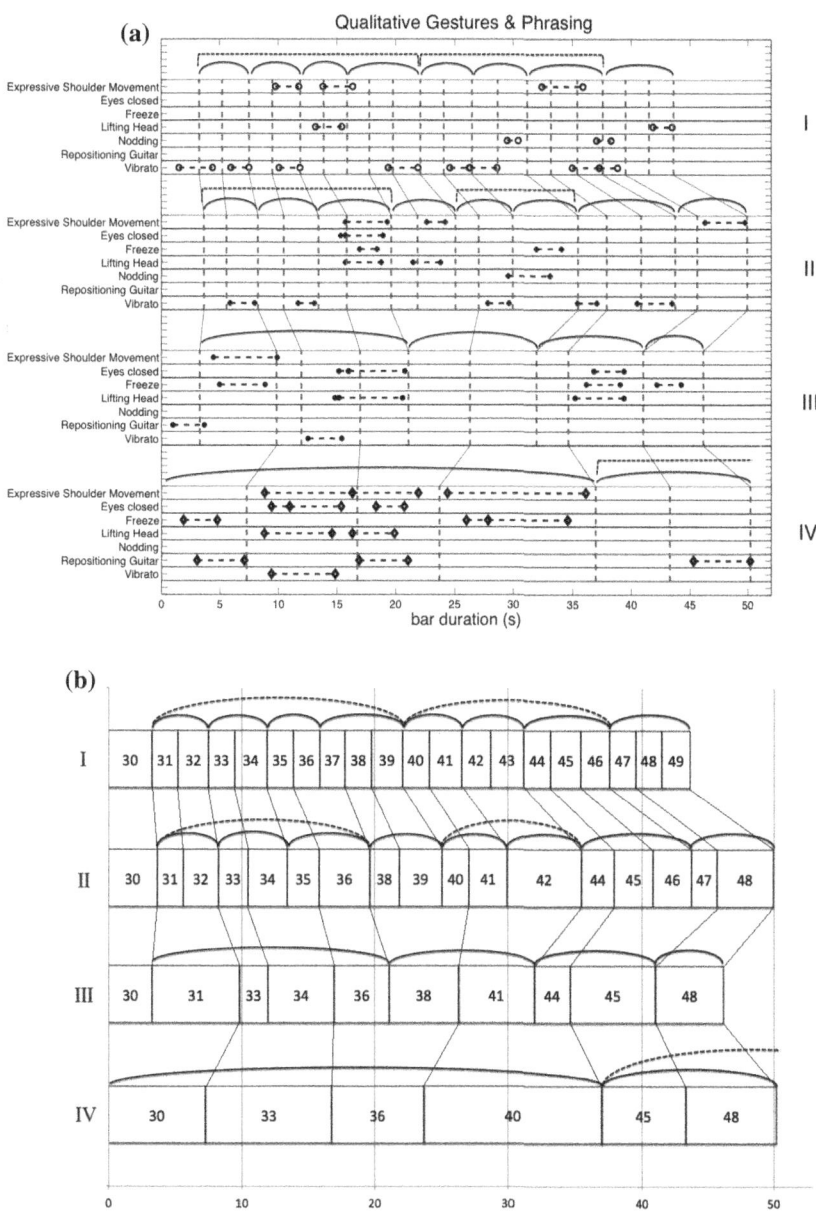

Fig. 9. (a) Perceived phrasing in bars 31–49 for each run-through with the duration of each bar. (b) Perceived phrasing in bars 31–49 for each run-through with the duration of each bar and a list of some annotated gestures.

patterns are consistent between the rounds. Notably, bar 36 is always shaped by a lifting of the head and, apart from in the first round, also with the eyes shut. The entire section is characterized by the code "expressive shoulder movements", especially in the section between bars 34 and 36, but these movements seem to be particular for the material at large, being connected to the shaping of phrases stretching over two or three bars. They occur frequently in the first two run-throughs when the material is largely continuous. Of more importance here is the introduction of new gesture material starting in the second round. In bars 37 and 43 we find the new code "freeze", which denotes a relative stillness and marks the first silent bars. The new pacing of the music is immediately reflected in the performer's choreography of movement. Interestingly, when the bars in the score become more cut out, the expressive shoulder movements are now, instead, aligned either with the "freeze" or the "lifting head" codes. Hence, the new shape of the music that emerges - both the shaping of the music in long lines and the later fragments between long silences - are clearly projected and connected through body movement.

The musical structure in terms of perceived phrasing is also reflected in the QoM pattern (Fig. 10). Consider bar 30–36 in the 2nd and 3rd run-through. In both cases these bars are connected in one big phrase, and despite the loss of musical material in the 3rd run-through, the movement pattern looks very similar. Also, the super phrase in bar

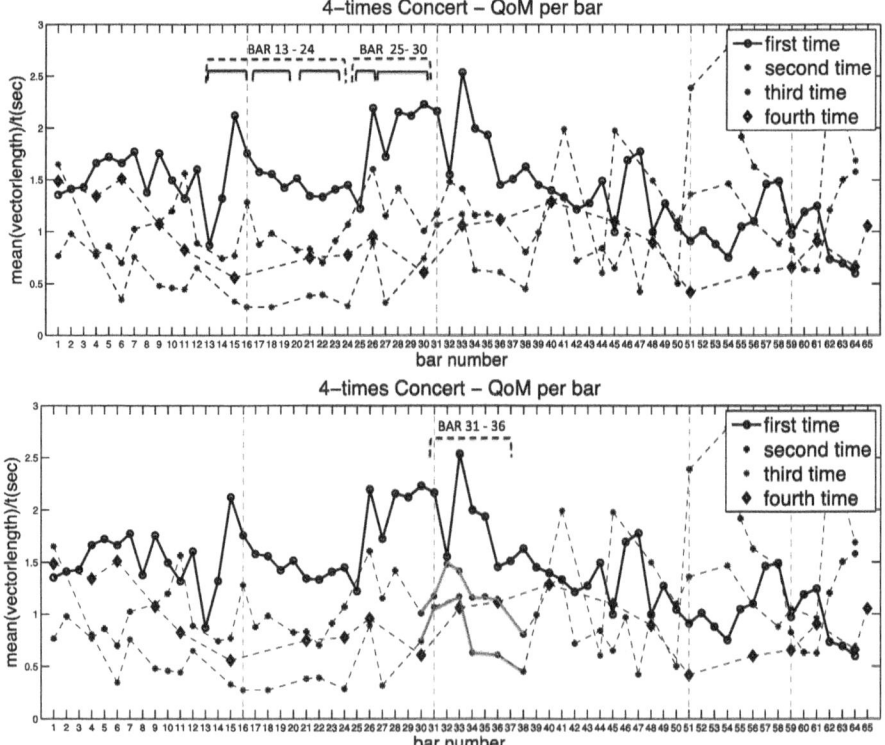

Fig. 10. QoM and perceived phrasing of the second and third run-through for bar 30–36 (top) and of the first run-through for bar 13–24 and bar 25–30.

13–24 and bar 25–30 in the first run-through show a similar profile, starting with a low QoM, and then a sudden increase. Remarkable as well: the 1st bar in the 1st and 2nd run-through belong to a super phrase, while in the later run-throughs, it stands on its own. When being the starting point of a super-phrase, there is a relatively low QoM, when standing alone, the QoM is relatively high.

Consolidation. To consolidate this mixed approach, the conclusions that were drawn from the different layers of analysis were discussed with the whole team. This last of the 'top-down' methods was necessary to verify the detected targets and to fully understand the observations made. The comparison of the timing in the different sections of the piece showed that there is a clear change between the second and the third run-through in the second section, which was clearly shorter. We can explain this by its musical content, as it consists of arpeggiated harmonics. The resonance of these tones is shorter than that of the chords, aggregates and fully-stopped tones used in the other sections. This forces the performer to compress the gaps, in order not to create excessively long silences.

Considering the musical targets, the viewpoint of the performer is fundamental. In the version discussed here, the reason bars like bar 15 and 59 are played in all the four run-throughs is because the performer deliberately chooses to do so, as they are of musical importance for the performer to structure the piece. Bars 26–28 by contrast seemed to be a questionable target. The performer reported that bar 26 and 28 are technically difficult bars with some artificial harmonics that demand rapid movements in both hands. The QoM does not indicate an expressive target here, but rather informs us of technical actions. When verifying this with the video recording, the increasing velocity in shoulder and wrist were caused mostly by the artificial harmonics to be played. Bar 30–33 also implies some technical difficulties, as the big shift in position on the fingerboard demands more physical action. The movements and bodily gestures are not unlike those of the way the musical shapes are disposed over the fret board and hence also in the trajectory of the left hand, but this contrasts with the general decrease in QoM during bars 41–51, where there are a lot of position shifts too.

5 Discussion and Conclusions

Establishing a Multimodal Framework for Analysis. The methodology developed in this paper provides a framework for the multimodal analysis of music performance. The bottom-up approach consisted of a timing analysis at different structural levels and an analysis of movement-data using low-level descriptors as QoM, velocity and acceleration. These descriptors are related to more high-level features as movement intensity and energy, but don't relate immediately to semantic descriptors or the performers' intentions. This might be considered as an important gap, as we often interact with and understand music at this level [4]. Therefore, the coding and annotations from the stimulated recall sessions and the perceived phrasing were added as a top-down approach. Next, the different analytical layers were compared and finally, the observations made were evaluated, which is crucial to get a reliable and meaningful interpretation of the data (Fig. 11).

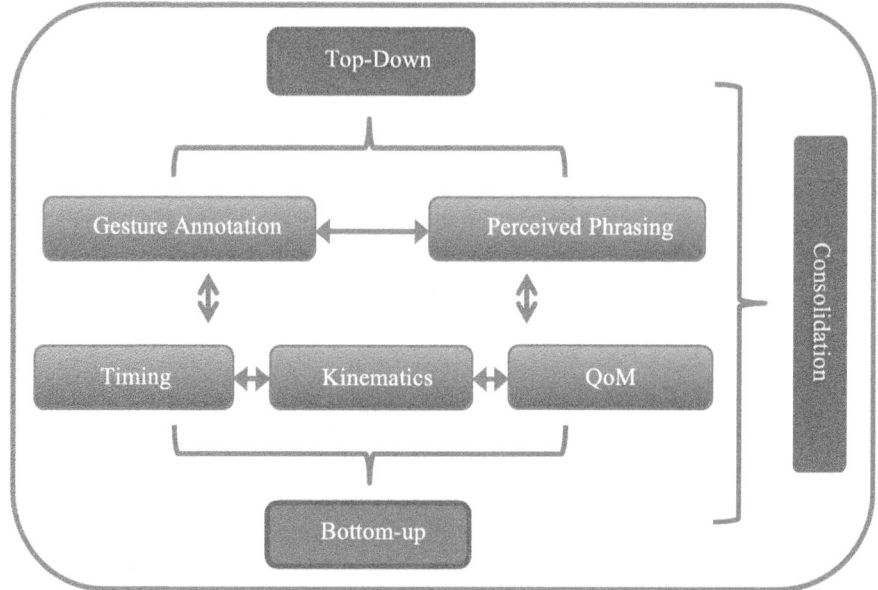

Fig. 11. Summary of analysis framework

During the process of analysis, some important observations were made that highlight the importance of a multimodal analysis when dealing with music performance. First of all, the findings from the analysis at different layers can reinforce each other. The compression of musical time that was observed in the different sections of the piece was nicely reflected by the changing QoM of the performer's body and the perceived phrasing, while the distribution of musical gestures along the piece reflected the change in musical material throughout the 4 repetitions of the piece. The mutual comparison of QoM, velocity and acceleration data with the annotated gestures on its turn, allowed identifying some important musical targets. The perceived phrasing also appeared to be a useful feature in the comparison of different modalities (timing, gestures, QoM) and highlights the importance of phrasing as a strategy of structuring the music by means of chunking and co-articulation for both performer and listener.

On the other hand, the multiple layers sometimes appeared to be contradictory. In some cases, the general body movement (QoM) showed a different behavior than the more detailed analysis of wrist and shoulder movements (e.g. bars 15–16 and 58–59). This means that different body parts are not engaged in the same way during performance, which is consistent with previous findings on violin/viola performances [24]. Also, the annotated gestures did not always reflect the change in QoM, for example an increase in QoM coinciding with annotated 'minimal movement'.

In the end, the viewpoint of the performer and composer appeared to be crucial for the interpretation of the analysis, e.g. some possible musical targets were discarded, as they were mere technical difficulties in the piece than real expressive targets. The collaboration between composer, performer and musicologists allows for the development of a methodology for performance analysis that helps interpreting the multiple data-streams, involving the expressive intentions that eventually lead to musical creativity and expressivity.

Future Work. The framework established here offers a valuable instrument for future analysis. Three other performances of the piece were recorded using the same set-up. Observations over the different performances could give additional information on how the musician applies body movements to structure and shape the performance and to communicate his intentions and the musical structure that emerge from the deconstruction of the piece to the audience. Moreover, a more detailed analysis of the expressive intentions of the performer as emerging from the score, the timing and characterization of gestures and performance cues at the note instead of the bar-level, together with a more thorough comparison of the different levels of analysis could provide a richer information and a better understanding of what we perceive as musical expressivity. If gestures are consistently related to certain materials one might be able to trace an 'expressive musical structure' from the mapping of the different layers of analysis.

This is also reflective of Lachenmann's idea that composition is a creative process of building an 'instrument', together with the performer, an idea that was also postulated by Clarke et al. [11]. The choreographic aspects of performance and the idea that bodily gestures *make* the music, is an idea worth to explore in the future. It would be wrong to think that the performer's movements are simply the result of emergent processes of embodiment, simply reflecting the music: in performance, the deliberate body strategies of the musician bear an explicitly choreographic aspect. On the one hand, these bodily gestures seem to be liberated from the music, but on the other hand, the music will get increasingly embodied. The musical performance is a result of the interplay between deliberate choices and intentions and spontaneous and unconscious behavior, and this is where the perspective of the performer is of key importance. In developing a theory on musical expression, the intentions of the performer, and hence it's subjectivity, are part of a crucial body of knowledge that is important in understanding the final realization and enactment of a performance. This seems rather trivial or obvious, but it is an aspect of performance that is often neglected or forgotten in research analysis, the more because this subjectivity is difficult to describe and access.

From this study, it is clear that the collaboration between musicians, performers and scholars should be encouraged in order to establish a corpus of studies that access expressive music performance from a multimodal perspective. The intriguing role gestures play in the shaping of a musical performance, and the interplay between musical timing, movement, expression and musical meaning is a rich field that can be explored and accessed in detail with the multimodal perspective established in this paper.

Acknowledgements. This study was partially realized under the FWO-project "Foundations of expressive timing control in music". Special thanks to Ivan Schepers, who helped developing the pressures sensors and mo-cap markers and Frank Desmet, who assisted in the analysis of the pressure sensors.

References

1. Godøy, R.I., Leman, M. (eds.): Musical Gestures: Sound, Movement, and Meaning. Routledge, New York (2010)
2. Windsor, W.L.: An ecological approach to semiotics. J. Theor. Soc. Behav. **34**, 179–198 (2004)
3. Clarke, E.: Ways of Listening: An Ecological Approach to the Perception of Musical Meaning. Oxford University Press, Oxford (2005)
4. Leman, M.: Embodied Music Cognition and Mediation Technology. MIT Press, Cambridge (2007)
5. Maes, P.-J., Palmer, C., Leman, M., Wanderley, M.M.: Action-based effects on music perception. Front. Psychol. **4**, 1008 (2014)
6. Davidson, J.W.: Qualitative insights into the use of expressive body movement in solo piano performance: a case study approach. Psychol. Music **35**, 381–401 (2007)
7. Wanderley, M.M., Vines, B., Middleton, W.N., McKay, C., Hatch, W.: The musical significance of clarinetists' ancillary gestures: an exploration of the field. J. New Music Res. **34**, 97–113 (2005)
8. Gritten, A., King, E.: Music and Gesture. Ashgate, Hampshire (2006)
9. Davidson, J.W.: Bodily communication in musical performance. In: Miell, D., Macdonald, R., Hargreaves, D.J. (eds.) Musical Communication, pp. 215–228. Oxford University Press, New York (2005)
10. Godøy, R.I.: Reflections on chunking in music. In: Schneider, A. (ed.) Systematic and Comparative Musicology: Concepts, Methods, Findings, pp. 117–132. Peter Lang, Frankfurt am Main (2008)
11. Clarke, E., Doffman, M., Timmers, R.: Creativity, collaboration and development in Jeremy Thurlow's *Ouija* for Peter Sheppard Skaerved. J. Roy. Music. Assoc. **141**, 113–165 (2016)
12. Desmet, F., Nijs, L., Demey, M., Lesaffre, M., Martens, J.-P., Leman, M.: Assessing a clarinet player's performer gestures in relation to locally intended musical targets. J. New Music Res. **41**(1), 31–48 (2012)
13. Godøy, R.I., Jensenius, A., Voldsund, A., et al.: Classifying music-related actions. In: Proceedings of the ICMPC-ESCOM 2012 Joint Conference: 12th Biennial International Conference for Music Perception and Cognition, 8th Triennial Conference of the European Society for the Cognitive Sciences of Music, pp. 352–357 (2012)
14. Thompson, M.R., Luck, G.: Exploring relationships between pianists' body movements, their expressive intentions, and structural elements of music. Music Sci. **16**(1), 19–40 (2012)
15. Fabian, D., Timmers, R., Schubert, E. (eds.): Expressiveness in Music Performance: Empirical Approaches Across Styles and Cultures. Oxford University Press, Oxford (2014)
16. Cycling '74: Max/MSP [Computer program] (2005). https://cycling74.com/products/max/
17. Troillard, C.: OSCulator [Computer program] (2012). http://www.osculator.net
18. Boersma, P., Weenink, D.: Praat: Doing Phonetics by Computer [Computer program] (2013)
19. Bloom, B.S.: Thought-processes in lectures and discussions. J. Gen. Edu. **7**, 161 (1953)
20. Jensenius, A.R., Wanderley, M.M., Godøy, R.I., Leman, M.: Musical gestures: concepts and methods in research. In: Godøy, R.I., Leman, M. (eds.) Musical Gestures: Sound, Movement, and Meaning, pp. 12–35. Routledge, New York (2010)
21. ResearchWare: HyperRESEARCH: Cross-Platform for Qualitative Analysis. [Computer program] (2015). http://www.researchware.com/products/hyperresearch.html
22. Burger, B., Toiviainen, P.: MoCap toolbox: a Matlab toolbox for computational analysis of movement data. In: Bresin, R. (ed.) Proceedings of the 10th Sound and Music Computing Conference Stockholm. KTH Royal Institute of Technology, Sweden (2013)

23. Dempster, W.T., Gaughran, G.R.L.: Properties of body segments based on size and weight. Am. J. Anat. **120**(1), 33–54 (1967)
24. Visi, F., Coorevits, E., Miranda, E., Leman, M.: Effects of different bow stroke styles on body movements of a viola player: an exploratory study. In: Proceedings of The joint ICMC|SMC|2014 Conference, Athens, Greece (2014)

3CMS: An Interactive Decision System for Live Performance

Rodrigo Schramm[1(✉)], Helena de Souza Nunes[1], Leonardo de Assis Nunes[2], Federico Visi[3], and Eduardo R. Miranda[3]

[1] Universidade Federal do Rio Grande do Sul, Porto Alegre, Brazil
{rodrigos,helena}@caef.ufrgs.br
[2] Universidade Federal da Bahia, Salvador, Brazil
leonardo.nunes@ufba.br
[3] Plymouth University, Plymouth, UK
{federico.visi,eduardo.miranda}@plymouth.ac.uk

Abstract. A machine system is designed to analyze the musical aspects during the live performance, allowing an interactive and dynamic flow of new expressions and also opening new compositional forms and multimodal methods. The focus of this approach is to measure the expressiveness from distinct characters during the performance of the musical piece while decisions are made by the machine. This multimodal approach is implemented in the musical piece *Três Microcanções de Câmara – Essência Pierrot, Atitude Arlequim, (In)Decisão Colombina* (3CMS), where audio features and body motion are used by the algorithm to choose a particular musical ending.

Keywords: Multimodal system · Machine decision · Micro song

1 Introduction

This work is situated in the vast interdisciplinary research context of expressiveness in music. The main purpose of this text is to explain the compositional process of the *Três Microcanções de Câmara – Essência Pierrot, Atitude Arlequim, (In)Decisão Colombina* (Three Chamber Micro Songs – Pierrot Essence, Harlequin Attitude, and Columbine [In]Decision, in this text abbreviated as 3CMS), which combines machine learning, pattern recognition, and musical production. From the technological point of view of this subject, there are several instances of analysis aided by computational algorithms as well as examples of artistic practice based on academic research. Camurri and colleagues carried out extensive research on using multimodal data for expressive content analysis and interactive implementations [4], with the particular focus on technologies and methods for the analysis of expressiveness in music and interactive performances involving body movement [3]. In terms of composition, an open-ended structure where multiple endings are selected during the performance through live EEG data processing was used by Miranda and Eaton [7]. Brain Computer Interfacing is also adopted for a variety of different tasks related to expressivity, such as detecting affective states and controlling electronic musical instruments [14]. Classification algorithms and machine learning have also been employed to interpret movement trajectories in musical performance [5], and several automated computer systems for expressive music performance have been developed over the past three decades [13]. In addition, movement and gestures are often taken into consideration in the analysis of musicians' expressivity [10] and the performer's movements are increasingly regarded as an expressive feature intertwined with other musical elements in the score [20].

From the artistic and musical point of view, the 3CMS is a musical piece for singer, piano, and computer, composed following the compositional method *Microcanções* CDG [17]. This work is a kind of Brazilian chamber song [2], containing many situations of love tensions in its narrative line. They are represented by a romance triangle among *Pierrot - Harlequin - Columbine*, in a contemporary perspective of *Commedia dell'Arte* [19]. These aspects inspired a conceptual map used in the developing process of the musical composition. The Brazilian modernist poem *Máscaras* [6] was an inspiration for the words and linguistic expressions, which were organized in the conceptual map, providing a potential material for a new poetic text. The expressive reading of this new and poetic text was analyzed by the PRAAT software tool [1], and supported by the concept of *Melodias Embrionárias* [12], conducting to the composition of the rhythmic and melodic structures of the song. These aspects also supplied the choreography and character expressiveness. All these elements are formalized in minimal songs, which contain a dense amount of information and rich performance possibilities. The piece 3CMS arises from the work of the composers. However, the interpreters can also improvise and create. The story line in this composition is presented in a specific form: (1) Introduction, which presents the three characters; (2) Three micromovements, where each of these characters are put in evidence, indicating their particular way to reach their love; and (3) Coda, where finally their fates are sealed. The characters' destiny is not always the same because it depends on their interrelationship during the musical performance. The machine will indicate the one who the expressiveness is the closest to the expected performance result, and then a real-time algorithm will place the final Coda to the interpreters. The Coda contains the music score from one of the three possible denouements based on the romantic relationship among the characters. The machine choice is presented live to the performers, on the last page of the score displayed on a screen.

Each particular musical ending is a consequence of the expressiveness performance of each character along the whole storyline. In this case, it is a consequence of the expressive evolution of the performance on stage, compared with a pre-established expressive pattern. Expressivity in performance is a central concept in this work. In the 3CMS approach, the interpreter is invited to extend the voice and gesture characteristics of *Pierrot*, *Harlequin* and *Columbine*, during the rehearsals. Such individual identities are learned by the machine as expressive patterns. On stage, the machine analyses these patterns, indicating the most expressive character as the one which the live performance part is the closest to the respective trained model. This work is a preliminary study which aims to establish a basis for future studies on expressivity analysis from live performances. Next, Sect. 2 presents the 3CMS music score, followed by the respective musical analysis in Sect. 3. Section 4 describes the proposed algorithm, Sect. 5 shows preliminary results and final considerations are drawn in Sect. 6.

2 Music Score

© Três Microcanções de Câmara (Introdução) - Vs2
Repertório CDG 2015
Reprodução autorizada mediante referência à fonte.

3CMS: An Interactive Decision System for Live Performance

I - Essência Pierrot

© Três Microcanções de Câmara (Essência Pierrot) - Vs2
Repertório CDG 2015
Reprodução autorizada mediante referência à fonte.

II - Atitude Arlequim

III- (In)Decisão Colombina

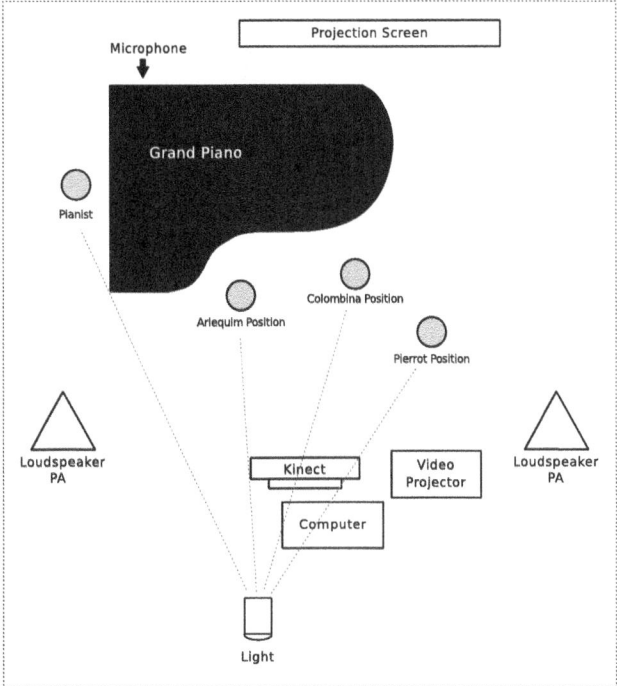

Fig. 1. Stage plot with the technological requirements for a live performance.

Detailed description of the technical requirements

Playback machine PC, including two channel audio system.
Kinect sensor (motion capture)
Public address audio system (stereo loudspeakers)
Video projector
Grand piano
One condenser microphone
One wireless headset microphone

3 Musical Analysis of the 3CMS Piece

The piece is inspired by the known plot of *Commedia dell'Arte*, as presented in the work of Del Picchia [6] and analyzed by Vendramini [19]. This adaptation of the classic love triangle to the contemporary scene is organized into five parts. In the Introduction are presented the *Leitmotiven* of each character: Pierrot (bar 2 and 3), Harlequin (bar 4) and Columbine (bar 6 and 7), all followed by fermatas. As indicated in the score, the pianist must play from memory, always turning his head and looking to the stage position, where the respective character is supposed to appear. Figure 1 shows the expected characters' places on the stage. The pianist's gesture accompanied by unmeasured silence serves to organize the listener's perception and enjoyment by giving him/her time to gain spatial and dramatic insight regarding the story that will unfold from there. This Introduction is then followed by three Micromovements, each of them referring to one of the three famous characters, and a Coda with three alternative endings. The main features of each character and the different moments of the story are translated into musical language through corresponding rhythmic-melodic, harmonic elaboration, tempo, dynamics and texture. The singer's performance includes different body posture and typical gestures for each character, as well as exchanging costumes and places on stage.

Pierrot is the focus of the first micromovement entitled *Essência Pierrot* (Pierrot Essence). He is a shy and dreamy character, whose inner potential has always been repressed. Columbine loves him because he is sweet; but so much sweetness also makes her life dull. He wears white because the color represents a completeness closed in itself: it is a color containing the sum of all light colors, not yet dispersed into a rainbow. This is the metaphor for his inability to formulate an appropriate solution for his conflict and to declare his love to Columbine. In *Essência Pierrot*, the *Leitmotiv* is written in the B key, providing fixed and stable harmonic support to the singer. Yes, internally, Pierrot is consistent; externally he appears simple and obvious. His melodic line, as the other characters', was developed from vocal inflections generated through expressive text declamations. He sings, in fact, justifying the "remaining intent" (bar 4); his voice is transformed into speech only at the end, when he recognizes his "tolerated pain" (bar 12). But the recurrence of triplets, in binary measure of simple time signature, in both voice and piano, brings the idea of ambiguity – another characteristic of his character. In the accompaniment, the triplets are revealed only when there are pauses in voice, indicating the alternation between submission and freedom, between desire and repression, also intrinsic to his character. In *Essência Pierrot*, there is a melancholic atmosphere of suffering, restraint and discretion marked by progress in quarter note 54 BPM. This also appears in the signal intensity that varies from p to mf. The tonal fields are determined by the chords: E/B and $F\sharp^7$ (bars 1 to 3; bars 12 to 15); $F\sharp^9/C\sharp$, $B^{maj7(add6)}/D\sharp$ (bar 6); $C\sharp^{7(omit3)}$, Bm^7, E^7/B (bar 7); $E^{maj7(9)}$, $F\sharp^9$ (bar 8); $G\sharp^{13}$, $A\sharp^{b5(b9)}$ (bar 9); $C\sharp m^9$, $D\sharp m^9$, $E^{maj7(9)}$, $F\sharp^9$ (bar 11); $B^{maj7(add6)}/D\sharp$ (bar 15). Such chords, though expanded, remain gravitating around an easily identifiable tonal center. However, when partially arpeggiated, they provide the listener only sparse fragments of the sonorities of the chords. They paint an almost impressionistic and inebriating atmosphere.

In contrast, Harlequin is the self-confident and bold character who takes initiative. He wears an attractive and colorful costume, just as extravagant as himself. He can also be aggressive and superficial. Columbine loves him because his exuberance; but she also fears him, since his attractive attitudes are the same that scare her. Based on this character, *Atitude Arlequim* (Harlequin Attitude) is the fastest micromovement of the work, starting with an acrobatic jump and a reverence gesture towards the public (bar 1). The progress eighth 150 BPM demonstrates his agility. He expresses himself mainly through body language, portraying his outgoing, bold and eccentric personality in choreographic movements. The vocal content is quite unstable, as his score explores alternating features of the spoken voice, sometimes simply surprising the listener ("scared ?! [bar 2]"); "Love Harlequin ?!" [bar 6]; and "thrill" [bar 8]). Through the combination of *mf* and *fff* intensities with the constant variation of the time signature (3/8, 6/8, 4/4, 2/4, 6/8, 3/4), the music score indicates, again, the chameleonic personality of Harlequin. In contrast to the previous micromovement, where a mild sonority represents the subtlety of Pierrot, *Atitude Arlequim* shows a chromatic and predominantly chordal harmony, alluding to the multicolored and most remarkable rags of his garments. There is no fixed tonal center; therefore, the different pitches of sound are organized under a post-tonal nature [18] using predominantly three scales for voice and piano: hexatonic (bar 1 and 8), two pentatonic whole tone (bar 6) and a mixed scale between diatonic B and mixolydian mode in B (bar 7 and 8). The used chords are: arpeggiated polychord F e F♯ (bars 1 and 8); Bb/Ab, F/E, $G^{(add6)}$/F, C^{maj7}/E, E/D (bars 3 and 9); $A^{(add6)}$ (bar 4), A♯m/G♯, E♯$^{\varnothing}$, $E^{6(♯4)}$, D♯$m^{maj7(♯4)}$ (bar 5); F♯^{9}, $B^{(add6)}$, G♯m^{11}, $E^{(add6)}$ (bar 7); $A^{(add9)}$ (bar 8); $Am^{(add9)}$/G, $Bb^{maj7(9)}$/F, $E^{(addb9)}$ (bar 10); $B^{b5(♯9/11)}$ (bar 11). The integration between singer and pianist seeks to symbolize Harlequin's either self-confident, happy or mocking laughter. They appear in his choreography, but are silent. His laughter sounds only on the piano: a sequence of chords that are played just after his surprising appearance (bar 3), setting the *Leitmotiv* of the character.

Columbine is a beautiful, capricious and vain character who now wants Pierrot, then wants Harlequin. Being sincere, the whole time, she desires both. Her life, then, has little meaning in itself. She seems to be the big star, but she is in fact fragile and insecure; she exists only in the pivot status of a love triangle whose dissolution would be a great risk for her. Representing her interior emptiness, *(In)Decisão Colombina* (Columbine [In]Decision) brings up the sound of a music box (bar 1 to 5), reproduced by medium-high register notes on the piano. This same gesture is composed of repetitions of the pentatonic scale of F♯ on the right hand; and a twelve-tone scale (not serial) as opposed left hand. Definitely, Columbine could be everything; but she is almost nothing. In the voice line, the same pentatonic scale motif from the piano is played in bar 5; a scale in the lydian mode in A is recited in the next bar (bar 6); after that, a scale in the aeolian mode D is sung (bar 7); and finally, a scale in the lydian mode B completes the melodic voice content of this third micromovement (bar 9 to 12). These melodic tours represent the fickle personality of Columbine. The rhythm of the micromovement also follows these inconsistencies. The changes in time signatures and motion, along with the figurations representing the *Leitmotiven* of the other characters, define her scenic appearance, now opting for one of them (6/8, bar 8 and 9), then for the other one (2/4, bar 10 to 12), or even none of them (bar 13). Initially, her scene brings the gestural expressions associated with Harlequin as Columbine sings "Your kiss is so hot" in *ritardando* followed by his *Leitmotiv* (bar 7 and 8). The harmonic identity gesture of Harlequin's laughter can be heard one octave higher, as a strident metaphor of a possible identification of Columbine with Harlequin. But she withdraws, frightened (bar 9). Then, Columbine, with a vague look, moves to Pierrot's stage position singing with a melancholic voice "The missing one makes me dream" - in an obvious expression of disappointment with Pierrot's shyness, accompanied by the piano playing his *Leitmotiv* (2/4, bar 10 to 12). Finally, defeated, she seems to give up: "Ah!" (bar 13). But this is when the machine assessment seals the fate of the characters, giving the story a temporarily definite end.

In the final page of the song, following the third micromovement, the three possible endings are exposed in the form of a Coda chosen by the algorithm. Each of these three endings hides, musically, the impossibility of a happy outcome. If the algorithm chooses ending number 1, the motif of Columbine is presented in agogic *molto rallentando*, indicating that the spring motor of the music box is loosing tension (bar 14 to 17). In other words, if Columbine predominated in the performance, her *Leitmotiv* will be repeated. It might seem as if her character won; however, she is alone. Neither Pierrot nor Harlequin were strong enough to conquer her choice; thus, loneliness imposes itself. Alone, Columbine loses purpose - which is exactly the need to decide between one of the two. If the machine leads to ending number 2, the Pierrot theme emerges, punctuated by the *Leitmotiv* of Columbine. This may seem as if the love between them won. However, in this case, the piano part is decomposed referring to a Pierrot that, despite having been the strongest during the performance, disappoints after being chosen. In this second possible ending, part of Columbine's theme in pentatonic scale - A♯, F♯, G♯, D♯, G♯ and F♯ - is transposed one whole tone lower, on the left hand of the piano (second half of bar 15). This transposition refers to the decay of the narrated story, in other words, to having chosen the most comfortable outcome. Finally, ending number 3 mixes Columbine's and Harlequin's themes representing that she has chosen him. In the higher notes played by the piano (bar 16), a transposition (a tritone below - E, C, D, A, D and C) of part of the music box melody in pentatonic blends with the harmonic gesture of Harlequin laughter. This is the sarcastic evidence of a tragic destiny.

There are three possible endings to the piece, each of them corresponding to the prevailing expressive power of one of the three characters throughout that particular performance. Codas are identified by the repetition of the corresponding *Leitmotiven*, as chosen by the algorithm, offering three different versions of the same story. Thus, this is an open work model where the performance itself, at the very moment it happens, provides relevant information regarding the decision on how the story is going to end. The ending is decided by the machine, based on the comparison between previous patterns and subsequent performances of the piece. In this model, the natural flow of events is modified according to the correspondence between the desired and the actual performance. In this context, using an algorithm is also an attempt to solve an insoluble conflict with mathematical and scientific logic. But, in fact, the love conflict represented by the three characters of *Commedia del' Arte* remains forever unsolved; after all, every possible outcome to every new particular story will always be unsatisfactory, unstable and incomplete. Columbine can not decide between Pierrot and

Harlequin because she wants both and dislikes the idea of having to pick one of them. However, both the paralyzed unconditionality of Pierrot and the exuberant braveness of Harlequin attract and repulses her at the same time. Paradoxically, the difference between them is precisely what ensures each of them their own sense and makes them an essential part of her. But the impossibility of having or not having them both leaves Columbine with three alternatives: choosing Pierrot and accepting being repeatedly disappointed and loosing her own youthful grace; choosing Harlequin and accepting a life in anguish oscillating between excitement and startle; or taking the choice to stay alone, until completely losing sense and willingness to live. All of the three endings are musically represented in the three possible Codas, each of them recovering the *Leitmotiv* of the corresponding character. The Pierrot Coda ends with an ethereal arpeggio; the Harlequin Coda, with a sudden sound movement; and the Columbine Coda resembles a fading music box. These possible solutions alleviate the intrinsic anguish of the characters; however, only for that particular narrative. In a new narrative, with a new performance, the outcome can be different. Thus, the temporarily definitive ending is also a definitely temporary ending.

4 Computing the Character Expressiveness

The proposed machine system is designed to analyze the musical aspects of the 3CMS during the live performance, allowing an interactive and dynamic flow of new expressions and also opening new compositional forms and multimodal methods. The focus of this approach is to measure the expressiveness from distinct characters during the performance of a musical piece. At the end, a machine decision is made by comparing the amount of expressiveness related to each of the possible characters. It is worth noting that in this work the concept of expressiveness arises from the performer's searches for the best way to convey his/her artistic ideas. This process works as an exploratory practice that happens repeatedly through several rehearsal sessions. The proposed approach is based on the assumption that the repeatedly rehearsal sessions converge to the model desired by the performer. A performance model (template) is learned by the machine during these rehearsals. After, on the live performance, the machine can evaluate the parts which are related to the each character, choosing the most expressive character as the one which is the closest to the learned model. Since the learned model is the reference for the performance, the character chosen by the machine (winner) will be also the most expressive.

To measure how close is the live performance from the desired expressiveness, the system combines several features captured from the musicians, dancers and actors, during the live performance on the stage. Each character is linked to time intervals in the piece, where these features will be extracted. These time intervals are represented by B^ω, where $\omega \in \{p, h, c\}$ stands for the characters Pierrot, Harlequin, and Columbine, respectively. Each interval B^ω is represented by a notation scheme on a particular staff in the music score, allowing the composer to experiment different combinations along the musical performance. The computer algorithm has its own staff (see music score in Sect. 2), where the temporal windows of evaluation are placed as musical notes. Each note sequence at each line/space in the "Machine" staff (the note pitch) is a time interval connected to a character ω.

Features are extracted from audio and video signals by the use of a set of signal processing techniques, and the comparison between the live performance and the trained model (desired expressiveness) is done jointly with a dynamic time warping algorithm (DTW). The DTW algorithm searches for the best alignment between the two feature sequences (model and live performances) that minimizes a cumulative cost. This cumulative cost is computed by evaluating a local cost function for each possible pair of features taking samples from each sequence. In this approach we implemented local cost functions that combine audio and motion features. Figure 2 illustrates the set of features implemented in this work:

1. CENS – Chroma Energy Normalized Statistics [16]: represents a condensed version of the pitch classes which are present in the audio signal. This chroma-based audio representation maps the amount of energy related to each musical note, projecting them into one octave. The chroma based features are less sensitive to timbre variation and has been used successfully in many problems of music synchronization [8] and audio matching [15]. The CENS estimates are used to compare how close is the performance of the music notes (piano and voice) to the trained model.
2. c^{3D} – 3D Point Cloud Distance: measures the distance between two body skeletons (3D point cloud) [16]. In our approach, all skeleton joints are translated accordingly to the body center (hip center), which turns the distance measure invariant to translations on the stage. Also, the distance measure is constrained to be invariant only to small rotations, so that the camera position should not affect significantly the results. This measure as well as the next two feature types (CI and QoM) are extracted using a motion capture device.

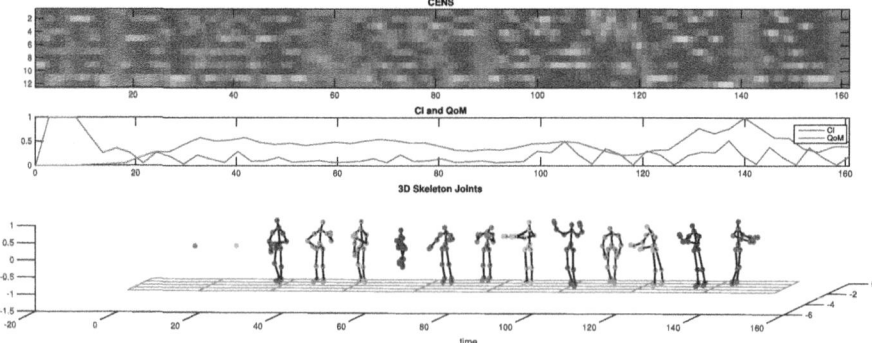

Fig. 2. An example of extracted features from the performance recording (Take 1).

3. CI – Contraction Index: quantifies how much is the contraction of the human body during the performance.
4. QoM – Quantity of Motion: measures the amount of body motion during the musical performance. Both CI and QoM measures have been widely used in multimodal embodied approaches to gesture mapping [21,22], including 3D expressive movements [9].

4.1 Learning the Character Expressiveness

The first step training our algorithm is the choice of the take that will be the reference for the expressive performance. This choice is made by the interpreter, which decides by his/her own audiovisual analysis the one that was closer to the desired performance. After, the take of reference is compared with the whole dataset, one by one, using the DTW algorithm with the above-mentioned local cost measures. In this approach, we decided to split the comparison into two distinct DTW estimates, one for audio and another for motion data, allowing the performer to experiment alternative configurations, varying the ratio between the audio and motion information.

The comparison between the sequence of reference and any other recording could be done straight with the DTW output distance. However, the boundary and step conditions of the DTW algorithm propagates accumulated costs that turns the final cost comparison unfeasible. Figure 3 illustrates this problem, showing the accumulated cost along the alignment path of the DTW algorithm between the reference recording and 3 other recording examples. Even when these performance examples are similar (according the interpreter opinion), the cost evolution has different levels at each character. For example, the takes number two and three (blue and green dotted lines) in Fig. 3a show a leap between the transitions among the characters Pierrot and Harlequin (around 62 seconds). These leaps happen because the performer is out of the stage (changing the costume) and the skeleton tracking introduces noise information. As a consequence, these localized errors in the cumulative cost curve have a high impact in the final and global DTW cost, causing an unfair comparison among the characters. Regardless the error propagation along the DTW path, we expect that the cost evolution of each character should follow a similar slope when the performance is similar to the reference model. Thus, instead the use of the global DTW cost, we propose a measure based on the robust linear fitting of the cumulative local cost curve, giving a more reliable similarity measure between the two sequences. Figure 3b and 3d show the fitting results (motion and audio data, respectively) for the Pierrot, Harlequin and Columbine.

Given the reference sequence and other input sequence for comparison, let D_a^ω and D_m^ω mean the DTW cumulative cost sequences related to audio and motion data, respectively. We compute the amount of character expressiveness by

$$\lambda(D_a^\omega, D_m^\omega) = \alpha C(D_a^\omega) + (1-\alpha)C(D_m^\omega) \tag{1}$$

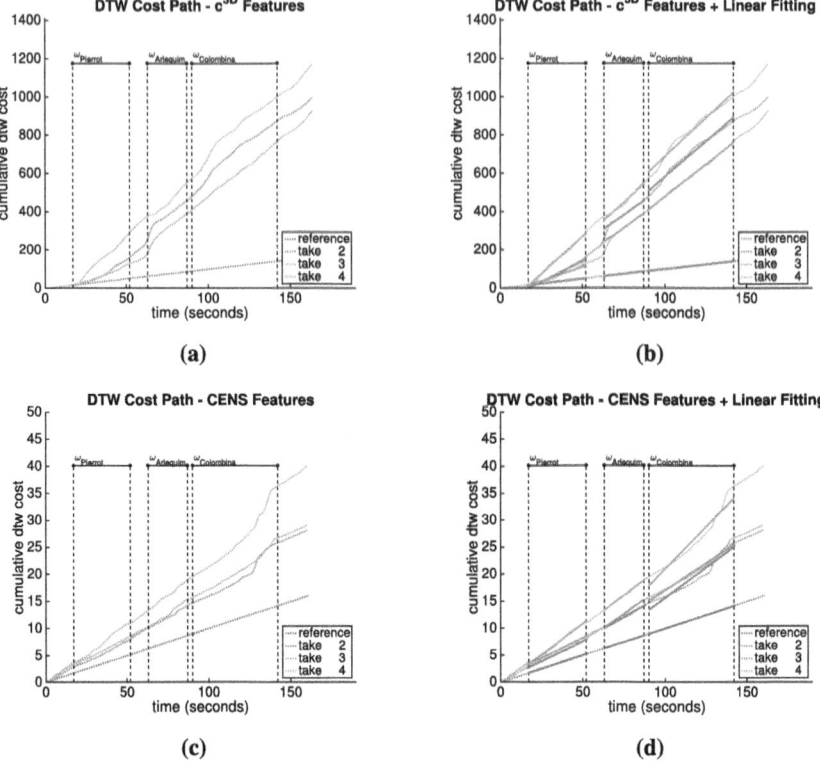

Fig. 3. (a) and (c) Show the cumulative cost of the DTW using c^{3D} and CENS features as local cost functions (dotted lines). (b) and (d) Illustrate the linear fitting (solid lines) achieved for each character. (Color figure online)

where

$$C(D^\omega) = R^2(D^\omega)\,e^{-\frac{\Phi(D^\omega)}{\mu_\Phi}} \quad (2)$$

is a function with exponential decay of the performance distance based on the linear fitting estimates:

$$\Phi(D^\omega) = 1 - \cos(\arctan(\theta(D^\omega))). \quad (3)$$

θ is the estimated tangent slope by a robust linear regression [11], and R^2 means the goodness of the fit, defined by

$$R^2(D^\omega) = 1 - \frac{\sum_{k=1}^{K}(d_k - \hat{d}_k)^2}{\sum_{k=1}^{K}(d_k - \overline{d})^2}, \quad (4)$$

where $\hat{d}_k$ is the predicted value with the linear fitting and $\overline{d}$ is the mean of the input costs values. μ_Φ is the average of Φ estimates related to the character ω, from all rehearsal recordings (training phase). Equation 3 estimates the angular slope distance between the reference and the evaluated cost sequences. The resultant distance measure is then mapped (Eq. 2) with an exponential decay, weighted by R^2 which penalizes the similarities in the case of bad fitting. Equation 1 combines the estimates from audio and motion, generating the final similarity measure. $\alpha \in [0,1]$ is a parameter that allows the performer to give the desired weight to each evaluated aspect (audio or motion).

4.2 Machine Decision

In previous section, it was described how the input feature sequences are mapped by the Eq. 1 into a real interval $[0,1]$. Values close to 1 indicate a high degree of similarity between the recorded performance and the reference model. In this approach, the machine decision is stated by choosing the character that has the higher similarity value among the all possibilities. This procedure allows the system to act as a state machine, changing the flow of musical execution or triggering new events. In the context of the 3CMS piece, there is only one decision which is made at the end of the third movement by:

$$mE = \operatorname*{argmax}_{\omega} \lambda(D_a^\omega, D_m^\omega), \tag{5}$$

with D_a^ω and D_m^ω estimated accordingly the time intervals specified in the music score.

5 Experiments

Several recordings from repeatedly rehearsals were captured using the technical requirements specified in Fig. 1. The audio and video (skeleton tracking) were captured using microphones and an RGB-D camera (Microsoft Kinect). Experiments were done to evaluate the proposed similarity measure (Eq. 1) regarding distinct local cost functions for the DTW sequence alignment. We did not verified if the machine decision is coherent with the interpreter and the audience opinions since it may be highly subjective. Instead, we did many comparisons of $\lambda(D_a^\omega, D_m^\omega)$ along several audiovisual recordings of the 3CMS piece. We used nine recordings of the rehearsal performances (the first eight takes are real attempts to reach the ideal model, and the take number 9 is a random performance). Figure 4 shows the pairwise DTW alignment between a reference take (1) and other takes (2, 3, 4, 5, 9). The DTW path is shown in red. An audiovisual analysis in these recordings validates the DTW alignments, that succeeded for all the proposed local cost functions (CENS, c^{3D}, CI, QoM, CI+QoM). Also, as expected, the alignment of the Take 9 (random performance) did not succeed well, confirming the discriminative power of the proposed local cost functions.

The feature combination was also evaluated regarding its influence in the final machine decision. c^{3D} feature had shown a great discriminative capability. This feature is very restrictive and can be used to make the system very rigorous, so that the performer is high penalized if he/she does not perform the gestures in

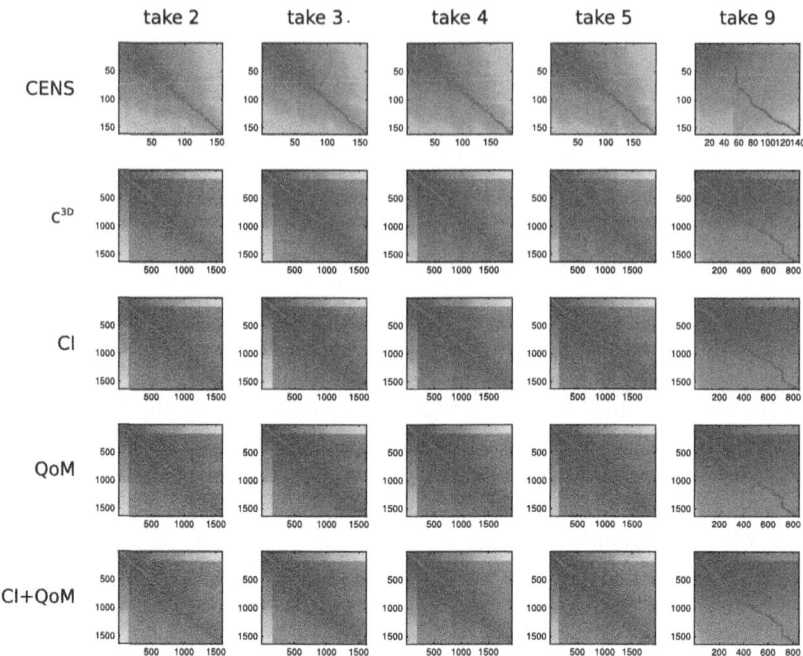

Fig. 4. DTW alignment of the performance recordings in comparison with Take 1. Takes in the range [2, 5] are recordings of rehearsals. Take 9 is a random performance. Each row represents a distinct local cost function.

the same way how he/she did during the rehearsals. We also investigate the CI and QoM features, which are alternative measures for less constraint movements, allowing the performer to have some degree of improvisation. Figure 5d shows that the QoM is not effective enough to distinguish outliers since the cumulative cost estimate of the Take 9 (random performance) falls inside the cluster of accumulated costs of valid performances recordings. CI feature appears to be more efficient than QoM, separating better the cumulative cost of the DTW. Figure 5f shows the Manhattan distance between the DTW warping paths on experiments using the c^{3D} feature as a reference for comparison with the features CI and QoM. Despite the bad discrimination power of the single QoM feature, the combination CI+QoM approximates better the DTW path of the c^{3D} feature. This indicates the possibility to replace the c^{3D} by the CI+QoM in the cases when is desired less constrained movements.

Table 1 shows the final machine decision for each take from our dataset regarding the proposed feature types in comparison with Take 1. Decisions are shown by the symbols "p", "h" and "c", which stand for the characters Pierrot, Harlequin and Columbine, respectively. Each character decision is presented with the respective similarity measure. In special, the last two rows of this table

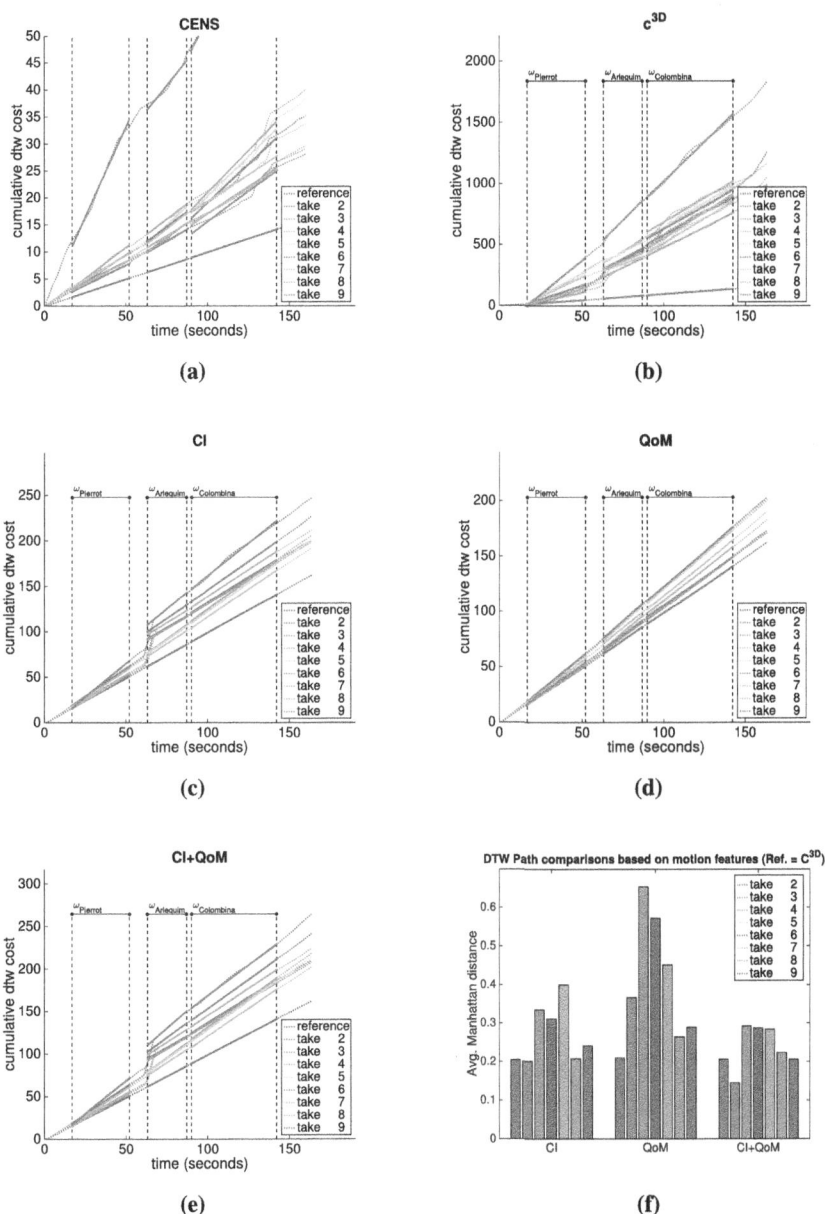

Fig. 5. (a) to (e) Comparisons of the cumulative cost of the DTW using distinct local cost functions (dotted lines). Linear fitting is represented by solid lines. (f) Comparisons of c^{3D} with CI and QoM through the Manhattan distance of the DTW path.

show very similar machine decisions, where there is only one difference on Take 4, corroborating to an alternative use of the CI+QoM in place of the c^{3D} feature.

Table 1. Machine decision based on individuals measures.

$\lambda(D_a^\omega, D_m^\omega)$	Feature type	Take 2	Take 3	Take 4	Take 5	Take 6	Take 7	Take 8	Take 9
$\alpha = 1.0$	CENS	h 0.94	h 0.93	h 0.63	h 0.77	h 0.76	h 0.83	h 0.92	p 0.04
$\alpha = 0.0$	c^{3D}	h 0.40	h 0.55	c 0.36	p 0.36	h 0.40	p 0.43	h 0.45	c 0.32
$\alpha = 0.0$	CI	h 0.88	h 0.88	h 0.35	h 0.36	p 0.38	p 0.54	h 0.84	c 0.07
$\alpha = 0.0$	QoM	h 0.91	h 0.98	p 0.17	p 0.32	c 0.14	p 0.47	h 0.77	c 0.96
$\alpha = 0.0$	CI+QoM	h 0.85	h 0.88	h 0.29	p 0.35	h 0.32	p 0.55	h 0.80	c 0.20
$\alpha = 0.5$	c^{3D}+CENS	h 0.40	h 0.55	c 0.36	p 0.36	h 0.40	p 0.43	h 0.45	c 0.32
$\alpha = 0.5$	CI + QoM + CENS	h 0.85	h 0.88	h 0.29	p 0.35	h 0.32	p 0.55	h 0.80	c 0.20

6 Conclusion

The musical elements of the piece 3CMS and the proposed approach for measuring the expressiveness of the performance are original contributions to the interdisciplinary field of computer music research.

The form of this musical composition includes an Introduction, three Micromovements, and a Coda. On each part, the same singer acts as one of the three characters: *Pierrot*, *Arlequim* or *Colombina*. The piece has also three possible endings, each one corresponding to a different character, according to his/her expressive power in the performance. The choice of the last part is not made directly by the performers on the stage, but it is a consequence of their live performance evaluated by an external machine. The proposed algorithm measures the degree of similarity between the trained patterns and the live performance. It is worth remembering that the expressive features of each character were recorded several times in order to build its individual pattern of expressiveness. During live performance, however, *Pierrot*, *Arlequim* or *Colombina* interpret their roles interacting with each other. External conditions have impact over all live performances. So, the interpreter of these three characters can approach or move away from the previously established patterns. This is an ideal artistic condition for the use of multimodal features and machine learning techniques. The described approach uses similarity measures based on CENS, c^{3D}, CI and QoM features. It was verified that all the recorded takes, which were deliberately close to the chosen reference, were effectively identified as similar by the algorithm; while the random performance was evaluated as largely distant from the desired pattern. Furthermore, the proposed similarity function has great discriminability power, which also allows the system to measure the variance of performances related to the same character. The set of analyses in our experiments also revealed that this approach can be configured to use two distinct combinations of audio and motion features. A more restrictive movement can be chosen with the features CENS+c^{3D}, which acts as a rigorous assessment system. Alternatively, a combination of CENS+CI+QoM can be used to give more freedom on the live performance, allowing some degree of improvisation.

In the future we plan to verify the coherence among the results obtained by the machine and human perception. This is also useful to further study the correlation between the audiovisual features and the notion of expressiveness.

References

1. Boersma, P., Weenink, D.: PRAAT: Doing Phonetics by Computer. Version 5.3.51. http://www.praat.org/
2. Borém, F., Cavazotti., A.: Entrevista com Luciana Monteiro de Castro, Mônica Pedrosa e Margarida Borghoff sobre o Projeto "Resgate da Canção Brasileira". In: Per Musi, no. 15, pp. 78–86, January 2007
3. Camurri, A., Volpe, G.: Multimodal analysis of expressive gesture in music performance. In: Solis, J., Ng, K. (eds.) Musical Robots and Interactive Multimodal Systems. Springer Tracts in Advanced Robotics, pp. 47–66. Springer, Heidelberg (2011)
4. Camurri, A., Volpe, G., De Poli, G., Leman, M.: Communicating expressiveness and affect in multimodal interactive systems. IEEE Multimedia **12**(1), 43–53 (2005)
5. Caramiaux, B., Wanderley, M.M., Bevilacqua, F.: Segmenting and parsing instrumentalists' gestures. J. New Music Res. **41**(1), 13–29 (2012)
6. Del Picchia, M.: Máscaras: o amor de Dulcinéia. Ediouro, Rio de Janeiro (1987)
7. Eaton, J., Miranda, E.: Real-time notation using brainwave control. In: Sound and Music Computing Conference 2013, Stockholm, Sweden (2013)
8. Ewert, S., Müller, M., Grosche, P.: High resolution audio synchronization using chroma onset features. In: Proceedings of IEEE International Conference on Acoustics. Speech, and Signal Processing (ICASSP), Taipei, Taiwan, pp. 1869–1872 (2009)
9. Fenza, D., Mion, L., Canazza, S., Rodà, A.: Physical movement and musical gestures: a multilevel mapping strategy. In: Proceedings of Sound and Music Computing Conference, Salerno (2005)
10. Glowinski, D., Baron, N., Grandjean, D., Ott, T., Shirole, K., Torres-Eliard, K., Rappaz, M.A.: Analyzing expressive styles and functions of bodily movement in violinist performance. Proceedings of 2014 International Workshop on Movement and Computing - MOCO 2014, pp. 154–155 (2014)
11. Holland, P.W., Welsch, R.E.: Robust regression using iteratively reweighted least-squares. Commun. Stat.: Theor. Methods **A6**, 813–827 (1977)
12. Kiefer, B.: Elementos da linguagem musical, 3rd edn. Movimento, Porto Alegre (1979)
13. Kirke, A., Miranda, E.R.: A survey of computer systems for expressive music performance. ACM Comput. Surv. **42**(1), 1–41 (2009)
14. Miranda, E.R., Castet, J.: Guide to Brain-Computer Music Interfacing. Springer, London (2014)

15. Muller, M., Ewert, S.: Towards timbre-invariant audio features for harmony-based music. IEEE Trans. Audio Speech Lang. Process. **18**(3), 649–662 (2010)
16. Müller, M.: Information Retrieval for Music and Motion. Springer, Berlin (2007)
17. Nunes, H.S.: A canção brasileira infantil na perspectiva da ficha cdg para análise e composição de canções. Revista Brasileira de Estudos da Canção **1**(1), 151–173 (2012)
18. Straus, J.N.: Introdução à Teoria Pós-Tonal. EDUFBA-UNESP, Salvador (2013)
19. Vendramini, J.E.: A commedia dell'arte e sua reoperacionalização. Trans/Form/Ação **24**(1), 57–83 (2001)
20. Visi, F., Coorevits, E., Miranda, E., Leman, M.: Effects of different bow stroke styles on body movements of a viola player: an exploratory study. In: Proceedings of joint ICMC—SMC—2014 Conference, Athens, Greece (2014)
21. Visi, F., Schramm, R., Miranda, E.: Use of body motion to enhance traditional musical instruments. In: Caramiaux, B., Tahiroglu, K., Fiebrink, R., Tanaka, A. (eds.) Proceedings of International Conference on New Interfaces for Musical Expression, Goldsmiths, pp. 601–604. University of London, London, 30th June - 03rd July 2014
22. Visi, F., Schramm, R., Miranda, E.R.: Gesture in performance with traditional musical instruments and electronics: use of embodied music cognition and multimodal motion capture to design gestural mapping strategies. In: Bevilacqua, F., Alaoui, S.F., Françoise, J., Pasquier, P., Schiphorst, T. (eds.) International Workshop on Movement and Computing, MOCO 2014, Paris, France, 16–17 June 2014, p. 100. ACM (2014)

Composition Tools

A Viewpoint Approach to Symbolic Music Transformation

Louis Bigo[1(✉)] and Darrell Conklin[1,2]

[1] Department of Computer Science and Artificial Intelligence,
University of the Basque Country UPV/EHU, San Sebastian, Spain
{louis.bigo,darrell.conklin}@ehu.es
[2] IKERBASQUE, Basque Foundation for Science, Bilbao, Spain

Abstract. This paper presents a general approach to the transformation of symbolic music. The method is based on viewpoints, which enable the representation of musical surfaces by sequences of abstract features. Along the transformation process, some of these sequences are conserved while some others are variable and can be replaced by generated ones. The initial piece is therefore seen as a template which is instantiated at each transformation. The method is illustrated in the paper with the particular case of transformations occurring at the harmonic level. New chord sequences are generated by sampling from a statistical model in a particular style. The pitch of the notes constituting the template piece are then transformed according to the generated chord sequence.

Keywords: Harmonic transformation · Viewpoints · Computer-aided composition · Harmonic analysis · Music generation · Statistical models · Computational creativity

1 Introduction

Music generation methods can be divided into two broad categories [9,11]. On one hand are *rule-based* methods that use hard coded rules and constraints for style emulation and algorithmic composition. On the other hand are *machine learning* approaches that generate musical objects by sampling from statistical models built from large corpora of music [6]. In this paper we propose a new approach to using statistical models for music generation, one guided by the transformation of a *template piece* from which intra-opus structural features are inherited. Generation by transformation has been investigated based on spatial representations [4] and audio content [2]. Some harmonic transformation methods have also been investigated to assist composition in the songwriting assistant system *Liquid Notes* [1]. A strong motivation of the transformational approach to music generation is to benefit from *conserved* high-level structures that are hard to generate. The generation can then be restrained to some *variable* musical objects, producing a transformation of the initial sequence that maintains its particular structural aspects.

An additional motivation for transformational approaches is to provide some tools to the composer along the creative process. A transformation system can indeed be used at any step of the composition process to provide some *alternative* realisations of an abstract musical idea.

This work uses the symbolic music representation method of *viewpoints* [8,9] for the formal representation of the conserved and variable aspects of a template piece. The general method is illustrated with the particular case of transformations occurring at the chord level. Pitches of notes are considered to be variable and are modified in order to fit with a generated chord sequence. Other aspects of the musical surface (rhythm, orchestration, etc.) are conserved and are left unchanged. The method presented here is used for the transformation of tonal sequences, and therefore requires a chordal analysis and key detection step.

The transformation algorithm can be summarized by three main steps. First, a harmonic analysis is performed on the template piece. Second, a new chord sequence is generated by random walk from a statistical model built from a corpus of chord sequences of a particular style. Finally, a new musical surface is produced by changing the pitch of every event of the template piece, constrained by the generated chords. Pitches are modified such that their harmonic function (e.g., chord note, passing note, etc.) and similarity with the template pitch sequence are conserved. The method therefore ensures that the register and the global melodic shape of the original piece are conserved.

This paper is structured as follows. The representation method of viewpoints is reviewed, with particular attention to harmonic viewpoints that are used in the steps of chord generation and pitch modification. Following this, the machine learning method for developing a statistical model of chord sequences is described, and the process for changing the notes of a piece is presented. Some transformation examples are illustrated using as a template an extract of Erik Satie's *Gymnopédie No. 1* (1888).

2 A Viewpoint-Based Method to Transform Musical Sequences

This section describes a general method for music transformation. A formalization of transformations based on viewpoint representations is introduced. The method is illustrated with the specific case of transformations occurring at the harmonic level which involves harmony-based viewpoints and generation of chord sequences in a particular style. Finally, a method to transform the template sequence according to a generated chord sequence is presented.

2.1 Viewpoint Representation for Transformations

The method of *viewpoints* is used to represent musical sequences. This representation method has already proven to be efficient in several fields like music prediction [9], music classification [8] and pattern discovery [7].

Musical sequences are represented at the surface level as sequences of events that have basic features including duration, onset time and additional values depending on the nature of the events (for example, note events include a pitch, chord events include a chord symbol, etc.). A *viewpoint* is a function mapping events to more abstract derived features. The function is partial, therefore it may be undefined ($\bot$) for some events. An event e is abstracted by application of a viewpoint τ to produce the abstract feature $\tau(e)$.

The application of k viewpoints $\tau_1, \ldots, \tau_k$ to an event sequence $e_1, \ldots, e_n$ may be represented as a $k \times n$ solution array where location (i, j) holds the value $\tau_i(e_j)$. The upper table of Fig. 1 illustrates such an array for a melody fragment extracted from the *Gymnopdie No. 1* of E. Satie. For better readability, only

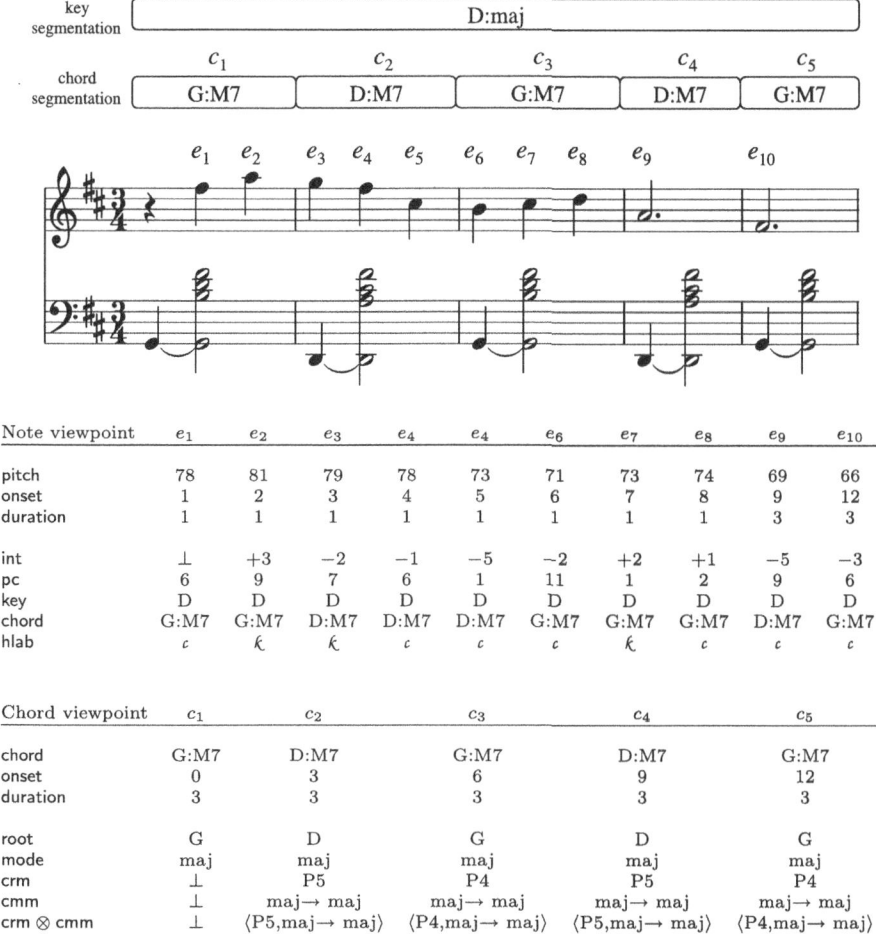

Fig. 1. Five measures extracted from the *Gymnopédie* No. 1 of E. Satie. A harmonic segmentation of the excerpt is provided above the score. The two tables below the score provide a viewpoint representation of the sequence of 10 events constituting the melodic fragment, and its associated sequence of five chords provided by the harmonic analysis. The top part of each table shows the basic viewpoints, the bottom the derived viewpoints used in this paper.

the notes of the melody part of the fragment (labeled by the events $e_1, \ldots, e_{10}$ on the upper staff) are represented with viewpoints. Values $\mathsf{int}(e_i)$ and $\mathsf{pc}(e_i)$ respectively correspond to the incoming pitch interval $\mathsf{pitch}(e_i) - \mathsf{pitch}(e_{i-1})$ and to the pitch class of the event $\mathsf{pitch}(e_i) \bmod 12$. Though not represented by viewpoints, the accompaniment (lower staff) is kept on the figure to provide the reader the harmonic context, which is necessary to compute harmonic based viewpoints introduced below.

Transformations. As previously mentioned, the notion of transformation requires a distinction between *conserved* and *variable* parts of an existing sequence. The process of transforming a sequence can then be seen as the task of modifying some of its describing viewpoint sequences while conserving some others. The choice of conserved and transformed viewpoints will be constrained by the dependencies between viewpoints. For example, modifying the pitch class of a note event will necessarily imply a modification of its pitch.

A strong advantage of this method, and also a major motivation of this work, is to enable the transformation of a musical sequence to be specified on higher musical levels (e.g., chords) than basic surface features (e.g., pitches). The process of transforming a musical sequence S can be described in 3 main steps (see Fig. 2):

- represent S by a set of viewpoint sequences V;
- produce an alternative set of viewpoint sequences V' by modifying some viewpoint sequences of V while conserving some others;
- generate a sequence of basic features S' that can be abstracted by the set of viewpoint sequences V'.

Note that because some viewpoint sequences in V are conserved, the transformed sequence S' has the same number of events as S. This general transformational approach is illustrated in the following with the specific case of transformation occurring at the harmonic level.

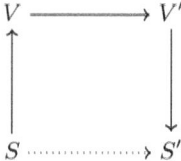

Fig. 2. An illustration of the transformation process applied on a musical sequence S abstracted by a set of viewpoint sequences V. V' is a transformation of V. A transformed musical sequence S' consists of any sequence that can be abstracted by V'. The dotted line between S and S' illustrates the transformation that is made indirectly through V and V'.

2.2 Harmony-Based Viewpoints

This section introduces harmony-based viewpoints necessary to process harmonic transformations. In order to be computed, harmonic viewpoints require a preliminary harmonic analysis to be processed on the musical sequence.

Harmonic Segmentation. Harmonic analysis includes as a first step the labelling of the sequence by chord and key segments. More specifically, a *chord segmentation* is a sequence of non-overlapping chord symbols, each labeled by a duration, that cover the time-line of a musical sequence. Additionally, a *key segmentation* is a sequence of keys, each labeled by a duration, covering the piece in the same way. The *harmonic segmentation* of a piece refers to the chord segmentation and the key segmentation resulting from the harmonic analysis of the piece. An harmonic segmentation is illustrated at the top of Fig. 1. Though the harmony of the musical excerpt of Fig. 1 is not ambiguous, in general there are no unique and exact methods for harmonic segmentation, in particular when inputs are MIDI files that do not include pitch spelling. These tasks are largely discussed within the music community and even when manually performed, they can produce different output depending on the analyst. Different methods trying to model this human cognitive ability have been investigated. These methods include an algorithm based on the spiral array [5], a dynamic programming approach [16] that processes chord and key segmentation based on Lerdahl's tonal distance [13] and the Melisma system [17].

The transformation method presented in this paper requires a chord/key segmentation of the input sequence to compute harmony based viewpoints. This segmentation constitutes an additional input to the transformation. Whether it is manually performed or automatically computed by one of the previous systems does not impact the functioning of the transformation method. To generate the transformations discussed in Sect. 3, both the algorithm described in [16] and some manual harmonic segmentation were used.

Chord and Key Viewpoints. A chord segmentation induces a viewpoint chord that returns for any note event e, the chord symbol of the chord segment in which e is included. The note viewpoint table of Fig. 1 represents the chord viewpoint sequence (chord) associated with the melodic extract, which in that case includes values G:M7 and D:M7. Note that a more accurate harmonic analysis would typically depict the degrees of these chords as IV and I respectively, showing thus the Lydian quality of the sequence. Although it is not the case in the harmonic transformations illustrated in this paper, the chord degrees could be conserved along the transformation by adding a chord degree viewpoint sequence to the conserved features of the transformation.

In this work, a note event is considered to be included within a segment if its onset is included in the segment. As a consequence, a note event that overlaps different segments will be systematically associated to the segment in which the event starts. Alternative segmentation strategies could be considered without affecting the functioning of the transformation method. In the same manner as chord segmentation, a key segmentation induces a viewpoint (key) that returns the key of the key segment that includes the event.

For an event e, the function $\mathsf{chord}_{\mathsf{pc}}$ returns the pitch class set associated with the chord symbol $\mathsf{chord}(e)$. Additionally, $\mathsf{key}_{\mathsf{pc}}(e)$ corresponds to the set of pitch classes that gathers all pitch classes composing the key $\mathsf{key}(e)$. For example, in Fig. 1, we have $\mathsf{chord}_{\mathsf{pc}}(e_6) = \{0, 4, 7, 10\}$ and $\mathsf{key}_{\mathsf{pc}}(e_3) = \{0, 2, 4, 5, 7, 9, 10\}$, respectively associated with the chord C:7 and the key F:maj.

Harmonic Label Viewpoint. A contribution of the paper is the introduction of the viewpoint hlab that attributes a harmonic label to every note event of the template piece. For any event e, $\mathsf{hlab}(e)$ is computed from the values $\mathsf{pc}(e)$, $\mathsf{chord}_{\mathsf{pc}}(e)$ and $\mathsf{key}_{\mathsf{pc}}(e)$.

Though the notion of harmonic label can be defined in different ways, in particular depending on the musical style, a simple specification is proposed to illustrate the method. Three possible harmonic labels can be attributed to an event, depending on if its pitch belongs to its relating chord and key regarding the harmonic segmentation. More formally, we propose the set of harmonic labels $\{c, k, o\}$ (c for "chord", k for "key" and o for "other") with:

$$\mathsf{hlab}(e_i) = \begin{cases} c \text{ if } \mathsf{pc}(e_i) \in \mathsf{chord}_{\mathsf{pc}}(e_i) \\ k \text{ if } \mathsf{pc}(e_i) \notin \mathsf{chord}_{\mathsf{pc}}(e_i) \text{ and } \mathsf{pc}(e_i) \in \mathsf{key}_{\mathsf{pc}}(e_i) \\ o \text{ if } \mathsf{pc}(e_i) \notin \mathsf{chord}_{\mathsf{pc}}(e_i) \text{ and } \mathsf{pc}(e_i) \notin \mathsf{key}_{\mathsf{pc}}(e_i) \end{cases}$$

On the example of Fig. 1, we have $\mathsf{hlab}(e_2) = k$ because $9 \notin \{2, 6, 7, 11\}$ and $9 \in \{0, 2, 4, 6, 7, 9, 11\}$. Figure 3 provides two additional examples of melodic fragments and their harmonic label sequences. The first one is extracted from the Piano Concerto No. 21 of W.A. Mozart. The harmonic segmentation of this fragment is easily performed thanks to the accompaniment part, which is not represented on the figure. The second one is extracted from the jazz standard *Take the "A" train*. The harmonic segmentation of this fragment is taken from the original lead sheet. The above definition of hlab consists for every event in a mapping between the 12 pitch classes and the set of harmonic labels. A different specification that would require octave information of the events to specify their harmonic function would also be possible. The harmonic label attributed to each note depends on the output of the harmonic segmentation and on the variety of chord types and keys supported by the harmonic segmentation system.

The set of possible harmonic labels could include a larger variety of values then the three above, as for example the notion of fundamental within a chord. Some harmonic labels can be specific to some musical style, for example the notion of *blue note* in jazz. The definition of the set of harmonic labels impacts the precision of the harmonic description of the sequence. As illustrated in Sect. 3, this aspect acts as an interesting parameter in the transformation process.

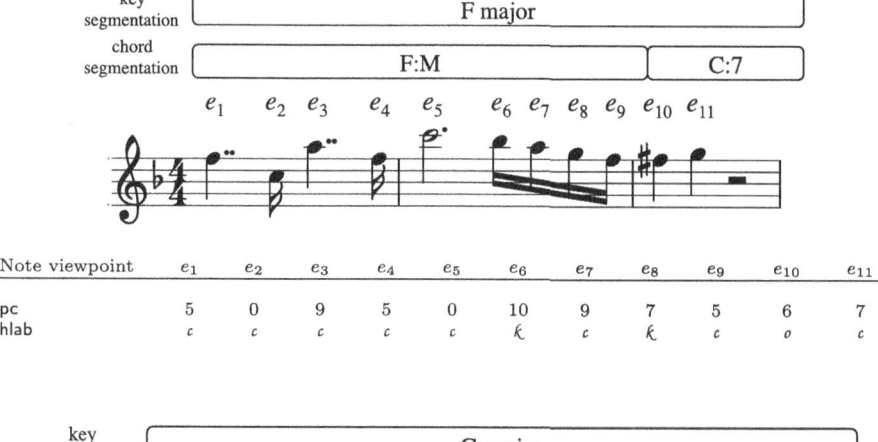

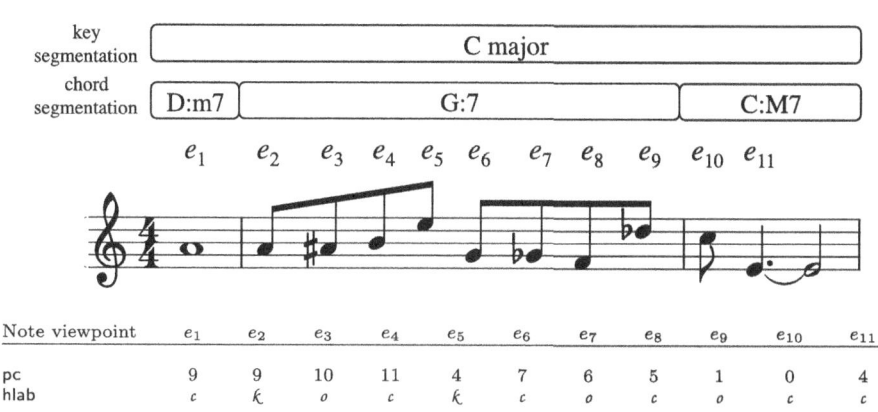

Fig. 3. Two examples of harmonic label sequences of melodic line fragments. The upper fragment is extracted from the second movement of the *Piano Concerto No. 21* of W.A. Mozart. The lower fragment is extracted from the jazz standard *Take the "A" train* from the pianist B. Strayhorn. For better readability accompaniment parts that are used to perform key and chord segmentation are not represented.

2.3 Conserved Viewpoints

The harmonic transformations presented in this work consist in (1) generating a new chords sequence and (2) transforming a musical sequence regarding the newly generated chord sequence. Though the pitches of the original note events are transformed, their harmonic label, onset and durations are conserved. More formally, an harmonic transformation of the musical sequence $e_1, \ldots, e_n$ is a sequence $e'_1, \ldots, e'_n$ that respects for every e':

- onset(e') = onset(e)
- duration(e') = duration(e)
- hlab(e') = hlab(e)

While the above viewpoints are conserved, the others are transformed. Section 2.4 presents a method to generate a new chord sequence $c'_1, \ldots, c'_m$ that has the same length than the chord segmentation $c_1, \ldots, c_m$ and where each chord c'_i is attributed the same onset and duration than its corresponding original chord c_i. Section 2.5 presents a method to generate an harmonic transformation of a musical sequence regarding the new chord sequence $c'_1, \ldots, c'_m$.

2.4 Chord Sequence Generation

The method for music generation using harmonic transformations relies centrally on the transformation of a template chord sequence into a new sequence. The task of chord sequence generation is stated simply as: given a statistical model over chord sequences, sample high probability sequences from the statistical model. This section describes the statistical modeling method used, and the corpus used to train the models.

A statistical model trained on viewpoint sequences from a corpus is used to generate new chord sequences. Here the method for using an abstract viewpoint to describe a first-order Markov model over chords is reviewed [8]. This method was also used recently to describe a statistical model for first-species counterpoint [12].

Let τ be a first-order viewpoint (i.e., computed from an event and its preceding event), and let $v = \tau(c_i \mid c_{i-1})$ be the feature assigned by τ to chord c_i, in the context of its preceding chord c_{i-1}. The probability $P(c_i \mid c_{i-1})$ of chord c_i following chord c_{i-1} can be written in the form

$$P(c_i \mid c_{i-1}) = P(c_i, v \mid c_{i-1}) = P(v) \times P(c_i \mid c_{i-1}, v)$$

with the first term $P(v)$ estimated as $c(v)/n$, where n is the number of chords in the corpus and $c(v)$ is the number of chords in the corpus having the feature v. To further reduce the number of parameters in the model simply to the possible values of τ, the second term $P(c_i \mid c_{i-1}, v)$ can be modelled with a uniform distribution over events having the feature v in the context of a given event c_{i-1} [8].

For a chord sequence $c_1, \ldots, c_m$, the *cross-entropy* of the sequence according to the statistical model is the mean negative log probability of the sequence:

$$- \log_2 \prod_{i=2}^{m} P(c_i \mid c_{i-1})/m$$

To generate chord sequences an iterated random walk procedure is used [12]. The first chord is fixed to a chosen starting chord, then random walk is used to generate a sequence of length m. This procedure is repeated multiple times with one of the low cross-entropy sequences retained. The random walk can be constrained to visit only tonal sequences that are composed by chords whose pitches belong to a unique tonality. Another possible constraint consists in generating sequences respecting a given structure (i.e., controlling how chords repeat along the sequence). The idea of constraining some chords along the generation process has also been explored by [10,14]. The structure constraint is interesting in our context of transformation since it enables the conservation of the harmonic structure of the template piece. It will be illustrated in the second example of Sect. 3.

The statistical model of chords is created by compiling statistics from a chord corpus. The musical style of the corpus impacts the chord generation and should thus be chosen carefully depending on the transformations that aim to be processed. The *Academic* subsection of the 9GDB chord sequence corpus [15] has been chosen to perform the transformations discussed in Sect. 3. This corpus contains the three subsections of classical, baroque, and romantic, and includes 235 chord sequences, reaching to total of 13027 chords.

This corpus was transformed by two steps: first, all chord extensions and slashes (chord inversion specification) were removed and chords were truncated to major, minor, augmented, suspended and diminished triads; second, runs of the same triad were collapsed to just one occurrence.

2.5 Template Transformation

This subsection describes a method to transform the template sequence, given as a MIDI file, to fit with a generated chord sequence.

MIDI Transformation. A MIDI file consists in a set of simultaneous tracks that can each provide a note event sequence $e_1, \ldots, e_n$ whose ordering corresponds to the ordering of their respective onset events within the MIDI track. However, two events e_i and e_{i+1} extracted from a polyphonic MIDI track can have the same onset time. As explained below, this property can have an important impact on a transformation.

For each track of the template MIDI file, a new sequence of events is computed with the method described below. Onsets and durations of the events are conserved but pitches are transformed. As a consequence, the MIDI file has the same structure before and after the transformation i.e., the same number of tracks, and the same number of events in each of these tracks.

Event Sequence Generation. A notable property of the harmonic transformations presented in this work is to conserve the harmonic label of the notes. The transformation consists then in generating a note event sequence $e'_1, \ldots, e'_n$ such that $\mathsf{hlab}(e'_i) = \mathsf{hlab}(e_i)$ for every event e_i.

For any original event e_i, we call the *event candidate set* A_i the set of all possible events having the same onset and duration as e_i and having a pitch respecting the harmonic label $\mathsf{hlab}(e_i)$. For every event of the original sequence, an event candidate set is built. A transformed sequence then results from the choice of one event in each successive candidate set.

Event Sequence Selection. Different strategies can be applied to select an event within a candidate set. To guide this selection, a score is calculated for any transformed sequence depending on its similarity with its original sequence regarding some arbitrary viewpoints.

Let $E' = e'_1, \ldots, e'_n$ be the result of a transformation of a sequence $E = e_1, \ldots, e_n$. The distance of the transformed sequence regarding a viewpoint τ corresponds to the mean distance, over the whole sequence, between $\tau(e_i)$ and $\tau(e'_i)$:

$$\delta_\tau(E', E) = \frac{\sum_{i=1}^n |\tau(e_i) - \tau(e'_i)|}{n}$$

For example, selecting an event sequence close from the original one in terms of pitches (i.e., minimizing δ_{pitch}) will tend to conserve the register of the original pitch sequence. On the other hand, selecting a sequence similar in terms of pitch interval (i.e., δ_{int} has a low value) will maintain the global pitch shape of the sequence. In the case of a polyphonic MIDI track, minimizing δ_{int} will tend to approximate both horizontal and vertical intervals of the original track.

This method only holds for numerical viewpoints. For non-numerical viewpoints, a specific notion of distance between $\tau(e_i)$ and $\tau(e'_i)$ would have to be defined. Note that τ should not belong to the viewpoints that are conserved along the note transformation process, otherwise, $\delta_\tau(E', E)$ would be zero. In the case of harmonic transformations presented here, it can be neither chord, hlab, onset nor duration.

In the following, we propose different strategies to generate sequences giving a low value to $\delta_\tau(E', E)$:

Greedy Algorithm. This strategy consists in selecting for each e_i a pitch in A_i that minimizes the local distance $|\tau(e_i) - \tau(e'_i)|$. Though very efficient, this algorithm provides only one solution that is not guaranteed to be optimal.

Viterbi Algorithm. This strategy consists in finding the sequence that minimizes $\delta_\tau(E', E)$. This task is achieved with dynamic programming [3]. If $\tau(e_i)$ is a 0-order viewpoint (i.e., $\tau(e_i)$ only requires e_i to be computed), the Viterbi algorithm will return the same sequence as the greedy algorithm. This is the case for the viewpoint pitch(e_i). However, first-order viewpoints (e.g., int(e_i) takes into account e_{i-1}) will benefit from the Viterbi algorithm to compute the sequence that minimizes $\delta_\tau(E', E)$.

Random Walk. A score is attributed to every event e of a candidate set A_i. This score is inversely proportional to the distance $|\tau(e_i) - \tau(e'_i)|$. An event is then randomly sampled from the set of candidate events, according to their relative score. This strategy has the advantage of providing a large number of solutions in efficient time.

3 Analysis of Transformed Sequences

This section illustrates our method by presenting and discussing different harmonic transformations of a template sequence corresponding to the five measures extracted from Erik Satie's *Gymnopédie No. 1* that are illustrated in Fig. 1. The chord sequences are generated from a statistical model built from the *Academic* subsection of the 9GDB chord sequence corpus [15] with chords truncated to major, minor, augmented, suspended and diminished triads as explained in Sect. 2.4. As a consequence, generated sequences only include these types of chords in these transformation examples. Generating more complex chords (e.g., including sevenths) would be possible but would require the statistical model to handle a more sophisticated chord representation.

Obviously these examples do not aim at producing anything comparable to the original sequence from an aesthetic point of view. In particular, the harmonic singularity of this piece, sometimes considered as post-tonal, did not influence these transformations since only onsets and durations of the original chords are conserved along the process. Furthermore, we choose to exemplify an harmonic transformation on an extract being both well-known and rhythmically simple, in order to illustrate more intuitively the effects of the transformations[1].

3.1 The Template Sequence

Figure 1 displayed at the beginning of the paper illustrates the score of the template sequence and the viewpoint representation of its melodic part. The events of the accompaniment part belong to a separate track which is not represented on the table for better readability. However, this track is transformed with the same method.

The preliminary harmonic segmentation of this template piece is not ambiguous. As shown under the score, it consists in an alternating of the chords G:M7 and D:M7 in the key of D major. The harmonic label sequence only provides values c and k which means that the fragment does not include any note outside the key of D major.

A less accurate harmonic analysis might have returned G:maj and D:maj for the two chords. As a consequence, the pitch class $F\sharp$ of e_1 would not be considered of being part of the chord $\mathsf{chord}(e_1)$ and $\mathsf{hlab}(e_1)$ would then have the value k instead of c. A transformation of the sequence would then assign to e'_1 a pitch not included in the generated chord $\mathsf{chord}(e'_1)$. This example typically illustrates how the harmonic analysis method impacts the transformation process. Interestingly, it does not seem obvious that the quality of the transformation is proportional to the accuracy of the harmonic analysis. In this example, forcing e'_1 to be out of the chord would produce a larger variety of transformed sequences, which can be interesting from a creativity point of view.

---

[1] The original excerpt and transformations are available at the address: https://soundcloud.com/harmonictransformations.

3.2 Transformation A

Figure 4 illustrates a first harmonic transformation of the fragment. The chord generation process has been performed with a filtration of tonal sequences, as explained in Sect. 2.4. The generation returns a low entropy triadic sequence in the key of D:maj (see bottom line of Fig. 4).

As explained in Sect. 2.3, the viewpoint sequence hlab is conserved throw out the transformation. The pitches of the events $e'_1, \ldots, e'_1$ are generated by computing the greedy solution minimizing local distance $|\mathsf{pitch}(e_i) - \mathsf{pitch}(e'_i)|$ tending thus to approximate the value of the pitches of the template sequence. The same algorithm has been applied to generate the event sequence constituting the accompaniment part. A notable property of this transformation is that some chords in the accompaniment part of the resulting score include fewer notes than in the template. This is the case for the chords appearing in bars 2, 3 and 5. This is due to a side effect of the strategy consisting in approximating the pitch value of the template notes: some simultaneous notes of the template piece have their pitch transformed into the same new pitch, producing identical events. This effect can be handled by approximating intervals between events rather than pitches, as proposed in the next example.

Another observation on the accompaniment part of this transformation is that the root note of the first chord D:maj is an F♯ which puts this chord in an inverted position contrary to the template in which all chords are in root position. Maintaining chord positions along transformation can be handled by adding the notion of chord fundamental in the set of available harmonic labels as illustrated in the next transformation example.

Fig. 4. A transformation of the extract of Fig. 1.

3.3 Transformation B

Figure 5 illustrates a second harmonic transformation of the fragment. The structure of the template chord sequence is conserved by applying a filter along the chord generation process as mentioned in Sect. 2.4. As a consequence, the generated sequence consists, as the original one, in two alternating chords. The pitches of the events $e'_1, \ldots, e'_n$ constitute the optimal solution (computed with the Viterbi algorithm mentioned in Sect. 2.5) minimizing the distance δ_{int} approximating thus the global pitch shape of the original sequence. Unlike in the previous transformation, simultaneous events will unlikely be transformed into identical events (i.e., having the same pitch) with this strategy. As a result, the number of notes in the chords in the accompaniment part is conserved. Furthermore, this transformation has been made while taking into account an additional harmonic label in the set presented in Sect. 2.2. This harmonic label specifies whether the pitch class of an event corresponds to the fundamental of its associated chord. This modification does not impact the transformation of the melodic part of the template because this part does not include any note whose pitch corresponds to the fundamental of its associated chord. However, the accompaniment part is affected and every chord is voiced in root position.

Fig. 5. A transformation of the extract of Fig. 1.

4 Conclusions

This paper presented a viewpoint approach to transform symbolic musical sequences. The method has been illustrated with the particular case of transformations occurring at the harmonic level and two examples of harmonic transformation have been discussed. Harmonic transformations can be controlled by a large set of variable components including the harmonic analysis system and the set of harmonic labels, the style and the complexity of the chords constituting the corpus which is learned by the statistical model, and the algorithm used to transform note event sequences.

The generic aspect of the viewpoint approach suggests a wider range of musical transformations that constitute future perspectives of this research. It is planed to explore rhythmic transformations in which onset and duration viewpoints sequences would be modified. The possibility to add or remove events from the original sequence is also part of future work.

Acknowledgments. The authors thank Dorien Herremans for valuable discussions and collaboration on this research. This research is supported by the project Lrn2Cre8 which is funded by the Future and Emerging Technologies (FET) programme within the Seventh Framework Programme for Research of the European Commission, under FET grant number 610859.

References

1. Liquid Notes. http://www.liquid-notes.com
2. Amatriain, X., Bonada, J., Loscos, A., Arcos, J.L., Verfaille, V.: Content-based transformations. J. New Music Res. **32**(1), 95–114 (2003)
3. Bellman, R.: Dynamic Programming, 1st edn. Princeton University Press, Princeton (1957)
4. Bigo, L., Ghisi, D., Spicher, A., Andreatta, M.: Spatial transformations in simplicial chord spaces. In: Proceedings of the Joint International Computer Music Conference — Sound and Music Computing, Athens, pp. 1112–1119 (2014)
5. Chew, E.: The spiral array: an algorithm for determining key boundaries. In: Anagnostopoulou, C., Ferrand, M., Smaill, A. (eds.) ICMAI 2002. LNCS (LNAI), vol. 2445, pp. 18–31. Springer, Heidelberg (2002)
6. Conklin, D.: Music generation from statistical models. In: Proceedings of the AISB Symposium on Artificial Intelligence and Creativity in the Arts and Sciences, pp. 30–35. Aberystwyth, Wales (2003)
7. Conklin, D.: Discovery of distinctive patterns in music. Intell. Data Anal. **14**(5), 547–554 (2010)
8. Conklin, D.: Multiple viewpoint systems for music classification. J. New Music Res. **42**(1), 19–26 (2013)
9. Conklin, D., Witten, I.: Multiple viewpoint systems for music prediction. J. New Music Res. **24**(1), 51–73 (1995)
10. Eigenfeldt, A., Pasquier, P.: Realtime generation of harmonic progressions using controlled Markov selection. In: Proceedings of ICCC-X-Computational Creativity Conference, pp. 16–25 (2010)
11. Fernandez, J.D., Vico, F.J.: AI methods in algorithmic composition: a comprehensive survey. J. Artif. Intell. Res. **48**, 513–582 (2013)
12. Herremans, D., Sörensen, K., Conklin, D.: Sampling the extrema from statistical models of music with variable neighbourhood search. In: Proceedings of the Joint International Computer Music Conference — Sound and Music Computing, Athens, pp. 1096–1103 (2014)

13. Lerdahl, F.: Tonal Pitch Space. Oxford University Press, Oxford (2001)
14. Pachet, F., Roy, P.: Markov constraints: steerable generation of Markov sequences. Constraints **16**(2), 148–172 (2011)
15. Pérez-Sancho, C., Rizo, D., Iñesta, J.M.: Genre classification using chords and stochastic language models. Connection Sci. **20**(2&3), 145–159 (2009)
16. Rocher, T., Robine, M., Hanna, P., Strandh, R.: Dynamic chord analysis for symbolic music. In: Proceedings of the International Computer Music Conference, Montreal, Quebec, Canada (2009)
17. Sleator, D., Temperley, D.: The Melisma music analyzer (2001). www.link.cs.cmu.edu/music-analysis

Balancing Audio: Towards a Cognitive Structure of Sound Interaction in Music Production

Mads Walther-Hansen[✉]

Department of Communication and Psychology,
Aalborg University, Aalborg, Denmark
mwh@hum.aau.dk

Abstract. This paper explores the concept of balance in music production and examines the role of conceptual metaphors in reasoning about audio editing. Balance may be the most central concept in record production, however, the way we cognitively understand and respond meaningfully to a mix requiring balance is not thoroughly understood. In this paper I treat balance as a metaphor that we use to reason about several different actions in music production, such as adjusting levels, editing the frequency spectrum or the spatiality of the recording. This study is based on an exploration of a linguistic corpus of sound engineering literature. Using this corpus, I show how corpus data may contribute to better understand the relation between embodied patterns of experience and hands-on interaction with sound.

Keywords: Embodiment · Sound and language · Sound interaction · Sound interfaces · Conceptual metaphors · Image schemas · Music production · Balance · Corpus linguistics

1 Introduction

Balance and related concepts, such as tension, release and stability are among the most important concepts in record production. A sound engineer may, for instance, refer to 'dynamic balance,' 'spectral balance,' 'colour balance,' 'wet/dry balance' or 'pan balance' when describing sonic qualities of a mix. However, few attempts have been made to understand how linguistic expressions, such as these, relate to underlying embodied structures that give rise to concrete actions in the act of recording, mixing, and mastering music.

In this paper conceptual metaphor theory [1–3] and corpus linguistics [4, 5] serve as a theoretical framework to understand the relation between how music producers and sound engineers imagine their mix and the operations they perform to achieve it. Previous studies have shown that the application of conceptual metaphors (also known as cognitive metaphors) in interface design allows for more intuitive interaction [6, 7]. Also, Droumeva et al. [8] have tested intuitive bodily responses to auditory balance. Their study has shown a link between body movements and perceived balanced/ unbalanced audio stimuli. This suggests a relationship between physical structures of balance and more abstract notions of auditory balance. Still, more research is needed to understand the complex ways in which conceptual metaphors are formed in our cognitive system and, accordingly, to understand what kinds of metaphorical structures are activated when interacting with sound.

Here I identify imagery in the conceptualization of sound mixing. I examine the cognitive structures sound engineers and music producers rely on when judging when a mix is balanced and how they respond meaningfully to an imbalanced mix. I support my claims with a study of a specialized linguistic corpus of sound engineering literature. The corpus has been designed specifically for this study.

The core design of mixing desks has not changed considerably since the early 1960s and the arrival of digital recording technology during the 1980s mainly resulted in a transference of this design to the digital domain. For this reason, interfaces for mixing are still mainly designed with the channel strip metaphor in mind.

In a recent paper, Gelineck et al. [9] have proposed a graphical user interface for sound mixing that uses the *stage metaphor* instead of the *channel strip metaphor*. In doing so, they aim to make a graphical interface design where sound sources are represented by objects that the user may move around on a 2-dimensional sound stage. This interface provides a tool to balance sounds across this virtual sound stage – to move a sound forward on the sound stage, the user drags the sound towards herself/himself and vice versa. The actual actions, then, and the position of the objects that represent the sound in the graphical user interface correspond to the location of sound on a perceived sound stage.

In this paper, I show that the sound stage [10] is insufficient to account for how music producers make sense of the mix. I claim instead that the mix is best realized as a 3-dimensional container where sounds with different *weights, shapes* and *sizes* are balanced by re-shaping them and re-locating them both vertically, horizontally and laterally.

Table 1. Composition of the corpus used in this study

Sub-corpus	Text type	Contents/subjects	Source	Words	Percentage of corpus
Sound on Sound Magazine	Written	Articles on music production, interviews technical reviews, tutorials, adverts	Web pages	13.211.540	71 %
Computer Music Magazine	Written	Articles on music production, technical reviews, tutorials, adverts	Digitized magazine	1.621.676	9 %
Various books on acoustics and music production	Written	Acoustics, sound engineering, digital audio	Digitized books	2.537.942	14 %
Audio tutorials and manuals	Written	Tutorials on sound engineering and technical manuals	Web pages	1.162.319	6 %
Total words				18.533.477	

Unlike most studies of conceptual metaphors, this study relies on actual citations found in natural language. In order to examine how the balance metaphor is represented in natural language, a specialized linguistic corpus of sound engineering literature was built (See Table 1). The corpus is analysed to determine recurrent linguistic patterns that may point to the operation of specific embodied schemas in the act of mixing music. I propose that these embodied schemas are formed through both previous sensorimotor experiences (bodily, everyday experiences) as well as through 'invented concepts' (learned from textbooks, operating audio equipment and so on). This paper, then, concludes with an outlook towards future research in the design of music production interfaces that more closely reflect how we make sense of music mixes.

2 Imagination and Metaphorical Mapping

This study builds on the notion that imaginative structures grow out of bodily experience. This central idea is founded on conceptual metaphor theory and the assumption that cognition is fundamentally metaphorical. According to this view, there is an underlying conceptual system behind our thoughts and actions that relies on concrete embodied experiences. It is these embodied experiences that allow us to extend the knowledge we have about the physical world to more abstract and complex experiences.

Since language is based on the same conceptual system as thought and action, we may gain access to the workings of our cognitive system by studying how experiences are conceptualized in language.

Linguistic metaphors may be seen as expressions of imagination as they invite the listener to think of something in terms of something else. Metaphors can also be creative and afford a new perspective on familiar experiences [11]. However, I will choose to focus more on the first use of metaphors in this paper.

But what does it mean that linguistic metaphors are expressions of imagination? Metaphors are fundamentally conceptual – something that exists at the level of thought rather than the level of language. However, it is these underlying conceptual metaphors that guide our thinking and reasoning and, therefore, also form the basis for our language. The main principle of conceptual metaphors is the mapping of perceptual domains from one domain (*a source domain*) to another (*a target domain*). Usually mappings go from a more concrete source domain (such as the act of shaping a physical object) to a more abstract target domain (such as the act of shaping sound). Since Lakoff and Johnson's book *Metaphors We Live By* [1] from 1980, conceptual metaphor theory has been the dominant position in cognitive linguistics. Several scholars have subsequently used these methods in the examination of specific domains, e.g., emotions [12], pictures [13], illness [14] and musical motion [15].

2.1 Audio Editing and Conceptual Metaphor Theory

In the present study, this idea is used to examine how sound engineers and music producers make sense of audio editing in terms of more concrete embodied experiences.

Music production involves rules and conventions for making a good sounding mix. However, these rules when brought together have complex relationships that can only really be understood through intuition. Like other art forms, music production involves imagining something beyond what is given to us in perception. Imagining something may be an act of creativity, as when envisioning a novel auditory structure, or it may simply be the recall of an aesthetic idea derived from the properties of a well-known auditory structure.

Imagining auditory structures is a perceptually messy process. A key problem is the fact that the auditory 'ideal' sound engineers aim to achieve is notoriously difficult to describe in words. This lack of suitable words does not mean, however, that imagination is not, or only partly in play, but that imagination goes beyond what we may conceptualize in language and that the link between imagination and conceptualization is a complex one.

Still, imagination is not completely unstructured. Kant [16] famously defined imagination as a faculty of the mind that forms schemas or general 'rules'. These schemas represent general aspects of experience and allow us to pair specific experiences with concepts that match related experiences.

Cognitive scientists have later refined this idea. They see these schemas as general knowledge structures shaped and created by recurrent bodily experiences. These patterns are often referred to as embodied schemas or image schemas [2, 17]. Image schemas emerge from interaction with the physical world (sensorimotor experiences) and are mapped onto more abstract experiences, such as responding to an unbalanced mix. In this way, these schemas connect experiences across different perceptual domains.

There is also an increasing academic interest in how image schemas serve to connect experiences across the senses and findings from these studies have found application in human-computer interaction design. While the connection between experiences of sound and image has been well-researched for decades – particularly in the domain of film [see 18] and computer game sound theory [19]. There is also work (although a lesser amount) done on the metaphorical connection between sound and haptics [20], sound and taste [21] and sound and odour [22, 23].

Visual and haptic feedback are usually the most important factors in sonic interaction design. Still, haptic feedback is often overlooked for practical purposes as there is little or no room for implementation of tactile feedback in most interfaces accessible to end-users, such as desktop computers and tablets. Here, I argue that haptic feedback – along with visual feedback – serves an important role when making sense of the actions one performs when editing sound. As I show in the concluding remarks, 3D interaction with haptic feedback is possible with current technology, however, further research is necessary to make these interfaces useable for interactive sound production.

3 Method

This study uses linguistic metaphors found in natural language as the main evidence of underlying cognitive structures. To perform the study, a linguistic corpus was composed. The use of linguistic corpora for the study of language – the field known as corpus linguistics [5] – is a means to provide empirical evidence for qualitative questions. Corpus linguistics has gained popularity in tandem with the increasing number of digitized texts available for researchers to compile corpora from and it has been applied in many areas of humanistic research – such as discourse analysis [24] and more recently in the study of metaphors [4, 25] – to produce new insights from 'big data'.

The corpus used in this study consists of 18.5 million words and is composed of sound engineering magazines, digitized books and tutorial articles on music production dating from 1994 to 2013. All texts are in British and American English. The corpus was analysed using Wordsmith Tools (Lexical Analysis Software Ltd.), an integrated suite of programs to analyse how words behave in large amounts of texts. In this study, Wordsmith was used to analyse the collocation of specific concepts. The composition of the corpus is outlined in Table 1.

The specialized corpus was composed in order to identify typical features used in the specialized language of audio professionals. A computer-generated analysis was made to find concepts that collocate with balance. However, in a corpus study of metaphors in naturally occurring language some manual analysis is necessary: firstly, because a computer-generated analysis does not distinguish between literal and metaphorical expressions and, secondly, because the pragmatic use of the word in context can only be accurately determined by humans.

The analysis of the data, therefore, included both bottom-up and top-down processes. Firstly, a search for "balance*" provided a list of concordance examples that were manually sorted in different ways in order for patterns to emerge more clearly – top-down (see Table 3). Secondly, to identify metaphorical expressions and the correspondent conceptual metaphors, a search for specific linguistic phrases was made based on potential linguistic realizations of conceptual metaphors. If these linguistic realizations were found, they formed part of the verification of the overall conceptual metaphor – bottom-up (see examples in Sect. 5).

4 The Balance Metaphor

4.1 The Bodily Experience of Balance

Arnheim [26] has provided one of the most elaborate accounts of the meaning of balance in experience. Arnheim focuses on visual perception and describes balance in paintings as an equal distribution of *weight* and *forces* across the picture frame. Any asymmetry in this distribution is perceived as *tension* as elements are striving towards a *restful* position. Talmy [27] later described these inherent *force tendencies* as a fundamental principle of all human experience. According to this view, perceptual entities have different *strengths* of *force tendencies* that come to determine the outcome of the experienced scenario.

Johnson [2] has made another important study in which he describes balance as a bodily activity that is not governed by a specific set of rules. Balance is something that is 'felt' bodily, a feeling we come to learn through acts of balancing (e.g., when learning to ride a bicycle or when learning how to properly hold a cup to drink from), where we learn to respond meaningfully to a lack of balance in order to restore balance. The claim is that there is a recurrent pattern in the experience of balance that connects seemingly different balancing acts. Usually this balance is not something that we are consciously aware during everyday experiences. Balance only becomes present when we experience a loss of equilibrium that requires a bodily response.

4.2 Balance in Music

Balance in music is often conceived of as the feeling of tension between tones [see 28]. One may even argue that in order for sound to be characterized as music, there must be some pattern of tension that causes one tone to lead to the next one. Larson and Johnson [15] have shown how listeners understand musical motion as a series of forces [see also 29]). The experience of musical forces is based on the logic of physical motion in actual space, where forces such as gravity and magnetism cause physical objects to move. Tension is, several scholars argue, the key concept to how we mentally organize the musical experience [30]. Similar to physical objects that have a tendency to move towards other objects or away from them, tones have an inherent tendency (depending on the musical patterns that come before and the cultural expectations of the listener) to move upwards, move downwards or to rest. In this way, tones 'strive' for locations that bring them into balance [see also 31]. In an earlier article, I proposed that these patterns of tension and release (force dynamic patterns) are profound timbral qualities of recorded sound and central to the experience of sound in general [32].

4.3 Balance in Music Production Literature

In music production, balance is often defined as the relative volume between several audio tracks [33]. This definition is clearly the most conventional, but it is also more generally understood as a felt sense of 'right' (balanced) and 'wrong' (unbalanced) in auditory experience. More importantly, though, the quality of a sound's spectromorphology can be conceived of in terms of a continuous flow of balanced and unbalanced experiences of the auditory stimuli. For this reason, we need an account of the recurrent embodied experience of balance that governs a number of decisions in music production beyond riding dynamic faders.

A keyword search in the corpus shows that the term 'balanc*' ('*' = wild card search) appears 9.401 times in the corpus. Based on a comparison with the British National Corpus (BNC) [34] balance* appears 3.37 times as often in music production literature than in a more general reference corpus. To demonstrate the typical context of balance in the corpus, words to the right of the phrase "balanc* the" are considered. There are 392 citations in the corpus containing "balanc* the". The most typical right collocates are listed in Table 2.

In Table 3, I have listed examples from a right-sorted collocation search (sorted alphabetically after words appearing in the first position to the right of "balanc* the". This concordance list hints at the varied meanings of balance. It is often necessary to access the source text to see the full context of the phrase and verify its meaning. Still, the list only allows us to see the context in which balance is explicitly stated. We may, however, use the list as a starting point for further investigation.

Table 2. Most significant right collocates

Levels	Image
Signals	Mix
Volume	Sound
Elements	Phases
Layers	Left and right side
Dynamics	High and lows
Tracks	Upper and lower register
Stereo	Frequency content
Tone	Thickness
Release	Wet and dry amount
Compressed and uncompressed signals	Clean and dirty levels

Table 3. Concordance examples

changes at 80Hz and 15kHz, for	*balancing the*	bass end and for
a setting I liked, it was easy to	*balance the*	clean and dirty levels,
is intended to help to counter-	*balance the*	darker, low-frequency
fully to the right, with nothing to	*balance the*	left side of the mix
allowing the system to actively re-	*balance the*	mid-range and upper harmonic
dull the mix is, and in turn how	*balanced the*	overall mix is
space in the construction is well	*balanced. The*	overall mix is tough and heavy
and we miss an opportunity to	*balance the*	stereo panorama
had a sort of hardness that	*balanced the*	thickness out better

In the following, I focus on some of the most frequent metaphorical uses of balance that emerged from the collocation searches. My interpretation of these metaphors follows from previous studies on conceptual metaphors – studies that rely mainly on intuition. I qualify this interpretation with a number of concrete realizations of conceptual metaphors from the corpus.

4.4 The Mix is a Seesaw

The left/right positioning of sound is not in itself metaphorical, as there is a literal change to the perceived location of sound in the lateral dimension when sounds are panned to one side. The balance schema emerges as a result of the metaphorical mapping of *forces* and *weights* onto individual sounds in the mix. Asymmetry and unbalance, for instance, often manifests itself as an uneven distribution of *forces* and *weights* across the lateral dimension.

To avoid this, *heavy* sounds (low frequency energetic and powerful sounds) are often panned centre (e.g. bass and kick drum), to serve as *anchor points* [35] while a number of *lighter* sounds may be positioned more freely in the lateral dimension. Also, lead vocals are often perceived as having a central *perceptual value* – Michel Chion [36] calls this enhanced perceptual value of vocal sounds *vococentrism* – and are therefore often found in centre position. This practice is so conventional that we only notice it when it is disturbed in some way, for instance by panning the voice hard to one side. These ways of balancing a mix make sense for the reason that a gravitational force of physical objects is mapped onto the sounds in the mix and because we think of the mix as a seesaw. This is represented in the Twin-Pan Balance Schema [2] (See Fig. 1).

Fig. 1. Twin-pan balance schema

The seesaw metaphor did not emerge with the advent of stereo recording, however, but developed with multitrack recording (16 and 24 tracks) in the early 1970s. Moore and Dockwray [37] show how production practices for locating sounds in the lateral dimension went through a number of phases before the practice with locating sound sources, such as vocals, kick drum and bass in centre position, became common practice.

The lateral balance may seem of little importance in many play-back situations, as listeners are seldom located in the stereo field's "sweet spot". However, the increasing use of headphones in playback has presented a need for more careful control with the lateral balance.

4.5 The Mix is a Container

The mix is a container in the sense that it contains sounds. The container schema is activated when we experience events where something is located within another thing.

Concrete events such as *in my car* or *outside the house* describe concrete experiences in the actual world. These experiences can be extended to abstract concepts such as *in love* or *out of touch* [2]. Similarly, we say that sounds are *in* the mix and that we *add volume* to a sound, which causes it to *take up* more space in the mix. This mode of conceptualizing defines sounds as physical elements organized in a container.

Mixing is organizing and balancing elements *inside* this container system to make the system appear right. We may compare this to the feeling of bodily imbalance when being ill. Illness is experienced as an abnormal state and something that should be restored to normal.

For the container to be in balance, all elements should co-exist in an appropriate way. If there is too much of something the container will overload. If there is too little, something is lacking, or if elements are not positioned correctly the balance is skewed relative to the central axis of the container. This form of balance is represented in the Equilibrium Schema [2] (See Fig. 2).

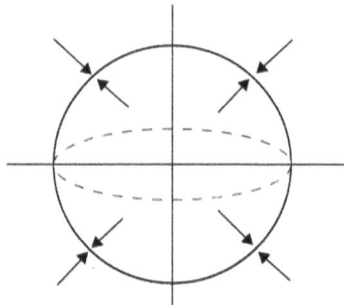

Fig. 2. Equilibrium schema

4.6 Verticality

The sounds that make up the content of the container are located in different positions *inside* the container. These positions may be experienced as a result of the physical acoustics of the sound, e.g. a sound arriving from the left or the right loudspeaker, or they may be non-physical, e.g. high and low sounds. The latter corresponds to Zbikowski's [38] studies where pitch relations between different musical pitches are characterized as *higher* and *lower*. These relationships build on an underlying Verticality Schema that structures the understanding of pitch on an up-down continuum (See Fig. 3).

Fig. 3. Verticality schema

Likewise, we use orientational metaphors to conceptualize where sound sources are in the container, and to make sense of tonal and timbral details by imposing a spatial structure onto the sound event. This is supported by the following expressions found in the corpus:

Add an 808 kick *underneath*
The snare is sitting *on top of* the kick drum

4.7 The Container Metaphor as a Master Metaphor

We have seen how the twin-pan balance schema works across the lateral dimension of a mix and how these experiences correspond to the unstable body-position we experience when we are about to fall over. Adding to this, the vertical axis of the body is seen to be in a perceived imbalance when you say that *the blood is rushing to your head* or that *you feel light-headed*. This physiological understanding of vertical equilibrium or disequilibrium corresponds to how one may imagine an inappropriate or appropriate distribution of sounds in the vertical dimension of a mix.

The container metaphor functions as a master metaphor that incorporates the verticality schema and the twin-pan balance schema into its substructure. Like the human body, the sound container behaves as a 'system' whose stability relies on the workings of several substructures.

5 Some Metaphorical Extensions of the Container Metaphor

A number of lexis from the corpus was selected for further examination. Patterns were then extracted from the computerized search to produce detailed and specified samples that were re-analysed manually. The words were categorized according to overall conceptual metaphors. As the field is highly complex the findings are in no way exhaustive. They should be seen as a way to get an idea of the complexity of the balance concept in music production, and as a starting point for further studies.

The data confirms how the mix is understood as a container that contains physical objects (sounds). This ontological metaphor has a practical value. Individual sounds within a mix are not discrete and clearly bounded entities, but metaphors allow us to imagine sounds as objects that can be handled, moved around and controlled. Balancing the mix involves modifying the properties of the sound, such as the *shapes*, and *sizes* and adjusting the *amount* and *location* of sounds within the container.

The container metaphor can be seen as a basic level metaphor that consists of three basic components; *an inside*, *an outside*, and a *boundary* between these positions [2]. More elaborate realizations of the mix are found in the conceptual metaphor THE MIX IS A PHYSICAL SPACE:

Metaphor
MIX IS A PHYSICAL SPACE

Citations from the corpus
The mix sounds way too *crowded*
Leave *room* for the kick to *occupy*
The snare *gets in the way* of the kick
I needed a longer reverb to *fill in* spaces
Keep a *hole open in the middle*
Clean up the mix

These citations describe different aspects of the mix, for instance, the relative position of the sounds and its internal state (e.g., *too crowded*).

THE MIX IS A LIVING ORGANISM is another frequent sub-metaphor detected in the corpus:

Metaphor	Citations from the corpus
THE MIX IS A LIVING ORGANISM	Make the mix *breathe*
	Squeeze the mix to *death*
	Make the mix come *alive*

The MIX IS A LIVING ORGANISM metaphor is used to make sense of the internal equilibrium of the mix. Living organisms maintain systemic balance by adjusting its physiological processes and we may promote this healthy state by making beneficial lifestyle choices. In the MIX IS A LIVING ORGANISM metaphor sounds are seen as elements that maintain the stability of the system. Any 'non-working' part will create systemic imbalance and the mix engineer must make sense of this imbalance to respond rationally. In the following examples, I show how responses to imbalances can show up as linguistic structures in corpus citations.

5.1 Push Pull

Push and *pull* are common force dynamic expressions found in the corpus. *Push* often occurs as a response to a sound being too loud or *jumping too much out of the mix*.

Some examples of responses found in the corpus are:

Push the sound back in the mix
Stick it back in
Tuck it back in

The image schematic structure of these responses show up as a trajectory moving away from the user, who *pushes* the sound back or *sticks* it in (See Fig. 4).

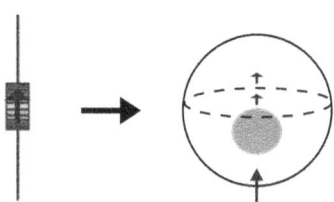

Fig. 4. Push

Conversely, *pull the sound out* means bringing it forward if it is too *soft* or otherwise *hidden* in the mix.

These metaphorical structures correspond to Gelineck's et al. [9] stage metaphor interface, where sounds are *pushed back* on the sound stage to turn them down.

5.2 The Channel Strip Metaphor

Interestingly, the schematic structure of *push* and *pull* responses does not correspond to the channel strip metaphor found on conventional mixing desks. Here you would need to pull the fader towards you to *push* a sound back in the mix and vice versa.

The lack of correspondence between the metaphor and the channel strip design seems to have a historical and a technological explanation. The recording engineer Tom Dowd is usually credited for being the first person to install channel strip faders on a mixing desk in the late 1950s [39, 40]. These faders replaced the typical rotary knobs and soon became part of the typical mixing desk design. The faders had a practical value as they made it possible to adjust the volume on several tracks at the same time with your fingers - when raising the faders sound levels increased and vice versa.

We have just seen that the fader design does not correspond to the metaphorical system argued for in this study. However, the fader design seems to make sense from a technological point of view. On analogue mixing desks, full gain is brought up to the faders. By raising the faders, you *open up* the signal flow and the sound is brought through. Conversely, turning the faders down gradually *closes* the signal flow. Also, the channel strip metaphor supports the connection between pushing the faders up and increasing the amount (the volume) of sound.

Clearly, the fader design has a logic structure from the point of view of sound engineers that grew up with analogue technologies. In many of today's digital audio workstations, however, end-users need to worry considerably less about the signal flow. For this reason, interface designs could easily be built more on how the auditory properties of the mix are conceived rather than the physical signal flow. Such a shift may be disturbing to sound engineers who were taught to think in terms of the functionality of the technology – and whose thinking is, therefore, largely influenced by 'learned metaphors'. However, interface designs based on embodied metaphors that are mapped from everyday sensorimotor experience have been shown to be much more intuitive to operate [41].

5.3 Open Up

Another common action is to *open up the sound*, or to help it to *cut through* the mix if it is too *tucked in* or *closed*. *Open up* is typically related to frequency balancing. In the metaphorical understanding of *open up* the force dynamic structure between the sound and that which *restricts* the sound from *coming out* is changed. Sounds are understood as entities that have a tendency to *come out*, unless restrained by an *external force*. This is further related to the metaphorical extension of *come out* meaning being accessible. Everything cannot get the same attention in the mix, and engineers often try to find a balanced position where the sound is neither *fully in* nor *fully out* as in the expressions: *Bring the vocal out a little bit more* or *bring the vocal out slightly*. We may thus think of a balanced state as between *out* and *in* and between *open* and *closed*.

While we may point to a schematic structure in our imagination for *open up*, there is no single action that translates this structure into practice. This shows that the cognitive structures that we use to make sense of balancing are often not directly related to the bodily actions we must perform, and the available interface controllers we must use, to bring it into practice.

6 Summary and Perspectives

The number of ways to create an appropriate balance may be infinite. There is no ideal configuration of sounds that make up a balanced mix in any context. We may, however, say something about the range of different embodied structures involved in creating a balanced mix and how we may respond meaningfully to imbalance.

In this paper, I have presented a corpus-based approach in an attempt to find new structural patterns in the understanding of audio editing. This investigation has provided examples of how basic structural aspects of the mix are conceptualized and how these structures point to a container system whose stability relies on proper handling of its component parts. I have proposed a number of conceptual metaphors and image schemas, such as the twin-pan balance schema, the equilibrium schema and the container schema that can serve as the basis for future designs of music production interfaces.

The goal of this research is to facilitate the development of new interfaces that allow for a more intuitive correspondence between how a mix is envisioned and how these visions are translated into practice. The paper has considered how the users of music production interfaces articulate and make sense of their interaction with sound, and I proposed that the container metaphor functions as a master metaphor for the act of balancing sound.

One means to implement this master metaphor in future designs would be to use current developments of 3D controllers and natural user interfaces (NUI) [42] that allow for 3D gestures. As 3D gestures are typically performed in mid-air with little tactile feedback, the implementation of force dynamic metaphors in such interfaces will prove difficult. Although current research has made tactile experiences in mid-air possible [43], the variety of tactile sensations these devices can make are still limited. Future research should seek to determine what kind of 3D interface technologies would be most suitable to test the actual functioning of the proposed conceptual metaphors.

Acknowledgments. The author would like to thank Mark Grimshaw and Justin Christensen for comments and suggestions on this paper.

References

1. Lakoff, G., Johnson, M.: Metaphors We Live By. The University of Chicago Press, Chicago (1980)
2. Johnson, M.: The Body in the Mind: The Bodily Basis of Meaning, Imagination, and Reason. The University of Chicago Press, Chicago (1987)
3. Kövecses, Z.: Metaphor: A Practical Introduction. Oxford University Press, Oxford (2002)

4. Deignan, A.: Metaphor and Corpus Linguistics. John Benjamins Publishing Company, Amsterdam (2005)
5. O'Keefe, A., McCarthy, M.: The Routledge Handbook of Corpus Linguistics. Routledge, London (2010)
6. Hurtienne, J., Blessing, L.: Design for intuitive use – testing image schema theory for user interface design. In: International Conference on Engineering Design, Paris, 28–31 August, pp. 1–12 (2007)
7. Hurtienne, J., Israel, J.H.: Image schemas and their metaphorical extensions: intuitive patterns for tangible interaction. In: Proceedings of 1st International Conference on Tangible and Embedded Interaction, New York, pp. 127–134 (2007). doi:http://dx.doi.org/10.1145/1226969.1226996
8. Droumeva, M., Antle, A., Corness, G., Bevans, A.: Springboard: exploring embodied metaphor in the design of sound feedback for physical responsive environments. In: Proceedings of the 15th International Conference on Auditory Display, Copenhagen, Denmark, 18–22 May, pp. 1–4 (2009)
9. Gelineck, S., Overholt, D., Büchert, M., Andersen, J.: Towards an interface for music mixing based on smart tangibles and multitouch. In: Proceedings of New Interfaces for Musical Expression, Daejeon, Korea, 27–30 May 2013
10. Moylan, W.: The Art of Recording: The Creative Resources of Music Production and Audio. Van Nostrand Reinhold, New York (1992)
11. Searle, J.: Metaphor. In: Ortony, A. (ed.) Metaphor and Thought, pp. 83–111. Cambridge University Press, Cambridge (1993)
12. Kövecses, Z.: Metaphor and Emotion: Language, Culture, and Body in Human Feeling. Cambridge University Press, Cambridge (2003)
13. Forceville, C.: Pictoral Metaphor in Advertising. Routledge, London (1996)
14. Gibbs, R.W.: Embodied metaphor in women's narrative about their experiences with cancer. Health Commun. **14**(2), 139–165 (2002)
15. Johnson, M., Larson, S.: "Something in the Way She Moves": metaphors of musical motion. Metaphor Symb. **18**(2), 63–84 (2003)
16. Kant, I.: Critique of Pure Reason, vol. 1781. Penguin Books, London (2008). (Trans. by. Weigelt, M.)
17. Oakley, T.: Image schemas. In: Geeraerts, D., Cuyckens, H. (eds.) The Oxford Handbook of Cognitive Linguistics, pp. 214–235. Oxford University Press, New York (2007)
18. Vernallis, C., Richardson, J., Gorbman, C. (eds.): The Oxford Handbook of New Audiovisual Aesthetics. Oxford University Press, Oxford (2013)
19. Grimshaw, M. (ed.): Game Sound. Technology and Player Interaction: Concepts and Developments, IGI Global, Hershey (2010)
20. DiFranco, D.E., Beauregard, G.K., Srinivasan, M.A.: The effect of auditory cues on the haptic perception of stiffness in virtual environments. In: Proceedings of ASME, Dynamic Systems and Control Division, DSC, vol. 61, pp. 17–22 (1997)
21. Simner, J., Cuskley, C., Kirby, S.: What sound does that taste? Cross-modal mapping across gustation and audition. Perception **39**(4), 553–569 (2010)
22. Belkin, K., Martin, R., Kamp, S.E., Gilbert, A.N.: Auditory pitch as perceptual analogue to odor quality. Am. Psychol. Soc. **8**(4), 340–342 (1997)
23. Grimshaw, M., Walther-Hansen, M.: The sound of the smell of my shoes. In: Proceedings of 10th Audio Mostly Conference, Thessaloniki, Greece. ACM Digital Library (2015). doi:10.1145/2814895.2814900
24. Bieber, D., Connor, U., Upton, T.A.: Discourse on the Move: Using Corpus Analysis to Describe Discourse Structure. John Benjamins Publisher, Amsterdam (2007)

25. Cameron, L., Deignan, A.: The emergence of metaphor in discourse. Appl. Linguist. **27**(4), 671–690 (2006)
26. Arnheim, R.: Art and Visual Perception: A Psychology of the Creative Eye. University of California Press, Berkeley (1954)
27. Talmy, L.: Force dynamics in language and thought. Cogn. Sci. **12**(1), 49–100 (1988)
28. Scruton, R.: The Aesthetics of Music. Clarendon Press, Oxford (1999)
29. Granot, R.Y., Eitan, Z.: Musical tension and the interaction of dynamic auditory parameters. Music Percept. **28**(3), 219–245 (2011)
30. Hjortkjær, J.: A cognitive theory of musical tension. Ph.D. thesis, University of Copenhagen, Copenhagen (2011)
31. Brower, C.: A cognitive theory of musical meaning. J. Music Theor. **44**(2), 323–379 (2000)
32. Walther-Hansen, M.: The force dynamic structure of the phonographic container: how sound engineers conceptualise the 'inside' of the mix. J. Music Mean. **12**, 89–115 (2014)
33. Wadhams, W.: Dictionary of Music Production and Engineering Terminology. Collier MacMillan Publishers, London (1988)
34. The British National Corpus, Version 3 (BNC XML Edition). Distributed by Oxford University Computing Services on behalf of the BNC Consortium (2007). http://www.natcorp.ox.ac.uk/
35. Hodgson, J.: Understanding Records: A Field Guide to Recording Practice. Continuum, New York and London (2010)
36. Chion, M., Gorbman, C.: The Voice in Cinema. Columbia University Press, New York (1999)
37. Moore, A., Dockwray, R.: The establishment of the virtual performance space in rock. Twentieth-Century Music **5**(2), 219–241 (2010)
38. Zbikowski, L.: Conceptual models and cross-domain mapping: new perspectives on theories of music and hierarchy. J. Music Theor. **41**(4), 193–225 (1997). Autumn
39. Tom Dowd and the Language of Music. Moormann, M. (Dir. Universal.) DVD (2003)
40. Daley, D.: The Engineers who Changed Recording: Fathers of Invention. Sound on Sound Magazine (October 2004)
41. Hurtienne, J., Blessing, L.: Design for intuitive use – testing image schema theory for user interface design. In: Proceedings of 16th International Conference on Engineering Design, Paris (2007)
42. Achintya, K.B.: Interactive Displays: Natural Human-Interface Technologies. Wiley, Hoboken (2014)
43. Sodhi, R., Poupyrev, I., Glisson, M., Israr, A.: AIREAL: interactive tactile experiences in free air. In: SIGGRAPH Conference Proceedings, Pittsburg (2013)

Conchord: An Application for Generating Musical Harmony by Navigating in the Tonal Interval Space

Gilberto Bernardes[1(✉)], Diogo Cocharro[1], Carlos Guedes[1,2], and Matthew E.P. Davies[1]

[1] Sound and Music Computing, INESC TEC, Porto, Portugal
{gba,diogo.m.cocharro,carlos.guedes,
mdavies}@inesctec.pt
[2] New York University Abu Dhabi, Abu Dhabi, United Arab Emirates

Abstract. We present Conchord, a system for real-time automatic generation of musical harmony through navigation in a novel 12-dimensional Tonal Interval Space. In this tonal space, angular and Euclidean distances among vectors representing multi-level pitch configurations equate with music theory principles, and vector norms acts as an indicator of consonance. Building upon these attributes, users can intuitively and dynamically define a collection of chords based on their relation to a tonal center (or key) and their consonance level. Furthermore, two algorithmic strategies grounded in principles from function and root-motion harmonic theories allow the generation of chord progressions characteristic of Western tonal music.

Keywords: Generative music · Harmony · Tonal pitch space

1 Introduction

Historically, Western tonal music has been subject to rigorous formalization, commonly expressed in a mathematical fashion. These formal tonal music frameworks are particularly adapted to computer modeling, which, in turn, can decisively contribute to machine musicianship [1]. A branch of this research is concerned with the automatic generation of harmony, which, within the Western tonal music context can be divided into two main problems: the automatic generation of chord progressions and the automatic harmonization of a given melody, of which the first concerns us here.

According to Wiggins [2], the automatic generation of musical harmony has been approached by different strategies, including (i) grammar-based systems [3], (ii) knowledge-based systems [4], (iii) biological-inspired algorithms [5, 6], (iv) constraint satisfaction systems [7] and (v) neural networks [8]. We extend Wiggins' taxonomy with a new category: statistical learning, which includes systems that generate harmony based on representations learned from musical examples [9, 10].

Central to this paper is the representation of the pitch configurations in generating musical harmony, especially through navigation in geometric pitch spaces, where neighborhood relations among the notes reflect perceptual or music theory properties.

The *Tonnetz* [11] is a planar representation of tonal pitch relations and one of the earliest examples of such geometrical spaces. Music theorists following the Riemann tradition adopted the Tonnetz to explain significant tonal pitch relationships, which are near one another in the space [12]. Chew's Spiral Array is another example of a geometric pitch space, which represents tonal pitch in a three-dimensional helix model and has been successfully applied to problems such as key estimation [13] and pitch spelling [14] from symbolic music data. Harte et al. [15] proposed the Tonal Centroid Space to estimate harmonic changes from musical audio by mapping 12-bin chroma vectors to the interior of a six-dimensional polytope. Recently, Bernardes et al. [16] presented a Tonal Interval Space, a twelve-dimensional space computed as the discrete Fourier transform of chroma vectors. While preserving the common-tone logic of the Tonnetz, the Tonal Interval Space overcomes an important limitation of the former by representing multi-level tonal pitch structures in the same space as unique vectors. Additionally, two important indicators can be computed from the space: tonal pitch relatedness and consonance.

Despite their intuitive and great explanatory potential, such spaces have yet to be widely applied to generative music. To the best of our knowledge, the only generative music systems built upon tonal pitch spaces were presented by: Behringer and Elliot [17] and Bigo et al. [18], who designed manually-driven generative systems based on the Tonnetz; Gatzsche et al. [19], who proposed a model for navigation on a three-dimensional space derived from Krumhansl and Kessler's [20] geometric representation of tonal pitch relations; and Chuan and Chew's [21] model for generating musical harmony through navigation in the Spiral Array.

Our approach to the automatic generation of musical harmony differs from, and extends previous research by proposing deterministic strategies for the real-time navigation in the Tonal Interval Space. We devise strategies to define spatial trajectories in the space for the generation of favorable chord progressions driven by principles from tonal harmony theories and build upon two main attributes of the space: tonal pitch relatedness and consonance. An important feature of our system is the possibility to modulate between keys—barely addressed in related software, yet a fundamental compositional strategy in tonal music.

Conchord, the prototype application of our model, was implemented for both Max [22] and Pure Data [23]. It allows expert and novice users to creatively explore musical harmony by assisting them in the automatic generation of 'generic' chord progressions characteristic of Western tonal music, rather than a specific response to a particular style or composer's idiom.

The main contributions beyond those in our previous work [24] include: (i) the use of a new set of weights in the Tonal Interval Space which better regulate the dimensions of the space for consonance measurements and (ii) the adoption of an algorithmic strategy to optimize the voice leading of selected chords given a user-defined pitch range.

The remainder of this paper is structured as follows. In Sect. 2 we present the architecture of Conchord, including the basic functioning of its component modules. In Sect. 3, we summarize the computation of the Tonal Interval Space in terms of its ability to measure tonal pitch relatedness among, and consonance level of, pitch configurations, in addition to the transposition invariance of tonal pitch directly mapped in the space. In Sect. 4, we describe the definition of a population of chords used during generation. In Sect. 5, we present the principles for optimal chord progression from two major harmony theories, which are then translated into spatial trajectories for the automatic generation of chord progressions in the Tonal Interval Space. In Sect. 6, we present an algorithmic strategy for unfolding selected chords represented by their component pitch classes to a user-defined pitch range while optimizing voice leading. In Sect. 7, we present the user interface of Conchord and the interaction design behind the application. In Sect. 8, we discuss the output of the system and finally, in Sect. 9, we state conclusions and future work.

2 Conchord: An Overview

Conchord is a system that automatically generates tonal harmony in real-time by navigation in a Tonal Interval Space, which places related pitch configurations at close distances. This property allows the definition of simple trajectories in the Tonal Interval Space driven by principles from function [25] and root-motion harmonic theories [26].

To enable navigation in the Tonal Interval Space and the generation of harmonic progressions, the system first populates the space with a collection of chords based on user input. These two main tasks are distributed into the following four modules of the system algorithmic chain: (i) initialization (ii) filtering, (iii) navigation/selection, and (iv) voice-leading (see Fig. 1).

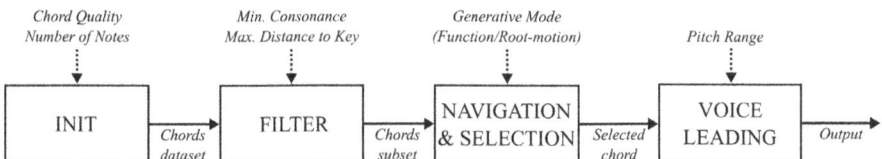

Fig. 1. Architecture of Conchord. The system modules are organized horizontally from left to right according to the information flow along with their input and output data.

The first module of the system automatically populates the Tonal Interval Space with a large set of chords based on user input specifying the chord quality and number of notes per chord. The second module is responsible for further constraining the chord dataset from the first module by filtering it according to two user-defined parameters: relatedness to a tonal center (or key) and consonance level. The resulting subset of chords is then stored into a database.

The third module comprises two generative algorithms for selecting favorable progressions among the (filtered) subset of chords through navigation in the Tonal Interval Space. The fourth and final module is responsible for organizing the voice leading of selected chords by unfolding its pitch class components into several pitch spacings and inversions over a user-defined pitch range. Then, a cost function ranks all generated solutions and outputs the candidate with the minimum cost for playback. Furthermore, this module allows the generation of chord progressions characteristic of

3 Tonal Interval Space

The backend of Conchord relies on a 12-dimensional (12-D) Tonal Interval Space [16]. It represents multi-level pitch configurations (i.e., pitch classes, chords, and keys) on a geometric space where indicators of tonal pitch relatedness and consonance can be computed.

In this space, pitch configurations are represented by Tonal Interval Vectors (TIVs), $T(k)$, computed as the DFT of 12-D chroma vectors $c(n)$ as follows:

$$T(k) = w(k) \sum_{n=0}^{N-1} \bar{c}(n) e^{-\frac{j2\pi k n}{N}}, \quad k \in \mathbb{Z} \quad \text{with} \quad \bar{c}(n) = \frac{c(n)}{\sum_{n=0}^{N-1} c(n)}. \quad (1)$$

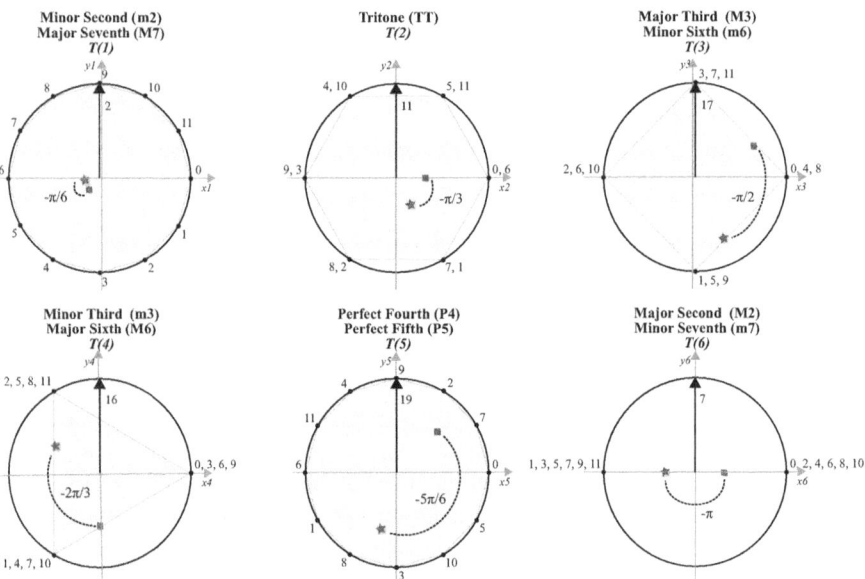

Fig. 2. Visualization of the Tonal Interval Space as six circles organized according to complementary intervals. Shaded grey areas denote the regions which TIVs can occupy for each circle. The plotted TIVs (square and star) correspond to the position of the C and C# major chords (pitch classes 0, 4, 7 and 1, 5, 8, respectively) in the space. The dashed circular lines indicate the angular rotation between C to C# major chords. The radii correspond to the weights of each complementary interval, $T(k)$, which for visualization purposes are all represented by identical size.

Here n is the chroma vector pitch class index up to $N = 12$, and $w(k) = \{2(m2/M7), 11(TT), 17(M3/m6), 16(m3/M6), 19(P4/P5), 7(M2/m7)\}$ are weights derived from empirical ratings of dyads' consonance used to adjust the contribution of each dimension k of the space. $T(k)$ uses $\bar{c}(n)$, which is $c(n)$ normalized by the DC component $T(0) = \sum_{n=0}^{N-1} c(n)$ to allow the representation and comparison of all levels of tonal pitch represented by $c(n)$ in the same space. In the standard DFT calculation, we set $k = 12$ however, in practice, we only need to calculate T for coefficients 1 to 6, thus excluding the DC component and symmetrical coefficients.

Following Harte et al. [15], we visualize the 12-D space as 6 circles, each representing one complex DFT coefficient (see Fig. 2), i.e. circle 1 has the real part of $T(1)$ on the x axis and the imaginary part of $T(1)$ on the y axis and so on.

3.1 Chroma Vector Representation of Multi-level Tonal Pitch

For the purpose of this paper, we restrict musical notation to symbolic representations, and hence we express the presence of input pitch classes in the chroma vector $c(n)$ by binary activations. Each of the 12 elements of the chroma vector corresponds to a pitch class of the chromatic scale, assuming equal temperament and enharmonic equivalence.

For example, the C major chord (pitch classes 0, 4, and 7) gives the chroma vector $c = \{1, 0, 0, 0, 1, 0, 0, 1, 0, 0, 0, 0\}$. Major keys are represented by their diatonic set of pitch classes (e.g., C major results in the chroma vector $c = \{1, 0, 1, 0, 1, 1, 0, 1, 0, 1, 0, 1\}$), and minor keys by the diatonic set of their natural minor scale (e.g., C minor results in the chroma vector $c = \{1, 0, 1, 1, 0, 1, 0, 1, 1, 0, 1, 0\}$).

A particularity of our approach is the use of the natural minor scale, which shares the same pitch classes as its relative major scale, instead of the harmonic minor scale commonly adopted to represent the minor region. In doing so, we systematize the method behind the computation of chord sequences in the major and minor regions. Therefore, for the remainder of this paper, we will primarily refer to the major mode; moreover, in Sect. 6, we further detail a strategy for adopting the harmonic minor scale.

Please note that in the chroma vector $c(n)$, and consequently in the TIV $T(k)$, no information about pitch height is encoded. Thus, the octave cannot be represented nor suggested by $c(n)$ with binary encoding because all the octaves are collapsed into one. Additionally, the information relative to chord inversions and the effect of the relative amplitude between pitch classes are lost.

3.2 Spatial Relations Among Multi-level Tonal Pitch Configurations

The TIVs, $T(k)$, of different chroma vectors are separated by some spatial distance in the Tonal Interval Space. In this section, we discuss how these spatial distances can be understood within the most salient hierarchical layers of the tonal system from lower to higher levels of abstraction (i.e., pitch classes, then chords, and finally keys or regions), as well as how the levels interconnect.

Similar to the pitch organization of the Tonnetz [11], the Tonal Interval Space places pitch class intervals understood as related within the Western tonal music context at close distances, i.e., minimizing distances for unisons over perfect fifth over major/minor thirds, etc.

For this work, the most relevant feature of the Tonal Interval Space's chordal level is how it minimizes distances among chords sharing common tones. The greater the number of common tones between chords, the closer they are in the space, thus favoring chord progressions with minimal displacement of moving voices (known as voice-leading parsimony).

At the regional level, our space minimizes distances for closely related regions, where each key is flanked by its relative, dominant and subdominant keys. Additionally, the diatonic pitch class set of a given region is in the neighborhood of its key TIV. In other words, in-key pitch classes are at a smaller distance to their respective key TIV than outside-the-key pitch classes. Table 1 further demonstrates this property of the Tonal Interval Space by showing the angular and Euclidean distances between C major region TIVs and all 12 pitch classes.

Table 1. Angular (θ) and Euclidean (d) distances between C major regions TIVs and the entire set of pitch classes. The diatonic pitch class set of each region are in bold.

	C	C#	D	D#	E	F	F#	G	G#	A	A#	B
θ	**1.22**	2.12	**1.09**	2.12	**1.22**	**1.40**	2.02	**1.15**	1.97	**1.15**	2.01	**1.40**
d	**30.9**	39.63	**29.50**	39.63	**30.91**	**32.79**	30.80	**30.07**	38.41	**30.07**	38.80	**32.79**

3.3 Transposition

The geometry of our space allows us to explain and directly map transposition-related pitch configurations by rotation of TIVs. Transposing a pitch configuration by p semitones result in rotations of $T(k)$ by $\varphi(p) = \frac{-2\pi kp}{N}$ radians. In other words, the angle of rotation of TIVs is systematic and different for each of the complex DFT coefficients (i.e., each of the 6 circles shown in Fig. 2). For example, transposing a pitch configuration one semitone up is achieved by rotating the six coefficients of the TIV by $-\pi/6$, $-\pi/3$, $-\pi/2$, $-2\pi/3$, $-5\pi/6$, and $-\pi$, respectively.

Denoting $T_p(k)$ as the transposed version of $T(k)$ we have

$$T_p(k) = |T(k)|e^{-\frac{j2\pi(k+p)}{N}}. \tag{2}$$

Rotating a TIV through all 12 semitones of the chromatic scale creates a concentric 'layer' containing all of its 12 possible transpositions. Therefore, pitch configurations sharing the same interval vector (e.g., chords with the same quality) are at the same distance from the center.

3.4 Measuring Consonance

Two important design principles of the Tonal Interval Space allow the computation of a tonal pitch consonance indicator from the space. They are the normalization by $T(0)$

and the weights $w(k)$ applied in Eq. (1). The former constrains the space to a limited area where all multi-level pitch configurations a chroma vector can represent exist. In the proposed visualization of the 12-D space shown in Fig. 2, this is equivalent to saying that all pitch configurations lie inside the 6 circles. The latter distorts the DFT coefficients to regulate the contribution of each interval according to empirical ratings of consonance. These two elements combined create a space in which pitch classes at the edge of the space and furthest from the center are considered the most consonant configurations, and a configuration with all 12 active pitch classes in the center of space is considered the most dissonant. These explicit design principles orders the norm of TIV, $\|T(K)\|$, for both dyads (i.e., P1 > P4/P5 > m3/M6 > M3/m6 > TT > M2/m7 > m2/M7) and common triads (i.e., major/minor > suspended fourth > diminished > augmented) according to empirical data derived from previous listening experiments [27–31].

Hence, we extrapolate the consonance measure $C(T)$ of the $\|T(K)\|$ by the norm $T(k)$, which can also be calculated as the Euclidean distance from the centre as follows:

$$C(T) = \|T(K)\| = \sqrt{T(k) \cdot T(k)} = \sqrt{\sum_{k=1}^{M}|T(k)|^2}. \tag{3}$$

4 Defining a Population of Chords

The first module of our algorithmic chain defines a population of chords to be used during generation by a twofold strategy. First, the system populates the space with a large set of chords with variable numbers of notes and qualities. Second, those chords that correspond to a pre-defined tonal center and minimum consonance level are retained and all others are discarded.

Conchord includes four options to initially populate the Tonal Interval Space with chords: (i) all m-note chords combinations without repetition from the set of 12 pitch classes; (ii) all major, minor, and augmented triads; (iii) all major, minor and half-diminished seventh chords; and (iv) the manual specification of chords.

After creating an initial population of chords, T_i, these are reduced to a subset of chords, Z_i, by applying user-defined constraints that regulate the chords' relation to a key and the chords' consonance. A maximal distance of the chords from a key TIV defines the key-relatedness constraint, and a minimum norm of the chords TIV defines the consonance constraint. In this way, the subset of chords, Z_i, meets both conditions simultaneously:

$$Z_i = T_i\{D_i < D_{max} \,\&\, C(T_i) > C_{min}\}, \tag{4}$$

where,

$$D_i = \sqrt{\sum_k \left[|T_{key}(k) - T_{chord}(k)|\right]^2}, \tag{5}$$

D_{max} is the maximum distance of chord TIVs, $T_{chord}(k)$, from a key TIV, $T_{key}(k)$, and C_{min} denotes the user-defined minimal chord consonance. Both constraints can be assigned using Conchord's interface as described in section. Typical ranges for these parameters are $11 < D_{max} < 33$ and $15 < C_{min} < 25$. The TIVs and the component pitch classes of the resulting subset of chords are then stored in a database.

The modulation between keys in the Tonal Interval Space combines the possibility to transpose keys by TIV rotation with the constraint-based strategies stated in (5). Given both the interval distance between a target and departure keys in semitones and their TIVs, we can modulate between them by defining an angular trajectory in the Tonal Interval Space that continuously discards and adds new chords to the chord database. This angular trajectory corresponds to the interpolation between target and departure key TIVs given by the smaller angular rotation (either clockwise or anti-clockwise) on each individual circle calculated using (3). The resulting trajectory enssures that overlapping and adjacent pitches and chords across regions favor a smooth transition between keys.

5 Chord Candidate Selection

This section details two algorithmic strategies for defining 'optimal' motions in the Tonal Interval Space among the database chords, Z_i. Chord selection occurs once every beat and is triggered by an internal clock adjusted to a user-defined tempo.

The algorithmic strategies for navigation in the Tonal Interval Space are driven by formalized principles from two theories of tonal harmony: function and root-motion harmonic theories (Sect. 5.1). The translation of formalized principles to trajectories in the Tonal Interval Space for the generation of favorable chord progressions is detailed in Sects. 5.2 and 5.3.

5.1 Theories of Tonal Harmony

Tonal harmony has been a frequently visited topic by music theorists since Rameau's original treatise [32]. Among the most widely accepted and popular theories of harmony we find: (i) scale-degree theories, which claim that each chord can resolve in its own characteristic way; (ii) function theories, which group chords into larger categories; and (iii) root-motion theories, which emphasize the intervals formed between successive chord-roots.

The principles for favorable chord progressions stated by the two latter theories will be presented next, with the aim of inferring formalisms which can then be translated into trajectories in the Tonal Interval Space. We do not address scale-degree theories because their underlying principles cannot be modeled in our space due to their asymmetric nature. For a comprehensive explanation of these theories please refer to [33].

Function Theories. Originated by Riemann [25], function theories examine and explain musical harmony according to two fundamental components: chord categories based on shared harmonic function and typical motions between these categories [34].

In detail, the first component groups chords together into three categories: (i) 'tonic,' (ii) 'subdominant,' and (iii) 'dominant' [25]. The tonic category comprises the tonic, mediant, and submediant degrees (the *I*, *iii*, and *vi* degrees); the subdominant category comprises the subdominant, supertonic, and submediant degrees (the *IV*, *ii*, and *vi* degrees); and the dominant category comprises the dominant, leading-tone, and mediant degrees (the *V*, *vii°*, and *iii* degrees). The second component of the function theory postulates normative patterns of functional progressions. According to Riemann [25], usual motions depart from the tonic to the subdominant to the dominant and then back to the tonic.

Root-Motion Theories. Following the seminal work of Rameau [32], root-motion theories have been extended by Schoenberg [26] and Meeus [35]. Root-motion theories claim that standard and common tonal progressions can be defined in terms of the intervals formed by the root of consecutive chords, emphasizing a set of 'optimal' or common chord root progressions, compared to 'atypical' sequences.

The guidelines for optimal chord progressions in terms of the type of root motion adopted here are based on Schoenberg [26], who distinguishes three root progression cases: 'ascending,' 'descending' and 'super-strong' progressions. In an ascending progression, the chord root moves a fourth up or a third down (e.g., *I–IV* and *I–vi*, respectively). In a descending progression the chord root moves up a fifth or a third (e.g., *I–V* and *I–iii*, respectively). Finally, in a super-strong progression a chord root moves a second up or down (e.g., *V–vi* and *V–IV*, respectively).

While encouraging the unreserved use of ascending root progressions, Schoenberg discourages the use of descending progressions—which should be treated as passing chords between ascending progressions—and the sparse use of super-strong progressions.

5.2 Angular Trajectories Driven by Harmonic Function Theory Principles

To define angular trajectories in the Tonal Interval Space that convey the harmonic function theory principles stated above, we first define three harmonic function regions—tonic, subdominant, and dominant—in the 12-D space. These harmonic function regions are represented by three vectors departing from the key TIV, $T_{key}(k)$, to the tonic, subdominant, and dominant TIVs, $T_i(k)$, respectively (represented in Fig. 3 as $\vec{T}_I$, $\vec{T}_{IV}$, and $\vec{T}_V$), such that

$$\vec{T}_i(k) = T_i(k) - T_{key}(k). \qquad (6)$$

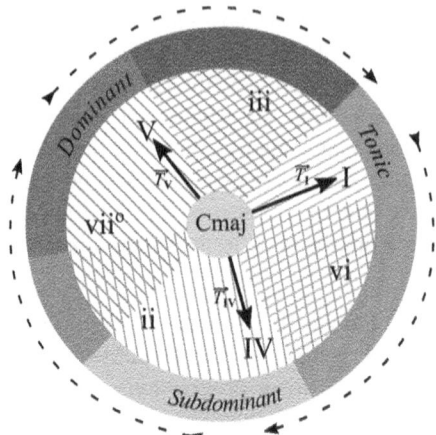

Fig. 3. 2-D visualisation of the 12-D representation of the C major key and its common component diatonic triads using nonmetric multidimensional scaling—Roman numerals label the harmonic function of each triad. The pattern regions denote three harmonic function categories (i.e., Tonic, Subdominant, and Dominant) and $\vec{T}_\text{I}$, $\vec{T}_\text{IV}$, and $\vec{T}_\text{V}$ their representative vectors. Dashed circular lines represent typical motions between harmonic function categories (i.e., Tonic to Subdominant to Dominant and back to Tonic).

For the purpose of visualization of the harmonic function categories regions we use a 2-D representation of the 12-D Tonal Interval space obtained by nonmetric multi-dimensional scaling[1] (MDS) as shown in Fig. 3.

Relying on the vector representations for the three harmonic function regions, we then define in the 12-D space favorable motions between them following Riemann [25]. To this end, we sequentially alternate between the target vectors $\vec{T}_{target}$ (i.e., $\vec{T}_\text{I}$, $\vec{T}_\text{IV}$, and $\vec{T}_\text{V}$) and randomly select a chord from the database within a $\pi/2$ angular distance, computed by the angle ϑ_i in Eq. (7). To perform this operation, all database chord candidates, $T_i(k)$, are first converted to vectors departing from the key TIV using Eq. (6).

$$\vartheta_i = \cos^{-1} \frac{\vec{T}_{target} \cdot \vec{T}_i}{\| \vec{T}_{target} \| \cdot \| \vec{T}_i \|}. \tag{7}$$

---

[1] Sheppard [36] and Kruskal [37] first used this method, which has been extensively applied to visualise representations of multidimensional pitch structures [38, 39]. Briefly, nonmetric MDS attempts to transform a set of n-dimensional vectors, expressed by their distance in the item-item matrix, into a spatial representation that exposes the interrelationships among a set of input cases. We use the smacof library [40] from the statistical analysis package 'R' to compute dimensionality reduction using a nonmetric MDS algorithm. More specifically, we use the function smacofSym, with 'ordinal' type and 'primary' ties.

5.3 Angular Trajectories Driven by Root-Motion Harmonic Theory Principles

We define root-motion motion between successive chords in a stochastic manner based on angular distances. Prior to selection, the system calculates the vectors departing from an assigned key TIV, $T_{key}(k)$, to the chord database TIVs, $T_i(k)$, and to an additional set of seven diatonic triads TIVs for each scale degree—referred hereafter as the target vector, $\vec{T}_I - \vec{T}_{vii°}$, where the chord database and target vectors are computed using (6).

At each new chord selection, a stochastic algorithm decides the next chord root following Schoenberg's suggestions for favorable chord-root progressions, i.e. favoring ascending progressions, over super-strong progressions, over descending progressions—according to heuristically assigned probabilities of 60 % (ascending), 20 % (super-strong), 10 % (descending) and 10 % (remaining in the same chord root).

Figure 4 shows the organization of the diatonic triad TIVs and their representative (target) vectors around the key TIV, as well as the probabilities of transition between them departing from the root of the tonic (left) and subdominant (right) degrees.

Then, given a chord root for the next progressions, the system identifies the corresponding triad with such a root and retrieves its representative target vector. Finally, the system computes in the 12-D space the angle ϑ_i between the target vector and the chord database vectors using (7), and randomly selects a chord from the set of database chord within the range $\pi/6$ around the target angle.

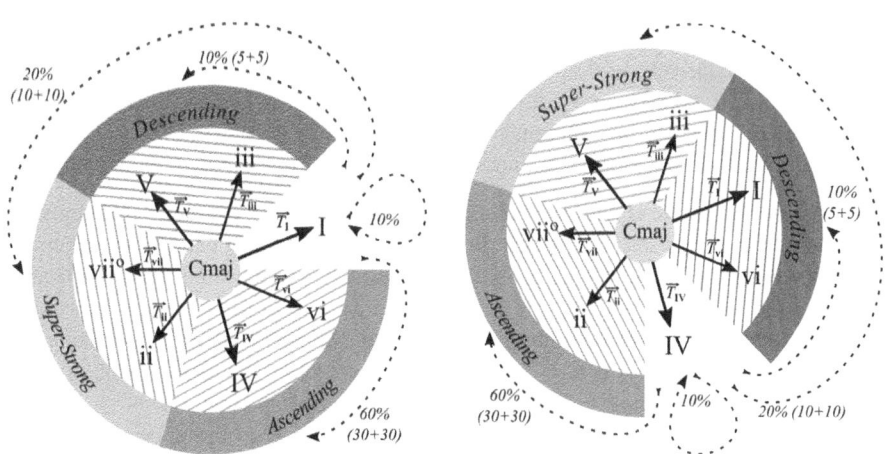

Fig. 4. 2-D visualisation of the 12-D representation of the C major key and its common component diatonic triads using nonmetric multidimensional scaling—Roman numerals label the harmonic function of each triad. The pattern regions organize and highlight the three root-motion progressions proposed by Schoenberg [26], departing from the tonic (left) and subdominant (right). Bold lines correspond to the vectors $\vec{T}_I - \vec{T}_{vii°}$ of common diatonic triads from their key TIV and dashed lines the probability of transitioning between root-motion cases.

6 Voice Leading and Playback

Voice leading is the term used to denote the horizontal motion of the individual parts (or voices) in harmony writing. The rules for voice leading together with the rules for harmonic progression establish the ground for successful musical harmony writing. Its importance is highlighted by Schonbrun [41, p. 174], who claims that 'good voice leading can take a simple chord sequence and transform it into a masterpiece'.

A vast amount of literature detailing objective rules for optimal voice leading exists [42]. The most common rules for voice leading found in music theory textbooks are drawn from, and meant for, four-part vocal music. Even though these rules can be applied to music outside this category, we should bear in mind that voice leading is highly linked and commonly adapted to the context of the piece, including style, orchestration, composer idiosyncrasies, etc.

We follow a strategy first detailed in [16] to enhance the voice leading of selected chords given their pitch class sets and a user-defined pitch range. The rules adopted here were selected from a large collection of voice leading rules framed for four-part vocal music in [42]. The selection criteria were based on the adaptability of the rules to general tonal music contexts other than vocal music, resulting in the following five rules:

1. Vertical (chord) spacings—intervals between parts should not exceed one octave, with the exception of the interval formed by the two lowest parts, in which no restriction is applied;
2. Avoid large horizontal (or melodic) leaps—adjacent chords should minimize the intervallic distance in each voice;
3. Avoid parallel octaves and fifths—intervals of the octave and fifth should not happen consecutively in the same parts;
4. Avoid hidden octaves and fifths—intervals of the octave and fifth should not happen consecutively in different parts;
5. Outer parts contrary motion—contrary motion between outer parts is encouraged.

Based on the above-stated rules, we devised an algorithmic strategy that finds the best voice leading for selected chords from a large set of chord candidates generated from unpacking the set of pitch classes to all possible inversions and vertical spacings within a user-defined pitch range. For example, a 3-note chord will result in a set of chord candidates which include the fundamental state as well as its two inversions (i.e. with the third and fifth on the bass). Additionally, for each of the three sets all possible chord spacings within the user-defined pitch range are instantiated.

All candidate chords generated are evaluated in relation to the previously played chord and are ranked using the set of points shown in Table 2. An algorithm assigns a cost for each of the five voice leading rules per chord candidate. Then, an overall cost per chord is computed by summing the five rule condition costs. Finally, the algorithm outputs the chord with the minimum (i.e., best) voice leading cost.

After a chord has been selected it is converted to MIDI note messages for playback using a synthesizer. For simplicity, we assign an arbitrary MIDI note velocity of 100 for all notes and set the duration to be equal to the length of each beat.

Table 2. Point assignments for voice leading rule conditions.

		1. Chord spacing	2. Melodic leap	3. Contrary motion	4. Parallel $5^{th}/8^{th}$	6. Hidden $5^{th}/8^{th}$
Cost	5	–	–	–	true	true
	2	>12	>8	–	–	–
	1	>3	>4	false	–	–
	0	=0	=0	true	false	false

Prior to the definition of the chord candidate that best fits the voice leading rules while in a minor key, a parallel operation shifts the seventh degree of the natural minor scale a semitone higher (e.g. on a minor scale, shifting the G natural to G sharp). While the use of the natural minor scale simplifies the generations and database construction, this additional processing allows the generation of chords characteristic of the harmonic minor scale, the most common scale for chord construction in minor keys.

7 User Interface

To allow users to interact with Conchord, we have created an interface for both Max [22] and Pure Data [23], of which a screenshot of the latter is shown in Fig. 5. Conchord's interface was designed to provide a simple, intuitive, and flexible experience for both expert and novice users. Despite minor cosmetic differences, the Max and Pure Data versions have identical functionality.

The interface is composed of three modules stacked vertically. The two upper modules are responsible for (i) setting the parameters for initializing and filtering out

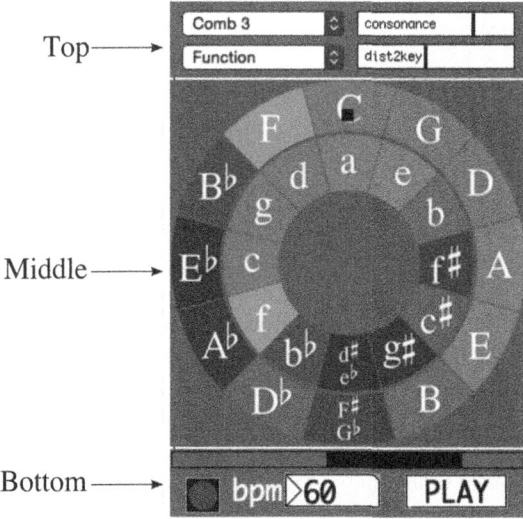

Fig. 5. Conchord interface developed for the PD programming environment.

the population of chords as detailed in Sect. 4 and for (ii) defining the generative strategy behind chord selection between function and root-motion harmonic theory principles. The lower module is responsible for controlling the playback as well as specifying the pitch range chords can occupy.

To initialize the Tonal Interval Space with a population of chords, the user must first define on the top-left menu of the uppermost module the type of chord aggregates initially generated by selecting one of following four predefined options: (i) 'Diatonic triads,' (ii) 'Diatonic tetrads,' (iii) 'Comb 3'—which stand for all 3-note chords combinations without repetition from the 12 pitch classes, and (iv) 'Comb 4'—which stands for all 4-note chords combinations without repetition from the 12 pitch classes. Then, the user should specify in the middle module a key among the 24 minor and major keys represented on a double circle of fifths, which mirrors the key organization of the Tonal Interval Space. The selected key will be then used to calculate the chord relatedness to a tonal center.

The first two top-left menu entries automatically initialize the Tonal Interval Space with the common diatonic triads and tetrads of a given key by populating the space with all major, minor and diminished chords and further filtering them according to pre-defined key-relatedness and consonance parameter values. Top-left menu entries three and four offer a greater degree of freedom and allow users to initialize the space with all combinations of 3- and 4-note chords, as well as the possibility to manually specify both filtering parameters. Furthermore, the space can also be populated by a set of chords manually chosen via a standard Max and Pure Data message format specifying their pitch class components. In the bottom-left menu of the top interface module, the user can define one of two 'Function and 'Root-motion' generative modes.

Finally, the bottom module of the interface includes parameters that regulate the pitch range chords can occupy, the tempo (in beats-per-minute), as well as start/stop and recording commands. The output format of the recoding is in the standard MIDI format, which can be further edited in traditional MIDI sequencers.

8 Results

This section discusses musical results generated by the two strategies implemented in Conchord, of which a transcription along with its function and root-motion harmonic analysis is shown in Fig. 6.

Figure 6 includes two staves, resulting from each generative strategy: the upper one corresponding to the harmonic function theory and the lower to the root-motion harmonic theory. Additionally, each stave is split into two parts, which differ according to the chord database. The first part only adopts common (major, minor and diminished) diatonic triads of the C major key. The second part remains in the key of C major, but adopts an extended degree of dissonance in relation to the core diatonic triads.

In the particular case of the harmonic function theory (upper stave of Fig. 6) the chord sequence follows the functional category motions proposed by Riemann [25], i.e. the normative patterns of functional progressions from the tonic (T) to the subdominant (SD) to the dominant (D) and back to the tonic. Additionally, the sequences of functional harmonic categories are not disturbed in the second part of the stave when

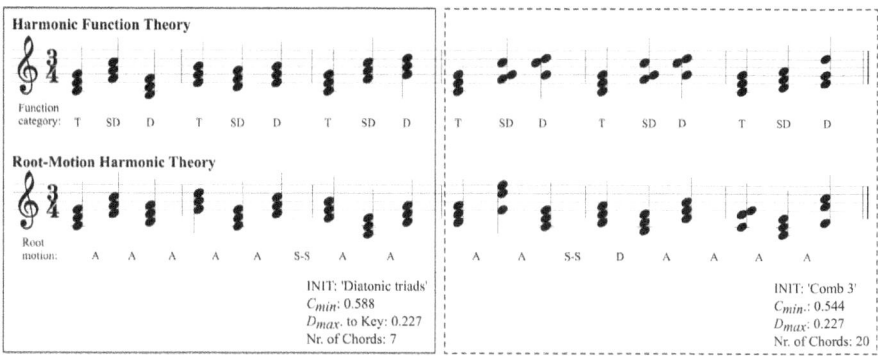

Fig. 6. Chord progressions generated with Conchord. The upper stave was generated using the harmonic function theory principles and includes an analysis of the chord's functional category (i.e., Tonic, SubDominant, and Dominant). The lower stave was generated according to root-motion theory principles and includes an analysis of the root-motion cases (i.e., Ascending, Descending, and Super-Strong). The bold square circumscribes the use of common diatonic triads of the C major key, and the dashed square remain in the key of C major but extends the database while adopting an extended degree of dissonance. To facilitate reading, chords were rearranged to their root position.

decreasing the level of consonance (which results in a higher degree of tonal ambiguity).

In the lower stave of Fig. 6, the chord progressions obey Schoenberg's [26] guidelines for favorable chord-root motions. Note that in the generated excerpt, ascending progressions occur 76 % of the time, super-strong progressions were explicitly restricted to 12 % and descending progressions or remaining in the same chord root to 6 % each. As in the function harmonic theory, decreasing the level of dissonance didn't disturb the expected the probability of occurrence of chord-root motions.

To summarize, the generated chord sequences demonstrate the efficiency of the algorithms, which convey the principles of the function and root-motion harmonic theories, as well as the behavior of the generative music algorithms under more dissonant and less representative chord aggregates of a tonal center. Several more musical examples generated by the system along with supplementary harmonic analysis and expanded use of generated chord progressions via arpeggiation and orchestration are available at: http://smc.inesctec.pt/technologies/conchord.

9 Conclusions and Future Work

In this paper we presented strategies for navigating in the Tonal Interval Space, a novel 12-D representation for the automatic generation of chord progressions based on harmonic theory principles. The primary contributions of our Tonal Interval Space in comparison to existing methods, notably those by Chew [13] and Harte et al. [15], are the possibility to explain the relations among pitch configurations at the three fundamental pitch, chord and key levels of Western tonal music in a single space, and to provide an indicator of the consonance of pitch configurations.

The algorithm and applications presented establish a novel approach to the real-time automatic generation of harmony driven by the tonal pitch organization of the Tonal Interval Space in combination with principles derived from function and root-motion harmonic theories. The algorithms convey the principles established by both theories, which have been modeled in existing generative music applications. The novelty of our approach relies on the highly flexible and dynamic specification of a chord database prior to generation based on user-defined chord parameters including: the number of notes, chord quality, relatedness to a key, and level of consonance, which in itself expands upon existing systems for the automatic generation of chord progression beyond the common four-voice setting and conventional use of simple triads.

While we only formalized principles for favorable chord progressions in this paper, many musical aspects such as rhythmic structure are not modeled currently. A more refined model will be addressed in future work by incorporating additional musical components, including the integration of the current algorithmic strategies within a metrical template. By doing so, we will also be able to more efficiently define strategies for selecting chords within the large chord categories considered by our system.

Acknowledgments. This research is financed by National Funds through the FCT - Fundação para a Ciência e a Tecnologia within post-doctoral grants SFRH/BPD/109457/2015 and SFRH/BPD/88722/2012.

References

1. Rowe, R.: Machine Musicianship. MIT Press, Cambridge (2001)
2. Wiggins, G.A.: Automated generation of musical harmony: what's missing. In: Proceedings of the International Joint Conference in Artificial Intelligence (1999)
3. Rohrmeier, M.: A generative grammar approach to diatonic harmonic structure. In: Proceedings of the 4th Sound and Music Computing Conference, pp. 97–100 (2007)
4. Pachet, F.: The MusES system: an environment for experimenting with knowledge representation techniques in tonal harmony. In: 1st Brazilian Symposium on Computer Music, pp. 195–201 (1994)
5. Phon-Amnuaisuk, S., Tuson, A., Wiggins, G.: Evolving musical harmonisation. In: Dobnikar, A., Steele, N.C., Pearson, D.W., Albrecht, R.F. (eds.) Artificial Neural Nets and Genetic Algorithms, pp. 229–234. Springer, Vienna (1999)
6. Navarro, M., Caetano, M., Bernardes, G., de Castro, L.N., Corchado, J.M.: Automatic generation of chord progressions with an artificial immune system. In: Johnson, C., Carballal, A., Correia, J. (eds.) EvoMUSART 2015. LNCS, vol. 9027, pp. 175–186. Springer, Heidelberg (2015)
7. Pachet, F., Roy, P.: Formulating constraint satisfaction problems on part-whole relations: the case of automatic musical harmonization. In: ECAI 98 Workshop on Constraints for Artistic Applications, pp. 1–11 (1998)

8. Gang, D., Lehmann, D., Wagner, N.: Harmonizing melodies in real-time: the connectionist approach. In: Proceedings of the International Computer Music Association, Thessaloniki, Greece, pp. 27–31 (1997)
9. Manaris, B., Johnson, D., Vassilandonakis, Y.: Harmonic navigator: a gesture-driven, corpus-based approach to music analysis, composition, and performance. In: Proceedings of the 9th AAAI Conference on Artificial Intelligence and Interactive Digital Entertainment, pp. 67–74 (2013)
10. Eigenfeldt, A., Pasquier, P.: Realtime generation of harmonic progressions using controlled markov selection. In: Proceedings of ICCC-X-Computational Creativity Conference, pp. 16–25 (2010)
11. Cohn, R.: Neo-riemannian operations, parsimonious trichords, and their "tonnetz" representations. J. Music Theory **41**(1), 1–66 (1997)
12. Cohn, R.: Introduction to neo-riemannian theory: a survey and a historical perspective. J. Music Theory **42**(2), 167–180 (1998)
13. Chew, E.: Towards a mathematical model of tonality. Ph.D. dissertation, MIT (2000)
14. Chew, E., Chen, Y.: Determining context-defining windows: pitch spelling using the spiral array. In: Proceedings of the International Society for Music Information Retrieval Conference (2003)
15. Harte, C., Sandler, M., Gasser, M.: Detecting harmonic change in musical audio. In: Proceedings of the 1st ACM Workshop on Audio and Music Computing Multimedia, pp. 21–26. ACM, New York (2006)
16. Bernardes, G., Cocharro, D., Guedes, C., Davies, M.E.P.: Harmony generation driven by a perceptually motivated tonal interval space. In: ACM Computers in Entertainment. ACM, New York (2015, in press)
17. Behringer, R., Elliot, J.: Linking physical space with the Riemann Tonnetz for exploration of western tonality. In: Hermida, J., Ferrero, M. (eds.) Music Education. Nova Science Publishers Inc, Hauppauge (2009)
18. Bigo, L., Garcia, J., Spicher, A., Mackay, W.E.: PaperTonnetz: music composition with interactive paper. In: Proceedings of the 9th Sound and Music Computing Conference, pp. 219–225 (2012)
19. Gatzsche, G., Mehnert, M., Stöcklmeier, C.: Interaction with tonal pitch spaces. In: 8th International Conference on New Interfaces for Musical Expression, Genova, Italy, pp. 325–330 (2008)
20. Krumhansl, C.L., Kessler, E.J.: Tracing the dynamic changes in perceived tonal organization in a spatial representation of musical keys. Psychol. Rev. **89**, 334–368 (1982)
21. Chuan, C.-H., Chew, E.: A hybrid system for automatic generation of style-specific accompaniment. In: Proceedings of the 4th International Joint Workshop on Computational Creativity, pp. 57–64. Goldsmiths, University of London (2007)
22. Pure Data. http://puredata.info
23. Max. https://cycling74.com
24. Bernardes, G., Cocharro, D., Guedes, C., Davies, M.E.P.: Conchord: an application for generating musical harmony by navigating in a perceptually motivated tonal interval space. In: Proceedings of the 11th International Symposium on Computer Music Modeling and Retrieval (CMMR), pp. 71–86 (2015)
25. Riemann, H.: Vereinfachte Harmonielehre. Augener, London (1893)
26. Schoenberg, A.: Structural Functions of Harmony, 2nd edn. W. W. Norton Inc., New York (1969). [1954], (Revised by Stein, L.)
27. Malmberg, C.F.: The Perception of consonance and dissonance. Psychol. Monogr. **25**(2), 93–133 (1918)

28. Kameoka, A., Kuriyagawa, M.: Consonance theory. Part I: consonance of dyads. J. Acoust. Soc. Am. **45**, 1451–1459 (1969)
29. Hutchinson, W., Knopoff, L.: The acoustic component of Western consonance. Interface **10**(2), 129–149 (1979)
30. Roberts, L.A.: Consonance judgements of musical chords by musicians and untrained listeners. Acta Acustica United Acustica **62**(2), 163–171 (1986)
31. Cook, N.D.: Harmony, Perspective, and Triadic Cognition. Cambridge University Press, New York (2012)
32. Rameau, J.-P.: Traité de l'Harmonie. Ballard, Paris (1722). Treatise on Harmony (trans: Gossett, P.) Dover, New York (1971)
33. Tymoczko, D.: Progressions Fondamentales, Fonctions, Degrés: Une Grammaire de l'Harmonie Tonale Élémentaire. Musurgia: Analyse et Pratique Musicales **10**(3–4), 35–64 (2003)
34. Agmon, E.: Functional harmony revisited: a prototype-theoretic approach. Music Theory Spectr. **17**(2), 196–214 (1995)
35. Meeus, N.: Toward a post-Schoenbergian grammar of tonal and pre-tonal harmonic progressions. Music Theory Online **6**(1) (2000)
36. Shepard, R.N.: Structural representations of musical pitch. In: Deutsch, D. (ed.) The Psychology of Music, pp. 335–353. Academic Press, New York (1982)
37. Kruskal, J.B.: Nonmetric multidimensional scaling: a numerical method. Psychometrika **29**, 28–42 (1964)
38. Krumhansl, C.L., Kessler, E.J.: Tracing the dynamic changes in perceived tonal organization in a spatial representation of musical keys. Psychol. Rev. **89**, 334–368 (1982)
39. Lerdahl, F.: Tonal Pitch Space. Oxford University Press, New York (2001)
40. De Leeuw, J., Mair, P.: Multidimensional scaling using majorization: SMACOF in R. J. Stat. Softw. **31**(3), 1–30 (2009)
41. Schonbrun, M.: The Everything Music Theory: Take Your Understanding of Music to the Next Level. Adams Media, Avon (2011)
42. Huron, D.: Tone and voice: a derivation of the rules of voice-leading from perceptual principles. Music Percept. **19**(1), 1–64 (2001)

Musical Variation and Improvisation Based on Multi-resolution Representations

Johan Loeckx(✉)

Artificial Intelligence Lab, Vrije Universiteit Brussel,
Pleinlaan 2, 1050 Brussel, Belgium
jloeckx@ai.vub.ac.be

Abstract. Musical creativity is one of the show pieces of Artificial Intelligence and during the last decades, many paths have been explored to capture musical style and to generate new music. One of the approaches exploits the similarities between music and language. In this paper, Fluid Construction Grammar, a state-of-the-art computational grammar is used to parse/analyse an existing piece, in order to create a variation on the song and generate an improvisation in the same style, using the same bi-directional grammar. A novel multi-resolution time representation to model musical melodies is presented.

Keywords: Fluid Construction Grammar · Improvisation · Musical style · Composition

1 Introduction

Many paths for representing and creating music have been explored in the last decades, including Hidden Markov Models [12], Machine Learning, Prediction Suffix Trees [9], n-gram models [13], schema-based approaches [6] and connectionist models [19]. Although a lot of these techniques have achieved many successes, most computational representations still lack the expressive power to model the complex subtleties and interactions in music. On of the running debates is the question what the analogies between music and language are [3] and whether paradigms and concepts of language can be successfully applied to music. In the past, for example, generative context-free grammars have been used [10,15], in which *constructions* (the rules of the grammar) are written in a generic form of recursive rewrite rules. The term "context-free" stems from the fact that the constructions can be applied *regardless of the context of their left-hand side*.

There are, however, some fundamental problems with these grammars in music as much as in language. First, music is heavily context-dependent. Though previous research efforts have attempted to generalize or extended these kinds of grammars to account for some of the context [14], they lack the intrinsic expressive power to model the complex context-aware interactions that constantly occur in music. Second, the single-aspect view on notes or degrees as atomic entity, combined with the limited expressive power of the rules, are not satisfying in the domain of music and multiple-viewpoint approaches are required [2]. For example, (a) the same note can have two degrees in a modulation sequence, depending whether you take the first or second key as a reference; (b) in a polyphonic piece, a note is both part of a "musical phrase" in the same voice (e.g. the highest note in the phrase) as part of a chord with regard to the other voices.

For this reason, the author opted for Fluid Construction Grammar (FCG), a state-of-the-art computational grammar that allows the expression of context in a sophisticated way and preserves the intrinsic multi-viewpoint nature of musical artefacts. In this paper, a novel methodology to create improvisations and variations on existing songs is proposed, based on a multi-resolution representation of music. This work is structured as follows. First, the concepts of Fluid Construction Grammar are introduced. Next, the methodology is explained and the implementation discussed. The approach is finally validated on two example, one for improvisation and one for variation.

2 Fluid Construction Grammar

2.1 Paradigm

Fluid Construction Grammar (FCG) is such a formalism that has repeatedly proved its power and flexibility in the domain of linguistics [4,17,20]. FCG was conceived in 1998 as an underlying formalism for modelling language evolution using language games played by autonomous robots [7]. It allows parsing a (natural language or musical) utterance into a semantic interpretation, and vice versa (during production), using the same bi-directional rule set of constructions. It uses as many as possible existing widely accepted notions in theoretical and computational linguistics, including but not limited to:

- *feature structures* for the representation of musical symbolic information;
- *abstract templates or constructions* for the representation of grammatical patterns;
- *general operators* for building up syntactic and semantic structures.

FCG represents all information during parsing and production using *transient structures*, which are extended coupled feature structures consisting of two sets of addressable units, called poles: a syntactical one that corresponds to structure and a semantic one that represents the "meaning" of a musical phrase. One of the strong point is that the feature structures provide information from different linguistic or musical perspectives. A note, for example, can have different viewpoints (an absolute pitch and a degree with respect to the key and chord) and relations, creating a sophisticated context to which constructions can refer.

A construction is an abstract schema that can be used to expand any aspect of a transient structure from any perspective and it can consult any aspect of the transient structure to decide how to do so. Constructions are not merely intended to be descriptive, they should support parsing and production processes as active computational entities. FCG-constructions use the same representation as transient structures, i.e. they are formulated in terms of named units, features and values. A construction may also introduce new units, and establish new relations between units. They are more abstract however than transient structures because its elements can be variables instead of concrete elements, and not all the features should be specified.

One of the main features of construction grammar is that the basic unit of grammar, the construction, deals not only with syntactic issues but also with semantics, pragmatics and meaning. In this sense, a construction is a pairing of form and meaning/function. It is important to note that the same construction can be used for parsing as well as production.

2.2 Differences with Context-Free Grammars

For those familiar with existing work on generative grammars for music production and representation, it is crucial to understand the fundamental differences between FCG and more "traditional" context-free grammars.

1. *FCG marks no sharp distinction between idiomatic and general rules:* a grammatical construction can be either highly specialised, e.g. applicable to a single case, or very abstract, covering a wide range of uses.
2. There is a *continuum in the hierarchy and domain of rules:* constructions can involve different levels of abstraction. For example, the same rule can for example apply to one note or to a motif and there no distinction in the formulation or processing of melodic or harmonic entries.
3. FCG allows *schematisation through variable binding and categorisation:* Grammatical constructions can be made more abstract (or schematic) than concrete instantiations of a musical phrase in three ways: parts of the structure can be left out (widening the context of application), variables can be used instead concrete instantiations and categories are introduced.
4. *Constructions can be combined* – several constructions all matching with different parts of the musical phrase – *or integrated*, using hierarchical constructions that combine partial structures into larger wholes.

2.3 Parsing and Producing Music

In comprehension or parsing, the transient structure starts from information derived from the input utterance and is progressively expanded using constructions until the meaning can be derived. In formulation, the transient structure contains initially the meaning to be expressed and then consecutive operations expand this structure until all the information is there to render an utterance. In this paper, we will not go deeper into detail into the semantics of music, which is a controversial topic on its own [8,11,16], but use a pragmatic interpretation that is not based on philosophical grounds but serves our purpose: to create a new song in the same (rhythmical) style; or to create the same song in a different style.

Fig. 1. Multi-resolution view on a simple melody. Layer 0 captures all fine-grained rhythmic information, while higher layers create rhythmic abstractions based on reduction. In this example reduction is obtained by selecting the "strong beat" at each layer, indicated by a cross, for each layer. The resolution (quantization) is indicated for each layer at the left. All different layers are stored simultaneously to create a multi-resolution representation of a musical phrase, model for a hierarchy of time and allowing to capture short-term details as well as long-term dependencies and discourse structures.

To facilitate further explanations, we'll briefly go into deeper detail on how the parsing process works and how FCG builds higher order abstractions when presented with a basic symbolic representation of a musical melody. Let us start from a simple list-based musical notation in which every extra level of brackets introduces a double timing resolution or quantization (e.g. from fourth to eighth note). Parsing the two bars at Layer 0 pictured in Fig. 1 to obtain the Layer 3 abstract representation, is achieved by executing following command in FCG/LISP:

```
(parse '(((1 2 3 4) 5 5 6 6) 5) *constructions*)
```

in which every number represents the degree of the note. The *constructions* variable contains a set of constructions (the grammar), which is essentially a set of templates that can be applied to the current *transient structure*. Applying such templates or constructions occurs in two phases. During *matching*, the features present in a template are matched with features in units in the transient structures; variables can represent any kind of structure (as everything is a list) and thus occur at different levels of the hierarchy. When the matching phase succeeded, the construction and transient structure are *merged* and all variables bound. New units can be created using the so-called "J" operator.

FCG is particularly suited for music because the complex short- and long-term and transversal interactions that frequently occur in music demand a representation that is able to capture these hierarchical elements while not being constrained by them [18]. More generally, music consists of many dependencies between different aspects and multiple views at different abstraction levels, as musical structures are not simple linear or purely hierarchical structures [2] but many sophisticated interactions between entities and across different levels of abstraction, occur [1].

3 Methodology and Results

Time to get to the core of our methodology. The creation of a new piece of music in the style of another, occurs in 4 phases:

1. *Abstraction:* in a first stage, a given song is being parsed by FCG to create a multi-resolution representation of the piece by progressively making more and more abstraction of time. Layer 0 corresponds to the original input.
2. *Parsing:* at each resolution, (grammatical) constructions are applied that transform the representation (Layer N) to a new one with higher resolution (layer $N-1$). It can be considered as a "trace" of how to arrive to the original song, starting from a time-abstracted representation. We define the set of applied generic constructions as *the musical style* of the song.
3. *Introduction of novelty:* In case of variation, a different set of constructions (different musical style) is applied to the highest abstracted song. In case of improvisation, a different abstract melody is used as input for the same construction set (style).
4. *Production:* The reverse process from parsing is applied (remember that all constructions are operational for parsing as well as production).

We'll now look into deeper detail into each of these phases. Figure 1 illustrates how a multi-resolution representation is derived. At each time-resolution or quantization-layer (indicated on the left), the amount of rhythmical information is reduced by summarizing two notes at layer N into one at layer $N+1$ (for example two eighth notes into one fourth). A rudimentary way to this is to withhold the strong beat only, as illustrated. Please note that this particular implementation is chosen only to illustrate the concepts and far too simplistic to yield satisfactory results in general. A better approach would be to capture relevant rhythmical and harmonic information, for example by means of melodic reduction [5].

In a second stage, constructions are applied that specify the transformation from one layer to the other in a generic manner. An example is given in Fig. 2. The two half notes C and E, summarized to C by the abstraction process, can be reconstructed by "interpolating" E between C and G. Please note that different constructions can apply to the same abstraction. Table 1 gives an overview of the implemented constructions in our example (that capture musical information).

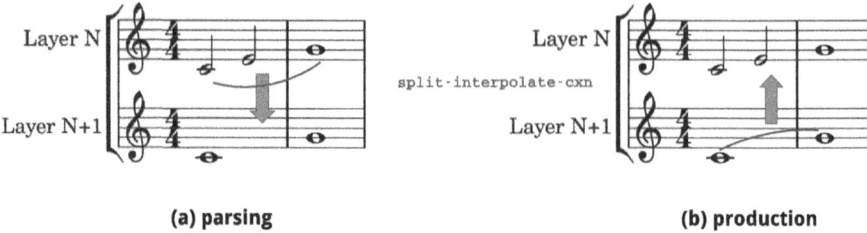

Fig. 2. The split-interpolate-cxn construction applied both in parsing and in production. During parsing, the construction creates a generic operator that can restore the abstraction performed by moving to a different resolution (higher layer or quantization). In production, application of the construction restores the lower layer representation. It is important to notice that the operator is a generic operator, which means that it can be applied to different notes as well. For example, in production, applying the same construction to the two whole notes of C and E at layer N, would yield the sequence C D E at layer $N-1$.

Table 1. List of bi-directional constructions, explained in the context of production. Please remark that the same constructions are used in parsing as well.

Name	Explanation
Hold	Keep a note (a whole stays a whole)
Split-interpolate	Insert the note in the middle of the two adjacent notes
Split-repeat	Repeat the note (e.g. a whole becomes two quarter notes)
Split-leadto	Fill in the note leading to the next note (a step below)
Split-movefrom	Split a note into the original note and a step above
Split-totonic	Add the tonic
Split-todominant	Add the dominant

In a third phase, novelty is introduced. In the case of improvisation (Fig. 3) in the style of a given song, the abstracted melody is altered, a different song is chosen or a completely new melody is generated. In the case of variation (Fig. 4), a different set of constructions is applied to the same abstracted melody. One is free to choose the starting resolution, depending on how close or far you want to deviate from the original song. Lastly, the grammar is applied in reverse direction (production), but using the same set of constructions. Figure 5 shows the LISP code for the split-interpolate construction, suitable for parsing as well as production. Note that variables in FCG are preceded by a question mark. As discussed above, each construction consists of two poles, a semantic one representing meaning and a syntactic one representing form. In *production*, the semantic pole is matched with the abstract representation and the transient structure is enriched with information from the syntactic pole. ?n3-1 and ?n3-2 represent two notes at layer 3, with degrees ?d3-1 and ?d3-2 respectively. If the

Fig. 3. The same style (set of constructions C), obtained from parsing an existing melody M is applied to a different abstract melody A′ to obtain an *improvisation* M′ in the same style as M. The grammar should be constructed in such a way that all relevant harmonic and melodic musicality is captured, so that any abstracted melody leads to a 'sensible' melody. One possibility is to start from the rules of counterpoint to express common musical knowledge.

semantic pole of the transient structure has been tagged with split-interpolate, the construction applies and the syntactic pole is constructed accordingly. In that case, two notes are constructed at layer 2 – indicated with (length 2) – and a degree equal to (?d3-1+?d3-2)/2. The calculation is performed by the :relation-interpolate? function. The footprints feature is used to keep track of all applied constructions. In parsing, the process is reversed and the syntactic pole is matched with the multi-resolution representation to enrich the semantic pole of the transient structure, in this case with the split-interpolate.

Fig. 4. The style extracted from melody M in Fig. 3 is applied to the time-abstracted version B of Frère Jacques without repeats (N), to yield a *variation* N′.

```
(add-cxn
  (make-cxn split-interpolate (:label transformation)
    (; Two adjacent notes
     (root
       (form (== (meets ?n3-1 ?n3-2))))

     ; At layer three, marked with split-interpolate
     (?n3-1
       (layer 3)
       (degree ?d3-1)
       (refinement split-interpolate))

     (?n3-2
       (layer 3)
       (degree ?d3-2)))|

<-->

    ((root
       (form (== (meets ?n3-1 ?n3-2) (meets ?n2-1 ?n2-2))))

     ; The note consist of two notes (subunits) at a lower layer
     (?n3-1
       (length 3)
       (footprints (==0 split-interpolate))
       (subunits (?n2-1 ?n2-2))
       (degree ?d3-1))

     (?n3-2
       (length 3)
       (degree ?d3-2))

     (?n2-1
       (length 2)
       (degree ?d3-1))

     ; the new note should be right in the middle
     (?n2-2
       (length 2)
       (degree (++ :relation-interpolate? (?d3-1 ?d3-2 ?d-new))))

     ((J ?n3-1)
       (footprints (== split-interpolate))))) *constructions*)
```

Fig. 5. LISP code for the FCG construction split-interpolate, musically illustrated in Fig. 2. The specification contains all required information for parsing (moving from the syntactic to the semantic pole) and production (reverse direction). The split-interpolate construction transforms a note at level N into two notes at level $N-1$ (smaller quantization level), in which the first note is equal to the original note and the second note interpolates between the first note and the next.

4   Conclusions and Future Work

First steps towards deeper symbolic representations of music for the modelling of style and generation of music were presented in this paper. The methodology has shown its capability to capture the style of a song and it was shown how a bi-directional grammar, representing a musical piece, can be derived from a multi-resolution representation. The approach builds a bridge between corpus-based and knowledge-based systems. Two examples were given, illustration variation and improvisation. A lot of improvements can be made to the proposed methodology. Currently, it only supports monophonic binary music in one key.

Also, the current grammar ignores chord structure, leading to "odd sounding" compositions. More research is to be done on the abstraction operator that constructs the multi-resolution representation, so it accounts for chord structure, the tonality of notes and syncopated rhythms.

Acknowledgements. This research has been supported by the EU FP7 PRAISE project #318770.

References

1. Alexander, C.: A city is not a tree. Architectural Forum (1965)
2. Conklin, D., Witten, I.H.: Multiple viewpoint systems for music prediction. J. New Music Res. **24**(1), 51–73 (1995)
3. Feld, S., Fox, A.: Music and language. Annu. Rev. Anthropol. **23**, 25–53 (1994)
4. Gerasymova, K., Steels, L., Van Trijp, R.: Aspectual morphology of russian verbs in fluid construction grammar. In: Proceedings of the 31th Annual Conference of the Cognitive Science Society, pp. 1370–1375. Cognitive Science Society gerasymova-09a. pdf Google Scholar (2009)
5. Gilbert, É., Conklin, D.: A probabilistic context-free grammar for melodic reduction (2007)
6. Gjerdingen, R.: Music in the Galant Style. Oxford University Press, Oxford (2007)
7. Hoffmann, T., Trousdale, G.: The Oxford Handbook of Construction Grammar. Oxford University Press, Oxford (2013)
8. Koelsch, S., Kasper, E., Sammler, D., Schulze, K., Gunter, T., Friederici, A.D.: Music, language and meaning: brain signatures of semantic processing. Nat. Neurosci. **7**(3), 302–307 (2004)
9. Lartillot, O., Dubnov, S., Assayag, G., Bejerano, G.: Automatic modeling of musical style. In: Proceedings of the 2001 International Computer Music Conference, pp. 447–454 (2001)
10. Lerdahl, F., Jackendoff, R.: An overview of hierarchical structure in music. Music Percept. **1**, 229–252 (1983)
11. Minsky, M.: Music, Mind, and Brain. Springer, Heidelberg (1982)
12. Pachet, F.: The continuator: musical interaction with style. J. New Music Res. **32**(3), 333–341 (2003)
13. Pearce, M.T., Wiggins, G.A.: Expectation in melody: the influence of context and learning. Music Percept. **23**(5), 377–405 (2006)
14. Rohrmeier, M.: A generative grammar approach to diatonic harmonic structure. In: Proceedings of the 4th Sound and Music Computing Conference, pp. 97–100 (2007)
15. Rohrmeier, M.A., Koelsch, S.: Predictive information processing in music cognition. a critical review. Int. J. Psychophysiol. **83**(2), 164–175 (2012)
16. Slevc, L.R., Patel, A.D.: Meaning in music and language: three key differences: comment on towards a neural basis of processing musical semantics by Stefan Koelsch. Phys. Life Rev. **8**(2), 110–111 (2011)
17. Steels, L.: Design Patterns in Fluid Construction Grammar, vol. 11. John Benjamins Publishing, Amsterdam (2011)

18. Steels, L., De Beule, J.: Unify and merge in fluid construction grammar. In: Vogt, P., Sugita, Y., Tuci, E., Nehaniv, C.L. (eds.) EELC 2006. LNCS (LNAI), vol. 4211, pp. 197–223. Springer, Heidelberg (2006)
19. Todd, P.M., Loy, D.G.: Music and Connectionism. MIT Press, Cambridge (1991)
20. van Trijp, R.: Feature matrices and agreement: a case study for German case. Des. Patterns Fluid Constr. Grammar **11**, 205 (2011)

Music with Unconventional Computing: Granular Synthesis with the Biological Computing Substrate *Physarum Polycephalum*

Edward Braund[✉] and Eduardo R. Miranda

Interdisciplinary Centre for Computer Music Research (ICCMR),
Plymouth University, Plymouth, UK
{edward.braund,eduardo.miranda}@plymouth.ac.uk

Abstract. This paper reports on the outcomes of an approach to granular synthesis using the biological computing substrate *Physarum polycephalum*. The plasmodium of *Physarum Polycephalum* is unicellular with a myriad of diploid nuclei, which moves like a giant amoeba in its pursuit of food. The organism is amorphous, and although without a brain or any serving centre of control, can respond to the environmental conditions that surround it. In the presented approach, we harness the organism's oscillatory behaviour and protoplasmic network configuration to produce and sequence sound grains. Such an approach is an extension to one of the author's previous musical works with *Physarum polycephalum*, which he presented in [13].

Keywords: Unconventional computing · Biological computing · Computer music · *Physarum polycephalum* · Bionic Engineering · Music · Granular synthesis

1 Introduction

Computers have been programmed to produce sound from the beginning of the 1950s [10]. Since, advances in computer science have had a significant impact on both the way audio media is consumed and produced. Therefore, it is likely that future computational advancements will change the field of music. Amongst computer scientists, there is a growing consensus that we will one day reach the limit of today's conventional computing paradigms, which are derived from the Turing machine [17] and von Neumann architecture [18]. We are interested in how the advancing field of unconventional computation may provide new pathways for music and related technologies.

In computer music, there is a tradition of experimenting with emerging technologies. Until recent years, developments put forward by the field of unconventional computation have been left unexploited, which is likely due to the field's heavy theoretical nature, complexity and lack of accessible prototypes. Uniquely, the biological computing substrate *Physarum polycephalum* requires comparatively fewer resources than most other unconventional computing substrates: the organism is cheap, openly obtainable, considered safe to use and has a robustness that allows for ease of application. It is for these reasons we have selected *Physarum polycephalum* to begin investigating how new, biological, computing schemes may provide innovative pathways for music. We have developed several projects that harness *Physarum polycephalum* for creative applications. These include sound synthesis [13], a biologically inspired step sequencer [7] and an analogue circuit for music generation [6] that encompasses biological components [9]. For a survey of unconventional computing in music see [8].

Physarum polycephalum (henceforth known as *P.polycephalum*) is an amorphous unicellular organism visible to the unaided human eye. *P.polycephalum*, during its vegetative plasmodium phase, creates an optimised network of protoplasmic veins connecting food sources (Fig. 1). The visual result of the organism's network is a planar graph where colonised food represent nodes and protoplasmic veins represent edges. The plasmodium feeds on micro-particles and creatures such as bacteria and spores and moves like a giant amoeba along gradients of attractants and repellents. The intracellular topology of plasmodia can be described as a network of biochemical oscillators [1]: waves of contraction or relaxation that collide inducing cytoplasmic streaming. Such intracellular activity produces fluctuating levels of electrical potential, typically in the range of ±50 mV, displaying oscillations at periods of approximately 50–200 s with amplitudes of 5–10 mV [2]. If recorded in isolated zones of colonisation over the duration of it being active, patterns emerge that correlate to spatial activity and environmental conditions. Adamatzky and Jones have examined such patterns and reported that they can be used to denote the plasmodium's behaviour and physiological state [2].

P.polycephalum's behaviour can be interpreted as computation [1]. Computational prototypes exploiting the organism's behaviour include robot control [16], logic gate schemes [3], route planning [15] and numerous others [1].

In this paper, we report on an approach to granular synthesis harnessing the plasmodium of *P.polycephalum*. This work is an extension to one of the author's previous projects, which he presented in [13]. In this project, the organism's electrical readings were recorded and subsequently scaled to control the frequencies and amplitudes of a group of oscillators within an additive granular synthesis framework. The results of this project were interesting and created a reasonable auditory representation of the organism's behaviour. However, results were hampered by the quantity of data generated by recording the organism's electrical activity. Such large amounts of data were compressed to render them usable, which was to the detriment of the relationship between the sound and the behaviour of the plasmodium. In this paper, we report on the outcomes of a different approach to sound synthesis with *P.polycephalum*, where we take advantage of the organism's oscillatory behaviour by regarding it as a granular audio oscillator that we can control via various methods of stimulation.

Granular synthesis is the rapid succession of short sound partials (typically 1–100 millisecond-long-sounds) referred to as grains that together form a larger sound object. Dennis Gabor inspired this method of sound synthesis with his

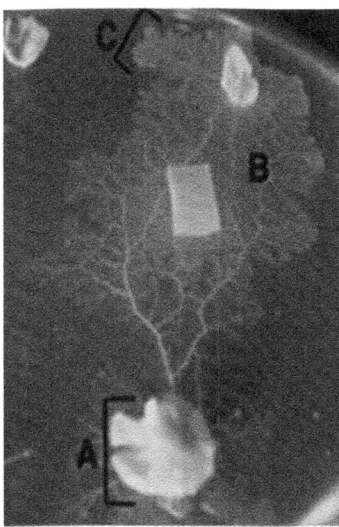

Fig. 1. A photograph of the plasmodium of *P.polycephalum* showing: (A) inoculation of plasmodium into the environment, (B) protoplasmic network connecting areas of colonisation and (C) a search front of pseudopods propagating along a gradient to food.

theory 'acoustical quanta', which proposed that complex sound events are made up of a myriad of simple sonic grains [11]. The first composer to approach granular synthesis for musical purposes was Xenakis [19] during the 1970s. Since, several different approaches to harnessing granular synthesis for music have been investigated. By way of related research into unconventional computing for granular synthesis, Miranda [14] experimented with using a cellular automata model of a reaction-diffusion computer to produce sequences of grains according to evolving chemical oscillations.

2 Methods and Materials

When conducting our research with the plasmodium of *P.polycephalum*, we adopt techniques from [1]. Here, we farm plasmodium in plastic containers on a moist, porous substrate. The farm is fed daily with oat flakes, moistened every other day and replanted onto a new substrate weekly. To inoculate plasmodium into an experimental arena, we take colonised oat flakes or heaps of pseudopods from the farm and position them as desired.

To measure the electrical activity of the plasmodium, we place bare wire electrodes coated with 2 % non-nutrient agar underneath sources of food (oat flakes). Electrodes do not touch and are electrically isolated from one another by a non-conductive plastic. In each experiment, we nominate one electrode the as a reference, and, as such, position the plasmodium on top. Figure 2 shows an experimental growth environment for our granular synthesis approach. Here, four electrodes are arranged on the vertices of a square, with a reference electrode

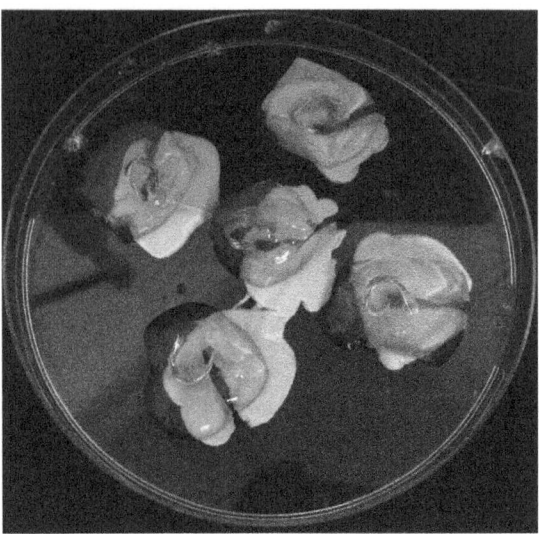

Fig. 2. A photograph of an example growth environment for the plasmodium to forage in. Shown is four measurement electrodes centred around a reference electrode.

positioned in the centre. In the context of this paper, such an arrangement represents four granular oscillators. Electrodes feed into an ADC-20 high-resolution data logger by Pico Technology, which sends measurements into custom software. All experiments take place in a 90 mm petri dish within a dark enclosure.

The behaviour of the plasmodium can be controlled by taking advantage of the organism's innate response to various stimuli. In unconventional computing studies, substances that result in attraction or repulsion are often used as a method of data input [1]. There are a number of substances that can act as attractants (e.g. glucose and various carbohydrates) and repellents (e.g. salt and metal ions). However, once positioned in the experimental arena, these substances create chemical traces that are difficult to remove. A more dynamic method of controlling behaviour is through various lighting techniques. The plasmodium of *P.polycephalum* exhibits negative phototaxis. That is, in the presence of certain light wavelengths, the organism diverts propagation to avoid the illuminated area [12]. Studies have identified that blue and white light affect the organism's oscillatory behaviour [4]. Thus, as we are harnessing the organism's oscillatory behaviour to produce sound directly, this provides appropriate means for a composer to fine tune and create variations in the final sonic result.

3 Granular Synthesis Engine

Due to *P.polycephalum* taking several days to span an environment, we designed custom software that implements our granular synthesis approach over the duration of the organism being active. Here, we take 100 samples from each electrode every second, which are then averaged to produce a single reading per second.

The software then transcribes these readings into audio buffers. At composer-defined intervals, each buffer is addressed to produce a sound grain, which are sequenced together in ascending order according to their running electrical potential average. Grain lengths are determined by scaling each electrode's potential difference value against the current average of all other electrodes, to a composer defined minimum and maximum grain length range. Each electrode's buffer is only addressed for grain creation if the organism is active in the respective area. Our software achieves this by reviewing each new measurement for oscillatory activity. Once initiated, the software automates the granular synthesis composition until the organism has exhausted all food sources and starts to fructify or progress into its dormant Sclerotium phase. Upon these conditions being met, the system halts and renders the resulting audio file. For our reference, images are taken of experiments at intervals of 5 min (see Fig. 3 for examples). Currently, we have designed the system to accommodate up to eight electrode inputs.

Fig. 3. Four sample images of the plasmodium's behaviour within the growth environment depicted in Fig. 2.

4 Results

Considering that the growth environment depicted in Fig. 2 illustrates a typical example of conditions for the plasmodium to forage in, on average it takes five days for experiments to complete. Shown in Fig. 4 is a set of graphs denoting the typical electrical activity produced by the setup depicted in Figs. 2 and 3. First, the plasmodium gradually propagates from the centre electrode to the measurement electrodes, which took two days to occur. When the plasmodium arrives at an electrode's site, readings show a quick rise followed by a sharp drop in potential. A clear example of this can be seen on electrode 4 in Fig. 4. Colonisation happened first at electrode 3, next at electrode 1 followed by electrode 2, and, finally, then electrode 4. Propagation to each of these electrodes came equally from the central inoculation electrode as well as neighbouring electrodes. This propagation behaviour configures a protoplasmic vein network that connects each of the colonised regions together. The resulting morphology impacts the electrical activity measured by each electrode. This is because of the cellular waves of contraction and relaxation that interact and proliferate across the organism. Such activity can result in a series of impulses that can spread a distance across the organism, according to the amplitude and conditions at other colonised regions. An example of which can be seen on electrodes 1 and 2 (marked by the rectangle). The Sclerotium phase is characterised by an increase in voltage (marked by the triangle). In this example, we experimented with using light to impact oscillatory behaviour. The effect of this can be seen on electrode 4 where 3 periodic bursts of light have caused spiking and an increase in amplitude (marked by the circle).

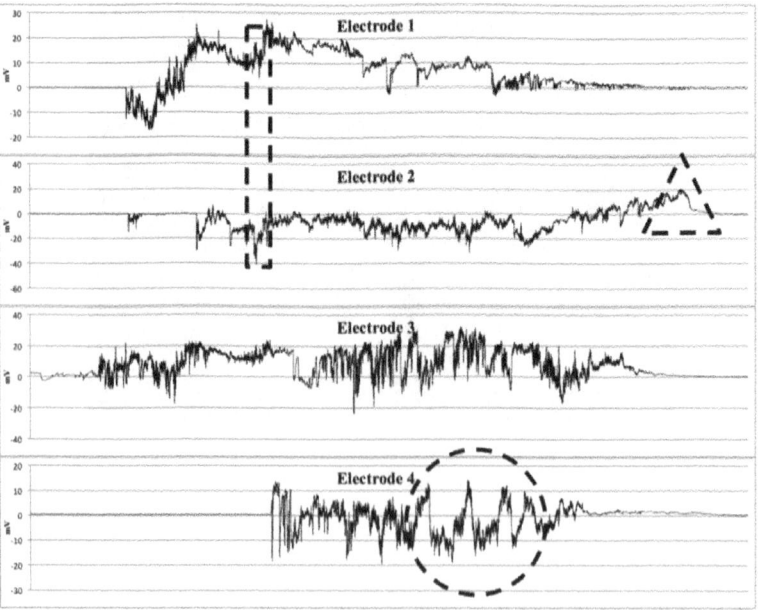

Fig. 4. Graphs depicting the electrical activity recorded on each of the electrodes within the growth environment shown in Fig. 2.

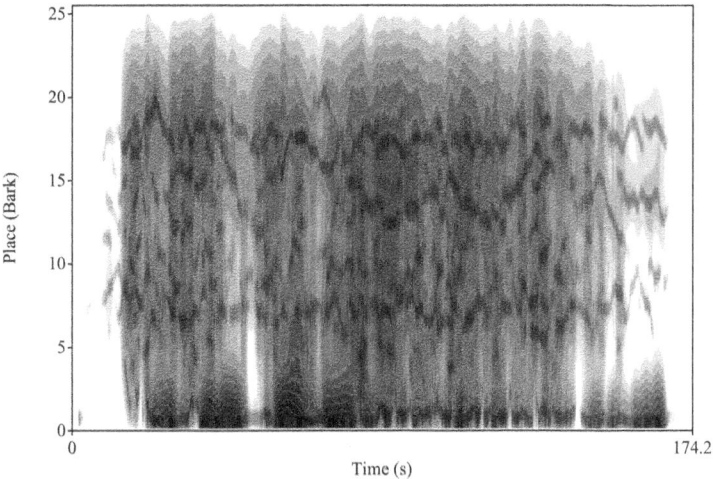

Fig. 5. A cochleogram of the granular piece produced by our system from the setup in Figs. 2 and 3, and graphs in Fig. 4.

Shown in Fig. 5 is a cochleogram of the granular piece produced by our system from the setup in Figs. 2 and 3, and graphs in Fig. 4. In this example, the system generated 174 s of audio material from five days of plasmodium electrical activity. Notice the dark lines in Fig. 5 and how they are morphologically related to the electrical plots displayed in Fig. 4. An audio example of granular synthesis material produced by the approach presented in this paper can be found at [5].

5 Discussions

Composing with granular synthesis can be extensive and a sonically detailed process. Compositions that conform to conventional musical theory have a temporal hierarchy of structure. Part of the compositional process is managing the interaction between structures on different time scales - from individual note level to the topmost level of a complete composition. When composing with granular synthesis, there are additional levels that go below note level to grain level. At grain level, there is a massive quantity of control data required to advance to higher perspective sound levels. For example, if each grain has n quantity of parameters (these often exceed double digits), and there is q amount of grains in a second long sound object, then n multiplied by q equals the amount of data needed to produce a second of audio. As such, composers wishing to adopt granular synthesis in their works often require algorithms that produce grains in accordance with global parameters.

The approach presented in this paper is useful for the composer wishing to use granular synthesis. This is because the approach automates the production of grains, and, by controlling the plasmodium's behaviour, the composer has a level of control over the sonic result. Moreover, by creating different arrangements of electrodes within an experimental arena, we can achieve a variety of audio densities and output lengths.

Currently, our approach takes several days to generate a few minutes of audio, which can make its employment tedious. In [13], we experimented with using a model of the organism to overcome this time constraint. Although this approximation is useable, it is simple in its assumptions and implementation and offers limited methods of interacting with behaviour. As such, to advance this paper's approach, we are experimenting with the plasmodium's vibrant intracellular activity. Here, we are looking into tracking the organism's shuttle streaming of biological components through a microscope camera (Fig. 6).

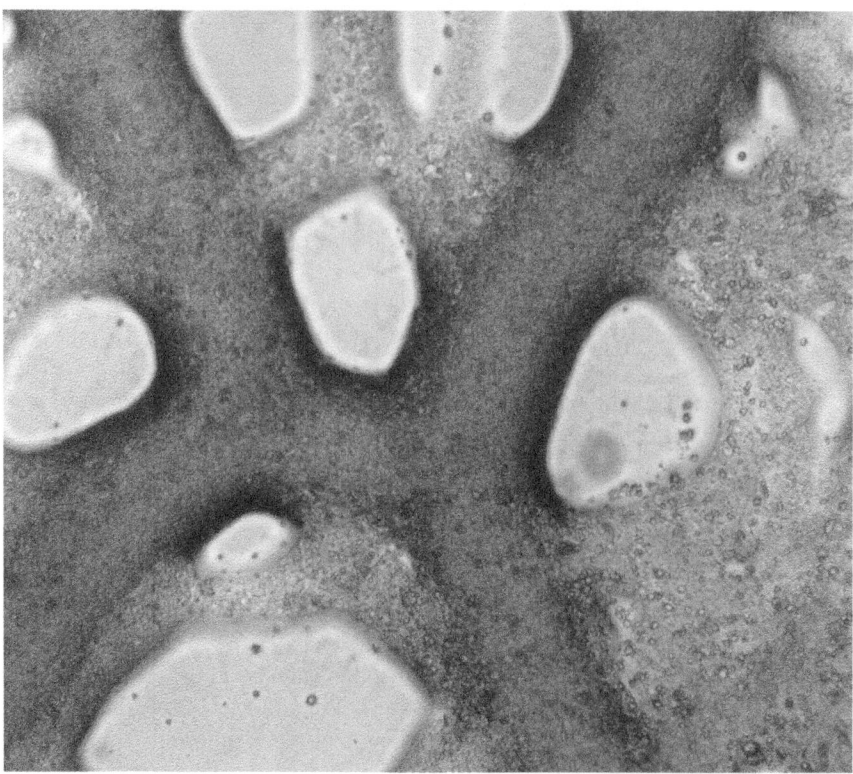

Fig. 6. A photograph of a protoplasmic vein junction under a microscope. We are currently investigating the feasibility of tracking the movement of intracellular components to control the parameters of audio synthesis frameworks.

6 Conclusion

This paper has presented an approach to granular synthesis using the biological computing substrate *P.polycephalum*. At this early stage in our research, we are spending a lot of time investigating and experimenting with how the application of *P.polycephalum* may be used to go beyond our standard offering in computer music. In the context of this paper, we are not concerned with the computational properties of *P.polycephalum*; rather, we are interested in building a sound/music-orientated understanding of its behaviour. For music, *P.polycephalum* is interesting because its behaviour can be controlled to produce variations of electrical activity (e.g., by using attractors or directing light on the organism), which consequently creates variations on the resulting audio. Methods of controlling and interacting with *P.polycephalum's* behaviour is incipient and an active area of research in laboratories worldwide. We are currently experimenting with musical ways that we can use *P.polycephalum's* behaviour in real-time.

References

1. Adamatzky, A.: Physarum machines: computers from slime mould, vol. 74, World Scientific (2010)
2. Adamatzky, A., Jones, J.: On electrical correlates of physarum polycephalum spatial activity: can we see physarum machine in the dark? Biophys. Rev. Lett. **6**(01n02), 29–57 (2011)
3. Adamatzky, A., Schubert, T.: Slime mold microfluidic logical gates. Mater. Today **17**(2), 86–91 (2014)
4. Block, I., Wohlfarth-Bottermann, K.: Blue light as a medium to influence oscillatory contraction frequency in physarum. Cell Biol. Int. Rep. **5**(1), 73–81 (1981)
5. Braund, E.: Physarm Polycephalum Granular Synthesis Example (2015). https://soundcloud.com/ed-braund
6. Braund, E., Miranda, E.: BioComputer music: generating musical responses with physarum polycephalum-based memristors. In: Computer Music Multidisciplinary Research (CMMR): Music, Mind, and Embodiment. Plymouth, UK (2015)
7. Braund, E., Miranda, E.: Music with unconventional computing: towards a step sequencer from plasmodium of physarum polycephalum. In: Johnson, C., Carballal, A., Correia, J. (eds.) Evolutionary and Biologically Inspired Music, Sound, Art and Design. LNCS, vol. 9027, pp. 15–26. Springer, Heidelberg (2015)
8. Braund, E., Miranda, E.R.: Unconventional computing in music. In: Proceedings of the 9th Conference on Interdisciplinary Musicology - CIM14, Berlin (2014)
9. Braund, E., Sparrow, R., Miranda, E.R.: Physarum-based memristors for computer music. In: Adamatzky, A. (ed.) Advances in Physarum Machines, vol. 21, pp. 755–775. Springer International Publishing, Heidelberg (2016)
10. Doornbusch, P.: The music of CSIRAC: Australia's first computer music. Common Ground (2005)
11. Gabor, D.: Acoustical quanta and the theory of hearing. Nature **159**(4044), 591–594 (1947)
12. Hato, M., Ueda, T., Kurihara, K., Kobatake, Y.: Phototaxis in true slime mold physarum polycephalum. Cell Struct. Funct. **1**(3), 269–278 (1976)

13. Miranda, E., Adamatzky, A., Jones, J.: Sounds synthesis with slime mould of physarum polycephalum. J. Bionic Eng. **8**(2), 107–113 (2011)
14. Miranda, E.R.: Granular synthesis of sounds by means of a cellular automaton. Leonardo **28**(4), 297–300 (1995)
15. Nakagaki, T., Yamada, H., Tóth, A.: Intelligence: maze-solving by an amoeboid organism. Nature **407**(6803), 470 (2000)
16. Tsuda, S., Zauner, K.P., Gunji, Y.P.: Robot control with biological cells. Biosystems **87**(2), 215–223 (2007)
17. Turing, A.M.: On computable numbers, with an application to the Entscheidungsproblem. Proc. Lond. Math. Soc. **42**(2), 230–265 (1936)
18. Von Neumann, J.: First draft of a report on the EDVAC. In: Randell, B. (ed.) The Origins of Digital Computers, pp. 383–392. Springer, Heidelberg (1982)
19. Xenakis, I.: Formalized Music: Thought and Mathematics in Composition, 6th edn. Pendragon Press, Hillsdale (1992)

Data Mining, Music Information Retrieval and Artificial Intelligence

Evaluation and Prediction of Harmonic Complexity Across 76 Years of Billboard 100 Hits

Kristoffer Jensen[1(✉)] and David G. Hebert[2]

[1] Aalborg University, A.C. Meyers Vænge 15, 2450 Copenhagen SV, Denmark
krist@create.aau.dk
[2] Grieg Academy, Bergen University College,
Lars Hilles Gate 3, 5015 Bergen, Norway
dgh@hib.no

Abstract. This study applies a novel computational strategy—Jensen Chroma Complexity (JCC)—to develop robust harmonic profiles of music recordings. This feature has been calculated on all US Billboard Top 100 hits across a 76-year period (n = 6,494). Results indicate a clear historical trajectory of harmonic profiles, with strong predictability. From the 1940s is a sustained increase in JCC that nearly doubles, peaking in the 1980s, and gradually decreasing into the 21st century. Each decade was also determined to correlate to a statistically distinctive harmonic profile. The findings presented here corroborate the effectiveness of JCC in generating robust harmonic profiles that enable identification of the approximate year in which a hit song was popularized.

1 Introduction

Using a pioneering technique called the Jensen Chroma Complexity (JCC), we traced harmonic profiles for the entire Billboard Top 100 popular song collection across what is now more than a 70-year period (1940–2015), consisting of 6,494 songs. Based on this meta-analysis using techniques that have until this point been unavailable due to technological limitations, we determined that the harmonic complexity of popular songs evolves in a predictable pattern, and that a song's likely year of origin can be automatically determined through this analysis.

Several previous studies have made use of the Billboard listings as a framework for evaluating broader changes in the social history of popular music in the USA. One such study [1] recently traced the emergence of rap music, while another [2] focused on hit songs by male duos, and yet another [3] examined the gender of hit song performers from the late 1990s onward. Other relevant studies have examined the role of Billboard and the hit song concept in the music industry [4–6]. Other studies have demonstrated various approaches to historiographic analysis of popular music [7, 8], which to some extent foreshadow aspects of the methods of the present study. Previous studies have also documented the extent to which particular approaches to mixing and mastering of studio recordings impact the reception of popular music [9], which is a topic we will discuss later in this article. Recent publications have advocated the need for new approaches in "computational ethnomusicology" [10] that might enable unprecedented insights into musical phenomena worldwide, including approaches that might entail rejuvenated form of comparative musicology, as we have argued in several conference presentations from 2012 through 2013 (RMA Music and Philosophy Study Group [11], Computer Music Multidisciplinary Research, [12], NNIMIPA [13]), and has since been taken up by other researchers [20, 22], as well as [19] who wrote:

> Although we considered investigating a larger collection of top US Billboard songs for each year (top 10, top 5, top 3), we ultimately decided to investigate the single top song from each year for logistic and theoretical reasons. First of all, having raters listen to nearly 500 songs for more than 24 h did not seem reasonable and may not have resulted in high-quality ratings. Second, and more importantly, using a combination or average of multiple song ratings to represent each year would assume that each song is preferred to the same extent, which is clearly not the case. In addition, by using only the top song from each year we can provide a tangible example of music listeners' preferences to illustrate our findings.

As the present study will demonstrate, pioneering computational techniques increasingly enable a large corpus of data to be evaluated in a meaningful way that previously had been unmanageable due to technological limitations.

Indeed, in reference to previous research [14], computational musicologists [24] (p. 1) have described how "One of the first publicly-available large-scale collections that has been analyzed by standard music processing technologies is the million song dataset. Among others, the dataset includes the year annotations and audio descriptions of 464,411 distinct music recordings (from 1955 to 2010)". Such approaches have been used more frequently for analysis of texts [18].

Some scholars within the fields of musicology and ethnomusicology have at times appeared to be suspicious toward all forms of quantification, which we consider to be an unhealthy view, for numbers are undeniably useful toward certain research objectives [10]. By using numbers, we are not implicitly suggesting that our methods are any more "scientific" than that of ethnographers or other qualitative researchers, but rather we are examining a different kind of question for which this kind of approach is inherently better suited. This study is exploratory in nature, so we merely seek to evaluate whether certain sonic patterns might reasonably be interpreted as predictable according to computational techniques, but in future studies we also test whether such patterns may relate in some way to notable historical developments.

2 Method

For the purposes of the present research study, a database of audio files was assembled consisting of individual sound recordings of the entire Billboard Top 100 across a 76-year period (1940–2015, n = 6494). This collection of the most popular songs in the USA offers 100 songs per year for most years (1956–2015); however from 1941 to 1955 only 30 songs per years are available, while only 44 songs are provided for the year 1940. Similar, albeit smaller, databases have been compiled and examined in various previous studies [14, 21]. One previous study [15] reportedly "compiled a corpus of songs selected from the Billboard charts spanning 1958 through 1991" that provided "manually-encoded annotations of rock songs, although the data in these corpora is limited primarily to harmonic and timing information" [22] (p. 188). Another very recent study offered insightful analysis of tendencies identified in a 200-song sample from a large corpus of popular songs that reportedly "contains harmonic and timing information, but it represents melodic information as well; to our knowledge, it is the first popular music corpus to do so". A previous related study also attained novel conclusions regarding harmonic tendencies across a 100-song sample of American popular music [16]. However, the uniqueness of the present study in relation to previous work is its use of computational strategies to evaluate harmonies across the entire Billboard corpus. The present study also extends upon previous work by one of the co-authors that examined bass loudness levels across entire Billboard 100 corpus [17].

2.1 Integrity of Database

Due to the unusually large scope of the current study, certain issues arise regarding the quality of data. These kinds of problems occur when the music has been digitized, post-processed or compressed to mp3 files. In particular, the compression issue has been discussed widely in the context of the "loudness war" [19]. However, many other modifications are also typically associated with the digitalization process. These modifications may be unintended, in the case of digitalization from vinyl, analogue tape or other, rendering cracking, hissing or other artifacts, or may be voluntary, as in the case of compression, or different kinds of filtering, etc.

Table 1 provides a list of common degradations and modifications to audio quality that tend to arise through various phases of the digitalization chain. The main confounding issue for large-scale analyses of this kind is associated with diverse approaches to compression that affect the loudness of songs. For instance, different versions (as obtained from the internet) of the same song may exhibit RMS variations of up to 10 dB even after normalization between ±1 of the audio. The same song found on different channels may thus be 10 dB louder. As a comparison, the full Billboard maximum RMS variation is 26 dB, so these variations are significant.

Table 1. Common modification artifacts in the digitization process.

Type	Loudness	Spectrum	Other
Digitization	NA	Missing treble	Clipping/Cracking
Compression	Increase	NA	Distortion
MP3 codec	No effect	Noise in treble	
Filtering	Increase	Increase treble	

This loudness modification influences perceptions of the relative loudness of harmonic components in relation to melody and other prominent musical elements. Normalization can also be a major factor in confounding measurements of this kind, for there is no simple answer to the question of how much normalization represents the most meaningful measurement, or to what extent multiple settings would be most effective. The solution to this problem is dependent both on the quality of the audio database, and the choice of features.

2.2 Chroma and Chromagram

The present study pioneers a new technique designed for robust and relevant computational analysis of harmonic complexity across a large corpus of digitized sound recordings. The Jensen Chroma Complexity measurement (JCC) is presented here as a way of applying the Chromagram measurement for meaningful analysis of a large corpus of digitized sound recordings. JCC is based on previous developments for computational harmonic analysis, including the Chroma, and the Chromagram, a measurement enabling comparison of Chroma to produce harmonic profiles of songs.

Another reason for our choice of analyzing chroma is that we regard harmonic complexity in western popular music to be both (1) more directly related to musical style and expression, and (2) less directly impacted by technological change than most other measurable aspects of musical sound (e.g. EQ, pulse/tempo, etc.). Bartsch and Wakefield [27] are generally credited with first developing the notion of chroma for "audio thumbnailing," a signal processing technique that enables examination of harmonic relationships in segments of sound recordings. Extending on the much earlier work of Shepard [25], their work advocated the analysis of "short, representative samples (or "audio thumbnails") of selections of popular music" (p. 15), and maintained "a chroma-based feature class can be used to capture harmonic relationships within a song. An examination of the chroma features themselves indicates that they do encode harmonic relationships to some extent" (p. 18). The procedures for chromagram analysis were subsequently developed [26], "the harmony feature (the chromagram) is based on the chroma," which is "calculated on … short-time Fourier transform (STFT)" (p. 2) and this measurement "gives rather precise information about the chroma of the notes played in the vicinity of the time location" (p. 4). The resulting approach, Jensen Chromagram Complexity (JCC), entails use of chroma-based signal analysis to produce visual mappings of the harmonic features of songs. However, for the purposes of the present study, in order to effectively map an unusually large corpus of audio files (in the thousands) across historical time, it was necessary to adopt a more reductive approach that would enable such a large set of data to be manageable, while at the same time produce an analysis that is independent, as much as possible, of the signal degradations shown in Table 1.

2.3 Examples of Chroma

Prior to explaining the precise nature of the JCC strategy devised for this study, some explanation seems necessary so readers understand how to meaningfully interpret chromagrams. What is displayed in a chromagram is the mean of pitches used—out of 12 possible chromatic pitches in the western system—across the entire song. In other words, a piece of 12-tone atonal music by Arnold Schoenberg, for example, would look essentially like a flat line in this kind of graph, while a very simple two chord song with a diatonic melody consisting of only a few notes would show much wider variation between certain notes (out of the 12 pitches) that are used very frequently versus others that are hardly (if ever) used at all. Therefore, although it might at first seem a bit counterintuitive, chromagrams with a relatively flat image are actually harmonically complex (in terms of how songs are traditionally conceived) since the 12 pitches are treated more equally than chromagrams in which there is much more distance between the most and least frequently used pitches. Still, it is important to keep in mind that the harmonic complexity represented by the melody tends to receive the greatest of emphasis in this system, rather than more subtle harmonies in the accompaniment. Moreover, like most any of the pioneering computational techniques for music analysis, chromagrams are imperfect and may be affected by "non-pitched" percussive sounds or thick timbres (such as heavy distortion in a guitar or overtones in an organ) that in human cognition are rarely recognized as functionally "harmonic" features of a song. Nevertheless, chromagrams may currently be among the most robust and musically relevant signal processing measurements yet devised for computational analysis of harmony.

To illustrate further, it may be useful to compare how the two examples of Stevie Wonder's "Don't You Worry Bout a Thing" and Billy Joel's "Just the Way You Are" are illustrated by the chromagram. For any musician who has ever attempted to improvise on either of these songs, it will be clear that both are relatively complex in terms of chord structure, for both use "jazzy" chords featuring extensions that would typically be regarded as "harmonically complex" relative to songs that have only standard major, minor, and seventh chords. However, if one focuses exclusively on the melody it becomes clear that Billy Joel's tune is relatively diatonic, repeating many of the same pitches without many unpredictable intervals or harmonic leaps. Stevie Wonder's song, on the other hand, uses many different pitches in its melody and entails complex interrelation of sections, between verse, chorus, and bridge. Therefore, a song such as Billy Joel's "Just the Way You Are" despite generally having rather complex jazz-influenced harmonies in the accompaniment will not be rated as complex according to the chromagram since its melody is essentially diatonic, while a song such as Stevie Wonder's "Don't You Worry About a Thing" which has a melody with a lot of unpredictable chromaticism receives a relatively more complex rating. Interestingly, visual inspection of the chromagrams across the entire Billboard 100 identified two of the most and least harmonically complex songs as from the same year, 1963. The least complex was an instrumental song, "Wild Weekend" by The Rebels, while the most complex was Andy Williams' "Can't Get Used to Losing You". These are shown in Fig. 1 along with "Don't You Worry Bout a Thing" and "Just the Way You Are". These songs have not been normalized for loudness.

As the above chart demonstrates, "Wild Weekend" clearly emphasizes 4 main pitches in a way that resembles "Just the way you are", putting the strength in the fundamental, the fifth and fourth degrees, while "Can't Get Used to Losing You" and "Don't You Worry Bout a Thing" more equally cover the entire set of 12 chromatic pitches.

The finding that "Wild Weekend" and "Can't Get Used to Losing You" were determined by chromagrams to represent the most extreme cases might be surprising considering the existence of hit songs in the Billboard 100 that have obvious harmonic complexity indicated within their melodies, such as the aforementioned "Don't You Worry Bout a Thing" by Stevie Wonder. However, if one takes a careful listen to "Can't Get Used to Losing You" with recognition of the parameters of chromagrams, this finding becomes more understandable, for "Can't Get Used to Losing You"

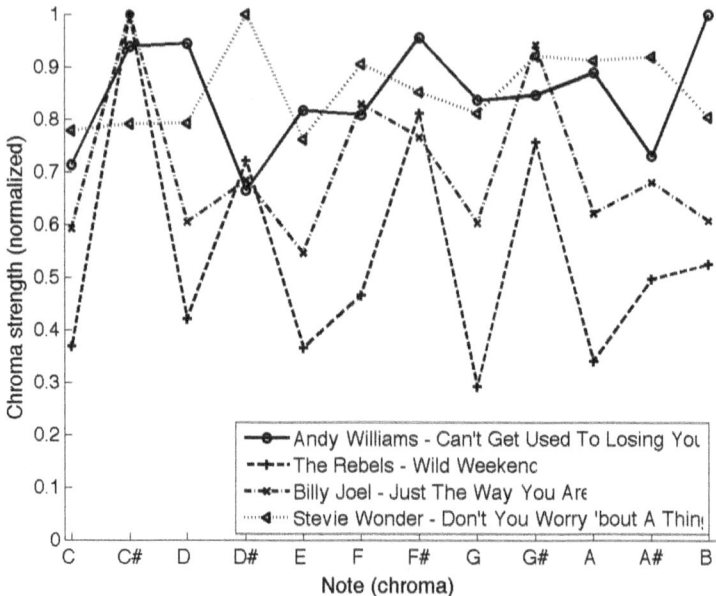

Fig. 1. Chroma of four songs.

actually has a melody that is unpredictable and covers a very wide range of pitches across the 12-note spectrum. Even a listen to just the first 30 s of the song reveals a remarkably unpredictable range of pitches and unusual chromaticism in the introduction and verses. Although a chorus eventually appears with the song's hook "I can't get used to losing you" that is mostly diatonic and fairly predictable, its actual melody treats each of the 12 chromatic pitches with approximately equal weight.

2.4 Jensen Chroma Complexity (JCC)

In order to enable efficient and manageable comparisons across a large corpus of data, a reductive approach has necessarily been undertaken in this study. In the field of music signal processing, chroma are widely regarded to be a relatively valid and robust strategy for representation of harmony. The JCC engenders an individual profile to evaluate the relative strength of each of the 12-chromatic pitches across each moment in a song (once every 125 ms, or 8 times per second). Averaging through calculation in relation to the mean and standard deviation leads to production of a single JCC profile score for each song. This measurement is appropriate for structural analysis and general music information retrieval purposes. As can be seen in Fig. 1 harmonically complex songs have more evenly distributed use of all twelve pitches, while harmonically simple songs have chroma featuring fewer strong pitches. In addition, it is clear that the songs have different loudness levels. The distribution of pitch use within the chroma is measured through the inverse of the standard deviation, while the loudness normalization is calculated via the mean of the chromas. The resulting Jensen Chroma Complexity is shown in Eq. (1) below.

$$JCC = \frac{\mu_c}{\sigma_c} \quad (1)$$

In the above equation, μ_c denotes the mean of the chroma, and σ_c denotes the standard deviation. Since the standard deviation is proportional to the mean of the chroma, multiplication by the mean normalizes for this effect, effectively nullifying all effects related to the *loudness war*. The resulting Jensen Chroma Complexity is an elegant, robust and manageable feature for the analysis of harmonic richness across a large data set. It is calculated elegantly (with minimal risk of bias), as compared to methods for calculating other musically relevant features, such as pitch or tempo estimations, which ensures the robustness of the measurement results. JCC is also largely resistant to postprocessing effects, as compared to, for instance, loudness measures. As an example, the four songs in Fig. 1 have the following JCC; "Can't Get Used To Losing You": 1.06, "Wild Weekend": 1.40, "Just The Way You Are": 1.17, and "Don't You Worry 'bout A Thing": 1.51. JCC can thus offer a useful representation of the holistic harmonic complexity of a song. In the next section, JCC is applied to illustrate the general evolution of harmonic complexity across historical time, which is merely one of its possible applications. It is also believed that JCC can be helpful in other music information retrieval tasks, such as song style identification, but for such purposes, the JCC would need to be combined with other measurements to ensure reliable results.

3 Result

Using advanced signal processing strategies, we generated chromagrams for all songs in the Billboard 100 across the 76-year period from 1940 to 2015, totaling 6494 songs (Table 2).

Table 2. Distribution of Billboard hits across the years.

Period (Years)	Number of songs per year
1956–2015	100 (n = 5900)
1941–1955	30 (n = 450)
1940	44 (n = 44)
Total	N = 6494

3.1 General JCC Evolution

The JCC in relation to each chromagram was then calculated as the mean from each frame of the audio, resulting in one JCC measure for each song. The resulting JCC is shown in Fig. 2 for all years in an error bar plot. It is clear that the JCC indicates a

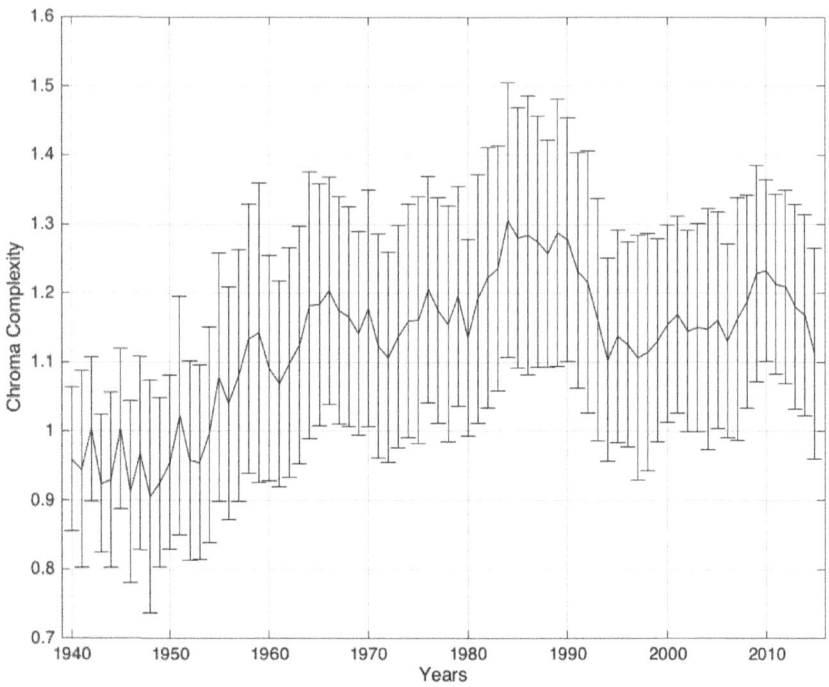

Fig. 2. Error bar plot of all JCC measures. The middle line denotes means for each year, and whiskers denote standard deviation.

continuous trajectory that increases significantly (from mean value 1 to mean value 1.8) from 1940 until around 1990, after which the value falls and stabilizes around 1.6.

3.2 Statistical Predictability

Based on these calculations, it appears that the JCC is an effective measurement for prediction of the year of origin for Billboard 100 songs. From 1940 to early 1950s there is one plateau of similar values, and a similar plateau is also found for the following decades. It is notable that a period from the mid-1980s through early 1990s shows a remarkable uniformity of JCC scores, while there is similarity in scores between the early 1980s and the years around 2000.

In order to test this predictability of the JCC, a two-sample Kolmogorov-Smirnov test was used. It returns a 1 if the null hypothesis—that data are from the same continuous distribution—is rejected, and 0 if not rejected (i.e. the JCC for the two years are coming from the same distribution). This enables us to identify, for each year, the other years to which it both is, and is not, significantly different. The standard signification level ($p < 0.05$) is used here. The complete overview of the year-to-year statistics is shown in Fig. 3. White color in this case indicates that the years on the x- and y-axes do not have the same distribution.

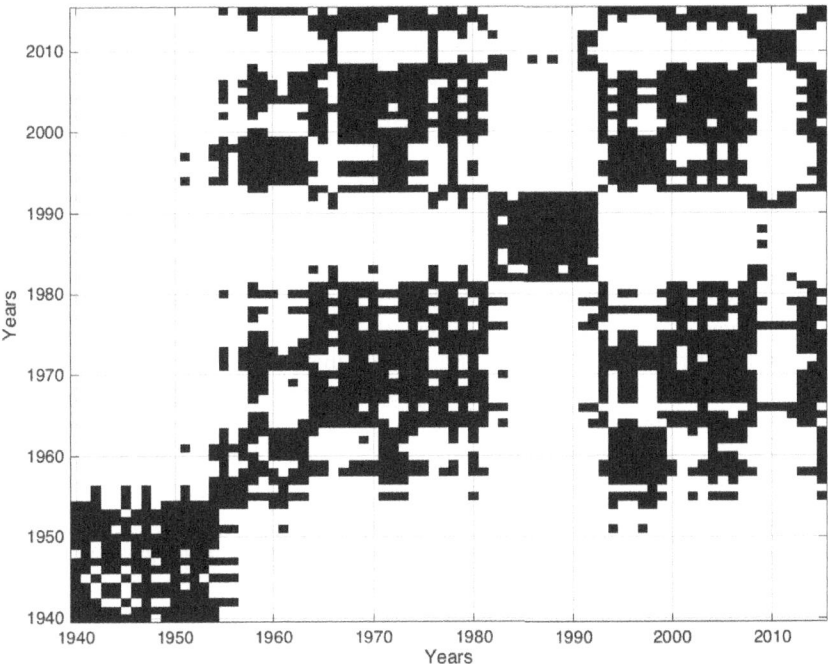

Fig. 3. Statistical signification for pair of year JCC measures having different distributions. Black indicates hypothesis of same distribution can not be rejected, and white indicates same hypothesis is rejected.

Overall, 77.88 % of the years measured are different when using JCC to separate years. Generally, we found that decades are the approximate unit of analysis by which shifts in harmonic tendencies are evident in this corpus. Specifically, several decade-like areas are clearly visible in Fig. 3: from 1940 to 1953, from 1954 to 1964, and from 1981 to 1993, while the decade of the 1970s is quite similar to the years between 1994 and 2008. In other words, based on these findings, JCC is sufficiently robust to demonstrate the notion that there is generally a "1960s sound" that is computationally distinguishable from that of the 1950s and 1970s in this corpus, and the same is roughly applicable to other decades, within the margin of a few years.

4 Discussion

It was satisfying to determine that the JCC measure offers a clear trajectory with strong predictability and significant correlation to specific decades, but we wondered whether JCC might also have potential application to broader forms of social inquiry. What, if anything, might JCC analysis suggest about relationships between music and society across historical time? Although the Billboard Top 100 corpus appears to offer the most useful representation of the popular culture consensus of notable songs in the US, few (if any) music experts would likely suggest that the songs in this corpus comprise the most important musical works of the 20th century. Similarly, upon considering historical relationships between music and society, we should keep in mind that expert historians are likely to disagree with the general public regarding which occurrences are most important. Music preference and participation are widely recognized as intertwined with identity, and in terms of historical understandings, several research studies have demonstrated the fundamental role of social memory in identity formation (Tavani et al. [31]), as well as profound cultural differences in how historical events are perceived (Liu et al. [28]). Various publications have also examined how university students and professional historians perceive the importance of particular historical events during the 20th century in the United States (Pennebakere et al. [30]; Time Editors [32]). However, what we regard as particularly relevant to any comparison with the Billboard Top 100 corpus is data regarding how the general population perceives its history. The most useful data for that purpose that we have identified comes from a Gallup poll (Newport et al. [29]). Its findings claim to show what "the people" of the US consider to be the 18 most significant events of the 20th century affecting the United States. Perhaps unsurprisingly, 7 of the 18 events on this list are wars or war-related events (Holocaust, atomic bombing of Japan, etc.). Others include assassinations (Kennedy), socioeconomic challenges (Great Depression), technological developments (Sputnik launch, lunar landing, Lindbergh's trans-Atlantic flight), legal developments (universal suffrage, Civil Rights), political shifts (fall of Berlin Wall, break-up of USSR), and major political scandals (Watergate, Clinton scandal, etc.). With cautious skepticism, it seemed appropriate to consider whether these events might in some way be correlated to our JCC data reflecting musical changes across historical time. Four of these 18 events were prior to the start of our Billboard 100 data (from 1940), and therefore cannot be compared: Women gaining the right to vote in 1920, World War I, US Depression in the 1930s, and Charles Lindbergh's transatlantic flight in 1927. The two lowest ranked events reported in the Gallup poll actually were rated as only "somewhat important" or "not important" by the majority of participants (Nixon and Clinton scandals), so we have elected to also remove them from consideration, leaving 12 of the 18 from the Gallup poll, as shown in Tables 3 and 4.

Table 3. Twelve major events since 1940, in perceived order of importance.

Rank	Event
1.	World War II
2.	Dropping the Atomic Bomb on Hiroshima in 1945
3.	The Nazi Holocaust during World War II
4.	Passage of the 1964 Civil Rights Act
5.	Landing a man on the moon in 1969
6.	The assassination of President Kennedy in 1963
7.	The fall of the Berlin Wall in 1989
8.	The breakup of the Soviet Union in the early 1990s
9.	The Vietnam War in the 1960s and early 1970s
10.	The launching of the Russian Sputnik satellites in the 1950s
11.	The Korean War in the early 1950s
12.	Persian Gulf War in 1991

Table 4. Twelve major events since 1940, in relative chronological order.

Rank	Event
1.	World War II
2.	The Nazi Holocaust during World War II
3.	Dropping the Atomic Bomb on Hiroshima in 1945
4.	The Korean War in the early 1950s
5.	The launching of the Russian Sputnik satellites in the 1950s
6.	The assassination of President Kennedy in 1963
7.	Passage of the 1964 Civil Rights Act
8.	The Vietnam War in the 1960s and early 1970s
9.	Landing a man on the moon in 1969
10.	The fall of the Berlin Wall in 1989
11.	The breakup of the Soviet Union in the early 1990s
12.	Persian Gulf War in 1991

Might any relationship be immediately apprehended between these historical events and the general trajectory of JCC? Recall that, as shown in Fig. 2, the JCC increases from around 1948 to 1958, followed by a small dip, then rising again until around 1966, where it decreases a bit and mostly stalls until 1980, when it rises again until 1985, and until 1991 it mostly remains on its one high plateau. Then, the JCC drops fairly steeply until 1994, where it stalls again with an increase around 2006 until 2010, when it again makes a steep decline. Based on the list of major historical events compiled here, we were unable to easily identify any likely correlations to the JCC, but in future studies we intend to cautiously test for possible correlations to more precise forms of social data than such a general list of major historical events allows.

5 Conclusion

This paper describes the feature estimation of large corpus of music across historical time. Such an endeavor puts high demands on the feature, as well as the database. A robust, manageable feature, the Jensen Chroma Complexity has been developed specifically for the demands of this study. It offers an elegant measure of the complexity of the chroma, which enables a single measure to represent the harmonic complexity of each song. The JCC remains robust in relation to common sound degradations, and it has been shown to render results in line with human expectations for select songs. A large database of 6,494 songs spanning 76 years has been assembled. The resulting JCC indicates a comprehensible trajectory that even enables predictability of the year of origin for each hit song with high precision. This work pioneers a novel approach to temporal music information retrieval through what we have shown to be a robust feature, the JCC.

Reflecting upon the broader significance of this study, we should also briefly note that an important difference between JCC and such commercial products as Shazam lies in the JCC's utility for production of robust harmonic profiles independent of any preexisting database. Shazam contrarily enables song identification by correlating an acoustic fingerprint to its catalogue of commercial recordings. In other words, JCC enables a form of computationally generated harmonic analysis that may ultimately be applied to even novel and archival recordings, while Shazam is a more general identification and information retrieval tool applicable only to song files in its massive commercial music database. Because JCC is able to analytically determine an approximate year of origin based on generation of harmonic profiles without reliance on direct correlation to a database, it offers an array of relatively promising future research applications, particularly in relation to music that has not been commercially released.

It is believed that the JCC can be useful for many other kinds of music information retrieval purposes, including analysis of novel and archival recordings. These promising results with only one feature for temporal prediction demonstrate the validity of JCC. Still, we acknowledge the need to combine JCC with other reliable measures of significant musical features—including rhythmic intensity—to develop a more complete understanding of the "big data" view of how popular music changes across time. In future studies, we intend to apply JCC to other genres and also courageously open the age-old "Pandora's Box" to evaluate possible correlations to social data in the hope of convincingly uncovering some of the ways that music may both shape and be shaped by society. Specifically, as computational techniques such as JCC are refined and repeatedly tested, we contend that a "Discursive Hypothesis" will ultimately be corroborated in sociomusicology: *because both music and language are cultural discourses (which may reflect social reality in similarly limited ways), a relationship may be identifiable between the trajectories of significant features of musical sound and linguistic discourse regarding social data.* In future studies, we will demonstrate how JCC can be used for such purposes.

References

1. Harrison, A.K., Arthur, C.E.: Reading Billboard 1979–89: exploring rap music's emergence through the music industry's most influential trade publication. Pop. Music Soc. **34**(3), 309–327 (2011)
2. Cooper, B.L.: Charting the success of male recording duos: Billboard recognition of country, pop, and R & B/rap pairs, 1944–2004. Pop. Music Soc. **33**(2), 237–257 (2010)
3. Lafrance, M., Worcester, L., Burns, L.: Gender and the Billboard top 40 charts between 1997 and 2007. Pop. Music Soc. **34**(5), 557–570 (2011)
4. Breen, M.: Billboard goes into technological overdrive to make radio hits. Pop. Music **9**(3), 369–370 (1990)
5. Christianen, M.: Cycles in symbol production?: a new model to explain concentration, diversity and innovation in the music industry. Pop. Music **14**(1), 55–93 (1995)
6. Hakanen, E.A.: Counting down to number one: the evolution of the meaning of popular music charts. Pop. Music **17**(1), 95–111 (1998)
7. Schurk, W.L., Lee, C.B.: Bumble boogie: 100 years of bee imagery in American sound recordings—a discography. Pop. Music Soc. **34**(4), 493–502 (2011)
8. Thornton, S.: Strategies for reconstructing the popular past. Pop. Music **9**(1), 87–95 (1990)

9. Doyle, P.: From 'My Blue Heaven' to 'Race with the Devil': echo, reverb and (dis)ordered space in early popular music recording. Pop. Music **23**(1), 31–49 (2004)
10. Tzanetakis, G., Kapur, A., Schloss, W.A., Wright, M.: Computational ethnomusicology. J. Interdiscipl. Music Stud. **1**(2), 1–24 (2007)
11. RMA Music and Philosophy Study Group conference, London (2013). http://www.musicandphilosophy.ac.uk/conference-2013/pre-conference-activities/. Accessed 9/3-2015
12. CMMR Computer Music Multidisciplinary Research conference, Marseille (2013). http://www.cmmr2013.cnrs-mrs.fr/. Accessed 9/3-2015
13. NNIMIPA Nordic Network for the Integration of Music Informatics, Performance and Aesthetics (NNIMIPA) (2013). http://www.nnimipa.org/. Accessed 9/3-2015
14. Bertin-Mahieux, T., Ellis, D.P.W., Whitman, B., Lamere, P.: The million song dataset. In: Proceedings of the International Society for Music Information Retrieval Conference (ISMIR), pp. 591–596 (2011)
15. Burgoyne, J., Wild, J., Fujinaga, I.: An expert ground truth set for audio chord recognition and music analysis. In: Proceedings of the 12th International Conference on Music Information Retrieval, Miami, FL, USA, pp. 633–638 (2011)
16. de Clercq, T., Temperley, D.: A corpus analysis of rock harmony. Pop. Music **30**(1), 47–70 (2011)
17. Jensen, K.: On the evolution of bass strength in popular music. In: Proceedings of the CMMR, Marseille, France, pp. 670–677 (2013)
18. Michel, J.-B., Shen, Y.K., Aiden, A.P., Veres, A., Gray, M.K., Pickett, J.P., Hoiberg, D., Clancy, D., Norvig, P., Orwant, J., Pinker, S., Nowak, M.A.: Quantitative analysis of culture using millions of digitized books. Science **331**, 176–182 (2011)
19. Pettijohn II, T.F., Sacco Jr., D.F.: Tough times, meaningful music, mature performers: popular Billboard songs and performed preferences across social and economic condition in the USA. Psychol. Music **37**, 155–179 (2009)
20. Savage, P.E., Brown, S.: Toward a new comparative musicology. Anal. Approaches World Music **2**(2), 148–197 (2013)
21. Schellenberg, E.G., von Scheve, C.: Emotional cues in American popular music: five decades of the top 40. Psychol. Aesthet. Creativity Arts **6**(3), 196–203 (2012)
22. Temperley, D., de Clercq, T.: Statistical analysis of harmony and melody in rock music. J. New Music Res. **42**(3), 187–204 (2013)
23. Vickers, E.: The loudness war: background, speculations and recommendations. Paper Presentation, Proceedings of the AES 129th Convention (Audio Engineering Society), San Francisco, CA, 4–7 November, pp. 1–27 (2010)
24. Serra, J., Corral, A., Boguñá, M., Haro, M., Arcos, J.L.: Measuring the evolution of contemporary western popular music. Sci. Rep. **2**, 521 (2012)
25. Shepard, R.: Circularity in judgements of relative pitch. J. Acoust. Soc. Am. **36**, 2346–2353 (1964)
26. Jensen, K.: Multiple scale music segmentation using rhythm, timbre and harmony. EURASIP J. Appl. Sig. Process. **1**, 68–74 (2007). Special Issue on Music Information Retrieval Based on Signal Processing
27. Bartsch, M.A., Wakefield, G.H.: To catch a chorus: using chroma-based representations for audio thumbnailing. In: Proceedings of the Workshop on Applications of Signal Processing to Audio and Acoustics, pp. 15–18 (2001)
28. Liu, J.H., et al.: Cross-cultural dimensions of meaning in the evaluation of events in world history?: perceptions of historical calamities and progress in cross-cultural data from thirty societies. J. Cross Cult. Psychol. **43**(2), 251–272 (2012)

29. Newport, F., Moore, D.W., Saad, L.: The most important events of the century from the viewpoint of the people. Gallup News Service (1999). http://www.gallup.com/poll/3427/most-important-events-century-from-viewpoint-people.aspx
30. Pennebaker, J.W., Páez, D., Deschamps, J.C.: The social psychology of history: defining the most important events of the last 10, 100, and 1000 years. Psicología Política **32**, 15–32 (2006)
31. Tavani, J.L., Collange, J., Rateau, P., Rouquette, M.-L., Sanitioso, B.R.: Tell me what you remember and I will know who you are: the link between collective memory and social categorization. Group Process Intergroup Relat., 1–18 (2015). doi:10.1177/1368430215596076
32. Time Editors 25 Moments that changed America. Time (2015). http://time.com/3889533/25-moments-changed-america/

Information Rate for Fast Time-Domain Instrument Classification

Jordan Ubbens(✉) and David Gerhard

Department of Computer Science, University of Regina, Regina, Canada
ubbens2j@uregina.ca

Abstract. In this paper, we propose a novel feature set for instrument classification which is based on the information rate of the signal in the time domain. The feature is extracted by calculating the Shannon entropy over a sliding short-time energy frame and binning statistical features into a unique feature vector. Experimental results are presented, including a comparison to frequency-domain feature sets. The proposed entropy features are shown to be faster than popular frequency-domain methods while maintaining comparable accuracy in an instrument classification task.

Keywords: Audio classification · Audio features · Audio signal processing · Time-domain methods

1 Introduction

Audio classification is a wide and diverse field which incorporates many subdomains including speech recognition and speaker verification, musical signal and musical instrument classification, digital foley, and others. Most audio classification systems require a number of preliminary steps before classification can take place, among them being auditory stream segregation and domain selection. Stream segregation is the process of separating a single auditory event from a collection or cluster of events that happen at the same time. This is a complicated, demanding, inexact, and error-prone area of research that will be beyond the scope of this paper. For the purposes of this paper, we are beginning with the assumption that all auditory events happen monophonically, in isolation and without noise.

A second and more practical requirement of most audio classification systems is some type of restriction of the relevant subdomain. In an ideal world, a single classification system would handle all forms of sound and produce all classification results at all levels, but in practice, systems designed for classification of a limited domain of sounds perform better than generalized systems. For the purposes of this paper, we will be restricting our focus to the classification of individual sounds generated by musical instruments.

In general, classification systems tend to proceed in a number of discrete and independent steps, each of which may be swapped out for alternative implementations of the same step. First, the audio is preprocessed in order to remove noise, constrain the frequency range, normalize the loudness, segment individual chunks of interest, or perform other tasks that are required to equalize the incoming data and allow the classification engine itself to focus on the task; optionally, the audio is broken into small frames (on the order of hundreds of samples) for time-restricted analysis; Second, a set of *features* are extracted from the audio signal which represent statistical, perceptual, physical or other traits of the sound itself. This process is performed in order to accomplish complexity reduction and represent the signal (or each frame of the signal) as a vector within a feature space; Third, these feature vectors are used to train a classification model in order to estimate parameters of the classification model which best represent the set of classes that correspond to the data under analysis, this training being either supervised (in which case the class is known *a priori*) or unsupervised (in which case the system discovers the inherent structure of clusters of data); and finally, the trained classification is verified against previously unseen signals.

This paper will consider the feature extraction phase, and make the assumption that the features presented herein can be applied to any standard classification process pipeline.

Although there are many ways to describe the wide variety of feature extraction systems in the literature and available off-the-shelf, one way of arranging these approaches, as applied to audio signals, is whether they are based in the *time domain* or the *frequency domain*. Time domain features are extracted from the time series of the audio waveform, and frequency-domain features are extracted from the frequency spectrum of the signal which must be calculated before the features can be extracted. Typically, this frequency spectrum is calculated using the Fast Fourier Transform (FFT) or the Short-Time Fourier Transform (STFT). Although well-studied time-domain features exist, to date, most systems have focused on frequency domain features, based on the assumption that more acoustically relevant information is available in the frequency domain than the time domain. The principal drawback of frequency domain features is that they require the calculation of, and transformation to, the frequency domain, before the feature extraction system can be applied. This additional computational cost has typically been seen as the "cost of doing business" when using frequency-domain features.

Time domain techniques, such as zero-crossing rate (ZCR) and power-based features, have been found to be useful for extracting some acoustically relevant information from certain classes of signals, but these techniques have not been reliable in all circumstances, and there are many examples of specific signals or situations which cause time domain techniques fail. Time domain features which are well-correlated with their spectral counterparts can be used to help avoid the large computational costs of FFT, as well as a number of other drawbacks that are incurred with the use of the FFT, as will be discussed in Sect. 2.2, including frequency blurring, reduced time resolution, and an artificial power-of-two requirement for frame sizes.

Powerful audio classifiers which operate in the time domain would be able to forego the conversion of the signal into the frequency domain using a transform such as STFT. The benefits would include reduced computation time and release from the power-of-two frame size requirement. This paper presents a description, examination, and evaluation of a novel time-domain feature: the use of Shannon entropy in conjunction with short-time energy, which we call the "Entropy Signature".

2 Background

Many candidate features have been explored with respect to audio classification. These features can be categorized as spectral features and temporal features, and many features can also be categorized as to whether they are based on perceptual or physical characteristics of the signal. Several studies have reviewed the performance of these features in instrument classification [3,5,6,9] and among the feature sets for audio classification, MFCCs remain one of the most popular "off-the-shelf" feature sets.

2.1 Spectral Features

Spectral features are the family of features which have seen the greatest success and attention in audio classification tasks. These features describe characteristics of the frequency spectrum after transforming the signal to the frequency representation. Spectral features are highly general, and perform well in several different domains, such as genre classification, where temporal features do not generalize.

Cepstral coefficients are an example of spectral features. They are calculated by taking the inverse Fourier transform of the log of the Fourier transform of the original signal. Features extracted from this cepstral process yield high rates of accuracy when applied to many audio classification problems. MFCC features are a variation on cepstral coefficients which relate to human perception by using the mel-frequency scale. MFCCs are known to be highly effective in instrument classification [5]. Other spectral features include the spectral centroid, which is a description of "brightness" [3]; spectral flux, a spectro-temporal feature describing the degree of spectral change [10]; spectral rolloff, which describes the right-skewedness of the spectrum; and bandwidth (or centroid width), which describes the frequency range.

2.2 The Cost of the Fourier Transform

Although common and effective, spectral features incur a number of inherent costs which are the result of the use of the Fourier transform or other spectral transforms for extracting the frequency content of the signal. These costs are typically accepted as fundamental to spectral analysis, but it is worth taking a moment to review these costs and remind the reader of the potential benefits of remaining in the time domain for feature extraction.

The first and most obvious of these costs is that the signal is typically segmented using a power-of-two frame size prior to analysis. Frames are a power of two number of samples in length (typically 512, 1024, or 2048), in order to optimize the computational efficiency and parallel nature of the Fast Fourier Transform algorithm. Although segmentation is critical for the analysis of signals which change their spectral content over time, being restricted to a power of two means the frame size cannot be chosen to fit the signal or the specifics of the domain. Different frame sizes can be chosen to focus on different features of the frequency spectrum, leading to what can be called "multidimensional analysis". The use of arbitrary frame sizes has increased in the recent past due to the increased computational resources available in modern computers, but this only serves to increase the relative cost of the spectral transform.

The second cost of the use of spectral transforms is the effect of windowing on the signal. Windowing a frame is the process of multiplying the frame content by a "window" which modifies the signal by reducing it to zero at the edges of the frame. Typical windowing functions include the Hamming window and the Parzen window. The act of windowing attempts to solve another inherent problem of the STFT which is that the fundamental frequency of the analysis window is almost always different than the fundamental frequency of the signal under analysis, which results in the spreading out, or blurring, of spectral peaks across adjacent frequencies. This is mediated, but not solved, by windowing, but the act of windowing the signal significantly alters the original spectral content as well, requiring an overlap between adjacent analysis frames.

The third problem inherent in short-time spectral analysis is the tradeoff between time resolution and frequency resolution of the analysis frame. The smaller the analysis window, the better the time resolution but the worse the time resolutions. In a kind of uncertainty principle, it is only possible to know the exact time of an audio event, or the complete spectral content of that event, but never both. To get better spectral information about a signal, one must use a larger frequency window, which blurs the information about when in the window a specific frequency event may have occurred.

Because of these drawbacks to frequency analysis, we wanted to re-visit the area of time-domain features and explore the development of new features that may have reasonable accuracy without the computational cost and conceptual drawbacks of STFT.

2.3 Time Domain Features

Features extracted in the time domain are not typically used in classification, although some such features do exist. Zero-Crossing Rate (ZCR) is one of the most common time domain features. ZCR is a measurement of how quickly the signal oscillates between positive and negative values. Short-time energy (STE) is a measurement of the signal's power over time. Although STE is not always valuable for audio classification on its own, there are some uses for statistics of the STE. Domain-specific time domain features, such as duration, have limited use here.

Temporal features describe how the signal evolves over time, both in the time-frequency domain as well as in the time domain. Some of these features have seen success in instrument classification, such as rise time [6]. Rise time characterizes the delay between the onset of a sound and the point of maximum amplitude. Temporal features can be used to detect modulation in frequency and amplitude, as well as onset asynchrony between different frequencies. The temporal envelope, including the amplitude envelope in the time domain, has been described as an important component of how information is encoded in the human auditory system [1].

2.4 Related Work

The feature we are proposing is based on an investigation of the entropy of the signal, and as such, it is worth reminding the reader of pertinent aspects of information theory.

Shannon entropy is a foundational concept in the field of information theory [11]. The entropy rate of a sequence of symbols (for instance, real numbers in a pulse-code modulated audio signal) is the average number of bits per symbol required to encode the sequence.

Shannon entropy appears in the audio classification literature in several different ways. Spectral entropy (also known as Wiener entropy, or spectral flatness) is an important feature which describes the tonality of a signal. A frequency spectrum with high entropy is said to be highly noise-like (as opposed to being highly tone-like). This feature has had success, for example, in environmental classification [2]. Other research has introduced the entropy of a signal's wavelet coefficients as a feature for musical genre classification [8].

The entropy of a signal in the time domain has other applications. In [7], the researchers found that the signal entropy with respect to time can function as an effective fingerprint for audio data, providing highly competitive accuracy in recognition tasks. Entropy has also been used to distinguish speech from singing as a measure of "regularity" [12].

3 Extracting Entropy Signatures

We propose a new time-domain feature set based on energy-indexed signal entropy. Because this method does not require a translation into the Fourier domain, computational cost can be kept to a minimum. As we will show in experimental results, the accuracy of the method remains comparable with traditional (slower) spectral techniques.

The method is based on calculating an entropy measurement for each frame of the signal, and relating this entropy to the energy of the signal itself. Statistics of entropy at each energy level are then assembled into a feature vector. Because the frames do not have to be windowed or a power of two (as in spectral transforms), minimal modifications are made to the signal in the process of extracting this new feature.

3.1 Feature Extraction Pipeline

A three-stage process pipeline is used to extract entropy features from an audio source. First, the signal is normalized and the *short-time energy* (STE) of the signal is calculated using Eq. 1. STE represents the energy level of the signal within a frame of sample size N, and the STE of the entire signal is the cumulative STE of each frame, taken over time [3]. STE is a framed physical feature commonly used in speech applications, such as speech/silence detection [4].

$$STE = \frac{1}{N} \sum_{n=1}^{N} x_n^2 \quad (1)$$

After calculating the STE, we calculate a "short-time entropy" signal for each frame as well. This is done on a sliding frame which is 128 samples long. The frame size corresponds to approximately 2 ms, and is not required to be a power of two. The hop size of the sliding frame is set at 1 sample, leading to significantly improved time resolution. Shannon entropy is calculated on the contents of the frame at each position, based on Eq. 2:

$$H(X)_t = - \sum_{x \in X} p(x) \log(p(x)) \quad (2)$$

where $H(X)_t$ is the value of the short-time entropy signal at frame position t, and X is the domain of values within the sliding frame. The most computationally expensive part of the calculation is maintaining the discrete probability distribution over X for each sliding step. We use a histogram method to use the result from the previous frame to recalculate the distribution for each new frame position (a requirement of the short time entropy calculation) and this histogram-based recalculation takes only two additional operations. We store calculated values in a lookup table, to be consulted by subsequent frames, as in [7]. This prevents unnecessary calls to the logarithm function. An example of the short time entropy extracted from a waveform can be seen in Fig. 1.

Finally, the mean and standard deviation of the entropy measurements are binned, using the corresponding STE of the signal, into ten energy levels. This gives us a unique vector which represents the signal's information rate as a function of signal power. We term this the signal's *entropy signature*. An entropy signature extracted from a musical instrument sample is shown in Fig. 2.

An intuitive and conceptual interpretation of this new feature is as follows: The time-domain energy of the signal corresponds to the loudness of the signal at that frame. The time-domain entropy (information rate) of the signal may be related to spectral content, with higher information rate relating to a more varied and complex spectrum, while a lower information rate may be related to a smoother, more frequency-sparse signal. Another interpretation of the entropy is as it relates to noise. Stochastic white noise is random and therefore cannot be predicted one frame to the next (or even one sample to the next). This is a very high-entropy signal because so much information must be encoded for each frame. A steady-state sinusoid, on the other hand, may be encoded very simply, as each frame is a perfect copy of the previous frame, requiring zero information.

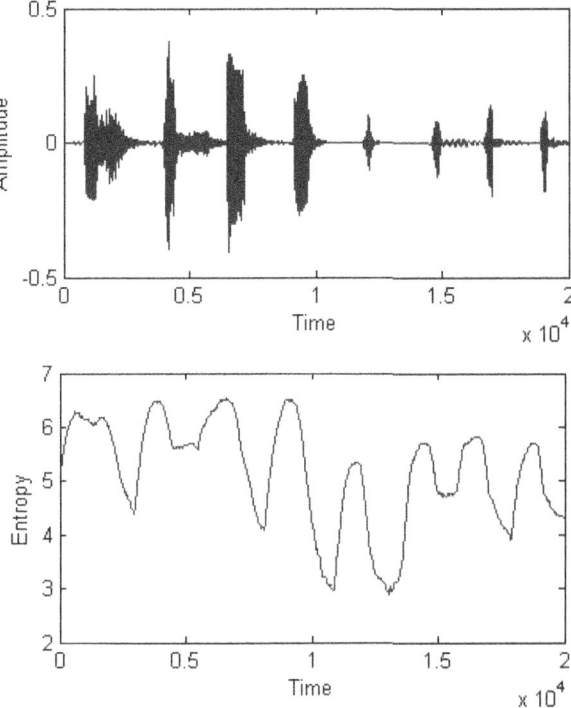

Fig. 1. Example of short-time entropy of a speech waveform: source signal (top) and short-time entropy (bottom)

In this way, the information rate can be seen as being related to the "noisiness" of the signal. The relationship between the loudness and noisiness of each frame is what makes up our new entropy-based feature vector.

3.2 Computational Complexity

The energy calculation and the entropy calculation used in the pipeline are both on the order of $O(n)$, meaning that the time complexity of the entire feature extraction pipeline remains at $O(n)$. Practical optimizations such as using the histogram method for maintaining the probability distribution over X and using a lookup table for values of $p(x)$ increase the efficiency of the implementation.

This is superior to traditional spectral feature methods, which require at minimum $O(n \cdot \log n)$ in order to transform into the spectral domain, before calculation of the feature set can even begin. Although FFT algorithms have been optimized over their long history, and many audio processing toolchains have hardware-level FFT algorithms baked into the chipset, a time domain method which is able to obviate the $O(n \cdot \log n)$ requirement for spectral processing is of potential interest. So far, no features which are informative enough to stand on their own have been found in the time domain and therefore $O(n \cdot \log n)$ stands as a theoretical prerequisite for feature extraction.

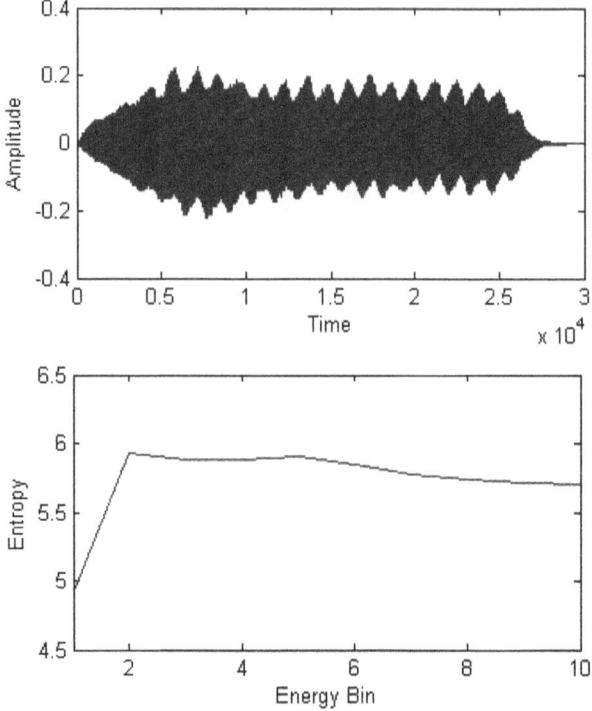

Fig. 2. An oboe sample (top) and corresponding mean entropy signature (bottom)

4 Comparing Entropy Signatures of Similar Classes

Since there are a variety of possibly confounding similarities to be seen in the waveforms of different instrument classes, it is worth examining some entropy signatures of instrument samples exhibiting physical similarities.

Figure 3 shows a sample of a bowed violin and the resulting entropy signature. This is compared to Fig. 4 which depicts the same instrument played in a different

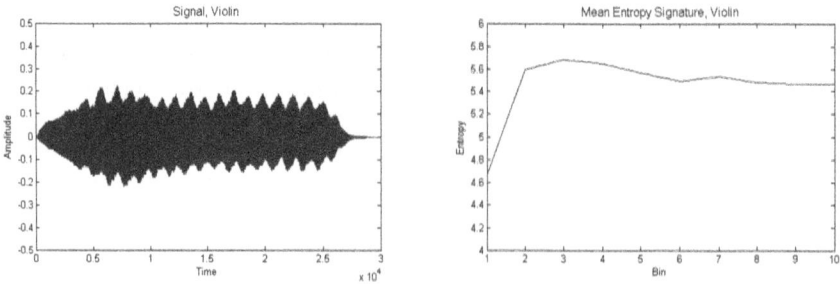

Fig. 3. A bowed violin sample (left) and corresponding mean entropy signature (right)

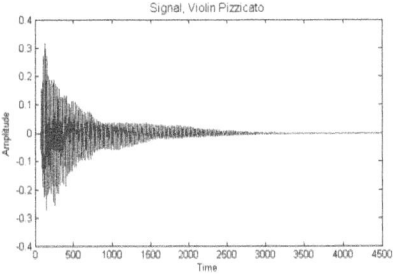 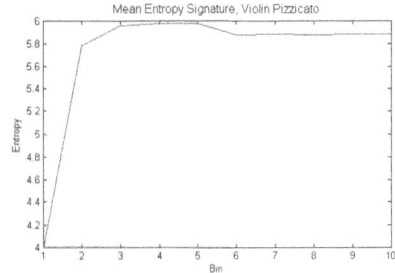

Fig. 4. A violin pizzicato sample (left) and corresponding mean entropy signature (right)

style (*pizzicato*, or plucking). Although the two classes are produced by the same instrument, they have different shapes and represent two different classes in the data set used for the experiments presented here.

The entropy signature of the pizzicato violin resembles that of the bowed violin, but exhibits a larger amount of entropy in the last nine bins.

Figure 5 shows the waveform and entropy signature of a tubular bell. Although the waveform of the tubular bell resembles that of the pizzicato violin sample, its entropy signature is distinctly different, with monotonically increasing entropy through the bins.

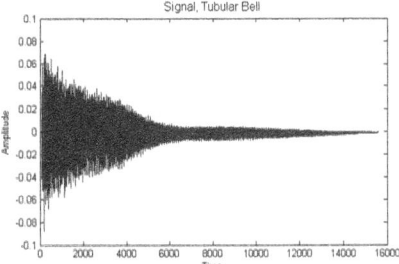 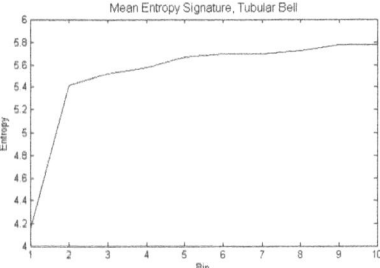

Fig. 5. A tubular bell sample (left) and corresponding mean entropy signature (right)

5 Experiments and Results

Pitched instrument samples from the *MuscleFish* audio classification dataset were used to evaluate the proposed entropy signature feature set. This dataset is comprised of 204 samples (sampled at 8 kHz) representing seven uneven classes. The audio classes include stringed instruments, brass, woodwinds, and bells.

The proposed entropy signature ("EntSig") feature set was tested in a multi-class classification task using three common classification algorithms: C4.5 decision trees, Naive Bayes, and Support Vector Machines (SVM). 10-fold cross-validation was used in each test. For comparison, cepstral and spectral feature sets were also extracted. Mean and standard deviation features were extracted for thirteen mel-frequency cepstral coefficients. MFCCs were chosen due to their continued popularity as an engineered feature for classification tasks. For the spectral feature set, mean and standard deviation were calculated for each of the root mean square (RMS), spectral centroid, bandwidth, and spectral flux. These particular features were selected because they are among the most descriptive spectral and physical (in the case of RMS) features for the instrument classification task [3]. These two popular frequency-domain feature sets provide a good benchmark for comparing our proposed time-domain method.

Table 1. Accuracy in the classification task (%)

Feature set	C4.5	N. Bayes	SVM
EntSig	70.59	68.14	73.53
Spectral	70.59	76.47	70.09
MFCC	71.56	85.78	87.74

The results of the classification experiments in Table 1 show that the proposed time-domain features are able to achieve classification performance which is comparable to the spectral feature set, outperforming the spectral features in the case of the SVM classifier. The EntSig features are comparable to the MFCC feature set when used with the C4.5 classifier, but fall as much as 17.64% behind MFCCs with other classifiers. Feature selection on the proposed 20-dimensional feature vector gives us the information gain measurements in Table 2.

Table 2. Information gain for EntSig features

EntSig mean		EntSig stdev.	
Bin	Information gain	Bin	Information gain
1	0.746	1	0.781
2	0.427	2	0.262
3	0.443	3	0.267
4	0.448	4	0.308
5	0.571	5	0.257
6	0.426	6	0.242
7	0.448	7	0.231
8	0.478	8	0.182
9	0.437	9	0.182
10	0.428	10	0

6 Conclusion and Future Work

In this paper, we have demonstrated a strictly time-domain feature set for instrument classification. In the experiments presented here, the proposed entropy features are able to match the performance of the spectral feature set (on average). This is an encouraging result for time-domain features, since frequency-domain methods are heavily optimized for the instrument classification task but continue to impose constraints including time complexity, spectral blur, and power-of-two frame size requirements. The time complexity of our proposed method is shown to be superior to frequency-domain methods. These experiments open up further discussion on the use of signal entropy for classification with many possible avenues for improvement.

Future work may focus on improving classification results with different window sizes and tests with non-uniform sizes of power bins and different audio domains. Adapting the size of the entropy window may also yield an advantage for different classes of audio.

References

1. Altaf, M., Juang, B.: Audio signal classification with temporal envelopes. In: IEEE International Conference on Acoustics, Speech and Signal Processing (ICASSP), pp. 469–472, May 2011
2. Delgado-Contreras, J., Garcia-Vazquez, J.: Classification of environmental audio signals using statistical time and frequency features. In: International Conference on Electronics, Communications and Computers (CONIELECOMP), pp. 212–216 (2014)
3. Deng, J., Simmermacher, C.: A study on feature analysis for musical instrument classification. IEEE Trans. Syst. Man Cybern. Part B: Cybern. **38**(2), 429–438 (2008)
4. Erdol, N., Castelluccia, C., Zilouchian, A.: Recovery of missing speech packets using the short-time energy and zero-crossing measurements. IEEE Trans. Speech Audio Process. **1**(3), 295–303 (1993)
5. Eronen, A.: Comparison of features for musical instrument recognition. In: IEEE Workshop on the Applications of Signal Processing to Audio and Acoustics, pp. 19–22 (2001)
6. Herrera-Boyer, P., Dubnov, S.: Automatic classification of musical instrument sounds. J. New Music Res. **32**(1), 3–21 (2003)
7. Ibarrola, A., Chavez, E.: A robust entropy-based audio-fingerprint. In: IEEE International Conference on Multimedia and Expo (ICME), pp. 1729–1732, July 2006
8. Lambrou, T., Kudumakis, P., Speller, R., Sandler, M., Linney, A.: Classification of audio signals using statistical features on time and wavelet transform domains. In: IEEE International Conference on Acoustics, Speech and Signal Processing (ICASSP), vol. 6, pp. 3621–3624, May 1998
9. Nielsen, A., Sigurdsson, S., Hansen, L., Arenas-Garcia, J.: On the relevance of spectral features for instrument classification. In: IEEE International Conference on Acoustics, Speech and Signal Processing (ICASSP), vol. 2, pp. 485–488, April 2007

10. Peeters, G., Giordano, B., Susini, P., Misdariis, N., McAdams, S.: The timbre toolbox: extracting audio descriptors from musical signals. J. Acoust. Soc. Am. **130**(5), 2902–2916 (2011)
11. Shannon, C.: A mathematical theory of communication. Bell Syst. Tech. J. **27**(3), 379–423 (1948)
12. Swe, E., Pwint, M.: An efficient approach for classification of speech and music. In: Huang, Y.-M.R., Xu, C., Cheng, K.-S., Yang, J.-F.K., Swamy, M.N.S., Li, S., Ding, J.-W. (eds.) PCM 2008. LNCS, vol. 5353, pp. 50–60. Springer, Heidelberg (2008)

Escaping from the Abyss of Manual Annotation: New Methodology of Building Polyphonic Datasets for Automatic Music Transcription

Li Su[✉] and Yi-Hsuan Yang

Center for Information and Technology Innovaiton, Academia Sinica,
128 Academia Road, Section 2, Nankang, Taipei 115, Taiwan
{lisu,yang}@citi.sinica.edu.tw
https://sites.google.com/site/lisupage/

Abstract. While recent years have witnessed large progress in the algorithm of automatic music transcription (AMT), the development of general and sizable datasets for AMT evaluation is relatively stagnant, predominantly due to the fact that manually annotating and checking such datasets is labor-intensive and time-consuming. In this paper we propose a novel note-level annotation method for building AMT datasets by utilizing human's ability in following music in real-time. To test the quality of the annotation, we further propose an efficient method in qualifying an AMT dataset based on the concepts of onset error difference and the tolerance computed from the evaluation result. According to the experiments on five piano solos and four woodwind quintets, we claim that the proposed annotation method is reliable for evaluation of AMT algorithms.

Keywords: Automatic music transcription · Multipitch estimation · Note tracking · Onset error difference

1 Introduction

Evaluating the performance of an automatic music transcription (AMT)[1] algorithm always requires a dataset containing music excerpts[2] in which every note has annotations of onset and pitch. A sizable dataset covering various classes of music and with accurate note-level annotation would be very helpful for AMT research. However, by now such a dataset is virtually unattainable since annotating the notes in polyphonic music is a tedious process, and there is no straightforward and efficient way of either creating ground truth for multiple-instrument music or checking whether the ground truth is correct [1,3]. Up to the present,

---

[1] In this paper we restrict the scope of AMT to the subtask of onset-only note tracking. Details can be found on the webpage of MIREX Multi-F0 Challenge [11].
[2] In this paper the term "music excerpt" means a segment (usually 20–30 seconds) of audio content taken from a longer music composition.

© Springer International Publishing Switzerland 2016
R. Kronland-Martinet et al. (Eds.): CMMR 2015, LNCS 9617, pp. 309–321, 2016.
DOI: 10.1007/978-3-319-46282-0_20

most AMT algorithms perform experiments only on piano data because it is relative easy to generate them by a MIDI-controlled piano [3]. Without an efficient method of note-level annotation, building sizable and general AMT datasets can be a boring job. Therefore, in comparison to the recent progresses of new AMT algorithms, the development of new and sizable datasets for AMT evaluation is quite slow and insufficient. The science on building an AMT dataset, including the scale, the efficiency and the quality of the annotations, is hardly questioned and investigated.

The purpose of this paper is not to introduce new AMT algorithms. In contrast, we concentrate on the methodology in building an AMT dataset. We expect that a good methodology should not only permit accurate note-level annotation, but also make it easy to build and extend the dataset. Moreover, its contents should be able to represent the music content encountered in real-world application. To discuss these requirements, we define the following criteria to evaluate the goodness of a dataset:

1. **Generality**: The form, genre or instrumentation of the music excerpts should be representative in the music universe and reveal the situations in real-world application. The dataset is not restricted to one class of instrument (e.g., piano solo only) or one specific form of music (e.g., woodwind quintet only). If we wish to apply the AMT algorithm for general online music contents, the dataset should contain real-world music played in real instruments by human and (sometimes) recorded in real environment rather than synthesized signals.
2. **Efficiency**: The annotation process should be fast rather than slow, knowledge intensive rather than labor intensive. Efficiency sometimes implies *scalability*, meaning that we can expand the dataset easily.
3. **Cost**: The cost of money and human resource for building the dataset should be minimized if possible.
4. **Quality**: The annotation should be accurate enough so as to evaluate the performance of an AMT algorithm in a proper manner. Although finding "correct" timing of the onsets and offsets is challenging, the annotation should be closed to the correct point so that the performance of an AMT algorithm can be evaluated accurately within a range of *tolerance* (e.g., in the standard of MIREX Multi-F0 Challenge, the tolerance is 50 ms.).

In terms of these criteria, the contributions of this paper are two-fold: A general, efficient and low-cost method for note-level annotation, and an efficient method in qualifying an AMT dataset. Given that the experience of annotating polyphonic music is actually similar to playing in an orchestra, the proposed annotation method utilizes the musician's technique and behavior by setting an interface (in this paper it is an electric piano with MIDI output) transferring the musician's playing into annotations.

Noticing that the evaluation procedure actually incorporates the concept of the *tolerance* to determine whether a note is correctly detected, we argue that the difference between detected note onset and the labeled note onset within the tolerance (named as *onset error difference*) could be a good indicator of the quality of an AMT dataset. Accordingly, we define criteria qualifying a dataset in terms of these quantities.

Section 2 reviews previous methods in building AMT datasets. Section 3 describes the proposed method, the technical details and experiment results on an AMT algorithm. Section 4 presents how we test the quality of this dataset. Section 5 concludes this paper.

2 Related Work

We categorize the previously proposed datasets available for AMT into 5 (overlapping) groups according to the method adopted to build the dataset: (1) the manual method, (2) the multi-track method, (3) the audio-score alignment method, (4) the autopiano method and (5) the synthesis method.

First, the manual method means that when building the dataset, we listen to the music excerpt and annotate every onset time and the corresponding note name of every note manually. This task is sometimes accomplished with the aid of audio visualization and musical signal analysis tools (e.g., Sonic Visualizer[3]) and music scores. One example using this method is the annotations of MIREX 2007 dataset, where the onsets and offsets are determined by setting an amplitude threshold [11]. The manual method is the most direct method and is available for all real-world music without any restriction of recording environment, instrument, etc., therefore it completely satisfies the merit of generality. However, this method is notoriously labor intensive, inefficient and challenging. Similarly, checking the annotations and improving the quality of the dataset are equivalently insufficient. Previous studies have also commented on this [3], [1].[4] Up to the present, there is still no sizable and fully manually-built dataset providing complete information for AMT.[5]

All the other four annotation methods are basically proposed to improve the efficiency of annotation at the cost of sacrificing generality. The multi-track method means that all the polyphonic music excerpts are mixed from separated parts of monophonic tracks. The monophonic tracks are easier to be labeled by the manual method or by single-pitch detection algorithm like YIN [4]. The greatest advantage of this method is that it downscales the complexity of annotating polyphonic music into monophonic music and is therefore relatively efficient. Another advantage is that we can produce a large variety of music excerpts by mixing the monophonic track in different ways and different polyphony levels. For example, when we have 5 separated parts of an excerpt of wood quintet, we can generate $2^5 - 1 = 31$ excerpts with number of sources ranging from 1 to 5. The drawback of the multi-track method is its high cost, as it often requires musicians specialized in various instruments, professional recording equipments

---

[3] http://www.sonicvisualiser.org/.
[4] To paraphrase J.P. Bello et. al [1]: "Hand-marking is a painful and time-consuming task that leaves no room for the cross-validation of annotations.".
[5] Some onset detection datasets are built fully in manual method, but the datasets do not provide pitch information [10,12].

and studio, etc. Examples of AMT datasets built in this way are MIREX 2007 [11] and Bach10 [6], etc.

The audio-score alignment method utilizes an audio-score alignment algorithm to align an music excerpt and its corresponding MIDI. Note-level annotation is thereby obtained from the aligned MIDI. One example using this method is the set of syncRWC annotations based on the alignment framework proposed by Ewert et al. [8]. This method is undoubtedly efficient and low-cost, but its scope is available for only those music pieces having well-edited MIDI files.

The autopiano method typically utilizes a MIDI-controlled piano (e.g., Yamaha Disklavier) to generate the music excerpts (played mechanically with the piano) from known note-level annotation (MIDI contents). Since it is easy to generate music excerpts in this way, many AMT studies perform experiments in this way, such as the datasets created by Dessein et al. [5], Poliner and Ellis [13], and the MAPS dataset by Emiya et al. [7]. Similarly, the method is efficient but not general as it is limited to only one instrument.

The most efficient way to generate an AMT dataset is using a synthesizer to generate music excerpts directly from the MIDI files. In addition, the quality of the annotations are *exact* since the onset and pitch of the audio part is just identical in the MIDI part. An example of such kind of dataset for AMT is the TRIOS dataset [2,9].[6] However, synthesized music excerpt is not able to represent lots of real-world audio contents. In most applications of AMT, such as the transcription in a live concert, the synthesized dataset is unsuitable for evaluation. It is worth mentioning that since the track information can be controlled in the multi-track and the synthesized methods, datasets built with these two methods can be used not only for AMT but also melody tracking and source separation.

From the discussion above, we found that current annotation methods cannot balance the tradeoffs among generality, efficiency and cost. Under some cases the quality can even not be controlled since we have to rely on the inefficient manual method to check the quality. Whenever we wish to verify whether a dataset is good, we always fall into "the abyss of manual annotation".

3 Proposed Method

3.1 Overview

Our task of annotating a note is to find the onset time and the note name[7] of the given given note event in the music excerpt and on the score sheet. This process is actually quite similar to the case when a musician plays music in an orchestra: the musician follows the mixture of music played by all other members in the

---

[6] http://c4dm.eecs.qmul.ac.uk/rdr/handle/123456789/27.
[7] In our scenario we just need to find the "note name" rather than the accurate "fundamental frequency". More specifically, we would not discriminate the fundamental frequencies of 440 Hz, 438 Hz or 442 Hz. Instead, we just need to identify "A4". In other words, our pitch detection task allows an error up to a half semitone ($\pm 3\%$).

orchestra, and plays his or her part together with all other members. When the musician is doing this, he or she is actually *annotating* (producing onsets and note names) his or her own part along with time.

To leverage this to note-level annotation work, we need to find an interface which transfers the musician's perception of note event and the behavior of playing into note-level annotation. An electric piano with MIDI output is the interface we want. A musician with both orchestra and piano playing experience would be able to do note-level annotation by "playing with the music excerpt". Providing score sheets, the musician can further follow every parts of the music excerpts fluently and without significant errors (Fig. 1).

1. Find a pianist with band/orchestral experience.
2. Prepare an electric piano with MIDI output. Prepare the score sheets of the music excerpt we want to annotate (If the musician is confident to find all parts in the music then the score sheet in not necessary).
3. Let the musician listen to the music, preview the score sheet, transpose the scores of transposing instruments (e.g., clarinet and horn in woodwind quintet) for playing piano, and practice.
4. Let the musician play the piano with the music following the score sheet. The piano therefore automatically records the information the musician follows in the format of MIDI. When annotating piano solo, the musician just plays the same thing as the audio contents. When annotating multiple-instrument music, the musician imagines he or she as a member in the music ensemble/orchestra and plays his or her own part (not necessary piano) with the full group. This process is then repeated part by part. For example, to annotate a string quartet, the musician plays the part of first violin solely with the audio, then the second violin, viola, and cello. The audio is played four times and the musician follows the music part by part, thereby completing the annotation of each part by recording it in the MIDI file.
5. Finally, the generated MIDI file is manually calibrated and checked if needed.

The proposed method can be used to annotate any real-world music with score sheets. Therefore, it is more general than the autopiano method (which is only for audio contents of piano), the synthesized method (which is only for synthesized audio contents) and the audio-score alignment method (because we can get score sheets for many kinds of music which has no available MIDI). The cost of the method is expected to be lower than the multi-track method. Also, this method can be used to improve the efficiency of the multi-track method.

3.2 Discussion

There are some potential restrictions of this method. First, an electric piano is limited in annotating some special music contents such as unusual playing techniques (e.g., slides in guitar or trombone) or voices with pitch variation smaller than a semitone. Therefore, we only choose the music excerpts without pitch variation smaller than a half tone. At the same time we also need to notice that using piano we can only annotate the pitch up to a level of half tone.

Second, in comparison to the scenario of playing in a real orchestra, our annotation scenario (Fig. 1) still lacks some critical information, such as the verbal communication or the gestures among the performers. Therefore, the musician may not be able to track the beats instantaneously and perfectly for tempo variation, such as tempo rubato, *accelerando* (gradually accelerating), *ritardando* (gradually slow down), and fast note sequences such as *trill* and *arpeggiato*. For the above cases, the annotation is more likely to incorporate the musician's own interpretation. To investigate what the above cases influences the musician's annotation, we consider some music excerpts with tempo variation and fast note sequences in the experiment.

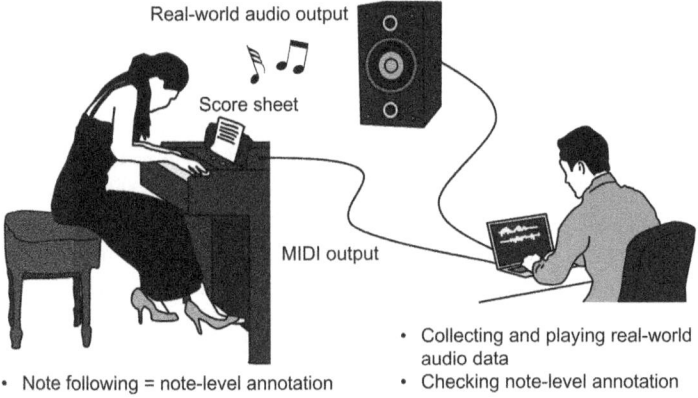

Fig. 1. The basic idea of the proposed method. In our scenario, a professional pianist follows and plays the music on an electric piano with MIDI output, thereby achieving the process of note-level annotation.

3.3 Experiment

The musician working at the creation of the dataset has more than 20 years of piano playing and teaching. The musician is also a professional clarinet player, and had more than 15 years of experience in orchestra. The musician is asked to play 9 musical excerpts including 5 piano solos and 4 woodwind quintets (flute, oboe, clarinet, horn and bassoon). Each excerpt has a length of 20 to 30 seconds. Detailed information is listed in Table 1. The music excerpts are selected arbitrarily from the recordings of professional classical music players. Some of the excerpts are relatively challenging for annotation due to the aforementioned situation: PS2, PS5 and WQ2 have significant tempo variation, PS4 has arpeggiato in the left-hand part, and WQ3 has some fast note groups including trill. PS3,

WQ1 and WQ4 have relatively stable tempo. Details of these music excerpts and the annotations are publicly available online.[8]

Table 1. The music excerpts used for the experiments. PS1 to PS5 are piano solo, and WQ1 to WQ4 are wood quintet.

No.	Composer	Name
PS1	L.V. Beethoven	Moonlight Sonata, Mov. 1, mm. 1–9
PS2	F. Chopin	Nocturne No 9, Op. 32–1, mm. 1–8
PS3	W.A. Mozart	Piano Sonata No. 16, KV545, Mov.1, mm. 1–12
PS4	J. Brahms	Waltz Op.39, No.15, mm. 1–16
PS5	R. Schumann	Scenes from Childhood, Op. 15:7 (Dreaming), mm. 1–8
WQ1	C. Nielsen	Quintet, Op. 43, Mov. 1, mm. 13–20
WQ2	A. Schönberg	Quintet, Op. 26, Mov. 4, mm. 18–27
WQ3	G.M. Cambini	Quintet, No. 1 in B-flat, Mov. 1, mm. 7–17
WQ4	F. Danzi	Quintet, op. 56 No. 1 in B-flat, mm. 1–12

The musician is asked to play with the audio as accurate as she can. Each excerpt is then checked by three amateur piano players with band experiences. The checking method is to play the audio excerpt and the annotated MIDI synchronously, and carefully find mismatch between the two. Mismatches are fixed and the audio and the MIDI are replayed and checked, until all mismatched have been fixed. Each excerpts is checked twice. Although it is hard to record accurate time spent on annotation and checking, in our experiment we found that, starting from previewing the scores to finishing the recordings, it takes about 75 min for the musician to finish a piano solo excerpt and 1.5 h to finish a woodwind quintet excerpt. Checking one music excerpt takes roughly from 15 min to more than 2 h.

3.4 Note-Level Evaluation

To get a brief picture of this new dataset, we use an AMT algorithm, the constrained non-negative matrix factorization (C-NMF) algorithm proposed by Vincent et al. [14][9] for our experiments. By default, it uses the NMF algorithm to learn one template per pitch adaptively from the signal being analyzed on-the-fly, with constraints that enforce harmonicity and spectral smoothness of the learned templates. Because the performance of C-NMF appears to be sensitive

---

[8] https://sites.google.com/site/lisupage/research/new-methodology-of-building-polyphonic-datasets-for-amt.
[9] http://www.irisa.fr/metiss/members/evincent/multipitch_estimation.m.

to the value of β for computing the β-divergence[10] and the value of ϑ for thresholding the activation patterns, we optimize the values of β and ϑ for each music excerpt independently and empirically by running a grid search.

We compare three different cases:

1. **Original**: The basic case, where the AMT algorithm is performed on the real-world music excerpts, and the F-scores are computed by taking the unchecked annotations generated by our musician as the ground truth.
2. **Checked**: The algorithm is also processed on the real-world music excerpts, but the ground truth is taken from the checked annotation.
3. **Oracle**: This is an ideal but unrealistic case, where the music excerpts are not the real-world ones, but the ones synthesized by the MIDI files of the unchecked annotation. The ground truth is also taken from the unchecked annotations. In this case, all annotations are considered perfectly matched to the audio contents, and the audio contents are clean and without noise or any real-world artifact. The synthesized audio contents are obtained from Edirol Hyper Canvas.[11]

These three cases will also be useful in the discussion in the next section.

We evaluate the performance of the algorithm in terms of note-level F-score. Here, a ground truth note is assumed to be correctly transcribed if the algorithm returns a note that is within a half semitone of that note, and the returned onset of the note is within $\pm\delta$ ms of the onset of the ground truth note. Here δ is called the *tolerance*; in MIREX $\delta = 50$ ms [11]. Note-level F-score is defined as $F = 2PR/(P+R)$, where $P = N_{TP}/(N_{TP}+N_{FP})$ and $R = N_{TP}/(N_{TP}+N_{FN})$ (N_{TP}, N_{FP}, N_{FN} are the number of true positives, false positives and false negatives, respectively).

Table 2 shows the results of each music excerpt by setting $\delta = 50$ ms. Each F-score is obtained from optimal β and ϑ. We can see that, when there is only one instrument (piano solo), the Oracle results outperform other cases from about 10 % (PS3) to even 47 % (PS2). For wind quintets the difference is smaller due to higher complexity of the audio signal, but the Oracle case is still better on

Table 2. Note-level evaluation results (F-scores in %).

No.	Original	Checked	Oracle	No.	Original	Checked	Oracle
PS1	41.18	42.62	73.96	WQ1	30.25	28.69	64.29
PS2	40.51	41.35	88.31	WQ2	23.85	22.12	32.73
PS3	76.16	76.16	85.45	WQ3	39.35	39.35	28.24
PS4	30.99	33.82	69.61	WQ4	40.87	38.79	41.47
PS5	32.67	35.33	70.31				

---

[10] The family of β-divergence includes the Euclidean distance ($\beta = 2$), Kullback-Leibler divergence ($\beta \to 1$) and Itakura-Saito divergence ($\beta \to 0$).
[11] http://www.roland.com/products/hq_hyper_canvas/.

average. The good performance of the Oracle reveals how good (and also how unrealistic) it would be if we use synthesized data in AMT evaluation.

Table 2 also indicates that the checked annotations do not necessarily lead to better F-scores. Specifically, the Checked case of the four wind quintets are even worse than the Original case, perhaps due to the systematic bias of human. In general, there is marginal improvement in F-scores after checking.

Two issues emerge. First, the F-score listed here still answer nothing specific about the quality of the dataset. High F-scores can be resulted from multiple factors: perhaps the annotation is accurate, perhaps the audio content is clean, perhaps the algorithm is good, or perhaps the specific excerpt is simple. More specifically, given one music excerpt, the F-score that can be obtained is jointly influenced by the algorithm and the annotation. Before we identify the errors stemming from these two sources we cannot make any conclusion.

Second, from the experiment we also learn that checking is not surely to make the data more reliable. It is likely that we are careless somewhere and we should have spent more time on the manual checking process so as to make them better. But should we keep spending time to improve the annotation manually and stay in the abyss of manual annotation?

These issues will be addressed in the next section.

4 Evaluating the Quality of an AMT Dataset

4.1 The Issue

Studies on AMT mostly concentrate only on the performance of the AMT algorithm rather than the quality of the AMT dataset. This is due to the fact that building a dataset of real-world music with exact annotation is nearly impossible, even when we use the tedious manual method – this is already not what we expect. In this section, we would like to answer the following two questions: (1) How to qualify a dataset in a general sense without manual checking? and (2) for the proposed method in Sect. 3, can we use the musician's original annotation for evaluation of AMT without manual checking?

The purpose of pursuing high quality annotation is not necessarily to make it as perfect as possible. Instead, our main purpose is to make the dataset able to reveal the performance of the AMT algorithm. Although we cannot build a dataset with exact annotation, we can argue that as the labels are closer to the exact ones, we can use smaller tolerance to evaluate the AMT algorithm. The conception of "good annotation" is inexact; it depends on the value of tolerance. The measure the quality of the dataset is a function of the tolerance.

Therefore, we are more interested in the relationship between the labeled onset and the detected onset, rather than the performance of the algorithm. For convenience in discussion, we define the *onset error difference* (denoted by ϵ) as the difference between the detected onset and the labeled onset given a finite tolerance window. Notice that ϵ can only be defined for TPs since FPs and FNs are not "detected" onsets.

4.2 Meanings of the Onset Error Difference

To investigate the meanings of ϵ, firstly we need to clarify where ϵ stems from. In general, ϵ is contributed by two sources: annotation error and algorithmic error, where the former is caused by the musician and the latter is the caused by the engineer who designs the algorithm. The two sources cannot be clearly separated. To simplify the problem, we assume that short-time onset error differences (e.g., $\epsilon < 50$ ms) are mostly caused by the annotation, whereas long-time onset error differences (e.g., $\epsilon > 200$ ms) are caused mostly by the AMT algorithm.[12] This assumption is reasonable since we do not expect a professional musician to make $\epsilon > 200$ ms. If ϵ is small for small tolerance δ then we are confident about the quality of the annotation.

The criteria of the quality of the dataset is described as follows by comparing the average onset error difference of the original case (ϵ_R), the checked case (ϵ_C) and the oracle case (ϵ_O) for all TPs in every music excerpt:

1. In the worst case, assuming ϵ is uniformly distributed in $[0, \delta]$,[13] then, for *usable* annotation, the averaged ϵ_R of a music excerpt should be smaller than $\delta/2$, especially for large tolerance window. Conversely, if $\epsilon_R > \delta/2$ for large δ, then we claim the annotation is surely unusable.
2. In the ideal case, ϵ_R should be as close to ϵ_O as possible. Here we further propose two criterions to test the closeness. The weak criteria states that, by defining $\Delta = \epsilon_R - \epsilon_O$, Δ should be less than 10 ms for $\delta = 50$ ms. The strong criterion states that through a two-tailed t-test, ϵ_R should *not* be significantly larger than ϵ_O for $\delta = 50$ ms. If the weak criterion is satisfied then we claim the annotation is *good*. If the strong criterion is satisfied then we claim the annotation is *high-quality*.[14]

4.3 Results

Figure 2 shows the results of the average onset error differences with various lengths of the tolerance under the three cases for each music excerpt.

For most excerpts, although the average ϵ_R and ϵ_C are slightly higher than $\delta/2$ (the diagonal thin line) for $\delta < 50$ ms, they are constantly smaller than $\delta/2$ for δ larger than 100 ms. As discussed earlier, ϵ_O mainly stems from the AMT algorithm rather than annotation for larger δ. Therefore, we may say that the proposed method is reliable. Table 3 lists the values of ϵ_R for $\delta = 50$ ms.

The other important issue is to see how close ϵ_R (and also ϵ_C) and ϵ_O are. Figure 2 shows that this depends on the music excerpts. For the excerpt with stable tempo (e.g., PS03), ϵ_R, ϵ_C and ϵ_O are generally small; ϵ_R is even smaller

---
[12] Also, we assume that FPs and FNs are also caused by the AMT algorithm.
[13] Obviously, the onset error difference is larger than zero and smaller than the tolerance δ.
[14] These criteria are arbitrary and are depending on how accurate we need for the annotation in real application.

Escaping from the Abyss of Manual Annotation: New Methodology   319

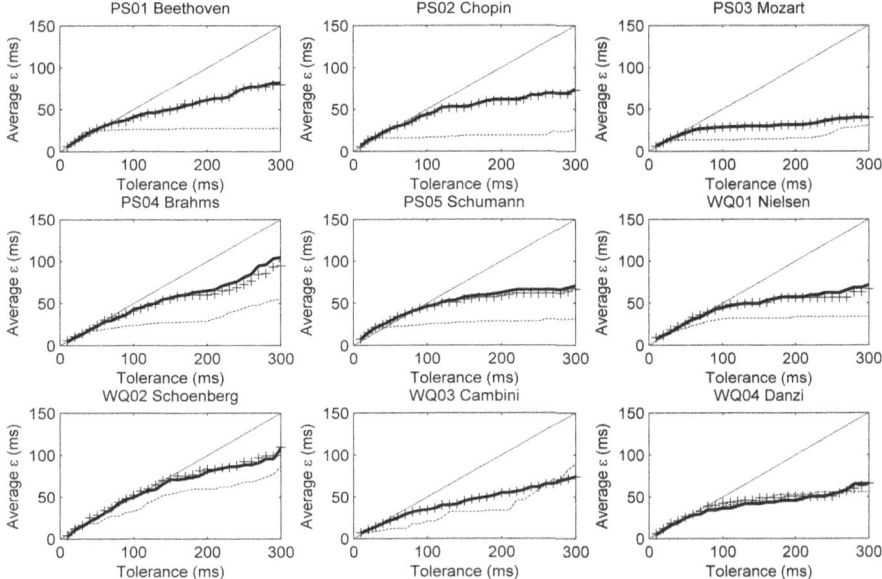

Fig. 2. Results of average ϵ_R, ϵ_C and ϵ_O with varying δ for each music excerpt. Grey thin line: baseline ($\delta/2$). Thick black line: ϵ_R. Thin black line with '+' marks: ϵ_C. Dash-dot line: ϵ_O.

Table 3. ϵ_R, Δ, p-value and the degree-of-freedom (d.f.) The unit of ϵ_R and Δ is in milliseconds.

No.	ϵ_R	Δ	p-value (d.f.)	No.	ϵ_R	Δ	p-value (d.f.)
PS1	27.1	2.12	1.63E-1 (171)	WQ1	26.4	6.39	2.51E-2 (106)
PS2	26.7	10.8	5.15E-8 (148)	WQ2	25.3	6.90	3.09E-2 (57)
PS3	21.8	8.18	4.66E-8 (278)	WQ3	21.8	9.99	5.26E-3 (81)
PS4	23.3	5.48	4.29E-3 (212)	WQ4	24.5	0.69	4.19E-1 (90)
PS5	28.8	6.78	8.72E-4 (137)				

than 50 ms for $\delta = 300$ ms. Not surprisingly, PS04 (arpeggiato in the left-hand part) and WQ02 (unstable tempo) have relatively high ϵ. In addition to the brief view of Fig. 2, Table 3 lists Δ and the p-value at $\delta = 50$ ms of every music excerpt for more detailed and rigorous comparison. Most music excerpts satisfy the weak criterion that $\Delta < 10$ ms excerpt for PS02. This is because the use of tempo rubato, a fermata and the term *stretto* in the sixth measure, and the term *poco ritenuto* in the seventh measure may have caused the musician unable to follow the music perfectly without any personal interpretation.

We also see that only PS1 and WQ4 satisfy the strong criterion, unfortunately. In fact, PS1 and WQ4 are both of slow and relative stable tempo (PS2 and PS5 are also slow but their tempo varies over time). Besides, the p-values of WQ01 and WQ02 are both near to 0.05.

Finally, by comparing ϵ_C and ϵ_R in Fig. 2 we found marginal improvement of checking. This result may stem from two reasons: the first is that the original annotation already "imprints" a position to the checking person and makes he or she believe the original annotation is correct. The second reason is that we do not pay enough labor and time in checking. However, we argue that the first is unavoidable while the second is unwanted. Therefore, to improve the quality, we opt for improving the technical details of our annotation scenario rather than pay more labor and time in calibration.

In summary, our proposed method can produce usable annotation for all music excerpts in the experiment. For music with slight tempo variation and medium speed, our method can produce good annotation. Moreover, for slow music excerpts with stable tempo, our method can produce high-quality annotation.

5 Conclusion

In this paper, we have firstly addressed the issue on how to build and qualify a sizable dataset for AMT without manual work. By clarifying the criteria for a good dataset, we have proposed a general, efficient and low-cost method for note-level annotation, and an efficient way to assess the quality of an AMT dataset. We have demonstrated the experiments, reported technical details and results, and verified its feasibility. For future work, we see two directions for improvement: the first is to test the quality of the offsets in addition to onsets and note names, and the second is to consider some scenarios for improving quality, e.g., collecting annotations from more than one musician. It is hoped that the presented methodology can help open the door of AMT research to more diverse training and test sets to cross the gap between scholarly curiosity to commercial applications.

Acknowledgments. The authors would like to thank Patricia Hsu for performing the experiment of the proposed annotating method. Also the authors thank Che-Yuan Kevin Liang, Yuan-Ping Chen and Pei-I Chen for checking the annotations. This work was supported by a grant from the Ministry of Science and Technology under the contract MOST 102-2221-E-001-004-MY3 and the Academia Sinica Career Development Program. Dr. Li Su was further supported by the postdoctoral fellowship from the Academia Sinica.

References

1. Bello, J.P., Daudet, L., Sandler, M.B.: Automatic Piano transcription using frequency and time-domain information. IEEE Trans. Audio Speech Lang. Process. **14**(6), 2242–2251 (2006)
2. Benetos, E., Cherla, S., Weyde, T.: An efficient shift-invariant model for polyphonic music transcription. In: 6th International Workshop on Machine Learning and Music (2013)

3. Benetos, E., Dixon, S., Giannoulis, D., Kirchhoff, H., Klapuri, A.: Automatic music transcription: challenges and future directions. J. Intell. Inf. Syst. **41**(3), 407–434 (2013)
4. Cheveigné, D.A., Kawahara, H.: YIN, a fundamental frequency estimator for speech and music. J. Acoust. Soc. Am. **111**(4), 1917–1930 (2002)
5. Dessein, A., Cont, A., Lemaitre, G.: Real-time polyphonic music transcription with nonnegative matrix factorization and beta-divergence. In: 11th International Society for Music Information Retrieval Conference, pp. 489–494 (2010)
6. Duan, Z., Pardo, B., Zhang, C.: Multiple fundamental frequency estimation by modeling spectral peaks and non-peak regions. IEEE Trans. Audio Speech Lang. Process. **18**(8), 2121–2133 (2010)
7. Emiya, V., Badeau, R., David, B.: Multipitch estimation of Piano sounds using a new probabilistic spectral smoothness principle. IEEE Trans. Audio Speech Lang. Process. **18**(6), 1643–1654 (2010)
8. Ewert, S., Müller, M., Grosche, P.: High resolution audio synchronization using chroma onset features. In: Proceedings of the IEEE International Conference on Acoustics Speech. and Signal Processing, pp. 1869–1872 (2009)
9. Fritsch, J.: High Quality Musical Audio Source Separation. Master thesis, Queen Mary Centre for Digital Music (2012)
10. Holzapfel, A., Stylianou, Y., Gedik, A., Bozkurt, B.: Three dimensions of pitched instrument onset detection. IEEE Trans. Audio Speech Lang. Process. **18**(6), 1517–1527 (2010)
11. MIREX 2014 Multiple Fundamental Frequency Estimation and Tracking Challenge. http://www.music-ir.org/mirex/wiki/2014:Multiple_Fundamental_Frequency_Estimation_%26_Tracking
12. MIREX 2014 Audio Onset Detection Challenge. http://www.music-ir.org/mirex/wiki/2014:Audio_Onset_Detection
13. Poliner, G., Ellis, D.: A discriminative model for polyphonic piano transcription. EURASIP J. Adv. Sig. Process. **8**, 154–162 (2007)
14. Vincent, E., Bertin, N., Badeau, R.: Adaptive harmonic spectral decomposition for multiple pitch estimation. IEEE Trans. Audio Speech Lang. Process. **18**(3), 528–537 (2010)

The Clustering of Expressive Timing Within a Phrase in Classical Piano Performances by Gaussian Mixture Models

Shengchen Li[1(✉)], Dawn A.A. Black[2], and Mark D. Plumbley[3]

[1] Queen Mary University of London, London, UK
shengchenli@hotmail.com
[2] Radioscape, London, UK
dawn.black@raioscape.co.uk
[3] University of Surrey, Guildford, Surrey GU2 7XH, UK
m.plumbley@surrey.ac.uk

Abstract. In computational musicology research, clustering is a common approach to the analysis of expression. Our research uses mathematical model selection criteria to evaluate the performance of clustered and non-clustered models applied to intra-phrase tempo variations in classical piano performances. By engaging different standardisation methods for the tempo variations and engaging different types of covariance matrices, multiple pieces of performances are used for evaluating the performance of candidate models. The results of tests suggest that the clustered models perform better than the non-clustered models and the original tempo data should be standardised by the mean of tempo within a phrase.

Keywords: Intra-phrase tempo · Model analysis · Classical piano performance · Model selection criteria

1 Introduction

Pianists typically vary the length of beats throughout classical piano performances. Such variations are known as expressive timing. Given the same piece of music, expressive timing is considered to contribute the expressive performances. To analyse the tempo variations in expressive performance, clustering of expressive timing in a unit of music is widely used by different researchers. For example, Rink et al. [22] analyse the beat timing of bars and classify these bars into four clusters using beat length distribution of each bar. They assert that musical structure and performed patterns are closely related. Repp [16] used Principal Component Analysis (PCA) to show different timing strategies and interpretations of the same piece and regarded them as different types of performances. Madsen and Widmer [11] defined common gestures of in expressive performances and made an "alphabet" to compare similarity between performers.

S. Li—Funded by Chinese Scholarship Council.

© Springer International Publishing Switzerland 2016
R. Kronland-Martinet et al. (Eds.): CMMR 2015, LNCS 9617, pp. 322–345, 2016.
DOI: 10.1007/978-3-319-46282-0_21

In additions to different clustering methods, the unit of length in each analysis varies between researches, e.g. half a bar [11], bar [22] and phrases [14]. In this paper, we show that it is useful to cluster tempo variations within a phrase.

Despite there are many works attempting clustering of tempo with a success, there is little evidence available to date to support the notion that it is useful to cluster expressive timing. In this paper, we demonstrate that it is useful to cluster intra-phrase expressive timing in performed music as a phrase can contain enough variations in expressive timing to enable us to perform an accurate analysis. Moreover, analysing expressive timing with the unit of a phrase can provide more samples of expressive timing than analysing with the unit of a performance with the same database of expressive timing information.

To support the notion that clustering expressive timing within a phrase is useful, we compare how non-clustered and clustered models are performed when candidate models are applied to fit the distribution of expressive timing within a phrase. Because of central limit theory [20, p. 204], which says that normal distributions can approximate the distribution of variable with sufficient large number of samples, we choose the Gaussian model — the most widely used non-clustered model [12, p. 39] — as the framework of candidate non-clustered models. Furthermore, the mixture of Gaussian models — the Gaussian Mixture Model (GMM) — is chosen as the framework of the candidate clustered models.

The process of comparing the performance of different models is known as model selection. Common methods [2, p. 36] used for model selection include model selection criterion, goodness-of-fit tests and cross-validation tests. We chose cross-validation as the primary measurement of model performance because cross-validation has been well studied as a basis for model selection [2, p. 36]. The use of model selection criteria is hence selected as our second evaluation of model performance for comparison purposes.

In this paper, we use a private database and a public database for analysis. For easier implementation by machines, the candidate pieces for analysis are preferred to have identical lengths for each phrase. Furthermore, to aid clustering, we want the candidate piece to be repetitive, as we anticipate the expressive timing in repetitive phrases to be similar to each other. Candidate piece for the private database we selected for this paper is the first 84 bars of *Islamey* [1], which contains only three themes repeated. To show that clustering the expressive timing is also helpful for the less repetitive candidate pieces, we also choose Chopin Mazurkas Op.24 No.2 (in short, Op.24/2) and Op.30 No.2 (in short, Op.30/2) to demonstrate the clustering of expressive timing within a phrase.

This paper is organised in the following way: we first introduce our database. Then, we introduce the clustered and non-clustered candidate models. Next, we test the cross-validation likelihood of the candidate models and examine the model selection criteria with *Islamey*. Finally, we investigate whether similar results can be repeated for the two Chopin Mazurkas.

2 Data Collection

In this paper, we use two databases: a private database and a public database. The private database consists of 25 performances[1] of *Islamey*. Unlike Mazurkas, which has a comprehensive but complicated music structure, the music structure of *Islamey* is simpler but the phrase lengths are consistent. The candidate piece in the private database is the first 84 bars of *Islamey* [1]. This section of *Islamey* has a four-bar coda and 40 two-bar phrases. In this database, we exclude the four-bar coda as the length of the coda differs from the other phrases, so in total we have 40 phrases for analysis in each performance.

The initial structure analysis was performed by the author (Shengchen Li) and verified by a professional composer. The analysis shows that there are only three themes for the two-bar phrases in the part of *Islamey* we considered and that two themes repeat ten times and one theme repeats twenty times. We show the results of the analysis of the music structure in Fig. 1. We anticipate the expressive timing in repetitive phrases would be similar in the same rendering, thus the expressive timing in the *Islamey* database may lead itself to clustering. In our *Islamey* database, we have 25 performances from different performers. As there are 40 phrases considered in each piece of performance, in total we have $40 \times 25 = 1000$ annotated phrases in the *Islamey* database.

The public database is the Mazurka dataset annotated by Sapp [18]. The database is used as the raw data in [18,21,22] and was created by the CHARM project.[2] The Chopin Mazurkas have 3-beat bars and the music structure information is included in the database for each candidate piece. Mazurkas are popular pieces amongst classical pianists, and thus for each piece in the Mazurka database, there are multiple performances from the same performer. There are five pieces of Mazurkas in the database: Op.17/4, Op.24/2, Op.30/2, Op.63/3 and Op.68/3. However, as we discussed, we want the phrase lengths in the candidate pieces to be consistent, consequently we only used the data from Op.24/2 and Op.30/2 in this paper.

According to the music structure analysis of *Islamey* and the music structure information provided for Chopin Mazurkas, all candidate pieces exhibit a hierarchical music structure. In defining the term *phrase* to specify the basic unit of music structure, we use the term, *higher-level phrase*, to specify a segment that contains several consecutive phrases.

---

[1] The performers include Abdel Rahmanel Bacha, Adam Aleksander, Alfred Brendel, Andrei Gavrilov, Arto Satukangas, Aya Nagatomi, Barbara Nissman, Boris Berezovsky, Eileen Joyce, Emil Gilels, György Cziffra, Idil Biret, Janö Jandó, Jie Chen, Jong-Gyung Park, Lang Lang, Michael Lewin, Michele Campanella, MikhailKollontay, Alvaro M. Rocha, Olga Kern, Philip Edward Fisher, Roger Wright, Rorianne Scherade and Saito Kazuya.

[2] www.charm.rhul.ac.uk.

The Clustering of Expressive Timing Within a Phrase by GMM 325

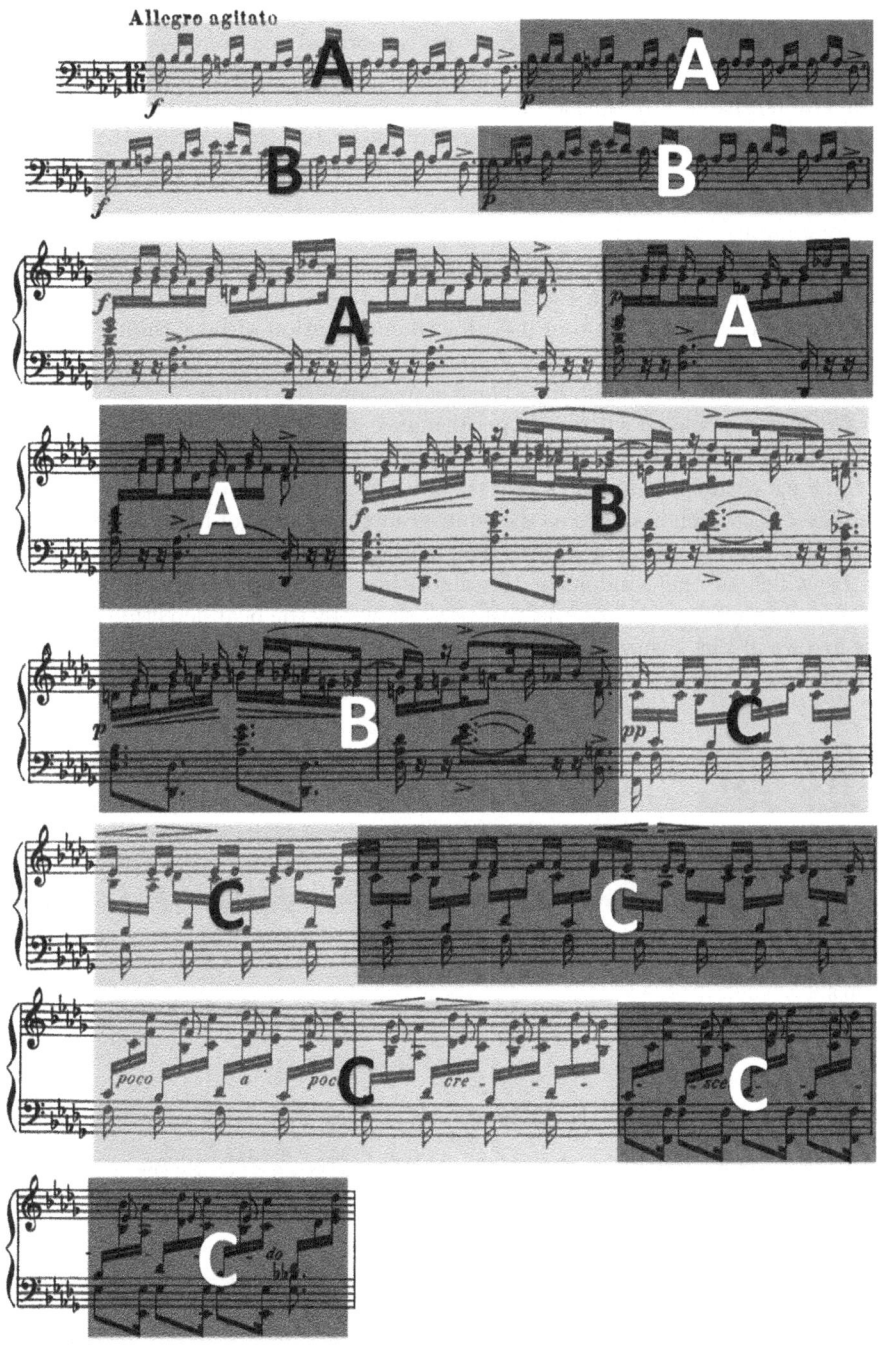

Fig. 1. The music structure analysis of the first twelve phrases in *Islamey*.

3 Data Annotation

Now we are going to introduce how we annotated our expressive timing in *Islamey*. Currently, the accuracy of automatic beat detection is still lower than human annotation in performed music. As a result, the popular method of beat tracking is to tap along with the performed music [10]. However, due to the perception process and possible delays from the devices [6], there are minor errors of beat timing in human annotation.

To minimise the error of annotation, we utilised a two-stage process for recording beat timing. This method makes use of the advantages of both human and machine annotation. In Fig. 2, we show the two-stage method for the annotation of beat timing. The tool used for the annotation of beat timing is Sonic Visualiser[3]. The y-axis shows the amplitude scale of waveforms in the L and R channel of the original audio file. The x-axis shows the timing.

We first tap along with each performance ten times. Then, the timing of each beat is utilised as the averaged timing of the ten different taps, as shown as the lines with spots in Fig. 2. We then use a beat detection function in Sonic Visualiser [5], which is shown as the contour at the bottom of Fig. 2. The contour is not smooth but rather it shows steps as the time span of each step is related to the width of the window in the algorithm. Then, we manually move the annotated beat timings to the nearest peak shown by the beat detection function. The arrows in Fig. 2 show such moves and the lines with stars label the final beat timing.

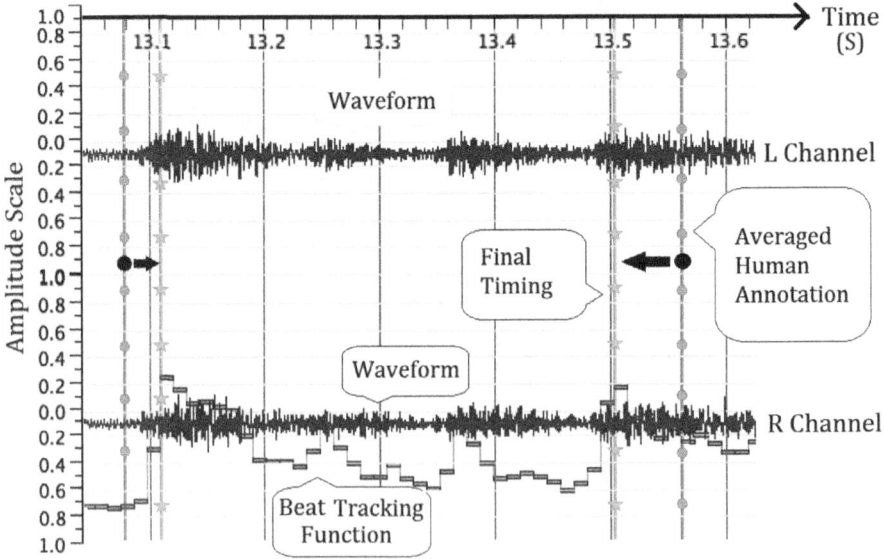

Fig. 2. The annotation of beat timing

---

[3] www.sonicvisualiser.org.

4 Pre-processing of Beat Timing

Although expressive timing is the subject of this paper, the term, *tempo*, is more commonly used by musicians. Tempo is defined as "the rate at which musical notes are played, expressed in score time units per real time unit" [8]. In this paper, we calculate the value of tempo using IBI. Here, we let a series of expressive timings on each beat in a performance be represented as $\{t_0, t_1, t_2, \ldots, t_n\}$, the tempo value can then be calculated as:

$$\tau_i = \frac{1}{t_i - t_{i-1}} = \frac{1}{\text{IBI}}. \tag{1}$$

In common practice, the unit of beats per minute (bpm) for tempo is used, so the conversion between beat timing and tempo can be written as:

$$\tau_i = \frac{60}{t_i - t_{i-1}} = \frac{60}{\text{IBI}}. \tag{2}$$

The exact timing of beats does not reflect the perception of tempo. As suggested by [3], we smoothed the raw tempo by averaging the three neighbouring beats. Here, we suppose $\{\tau_1, \tau_2, \ldots, \tau_n\}$ represents the tempo values of each beat in a performance, the smoothed tempo values are then represented as $\{\bar{\tau}_1, \bar{\tau}_2, \ldots, \bar{\tau}_n\}$, where

$$\bar{\tau}_i = \frac{\tau_{i-1} + \tau_i + \tau_{i+1}}{3}. \tag{3}$$

Although all our tempo values are taken from the same piece (*Islamey*), different performers will play at a different overall tempo throughout different phrases. We regard such differences as speed bias. This prevents the direct comparison of phrases such that the expressive timing of different phrases are clustered according speed bias rather than the changes of beat timing. To remove the possible effects of speed bias, we introduce a standardisation process to remove the speed bias. The standardisation process intends to remove, or minimise the difference of overall tempo throughout different phrases.

In previous works [7,13], a logarithm was used to standardise tempo variations. The standardisation process minimises the difference in global tempo across different performances. We therefore also try a logarithm (LOG) standardisation process. Moreover, in statistics, a standard way to normalise the differences between means in samples is to use standard scores [20, p. 101], which standardise the mean and variance of data to a specific value. We propose this as a candidate standardisation method MVR (Mean-Variance Regulation). Additionally, a previous work suggested that the tempo variations within a phrase are effected by the global tempo [15]. Therefore, we consider two other methods that investigate if the tempo variations within a phrase are proportional to other hyper-parameters (such as the mean and range of tempo variations within a phrase). The first method we propose is Mean Regulation (MR), which forces the mean tempo value in each phrase to be 1. Another method we proposed is Range Regulation (RR), which forces the range of tempo in each phrase to a specific value.

We introduce the implementation of four standardisation methods: RR, MR, MVR and LOG. Here, we give mathematical definitions of these methods. Let $\vec{T} = (\tau_1, \tau_2, \ldots, \tau_n)$ and $\vec{T}_s^{(\mathbf{X})} = (\tau_1^{(\mathbf{X})}, \tau_2^{(\mathbf{X})}, \ldots, \tau_n^{(\mathbf{X})})$ represent original and tempo variation standardised by method $\mathbf{X}$, respectively, so we can give a mathematical representation of each standardisation method.

LOG-Scaling (LOG) Standardisation

This method log scale tempo variations within each phrase. As the logarithm is a non-linear transform, the range of overall tempo throughout different phrases is mapped to a smaller range after scaled by logarithm. The mathematical representation of LOG standardisation is:

$$\boldsymbol{T_s}^{(\text{LOG})} = log_2(\boldsymbol{T}). \tag{4}$$

Mean-Variance-Regulation (MVR) Standardisation

This method is a common method used in statistics. We force the tempo variation in each phrase to have a mean of 0 and a variance of 1. This methods is known as normalisation in signal processing and statistics. It is also called standard score in statistics [20, p. 101]. The mathematical representation of MVR is:

$$\tau_j^{(\text{MVR})} = \frac{\tau_j - mean(\boldsymbol{T})}{std(\boldsymbol{T})} \text{ for } j = 1, 2, \ldots, n. \tag{5}$$

Mean-Regulation (MR) Standardisation

This method forces the mean value of tempo variation within each phrase to 1, which ensures differences of global tempo between phrases are removed. The degree of stretching of tempo variations is set to the mean of each tempo curve. This method assumes that the degree of tempo variation is related to the global tempo and hence can be taken as a simpler version of the standard score that is used in statistics [20, p. 101]. The MR standardisation can be represented as:

$$\tau_j^{(\text{MR})} = \frac{\tau_j}{mean(\boldsymbol{T})}, \text{ for } j = 1, 2, \ldots, n. \tag{6}$$

Range-Regulation (RR) Standardisation

The range of tempo variation within each phrase is regulated to a specific value in this standardisation method. Unlike the other standardisation methods, RR forces the range of variations to an absolute unified value. By unifying the range of tempo variations in each phrase, the differences in standardised global tempo between phrases are minimised. The RR standardisation can be represented as:

$$\tau_j^{(RR)} = \frac{\tau_j - min(\boldsymbol{T})}{max(\boldsymbol{T}) - min(\boldsymbol{T})} \text{ for } j = 1, 2, \ldots, n. \qquad (7)$$

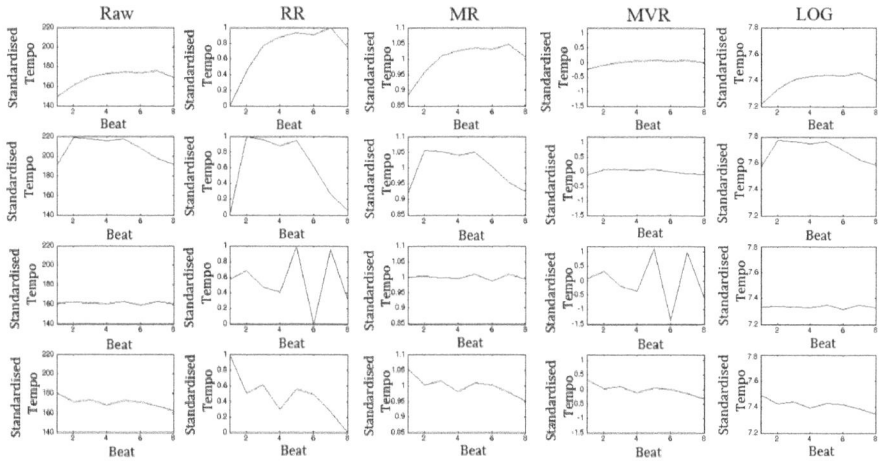

Fig. 3. Comparison of the standardisation methods applied to different types of tempo variations (from top to bottom: accelerating type, symmetric type, constant type and decelerating type). The vertical axes in all the diagrams are the standardised tempo values (by definition of (7), (6) and (5), there are no units for the values of the standardised tempo. We omit the units for the standardised tempo of the LOG method for comparison purpose).

In Fig. 3, we show some examples of standardisation. The standardisation methods employed from left to right are: none (original tempo variations), RR, MR, MVR and LOG. The four sample tempo variations represent four easily identifiable types of tempo variations within a phrase. If the tempo in a phrase keeps speeding up, we identify the tempo variation as 'accelerating'. If the tempo in a phrase speeds up and then slows down, we call the type of tempo variation a 'symmetric type' of tempo variations within a phrase. If the tempo in a phrase has varied across a minor range, we classify the tempo variation as 'constant'. Finally, if the tempo in a phrase slows down, we classify the tempo variations as 'decelerating'.

According to the mathematical definitions of the standardisation methods, we can see that the differences in the global tempo are eliminated by the MR and MVR methods only. The LOG and RR methods only reduce such differences. Moreover, the RR and MVR methods tend to even out the range of tempo variations across phrases. The MR method stretches the tempo variations in each phrase slightly. The LOG method is a non-linear transformation, the shape of tempo variations changes very little, while the variations are slightly magnified. The resulting standardised tempo variations by MVR introduces various results. As shown in the fourth column in Fig. 3, the more variant tempo curves are flattened and the less variant tempo curves are amplified. However, as we are uncertain about which aspect affects the clustering of expressive timing, we also compared the experimental results with different standardisation methods employed in further experiments.

5 Mathematical Models

In our *Islamey* database, there are 25 performances and each performance comprises 40 phrases for analysis (*see Sect.* 2). In each phrase, there are only eight beats. As a result, the data we use for model analysis comprises 1000 samples of an eight-point vector. If we consider each eight-point vector as a point in eight-dimensional space, the candidate mathematical models predict the distribution of expressive timing in an eight-dimensional space. We used the Gaussian distribution as a non-clustered model and the GMM as a clustered model.

5.1 Non-Clustered Models

To build the Gaussian model, we need to train the mean and covariance matrix of the model. In this paper, there are two different conditions for the mean and two different conditions for the covariance matrix. By combining the conditions for mean and the conditions for covariance, we obtained four candidate non-cluster models.

Besides the mean of the Gaussian model in the normal case [12, p. 38], we propose a restricted version of mean as a series of constant values because in piano practice, using metronome to keep a constant tempo is considered a useful way to practise (in Prelude of [9]). As a result, if the mean is restricted, we only use the covariance matrix to fit the tempo variations within a phrase. We use the letter 'C' to represent the models with constant mean in context and the letter 'N' to represent the models that use the normal mean. Consequently, herein, the models with a constant mean are called 'C models' and the models with no restrictions on the mean are called 'N models'.

We propose two versions of the covariance matrix. The normal definition of the covariance matrix in Gaussian models has no restrictions. For comparison, we propose a restriction of the diagonal covariance matrix in other to investigate whether the tempo variation on each beat is related to the tempo variations on other beats. With the diagonal covariance matrix engaged, a multivariate Gaussian model can be written as the product of multiple Gaussian models, which suggests that the variances of each beat are independent of each other. We use the letter 'F' to represent the covariance matrix without restrictions and the letter 'D' to represent the models with a restricted covariance matrix. The restriction of the covariance matrix also has a musical significance as the restricted diagonal covariance matrix assumes the tempo variation on each beat is independent of tempo variations on other beats.

Combining the conditions for the mean and the covariance matrix in the Gaussian model gave us four types of non-clustered candidate models: CD models, CF models, ND models and NF models. Next, we give the mathematical definitions of the candidate models. However, before giving the definitions, we need to define some notations.

We use $\mathcal{N}$ to represent the Gaussian (Normal) distribution, $\vec{T_n}$ to represent the standardised tempo within a phrase, $\vec{\mu}$ to represent the mean of the Gaussian distribution and Σ to represent the covariance matrix. As we propose two types of means and covariance matrices, we use $\vec{\mu_c}$ and $\vec{\mu_n}$ to represent the means of the C and N models, receptively. Now if we let $\vec{T_i} = (\tau_{i1}, \tau_{i2}, ..., \tau_{ik})$ represent the standardised tempo variations in phrase i that has k beats, if there are l phrases in the database, then $\vec{\mu_c} = (\bar{\tau}, \bar{\tau}, ..., \bar{\tau})$, $\vec{\mu_n} = (\bar{\tau}_1, \bar{\tau}_2, ..., \bar{\tau}_k)$, where $\bar{\tau} = \frac{1}{nl} \sum_{i=1}^{k} \sum_{j=1}^{l} \tau_{ij}$ and $\bar{\tau}_i = \frac{1}{l} \sum_{j=1}^{l} \tau_{ij}$. For the covariance matrix, we use Σ^{full} to represent the covariance matrix in the F model and Σ^{diag} to represent the covariance matrix in the D model. If we use σ_{kl}^2 to represent the covariance of beat k and beat l, thus σ_{kk}^2 represents the variance of beat k. We have

$$\Sigma^{diag} = \begin{pmatrix} \sigma_{11}^2 & 0 & \cdots & 0 \\ 0 & \sigma_{22}^2 & \cdots & 0 \\ \vdots & \vdots & \ddots & \vdots \\ 0 & 0 & \cdots & \sigma_{nn}^2 \end{pmatrix} \text{ and } \Sigma^{full} = \begin{pmatrix} \sigma_{11}^2 & \sigma_{12}^2 & \cdots & \sigma_{1n}^2 \\ \sigma_{21}^2 & \sigma_{22}^2 & \cdots & \sigma_{2n}^2 \\ \vdots & \vdots & \ddots & \vdots \\ \sigma_{n1}^2 & \sigma_{n2}^2 & \cdots & \sigma_{nn}^2 \end{pmatrix}.$$

With the annotation introduced, we now define the four candidate models in (8), (9), (10) and (11), e.g.

$$p(\vec{T_n}) = \mathcal{N}(\vec{T_n}|\vec{\mu_c}, \Sigma^{diag}) \tag{8}$$

$$p(\vec{T_n}) = \mathcal{N}(\vec{T_n}|\vec{\mu_c}, \Sigma^{full}) \tag{9}$$

$$p(\boldsymbol{T_n}) = \mathcal{N}(\vec{T_n}|\vec{\mu_m}, \Sigma^{diag}) \tag{10}$$

$$p(\boldsymbol{T_n}) = \mathcal{N}(\vec{T_n}|\vec{\mu_m}, \Sigma^{full}). \tag{11}$$

5.2 Clustered Models

A straightforward way to build a clustered model is to mix several non-clustered models [12, p. 340]. In this research, we combine several Gaussian models for non-clustered models to form the clustered models. The combination of several Gaussian models are called Gaussian Mixture Models (GMM). We recall that the definition of GMM with A Gaussian components for the distribution of multivariate variable $\boldsymbol{T}_i$ is

$$p(\boldsymbol{T}_i) = \sum_{a=1}^{A} \pi_a \mathcal{N}(\tau_i|\mu_a, \Sigma_a). \tag{12}$$

There are three variables in GMM: the means of the Gaussian components μ_a, the covariance matrix of each Gaussian component $\boldsymbol{\Sigma}_a$ and the weight of each Gaussian component π_a. As we would like to observe the centroids of each resulting cluster, we do not restrict the mean of each Gaussian component. Moreover, since we have background knowledge about the weight of each Gaussian component, we cannot set restrictions on the weight. Therefore we propose some restrictions to the covariance matrices in GMMs only.

Similar to the case in non-clustered Gaussian models, we can restrict the covariances to be diagonal or not (namely to use $\boldsymbol{\Sigma}^{diag}$ and $\boldsymbol{\Sigma}^{full}$ in the proposed models, respectively). Again we use letter 'D' to represent the covariance matrices that are restricted to the diagonal and we use letter 'F' to represent the covariance matrices without restrictions. The musical significance of the restrictions of covariance matrices remain the same.

Furthermore, we want to investigate if the variance on each beat or the covariance between beats are independent to the tempo variations within a phrase. According to the definition of GMM [12, p. 341], for each Gaussian component, there is a covariance matrix. We want to test if each covariance matrix is independent to each Gaussian component, thus we propose restricting the covariance matrix of each Gaussian component to be the same for comparison. We use letter 'S' to represent the restriction that the covariance matrices of all the Gaussian components are the same and the letter 'I' to represent the normal GMM without restriction on the covariance matrices. Similar to the case of covariance matrices, we call the models with shared covariance matrices as S models and the models with independent covariance matrices as I models.

Combining the two types of restrictions we proposed for the covariance matrices in GMMs, we obtain four types of GMMs with various Gaussian components. If we use the letter $\mathcal{M}$ to represent the GMMs, the four types of GMMs are $\mathcal{M}_{SD}$, $\mathcal{M}_{SF}$, $\mathcal{M}_{ID}$ and $\mathcal{M}_{IF}$. We use a superscript to represent the number of Gaussian components, and the standardisation method used is included in brackets. For example, $\mathcal{M}_{SD}^{(2)}(RR)$ means a two-component GMM whose covariance matrix is diagonal and shared by Gaussian components, where the input data is standardised by RR. With the similar form of GMM definition in (12), the four candidate types of GMM are defined in (13), (14), (15) and (16) for the SD, SF, ID and IF models, respectively.

- GMM with shared diagonal covariance matrix $\mathcal{M}_{SD}^{A}$:

$$p(\tau_i) = \sum_{a=1}^{A} \pi_a \mathcal{N}(\tau_i | \mu_a, \boldsymbol{\Sigma}_a^{diag}), \text{ where } \Sigma_1^{diag} = \Sigma_2^{diag} = \ldots = \Sigma_n^{diag} = \Sigma^{diag}.$$
(13)

- GMM with shared full covariance matrix $\mathcal{M}_{SF}^{A}$:

$$p(\tau_i) = \sum_{a=1}^{A} \pi_a \mathcal{N}(\tau_i | \mu_a, \boldsymbol{\Sigma}_a^{full}), \text{ where } \Sigma_1^{full} = \Sigma_2^{full} = \ldots = \Sigma_n^{full} = \Sigma^{full}.$$
(14)

- GMM with independent diagonal covariance matrices $\mathcal{M}_{ID}^{A}$:

$$p(\tau_i) = \sum_{a=1}^{A} \pi_a \mathcal{N}(\tau_i|\mu_a, \Sigma_a^{diag}). \tag{15}$$

- GMM with independent full covariance matrix $\mathcal{M}_{IF}^{A}$:

$$p(\tau_i) = \sum_{a=1}^{A} \pi_a \mathcal{N}(\tau_i|\mu_a, \Sigma_a^{full}). \tag{16}$$

The term Σ^{diag} and Σ^{full} are defined in Sect. 5.1.

The resulting GMMs can be used for the clustering of tempo variations. Each Gaussian component models a single cluster. A sample belongs to a cluster that has the maximum posterior probability for the respective Gaussian component [12, p. 342].

5.3 Remaining Model Parameters

To test the proposed models, two other parameters need to be determined. The first is the standardisation method for tempo variations within a phrase. The other is the number of Gaussian components in the proposed models. We choose powers of 2 as possible numbers of Gaussian components (i.e. 2, 4, 8, 16, 32, 64, 128 and 256). We stop at 256 because the next possible number is 512 and the IF model would then have 47,736 parameters to be trained with 1000 samples, which has even more parameters than samples. Moreover, as the training process of GMMs is computationally expensive, training a 512-component GMM requires too much time, considering the computational power we have at our disposal.

The method we used for training a GMM is the Expectation Maximum method [12, p. 350]. Since the initial parameter settings may lead to different resulting models in the EM algorithm, we repeat the training process of EM 1000 times for each type of GMM. In each training process, we start the training process with a different random initial value. Each resulting model is then evaluated by the model likelihood for the training dataset. The final result of each type of GMM is the model that has the highest model likelihood during the training process.

6 Model Evaluation Methods

We use cross-validation and model selection criteria to evaluate the candidate models independently. Cross-validation is known as "a basis of model selection" [2, p. 36]. However, cross-validation is a computationally expensive method, the use of model selection criteria is sometimes used as an alternative method for model selection [2, p. 37]. In this paper, we use both methods for model selection and examine how well they perform.

One of the commonly used variants of cross-validation is five-fold validation, where all data in divided into five parts. Each part is formed by random renditions and acts as the testing set once. All the remaining data forms the training set. Certain criteria are selected to assess how well the resulting models predict the testing set. In this paper, we use the model likelihood to evaluate the candidate models. If we present our dataset as $T = \{\vec{T_1}, \vec{T_2}, \ldots, \vec{T_n}\}$, then the model likelihood is $\mathcal{L} = p(\theta|T_n)$, where θ represents the parameter set of the candidate model $\mathcal{M}$. A better model should have a higher likelihood [12, p. 321]. Here for the convenience of presentation and the accuracy of computation, we show the logarithm scaled likelihood (known as the log-likelihood), unless specified otherwise.

A model selection criterion is a mathematical selector designed for selecting the most appropriate model to fit a set of data. A particular strength of the use of model selection criteria is that all the data can be used for training. However, different model selection criteria have different strengths when used to select models. In this experiment, we use two classical model selection criteria, Akaike's Information Criterion (AIC) and Bayesian Information Criterion (BIC), [4, ch. 2–3] to test the performance of the resulting models. The definition of AIC and BIC can be written as:

$$AIC = 2 * o(\theta) - 2 * \text{likelihood} \qquad (17)$$

$$BIC = log(N) * o(\theta) - 2 * \text{likelihood} \qquad (18)$$

where $o(\theta)$ represents the number of parameters in the candidate model and the dataset has N samples in total. However, the model selection criteria can only evaluate the candidate models that fit the same set of data [2, p. 80]. After the pre-processing, the data of expressive timing are essentially different data as the original performance data are now scaled according to different factors. As a result, the model selection criteria can only be used to compare different settings of GMMs rather than to compare different standardisation methods.

7 Results

7.1 Cross-Validation Tests

In this section, we compare the clustered and non-clustered models in the cross-validation tests. Using the best clustered models according to log-likelihood in cross-validation test, we then discuss which type of covariance matrix and which standardisation methods are the most suitable for clustering expressive timing within a phrase.

First, we compare the clustered and non-clustered models. For clustered methods, we select a GMM with two components to enable a simpler comparison. The results shown in Table 1 are negative cross-validation log-likelihood, thus a more negative value means a better model performance.

Table 1. Cross-validation tests of non-clustered and clustered models with *Islamey* database, where the statistics are negative log-likelihood per sample and a more negative value means better model performance. RR, MR, MVR and LOG are standardisation methods defined in Sect. 4, while $\mathcal{M}$ means GMM as defined in Sect. 5.1. The definitions of CD, ND, CF, NF are in Sect. 5.2.

Neg. Likelihood \ Stand. Model	RR	MR	MVR	LOG
CD models	2.53	-6.44	10.57	-10.02
ND models	1.79	-7.22	9.80	-10.46
$\mathcal{M}^2_{SD}$	1.51	-7.60	9.65	-11.30
$\mathcal{M}^2_{ID}$	-2.69	-8.07	9.40	-11.49
CF models	2.41	-16.24	-0.87	-11.61
NF models	1.57	-16.73	-1.59	-12.14
$\mathcal{M}^2_{SF}$	1.38	-16.85	-1.64	-12.33
$\mathcal{M}^2_{IF}$	-2.81	**-17.29**	-1.90	-12.97

In Table 1, we notice that for the RR, MR and MVR standardisation methods, the constraints for the covariance matrices have major effects on the cross-validation log-likelihood test. In general, F models have better performance than D models. However, under the same type of covariance matrices, the clustered models perform better than the non-clustered models. For LOG standardisation methods, the clustered models outperform non-clustered models regardless of covariance matrix regulation. For comparison between standardisation methods, the MR and LOG methods outperform the other standardisation methods.

Table 2. The best performance of GMMs under different settings of covariance matrices and standardisation methods. The numbers in brackets besides the negative model log-likelihood are the number of Gaussian components in the best performed models under different settings. A more negative value means a better performance for the resulting model.

Neg. Like. \ Stand. Model	RR	MR	MVR	LOG
SD	0.82(32)	-7.90(8)	9.27(16)	-12.36(16)
SF	0.81(16)	-17.03(16)	-1.81(16)	-12.53(16)
ID	-11.20(128)	-8.37(8)	8.94(16)	-12.89(16)
IF	-6.02(8)	**-17.35(2)**	-2.05(4)	-13.05(4)

In Table 2, we show the best performances of different types of GMMs with different standardisation methods engaged. In brackets, we show the number of Gaussian components in the best performed GMM. We confirm the results in Table 1 (that $\mathcal{M}_{IF}$(MR) has the best performance). D models and F models have similar results when the data is LOG standardised. Moreover, in general, with the same conditions for all the other parameters, F models are usually better than D models and I models are usually better than S models. These results suggest that the tempo difference on each beat is dependent on each other and the covariance between beats in a phrase changes with the shape of tempo variations within the phrase.

From Table 2, we also see that for different types of GMMs with different standardisation methods engaged, the number of Gaussian components in the best performed models varies within a certain range. In 8 out of 16 cases, the best performing models have 16 Gaussian components, which suggests there are close to 16 clusters for the tempo variations within a phrase in the performance of *Islamey*. We discuss the number of Gaussian components in the best performed models further in Sect. 9.

7.2 Comparison Between Cross-Validation and the Model Selection Criteria

In this section, we use the model criteria AIC and BIC to evaluate the clustered models. From Table 1, the model likelihood in the cross-validation test has clearly shown that the clustered models outperform the non-clustered models, henceforth we no longer consider non-clustered models. In Table 3, we list three parameters for the evaluation of clustered models: negative cross-validation log-likelihood, AIC and BIC. All the parameters use a more negative number to indicate a better performance of candidate model. The candidate models combine all possible variants of covariance matrices and Gaussian components. The GMMs are denoted as IF, SF, ID, SD in order.

Next, we examine how well the cross-validation test and the model selection criteria are correlated. As we used the negative log-likelihood for measuring the performance of candidate models in the cross-validation test and as the model selection criteria we selected in this paper is based on a negative model likelihood, the agreement between cross-validation and the model selection criteria should show a strong positive correlation. The measure of correlation we selected is Spearman's rho [19]. This measurement of correlation is not dependent on the linear relationship between two variables for a strong correlation.

We use Spearman's rho to correlate the model selection criteria (AIC and BIC) and the negative log-likelihood in the cross-validation test which results in varying the number of Gaussian components in candidate GMMs under the same standardisation methods and the same type of model. For example, if we correlate the first column (X under SD) and the third column (BIC under SD), the resulting correlation shows how well BIC and the cross-validation agree (the value is shown as the sixth column in the fourth row, namely MR-SD under BIC, in Table 4). The correlations between the model selection criteria and cross-validation under all circumstances are illustrated in Table 4.

From Table 4, we notice that the BIC has a strong positive correlation with the negative cross-validation log-likelihood. The numbers shown in bold indicate

Table 3. The negative cross-validation log-likelihood and the model selection criterion with best standardisation MR applied. The N represents the number of Gaussian components in GMMs. The X represents the negative cross-validation log-likelihood.

	SD			SF			ID			IF		
	X	AIC	BIC	X	AIC	BIC	X	AIC	BIC	X	AIC	BIC
N=2	−7.51	−13.51 × 10^3	−5.42 × 10^3	−16.84	−31.96 × 10^3	−23.74 × 10^3	−8.14	−14.40 × 10^3	−6.27 × 10^3	−17.35	−32.78 × 10^3	−24.3 × 10^3
N=4	−7.79	−13.94 × 10^3	−5.76 × 10^3	−16.96	−32.12 × 10^3	−23.81 × 10^3	−8.31	−14.80 × 10^3	−6.51 × 10^3	−17.29	−32.87 × 10^3	−24.03 × 10^3
N=8	−7.90	−14.34 × 10^3	−5.99 × 10^3	−17.00	−32.29 × 10^3	−23.80 × 10^3	−8.37	−15.06 × 10^3	−6.43 × 10^3	−17.08	−32.90 × 10^3	−23.17 × 10^3
N=16	−7.89	−14.72 × 10^3	−6.02 × 10^3	−17.03	−32.44 × 10^3	−23.60 × 10^3	−8.31	−15.26 × 10^3	−5.97 × 10^3	−16.45	−32.91 × 10^3	−21.42 × 10^3
N=32	−7.86	−15.05 × 10^3	−5.64 × 10^3	−16.95	−32.52 × 10^3	−22.97 × 10^3	−8.02	−15.44 × 10^3	−4.81 × 10^3	−14.20	−33.12 × 10^3	−18.09 × 10^3
N=64	−7.51	−15.16 × 10^3	−4.33 × 10^3	−16.59	−32.52 × 10^3	−21.55 × 10^3	−7.46	−15.58 × 10^3	−2.28 × 10^3	−8.54	−34.37 × 10^3	−12.28 × 10^3
N=128	−6.64	−15.07 × 10^3	−1.41 × 10^3	−15.49	−32.14 × 10^3	−18.35 × 10^3	−5.78	−15.82 × 10^3	2.81 × 10^3	25.85	−42.61 × 10^3	−6.38 × 10^3
N=256	−4.19	−14.51 × 10^3	4.80 × 10^3	−13.12	−31.15 × 10^3	−11.70 × 10^3	−1.28	−17.73 × 10^3	11.59 × 10^3	1.06 × 10^3	−63.85 × 10^3	0.64 × 10^3

Table 4. The correlation between the model selection criteria and the negative cross-validation likelihood. The bold numbers mean the correlation between the model selection criteria and the negative cross-validation log-likelihood is strong enough to pass a significance test.

	AIC				BIC			
	SD	SF	ID	IF	SD	SF	ID	IF
RR	0.33	0.05	**0.83**	−0.74	**0.95**	**0.98**	**0.83**	**0.81**
MR	−0.26	0.40	−0.83	−1.00	**0.95**	**0.78**	**0.95**	**1.00**
MVR	−0.31	0.12	−0.60	−0.74	**0.90**	**0.83**	**0.83**	**0.76**
LOG	0.40	0.19	−0.57	−0.98	**0.95**	**0.81**	**0.98**	**0.98**

that the negative cross-validation log-likelihood test has a significant positive correlation with the BIC according to significance test in statistics [20, p. 246].

In Tables 3 and 4, we can see that the best model in the cross-validation test $\mathcal{M}_{\text{IF}}(\text{MR})$ has the best performance. Moreover, BIC can best predict the model performance when a different number of Gaussian components is employed. The results suggest that the model $\mathcal{M}_{\text{IF}}(\text{MR})$ is the best model for clustering expressive timing in a phrase among the candidate models.

8 Application to Chopin Mazurkas

As *Islamey* is annotated by one of the author and the periodicity of melody in *Islamey* may influence the clustering process, we also apply the proposed experiment to Chopin Mazurkas to investigate whether the conclusion with *Islamey* is still valid. The Mazurka database has been used before [18,22] and has already been annotated by other researchers, so we can confirm the annotation process may not limit the generality of the proposed experiment.

In [17], Sapp annotated five pieces of Chopin Mazurkas with various numbers of renditions. However, the proposed experiment requires that the lengths of phrases in a candidate piece be identical throughout the piece. Amongst the Mazurkas annotated by Sapp, two pieces of Mazurkas — Op.24/2 and Op.30/2 — have identical lengths of phrases throughout the piece. Consequently, we choose these two Mazurkas as the new candidate pieces for analysis. In Mazurka Op.24/2, there are 30 phrases that are 12-beats long and there are 64 pieces of performances in the database. As a result, we have $30 \times 64 = 1920$ samples in this model analysis. For Mazurka Op.30/2, there are only 8 24-beat phrases so we have only $8 \times 34 = 272$ samples if we take the phrases with full length in the experiment. As a result, in this experiment we use the phrases with half of the full length. In other words, we have 544 samples of 12-beat phrases for Mazurka Op.30/2 in this experiment.

8.1 Cross-Validation Tests

First, we compare the clustered models and non-clustered models in Tables 6 and 5, where we present the performance of the candidate models. Similar to the case of *Islamey* in Table 1, we notice that if a standardisation method is engaged and the same restriction is applied to the covariance matrix, the clustered models outperform the non-clustered models for both pieces of Mazurkas.

Next, we compare the best performing model under the proposed clustered models and the proposed standardisation methods. We list the best performance of models under different settings of covariance matrices and standardisation methods in Tables 7 and 8. From the results, we can see that the best performance

Table 5. Cross-validation tests of non-clustered and clustered models with candidate piece Chopin Mazurkas Op.24/2, where the statistics are negative log-likelihood per sample and a more negative value means better model performance. RR, MR, MVR and LOG are standardisation methods defined in Sect. 4, while $\mathcal{M}$ means GMM as defined in Sect. 5.1. The definitions of CD, ND, CF, NF are in Sect. 5.2.

Neg. Likelihood \ Stand. Model	RR	MR	MVR	LOG
CD models	3.89	-3.36	16.87	-9.85
ND models	1.96	-4.61	14.89	-10.41
$\mathcal{M}_{SD}^2$	1.32	-5.61	14.16	-11.87
$\mathcal{M}_{ID}^2$	-1.65	-5.68	13.99	-12.38
CF models	3.09	-14.90	4.90	-13.12
NF models	0.77	-16.05	2.58	-14.11
$\mathcal{M}_{SF}^2$	0.62	-16.16	2.43	-14.38
$\mathcal{M}_{IF}^2$	-2.58	**-17.72**	1.82	-15.96

Table 6. Cross-validation tests of non-clustered and clustered models with candidate piece Chopin Mazurkas Op.30/2, where the statistics are negative log-likelihood per sample and a more negative value means better model performance. RR, MR, MVR and LOG are standardisation methods defined in Sect. 4, while $\mathcal{M}$ means GMM as defined in Sect. 5.1. The definitions of CD, ND, CF, NF are in Sect. 5.2.

Neg. Likelihood \ Stand. Model	RR	MR	MVR	LOG
CD models	3.15	-3.80	15.48	-9.09
ND models	2.50	-4.48	14.67	-9.55
$\mathcal{M}_{SD}^2$	-1.44	-8.06	10.51	-11.60
$\mathcal{M}_{ID}^2$	-2.77	-8.31	10.31	-11.68
CF models	-6.56	-24.29	-5.02	-21.55
NF models	-8.04	-25.08	-5.93	-22.70
$\mathcal{M}_{SF}^2$	-8.57	-25.20	-6.33	-22.94
$\mathcal{M}_{IF}^2$	-12.77	**-25.82**	-7.04	-23.82

Table 7. The best performance of different types of GMMs with different standardisation methods engaged for candidate piece Chopin Mazurka Op.24/2. The numbers in brackets are the number of Gaussian components. A more negative value means a better model performance.

Op.24/2	RR	MR	MVR	LOG
SD	−4.33(128)	−15.34(64)	8.09(16)	−20.32(64)
SF	−6.02(32)	−27.52(32)	−3.86(64)	−25.68(64)
ID	−16.16(128)	−16.04(32)	7.17(64)	−20.98(64)
IF	−14.44(8)	−28.85(8)	−5.29(4)	−26.83(4)

of the proposed models are $\mathcal{M}_{\text{IF}}(\text{MR})$ for both Mazurkas. For the candidate pieces, F models outperform D models and I models outperform S models. Both conclusions agreed with the conclusions we drew with the *Islamey* database.

Table 8. The best performance of different types of GMMs with different standardisation methods engaged for candidate piece Chopin Mazurka Op.30/2. The numbers in brackets are the number of Gaussian components. A more negative value means a better model performance.

Op.30/2	RR	MR	MVR	LOG
SD	−6.16(64)	−12.29(32)	5.51(64)	−17.43(32)
SF	−9.60(8)	−25.71(16)	−7.50(16)	−23.78(8)
ID	−14.22(16)	−13.21(16)	4.60(16)	−17.50(32)
IF	−16.47(4)	−25.99(4)	−8.09(4)	−24.69(4)

On the other hand, we noticed that the number of Gaussian components differs from piece to piece in the best performed models when the type of covariance matrix and the standardisation methods are the same. For Mazurka Op.24/2 (Table 7), 6 out of 16 best performing models have 64 components. However, for Mazurka Op.30/2 (Table 8), only 2 out of 16 best performed models have 64 Gaussian components. We show the comparison of the number of Gaussian components in the best performed models for each candidate piece in Sect. 9 in order to investigate the number of Gaussian components in the best performing models.

8.2 Comparison Between the Model Selection Criteria and Cross-Validation

Next, we investigate if the model selection criteria can predict the results of the cross-validation tests. In Tables 9 and 10, we show the correlation between the model selection criteria and the negative cross-validation likelihood for both

Table 9. The correlation between the model selection criteria and the negative cross-validation likelihood with candidate piece Chopin Mazurka Op.24/2. Positive correlations are expected.

	AIC				BIC			
	SD	SF	ID	IF	SD	SF	ID	IF
RR	**0.83**	0.19	**0.86**	−0.69	**0.76**	**0.78**	**0.90**	**0.83**
MR	**0.93**	0.10	0.57	−0.74	**0.67**	**0.71**	**0.67**	**0.90**
MVR	**0.83**	0.19	0.57	−0.67	0.62	0.55	**0.67**	0.21
LOG	0.86	0.33	0.57	−0.83	**0.86**	**0.62**	**0.76**	**0.97**

Table 10. The correlation between the model selection criteria and the negative cross-validation likelihood with candidate piece Chopin Mazurka Op.30/2. Positive correlations are expected.

	AIC				BIC			
	SD	SF	ID	IF	SD	SF	ID	IF
RR	−0.17	−0.62	−0.40	−0.95	**1.00**	**0.95**	0.17	0.23
MR	0.02	−0.45	−0.31	−0.90	**0.90**	**0.93**	0.24	**0.64**
MVR	−0.10	−0.67	−0.43	−0.90	**0.98**	**0.98**	0.31	0.12
LOG	−0.10	−0.69	−0.33	−0.86	**1.00**	**0.98**	0.28	0.60

Mazurkas. We find that, in some cases, BIC fails to show a significant correlation with the cross-validation likelihood. However, the model we suggested in the *Islamey* $\mathcal{M}_{\mathrm{IF}}(\mathrm{MR})$ dataset shows a significant positive correlation in both Mazurkas. Thus, we conclude that $\mathcal{M}_{\mathrm{IF}}(\mathrm{MR})$ (Gaussian Mixture Model with Independent Full Matrix and with Mean Regulation Standardisation method applied) is the best model among the candidate models as this model have a high log-likelihood in cross-validation tests and the BIC can be potentially used to evaluate the candidate models under the engagement of standardisation methods and the engagement of covariance matrices of $\mathcal{M}_{\mathrm{IF}}(\mathrm{MR})$.

9 Discussion

In this paper, we investigate how mathematical models predict the distributions of expressive timing within a phrase. The results support the following statistical conclusions:

1. Clustered models outperform non-clustered models for predicting tempo variations distribution on the data we tested.
2. The best model in the cross-validation tests is $\mathcal{M}_{\mathrm{IF}}(MR)$ on the data we tested. More generally, the model with full covariance matrices is better than the model with diagonal covariance matrices. The model with independent

covariance matrices for each Gaussian component is better than the model that has a shared covariance matrix for each Gaussian components.
3. The number of Gaussian components in the best performing models varies according to the different pieces.
4. Compared with AIC, BIC predict the log-likelihood in cross-validation tests better.

In Tables 1, 5 and 6, we can see that if the standardisation method and the covariance matrix are engaged, the clustered models outperform the non-clustered models. From Tables 1, 2, 5, 6, 9 and 10, we can find a general conclusion that for the data we tested, F models outperform D models. Moreover, on average, the order of standardisation methods is MR, LOG, RR and MVR for the performance of the best performing models. For clustered models, I models outperform S models. For non-clustered models, N models outperform C models. Summarising the above conclusions, according to the data we tested, the model we suggest for modelling expressive timing within a phrase is the Gaussian Mixture Model with Independent Full covariance matrices and the engaged standardisation method is Mean Regulation ($\mathcal{M}_{IF}(MR)$).

Next we discuss how many Gaussian components are contained in the best performing models. In fact, if we compare Tables 2, 7 and 8, the number of Gaussian components in the best performing models differ from piece to piece. In Table 11, we count the number of times that each number of Gaussian components appeared in the best performing GMMs in the cross-validation likelihood tests with each proposed models and standardisation method engaged. From the table we can see that the number of Gaussian components in the best performing models differ from piece to piece. The reason for such difference needs further investigation.

Table 11. The count of the number of times that each number of Gaussian components appeared in the best performing GMMs in the cross-validation likelihood test with each proposed model and standardisation method engaged.

	Islamey	Op.24/2	Op.30/2
N=2	1	0	0
N=4	2	2	4
N=8	3	2	2
N=16	8	1	5
N=32	1	3	3
N=64	0	6	2
N=128	1	2	0
N=256	0	0	0

To compare the model selection criteria and the negative cross-validation log-likelihood, we use Spearman's rho [19] to measure the correlation between model selection criteria and the negative cross-validation log-likelihood. Spearman's rho does not demand a linear relationship to have a higher correlation. From the correlation coefficient and the significance tests, the BIC and negative log-likelihood in cross-validation test are more correlated according to Spearmean's rho. By this result, we can assert that the BIC can better predict the model performance in terms of negative cross-validation log-likelihood test than the AIC.

10 Conclusions

In this paper, we used a model selection test to show that the tempo variations within a phrase can be clustered. We first introduced the pre-processing of the performance data. The smoothing was introduced for approximating human perception and the standardisation was used for removing the speed differences between phrases.

We proposed a few different mathematical models including clustered and non-clustered models. The frameworks of all the models were based on the Gaussian model, which is a widely used model for multivariate distribution. We regulated the covariance matrix and the mean of the non-clustered candidate models. For the clustered candidate models, we proposed a mixture of non-clustered models, GMM, and constricted the covariance matrices in GMM by two ways. We use the Expectation Maximum (EM) algorithm to train the proposed models with the candidate pieces.

To compare the performances of the candidate models, we used cross-validation tests to compare the performances of the proposed models. The database was divided into two datasets: the training and the testing dataset. The proposed models were trained by the training dataset with EM. Then the candidate models were evaluated by testing how likely the testing dataset was observed by the resulting models. This procedure was defined as the cross-validation test. We then evaluated the candidate models by showing how well the model selection criteria predicts the performance in cross-validation tests of the candidate models.

Next, we repeated all the proposed experiments for the exemplar piece *Islamey* to two Chopin Mazurkas. The Chopin Mazurkas have a more complicated music structure and possibly more varieties in expressive timing. The validation of the proposed algorithm with the Chopin Mazurkas could be possibly considered as evidence of potential generalisation of the proposed algorithm.

From the results of the cross-validation likelihood tests, the model suggested for clustering expressive timing is the GMM with independent full covariance matrices and mean regulation standardisation ($\mathcal{M}_{\text{IF}}(\text{MR})$). This result was confirmed by two pieces of Chopin Mazurkas and our private *Islamey* database. It would be interesting to test if this conclusion can be generalised to other databases.

References

1. Balakirev, M.: Islamey, Op. 18. D. Rahter, Hamburg (1902). http://imslp.org/wiki/Islamey,_Op.18_(Balakirev,_Mily)
2. Burnham, K.P., Anderson, D.R.: Model Selection and Multimodel Inference - A Practical Information-Theoretic Approach, 2nd edn. Springer, Berlin (2002)
3. Cambouropoulos, E., Dixon, S., Goebl, W., Widmer, G.: Human preferences for tempo smoothness. In: Proceedings of the VII International Symposium on Systematic and Comparative Musicology and III International Conference on Cognitive Musicology, pp. 18–26 (2001)
4. Claeskens, G., Hjort, N.L.: Model Selection and Model Averaging. Cambridge University Press, Cambridge (2008)
5. Davies, M.E.P., Plumbley, M.D.: Context-dependent beat tracking of musical audio. IEEE Trans. Audio Speech Lang. Process. **15**(3), 1009–1020 (2007)
6. Degara, N., Rua, E.A., Pena, A., Torres-Guijarro, S., Davies, M.E.P., Plumbley, M.D.: Reliability-informed beat tracking of musical signals. IEEE Trans. Audio Speech Lang. Process. **20**(1), 290–301 (2011)
7. Desain, P., Honing, H.: Does expressive timing in music performance scale proportionally with tempo? Psychol. Res. **56**, 285–292 (1994)
8. Dixon, S.: Automatic extraction of tempo and beat from expressive performances. J. New Music Res. **30**(1), 39–58 (2001)
9. Franz, F.: Metronome Techniques: Being A Very Brief Account of the History and Use of the Metronome with Many Practical Applications for the Musician. Printing-Office of The Yale University Press, New Haven (1947)
10. Grosche, P., Muller, M., Sapp, C.S.: What makes beat tracking difficult? A case study on Chopin Mazurkas. In: Proceedings of the International Conference on Music Information Retrieval (ISMIR), pp. 649–654 (2010)
11. Madsen, S.T., Widmer, G.: Exploring pianist performance styles with evolutionary string matching. Int. J. Artif. Intell. Tools **15**(4), 495–514 (2006)
12. Murphy, K.P.: Machine Learning: A Probabilistic Perspective. The MIT Press, Cambridge (2012)
13. Repp, B.H.: Diversity and commonality in music performance: an analysis of timing microstructure in Schumann's "Träumerei". J. Acoust. Soc. Am. **92**, 2546–2568 (1993)
14. Repp, B.H.: Expressive timing in Schumann's Träumerei: an analysis of performances by graduate student pianists. J. Acoust. Soc. Am. **5**, 2413–2427 (1995)
15. Repp, B.H.: Quantitative effects of global tempo on expressive timing in music performance: some percepeptual evidence. Music Percept. Interdisc. J. **13**, 39–57 (1995)
16. Repp, B.H.: A microcosm of musical expression. I. Quantitave analysis of pianists' timing in the initial measures of Chopin's Etude in E major. The. J. Acoust. Soc. Am. **104**, 1085–1100 (1998)
17. Sapp, C.: Comparative analysis of multiple musical performances. In: Proceedings of the International Conference on Music Information Retrieval (ISMIR), pp. 497–500 (2007)
18. Sapp, C.: Hybrid numeric/rank similarity metrics for musical performance analysis. In: Proceedings of the International Conference on Music Information Retrieval (ISMIR), pp. 501–506 (2008)
19. Spearman, C.: The proof and measurement of association between two things. Am. J. Psychol. **15**(1), 72–101 (1904)

20. Spiegel, M.R., Stephens, L.J.: Schuaum's Outlines: Statistics. McGraw-Hill Education, New York (2011)
21. Spiro, N., Gold, N., Rink, J.: Plus ça change: Analyzing performances of Chopin's Mazurka Op. 24 No. 2. In: Proceedings of International Conference on Music Perception and Cognition (ICMPC), pp. 418–427 (2008)
22. Spiro, N., Gold, N., Rink, J.: The form of performance: analyzing pattern distribution in select recordings of Chopin's Mazurka op. 24 no. 2. Musicae Sci. **14**(2), 23–55 (2010)

Modeling Affective Responses to Music Using Audio Signal Analysis and Physiology

Konstantinos Trochidis[✉] and Simon Lui

Department of Information Systems Technology and Design, Singapore
University of Technology and Design, 8 Somapah Road, Building 1, Level 5,
Singapore 487372, Singapore
{Konstantinos,Simon_Lui}@sutd.edu.sg

Abstract. A key issue in designing personalized music affective applications is to find effective ways to direct emotion by music selection with appropriate combination of acoustic features. The aim of this study is to understand the dynamic relationships between acoustic features, physiology and affective states. To model these relationships we used a multivariate approach including continuous measures of emotions from behavioral, subjective and physiological responses. Classical music excerpts taken from opera overtures were used as stimuli to induce emotional variations across time between neutral and intense emotional states. Continuous ratings of arousal and valence along with cardiovascular, respiratory, skin conductance and facial expressive activity were recorded simultaneously. Results show that parts of the music with higher loudness and pulse clarity induced higher ratings of arousal, sympathetic activation and increased cardiorespiratory synchronization. In contrast, pleasant and calming parts with major mode and prominent key strength induced higher ratings of valence, parasympathetic activation and increased facial activity.

Keywords: Musical emotion · Emotion recognition · Acoustic features · Physiological responses · Affective computing

1 Introduction

Music by its nature has the ability to communicate strong emotions in everyday experiences. Emotions expressed or induced by music is one of the central aspects in music listening and is the main reason why music appeals to people. Given the important role of emotion in music listening, there has been intensive research on the field during the last two decades, which contributed to important developments. A large number of research approaches have been used to gain a better understanding of features and processes related to musical emotions.

Musical characteristics, such as tempo, mode, loudness, pitch, timbre, and so on, are inherent properties of the musical structure, and their influence on emotional responses to music has been shown [1]. Many studies explored the relationship between acoustic features and musical emotions [2–4]. Most of them try to extract low- and high-level acoustic features representing various music descriptors (timbre, dynamics, pitch, melody, harmony) and correlate them with emotional ratings from participants. On the other hand, there is a large amount of studies establishing the relationship between physiological changes and musical emotions during music listening [5]. Research on physiological effects of music includes mainly changes in heart rate, respiration, skin conductance and muscle tension [6–9]. Most of the existing studies consider acoustic features and physiological responses separately. Few studies combined both modalities to improve emotion recognition, which indicated that merging acoustic and physiological modalities substantially improves prediction of participants' ratings of felt emotion [10, 11]. The relationship, however, between music features, physiological responses and affective states remains unexplored. Thus, there are no reliable criteria to select audio features based on psychological or physiological research. Furthermore, audio features are usually extracted using short music segments neglecting the temporal dynamics. Music, however, by its very nature changes over time and consequently emotions communicated by music change also over time. The dynamic aspects of music emotions, however, remain poorly understood. The investigation of emotional responses as a dynamic process and their relation to audio features over time requires a methodological approach that can reflect the dynamics of unfolding emotional events. In the present work, we investigate the relationship between acoustic features and musical emotions incorporating physiological measures. A multivariate approach is used including continuous second-by-second measures of emotions from behavioral, subjective and physiological responses from listeners. We focused on 5 musical characteristics: loudness, brightness, pulse clarity, mode and key clarity which are known to explain a large amount of musical variability. Furthermore, we incorporated physiology to effectively validate the responses found by subjective feeling reports from listeners. As a result, we expect to gain better insight into the relationship between audio features and music emotion and be able to effectively use music features to direct affective states.

Aims of the Study. The primary aim of this study is the development of an accurate and robust model for mapping the relationships between physiology and affective states. A multivariate approach is used including continuous measures of emotions from behavioral, subjective and physiological responses from listeners. To this end, instead of using only monovariate physiological measures, including skin conductivity, heart or respiration rate, bivariate measures related to cardio-respiratory synchronization were also employed. These measures reflect the coherence within the peripheral physiological system during emotion elicitation and therefore, can be used for more accurate emotion detection.

A second aim of this paper is to build a model that links musical features, physiology and affective states in order to systematically investigate their underlying relationships. In this context, we focused on 5 musical characteristics: loudness, brightness, pulse clarity, mode and key clarity, which are known to explain a large amount of musical variability [12]. Furthermore, we incorporated physiological and behavioral responses to effectively validate the responses found by subjective feeling reports from listeners.

Combining audio and physiology modalities improves music selection based on music retrieval and evaluation of the system by using affective detection and physiology. This approach can be incorporated in the development of robust affective music applications to enhance personalization and direct users current affective state.

2 Methods

Participants. Twenty-eight non-musicians students from SUTD were recruited as participants (14 males and 14 females). The mean age was 25 years old. All participants reported no hearing problems and that they liked listening to Classical music. In accordance with the requirements of Singapore University of Technology and Design Research Ethics Board, which certified this study, written informed consent was obtained from each participant prior to the experiment. No symptoms of cardiovascular, mental, or neurological disorders were reported by any of the 28 participants.

Stimuli and Apparatus. Two musical excerpts with duration of 10 min each taken from Classical music overtures were selected as stimuli (William Tell by Rossini and Prince Igor by Borodin). The excerpts were selected to elicit a variety of emotional reactions along both the two-dimensional emotion space formed by the dimensions of arousal and valence. The stimuli were presented to the participants in a randomized order. The experimental session was programmed and run using an emotion tracking application programmed on a Macintosh workstation.

By moving the index finger of their dominant hand using a track-pad to move to a two dimensional emotion space from left to right, participants were instructed to indicate how positive the effect of the music was (left = negative and unpleasant; right = positive and pleasant).

By moving their finger from top to bottom, participants indicated the degree of their emotional arousal while listening to the music (top = excited; bottom = calm). Participants were instructed to rate their current emotional state on both dimensions simultaneously, with the finger position at each moment reflecting their emotional response to the piece as they were listening. They were also asked not to rate emotions recognized, but only their own emotional response.

The stimuli were presented over Sony BM6A headphones. Audio signals were sampled at 44.1 kHz with 16-bit resolution. We used two ProComp SA9309 M sensors (Thought Technology, Inc., Montreal, QC) to measure skin conductance (galvanic skin response, or GSR), which were attached to the index and ring fingertips of the non-dominant hand. ECG signals were recorded with three electrodes attached to the participant's chest in a triangular configuration (three leads situated on the upper left and upper right chest, and on the left lower ribcage). Recording of respiratory signals was achieved using a ProComp SA9311 M respiration stretch sensor (Thought Technology, Inc., Montreal, QC) strapped around the chest just below the pectoral muscles with Velcro. Expressive muscle activations were measured using one electromyography (EMG) electrode (MyoScan-Pro surface EMG sensors) placed on the zygomaticus major (associated with smiling) muscles. EMG electrode was placed on the side of the face contralateral to the dominant hand (with positive and negative electrodes aligned with the respective muscles and the reference electrodes placed on the cheek bone). The signals were collected using the ProComp Infiniti Unit. Signal amplitudes were registered in 16-bit integer format on a hard drive at a rate of 256 Hz with time stamps.

Procedure. To begin, the experimenter first attached the sensors to the participant's skin. Once comfortably installed, they were instructed to sit back and relax and to stay still and awake during the experiment. Once the experimenter left the room, each participant was introduced to the experiment by reading instructions of the experimental procedure in the screen from the emotion tracking application run on the computer. Subsequently, the music was presented to participants randomized in the following manner. Before and between the music pieces, a two-minute physiological baseline activity without any stimulation was recorded. Before beginning the experiment, a practice trial of one minute using a musical excerpt by Bela Bartok was presented to familiarize the participants with the experimental task and the continuous rating procedure.

3 Audio Feature Extraction

A theoretical selection of musical features was made based on musical characteristics such as dynamics, timbre, harmony, rhythm using the MIR Toolbox for MATLAB [13]. A total of 5 descriptors related to these features were thus extracted from the musical excerpts.

Dynamics. We computed the RMS amplitude to examine whether the energy is evenly distributed throughout the signals, or to determine whether certain time points are more contrasted than others.

Timbre. Brightness was computed as the relative amount of spectral energy above a certain cut-off frequency (1500 Hz).

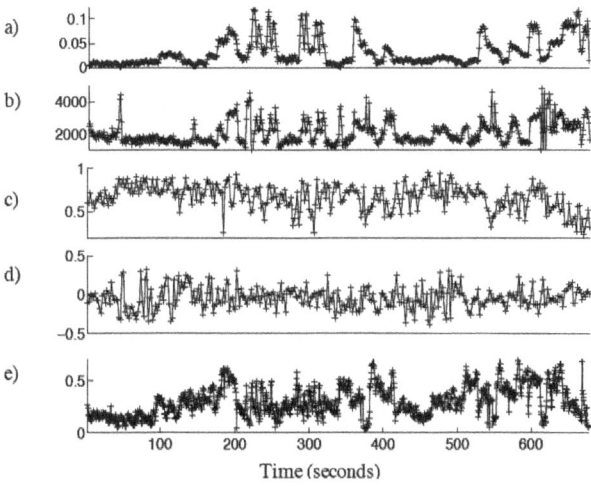

Fig. 1. Time-series of the 5 audio features extracted (a) Loudness (b) Brightness (c) Key Clarity (d) Mode (e) Pulse Clarity

Tonality. The signals were also analyzed according to their harmonic characteristics. A chromagram representing the distribution of pitch-classes is created. The key strength computed the cross-correlation of the chromagram with each possible major or minor key. The key clarity is the key strength of the key with the highest key strength out of all 24 keys. To model the mode of each piece, a computational model that distinguishes major and minor excerpts was employed. It calculates an overall output that continuously ranges from zero (minor mode) to one (major mode) [13].

Rhythm. The Pulse Clarity, a measure of the rhythmical and repetitive nature of a piece, was estimated by the autocorrelation of the onset detection curve of the signal. Figure 1 shows an example of the time course of the five audio features considered in the study.

4 Data Analysis of Physiological and Behavioral Measures

Preprocessing of all physiological and behavioral continuous signals recorded with a sample rate of 256 Hz was done in MATLAB (The Mathworks, Version 7.14.0.739). For each piece we extracted the physiological data using a frame size of 30 s with an overlap of 10 s. All signals were filtered in order to remove extraneous information, using a linear-phase filter based on the convolution of a 4th-order Butterworth filter impulse response. Subsequently, ECG signals were band-pass filtered (1–30 Hz), respiration activity was low-pass filtered (1 Hz), and skin conductance level was low-pass filtered (0.3 Hz). We subtracted all the physiology values in the music listening condition from the baseline physiology values, because we were interested in comparing the change in reactivity from the baseline condition during music listening.

Heart-Rate Variability Analysis. To quantify HRV, a series of R peaks were derived from the ECG signal. The ECGs were further filtered (passband was set to 1–30 Hz) to remove power line noise, baseline wander and muscle noise, but to preserve most of the spectral components of the QRS complexes. To avoid phase shifting, the signal peak filtering was performed with a linear-phase filter constructed from the convolution of a 4th-order Butterworth filter impulse response convolved with itself in reverse time. An adaptive derivative-based algorithm to detect the QRS complex was applied to construct the IBI time series consisting of inter-beat intervals that were subsequently obtained as differences between successive R-peak occurrence times. The HRV analysis measured six parameters: two time-domain measures and four frequency-domain measures. The two time-domain measures were mean heart rate (HR) and the square-root difference in the R-R interval (RMSSD). Frequency-domain measures included mean high-frequency power (absHF), mean low-frequency power (absLF), and the ratio of low-frequency to high-frequency power (LF/HF ratio). We obtained frequency-domain measures from the IBI time series by applying Fast Fourier Transform (FFT) over the time series. The calculated frequency spectrum was divided into two spectral bands: low frequency (LF, 0.04–0.15 Hz), and high frequency (HF, 0.15–0.4 Hz).

EMG Analysis. The MyoScanPro EMG sensor automatically converted the signal to a root mean square signal (after an internal analog rectification), which was therefore not preprocessed any further (capturing EMG activity at frequencies up to 500 Hz).

Continuous Ratings Analysis. We removed any individual differences in scale use by individual range normalization dividing each participant's rating by his or her individual range of ratings over the entire experiment and then subtracting each participant's resulting minimum rating value over the entire experiment, creating a range for each participant from 0 to 1.

Cardio-Respiratory Coupling Analysis. In previous studies heart and respiration rates are considered separately as monovariate measures of physiological activity during music listening. In our study, the cardiorespiratory synchronization is introduced as a bivariate measure of their interaction that better reflects the emotional state. Considering the cardiac and respiratory system as two coupled oscillators, we denote the phase of the heart as ϕ_h and the phase of respiration rate as ϕ_r respectively.

Assuming m heartbeats occur within n heart or respiratory cycles, synchronization is understood as phase locking of the corresponding phases given by:

$$|m\phi_h - n\phi_r| < const \tag{1}$$

where m and n are integers denoting the cardiac and the respiratory cycles, respectively. In other words, if the instantaneous phase difference between the oscillators remains constant within a given threshold, the oscillators are considered to be synchronized in their phase modulations.

To assess and quantify the cardio-respiratory synchronization, the synchronization index γ was employed which measures the degree of phase locking (synchronization) and calculated as:

$$\gamma = \left\| \frac{1}{M} \sum_{j=1}^{M} e^{i\theta(tj)} \right\|^2 \tag{2}$$

where $\theta(t_j) = m\phi_h(t_j) - n\phi_r(t_j)$ is the phase difference, t_j is the time point for $j = 1, \ldots, M$, and M is the number of sampling data points in the given time interval. This method is based on a mathematical model proposed in earlier studies [14].

If both oscillators are synchronized, $\gamma = 1$, whereas the completely desynchronized case yields $\gamma = 0$.

To detect synchronization for different $m:n$ ratios, this method has to be applied for each desired $m:n$ ratio. In practice, synchronization is present if γ exceeds a pre-defined threshold $\gamma \geq thres_\gamma$.

The study was carried out for the following $m:n$ ratios: n = 1; m = 2, ... 8 and n = 2; m = 5, 7, 9, 11, 13 (Fig. 2).

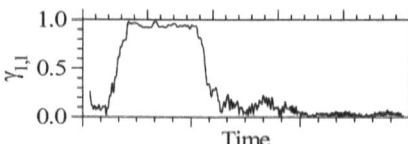

Fig. 2. Time-course of the synchronization index γ. The plateau close to 1 represents a period of synchronization, whereas the sections close to 0 represent periods of de-synchronization.

5 Results

For testing of significance on listener's responses, we employed a hierarchical linear modeling approach using the MIXED procedure in SPSS Statistics (IBM, Version 21). Estimation of parameters was based on restricted maximum likelihood. Beside fixed effects coefficients, the models included an intercept and a first-order autoregressive residual covariance structure (AR1).

William Tell – Gioachino Rossini. Figure 3 presents the evolution over time of experienced arousal, audio features and physiological responses related to arousal. It can be seen that the corresponding time-series exhibit synchronous changes overtime indicating that arousal can be described using audio descriptors such as loudness, pulse clarity, brightness and physiological measures such as skin conductance (SC) and cardiorespiratory synchronization index (CRS).

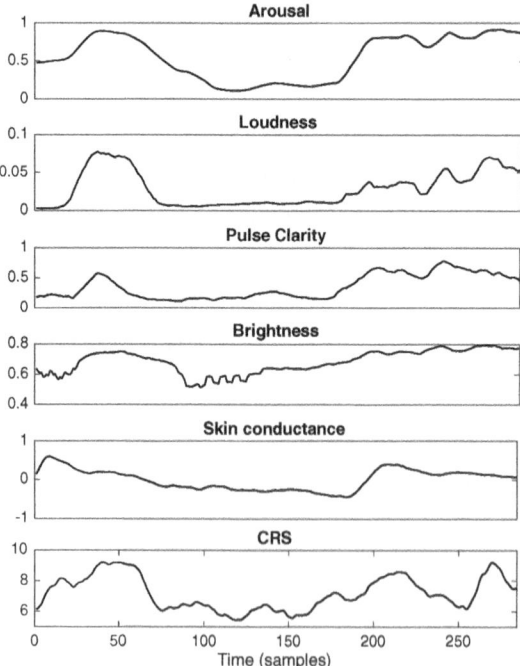

Fig. 3. Evolution over time of experienced arousal, audio features and physiological responses

The results of the statistical analysis are summarized below.

Subjective Arousal Scores: There was a positive effect of loudness ($b = 4.96$, $t = 27.637$, $p < 0.01$), brightness ($b = .93$, $t = 13.718$, $p < 0.01$) and pulse clarity ($b = .7$, $t = 26.304$, $p < 0.01$) features on arousal. Participants responded with increased arousal ratings in louder, brighter and prominent beat sections of the pieces. On the other hand, there was a negative effect of mode ($b = -.85$, $t = -12.690$, $p < 0.01$) indicating that as the piece became less major the ratings reported were more arousing.

SCL Scores: There was a positive effect of pulse clarity ($b = .25$, $t = 2.469$, $p < 0.01$). No other effects were found.

Cardiorespiratory Coupling: For the cardiorespiratory data there was a positive effect of pulse clarity ($b = 1.73$, $t = 2.021$, $p < 0.05$) and loudness ($b = 19.32$, $t = 3.337$, $p < 0.01$). Participants responded to increases in loudness and pulse clarity with higher prominence of 3:1 cardiorespiratory synchronization ratio.

HRV Scores: There was a negative effect of pulse clarity ($b = -11$, $t = -5.237$, $p < 0.01$) with increased parasympathetic activity in less beat prominent parts of the music.

Figure 4 presents the evolution over time of experienced valence, audio features and physiological responses related to valence. It follows that valence can be described

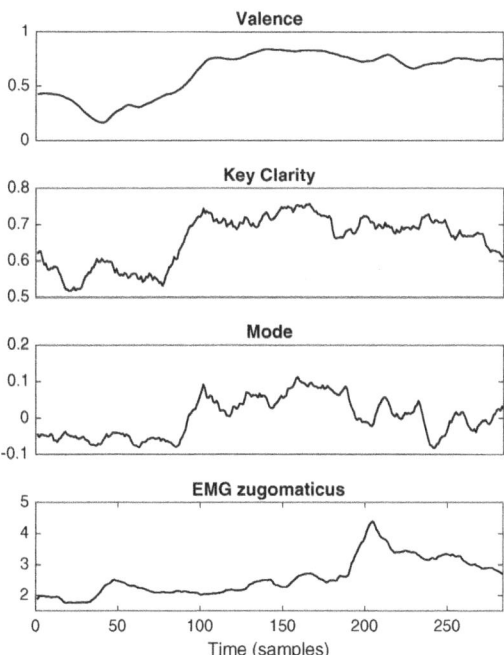

Fig. 4. Evolution over time of experienced valence, audio features and expressive responses

using audio descriptors such as key clarity and mode and expressive responses such as electromyogram (EMG).

The results of the statistical analysis are summarized below.

Subjective Valence Scores: There was a positive effect of key clarity ($b = .19$, $t = 2.546$, $p < 0.01$) and mode ($b = .42$, $t = 6.991$, $p < 0.001$) features on valence. On the other hand, there was a negative effect of pulse clarity ($b = -.15$, $t = -5.676$, $p < 0.01$) and loudness ($b = -.83$, $t = -4.496$, $p < 0.01$) indicating that as the piece became less beat prominent and less loud the ratings reported were more positive.

EMG Zygomaticus Scores: There was a positive main effect of pulse clarity ($b = .75$, $t = 27.637$, $p < 0.01$) and mode ($b = .35$, $t = 4.427$, $p < 0.01$) features associated with increased facial expressive activity.

Prince Igor – Alexander Borodin. The analysis of William Tell overture described above was carried out also for Prince Igor overture. The results of the analysis are quite similar and are summarized in the following paragraphs.

Subjective Arousal Scores: There was a positive effect of pulse clarity ($b = .27$, $t = 6.224$, $p < 0.01$) and loudness ($b = 6.03$, $t = 32.887$, $p < 0.01$) features. Participants responded with increased arousal ratings in loud and more prominent beat sections of the pieces. On the other hand, there was a negative effect of mode ($b = -21$, $t = -2.369$, $p < 0.05$) indicating that as the piece became less major the ratings reported were more arousing.

Subjective Valence Scores: There was a positive effect of key clarity ($b = .73$, $t = 10.148$, $p < 0.01$) and mode ($b = .17$, $t = 2.386$, $p < 0.05$) features. Participants responded with increased positive ratings in more major and key prominent parts of the pieces. On the other hand, there was a negative effect of loudness ($b = -1.64$, $t = -7.746$, $p < 0.01$) indicating that as the piece became less loud the ratings reported were more positive.

SCL Scores: There was a positive effect of pulse clarity ($b = .47$, $t = 4.559$, $p < 0.01$). No other effects were found.

Cardiorespiratory Coupling: For the cardiorespiratory data there was a positive effect of loudness ($b = 13.57$, $t = 2.673$, $p < 0.01$) and pulse clarity ($b = 2.46$, $t = 2.208$, $p < 0.05$). Participants responded to increases in loudness and pulse clarity with higher prominence of 3:1 cardiorespiratory synchronization ratio.

HRV Scores: There was a positive effect of mode ($b = .02$, $t = 2.302$, $p < 0.05$) with increased parasympathetic activity in major parts of the music.

6 Discussion

The results show that all music features (loudness, pulse clarity, brightness, mode and key clarity) influence both subjective and physiological measures of emotion. It is shown that arousal is positively related to loudness, pulse clarity and brightness, whereas valence is positively related to key clarity and mode. The relationships found between music features and emotion dimensions are in agreement with existing studies [1]. Minor mode is known to be associated to negative valence. In our study we found that minor mode (less major) is related to higher arousal. This finding has been also observed in previous studies [15]. A possible explanation for this result is the long duration music pieces used in our study where the music features are present and evolve in time.

In relation to physiological measures, it was found that SCL is positively associated to pulse clarity, i.e. beat prominent segments of music. Additionally, we found that EMG activity relates positively with both pulse clarity and mode, whereas HRV increases with increasing mode. Overall, the results are consistent with existing studies [8].

The correlations between the audio features and physiological measures related to arousal are high and explain the high accuracy of arousal recognition. On the contrary, the correlations between audio features and physiological measures related to valence are moderate to low explaining the low accuracy of valence recognition. It seems that, physiological reactions in the autonomous nervous system are more sensitive to changes in arousal than to changes in valence. Thus, new physiological measures out of the autonomous nervous system have to be found that are better related to valence. Based on these measures, new audio features could be found that better describe valence. Considering the cognitive nature of valence, a good candidate is responses from the central nervous system related to encephalogram (EEG). This should be further investigated in future research.

In our study, instead of using monovariate measures of heart and respiration rates we employed the cardiorespiratory synchronization as a bivariate physiological measure of affect. We found that cardiorespiratory synchronization increases with increasing pulse clarity and loudness. During strong beat and loud music segments, the heart and respiration oscillators become stronger phase locked. In addition to its importance as a bivariate physiological measure of affect, cardiorespiratory synchronization may be related to rhythmic entrainment mechanism of emotion elicitation [12]. Rhythmic entrainment is the process where an emotion is induced by a piece of music because the strong external rhythm of music interacts with and synchronizes to internal heart or respiration rhythms producing increased arousal.

The results of this study may also have implications in music psychology for the definition of emotion and the understanding of the underlying production mechanisms and to affective computing applications by facilitating the recognition of affective states using physiology.

7 Conclusions

The aim of this paper was to investigate the dynamic relationships between acoustic features, physiology and affective states. The results are consistent with existing studies and show that parts of the music with higher loudness and pulse clarity induced higher ratings of arousal, sympathetic activation and increased cardiorespiratory synchronization. In contrast, parts within the pieces with major mode and prominent key strength induced higher ratings of valence, parasympathetic activation and higher levels of facial activity. A novelty of our study is the employment of cardiorespiratory synchronization as a bivariate physiological measure of affect, which may be related to rhythmic entrainment mechanism of emotion elicitation. Future work will examine methods to capture response coherence among different emotional components including behavioral, physiological and neural responses. Practical implications of this work may include the development of affective music retrieval systems, design of music-computer interfaces and music therapy applications.

Acknowledgments. This work is supported by the SUTD-MIT International design center (IDC) Research Grant (IDG31200107/IDD11200105/IDD61200103). The authors thank Hải Lê Vũ for valuable technical assistance during the experiments.

References

1. Gabrielsson, A., Lindstroem, E.: The role of structure in the musical expression of emotions. In: Juslin, P.N., Sloboda, J.A. (eds.) Handbook of Music and Emotion: Theory, Research, Applications, pp. 367–400. Oxford University Press, New York (2010)
2. Eerola, T., Lartillot, O., Toiviainen, P.: Prediction of multidimensional emotional ratings in music from audio using multivariate regression models. In: Proceedings of the International Conference for Music Information Retrieval (ISMIR) (2009)
3. Fornari, J., Eerola, T.: The pursuit of happiness in music: retrieving valence with contextual music descriptors. In: Ystad, S., Kronland-Martinet, R., Jensen, K. (eds.) CMMR 2008. LNCS, vol. 5493, pp. 119–133. Springer, Heidelberg (2009)
4. Trochidis, K., Delbé, C., Bigand, E.: Investigation of the relationships between audio features and induced emotions in Contemporary Western music. In: Proceedings of the 8th Sound and Music Computing Conference (2011)
5. Hodges, D.A.: Psychophysiological responses to music. In: Juslin, P.N., Sloboda, J.A. (eds.) Handbook of Music and Emotion: Theory, Research, Applications, pp. 279–311. Oxford University Press, New York (2010)
6. Krumhansl, C.: An explanatory study of musical emotion and psychophysiology. Can. J. Exp. Psychol. **51**(4), 336–352 (1997)
7. Gomez, P., Danuser, B.: Relationships between musical structure and physiological measures of emotion. Emotion **7**(2), 377–387 (2004)
8. Nyklicek, I., Thayer, J., Van Doornen, L.: Cardiorespiratory differentiation of musically-induced emotion. J. Psychophysiol. **11**, 304–321 (1997)
9. Khalfa, S., Roy, M., Rainville, P., Dalla Bella, S., Peretz, I.: Role of tempo entrainment in psychophysiological differentiation of happy and sad music? Int. J. Psychophysiol. **68**(1), 17–26 (2008)
10. Coutinho, E., Cangelosi, A.: Musical emotions: predicting second-by-second subjective feelings of emotion from low-level psychoacoustic features and physiological measurements. Emotion **11**(4), 921 (2011)
11. Trochidis, K., Sears, D., Trân, D.-L., McAdams, S.: Psychophysiological measures of emotional response to Romantic orchestral music and their musical and acoustic correlates. In: Aramaki, M., Barthet, M., Kronland-Martinet, R., Ystad, S. (eds.) CMMR 2012. LNCS, vol. 7900, pp. 44–57. Springer, Heidelberg (2013)
12. Juslin, P.N., Sloboda, J.A.: Handbook of Music and Emotion: Theory, Research, Applications. Oxford University Press, Oxford (2010)

13. Lartillot, O., Toiviainen, P.: MIR in Matlab (II): a toolbox for musical feature extraction from audio. In: International Conference on Music Information Retrieval, Vienna (2007)
14. Rosenblum, M., Pikovsky, A., Kurths, J., Schäfer, C., Tass, P.A.: Phase synchronization: from theory to data analysis. Handb. Biol. Phys. **4**, 279–321 (2001)
15. Van der Zwaag, M., Westernik, H.D.M., Van der Broek, E.: Deploying music characteristics for an affective music player. In: 3rd International Conference on Affective Computing and Intelligent Interaction and Workshops, Amsterdam, Netherlands (2009)

A New Look at Musical Expectancy: The Veridical Versus the General in the Mental Organization of Music

Emery Schubert[1(✉)] and Marcus Pearce[2]

[1] Empirical Musicology Laboratory, The University of New South Wales,
Kensington, Australia
e.schubert@unsw.edu.au
[2] Queen Mary, University of London, London, UK
marcus.pearce@qmul.ac.uk

Abstract. This paper takes a step back from what we label 'problem solving' approaches to the psychology of music memory and processing. In contrast with generalised expectation theories of music processing, a hypothesis is proposed which is based on the idea that mental representations of music are largely based on a large library of individual pieces: Case-based memory. We argue that it is the activation of these memories that forms the critical aspect of musical experience. Furthermore, a specific hypothesis is proposed that it is possible to represent any new piece of music through the chaining together of different, pre-existing veridical segments of music, in contrast with 'problem solving by generalization' which determines expectation based on statistical/stylistic/schematic factors. By adjusting segment length, or by forming new segments through repeated listenings, new music can be absorbed into an existing, growing mental database by chaining together existing veridical segments that match the incoming stimulus.

Keywords: Music processing · Veridical memory · Schematic expectation · Exemplars · Prototypes, musical experience, problem solving, spreading activation

1 Introduction

Current, established theories of music perception tell us that when we perceive music, the music signal is compared against certain principles and processes which lead to particular expectations. These expectations are then compared with the actual incoming signal and so the incoming signal is either processed as being a violation (generating, for example, surprise) or fulfillment of the expectation. Schema theory is an example of such an established perspective. Schema theory posits that through much previous

---

This paper is based on Schubert, E., & Pearce, M. (2015). Veridical Chaining: A case-based memory matching approach to the mental organization of music. In M. Aramaki, R. Kronland-Martinet & S. Ystad & (Eds.), 11th International Symposium on Computer Music Multidisciplinary Research (CMMR) (pp. 428–440).

© Springer International Publishing Switzerland 2016
R. Kronland-Martinet et al. (Eds.): CMMR 2015, LNCS 9617, pp. 358–370, 2016.
DOI: 10.1007/978-3-319-46282-0_23

exposure, regularities in the 'way that music tends to go' are formed. For example, when a melody reaches the seventh scale degree there is an expectation that the note which follows will be the eighth scale degree. Such an approach to music perception sees musical processing as a problem solving task, with the problem being to determine whether the music fulfills or does not fulfill (or partially fulfills) expectation. Bhuracha [1–4] among others has drawn our attention to another way in which expectation is assessed, namely through comparison with the veridical. That is, when listening to a well known tune, upon listening to the nth note of the tune the next note $(n + 1)$ that is expected is the next note of the tune itself, and this will not necessarily be the statistically more likely note that schema theory predicts. We can think of this as 'case-based' matching to distinguish it from the general, emergent rules of schema theory. Whether note $n + 1$ violates a schematically driven expectation or not, the veridical expectation will always follow the specific case stored in memory, what we will refer to as the 'mental representation' of the tune (or music).

While veridical and schematic expectancy are both fairly well understood phenomena, schema and other 'problem solving by generalization' (PSBG) theories have occupied the bulk of research attention on the mental organization of music. This is reflected in the computational models of music, which can consist of training a programming architecture, such as a neural network, with a music corpus, and then testing how the network deals with a new stimulus [e.g. 5–9]. For example, statistical analysis of note-to-note transition is one computational way of estimating expectancy. High note-to-note pitch transition probability that emerges in the test corpus (because of frequent occurrence) will mean that in the typical test piece the recurrence of that transition will be highly expected. This is why note-to-note transition probabilities are an example of PSBG theory.

Veridical expectation receives understandably less attention in computational modeling of music because the output decision-making is trivial. If a known piece is being processed, its veridical memory at any point, such as note n, provides a 100 % accurate prediction of what is expected at the next note $(n + 1)$ of that piece. And if the incoming signal *is* that piece, there will be a perfect match, with complete expectancy fulfilled. Any perceived departure from the individual piece will be a 'perfect' mismatch from the veridically stored version. Expressive variation, embellishment, error and musical variation is considered later in this paper, but for now we consider veridicality in a strict sense, as though a precisely repeatable sound-recording.

Computational modeling of schematic expectancy presents interesting challenges in both computer science and music psychology. Such computational models provide a workspace where a large corpus generates a particular kind of complex, non-linear behavior, particularly where a musical progression presents an ambiguous set of possibilities, and the solution (e.g. determining the next note) is not well defined.

Despite the apparent triviality, veridical expectancy *is* subjected to statistical analysis. Some researchers have investigated how long it takes (usually in terms of time or as a function of number of notes) before the listener is certain of the identity of a particular unfolding melody. For example, Huron [10, pp. 221–224] played a set of notes that made up a sequence of a familiar tune. Huron wanted to know how many notes were required before the participant was confident about the identity of the tune. The sequence of notes presented commenced with the first note only in one trial, the first two notes in another trial and so on. For each trial, within each familiar stimulus, the proportion of participants who could correctly identify the melody was calculated. Of the four excerpts reported, more than 50 % of participants identified the 'correct' melody by the fourth note in three out of the four pieces tested. The length of the sequence required for recognition of the familiar melody is a function of several variables; It is not a universal 'four notes' principle. Obviously the individual's personal familiarity with the actual piece is critical. But also critical is how many other tunes share the pattern. Huron refers to two pieces in particular, where the opening notes are identical in terms of tone-rhythm pattern: *O Christmas Tree* (*O Tannenbaum*) and *Here Comes the Bride*. Up to the onset of the fourth note, the tone-rhythm pattern is identical for each (assuming they are transposed to the same key). Greater than 50 % correct identification was reported after three notes for *Here Comes the Bride* and after five notes for *O Christmas Tree*. While it may seem strange that such high confidence could be reported for the first three notes of Here Comes the Bride even though the tone-rhythm pattern is still identical to O Christmas Tree, the metric accent, and other musical feature variables provide additional cues that help to distinguish the pieces (a matter to which we will return).

Nevertheless, the point is that after the presentation of a certain amount of information a veridical mental representation is 'primed'. Once the recognition reaches 100 % the computational question becomes less interesting because the 'problem' (of what is the next most likely note) has been solved for each subsequent note. That is, as per another stimulus used by Huron in the study, after hearing the semiquaver (sixteenth note) sequence E5, D#5, E5, D#5, E5, B4 with a piano timbre, the listener familiar with the piece will then expect the specific piece, or case, of Beethoven's *Fur Elise*. And as long as that is what the listener continues to hear, the expectancy will be perfectly predicted by the veridically encoded mental representation.

2 Veridical Processing Is Ordinary

The veridical matching of incoming stimulus with memory is a very normal, day-to-day kind of processing. In fact, it is an essential part of consciousness and identity. We know who we are and where we are because we recognize specific instances of our home, furniture, foods we eat, clothes we wear, Uncle Ling who lives down the road, the path we take to go to the park, school or work, and so on. Although humans have an astounding ability to process new situations based on previous information, the veridical, exemplar, case-based memory is fundamentally important, too. And the two ways of processing need not be mutually exclusive.

In the case of music, a typical individual raised in Western culture has a high level of familiarity with a large mental library of individual pieces from at least their adolescence [11, 12], and like aspects of everyday life, this familiarity plays in important role in forming one's identity [e.g. 13, 14]. Huron even claims that "[m]ore than 99 % of all listening experiences involve listening to musical passages that the listener has heard before" [10, p. 241]. With such prevalence of familiarity with individual musical cases, as distinct from general principles of how music unfolds, it surprising that apart from the work of a few, such as Bharucha and Huron—both cited above, more attention is not paid to the processing of veridical musical information and its fundamental role in the mental organization of music.

If the announcer on a radio station says that the next piece is Beethoven's *Fifth Symphony*, the Beatles' *Penny Lane*, Dave Brubeck's, *Take Five*, Danny Elfman's *The Simpsons Main Title Theme*, Nirvana's *Smells Like Teen Spirit, Happy Birthday* or *Twinkle Twinkle Little Star*, then those familiar with the piece will have an expectation of what is about to come [for more detailed discussion, see 10]. And unless the presenter made an error or was joking, or if the listener had to stop listening, the expectation will be fulfilled. Even the announcement of the piece may initiate a mental rehearing, before the first note is sounded (as may well be the case now for the reader for one of the above examples). Furthermore, even without the announcement, the first few seconds, and even less [15–17] can be enough to initiate the expectation of what is to come – the actual music piece itself.

In this paper, we will argue that closer analysis of how veridical data is organized mentally will give insight into (1) the nature of musical experience and (2) how musical memories may be organized in a way that contrasts with PSBG theories. As an alternative to PSBG theories, we will build on a 'case-based memory matching' theory of music from which we present the 'veridical chaining' hypothesis of musical organization [18]. To simplify the examples we will refer largely to tone-rhythm pattern coding. But the discussion applies to all aspects of music, including rhythm, timbre, timing and loudness. Timbre and timing are important factors too, but tone-rhythm is easier to use for illustrative purposes through the convenience of Western music notation.

3 Musical Problem Solving or Musical Experience?

While schema theory and other theories applying a PSBG approach have made great strides in understanding how the mind processes music, the assumption or inference that music listening is a problem-solving task has some limitations. It suggests, and in many theories explicitly states, that the comparison of an incoming piece against a generalized prediction is what generates the aesthetic or affective experience, making the prediction process fundamentally important [19]. Perhaps the most well known instance of this perspective is Meyer's theory of expectancy in which he argued that "[e]motion or affect is aroused when a tendency to respond is arrested or inhibited" [20, p. 14]. In contrast, author ES has argued elsewhere that the activation of mental representation generates affect [21–23]. The idea is based on Martindale [24–27], where the activation of cognitive units generates pleasure [for more detailed discussion, see 21, 22, 28, 29]. The point of this approach that is in sharp contrast to (though not mutually exclusive from) PSBG theories is that the pleasure in response, or attraction we have, to music is not a result of (necessarily) a result of the problem solving process, but the mere activation of (existing) mental representations. 'Affect through activation', as it may be thought of, makes the role of veridical storage and activation critical to musical experience, and therefore to the music listening experience. This is in concert with the view of Stephen Davies who near the opening of his book on *Musical Meaning and Emotion* states:

I do not believe music is a symbol system that conveys a semantic meaning, or quasi-semantic meaning, content. But I am not embarrassed to use the term "meaning" here because I think both that music can and should be understood to be appreciated and that it is created to be so. That composers intend to make something that invites attention, engagement, and consideration rather than aiming to stimulate mindless reflex, and that they succeed in producing works rewarding in just this way, suggest to be that we might reasonably talk of music's meaning what is grasped by the person who understands it. [30, p. ix]

If the role of veridical activation is crucial to musical experience, we can reconceptualise our understanding of the mental organization of music. In what follows, such an reconceptualisation is proposed.

4 Case-Based Memory (CBM) Matching

As a point of departure from PSBG theories of music processing, we will use case-based memory [31] matching as a starting point of hypothesizing how music is organized in memory. Case-based memory is an outgrowth of the Script theory which focuses on the role of procedural knowledge in problem solving in psychology and artificial intelligence research [32–35]. It is more commonly referred to as case-based 'reasoning' [34, 35] but in this paper we use of the term 'memory' deliberately because of our emphasis on activation (of memory) rather than problem solving. Consider an approach to computational language translation of natural language text (e.g. from English to Cantonese) called translation memory [36]. This is a text translation system that accesses large databases of text, and finds the closest match to the target text. If one or more exact matches are found, the target text in the corresponding rows of the database are retrieved. If a match is not found, the next best match is selected, if available, and further processing takes place before a possible solution is found. Immediately, in this example, it is clear that text translation *is* a problem solving task. And while we have argued above that music is primarily a mental activity, rather than problem solving task, the simple computational example of translation memory is still informative. In music, the process of finding and activating the match is in itself sufficient to initiate a musical experience. Returning to the discussion of Huron's veridical memory recognition task, consider now the melody in Fig. 1 in quadruple meter.

Those who are able to imagine the three note melody may instantly start thinking about the song *Yesterday* by Lennon and McCartney. We may even start hearing the next notes of the melody as shown in Fig. 2. In fact, we may even hear the guitar timbres, and McCartney's voice, as we imagine the piece triggered by the three notes of Fig. 1. This is an explicit example of veridical activation. It is achieved by having a 'perfect' match from a segment of the incoming music (as decoded from a music score

Fig. 1. Opening notes of a well-known tune.

Fig. 2. A possible continuation of the melody in Fig. 1.

in this case) with memory store. It can therefore be thought of as direct memory addressing that is fundamental to memory organization in microprocessors and the translation memory approach. The returned data are the next notes in the sequence, and in fact the piece itself. In the case of translation memory it is the translated text. There is no need for recourse to PSBG of expectation. We do not need to look at note-to-note transition probabilities. Expectation and implication theories argue that when a PSBG outcome is not achieved, surprise results. CBM, on the other hand, predicts that any digression from the veridical will be unexpected. But importantly, if the digression has not been previously encoded, it will not be perceived as a musical experience because no activation takes place at the point [see also 29].

The activation of the memory that matches with the musical extract is linked to other, previously encoded data. These data can be classified into two broad kinds: intramusical and extramusical [20, 37]. Extramusical links refer to activation of representations consisting of connections outside the music itself, such as thoughts, situations, images, designations, ideas as so on [see, for example 12, 38, 39, Chapter 8]. Intramusical connections are those made to other musical segments, both within the piece being sounded (intraopus) and to other pieces (extraopus) [40]. All of these links can be activated through the principle of spreading activation [41, 42], and the repeated activation of these links binds them together into new veridical stores [e.g. 43].

Of interest here is the activation of the intraopus links. Just as with the lookup table pertaining to the translation memory discussed above, the returned value from the intraopus perspective is the next note or group of notes. That is, the next contiguously coded 'fragment' becomes primed (we could also say 'expected'), and then when that fragment of music is sounded, it acts as the index for priming the next contiguous segment after that one, and so on, recursively. If we take our starting point as recursive activation of a memory as a result of the temporally unfolding, continuing matches with the sounded music, we are able to generate hypotheses about how new pieces of music may be processed, putting aside (for now) the PSBG approaches. One hypothesis which we now discuss consists of online segmentation of the incoming piece in such a way that matches for each segment can be found, and then chained together.

5 Veridical Chaining

When a new piece of music is auditioned, our mental network will try to find a match with an existing representation. If a match is not found, the incoming musical stream will be broken into smaller segments until a match is found. Note that, for now, we are avoiding reference to statistically 'best', 'approximate', 'similar' or 'nearest neighbour' match which are hallmarks of PSBG approaches. The match, for the purpose of the current hypothesis, must be 'exact'. In the case of a tone-rhythm pattern, a downward segmenting size adjustment of the incoming stream continues until some match is found, or until the segments become too small to process. In the case of no matching segments, the stimulus (or that part of it) will not activate a mental representation. With sufficient repetition, however, a new mental representation will form: a representation of the new segment or piece, commensurate with the principle of mere exposure [44, 45].

If a particular segment *has* been encoded previously, that pre-encoded segment will be activated, and activation will also prime segments to which it was previously linked. If, on the other hand, there is no match, there will be no phenomenal recognition or 'sounds like' or 'ah, I know this piece' experience.

As a simple example, suppose a new piece of music consists of two segments (for example, two phrases of music) and each segment has a unique but non-overlapping match in the existing memory (mental representation) network. That is, if a short piece of familiar music can be described as consisting of two phrase sequences, say AB, and another familiar piece as XY, then a new piece consisting of AY will be easily encoded because of its matches with the two previously distinct pieces, but will activate the mental representations of both those pieces. The process is dynamic and interactive, and so all represented stimuli containing some segmental match can be affected by the intrusion of the new piece. This is the basic groundwork which presents an alternative to PSBG, and can be summarized as *veridical segment cross-chaining of existing mental representation segments*, or for ease of reading, 'veridical chaining' [18]. In the example, over time, with further exposure, a new link forms connecting the pre-existing segment A with the pre-existing segment Y. When well learnt, the auditioning of segment A will prime both segments B and Y, since there are links to both through the chaining process.

Consider *Twinkle Twinkle Little Star* (TTLS) and *Baa Baa Black Sheep* (BBBS). Ignoring the words and transposing into the same key, each melody will activate the same segment in the opening bar. For the purpose of understanding veridical chaining, let's make the assumption that the listener whose mental network we are investigating has only encoded one piece of music in autobiographical time, and that she has heard the piece sufficiently frequently to have a mental representation of the piece. The mental representation is shown in Fig. 3 in Western musical notation for convenience. Suppose now that the individual is exposed to the tune in Fig. 4.

Under the assumption of case-based memory matching, the first bar will present a perfect match, and therefore activate the mentally represented first bar. However, during this time, the second bar will become primed and therefore expected, assuming that the listener has (incorrectly) recognized the tune as TTLS. When the second bar actually begins sounding there will no longer be a case-based match. Again, we must emphasize that we are taking an 'extreme', veridical perspective. It is obvious to us that the quaver (quarter note) pattern in the second bar of BBBS is an embellishment of the

Fig. 3. Opening four bars for the melody of *Twinkle Twinkle Little Star*.

A New Look at Musical Expectancy: The Veridical Versus the General   365

Fig. 4. Opening four bars for the melody of *Baa Baa Black Sheep*.

same point in TTLS. But for the purpose of illustration, and on the basis that only 'perfect' matches are possible, similarity is not enough. A 'perfect' match is the requirement.

The way the network will process the new piece according to case-based memory matching is illustrated in Fig. 5. Strictly speaking, the hypothetical individual who only has one piece stored in memory will have that piece primed as soon as the first note is heard (because there is only one solution after hearing one note). The illustration however shows that it takes three 'steps' (notes) to be sounded before the individual 'recognises' (and hence activates) a mental representation (time steps 3 to 5). This is to keep the process more in line with the findings reported by Huron, discussed earlier. But the specifics are not so important here. The important point in the hypothetical example occurs at time step 6, where the melody ceases to (perfectly) match that stored in memory. At that point, no activation is taking place, although some residual priming may remain for the representation of the initially primed piece.

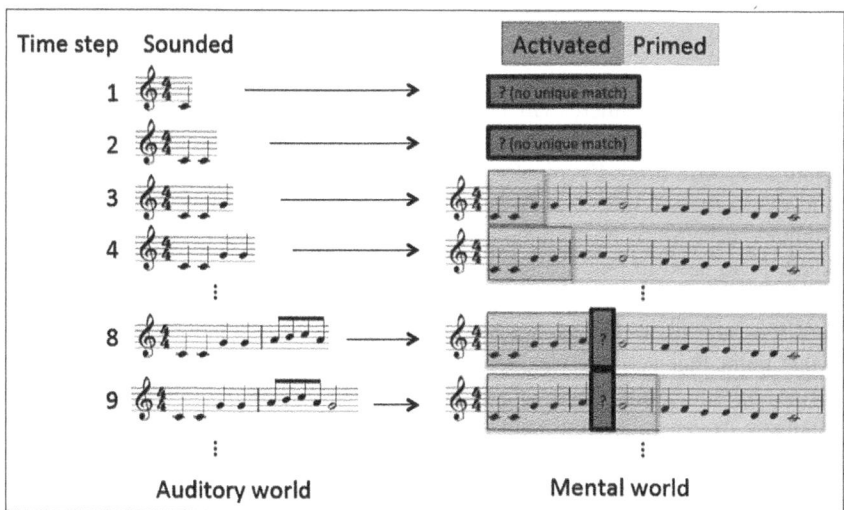

Fig. 5. Case-based memory matching for a new, incoming piece (BBBS) when the only available veridical memory is TTLS. Blue shading indicates activated mental representation. Green shading indicates mental representation primed as a result of the activated mental representation. Red shading indicates a mismatch – no activation. The hypothetical individual has only one piece of music in memory, meaning that the opening notes (time steps 1 and 2) will match TTLS. No 'unique' match indicates the more general case when the individual has more pieces mentally represented. Time steps are in units of unfolding notes. (Color figure online)

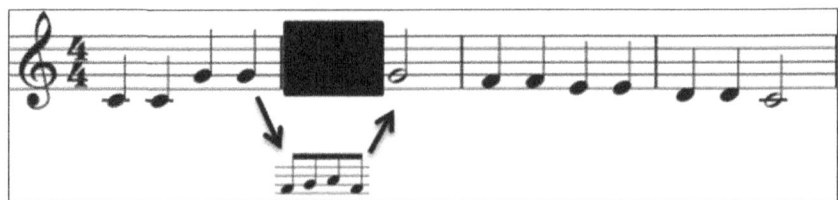

Fig. 6. Example of a veridical chain formed using an existing representation of a previously known piece, and the linking to a segment that diverged (had no match) from the original. The new piece is heard sufficiently frequently and this leads to the chaining of the links to form a new, veridical mental representation.

If we now suppose that the individual becomes frequently exposed to BBBS, then the TTLS network will still be utilized, but eventually a new segment will form, consisting of the quaver passage. The new passage is accessed by a link from the first bar of TTLS, and then, after the activation of the new segment, a link will return and continue the activation of the remainder of TTLS, as shown in Fig. 6. The 'chaining' together of old segments in the processing of new, incoming music, is the basis of the veridical chaining hypothesis.

As the individual hears more and more pieces of music, more and more mental representations are developed. An extreme interpretation of veridical chaining is that the music will always be parsed so that there are matches with an existing mental representation or portions thereof, and if no representation is available, no activation takes place. If there is no match regardless of segment length, repeated listening is necessary to form a new mental representation of that segment. As the mental database becomes large enough, there will be more and more opportunity for new pieces to generate links across different segments of pre-existing memories simply because there are more to choose from. Eventually, the matching of segments, such as the first three of four notes reported in the study conducted by Huron, will open up a vast range of possibilities, because so many notes will contain those segments. The extreme view is that there is no need to find a solution that is similar in the sense of PSBG, should an exact match not be found. But on the other hand, once a segment becomes small enough, it is very likely that an exact match can be found, just not a unique solution. It is at this point that veridical segmentation melds with many PSBG models because numerous, minute combinations of veridical segments are able to give the appearance of schematic or generalized principles. This can be demonstrated through the calculus principles of limiting sums and integration [e.g. 46].

Recent PSBG approaches use probabilistic models that store a complete record of every musical sequence ever experienced [49]. This is achieved efficiently using suffix tree representations [49–52]. In these models, new musical sequences are matched with previously heard sequences by following the appropriate transition in the suffix tree as each consecutive note is heard. Expectations are generated probabilistically through analysis of the frequency with which different notes have followed the context in the model's previous experience. When they encounter a context that has not been heard before, these models generalize by generating expectations using a shorter suffix of that context that have not been heard before. Therefore, such models may prove capable of integrating veridical chaining with PSBG, since they store veridical representations of every musical sequence experienced but also generate schematic expectations by generalizing to lower-order contexts. This is an important topic to be developed in future research.

We conclude this section by noting that it has been established in the literature for some time [e.g. 47] that when a prototype representation is established, the individual exemplars related to that prototype are also activated, and the degree to which either an exemplar versus a generalized prototype can be activated is a matter of some debate. For example, some research has suggested that when our mental database is large enough, activation of an exemplar is a more efficient way of identifying the category to which the stimulus belongs than is the prototype [48]. The role of the exemplar, or the veridical, in psychological perception is therefore difficult to ignore in cognitive science in general.

6 Evidence for Veridical Chaining

While evidence for veridical chaining is drawn mainly from script, prototype and case-based reasoning theory, there have been few studies in music perception that directly test case-based (veridical) memory coding, and the segmenting of a music stream. Two possible exceptions are briefly outlined here. Justus and Bharucha [53] compared responses to mistuned versus in-tune final chords after being primed with a schematically probable chord, or a schematically improbable chord. Relatively fast, accurate response in identifying the mistuned chord in the harmonically close chord target condition versus distant chord target was taken as evidence that schematic processing is favoured over veridical. The veridical condition had each trial consisting of a 'preview' prime-target followed by the trial prime-target pair, but in the trial the target on the second occasion might be in tune or out of tune—that is, congruent or incongruent with the first pair.

Similar results were reported by Tillmann and Bigand [54], with schematic expectancy better explaining faster and more accurate responses. The researchers used chord sequences, with manipulation of the final chord while participants performed a timbre judgement task on the final chord. Exposition phases were manipulated with the goal of generating schematic (Experiment 1) and veridical (Experiment 2) mental organization of chord sequence materials.

These studies, and others, generally assume that veridical coding can be achieved by a fairly short period of repeated exposure. However, veridical memories of the kind we have been discussing are all firmly established in long term memory, and may well consist of exposure over several days, weeks and years. Hence it may be wise to distinguish between 'long term veridical memory' and 'short term veridical memory', the latter being more convenient and pragmatic to test under well-controlled experimental conditions. In the Tillman and Bigand study, when the group was trained with harmonically related material (prior to test trials), they were overall faster. Perhaps one measure in their design that could have demonstrated 'long-term' veridical coding would be if reaction time for the repeated exposure group had reached the same level as the group receiving unrelated, but similar (generalized) examples, where a schematic coding may emerge – short term schematic preparation. That is, the repetition phase would need to be extended until this condition was met (an experimentally problematic design). Another alternative would be to retest recognition of items from the exposure phase, but do so at a much later time (weeks or months later) to determine if the pieces had indeed formed a long lasting veridical memory, and hence, mental representation. In other words, we have not cited a study where *long-term* veridical memory generated expectancy has been tested on an equal footing with schematically generated expectancy. The veridical chaining hypothesis presents one impetus for designing such a study.

7 Conclusion

This paper presented the view that the activation of musical exemplars *is* the fundamental act of the musical experience, and that veridical chaining allows this simple principle to be retained. We do not want to dogmatically replace or denigrate PSBG approaches. But we do want to point out that case-based memory matching, and the veridical chaining hypothesis shifts the focus of understanding musical experience to the 'act of activation', rather than problem solving. In this regard, veridical chaining plays an important role in questioning the implied or inferred aspects of music processing that are now considered mainstream in music psychology and computational modeling of music perception. Our provocative angle here is that if a stream of incoming music is processed, why would it not first 'match' (activate) a previously encoded instance of itself? A sound recording should be able to do this because each replay of that recording is essentially identical, and so matching with the memory of the individual who has 'grown up' (*vis-à-vis* long term veridical memory) with that recording. The veridical chaining hypothesis will be expanded in the future. The aim of this paper was to introduce the principle of veridical chaining as an alternative to PSBG explanations of music processing and highlight its potential utility.

Acknowledgments. This research was supported by a Fellowship from the Australian Research Council (FT120100053) held by author ES.

References

1. Bharucha, J., Curtis, M., Paroo, K.: Varieties of musical experience. Cognition **100**, 131–172 (2006)
2. Bharucha, J.J.: Tonality and expectation. In: Aiello, R., Sloboda, J.A. (eds.) Musical Perceptions, pp. 213–239. Oxford University Press, London (1994)
3. Bharucha, J.J., Todd, P.M.: Modeling the perception of tonal structure with neural nets. Comput. Music J. **13**, 44–53 (1989)
4. Bharucha, J.J.: Music cognition and perceptual facilitation: a connectionist framework. Music Percept. **5**, 1–30 (1987)
5. Pearce, M.T., Wiggins, G.A.: Improved methods for statistical modelling of monophonic music. J. New Music Res. **33**, 367–385 (2004)

6. Pearce, M.T., Wiggins, G.A.: Expectation in melody: the influence of context and learning. Music Percept. **23**, 377–405 (2006)
7. Wiggins, G.A., Pearce, M.T., Müllensiefen, D.: Computational modelling of music cognition and musical creativity. In: Dean, R. (ed.) Oxford Handbook of Computer Music and Digital Sound Culture, pp. 383–420. Oxford University Press, Oxford (2009)
8. Temperley, D.: The Cognition of Basic Musical Structures. MIT Press, Cambridge (2001)
9. Temperley, D.: A probabilistic model of melody perception. Cogn. Sci. **32**, 418–444 (2008)
10. Huron, D.: Sweet Anticipation: Music and the Psychology of Expectation. MIT Press, Cambridge (2006)
11. Folkestad, G.: Digital tools and discourse in music: the ecology of composition. In: Hargreaves, D.J., Miell, D.E., MacDonald, R.A.R. (eds.) Musical Imaginations, pp. 193–205. Oxford University Press, Oxford (2012)
12. Hargreaves, D.J.: Musical imagination: perception and production, beauty and creativity. Psychol. Music **40**, 539–557 (2012)
13. MacDonald, R.A., Hargreaves, D.J., Miell, D.: Musical identities. In: Hallam, S., Cross, I., Thaut, M. (eds.) The Oxford Handbook of Music Psychology, pp. 462–470. Oxford University Press, Oxford (2009)
14. Lamont, A.: Musical identities and the school environment. In: MacDonald, R.A.R., Hargreaves, D.J., Miell, D. (eds.) Musical Identities, pp. 41–59. Oxford University Press, Oxford, UK (2002)
15. Gjerdingen, R.O., Perrott, D.: Scanning the dial: the rapid recognition of music genres. J. New Music Res. **37**, 93–100 (2008)
16. Plazak, J., Huron, D.: The first three seconds. Musicae Sci. **15**, 29–44 (2011)
17. Schellenberg, E.G., Iverson, P., Mckinnon, M.C.: Name that tune: identifying popular recordings from brief excerpts. Psychon. Bull. Rev. **6**, 641–646 (1999)
18. Schubert, E.: Reconsidering expectancy and implication in music: the veridical chaining hypothesis. In: Ginsborg, J., Lamont, A. (eds.) Ninth Triennial Conference of the European Society for the Cognitive Sciences of Music, RNCM, Manchester, UK (2015)
19. Narmour, E.: The top-down and bottom-up systems of musical implication: building on Meyer's theory of emotional syntax. Music Percept. **9**, 1–26 (1991)
20. Meyer, L.B.: Emotion and Meaning in Music. University of Chicago Press, Chicago (1956)
21. Schubert, E.: Enjoyment of negative emotions in music: an associative network explanation. Psychol. Music **24**, 18–28 (1996)
22. Schubert, E.: Loved music can make a listener feel negative emotions. Musicae Sci. **17**, 11–26 (2013)
23. Schubert, E., North, A.C., Hargreaves, D.J.: Toward a theory of music aesthetics: the affect-space framework. Psychology of Aesthetics, Creativity, and the Arts (submitted)
24. Martindale, C., Moore, K.: Priming, prototypicality, and preference. J. Exp. Psychol. Hum. Percept. Perform. **14**, 661–670 (1988)
25. Martindale, C.: Aesthetics, psychobiology, and cognition. In: Farley, F.H., Neperud, R.W. (eds.) The foundations of Aesthetics, Art, & Art Education, pp. 7–42 (1988)
26. Martindale, C.: The pleasures of thought: a theory of cognitive hedonics. J. Mind Behav. **5**, 49–80 (1984)
27. West, A., Moore, K., Martindale, C., Rosen, K.: Prototypicality and preference. Bullet. Br. Psychol. Soc. **36**, A138–A138 (1983)
28. Schubert, E., Hargreaves, D.J., North, A.C.: A dynamically minimalist cognitive explanation of musical preference: is familiarity everything? Front. Psychol. **5**, 38 (2014)
29. Schubert, E.: The fundamental function of music. Musicae Sci. **13**, 63–81 (2009–2010)
30. Davies, S.: Musical Meaning and Expression. Cornell University Press, Ithaca (1994)

31. Hammond, K.J., Seifert, C.M.: A cognitive science approach to case-based planning. In: Chipman, S., Meyrowitz, A.L. (eds.) Foundations of Knowledge Acquisition: Cognitive Models of Complex Learning, vol. 194, pp. 245–267. Springer, Berlin (1993)
32. Tomkins, S.S.: Script theory: differential magnification of affects. In: Howe, H.E., Dienstbier, R.A. (eds.) Nebraska Symposium on Motivation, vol. 26, pp. 201–236. University of Nebraska Press, Lincoln (1979)
33. Schank, R.C., Abelson, R.P.: Scripts, Plans, Goals and Understanding: An Inquiry into Human Knowledge Structures. Lawrence Erlbaum, Hillsdale (1977)
34. Riesbeck, C.K., Schank, R.C.: Inside Case-Based Reasoning. Lawrence Erlbaum Associates, Hillsdale (1989)
35. Kolodner, J.: Case-Based Reasoning. Morgan Kaufmann, San Mateo (1993)
36. Somers, H.: Translation memory systems. In: Somers, H. (ed.) Computers and Translation: A Translator's Guide, pp. 31–48. Benjamins, Amsterdam (2003)
37. Finnäs, L.: How can musical preferences be modified - a research review. Bullet. Counc. Res. Music Educ. **102**, 1–58 (1989)
38. Hargreaves, D.J., Hargreaves, J.J., North, A.C.: Imagination and creativity in music listening. In: Hargreaves, D., Miell, D., MacDonald, R. (eds.) Musical Imaginations: Multidisciplinary perspectives on creativity, performance and perception, pp. 156–172. Oxford University Press, Oxford (2012)
39. Dowling, W.J., Harwood, D.L.: Music Cognition. Academic Press, London (1986)
40. Narmour, E.: The Analysis and Cognition of Basic Melodic Structures: The Implication-Realization Model. University of Chicago Press, Chicago (1990)
41. Bharucha, J.J., Stoeckig, K.: Priming of chords: spreading activation or overlapping frequency spectra? Percept. Psychophys. **41**, 519–524 (1987)
42. Collins, A.M., Loftus, E.F.: Spreading activation theory of semantic processing. Psychol. Rev. **82**, 407–428 (1975)
43. Oja, E.: Simplified neuron model as a principal component analyzer. J. Math. Biol. **15**, 267–273 (1982)
44. Zajonc, R.B.: Attitudinal effects of mere exposure. J. Pers. Soc. Psychol. **9**, 1–27 (1968)
45. Zajonc, R.B.: Mere exposure: a gateway to the subliminal. Curr. Dir. Psychol. Sci. **10**, 224–228 (2001)
46. Stewart, J.: Calculus, Concepts and Contexts. Brooks, Brooks/Cole, Belmont (2009)
47. Smith, E.R., Zarate, M.A.: Exemplar and prototype use in social categorization. Soc. Cogn. **8**, 243–262 (1990)
48. Griffiths, T.L., Canini, K.R., Sanborn, A.N., Navarro, D.J.: Unifying rational models of categorization via the hierarchical Dirichlet process. In: Proceedings of the 29th Annual Conference of the Cognitive Science Society, pp. 323–328 (2007)
49. Pearce, M.T.: The construction and evaluation of statistical models of melodic structure in music perception and composition. Doctoral dissertation, Department of Computing, City University, London, UK (2005)
50. Bunton, S.: Semantically motivated improvements for PPM variants. Comput. J. **40**(2/3), 76–93 (1997)
51. Cleary, J.G., Teahan, W.J.: Unbounded length contexts for PPM. Comput. J. **40**(2/3), 67–75 (1997)
52. Ukkonen, E.: On-line construction of suffix trees. Algorithmica **14**(3), 249–260 (1995)
53. Justus, T.C., Bharucha, J.J.: Modularity in musical processing: the automaticity of harmonic priming. J. Exp. Psychol. Hum. Percept. Perform. **27**, 1000–1011 (2001)
54. Tillmann, B., Bigand, E.: Musical structure processing after repeated listening: schematic expectations resist veridical expectations. Musicae Sci. **14**, 33–47 (2010)

Music Analysis, Music Generation and Emotion

Emotional Experiences of Ascending Melodic Lines

Hans T. Zeiner-Henriksen[✉]

Department of Musicology, University of Oslo, Oslo, Norway
h.t.zeiner-henriksen@imv.uio.no

1 Introduction

Music has the ability to cause intense emotional experiences with perceptible physical reactions as their outcome [1–3]. "Chills" or "goose bumps" have been found to be reliable indicators of emotional peaks in music listening through the combination of self-reporting methods and the concrete measurements of physical reactions [4–6]. In this way it is possible to identify musical passages that are especially effective at producing emotional peak experiences [5]. These experiences can be evoked in many ways and are often connected to music on a highly subjective level [7]. Nevertheless, large groups of listeners often seem to agree on the effectiveness of certain music and even specific passages in this regard [5, 6, 8].

The role of dopamine activity points to a specific cerebral process occurring while emotions are aroused [9]. But how an abstract acoustic musical signal can initiate this process is less clear. Several psychological mechanisms are suggested to explain the relationship between music and emotions [7]. These range from universal reflexes and imitation and entrainment mechanisms, to intricate intellectual processes of evaluation, association, imagery and expectation.

This study focuses on ascending melodic lines; a musical feature that I often find present during strong emotional experiences with music. I have also found ascending melodic lines frequently present in musical examples that are identified as especially effective when music evokes emotions [5, 8, 9]. However, in the literature on music and emotion this feature is seldom mentioned as having any particular significance.

Some of the pivotal scholars within the field have to a certain extent implied a connection between directions in music and emotional content: Deryck Cooke points to a basic set of melodic lines that convey specific emotional meaning, including several ascending and descending lines [10], Peter Kivy's contour theory suggests that emotional expressiveness lies in its resemblance of the contour of human emotion [11], while Leonard Meyer believes that audiences have problems to respond emotionally to avant-garde music because the large descending skips and intervals make it difficult to experience motorically [12]. In a methodical study, Zohar Eitan demonstrates that directions and contours in music are not coincidental [13]. He focuses on the position of the highest pitch in music composed by Joseph Haydn, Frederic Chopin and Alban Berg, and especially the two last composers have as part of their tonal language lots of ascending melodies that ends on climatic high points.

This study is mainly focused on popular music, where there are many indications of the significance of directions in music; almost all modulations are upward movements, in pop songs vocal lines very often ascends from the verse up to the refrain, while build-ups in electronic dance music almost always are structured with ascending melodies and upwards pitch movements up to the climax (the bass drop). Ragnhild T. Solberg suggests that such ascending lines in a build up can evoke intense emotional experiences among the dancers/listeners [14].

To test if passages with ascending melodic lines can be effective in evoking emotions, I have conducted a study combining self report and measuring of skin conductance with the assistant of master student Stian Omdahl. He both completed some of the individual tests and helped analyse the results. The study was part of the research project "Music, Motion and Emotion. Theoretical and Psychological Implications of Musical Embodiment", founded by the Research Council of Norway and led by professor Hallgjerd Aksnes at the Department of Musicology at the University of Oslo.

2 Method

2.1 Participants

10 respondents were recruited from the Department of Musicology at the University of Oslo and 14 were recruited outside of the institute; 12 with more than five years of musical training and 12 with less than five years of musical training – a composition of respondents that parallels similar studies [15]. 50 % of the respondents were male and 50 % were female. The average age was 25.5 (Range = 20–40, SD = 5,54).

2.2 Materials

The 24 respondents were asked to bring one example of music that often gave them strong emotional experiences. In addition we prepared an eight minutes long sound file with excerpts from four different musical pieces with certain passages that included ascending melodic lines and pitch movements.

1. Christel Alsos: *Finding Gold* (2010) (0:00–1.30)
2. Gustav Mahler: *Adagietto* (*Symphony no. 5 in C sharp minor, IV*, recording by New Philharmonia Orchestra, (0:00–1:25)
3. Sigur Rós: *Varúð* (2012) (1:55–5:33)
4. Josh Groban: *You Raise Me Up* (2003) (2:30–3:45).

The majority of studies on how music evokes emotions are carried out solely with the use of classical music. The inclusion here of extracts from popular music resulted in a better match between the self-selected and the pre-prepared material.

2.3 Equipment

The respondents listened to the music with a pair of Ultrasone HFI-2200 ULE headphones connected to a computer. To record skin conductance we used the Q-sensor from Affectiva. It is a small, practical device that sends data via Bluetooth providing real time monitoring and stores everything internally as well. The sensor records skin conductance, skin temperature, movement (with a 3-axis accelerometer), and event markers. The Q software represents the data in comprehensible graphical user interfaces.

2.4 Procedure

The respondents were tested one by one, seated in a small room with a computer and the headphones. The Q-sensor was strapped around the non-preferred hand of the respondents, with the sensor's two electrodes pressed against the palm on the opposite side of the thumb. After the sensor data was checked and the respondents had worn the sensor for about five minutes the test started with the self-selected music. The sensor has a large round button in the middle that records event markers, and the respondents were asked to press this button if they sensed any type of physical reaction while listening to the music (chills, goose bumps, thrills, shudders, etc.). After having listened to their self-selected music (maximum 4 min), the same procedure was repeated with the pre-prepared track. The respondents were alone in the room when they listened to the music.

3 Results

3.1 Self-selected Music

The 24 respondents had chosen music of many different genres:

All but one respondent pushed the button one or more times during the first listening session to report some sort of physical reaction. The mean number (M) of entries was 6.08 (SD = 4.2), (M males: 4.9, M females: 7.3). The group of respondents with less than five years of musical training had a total of 76 marker entries (M = 6.3), while the group with more than five years of musical training had a total of 70 (M = 5.8). The students recruited from the Department of Musicology selected music from a wider range of genres (rock, choir music, indie pop, classical, electronica, jazz and reggae) (Table 1).

The marker entries were used to identify the specific places in the music where the respondents had reported physical reactions. These places where analyzed and categorized according to the musical features that were present – in a similar manner as has been done in earlier studies [8, 16].

Of the thirteen respondents that reported physical reactions at places where *Ascending melodic lines or pitch movements* were identified, ten are also present in the second category *High pitches*. Seventeen of the identified places are the same for these

Table 1. Overview of the self-selected music, categorized according to genre. The marker entries (M.E.) show how many times the respondents have pushed the sensor button. The S/MT-colon shows the sex of the respondent (Female/Male) and if he or she has more or less than five years of musical training (±5).

Genre:	Group/artist/composer:	Title:	M.E.	S/MT
Rock:	U2	Where the Streets Have No Name (live)	8	M/-5
	Nickelback	Lullaby	9	F/-5
	Dream Theater	The Count of Tuscany	4	M/-5
	Guns'n'Roses	Sweet Child of Mine	2	M/+ 5
Singer-songwriter:	First Aid Kit	Lion's Roar	1	F/+ 5
	Salem Al Fakir	Astronaut	2	M/-5
	Melissa Horn	Kungsholmens Hamn	11	F/+ 5
Pop:	DJ Sammy, Yanou & Do	Heaven – Yanou's Candlelight Mix	9	F/-5
	Celine Dion	My Heart Will Go On	10	M/-5
	Michael Jackson	Speechless	2	F/-5
Electronic dance music:	Moby	Lift Me Up (2006 Remaster)	10	F/-5
	Ocean Lab	Sirens of the Sea (Above and Beyond Club Remix)	0	M/-5
Choir music:	Grex Vocalis	E. Grieg: Hvad est du dog skjøn	10	F/+ 5
	Oslo Kammerkor	Ned i vester i soli glader	3	F/+ 5
Indie pop:	Coldplay	Yes	1	F/+ 5
	Kashmir	The Aftermath	7	M/+ 5
Classical:	J. Sibelius	Symphony nr. 7 (from start)	11	M/ + 5
	F. Chopin	Nocturne nr. 2, op. 29, andante	3	M/-5
Electronica:	Björk	Hidden Place	5	M/+ 5
Film score:	Hans Zimmer	Time ("Inception")	3	M/-5
Rap:	Timbuktu	Plotten Tjoknar	8	F/+ 5
Jazz:	Clockwork	Valseri	7	F/+ 5
Reggae:	Kultiration	Harmoni	4	M/+ 5
Afghan pop:	Moein	Bahaneh	16	F/-5

two categories (having both ascending melodic lines or pitch movements and especially high pitches). Several other identified places also include more than one musical feature. Seven identified places lacked any distinct musical feature and have not been categorized. Some of the respondents have pressed the button several times during short time spans (5–10 s.) increasing the number of M.E.s connected to the same musical features.

Compared to the straightforward recording of marker entries, there are several more elements of uncertainty connected to the recording of skin conductance [17]. The electric flow within human tissue does not behave homogenously. It is influenced by skin conditions and reactionary patterns of the individual. The skin conductance data of some of the respondents were, for example, very sensitive to movement, while other's were not (a correlation that was exposed by the sensor's accelerometer). The baseline level that is often used as a starting point in skin conductance measuring was also difficult to use, since the activity of music listening itself in most cases influenced the skin conductance level considerably.

Table 2. Overview of musical features present in the music at the places where the respondents reported a physical reaction by pressing the sensor button. The marker entries (M.E.) show the total number of places, while the Resp.-colon shows the number of discrete respondents (since many reported several times during the same music). The M.S.C. shows the mean number of corresponding increase in skin conductance levels.

Musical feature	M.E.	Resp.	M.S.C.
Ascending melodic lines or pitch movements	48	15	1.9
High pitches	39	14	1.6
Crescendos	31	9	1.7
Rhythmic groove	15	5	0.8
Entrance of new element	14	8	1.4
Increased rhythmic density	13	7	1.3
Musical theme	10	7	1.4
Sudden rhythmic break	9	5	1.0
Return to earlier element	5	3	2.2
Decrescendos	4	2	2.0
Descending melodic lines	3	1	1.6
Rhythmic displacement	2	2	1.0

Nevertheless, there were several cases of clear correspondence between a self-reported marker entry and considerable increase in skin conductance level. To obtain a systematic result, all the places where the respondents had pushed the sensor button were graded from 0 to 3 – with 0 meaning no increase and 3 meaning a considerable increase. This grading was based on the increase in microsiemens = μs in relation to the mean level of 10 s. Preceding and succeeding the marker entry. The result showed primarily to what extent the skin conductance data matched the marker entries for the various respondents and gave us an indication of how reliable the skin conductance data was for the 24 individuals. These findings were subsequently used to evaluate the results of the second part of this study (Table 3).

The grading of the corresponding increase in skin conductance levels was also used to study differences in relation to the musical features. The result is displayed above in Table 2 (M.S.C.). Slightly smaller numbers for the features connected to groove and rhythm was the most significant finding.

Table 3. Overview of the degree of correspondence between marker entries and the increase of skin conductance levels.

Correspondence	Total	Female	Male
Mean number between 2.5 and 3.0 (very good correspondence)	3	2	1
Mean number between 2.0 and 2.4 (good correspondence)	5	1	4
Mean number between 1.5 and 1.9 (some good matches)	4	2	2
Mean number between 1.0 and 1.4 (a few good matches)	6	4	2
Mean number between 0.5 and 0.9 (bad correspondence or deficient readings)	2	1	1
Mean number between 0.0 and 0.4 (very bad correspondence or deficient readings)	3	2	1

The figure below shows a very clear example of correspondence between increase in skin conductance level and marker entries. The respondent (male 21) has pushed the sensor button as many as eight times during a period of 22 s while the skin conductance level gradually increases from 3.4 μs up to 4.9 μs. The self-selected music is Celine Dion's *My Heart Will Go On*, and the section (from 3:17 to 3:39) where this occurs includes a modulation up a major third (from C# minor to F minor), an ascending melody played by a flute and a powerful crescendo (Fig. 1).

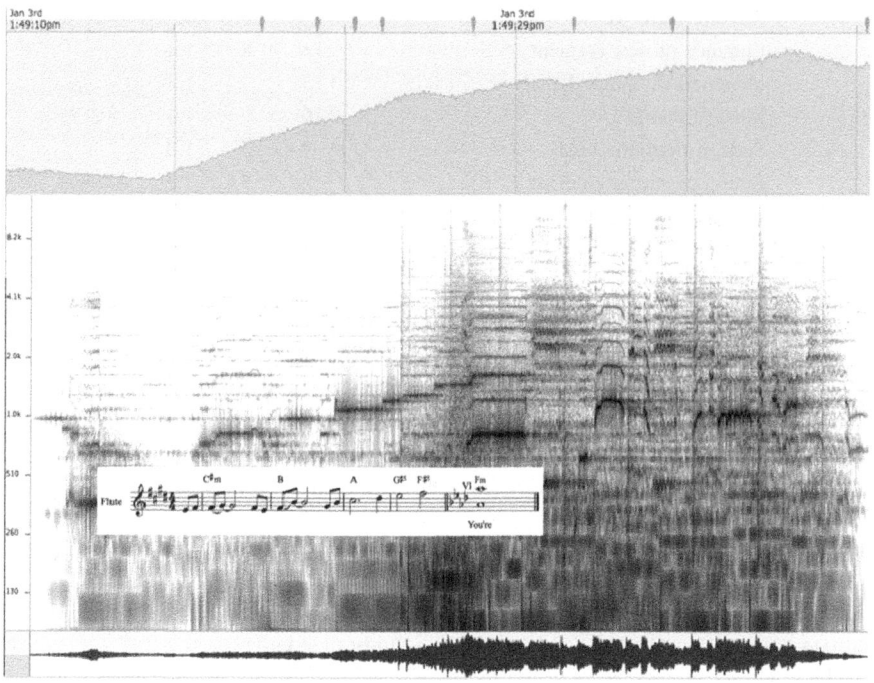

Fig. 1. On top is an excerpt from the display of skin conductance data from the Q software. Below are a sonogram and an amplitude presentation from Celine Dion's *My Heart Will Go On* (3:17–3:39). Eight marker entries are displayed above the skin conductance data. An ascending melody played by a flute is present from around 800 Hz and up to 2 kHz in the sonogram and is displayed also with inserted notation. A crescendo is seen around the middle of the figure in both the sonogram and the amplitude presentation.

3.2 Pre-prepared Track

21 of the 24 respondents (87.5 %) pushed the sensor button during listening to the pre-prepared track. Four of these had pushed the button twice, while the rest (71 %) had more than two entries. The three respondents who did not have any marker entries did neither have many for their self-selected music (M = 1).

Six places or passages on the pre-prepared track were identified through the concentration of marker entries from the various respondents. These places were checked for increase in skin conductance level for all respondents (also for those who had not pushed the sensor button), and – similar to the procedure with the self-selected music – they were graded from 0 to 3 according to the amount of increase. The skin conductance measuring collapsed for five of the respondents at some point during the listening of the pre-prepared track making the total number of respondents gradually smaller (Table 4).

Table 4. Overview of the six places/passages in the pre-prepared track where the highest numbers of respondents pushed the marker button. The M.E.-colon shows the number of marker entries. The following M.S.C.-colon shows the mean number of increase in skin conductance for the places where marker entries have been entered. The S.C.inc.-colon shows the number of respondents that had an increase in skin conductance level (+ the total number of respondents). The second M.S.C-colon shows the mean number of increase in the total number of increase-cases and the Corr.-colon shows the number of correspondences between marker entries and increase in SC-levels.

Music – place/passage	M.E.	M.S.C.	S.C.inc.	M.S.C.	Corr.
1. Christel Alsos: *Finding Gold* (0:22–0:27)	8	0.8	11 (T:22)	1.5	6
2. Christel Alsos: *Finding Gold* (0:46–0:52)	9	1.3	12 (T:22)	1.5	6
3. Christel Alsos: *Finding Gold* (1:18–1:25)	6	1.7	8 (T:22)	2.1	5
4. Gustav Mahler: *Adagietto* (0:34–0:40)	7	1.0	9 (T:21)	1.4	6
5. Sigur Rós: *Varúð* (2:58–3:03)	14	1.1	8 (T:21)	2.1	7
6. Josh Groban: *You Raise Me Up* (3:16–3:20)	5	1.4	10 (T:19)	1.9	3

4 Musical Analysis

The following analysis is an attempt to expose the most significant musical features of the eight passages as to why they have been selected by the respondents.

4.1 Christel Alsos: *Finding Gold* (0:22–0:27 and 0:46–0:52)

This song has a simple rhythmic foundation of tuned toms and repeated piano chords. The Norwegian female singer is recorded and mixed very close so that details like her intakes of breath are heard very clearly. In both passage 1 and 2 she sings an ascending stepwise melodic line twice that ends with a portamento up to the note A. This note is held with a modest vibrato. The line is song twice with different lyrics in both passages. The second passage has a bass guitar, a cymbal and – most prominent – a second voice that adds more harmonies and support to the ascending melodic line. The marker entries and increases in skin conductance levels are mostly found during the last sustained note of this melodic line. Five (21 %) of the respondents reported that they had heard the song before.

Musical features: Ascending melodic line and pitch movement (portamento) and high notes (Fig. 2).

Fig. 2. An ascending melodic line from the verse of Christel Alsos: *Finding Gold* (0:21–0:26).

4.2 Christel Alsos: *Finding Gold* (1:18–1:25)

The chorus of *Finding Gold* is an ascending movement of a melodic motive with ascending intervals. Strings and el. guitar is added to the arrangement and a slow gradual crescendo builds up to the highest pitch (G). The song returns to the verse with a sudden decrescendo. The marker entries and increases in skin conductance levels are mostly found during the last sustained note and at the decrescendo.

Musical features: Ascending melodic line, high notes, crescendo, decrescendo and increased rhythmic density (Fig. 3).

Fig. 3. The vocal line of the chorus of Christel Alsos: *Finding Gold* (1:03–1:22).

4.3 Gustav Mahler: *Adagietto* (Bar 4–6) (0:34–0:40)

This is probably Mahler's most famous orchestra music, and it is often used in studies to represent typical sad music [18, 19]. It has a very slow tempo and the passage in question has an ascending melodic line played legato by strings stepwise from G and up to a sustained C (chord: F/3), before a repeated C takes us further up to a sustained D (chord: Fm6/3) while the bass descends a semitone (from A to Ab). The marker entries and increases in skin conductance levels are mostly found during or soon after the second sustained high note. Seven (29 %) of the respondents reported that they had heard this music before.

Musical features: Ascending melodic line and high notes (Fig. 4).

Fig. 4. The principle line from Gustav Mahler: *Adagietto* (bar 4–6) (ca. 0:30–0:40).

4.4 Sigur Rós: *Varúð* (2:58–3:03)

Varúð (transl.; Caution) is a 6.30 min long song by the Icelandic group Sigur Rós. It is slow and atmospheric and has a long build-up section towards the end. The male vocalist often uses a self-invented unintelligible language (Vonlenska), but this song is in standard Icelandic. He uses falsetto voice the whole time. The passage in question is a typical climax point with a distinct crescendo and an ascending melodic movement supported by an ascending chord progression (G♭ – A♭ – B♭m), performed by vocals, strings and various keyboard/synthesizer sounds. The melodic climb is executed with clear portamento effects and mixed with a lot of reverb and echo (both visible on the sonogram) (Fig. 5).

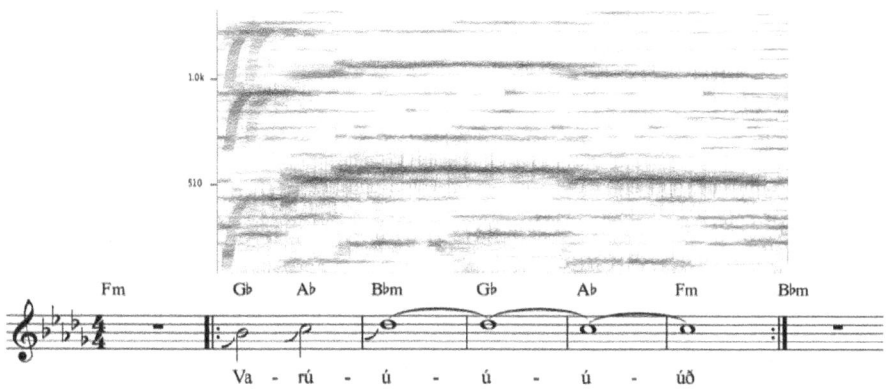

Fig. 5. A sonogram and notation of the chorus of Sigur Rós: *Varúð* (2:52–3:26). The portamentos up to the first pitch can be seen at the start of the sonogram.

While only the first and third beats of the bar is marked in the ascend, all four are marked when it has reached the highest pitch. In a review of the album, journalist Wyndham Wallace writes; "The album's highlight is Varúð, an elegiac, spectral hymn whose chorus ascends heavenwards in the traditional Sigur Rós manner" [20]. The marker entries and increases in skin conductance levels are mostly found in the section that follows the ascend. Nine (39 %) of the respondents reported that they had heard the song before.

Musical features: Ascending melody and pitch movement, crescendo, high notes, and increased rhythmic density.

4.5 Josh Groban: *You Raise Me up* (3:17)

This song is written by the Norwegian composer and songwriter Rolf Løvland and is often used in weddings, funerals and similar occasions. The most famous version is the recording by the American singer Josh Groban from 2003, with piano, strings, bass and a solo fiddle during the first part of the song. The passage in question is the beginning of the last chorus. At this point the song seems to end with a traditional closure, but then continues with full power, introducing drums and a choir, while modulating up a semitone. The chorus starts with an ascending melodic line, and the highest pitch (F#) is established also by an arpeggiated harp-chord (as can be seen circled in the sonogram below) (Fig. 6).

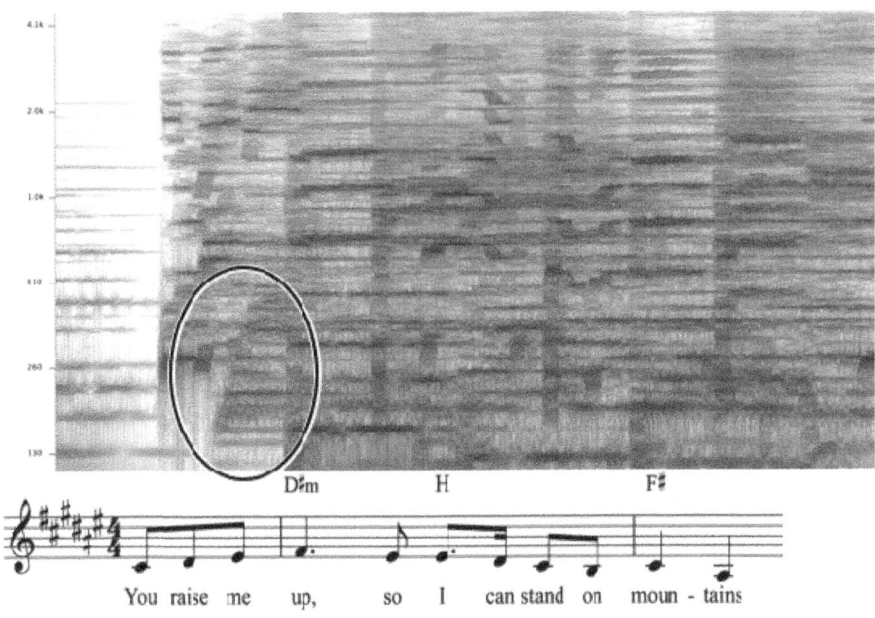

Fig. 6. A sonogram and notation of the last chorus of Josh Groban: *You Raise Me Up* (3:12–3:22). In the sonogram the arpeggiated harp-chord is circled.

The marker entries and increases in skin conductance levels are mostly found right after the ascend have reached the highest pitch (F#). All but one respondent reported that they had heard the song before.

Musical features: Ascending melody, arpeggio, crescendo, entrance of new element and high notes.

5 Discussion

The engagement of the motor system has been suggested as having an important role in music listening [21], but it is not often brought into discussions on music and emotions. In his influential book *Emotion and Meaning in Music* from 1956, Leonard Meyer included a subchapter on motor behaviour, but concluded that no special attention was needed since he saw it merely as a product of mental activity [22]. More recent contributions to the interdisciplinary field of embodied cognition have offered theoretical bases where the influence of the body on cognitive activity is taken into consideration [23]. These suggest an interdependent relationship between music perception and corporeal movement. They offer explanations for the dynamic system of rhythmic entrainment [24, 25], processes of imitation and gesturing in music [26], and the metaphoric relation between up and down in music and actual vertical directions [27–29].

There is no actual up or down in the acoustic musical signal we perceive, thus, the understanding of directions in music lies somehow in our "intellectual" understanding [30]. The metaphor theory of linguist George Lakoff and philosopher Mark Johnson suggests that our understanding of basic metaphors (such as up and down) is shaped through corporeal experiences [28]. Motor schemas and image schemas are formed when we sense correspondences between, for example, an ascending pitch-movement and an upward movement. Thus, the "intellectual" understanding of directions in music can be deeply influenced by and fundamentally connected to corporeal up- and down-movements.

Alicia Peñalba Acitores argues for proprioception as a bodily source of our perceptual awareness of musical material. She questions especially the connection between the up-down schema and musical pitch, and claims that "going up and down with melodies, travelling along a path with themes" are some of the actions music offers [31].

Proprioception is our sensing of the position and the movements of our body. We have receptors in muscles, skin and in our inner ear that provides the brain continuously with information on the state of our body. When we listen to music, contractions and relaxations of muscles, subtle corporeal movements and even small changes in our breathing patterns are sensed by our proprioceptive system. This information most likely influences our experience. An ascending melodic line may coincide with an inhale and a contraction of muscles that last until a high note is released or the music continues with a descend.

The focus on musical expectancy in the literature on music and emotions has been considerable [22, 32, 33]. But how emotional tension has been caused by expected musical continuation that has either been fulfilled or violated, has been theorized without discussions of the involvement of the body. A corporeal tension building may work within the same basis of expectancy, but by bringing in the proprioceptive system, an important link between the human motor system and our emotions may be identified.

The results of this study do not directly imply that corporeal engagement has been activated. Muscle activity or movement patterns were not investigated. But the magnitude of ascending melodies or pitch movements connected to physical reactions can be explained through the presence of a body in the listening situation – a body that experiences the directions in music through muscular tension and relaxation.

The examples from the pre-prepared track not only have ascending melodies; the portamentos (4.1, 4.4) and the arpeggio (4.5) also communicate a strong sense of direction upwards. Contrary to setting the pitch directly, the glide upwards may help to bring the listener up to the higher pitch. Mark Johnson describes the tension felt when listening to the ascending octave leap in Judy Garland's performance of "(Somewhere) Over the Rainbow" [29]. She glides from the lower note up to the higher in a slow, continuous movement. Moreover, the crescendo (4.2, 4.4, 4.5) is associated with vertical directions, as well (low and high volume). It corresponds systematically in the examples with gradually higher volume following ascending melodies or pitch movements.

It can be argued that the musical excerpts from the pre-prepared track were specifically chosen to produce particular bodily sensations, and that other music would have produced other results. These excerpts could have been tested side-by-side with other musical features to compare the effects. However, there were several passages without ascending melodic lines in the pre-prepared track and the magnitude of marker entries found at places with similar musical features in the self-selected material demonstrates their significance. Several of the places marked by the respondents are in many ways similar to the passages in the pre-prepared track with ascending melodic lines or pitch movements, high notes, and crescendo effects. Interestingly, these range across a multitude of very different musical genres; ex; Björk: *Hidden Place* 0:50–0:52, Celine Dion: *My Heart Will Go On* 3:15–3:32, Nickelback: *Lullaby* 0:07, Dream Theater: *The Count of Tuscany* 2:28–2:36, Guns'n'Roses: *Sweet Child o' Mine* 4:03–4:08, Grex Vocalis: *Hvad est du dog skjøn* 3:25–3:36, Moein: *Bahaneh* 2:37–2:45.

The introduction of a random ascending melodic line will of course not guarantee any form of reaction. Music is a highly complex form of communication with many aspects involved, and composers and performers have to know how to push the right buttons. Furthermore, since the experience of directions in music is formed through a lifelong involvement with music, the result is highly individual [34]. Nevertheless, as I argue here, corporeal engagement in music listening may stand as a common foundation for, at least, how many humans react, and may also have a vital role when music causes intense emotional experiences. To better understand these processes, the combination of perception and proprioception should be taken into consideration.

References

1. Goldstein, A.: Thrills in response to music and other stimuli. Physiol. Psychol. **18**, 126–129 (1980)
2. Panksepp, J.: The emotional sources of "chills" induced by music. Music Percept. **13**(2), 171–207 (1995)
3. Gabrielson, A.: Strong experiences with music. In: Juslin, P.N., Sloboda, J.A. (eds.) Handbook of Music and Emotion: Theory, Research and Applications, pp. 547–574. Oxford University Press, Oxford (2010)

4. Rickard, N.S.: Intense emotional responses to music: a test of the psychological arousal hypothesis. Psychol. Music **32**, 371–388 (2004)
5. Guhn, M., Hamm, A., Zentner, M.: Physiological and musico-acoustic correlates of the chill response. Music Percept. **24**, 473–483 (2007)
6. Grewe, O., Kopiez, R., Altenmüller, E.: Chills as an indicator of individual emotional peaks. Ann. N.Y. Acad. Sci. **1169**, 351–354 (2009)
7. Juslin, P.N., Liljeström, S., Västfjäll, D., Lundqvist, L.-O.: How does music evoke emotions? exploring the underlying mechanisms. In: Juslin, P.N., Sloboda, J.A. (eds.) Handbook of Music and Emotion: Theory, Research and Applications, pp. 605–642. Oxford University Press, Oxford (2010)
8. Sloboda, J.A.: Musical structure and emotional response: some empirical findings. Psychol. Music **19**, 110–120 (1991)
9. Salimpoor, V.N., Benovoy, M., Larcher, K., Dagher, A., Zatorre, R.J.: Anatomically distinct dopamine release during anticipation and experience of peak emotion to music. Nat. Neurosci. **14**, 257–262 (2011)
10. Cooke, D.: The Language of Music. Oxford University Press, Oxford (1959)
11. Kivy, P.: The Corded Shell: Reflections on Musical Expression. Princeton University Press, Princeton (1980)
12. Meyer, L.: Music and emotions: distinctions and uncertainties. In: Juslin, P.N., Sloboda, J.A. (eds.) Music and Emotion: Theory and Research, pp. 341–360. Oxford University Press, Oxford (2001)
13. Eitan, Z.: Highpoints: A Study of Melodic Peaks. University of Pennsylvania Press, Philadelphia (1997)
14. Solberg, R.T.: Waiting for the bass to drop: correlations between intense emotional experiences and production techniques in build-up and drop sections of electronic dance music. Dancecult: J. Electron. Dance Music Culture **6**(1), 61–82 (2014)
15. Waterman, M.: Emotional responses to music: implicit and explicit effects in listeners and performers. Psychol. Music **24**(1), 53–67 (1996)
16. Schubert, E.: Modelling perceived emotion with continuous musical features. Music Percept. **21**(4), 561–568 (2004)
17. Grimnes, S., Martinsen, Ø.G.: Bioimpedance and Bioelectricity Basics, 2nd edn. Academic Press, Oxford (2008)
18. Gomez, P., Danuser, B.: Relationships between musical structure and psychophysiological measures of emotion. Emotion **7**(2), 377–387 (2007)
19. Riener, C.R., Stefanucci, J.K., Proffitt, D.R., Clore, G.: An effect of mood on the perception of geographical slant. Cogn. Emot. **25**(1), 174–182 (2011)
20. Wallace, W.: Sigur Rós Valtari Review. BBC Review (2012). http://www.bbc.co.uk/music/reviews/4z8r
21. Zatorre, R.J., Chen, J.L., Penhune, V.B.: When the brain plays music: auditory-motor interactions in music perception and production. Nat. Rev. Neurosci. **8**, 547–558 (2007)
22. Meyer, L.B.: Emotion and Meaning in Music. The University of Chicago Press, Chicago (1956)
23. Shapiro, L.: Embodied Cognition. Routledge Press, New York (2011)
24. Thelen, E., Smith, L.B.: A Dynamic Systems Approach to the Development of Cognition and Action. The MIT Press, Cambridge (1994)
25. Kelso, J.A.S.: Dynamic Patterns: The Self-Organization of Brain and Behaviour. The MIT Press, Cambridge (1995)
26. Godøy, R.I., Leman, M.: Musical Gestures: Sound, Movement, and Meaning. Routledge Press, New York (2010)

27. Lakoff, G., Johnson, M.: Metaphors We Live By. The University of Chicago Press, Chicago and London (1980)
28. Lakoff, G., Johnson, M.: Philosophy in the Flesh: The Embodied Mind and Its Challenge to Western Thought. Basic Books, New York (1999)
29. Johnson, M.: The Meaning of the Body: Aesthetics of Human Understanding. The University of Chicago Press, Chicago and London (2007)
30. Cox, A.W.: The mimetic hypothesis and embodied musical meaning. Music Sci. **5**(2), 195–212 (2001)
31. Acitores, A.P.: Towards a theory of proprioception as a bodily basis for consciousness in music. In: Clarke, D., Clarke, E. (eds.) Music and Consciousness: Philosophical, Psychological, and Cultural Perspectives, pp. 215–230. Oxford University Press, Oxford (2011)
32. Huron, D.: Sweet Anticipation: Music and the Psychology of Expectation. The MIT Press, Cambridge (2006)
33. Huron, D., Margulis, E.H.: Musical expectancy and thrills. In: Juslin, P.N., Sloboda, J.A. (eds.) Handbook of Music and Emotion: Theory, Research and Applications, pp. 605–642. Oxford University Press, Oxford (2010)
34. Walker, R.: The effects of culture, environment, age, and musical training on choices of visual metaphors for sound. Percept. Psychophys. **42**(5), 491–502 (1987)

σGTTM III: Learning-Based Time-Span Tree Generator Based on PCFG

Masatoshi Hamanaka[1](✉), Keiji Hirata[2], and Satoshi Tojo[3]

[1] Kyoto University, Kyoto 606-8501, Japan
hamanaka@kuhp.kyoto-u.ac.jp
[2] Future University Hakodate, Hakodate, Japan
hirata@fun.ac.jp
[3] JAIST - Japan Advanced Institute of Science and Technology,
1-1 Asahidai, Nomi, Ishikawa 923-1292, Japan
tojo@jaist.ac.jp
http://gttm.jp/

Abstract. An automatic analyzer based on the generative theory of tonal music (GTTM) for acquiring a time-span tree is described. Although an analyzer based on GTTM was previously reported, it requires manually manipulating 46 adjustable parameters on a computer screen in order to analyze a time-span tree properly. We reformalized the time-span reduction in GTTM on the basis of a probabilistic model called probabilistic context-free grammar, which enables acquiring the most likely time-span tree. Applying leave-one-out cross validation over 300 datasets revealed that the new analyzer outperformed our previously developed GTTM analyzer.

Keywords: Generative theory of tonal music (GTTM) · Probabilistic context-free grammar (PCFG) · Time-span tree · Automatic time-span tree analyzer (ATTA) · Full-automatic time-span tree analyzer (FATTA) · σGTTM

1 Introduction

This article describes a method for automatically generating a time-span tree based on the generative theory of tonal music (GTTM) [16]. The methods main advantage is that it is based on probabilistic context-free grammar (PCFG) [1] and therefore enables acquiring a model that makes it possible to generate a time-span tree by statistically learning training data that has been analyzed manually by a musicologist.

Generally, a piece of music will have more than one interpretation, and such ambiguity is a major obstacle when implementing music theory on a computer. A probabilistic model is suitable for constructing a music analyzer that handles such ambiguity. In other words, introducing a probabilistic model into a musical analyzer enables comparing the likelihood of one interpretation to other interpretations. One such probabilistic model we introduce here is PCFG, which is used for syntactic analysis of natural language.

This model consists of multiple production rules, each of which is associated with a probability. The probability of a sentence is derived from the product of the probabilities of applied rules for generating the sentence. Finding a rule set that can generate the sentence is called "parsing," and a tree structure that indicates the parse result is called a "parse tree."

The time-span tree is a result of analysis by GTTM, which is a binary tree in which each leaf connects a note lined in time order. Each non-terminal node between the root and leaves has labels that indicate which note is salient between two notes that connect directly to the node. Therefore, a time-span tree can acquire a reduced melody by omitting non-salient notes.

A time-span tree is a "reduction tree" (and required to be binary, by GTTM), in that the terminal nodes correspond to individual notes, and the non-terminal nodes are represented by the note that is structurally more salient between the notes associated with the two child nodes. By picking up the notes at intermediate levels, we obtain a "reduced melody" of the original.

In this study, we regard the time-span tree as a parse tree of a melody. Because parsing and generating are inverse processes, we can generate a melody by using PCFG. In other words, after generating a melody by PCFG, the reduction process is an inverse problem of the generation. The probabilities of the PCFG rules are learned by using training data that had been analyzed manually by a musicologist after setting 645 PCFG rules.

Then we calculated the probability of each parse tree of all the well-formed time-span trees and selected the tree with the maximum probability value as a solution to the inverse problem. We applied leave-one-out cross validation over 300 datasets. The results indicated an average accuracy of 0.76, which outperformed our previously developed GTTM analyzer.

2 Related Work

We briefly look back on cognitive music theories and our constructed GTTM music analyzers. The implication-realization model (IRM) proposed by Eugene Narmour abstracts and expresses music according to symbol sequences derived from musical scores [20,21]. Recently, IRM has been implemented on computer and can be used to acquire the chain structures of IRM from a score [27]. Schenkerian analysis is used to analyze the deeper structures called "Urlinie" (fundamental line) and "Ursatz" (fundamental structure) from the music surface [24]. Short segments of music can be analyzed using Schenkerian analysis on a computer [18]. Other music theories suited for computer implementation have also been proposed [15,26].

The main advantage of analysis by GTTM is that it can acquire the tree structures called time-span and prolongation trees. The time-span and prolongation trees provide a summarization of a piece of music, which can be used as the representation of an abstraction [11]. It can also be used for performance rendering [10] and reproducing music [12]. Additionally, the time-span tree can be used for melody prediction [5] and melody morphing [6].

Some other studies have applied PCFG to analyze music, for example, chord analysis for jazz [2], analysis of the metrical structure [25], and automatic transcription [13]. These studies [2,13,25] show the usefulness of using PCFG in musical analysis. GTTM [16] has a concept of reduction that is an inverse process of generation; however, no one has yet regarded a time-span tree as a parse tree or estimated the most likely time-span tree.

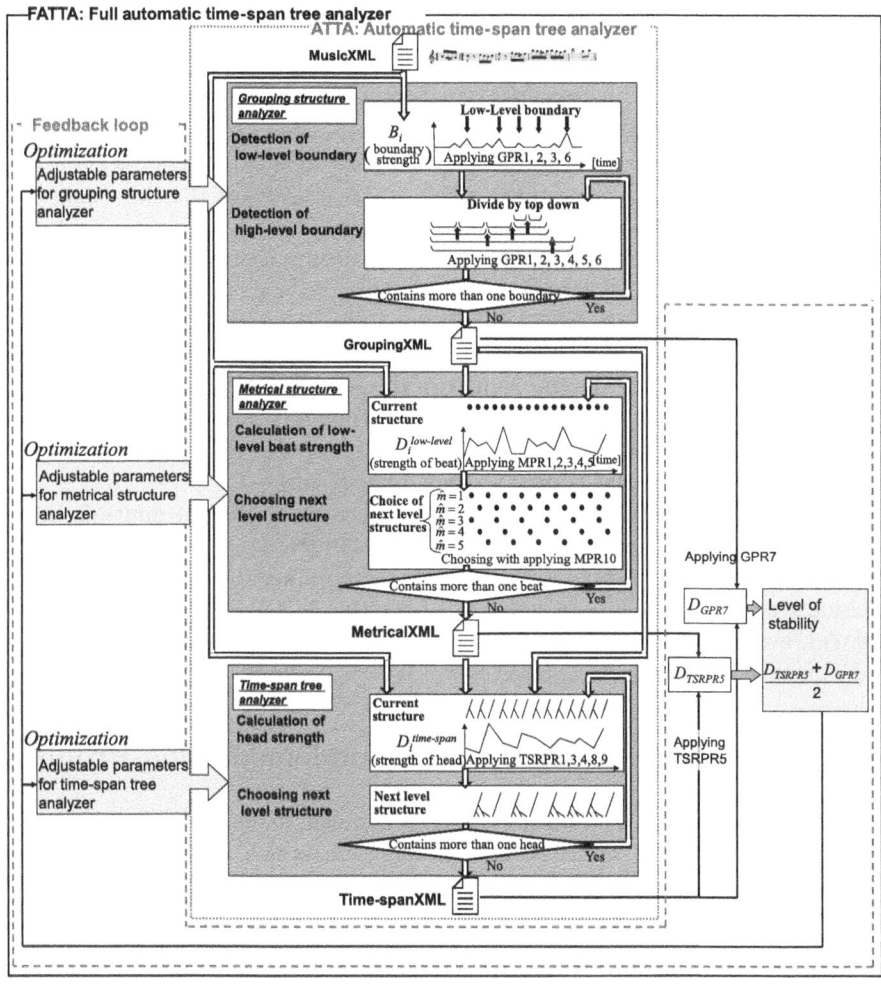

Fig. 1. Processing flow of ATTA and FATTA.

We constructed four types of GTTM analyzers: ATTA, FATTA, σGTTM, and σGTTMII. Figure 1 shows the processing flow of ATTA and FATTA. We extended the original theory of GTTM with a full externalization and parameterization and proposed a machine-executable extension of GTTM called exGTTM [3]. The externalization includes introducing an algorithm to generate a hierarchical structure of the time-span tree in a mixed top-down and bottom-up manner, and the parameterization includes introducing a parameter for controlling the priorities of rules in order to avoid conflict among the rules, as well as parameters for controlling the shape of the hierarchical time-span tree. We implemented exGTTM on a computer called ATTA (automatic time-span tree analyzer), which can output multiple analysis results by configuring the parameters.

Although ATTA has adjustable parameters for controlling the weight or priority of each rule, these parameters have to be set manually. This takes a long time because finding the optimal values of the settings themselves takes a long time. We discuss the problem of ATTA in detail in Sect. 3.3.

FATTA (full-automatic time-span tree analyzer) can automatically estimate the optimal parameters by introducing a feedback loop from higher-level structures to lower-level structures on the basis of the stability of the time-span tree [4]. Without manual configuration FATTA can output only one analysis result, which makes its performance insufficient for analyzing time-span trees.

We also developed σGTTM, a system that can detect the local grouping boundaries in GTTM analysis, by combining GTTM with statistical learning [19]. The σGTTM system statistically learns the priority of GTTM rules from 100 sets of scores and grouping structure data analyzed by a musicologist; it does this by using a decision tree [22]. Its performance results are good for most of the pieces but very insufficient for some. It can construct only one decision tree from 100 datasets and cannot output other results.

The σGTTM II system assumes that a piece of music has multiple interpretations, and thus it constructs multiple decision trees (each corresponding to an interpretation) by iteratively clustering the training data and training the decision trees. The system outperformed both the ATTA and σGTTM systems [14]. However, σGTTM and σGTTM II are only suitable for grouping structures and cannot acquire time-span trees.

3 Time-Span Reduction and Its Implementation Problem

We use the grouping and metrical structures of music to derive a time-span tree. Figure 2 illustrates how metrical and grouping structures, and time-span trees are graphically presented for a given note sequence.

The grouping structure is intended to formalize the intuitive belief that tonal music is organized into groups that are in turn composed of subgroups. These groups are graphically presented as several levels of arcs below a music staff. The metrical structure describes the rhythmic hierarchy of the piece by identifying the position of strong beats at different levels such as those of a quarter note, half note, a measure, two measures, and four measures. Strong beats are illustrated as several levels of "dots" below the musical staff. The time-span tree is a binary tree, which is a hierarchical structure describing the relative structural importance of notes that differentiate the essential parts of the melody from the ornamentation. For example, the left side of Fig. 3 depicts a simple note sequence and its tree. The time span (designated as ←—→) is represented by a single note, called a head, which is designated here as "C4." In the tree, the salient notes are connected to a branch nearer to the root of the tree. In contrast, the nonsalient (ornament) notes are connected as a sub-tree. We hereafter call the "primary" (salient) notes the main tree and the "secondary" (nonsalient) notes the sub-tree (Fig. 4).

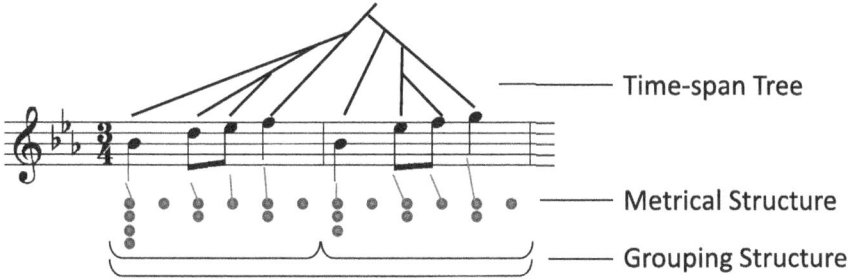

Fig. 2. Time-span tree, metrical structure, and grouping structure.

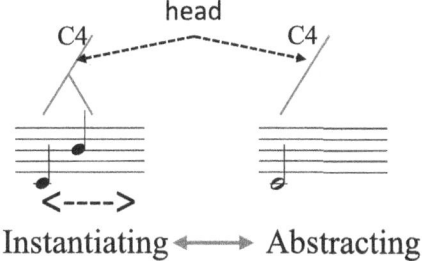

Fig. 3. Subsumption relation of melodies.

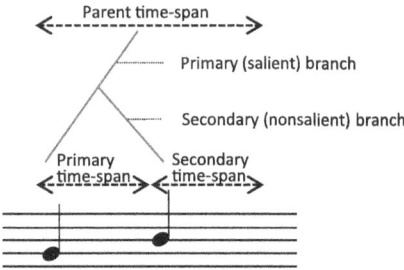

Fig. 4. Primary and secondary time-span trees.

3.1 Time-Span Segmentation

Before the time-span reduction, the time-span segmentation divides the entire piece into hierarchical time spans. We show the division procedure in Fig. 5, which involves the following steps:

1. Regard all of the resultant groups of grouping analysis as time spans.
2. Divide a time span into two spans before the strongest beat when a time span in the lowest level includes more than one note. When the strongest beat is the first note in the time span, divide the time span into two spans before the second strongest beat.
3. Repeat 2 recursively.

In [16], there are two rules for time-span segmentation, which are called segmentation rule 1 and segmentation rule 2. The former corresponds to (1) and the latter to (2).

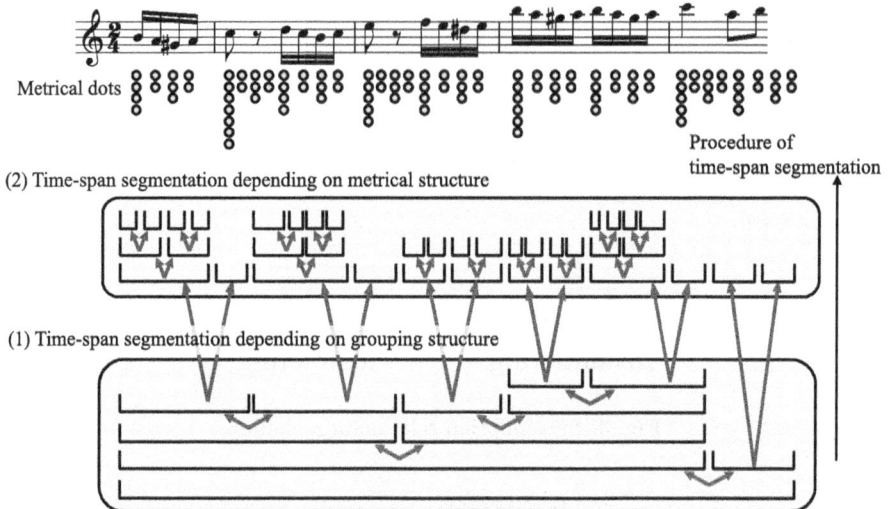

Fig. 5. Time-span segmentation.

3.2 Time-Span Reduction

As a result, a music piece is formed into a binary tree, at each node of which the more important branch extends upward as a head note. The selection of a head at each node is hierarchically computed from the lower level. Therefore, heads are selected from leaves to root branches.

Nine rules are defined for the time-span reduction preference rules that indicate superiority of one tree over another. These rules consist of local rules and global rules.

For example, both TSRPR1 and TSRPR5 are rules related to the metrical structure. However, TSRPR1 is a local rule and TSRPR5 is a more global rule.

> **TSRPR1 (Metrical Position)** Of the possible choices for the head of a time-span tree T, prefer a choice that is in a relatively strong metrical position.
> **TSRPR5 (Metrical Stability)** In choosing the head of a time span T, prefer a choice that results in a more stable choice of metrical structure.

The biggest problem when implementing time-span reduction on computer is that there is little information on how to combine local and global rules and how to construct hierarchical time span trees.

3.3 Problems of Time-Span Reduction in ATTA

Parameters must be adjusted to control the strength of each time-span preference rule in order to overcome the problem in Sect. 3.2. A hierarchical time-span tree is constructed by iterating the calculation of the plausibility of the head for the current heads and choosing the next level heads (Fig. 6).

However, the performance of time-span reduction in ATTA was not sufficient. We investigated some pieces of music for which the time-span reduction performance was not very good, and the results indicated that many of them had a weak beat that becomes a head (primary) near the leaves of the tree and a strong beat that becomes a head near the root of the tree.

Figure 7 is a typical example of a piece of music and analysis results for it provided by a musicologist. In GTTM, there are two time-span reduction preference rules for a metrical structure as described in Sect. 3.2. In this figure, circles indicate rules that are stated (near the root of the tree but not near the leaves of the tree) and x marks indicate those that are not stated. ATTA cannot perform well in songs where the importance of the rules differs depending on whether the branching is near the leaves or the root of the tree.

The essential cause of this problem is context dependency. That is, the information dealing with a time-span tree near the leaves and near the root is different in itself. For example, the metrical structure does not have any effect near the root of the tree as described in the previous paragraph. For another example, note information near the leaf is a single note and near the root is a chord.

We can consider two ways of managing the context dependency and solving the problem. The first one is to introduce a more adjustable parameter that enables us to control the strength of rules at each level of the time span. However, this idea is not practical because it is difficult to adjust each parameter manually. The second way is to introduce a probabilistic model that can learn the strength of rules at each level of the time span, as described in the next section.

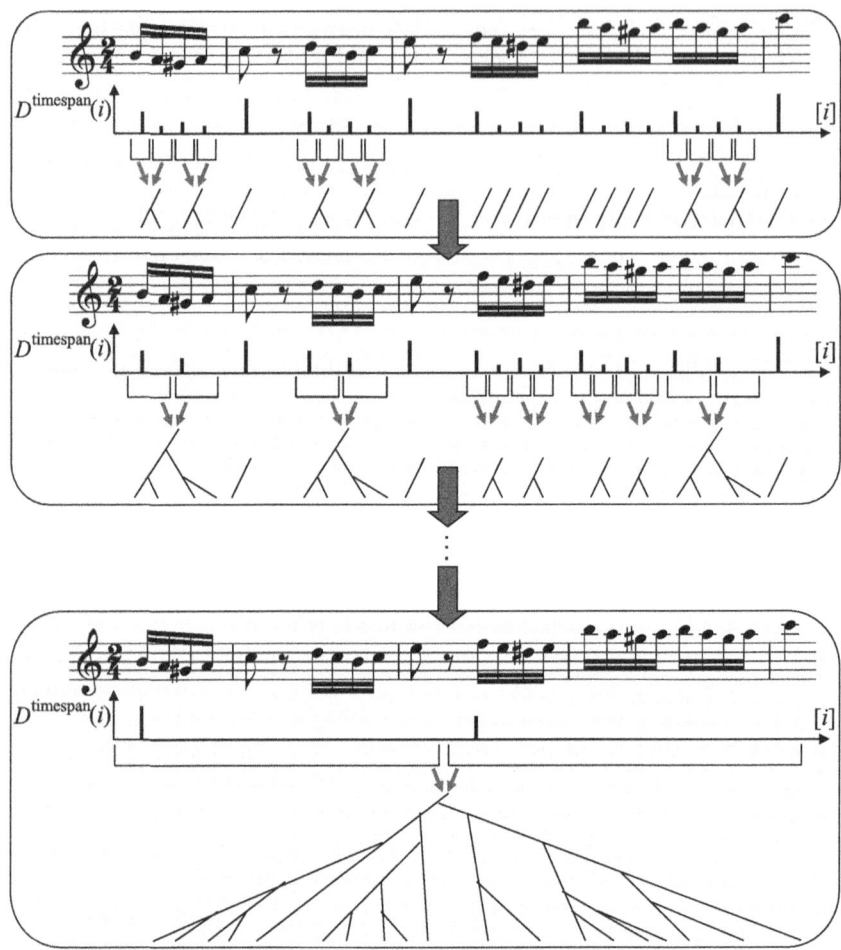

Fig. 6. Selecting the next-level heads in the time-span reduction.

4 σGTTMIII: Learning-Based Time-Span Tree Generator

In order to manage the context dependency, in this section we propose σGTTMIII, which introduces probabilistic context-free grammar that enables differential analysis depending on each level of the time span by properly using the rules of each level.

The time-span tree can extract a reduced melody by reducing ornament notes. An example of time-span reduction is shown in Fig. 8. The time-span tree in the figure is from melody A, which embodies the results of GTTM analyses. We can obtain a reduced melody B by slicing the tree in the middle and omitting

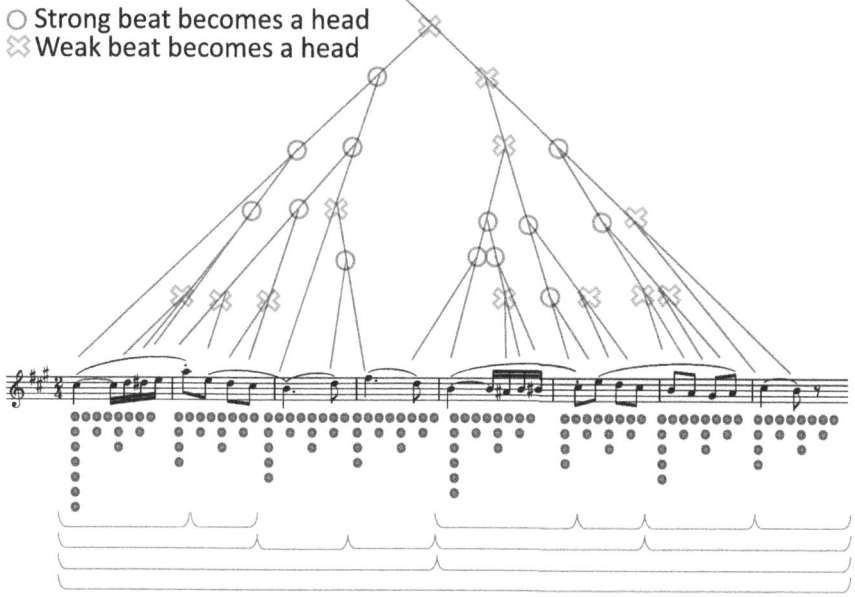

Fig. 7. Example of a piece that does not give good performance.

Fig. 8. Time-span reduction.

notes that are connected to branches under line B. In the same manner, if we slice the tree higher up at line C, we can get a more abstracted melody C.

If we apply this reduction process in the inverse direction, we can use it as a generation process as follows (Fig. 9).

1. Identify the note in which the time span (length) is the same as the whole piece of music.
2. Separate the time span of the note and make a primary note and a secondary note.
3. Repeat 2 recursively when a time span has more than one note.

By expressing the above generation process using a probabilistic model, we can acquire the most likely time-span tree.

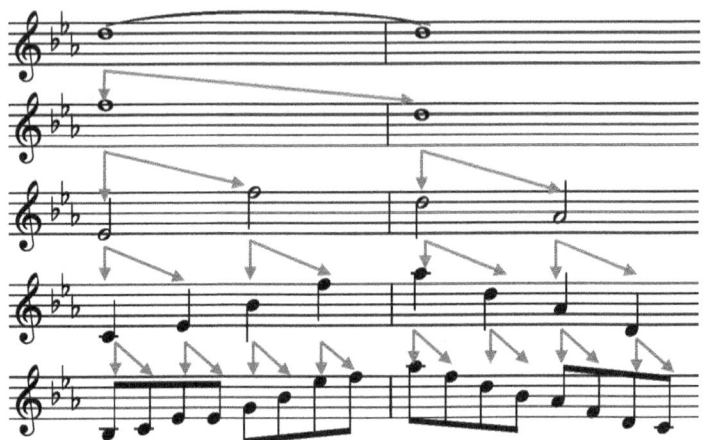

Fig. 9. Generation process of note sequence.

4.1 Training Data

The training data we used for the probabilistic model was a musical structural database based on GTTM that we constructed [8,16].

We collected 300 8-bar-long monophonic[1] classical music pieces that included notes, rests, slurs, accents, and articulations entered manually using music notation software called "Finale" [17]. We exported the MusicXML by using a plugin called "Dolet." The 300 pieces and 8 bars were selected by a musicologist [23].

We asked a musicology expert to manually analyze the score data faithfully with regard to GTTM by using the manual editor in the GTTM analysis tool (Fig. 10) in order to assist in editing the grouping structure, metrical structure, and time-span tree. Three other experts crosschecked these manually produced results.

The analyzer and database can be downloaded at http://www.gttm.jp/.

---

[1] Although the theory accepts homophonic music, we first restricted our target music to monophonic music. Recently, we attempted to develop a time-span tree analyzer for polyphonic music [7].

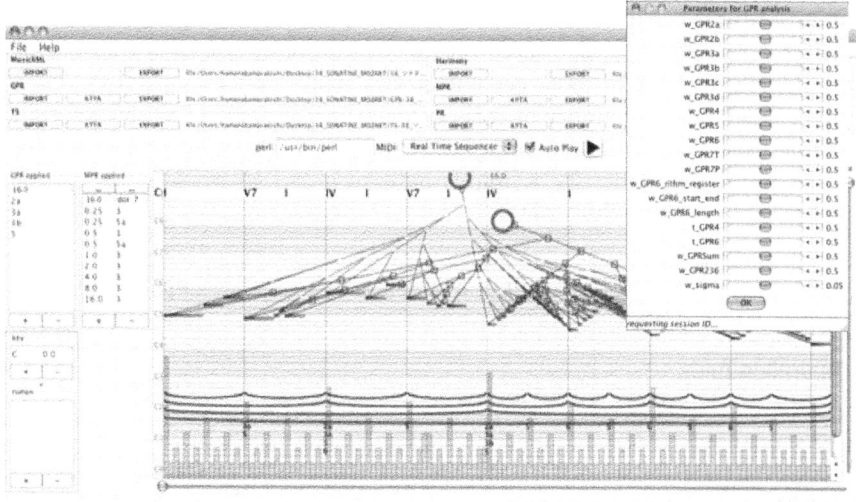

Fig. 10. Interactive GTTM analyzer.

4.2 PCFG Model for Generating Time-Span Tree

We introduce here a probabilistic context-free grammar (PCFG), which we used to construct a probabilistic generation model of a melody. The PCFG has multiple production rules with probabilities that can represent the separation of primary and secondary notes in each node of a time-span tree.

The PCFG of G can be defined by a quintuple:

$$G = \{T, M, S, R, P\} \tag{1}$$

where T is the set of terminal symbols, M is the set of non-terminal symbols, S is the start symbol, R is the set of production rules, and P is the set of probabilities on production rules.

T: terminal symbols. Notes are the terminal symbols.
M: non-terminal symbols. Time spans are the non-terminal symbols.
S: start symbol. The start symbol of PCFG is a time span that has the length of an entire piece of music without any rests, which means the length of the timespan of the whole piece.
R: production rules. There are two kinds of production rules. The first kind involves a time span from which two time spans are generated. There are several rules hat generate two time-spans from one time-span. We call this rule the time-span separation rule. The sum of the length of two time spans is the same as the length of the original time span. The second kind involves a time span to generate a note, which we call the note production rule. The length of the original time span and the length of the generated note are the same (Fig. 11).

***P*: probabilities of production rules.** Each production rule has a probability (Fig. 11). For example, the probability of generating a time span that has the length of the 32nd note generating the 32nd note is almost 1.00. On the other hand, the probability of generating a time span that has the length of a double note generating a double note is almost 0.00 because there are many other production rules for a double note such as two whole notes or a half note with a dotted whole note.

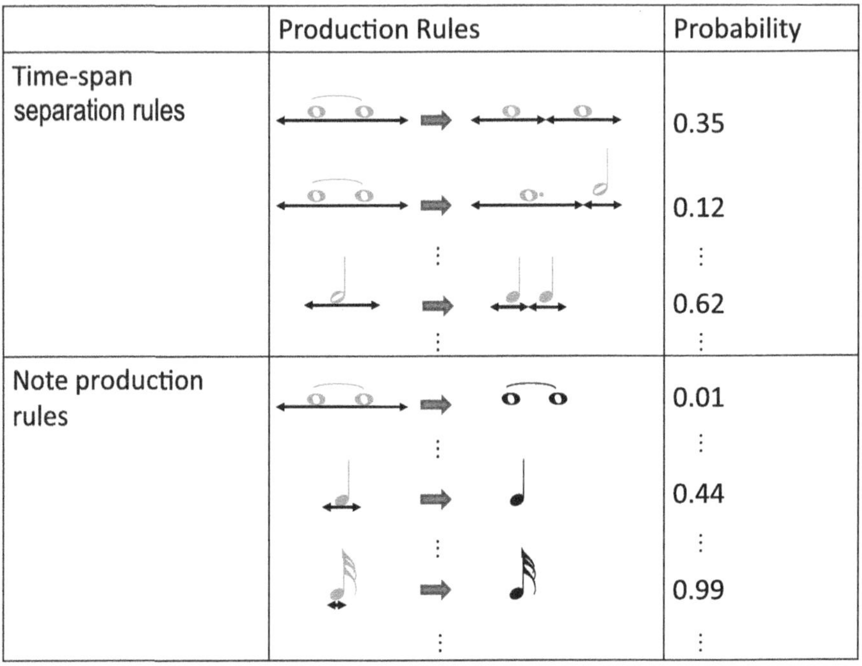

	Production Rules	Probability
Time-span separation rules		0.35
		0.12
	⋮	⋮
		0.62
	⋮	⋮
Note production rules		0.01
	⋮	⋮
		0.44
	⋮	⋮
		0.99
	⋮	⋮

Fig. 11. Examples of production rules and their probabilities.

4.3 Design Rules of PCFG for Generating Time-Span Tree

We have so far only discussed the length of a note in the basic PCFG model described in Sect. 4.2. Other relevant information is as follows.

Primary and secondary. When two time spans are generated according to the time-span separation rules, one becomes a primary time span and the other becomes a secondary time span.
Pitch. When the primary and secondary time spans are generated, the primary pitch will be inherited and the secondary pitch will be generated.
Order of time spans. There are two orders when primary and secondary time spans are generated. In one, the primary time span is before the secondary time span. In the other, the secondary time span is before the primary time span.

Numbers of dots. As described in Sect. 3.2, the metrical structure strongly affects the generation of the time span. Therefore, the numbers of dots in the primary and secondary time spans should be included in the model.

Use of the above information in the naive implementation of the rules of PCFG results in too many rules, and the probability of most of them is zero because we have limited numbers of training datasets. We solve this problem of space training data by abstracting the rules as follows.

3 types of pitch change. We graded the changes in the pitch of primary and secondary time spans as up, down, or the same.
7 types of duration ratio. We graded the length ratio of primary and secondary time spans as the one closest to 4 times, 3 times, 2 times, 1 time, 1/2 time, 1/3 time, and 1/4 time.
2 orders of time spans. One order is that the primary time span is before the secondary; the other is that the secondary time span is before the primary.
3 types of numbers of dots. We graded the dots of primary and secondary time spans in three groups: primary has more dots than secondary, secondary has more dots than primary, and primary and secondary have the same number of dots.
5 types of head time-span length. We graded the length of the time span before separating it into primary and secondary as the one closest to sixteenth, eighth, quarter, half, whole, and double time.

We established 645 PCFG rules in total, which consist of $630 (= 3 \times 7 \times 2 \times 3 \times 5)$ time-span separation rules and $15 (= 5 \times 3$ types of numbers of dots) note production rules.

4.4 Generation of Time-Span Tree by Using PCFG

The probability of each PCFG rule was achieved using supervised learning by counting 19,296 nodes of 300 time-span trees in our database. Calculating the production rule probabilities consists of three steps. First, calculate the frequencies at which the production rules appear. Then, sum the frequencies of production rules for which the length of the original time span is the same. Finally, as a normalization process, divide the probability of each production rule by the frequency of the rules by the summation of the frequencies of production rules for which the length of the original time span is the same.

After calculating the probability of each production rule, we were able to obtain the most likely time-span tree for each music piece by calculating the probability of each parse tree of all the well-formed time-span trees and selecting the tree with the maximum probability value (Fig. 12). Generating all the well-formed time-span trees requires grouping and metrical structures. For this purpose we can use the analysis results of our GTTM analyzers such as ATTA or σGTTMII. In the experiment reported in Sect. 5, we used the correct data of grouping and metrical structures in the GTTM database.

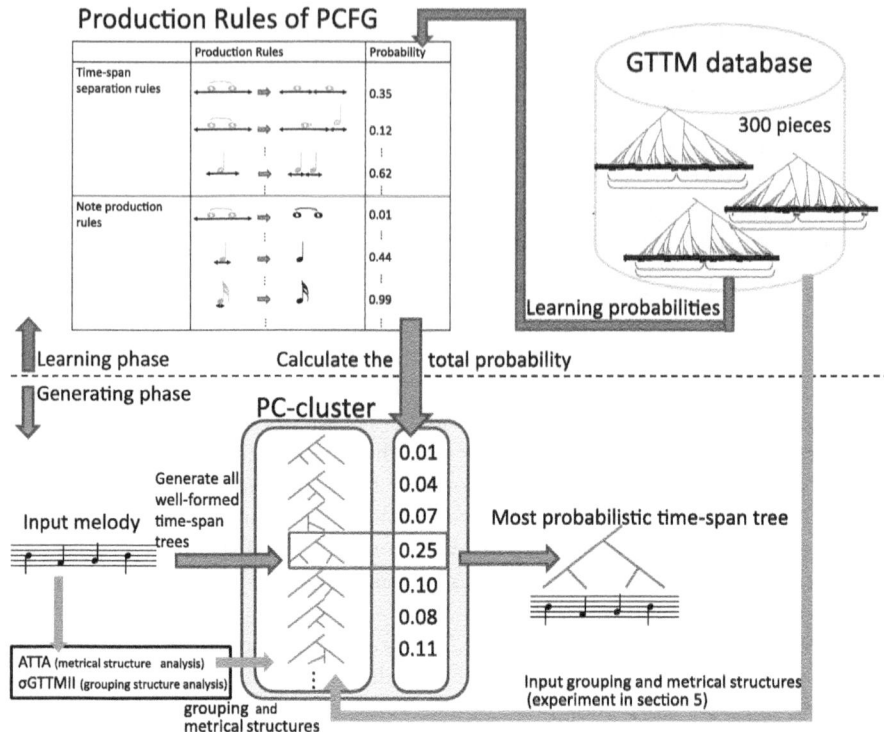

Fig. 12. Overview of σGTTMIII.

Generating all the well-formed time-span trees requires substantial computing time because the combinations of trees increase exponentially when the numbers of notes increase. To reduce the computing time, we parallelized eight processes for generating time-span trees for each piece of music. Using the PCFG, we needed three weeks to acquire plausible time-span trees of 100 pieces of music in the GTTM database using a PC cluster (16 machines of Intel Xeon E5-2430@2.00 GHz 12 core). The computing time depended on the musical pieces; the longest was two weeks, and the shortest one was two minutes[2].

5 Experimental Results

We evaluated the performance of σGTTMIII by leave-one-out cross validation in order to compare its accuracy with that of ATTA, a previously developed time-span tree analyzer [3]. We used the same 100 pieces of music as used to evaluate ATTA, and they were numbered from 1 to 100 in the 300-piece database. In other words, we used 299 pieces to calculate the probabilities of product rules

---

[2] Although we can use the Viterbi algorithm, in the experiment we did a full search. In future we plan to implement the Viterbi algorithm to reduce the computing time.

and evaluate one piece. Then we iterated this evaluation a hundred times for the 100 pieces and calculated the average accuracy.

When calculating the accuracy, we did not consider the possibility that a low-level error would propagate up to a higher level; we counted wrong answers without regard to the differences in time-span levels.

$$Accuracy = \frac{\text{Numbers of matched nodes in the time-span tree}}{\text{Numbers of nodes in the time-span tree}} \quad (2)$$

The results of our experiments are given in Table 1. ATTA has two kinds of results because the accuracy of ATTA varies depending on its adjustable parameters.

Table 1. Accuracies of ATTA and σGTTMIII.

Melodies	Baseline performance of ATTA	ATTA with configured parameters	σGTTMIII σGTTMIII σGTTMIII
1. Moments Musicaux	0.71	0.84	0.88
2. Wiegenlied	0.54	0.69	0.78
3. Traumerei	0.50	0.63	0.84
4. Sinfonie Nr.9 d moll Op.125 4.Satz An die Freude	0.22	0.48	0.68
5. The Nutcracker Suite Op.71a No.8 Waltz of the Flowers	0.42	0.91	0.72
	⋮	⋮	⋮
Total (100 melodies)	0.44	0.60	0.76

It took us an average of about 10 min per piece to find the plausible tuning for the set of parameters. The σGTTMIII outperformed ATTA in average accuracy in both the baseline and after tuning the parameters. It also outperformed the baseline performance of ATTA for all the pieces. After the parameters were tuned, ATTA outperformed σGTTMIII in a few of the pieces.

We investigated the pieces for which ATTA outperformed the σGTTMIII; the results indicated that those pieces applied many rules and the shape of the time-span tree changed very diversely when the parameters corresponding to those rules were changed. However, it is difficult to tune the parameters properly if the person who tunes them is not a musicologist. By learning the probabilities of production rules, σGTTMIII enables acquiring a time-span tree with high accuracy.

6 Conclusion

We described σGTTMIII, a time-span tree generator based on probabilistic context-free grammar (PCFG). We set 645 rules for generating time spans and after carrying out supervised learning of the PCFG rules, σGTTMIII outperformed the previous time-span tree analyzer ATTA in terms of average accuracy.

This is the first example of introducing PCFG into the generative theory of tonal music (GTTM) for learning the production rules of each level of a time span and its probabilities. In the future we plan to achieve unsupervised learning of rules to improve the accuracy. We also plan to analyze music pieces longer than 8 bars as a means to investigate in detail why σGTTMIII works well.

Some applications such as melody morphing or melody summarization require the use of a time-span tree [5,6,10–12]. For example, Fig. 13 shows a demonstration system for a melody morphing method that changes the morphing level of each half bar by using the values from the accelerometer in the iPad/iPhone/iPod Touch[3] [9]. However, such applications are not practical because the accuracy of the previous time-span analyzer is not sufficient and requires manual parameter tuning. We therefore plan to construct an application for automatic melody morphing or summarization.

Fig. 13. ShakeGuitar.

Acknowledgments. This work was supported in part by JSPS KAKENHI Grant Numbers 23500145, 25330434, and 25700036 and PRESTO, JST.

References

1. Charniak, E.: Tree-bank grammars. In: Proceedings of the Thirteenth National Conference on Artificial Intelligence, AAAI 1996, pp. 1031–1036 (1996)
2. Granroth-Wilding, M., Steedman, M.: Statistical parsing for harmonic analysis of jazz chord sequences. In: Proceedings of the International Computer Music Conference, pp. 478–485. International Computer Music Association (2012)

---

[3] When the user stops moving the iPhone/iPod Touch, the unit plays the backing melody of "The Other Day, I Met a Bear (The Bear Song)". When the user shakes it vigorously, it plays heavy soloing. When the user shakes it slowly, it plays a morphed melody between the backing and heavy soloing. The ShakeGuitar can be downloaded at http://gttm.jp/hamanaka/en/shakeguitar/.

3. Hamanaka, M., Hirata, K., Tojo, S.: Implementing 'a generative theory of tonal music'. J. New Music Res. **35**(4), 249–277 (2006)
4. Hamanaka, M., Hirata, K., Tojo, S.: FATTA: full automatic time-span tree analyzer. In: Proceedings of the 2007 International Computer Music Conference (ICMC 2007), pp. 153–156 (2007)
5. Hamanaka, M., Hirata, K., Tojo, S.: Melody expectation method based on GTTM and TPS. In: Proceedings of the 2008 International Society for Music Information Retrieval Conference (ISMIR 2008), pp. 107–112 (2008)
6. Hamanaka, M., Hirata, K., Tojo, S.: Melody morphing method based on GTTM. In: Proceedings of the 2008 International Computer Music Conference (ICMC 2008), pp. 155–158 (2008)
7. Hamanaka, M., Hirata, K., Tojo, S.: Time-span tree analyzer for polyphonic music. In: 10th International Symposium on Computer Music Multidisciplinary Research (CMMR 2013), pp. 886–893 (2013)
8. Hamanaka, M., Hirata, K., Tojo, S.: Music structural analysis database based on GTTM. In: Proceedings of the 2014 International Society for Music Information Retrieval Conference (ISMIR 2014), pp. 325–330 (2014)
9. Hamanaka, M., Yoshiya, M., Yoshida, S.: Constructing music applications for smartphones. In: Proceedings of the 2011 International Computer Music Conference (ICMC 2011), pp. 308–311 (2011)
10. Hirata, K., Hiraga, R.: Ha-hi-hun plays Chopin's etude. In: Working Notes of IJCAI 2003 Workshop on Methods for Automatic Music Performance and their Applications in a Public Rendering Contest, pp. 72–73 (2003)
11. Hirata, K., Matsuda, S.: Interactive music summarization based on generative theory of tonal music. J. New Music Res. **5**(2), 165–177 (2003)
12. Hirata, K., Matsuda, S.: Annotated music for retrieval, reproduction. In: Proceedings of the 2004 International Computer Music Conference (ICMC 2004), pp. 584–587 (2004)
13. Kameoka, H., Ochiai, K., Nakano, M., Tsuchiya, M., Sagayama, S.: Context-free 2d structure model of musical notes for Bayesian modeling of polyphonic spectrograms. In: Proceedings of the 2012 International Society for Music Information Retrieval Conference (ISMIR 2012), pp. 307–312 (2012)
14. Kanamori, K., Hamanaka, M.: Method to detect GTTM local grouping boundarys based on clustering and statistical learning. In: Proceedings of the 2014 International Computer Music Conference (ICMC 2014), pp. 1193–1197 (2014)
15. Lerdahl, F.: Tonal Pitch Space. Oxford University Press, Oxford (2001)
16. Lerdahl, F., Jackendoff, R.: A Generative Theory of Tonal Music. Cognitive Theory and Mental Representation. MIT Press, Cambridge (1985)
17. MakeMusic: Finale (2015). http://www.finalemusic.com/
18. Marsden, A.: Software for Schenkerian analysis. In: Proceedings of the 2004 International Computer Music Conference (ICMC 2011), pp. 673–676 (2011)
19. Miura, Y., Hamanaka, M., Hirata, K., Tojo, S.: Decision tree to detect GTTM group boundaries. In: Proceedings of the 2009 International Computer Music Conference (ICMC 2009), pp. 125–128 (2009)
20. Narmour, E.: The Analysis and Cognition of Basic Melodic Structures: The Implication-realization Model. University of Chicago Press, Chicago (1990)
21. Narmour, E.: The Analysis and Cognition of Melodic Complexity: The Implication-Realization Model. University of Chicago Press, Chicago (1992)
22. Quinlan, J.: C4.5: Programs for Machine Learning. Machine Learning. Morgan Kaufmann, Elsevier Science, San Mateo (2014)

23. Recordare: Musicxml 3.0 tutorial (2011). http://www.musicxml.com/wp-content/uploads/2012/12/musicxml-tutorial.pdf
24. Schenker, H.: Der frei Satz. Universal Edition, Vienna. Published in English as Free Composition, Translated and Edited, Longman, New York (1979)
25. Tanji, M., Ando, D., Iba, H.: Improving metrical grammar with grammar expansion. In: Wobcke, W., Zhang, M. (eds.) AI 2008. Lecture Notes in Artificial Intelligence (LNAI), vol. 5360, pp. 180–191. Springer, Heidelberg (2008). doi:10.1007/978-3-540-89378-3_18
26. Temperley, D.: The Cognition of Basic Musical Structures. MIT Press, Cambridge (2004)
27. Yazawa, S., Hamanaka, M., Utsuro, T.: Melody generation system based on a theory of melody sequences. In: Proceedings of International Conference on Advanced Informatics: Concepts, Theory and Applications, pp. 347–352 (2014)

BioComputer Music: Generating Musical Responses with *Physarum polycephalum*-Based Memristors

Edward Braund[✉] and Eduardo R. Miranda

Interdisciplinary Centre for Computer Music Research (ICCMR),
Plymouth University, Plymouth, UK
{edward.braund,eduardo.miranda}@plymouth.ac.uk

Abstract. This paper introduces *BioComputer Music*, an experimental one piano duet between pianist and plasmodial slime mould *Physarum polycephalum*. This piece harnesses a system we have been developing, which we call *BioComputer*. *BioComputer* consists of an analogue circuit that encompasses components grown from the biological computing substrate *Physarum polycephalum*. Our system listens to the pianist and uses the memristive characteristics of *Physarum polycephalum* to generate a musical response that it plays through electromagnets placed on the strings of the piano. Such electromagnets set the strings into vibration, producing a distinctive timbre. *Physarum polycephalum* is an amorphous unicellular organism that has been discovered to exhibit memristive qualities. The memristor changes its resistance according to the amount of charge that has previously flown through. In this paper, we introduce the general concepts, technology and musical composition behind the *BioComputer Music* piece. We also discuss our rationale for using *Physarum polycephalum*.

Keywords: *Physarum polycephalum* · Memristors · Unconventional computing for music · Computer music · Biomusic · Biological engineering · Biological computing

1 Introduction

The field of computer music has evolved in tandem with advances made in computer science. We are interested in how the field of unconventional computation [4] may provide new pathways for music and related technologies. In computer music, there is a tradition of experimenting with emerging technologies. Until recent years, developments put forward by the field of unconventional computation have been left unexploited, which is likely due to the field's heavy theoretical nature, complexity and lack of accessible prototypes. Uniquely, the biological computing substrate *Physarum polycephalum* requires comparatively fewer resources than most other unconventional computing substrates: the organism is cheap, openly obtainable, considered safe to use and has a robustness that allows for ease of application. It is for these reasons we have selected *Physarum polycephalum* to begin investigating how new, biological, computing schemes may offer new pathways for music. For a survey of unconventional computing in music see [9].

The plasmodium of *Physarum polycephalum*, henceforth known as *P.polycephalum*, is an amorphous unicellular organism (visible to the human eye) with a myriad of diploid nuclei. The plasmodium inhabits dark, cool and moist environments and feeds on micro-particles and creatures such as bacteria and spores. It propagates along gradients of stimuli while building a route-efficient network of protoplasmic veins connecting foraging efforts and areas of colonisation (Fig. 1). The visual result of the organism's network is a planar graph where colonised food sources represent nodes and protoplasmic veins represent edges. The intracellular activity of *P.polycephalum* can be described as a network of biochemical oscillators [27]: waves of contraction colliding. This contraction behaviour induces shuttle streaming, which switches direction approximately every minute.

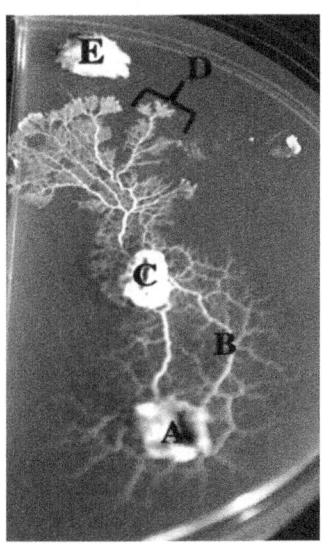

Fig. 1. A photograph of plasmodium of *P.polycephalum* showing: (A) inoculation of plasmodium into the environment, (B) protoplasmic network connecting areas of colonisation, (C) colonised food sources, and (D) extending pseudopods forming a search front along a gradient to food (E).

P.polycephalum's behaviour can be interpreted as computation [1]. Computing prototypes exploiting *P.polycephalum*'s behaviour include robot control [25], logic gate schemes [3], route planning [2,24] and numerous others [1]. We have developed several projects that harness the behaviour of *P.polycephalum* for music. These include sound synthesis [5–7,21], a biologically inspired step sequencer [8] and contemporary composition [19].

In this paper, we give an overview of the music and technology behind the composition *BioComputer Music*. *BioComputer Music* is an innovative duet between pianist and an analogue circuit, which encompasses components grown from the plasmodium of *P.polycephalum*. This composition marks the beginning of our initial experimentation and research into building analogue hardware-wetware with *P.polycephalum* for music. The piece is to be premièred at the 2015 Peninsula Arts Contemporary Music Festival, Plymouth University, UK. This paper is structured as follows. First, we introduce the background information regarding the technology side of the composition. Then, we present the software and accompanying hardware-wetware that makes up the technology. Next, we discuss the *BioComputer Music* composition, offering our artistic motives behind the music. Finally, the paper ends with final remarks on using the presented technology to compose music and how we plan on progressing our work in the future.

2 Background Information

First, we give an overview of some underlying concepts behind the technology used for *BioComputer Music*, the first of which is the memristor. Memristors are the fourth fundamental passive circuit component that relates magnetic flux linkage and charge. The memristor's existence was originally theorised by Chua in 1971 [11] but was not physically discovered until 2008 [23]. A memristor alters its resistance as a function of the previous charge that has flown through it. The current versus voltage characteristic of a memristor, when applied with an AC voltage, is a pinched hysteresis loop - a Lissajous figure formed by two perpendicular oscillations. Hysteresis is where the output of a system is dependent on both its current input and history of previous inputs. In an ideal memristor, this figure is observed as a figure of 8 where the centre intersection is at zero volts and current (Fig. 2). For an excellent introduction to memristors see [16].

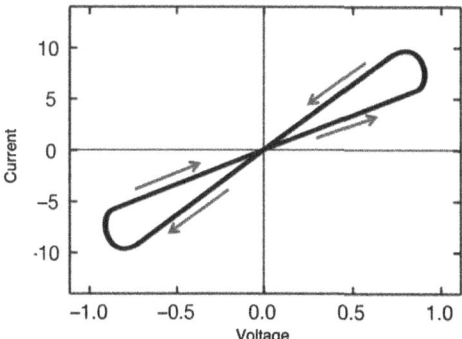

Fig. 2. Example of hysteresis in an ideal memristor (arbitrary values used).

We believe that the memristor's nonlinear ability to alter its resistance as a function of both its current input and history of previous inputs, holds potential for music generation. Unfortunately, until recently, we have been unable to explore such potential due to the component not yet being commercially available. There has, however, been one investigation using a simulation of a memristor network under a DC voltage [13] to generate music [14]. Other labs have also been restricted in their memristor interests due to this lack of accessibility. As a result, researchers have been looking past conventional electrical engineering approaches and have found that a selection of organic systems exhibit memristive characteristics. Examples include human blood [17], human skin [15] and Aloe Vera plants [26].

In 2009, Pershin et al. [22] published a paper that described the plasmodium's adaptive learning behaviour in terms of a memristive model. Shortly after, Gale et al. [12] demonstrated in laboratory experiments that the protoplasmic tube of *P.polycephalum* showed I-V profiles consistent with memristive systems. These discoveries have conveniently allowed us to coincide our musical research interests in memristors and unconventional computing with *P.polycephalum*. Moreover, it has gifted us with an early opportunity to investigate how some of the memristor's characteristics may provide new pathways for music before they are made widely accessible.

In *BioComputer Music*, we experiment with the plasmodium's memristive characteristics - its nonlinear ability to alter its resistance as a function of the previous input - to generate musical accompaniments. Here, we have designed a system that transcribes a pianist's performance into MIDI note information. The result of such transcription is subsequently scaled into voltages that together fabricate a discrete waveform that passes through a *P.polycephalum* protoplasmic tube. We then take an instantaneous resistance measurement at each voltage step and, using mapping/sonification techniques, transcribe the evolved output to musical notes, which the system then plays through electromagnets arranged above the piano's strings. In the following section, we give an overview of the *BioComputer Music* system.

3 The *BioComputer Music* System

The *BioComputer Music* system consists of two parts, hardware-wetware and software. First, we explain the hardware, which consists of eight protoplasmic tubes (henceforth referred to as components) grown from plasmodium, two electrical measurement instruments, USB relay boards and twenty-four electromagnets.

We use eight components for our system as successive applications of voltage cause the organism to retire the grown component and forage for food elsewhere. Thus, to reduce the stress imposed on each protoplasmic tube, our system alternates between eight. We have noticed that excessive use of any single *P.polycephalum* component causes the overall resistance to increase. Furthermore, after approximately 4 min of successive voltage application, the component begins to dry up. As such, we alternate between components approximately once every 3 min. Note, we are aware that findings from [12] indicate that hysteresis loops vary heavily in magnitude from organism-to-organism and are often asymmetric (see Fig. 3 for examples). We believe that such asymmetry is due to the organism producing an internal current source, which, dependent on the direction of flow, will oppose or add to driven current [10]. In most electrical engineering situations, this would be detrimental to applications. For music generation, such variation can be desirable and even sought after: composers are known to use a wide span of different processes (e.g. stochastic) to evolve their compositions. As such, we are not concerned about the stability of hysteresis at this point; rather, we are keen to investigate this quality as a stylistic trait of using *P.polycephalum*. However, methods of improving stability may be a future area of research when silicon memristors become accessible, as some level of repeatability in hysteresis will widen the application and usability of our system (e.g. performers wanting to perform a composition consistently).

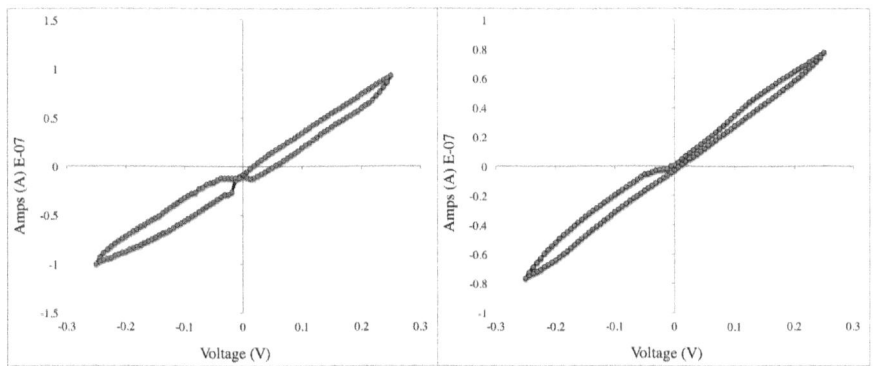

Fig. 3. Two examples of *P.polycephalum* hysteresis recorded at ICCMR labs under a fabricated AC voltage waveform of 160 steps, voltage range of ±250 mV and a step dwell time of 2 s.

To produce the plasmodium for this project, we adopt techniques from [1]. Here, we farm the organism in plastic containers on a moist, porous substrate. The farm is fed daily with oat flakes and replanted approximately once a week. *P.polycephalum* components consist of two electrodes linked via a protoplasmic tube. Electrodes are comprised of a circle (roughly 2 cm in diameter) of tinned copper wire (16 stands at 0.2 mm) filled with a 2-percent non-nutrient agar. To grow the components, we place a colonised oat flake from our farm on one of the electrodes and a fresh oat flake on the other. This arrangement causes the plasmodium to propagate along a chemical gradient to the fresh oat, resulting in a protoplasmic tube linking the two electrodes (Fig. 4). To house eight of these components, we divided two 120 mm square Petri dishes into four sections (Fig. 5). During the *BioComputer Music* piece, humidity is kept high for the components by fixing a moist cloth on the lid of each dish.

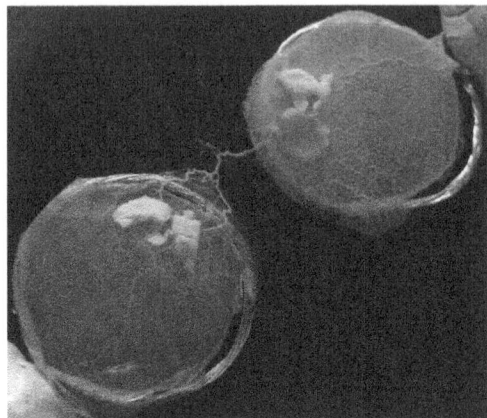

Fig. 4. A *P.polycephalum* component grown between two electrodes comprised of a circle (approximately 2 cm in diameter) of tinned copper wire (16 stands at 0.2 mm) filled with a 2-percent non-nutrient agar.

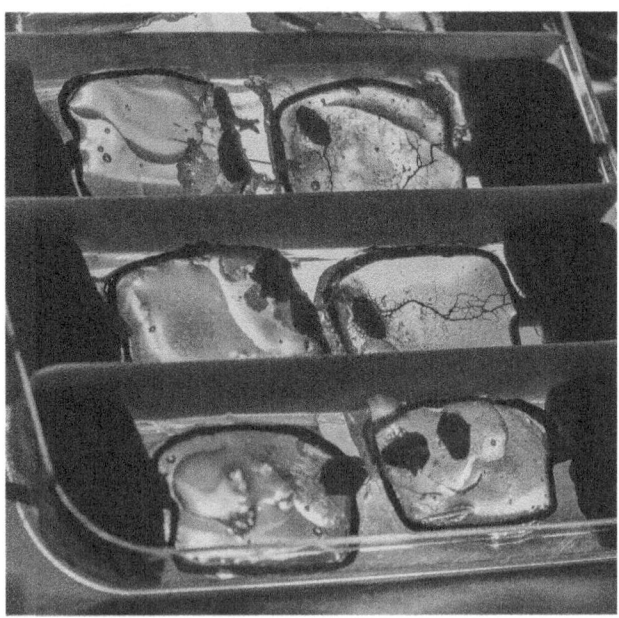

Fig. 5. Four components grown from the plasmodium of *P.polycephalum* housed in a 120 mm square Petri dish.

Two eight-channel USB relay boards facilitate alternation between each component. Here, the first board regulates which component is applied with a voltage from a Keithley 230 programmable voltage source while the second controls which component's output is being measured by a Keithley 617 programmable electrometer. We interface with each of the Keithley instruments using a Prologix GPIB USB controller.

To enable the *BioComputer Music* system to accompany the pianist, we furnished twenty-four of the piano's strings with electromagnets (Fig. 6). These operate by exciting the strings with an audio signal sent by our software. Currently, the system is restricted to only having up to six magnets active simultaneously.

Fig. 6. A photograph of twenty-four electromagnets furnished above the strings of a grand piano.

The software side of the *BioComputer Music* system is designed in Max by Cycling 74. Our software is primarily intended to act as a translator between the pianist, hardware and electromagnets. Before the *BioComputer Music* system can be used, the software needs to be informed of which strings the electromagnets are positioned above. This information notifies the software of the notes that it has available to play. Furthermore, within the software, there are banks of performer-switchable presets (made switchable via an iPad). These allow the performer to define the following parameters: what notes are active out of the available twenty-four, minimum and maximum note duration range, accompaniment speed factor and electromagnet excitation source. We discuss the function of each of these parameters below. When in use, the software is operating in either listening or playing mode. When listening, the pianist is inputting into the system. Conversely, when in playing mode, the system outputs its response to the input. In this mode, the software no longer listens to the performer but instead feeds back the newly generated notes into the hardware.

When listening, the software takes an audio feed from a microphone positioned above the strings of the piano. This audio signal is transcribed into MIDI note information via an FFT process, with the aid of piano-specific pitch templates. Once transcribed, the MIDI data is passed through an algorithm that serves two functions. The first is to transpose the detected pitches to the notes the performer has made available to the system. For example, if E3 is detected, but only E2 is available, the algorithm will alter the MIDI note to E2. The second function: if a pitch is detected but is not offered and there is not an equivalent available in another octave, the pitch is removed. This algorithm is necessary as allows the performer to input into the system while playing the full piano range, not just the notes furnished with electromagnets.

Following the pitch recognition and transposition processes, notes are transcribed into voltage values. The software does this in batches of either ten notes or ten second's worth of notes, whichever occurs first. Initially, each note available within the active preset is assigned a voltage value in the range of 100–240 mV. For this project, notes are assigned in ascending order according to pitch. Our rationale for assigning voltages this way is simplicity at this early stage of using *P.polycephalum* components for music generation. In the future, we will look to experiment with assigning voltage values in a more meaningful fashion; for example, assigning voltages according to the number of times a note occurs. Moreover, we are currently researching into the organism's conductance profile under different voltage scenarios to take better musical advantage of *P.polycephalum* memristive characteristics [10].

Once assigned, the software translates each MIDI note into their respective voltage value to create a list, which the system uses to fabricate a complex symmetrical voltage waveform with a step dwell time of 2-s. Here, the first quarter of the wave steps through the list in order. The second quarter steps through the list in reverse order. The second half of the wave then replicates the first half but in the negative voltage domain (Fig. 7). To make the waveform symmetrical, we assign the node, crest and trough of the fabricated waveform 0 mV, 250 mV and −250 mV respectively. This process creates a fabricated waveform with the voltage range of ±250 mV, which we chose as in our experimentation we found that it produced the best results in terms of hysteresis and did not damage the organism. We create waveforms in this fashion as we are keen to experiment with the asymmetrical nature of the organism's hysteresis. Once fabricated, the software communicates the waveform to a Keithley 230 voltage source, which it subsequently transmits to the currently addressed *P.polycephalum* component.

Interfacing with the Keithley 617 programmable electrometer, the software measures the instantaneous resistance response at each voltage step (node, crest and trough voltages are not measured). Shown in Fig. 8 is a set of graphs denoting the instantaneous resistance measurements for each quarter of a fabricated waveform. Such measurements are subsequently transcribed back into MIDI note form using a mapping/scaling technique derived from the note-voltage transcription stage: available notes are arranged in ascending pitch order with higher notes

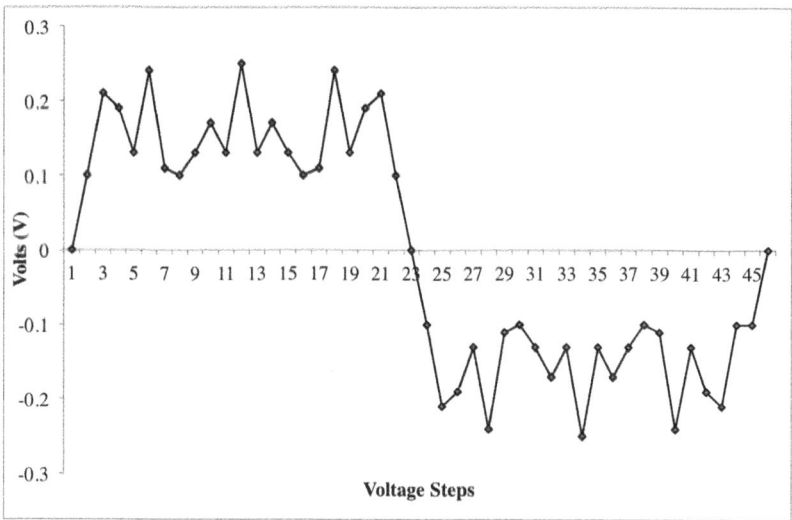

Fig. 7. An example of a voltage waveform fabricated from transcribed MIDI note data.

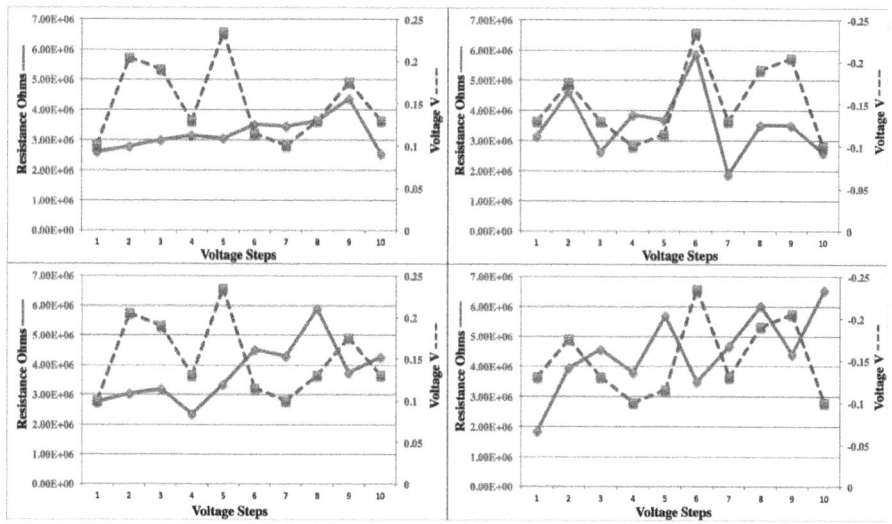

Fig. 8. Four graphs representing the *P. polycephalum* component's resistance at each voltage step. The red dashed line represents input voltage, while the blue solid line represents resistance. The voltage waveform used to create these graphs is shown is Fig. 7. (Color figure online)

being chosen by higher levels of resistance. This process is depicted in Fig. 9. Each wave cycle generates four times the length of the input. The sequence of notes produced by the second and fourth quarter of the waveform are reversed; thus arranging them into the correct order.

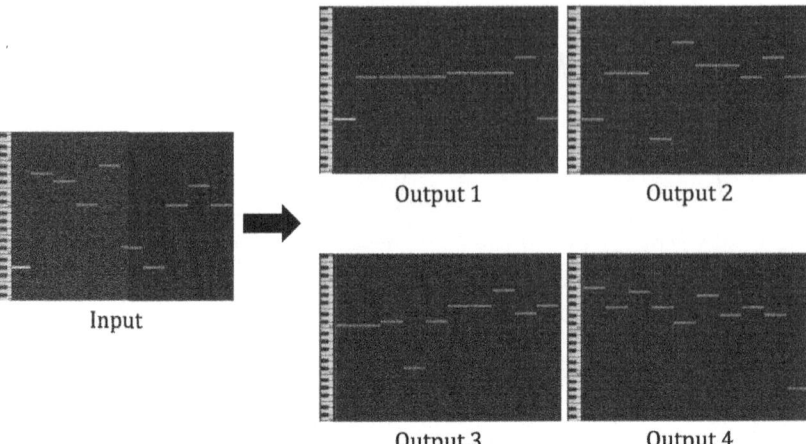

Fig. 9. An example of the *BioComputer Music* system's response to an input. Shown on the left is the input sequence of notes which our software transcribes into voltages and sends through a *P.polycephalum* component. On the right, is the a component's response to the input (note that 2 and 4 have been reversed as explained). This is the musical result of the voltage and resistance depicted in Figs. 7 and 8 respectively. Note, this figure uses a MIDI grid of 3 and a half octaves, only 10 notes within this range were available for the system to use.

At this stage of implementation, due to current resource constraints, the *BioComputer Music* system only uses the *P.polycephalum* components to generate lists of notes. To produce rhythmic structure, we apply a conventional second order Markov chain, which uses the transcribed MIDI data as input before the filtering/transposition algorithm. The output of this Markov chain is altered using the performer's speed factor parameter. To discern note durations, we use a Gaussian distribution, which operates within the performer's minimum and maximum range. We are currently looking into feasible methods of generating both rhythm and duration from *P.polycephalum* components and anticipate that we will have an autonomous *P.polycephalum* music generation system shortly.

As a result of using a voltage step dwell time of 2-s, the system can only generate notes at 2-s intervals. For this reason, the note generation process starts in concurrence with the performer inputting data while in listen mode. The software places these notes into a buffer until the system is put into play mode, upon which the buffer's contents is translated into commands and sent to the electromagnet hardware. If the system is placed into play mode but is yet to process the entire input, it will continue to generate notes until it has processed the entire input. However, if the buffer's contents are exhausted before processing the entire input, the system will calculate the time needed to finish and will fill the time-lapse by repeating previously generated sequences. Conversely, if the system finishes processing the input, it will begin to process the notes it has already generated.

The electromagnets function by exciting their respective piano string using an audio signal sent from our software. This signal is defined in the performer presets and can take the form of a combination of wavetable oscillators, each automatically set at the respective string's harmonics, or a sound sample loaded into a buffer. For detailed information regarding the electromagnet side of the *BioComputer Music* system, please refer to [18].

As a summary, the musical result of the *BioComputer Music* system is as follows. If a repetitive sequence of notes is input, then the fabricated waveform may become increasingly directional, resulting in decreased changes in resistance. Moreover, if the performer only plays one note, after the initial change in resistance, over time the organism will essentially become an ordinary resistor. Thus, the resistance measurement will remain the same, resulting in the system playing the same note with no variation. Conversely, under an extremely dynamic input, changes in resistance are likely to be higher, resulting in an output containing a wider span of notes.

4 The *BioComputer Music* Composition

A recording of the *BioComputer Music* piece can be found at [20]. For the composition of *BioComputer Music*, we explored the notion of interactivity between a composer/performer and the *BioComputer* system. We wanted to compose a piece that sounded as if the performer asks questions to *BioComputer*, which in turn answers them. This is a very traditional musical form, which originated from ecclesiastical music where the leader of a ceremony sings a prayer in alternation with a chorus. However, we wanted to be surprised by *BioComputer's* responses, which will vary from performance to performance, but within a certain boundary of constraints (composer presets). Therefore, the piece consists of materials notated on a musical score for the pianist to play when the system is in listening mode. Once a section is played, the performer switches the system into playing mode and *BioComputer* system plays its response for a given period until the performer switches it back to listening mode and plays another section of the music, and so on. There are occasions where the pianist plays alongside the *BioComputer* system, but the latter does not listen to this because it would be in player mode.

An excerpt of the score is shown in Fig. 10. In section 10, at the top stave, the symbol Bioset 8 is instructing the performer to switch the *BioComputer* system to player mode. While it is in player mode the performer plays three chords. At the bottom stave, the passage before section 11 is played on the piano while *BioComputer* is in listening mode. This section will then be processed by the system; that is, it will serve as seeds for *BioComputer* to produce a response as soon as the performer switches it to player mode, indicated by the symbol Bioset 9.

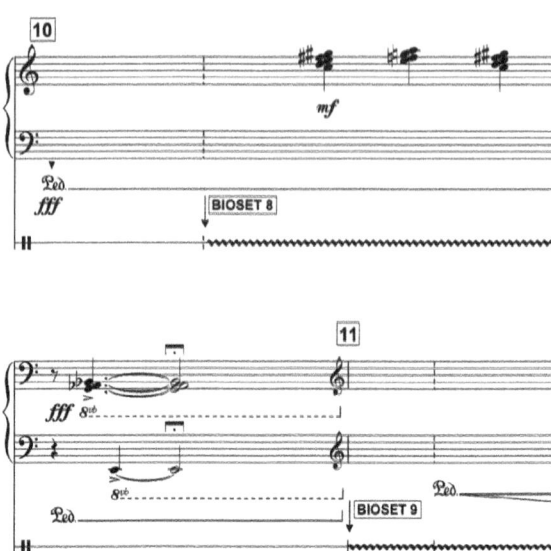

Fig. 10. An excerpt of the musical score for the composition *BioComputer Music*.

5 Final Remarks

To the best of our knowledge, *BioComputer Music* is the first musical composition that harnesses biological circuit components to generate music. *BioComputer Music* is an exciting new development for music not only regarding technological novelty, but also in terms of approaches to creativity. In tandem with the scientific research, we also have been looking into how such new technology might lead to new approaches to musical composition. In terms of compositional practice, the *BioComputer* system has enabled us to revisit a few concepts that we have explored in previous compositions, but from a different perspective. One of them is the notion of musical interaction with a non-deterministic machine. We used to spend a great deal of time programming digital computers with artificial intelligence to interact with a performer in interesting ways. By interesting ways we mean in ways that are surprising and engaging, but not completely by accident. *BioComputer* makes this task much easier to achieve: it is a nonlinear machine in its own right and displays an intriguing level of intrinsic intelligence, which does not require much programming. It is ideal to develop the sorts of musical systems that we are interested in composing for.

In regards to our research into music with unconventional computing, the *BioComputer* system marks the beginning of a new avenue. Until now, in our research with *P.polycephalum*, we have been using behavioural data that takes several days to gather. The outcomes of these studies are interesting in their own right, but our ultimate goal is to be able to harness *P.polycephalum* for near real-time musical applications. *BioComputer Music* is a large step towards reaching our goal. Although the system behind the piece is our first implementation, the musical result is both engaging and interesting. Of course, there are several areas we need to develop. Foremost, we intend to review our method of transcribing notes into voltages. Here, we are researching and experimenting with the most meaningful and interesting way of taking advantage of the *P.polycephalum* component's nonlinear conductance profile. Also, we are working towards developing feasible methods of generating note duration and rhythmic structure with *P.polycephalum* components. Shown in Fig. 11 is a new prototype we are developing, where an additional two Petri dishes are used to generate note duration and rhythmic structure.

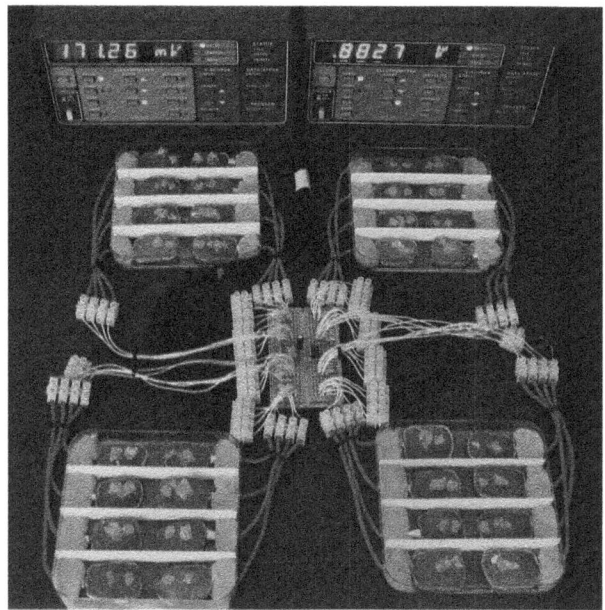

Fig. 11. We are already designing future versions of the *BioComputer Music* system. Shown in this picture is a new prototype where an additional two Petri dishes are used to generate note duration and rhythmic structure.

As we move on to work with living matter in computing technology, essentially we will be harnessing the intelligence of such organisms to compose music with. Undoubtedly, new forms of music making will emerge from Unconventional Computing. *BioComputer Music* is only a glimpse of what is to come.

References

1. Adamatzky, A.: Physarum Machines: Computers from Slime Mould, vol. 74. World Scientific, Singapore (2010)

2. Adamatzky, A.: Physarum machines for space missions. Acta Futur. **6**, 53–67 (2013)
3. Adamatzky, A., Schubert, T.: Slime mold microfluidic logical gates. Mater. Today **17**(2), 86–91 (2014)
4. Adamatzky, A., Teuscher, C.: From Utopian to Genuine Unconventional Computers. Luniver Press, Beckington (2006)
5. Braund, E.: Unconventional computer music with physarum polycephalum. Master's thesis, Interdisciplinary for Computer Music Research (ICCMR), Plymouth University (2013)
6. Braund, E., Miranda, E.: Music with unconventional computing: towards a platform for physarum polycephalum sound synthesis (2013)
7. Braund, E., Miranda, E.: Music with unconventional computing: a system for physarum polycephalum sound synthesis. In: Aramaki, M., Derrien, O., Kronland-Martinet, R., Ystad, S. (eds.) CMMR 2013. LNCS, vol. 8905, pp. 175–189. Springer, Heidelberg (2014)
8. Braund, E., Miranda, E.: Music with unconventional computing: towards a step sequencer from plasmodium of *physarum polycephalum*. In: Johnson, C., Carballal, A., Correia, J. (eds.) EvoMUSART 2015. LNCS, vol. 9027, pp. 15–26. Springer International Publishing, Switzerland (2015)
9. Braund, E., Miranda, E.R.: Unconventional computing in music. In: Proceedings of the 9th Conference on Interdisciplinary Musicology - CIM 2014, Berlin, Germany (2014)
10. Braund, E., Sparrow, R., Miranda, E.R.: Physarum-based memristors for computer music. In: Adamatzky, A. (ed.) Advances in Physarum Machines, vol. 21, pp. 755–775. Springer International Publishing, Switzerland (2016)
11. Chua, L.: Memristor-the missing circuit element. IEEE Trans. Circuit Theory **18**(5), 507–519 (1971)
12. Gale, E., Adamatzky, A., de Lacy Costello, B.: Slime mould memristors. BioNanoScience **5**, 1–8 (2014)
13. Gale, E., de Lacy Costello, B., Adamatzky, A.: Observation, characterization and modeling of memristor current spikes (2013). arXiv preprint: arXiv:1302.0771
14. Gale, E., Matthews, O., de Lacy Costello, B., Adamatzky, A.: Beyond Markov chains, towards adaptive memristor network-based music generation (2013). arXiv preprint: arXiv:1302.0785
15. Johnsen, G.K., Lütken, C.A., Martinsen, O.G., Grimnes, S.: Memristive model of electro-osmosis in skin. Phys. Rev. E **83**(3), 31916 (2011)
16. Johnsen, G.K.: An introduction to the memristor-a valuable circuit element in bioelectricity and bioimpedance. J. Electr. Bioimpedance **3**(1), 20–28 (2012)
17. Kosta, S.P., Kosta, Y.P., Bhatele, M., Dubey, Y.M., Gaur, A., Kosta, S., Gupta, J., Patel, A., Patel, B.: Human blood liquid memristor. Int. J. Med. Eng. Inform. **3**(1), 16–29 (2011)
18. McPherson, A.: The magnetic resonator piano: electronic augmentation of an acoustic grand piano. J. New Music Res. **39**(3), 189–202 (2010)
19. Miranda, E.: Harnessing the intelligence of physarum polycephalum for unconventional computing-aided musical composition. IJUC **10**(3), 251–268 (2014)
20. Miranda, E.: Biocomputer Music. http://tinyurl.com/kszgm3r. Accessed 12 Feb 2015
21. Miranda, E., Adamatzky, A., Jones, J.: Sounds synthesis with slime mould of physarum polycephalum. J. Bionic Eng. **8**(2), 107–113 (2011)
22. Pershin, Y.V., La Fontaine, S., Di Ventra, M.: Memristive model of amoeba learning. Phys. Rev. E **80**(2), 21926 (2009)

23. Strukov, D.B., Snider, G.S., Stewart, D.R., Williams, R.S.: The missing memristor found. Nature **453**(7191), 80–83 (2008)
24. Tero, A., Kobayashi, R., Nakagaki, T.: Physarum solver: a biologically inspired method of road-network navigation. Phys. Sect. A **363**(1), 115–119 (2006)
25. Tsuda, S., Zauner, K.P., Gunji, Y.P.: Robot control with biological cells. Biosystems **87**(2), 215–223 (2007)
26. Volkov, A., Reedus, J., Mitchell, C.M., Tucket, C., Forde-Tuckett, V., Volkova, M.I., Markin, V.S., Chua, L.: Memristors in the electrical network of Aloe vera L. Plant Signal. Behav. **9**(4), e29056 (2014)
27. Wohlfarth-Bottermann, K.E.: Oscillatory contraction activity in physarum. J. Exp. Biol. **81**(1), 15–32 (1979)

'Understood at Last'?: A Memetic Analysis of Beethoven's 'Bloody Fist'

Steven Jan[✉]

University of Huddersfield, Queensgate, Huddesfield HD1 3DH, UK
s.b.jan@hud.ac.uk

Abstract. As a singular moment in the western canon, the opening of the recapitulation in the first movement of Beethoven's Ninth Symphony has prompted a variety of structural and expressive readings. This paper explores its intertextual connections with Mozart's *Don Giovanni* from a memetic perspective, outlining certain extra-musical interpretations, including some related to Susan McClary's controversial reading of the passage, one might infer from the strong musical connections.

Keywords: Beethoven · Ninth Symphony · Mozart · *Don Giovanni* · Memetics

1 Introduction

Of the myriad exemplars of sonata forms in the canon, the opening of the recapitulation in the first movement of Beethoven's Ninth Symphony is arguably the most audacious. This moment – bb. 301–*c*. 329 – has stimulated comment from a variety of perspectives, from the formal ('introversive' semiosis) to the hermeneutic ('extroversive' semiosis) [1]. Apropos the former perspective, Hopkins asserts that 'if the orchestra broke off abruptly on the final semiquaver of b. 300, not one in a thousand musicians would accurately predict the ensuing harmony. It is one of the supreme surprises of the entire repertoire …' [2]. Leaving aside the not insignificant fact that there are probably considerably fewer than one thousand syntactically legitimate two-chord progressions of which the first element is a $\text{vii}^{\sharp 4}_3$ (bb. 299–300), the passage is certainly highly arresting, counting as one of the most awe-inspiring moments in Beethoven's music and indeed in Western musical literature as a whole. Apropos the latter perspective, the passage has motivated readings of potential extra-musical meanings since the early-nineteenth century, ranging from images of war, cosmic conflict and, most recently and controversially, of sexual violence. It is the latter interpretation, proposed and then to some extent tempered by Susan McClary, which is most relevant to my argument here and which will be explored, extended and focused in Sect. 3.

I attempt here to sketch a fresh reading of the symphony, albeit one that draws in part from existing accounts; and I invoke the theory of memetics [3], and other approaches, not only to support my interpretations, but also to exemplify the virtues of a memetic approach. Memetics allows the formalization of intertextual relationships between the symphony and a work which I argue is to some extent a source for Beethoven's passage, namely Mozart's *Don Giovanni*. This is a work whose iconicity was growing in the first decades of the nineteenth century and whose prevailing tonic, and a topos of *Sturm und Drang*, is shared with the first movement of Beethoven's symphony [4]. The hypothesized linkage with *Don Giovanni* leads me to contend (Sects. 2 and 4) that, from an introversive perspective, Beethoven's passage is not as singular and unmotivated as Hopkins argues; and that, from an extroversive perspective, its connection to a work with an explicit text-content allows the formulation of arguably more secure expressive/connotative readings of Beethoven's passage than have hitherto been advanced (Sects. 3 and 5).

Memetics encourages fruitful cross-linkages between theory, analysis, cognitive science and evolutionary theory (not all of which can be explored here). It provides a *comitium*, a meeting place, within which a variety of perspectives on musical material from ostensibly different and seemingly exclusive disciplinary perspectives can be reconciled by an appeal to the question 'what aspects of the lower-level perspectives contribute to an understanding of the meta-theoretical Darwinian forces driving pattern recurrence and similarity?'. A concrete illustration of this will be given in due course.

It might be argued that the longer a duplicated passage, the less likely it is to be memetic, as if quotation does not constitute replication. Clearly there is a continuum of meme-length, at the 'short' end of which are passages of low salience but high replicative stability over time, and at the 'long' end of which are passages of high salience and low replicative stability over time [5]. From a Darwinian standpoint – from the 'memes' eye view' [6] – whether the passage replicated is a small and generic fragment or a longer and more recognizable quotation is arguably immaterial. What matters from this perspective is the survival by replication of the meme. Whether this is the result of the unreflective incorporation of a generic figure into a work or of a conscious decision by a composer to incorporate a distinctive antecedent pattern from a work of his/her immediate cultural context, for whatever motive, is strictly irrelevant from the meme's (metaphorically) selfish perspective [3].

When there is evidence of quotation and/or a specific collection of memes replicated, such that the antecedent work is clearly referenced, then it is normally the case that an imaginative or conceptual (subtextual) transfer between the 'source' and 'destination' work is intended – not necessarily consciously – by the composer. The often unpalatable assertion that free will is dissolved by memetics implies that it is the 'selfplex' of the composer which is creating the selective environment within which this transfer is motivated and mediated, not some unitary Cartesian self, with all the implications of agency and intentionality this carries [7].

2 A Memetic Analysis, Part I

To illustrate the hypothesized introversive correspondences, Example 1 xv shows bb. 299–329 of the first movement of the Ninth Symphony on a 'meme *particella*', passages posited as antecedent coindexes (precursors) to Beethoven's passage being shown on the smaller staves above and below it.[1] The latter are labelled chronologically and according to their sequential order in *Don Giovanni*. These inter-work relationships will

---

[1] High-resolution versions of the examples and figures in this paper are available at https://hud.academia.edu/StevenJan.

be considered in detail (here and in Sect. 4), in order to provide a foundation for the more speculative excursions of Sects. 3 and 5.

Example 1 Musemes in Mozart's *Don Giovanni* K. 527 (1787/8) and Beethoven's Ninth Symphony, Op. 125 (1824), I.

'Understood at Last'?: A Memetic Analysis of Beethoven's 'Bloody Fist' 423

The start of the recapitulation recomposes the exposition's opening dominant-orientated material, Example 1 xiv, giving it a new tonic-major orientation. By the beginning of the recapitulation the range of interpretations of the opening has narrowed considerably: it is retrospectively recoded (certainly by many listeners) as a V_3^6 with a missing/implicit third and the recapitulation is heard as beginning with D major as either I_3^6 or as V_3^6 of iv. Aurally, this D major is redolent of the climax of the Act II finale of *Don Giovanni* in its 'cold pitiless majesty' [8], where, as Giovanni is dragged down to hell, an austere *stile antico* cadence (bb. 592–3) resolves onto a luminous, quasi-baroque *Tierce de Picardie*, Example 1 xiii. This may be heard, as with most tonic-major conclusions of minor-key movements, as oscillating between functioning as a I and as a V of iv.

Additionally, and for all its epic scale and intensity, the opening of Beethoven's recapitulation draws upon a typical *recitativo secco* harmony and chord-disposition, the third of the D major chord appearing in the bass and the tonic and dominant degrees sounding above. Beethoven's *tutti* orchestration and *ff* dynamic transform one of the oldest sonorities and textures in tonal music, and illustrate how secondary parameters [9] can contribute markedly to the prominence of the figuration in a passage while paradoxically blurring their stylistic origins. The structural locus contributes a further saliency effect, the constituent patterning being greatly intensified by its placement at this most pregnant formal juncture of the movement.

In co-adaptation with this harmony, the figuration in bb. 301ff. – specifically the falling $\hat{1}$–$\hat{5}$–$\hat{1}$ pattern marked 'Museme (musical meme) *a*' in Example 1 xv – while amorphous in character, draws upon certain allele-classes (sets of functionally/structurally analogous musemes) commonly replicated in recitatives whose constituent musemes incorporate pitches oscillating between $\hat{1}$ and $\hat{5}$ of the prevailing harmony and rhythmic patterns of short/weak-to-long/strong note values (generally reflecting stressed second syllables in Italian). Example 1 iv shows the recitative before No. 2 of *Don Giovanni*, where Donna Anna, having earlier left her father in order to summon assistance, returns with Don Ottavio to the Commendatore's lifeless body. It contains three motions between a^1 and d^2, two rises (bb. 1 and 3) and a fall (b. 2), and of course it is largely based on a D major $^6_3$ chord. Similarly, bb. 7–10 of the recitative before No. 13 (Example 1 vi), in which Zerlina and Masetto argue before the arrival of Don Giovanni, has the same harmonic underpinning and similar melodic gestures. Obviously one may find countless similar passages in different keys in this and other late-eighteenth-century operas; and neither of these two recitatives contains an exact antecedent coindex of Museme *a*. But the posited link with *Don Giovanni* is strengthened when several other connections with the opera are considered. Primary among these is the clear possibility that Museme *a* might derive from the opening bars of the Overture to *Don Giovanni*, Example 1 i, which outlines Museme *a* over a $i-V^6_3-i$ harmonic progression. These bars, as is made explicit when they are reworked at the Commendatore's return in the 'retribution' scene, No. 24.5 (Example 1 ix), adopt a similar *recitativo* (here *accompagnato*) texture. In accordance with the large-scale structural symmetry underpinning the opera [10], No. 24 also begins with this museme (bb. 1–3), foreshadowing the larger contour of the melody sung by Giovanni at 'Già la mensa è preparata' (bb. 5–7, 17–19), Example 1 viii.

Museme *a* illustrates the point made in Sect. 1 regarding the power of memetics to bring together a range of perspectives under a single Darwinian framework. A three-note museme, it conforms to Narmour's notion of 'Process' (see the brackets on Example 1 xv), whereby the implication of the fourth d^3-a^2 is for further continuation in the same direction via an interval of similar size [11]. This implicative force counteracts the internal segmentational pressure of the rest at b. 4 (Overture) and b. 436 (No. 24) in Mozart's passages, subordinating it to the segmentational force of the initial and terminal node d^3 and d^2 and thereby binding the elements of the museme together to form a single psychological unit capable of serving as a unit of selection. These 'innate' attributes are mediated by enculturated judgements, meaning that the a^2, as a contextually determined $\hat{5}$, will tend to resolve to d^2, as $\hat{1}$, and not, for instance, to $e\flat^2$, the rather less normative $\flat\hat{2}$; and that the d^2 will be perceived as a point of tonal/stylistic closure.

Having identified a unit via the invocation of music-psychological and music-theoretical criteria, those attributes which relate to its salience may be considered. While the quantification of a museme's salience is complex [5], any given museme has an equal, greater or lesser salience than any other, and this fact will, on Darwinian principles, determine the museme's relative predominance in the wider population of musemes. Were one to quantify the salience of every museme in relation to every other, then the index of this salience would, *ceteris paribus*, be directly proportional to the relative distribution of each museme. In the case of Museme *a*, for example, and on the basis that (as a Process) $i - rp = x.(y - x)$, Jan's metric gives a value of 5.2; whereas for Museme *c*, and on the basis that (as a 'Retrospective Reversal' [11] followed by two Processes (see the brackets on Example 1 iii)) $i - rp = (x.(y - x)) + (x.(y - x)) + (x.(y - x))$, it gives a value of 9.4 [5]. This suggests that, again *ceteris paribus*, Museme c is c. 1.8 times more salient, and was therefore c. 1.8 times more predominant in its meme pool, than Museme a. Such 'population-memetics' determinations can, in principle, help finesse traditional musicological discussions of style change in historical contexts by fostering understanding of why particular patterns and processes predominate in certain music-historical periods.

Beethoven's harmonic progression across bb. 300–301 – vii$^{\sharp 4}_3$–I$^6_3$, labelled 'Museme b' in Example 1 xv – is closely related to the opening of No. 24.5 in *Don Giovanni*, Example 1 ix. The harmonic function and inversion of the diminished seventh of Mozart's 'Commendatore' progression is different to Beethoven's (it is vii$^{\sharp 6}_5$/V–V$^6_3$ in Mozart as against yvii$^{\sharp 4}_3$–I$^6_3$ in Beethoven), but the two Museme b progressions in Example 1 ix and xv may be regarded as the same museme if Beethoven's is heard as resolving onto the dominant of iv – an implication which is followed up explicitly in the subdominant gravitation of his bb. 322–6. As discussed above apropos the climax of No. 24, the same flatwise gravitation is also found in b. 3 of Example 1 iv and b. 10 of Example 1 vi. In the former, as Ottavio takes over, the preceding D major harmony is retrospectively reinterpreted, as is often the case with major $^6_3$ chords in recitatives, as a local dominant. Indeed, his phrase in bb. 56–8 of the following Recitative of No. 2, Example 1v, moves from dominant-functioning D major harmony to G minor, and might be regarded as another instance of Museme a.

As shown in Example 1 xv, the bass figure in Beethoven's bb. 318–22 marks the intersection of two distinct musemes with antecedents in *Don Giovanni*. That marked 'Museme c', a figure which outlines the scale degrees $\hat{5}$–$\hat{1}$–$\hat{7}$–$\hat{6}$–$\hat{5}$–$\hat{4}$ in D minor or $\hat{2}$–$\hat{5}$–$\hat{4}$–$\hat{3}$–$\hat{2}$–$\hat{1}$ in G minor, might be traced back to a figure sung by Giovanni in No. 1 at 'di pugnar teco', Example 1 iii, where he attempts to evade a conflict with the Commendatore. In its tonality of G minor, Mozart's passage anticipates Beethoven's swerve to this key in bb. 320–22 on his repetition of Museme c. This second occurrence of Museme c is marked by infilling of the fourth a–d^1, first with semiquavers and then, at the start of an abortive third statement (b. 322), with a Mozartean triplet 'roulade' upbeat figure. This is the only such pattern in the whole of Beethoven's first movement; the simple triplet figure, ♪♫, by contrast, is common (see b. 19 and the derived bb. 55f). This roulade connects Beethoven's pattern with a recurrence of the same museme from Giovanni's final encounter with the Commendatore, at his renunciation of the opportunity of repentance at 'Ho fermo il core in petto: non ho timor, verrò!', Example 1 xii (roulades boxed). Both Mozartean instances of Museme c are therefore associated with the idea of Giovanni attempting to exert control over the situations in which he finds himself in conflict with the Commendatore, the first concerning his physical safety, the second that of his immortal soul.

Overlapping with Museme c, the pattern marked 'Museme d' traces a familiar galant-Mozartean arc, found in *Don Giovanni* at bb. 6–7 of No. 24, Example 1 viii, even hinting at the relative major key in Beethoven's passage despite the prevailing tonic-minor context. This pattern, $\hat{5}$–$\hat{5}$–$\hat{4}$–$\hat{3}$–$\hat{2}$–$\hat{1}$, or its lower-third shadow $\hat{3}$–$\hat{3}$–$\hat{2}$–$\hat{1}$–$\hat{7}$–$\hat{1}$ (these strictly two musemes, owing to their different intervallic sequence), is arguably emblematic of Giovanni's worldly pomp and arrogance and occurs throughout the opera in passages sung by or about him. A subtype of the 'Cadence Galante' [12], it is one of the Don's distinctive musical fingerprints and it resonates obstinately at the centre of Beethoven's passage, resisting the encompassing tumult.

These two musemes also offer evidence in support of certain neurobiological theories of information encoding. That advanced by William Calvin, the Hexagonal Cloning Theory (HCT), proposes a theory of neuronal 'minicolumns' distributed regularly across the surface of the neocortex and organized into resonating triangular arrays in response to perceptual stimulation or memory recall [13, 14]. These arrays are hypothesized to be organized into hexagonal plaques, each encompassing a set of coordinated attributes, such as the constituent pitches of a museme [15]. Copying of these hexagons over the surface of cortex occurs according to Darwinian principles, the 'victorious' configuration representing the best fit with incoming perceptual data or the details of a recognized or remembered pattern. Within a given region of neocortex, several potential arrays, and their associated hexagonal overlays, may be supported by embedded 'attractors' in the neuronal connectivity. This would help account for the overlapping encoding of Musemes c and d, as two notionally discrete musemes which nevertheless share certain pitches [16]. The HCT will be invoked again in Sect. 5, because it can illuminate the mechanisms underpinning extroversive mappings between musemes and verbally-tokened concepts.

A few bars after the co-statement of Musemes c and d, the descending diminished seventh line of Beethoven's bb. 327–9, marked 'Museme e' in Example 1 xv, is a replication of the same museme as underpins bb. 177–80 of No. 13's 'Bisogna aver coraggio', the trio of encouragement sung by the masked Anna, Ottavio and Elvira (Example 1 vii), albeit with the mutation of Mozart's antepenultimate $\natural\hat{2}$ to $\flat\hat{2}$ in Beethoven. This chromaticism might appear to be tonal flotsam impelled by the mutational pressure of the preceding wave of subdominant harmony, but it also relates to similar passages from other places in *Don Giovanni*. Such other antecedent coin-dexes (all diminished-seventh-outlining musemes, with or without $\flat\hat{2}$; some perhaps best regarded as belonging in separate but overlapping allele-classes [16]), include Leporello's phrase at 'Ah padron, siam tutti morti!', bb. 449–51 of No. 24, Example 1 x, with its distinctive falling diminished seventh contour and $\flat\hat{2}$; and the Commendatore's following 'Non si pasce di cibo mortale', bb. 454–9, Example 1 xi. The falling diminished-fifth museme at the start of the second group of the Overture, Example 1 ii (expandable to a seventh by the operation suggested on the example), is also similar in contour to Beethoven's line; the diminished-fifth figure might be regarded as an exemplar of a subset class of the diminished-seventh-progression allele-class(es).

3 Interpretations of Extra-Musical Meanings

It is perfectly possible that the connections discussed in Sect. 2 inhere purely in the realm of style and patterning. That is, Beethoven may have simply seen elements of Mozart's opera as offering solutions to the compositional problems which faced him in the first movement of the Ninth Symphony, prompted perhaps by the cueing effect of the shared tonic. But if *Don Giovanni* were indeed one source of Beethoven's passage, then we might wonder whether the shared tonality and musemic replication were motivated by Beethoven's having intended a semiotic or referential connection by means of alignments between 'verbal-conceptual memes' and musemes. To begin to address this, Table 1 summarizes the attributes and locations of Musemes *a–e* in both works, together with their explicit text-associations in *Don Giovanni* (translations are from [17]). Bracketed terms in italics are implicit high-level concepts inferred from the explicit text content of the opera and are discussed further in Sect. 5. A 'Museme *f*' is also listed in Table 1, and will be discussed in Sect. 4.

Table 1. Musemes *a–f* in Mozart's *Don Giovanni* and Beethoven's Op. 125, I

	Attributes	Number and Bars in *Don Giovanni*	Explicit and Implicit Text content in *Don Giovanni*	Bars in Op. 125, I
a	$\hat{1}$–$\hat{5}$–$\hat{1}$ recitative figure	Overture: 1–4 No. 24: 433–6	– 'Don Giovanni, a cenar teco'/'Don Giovanni, you invited me to dine with you' (*hedonism, retribution*)	301–3, and *passim*
b	vii$^{\#6}_5$/V–V$^6_3$ or vii$^{\#4}_3$–I$^6_3$ harmonic progression	No. 24: 433–6	'Don Giovanni, a cenar teco'	299–301
c	$\hat{5}$–$\hat{1}$–$\hat{7}$–$\hat{6}$–$\hat{5}$–$\hat{4}$ in i or $\hat{2}$–$\hat{5}$–$\hat{4}$–$\hat{3}$–$\hat{2}$–$\hat{1}$ in iv melodic figure	No. 1: 145–6 No. 24: 514–15	'[Va, non mi degno] di pugnar teco'/'[Go, I don't want] to fight with you' (*evasiveness*) '[Ho fermo il cuore in petto:] non ho timor: [verrò!]'/'[My heart is beating steadily] I'm not afraid. [I'll come!]' (*masculine resistance*)	318–20
d	$\hat{5}$–$\hat{5}$–$\hat{4}$–$\hat{3}$–$\hat{2}$–$\hat{1}$ or $\hat{3}$–$\hat{3}$–$\hat{2}$–$\hat{1}$–$\hat{7}$–$\hat{1}$ melodic figure	No. 24: 6–7 No. 24: 18–19	'Già la mensa è preparata'/'The table is already prepared' (*appetite/excess/hedonism*)	318–20
e	sometimes infilled falling $\hat{6}$–($\natural\hat{2}/\flat\hat{2}$)–$\#\hat{7}$ melodic figures	Overture: 77–8 No. 13: 176–80 No. 24: 449–50 No. 24: 455–9	– 'Bisogna aver coraggio'/'We must be courageous' (*retribution*) 'Ah padron! Siam tutti morti!'/'Oh master! We're all going to die!' (*retribution*) 'Non si pasce di cibo mortale, chi si pasce di cibo celeste'/'No nourishment from mortal food for one who is nourished by celestial food' (*higher purpose*)	327–9
f	V^7/♭II versus G^6 harmonic museme	Overture: 27–9 No. 2: 36–42 No. 24: 538–40	– '[Caro padre!] Padre amato! Io manco [, io moro.]'/'[Dear father!] Beloved father … I am fainting. [I am dying.]' (*Anna as victim*) 'Pentiti! – No!'/'Repent! – No!' (*retribution; aggressive resistance*)	312–26

There is no obvious 'episodic' plot arc in Beethoven's passage, in the sense that arranging the associated textual content of Mozart's musemes in the order in which they are replicated by Beethoven does not describe or re-enact a coherent chronological or linear narrative. Rather, the connection appears more 'semantic' [15], in the sense that the primary conceptual topos of *Don Giovanni*, the notion of vengeance or retribution, together with various ancillary ideas, is generically attached to Beethoven's passage by virtue of the strong Museme *a*, *b* and *c* connections. In Mozart, these patterns highlight encounters between the Don and the Commendatore, and thereby articulate the conflict between the desire for liberty and the necessity for order.

If we take Anna's account of her encounter with Giovanni at the start of the *Introduzione* at face value, the hypothesized connections between the symphony and the opera align with McClary's controversial 'rape' metaphor for Beethoven's passage – indeed it recuperates her original reading, despite her strategic retreat from that interpretation. McClary argues that 'the point of recapitulation ... unleashes one of the most horrifyingly violent episodes in the history of music' [18], coded as a specifically sexual violence in her initial reading. This was outlined in [19], in which she spoke of 'the throttling, murderous rage of a rapist incapable of attaining release'. In the article's later reprint, in [18], McClary excised this passage and foregrounded violence rather than (failed) rape [20]. Nevertheless, the interpretation of sexual violence is sustained by McClary's re-citation in the reprint of Rich's poem 'The Ninth Symphony of Beethoven Understood at Last as a Sexual Message' (1972), with its arresting imagery of rage and incipient sexual violence; and it is to that first reading, despite its subsequent partial renunciation by McClary, to which I primarily refer here [18, 21]:

A man in terror of impotence
or infertility, not knowing the difference
a man trying to tell something
howling from the climacteric
music of the entirely
isolated soul
yelling at Joy from the tunnel of the ego
music without the ghost
of another person in it, music
trying to tell something the man
does not want out, would keep if he could
gagged and bound and flogged with chords of Joy
where everything is silence and the
beating of a bloody fist upon
a splintered table.

To expand upon this network of connections between *Don Giovanni*, Beethoven's movement, and McClary's (first) reading of Beethoven's passage, one might ask whether Beethoven's own personal circumstances in the early 1820s motivated an imaginative transfer of the semantic constellation of the opera to the implicit narrative of the symphony movement, the musical threads tacitly linking *ars* and *vita*. It is not beyond probability that, if the first movement of the Ninth Symphony were indeed associated by Beethoven via the *Don Giovanni* connection with notions of transgression and violent retribution, then the focus of his various tensions was his sister-in-law, Johanna van Beethoven. Long an object of stony disapproval, Beethoven came to regard her as his greatest adversary and, rightly or wrongly, the wellspring of his misery. Even though their legal conflict over the custody of his nephew Karl had been formally resolved in Beethoven's favour in July 1820, Karl continued to see his mother surreptitiously and, in the composer's view, came to be depraved and corrupted by her malign influence [22].

Is it conceivable that Beethoven regarded himself as in some sense a Don Giovanni figure in relation to his sister-in-law? If so, there are two scenarios through which this transference might have been channelled. Either he saw himself as exacting revenge – in a distortion of the opera's theme of retribution *for* sexual and physical violence –

through imagined sexual and physical violence on his Joh/Anna. Or, alternatively, he perhaps felt that he himself deserved punishment, imaginatively through musical cross-association, for a similarly imaginary violation of Joh/Anna. For both of these horrible scenarios, we might also ask – despite the consensus that the underlying motivation for rape often stems from a quest for power and control – whether the violence was perhaps motivated by an underlying desire, a sublimated eroticism, on Beethoven's part? Whatever the details of Beethoven's psycho(path)logy, one overarching interpretation of the evidence discussed is that while he could never enact physically or sexually his feelings of violence against (or his desire for) his sister-in-law, he could certainly play them out imaginatively in music, by means of memetic transference from an antecedent work which develops many of the same themes. In this sense, from Mozart's musemes' eye view, their association with verbal-conceptual memes relevant to Beethoven's biographical and psychological circumstances conferred upon them a clear selective advantage.

Fink defends and expands upon McClary's critique, situating it in respect to a dialectic of 'romantic-modern' *versus* 'postmodern' sublimity. The former encompasses situations where 'unpresentable content [is] mediated by the power of formal presentation'; the latter addresses 'the traumatic moment where the unpresentable breaks through into presentation itself', and thereby defies attempts at the 'beautification' of the unpresentable in romantic-modern sublimity through the rationalization afforded by formal analysis. Such rationalization reaches its apotheosis, according to Fink, in Schenker's structuralist monograph on the symphony of 1912 [20, 23]. Fink argues that the 'unpresentable', the violence of the moment of recapitulation, has been articulated by a variety of metaphors in the critical literature on the symphony since the late 1830s, these coalescing around two predominant (in my terms) verbal-conceptual memeplexes [5]. One articulates Faustian notions of the *Erdgeist* (a fearsome, blazing spectre), and the other concerns ideas of storm, chaos and apocalypse, with both crystallizing in the account given by Marx [20]. Fink maintains that McClary's original 'rape' metaphor aligns broadly with both of these traditions – encompassed by the idea of 'Beethoven Antihero, the Faustian purveyor of sublime eroticized violence' – by virtue of McClary's metaphor adopting a female subject-position with respect to the brutality [20].

In a similar (albeit not gendered) vein, Chua discusses Beethoven's passage in the light of Adorno's critique of the 'coldness' of modern society and his reading of the opening of the recapitulation as representing 'a steely vision engaged in some kind of staring contest with fate' [24]. The formal requirement of the recapitulation represents an authoritarian and repressive force, perhaps none more so than in Op. 125, I; but the violence of repression motivates resistance because '[t]he "shudder" of the recoiling subject in such moments of structural necessity produces a counterforce that stares fate in the face … it shakes the "I" into an awareness of an ethical sublimity within itself that can withstand the limits imposed by an authoritarian world' [24]. The resistance is embodied by an attenuation of the unity of purpose and texture normal at this formal axis and expected on the basis of the 'unison [*sic*] haze' of the opening of the exposition [24]. Specifically, the bass line of bb. 312ff. acts as a 'rogue element', destabilizing the tonality with 'unorthodox' voice leading [24]. It 'refuses to align itself with the forces above it', thereby counteracting the normal hegemony of the principal theme at this point of the form [24]. It is not difficult to equate the rogue element with Don Giovanni/Beethoven who – while convincing himself of his 'ethical sublimity' – rails against (in the first scenario hypothesized above), or subliminally welcomes (in the second), the constraints of society and their immuring of his desire to settle the score, as it were, with Joh/Anna.

4 A Memetic Analysis, Part II

For Fink, the locus of the 'traumatic moment', the place 'where the unpresentable breaks through into presentation itself', is bb. 312–15 (Example 1 xv), in which a notated dominant seventh in E♭ major is heard to function as a German sixth. Its treatment is irregular in that, apart from the 'incorrect' notation, it is initially presented in the 'wrong' inversion (♯iv$^{\#4}_2$, last quaver beat of b. 312), and then resolved – via Chua's 'unorthodox' voice leading [25] – not to a chord of dominant function (i$^6_4$ or V) but to a tonally unsatisfying i$^6_3$ (b. 315), which might tentatively be aligned with Rich's image of the 'terror of impotence'. One might categorize it as an example of harmonic ellipsis, broadly related to certain 'elliptical retransitions' in Haydn. In these, various anticipated harmonies are omitted in order to engender puzzling and witty effects [26].

This progression is similar in technique and effect to that of bb. 34–5 of the first movement, where a i$^6_4$ resolves to a i$^5_3$ without an intervening V$^5_3$. Several other examples of this type of ellipsis may be found in music of Beethoven's third period, as can converse cases where a V resolves first to a I$^6_4$ then to a I$^5_3$ (the latter such as in bb. 2–3 and 26 of the third movement of Op. 125). Moreover, the lead-up to this non-cadence (bb. 31–3) mirrors passages sung by Anna from No. 2 of *Don Giovanni*, 'Ma qual mai s'offre' (bb. 39–40, of which more presently) and from No. 23, 'Crudele! Ah no, mio bene!' (bb. 14–15) in its vii^7/iv–vii^7/V(–i$^6_4$) progression.

While not observed by Fink, the treatment of the augmented sixth chord is a manifestation of yet another memetic connection with *Don Giovanni*, because a distinctive harmonic fingerprint of the opera is its play with the notation and resolution of the pitch collection B♭–D–F–G♯/A♭, its spelling as a German sixth leading to i$^6_4$ in D minor, and as a dominant seventh of the Neapolitan leading to ♭II$^6_{♭4}$. Rushton's analysis of three passages involving these progressions is paraphrased in Example 2 [10]. This abstracts material from the Overture (Example 2 ii), the accompanied recitative of No. 2 (iii) and No. 24 (iv) of *Don Giovanni*; together with the start of the recapitulation of Beethoven's symphony movement (v). It also shows material from Mozart's Sonata in C minor K. 457 (1785), I (i), transposed for ease of comparison, which prefigures Mozart's treatment of this harmony in *Don Giovanni* [27].

Example 2 $V^7/\flat II$ versus G^6 harmonic museme in *Don Giovanni* and Op. 125, I.

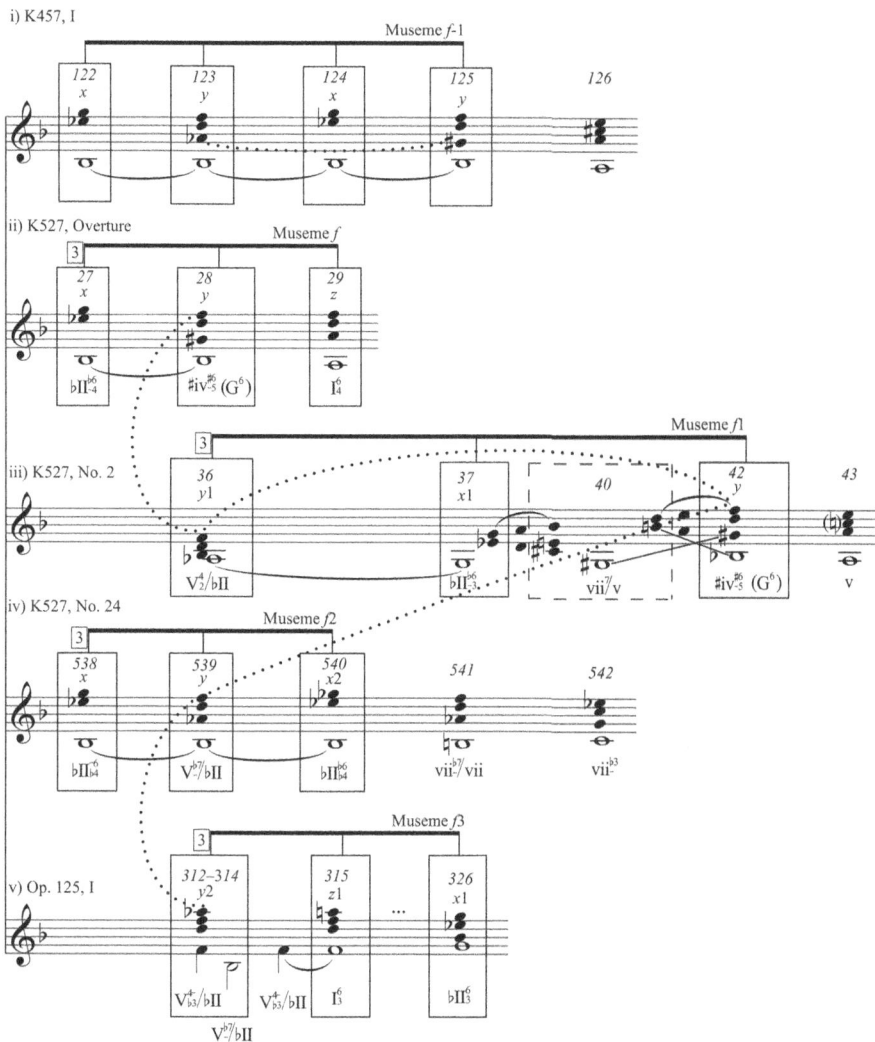

Specifically, the 'fingerprint' involves the three harmonies marked x ($\flat II^6_4$), y ($\sharp iv^{\sharp 6}_5/G^6$) and z (i^6_4), which are presented in the Andante of the Overture in their 'canonical' x–y–z form (the Sonata movement presents x–y–x–y); mutated to y^1–x^1–y in the recitative of No. 2, where Anna sings of her love for her father before fainting (with a pre-figuration of the 'Crudele!' vii^7/iv–vii^7/V progression in bb. 39–40, shown in the dotted box in Example 2 iii); further mutated to x–y–x^2 in No. 24, where Giovanni refuses for the last time to repent before the statue of the Commendatore withdraws, leaving Giovanni to his fate; and then, in Beethoven, mutated yet again to y^2–z^1–x^1.

The three chords constitute a distributed harmonic museme, labelled 'Museme *f*' in Example 2, one relatively impervious to the sequential permutation and mutation of its component elements. One might more correctly describe it as a discontiguous harmonic museme held together by a 'musico-operational/procedural' museme – a set of operations, possibly articulable verbally-conceptually, which affect musemes in specific ways and which make a distinction between a generic procedure and a specific material substrate – the latter regulating the G♯/A♭ enharmonic 'trick'. In Beethoven, the museme is able to retain its identity and connection with its antecedents, despite undergoing radical mutation and temporal extension. The posited Museme *f* connection with *Don Giovanni*, particularly when considered in the light of the links engendered by Musemes *a–e*, appears a more convincing reading of Beethoven's passage than Fink's comparison of it with the undoubtedly similar bb. 174–200 of the Gloria of the *Missa Solemnis* (which may of course also have been influenced by aspects of *Don Giovanni*) [20].

5 Towards a Musico-Conceptual Synthesis

The foregoing sections have presented evidence of connections between Mozart's *Don Giovanni* and the first movement of Beethoven's Ninth Symphony, and have attempted to use them as evidence in support of a memetic view of musical structure and of a particular reading of the opening of Beethoven's recapitulation which aligns it with the notions of vengeance and retribution through sexual violence. But it might be argued that the mediation between the purely musical (the introversive) and the semantic (the extroversive) here is largely informal. One way of formalizing the linkage would be to invoke the notion of the 'conceptual integration network' (CIN) [28].

This proposes that even notionally 'absolute' music can be treated as an instance of multimedia, in that it integrates a number of spaces: a 'music space' (encompassing a 'selection of attributes from the musical trace'); a 'text space' (encompassing either the explicit text of a vocal work, or an implicit/inferred verbal-conceptual abstract or image in the case of an instrumental composition; the latter constitutes 'a discovery within the music of these qualities, in the sense that the interpretation builds upon the music's semantic potential'); a 'generic space' (characterized by an 'enabling similarity', meaning 'there must be common attributes presented by the various media in question … in the absence of which there would be no perceptual interaction between them'); and a 'blended space' ('in which the attributes unique to each medium are combined, resulting in the emergence of new meaning') [25, 28].

In the case of memetic relationships between two works, it is logical to extend Cook's model to represent connections, and therefore semantic transference, between two CINs. Figure 1 (after [25]) shows such a composite CIN, formed of networks for *Don Giovanni* and the first movement of the Ninth Symphony, and a 'meta-blended space' arising from their interaction. The CIN for *Don Giovanni* identifies the text space concepts of aggressive and hedonistic masculinity, Anna as the object of desire and violence, and punishment for the transgression of societal and class norms (these concepts being derived from the italicized terms in Table 1); the music space elements of Musemes *a–f* and the bold D major/minor sonorities; the generic space concepts of

'Understood at Last'?: A Memetic Analysis of Beethoven's 'Bloody Fist'   433

resoluteness, fearless audacity, and terror; and the blended space concepts of vengeance and retribution, and fratricide. The CIN for Op. 125, I is adapted from that abstracted by Cook from McClary's (revised) reading [25]. It identifies the music space elements of Musemes *a–f* and the bold D major/minor sonorities; the text space concepts (from McClary) of 'violence, mindlessness, the maintenance of identity, and desire'; the generic space concepts of forcefulness, power and violence; and the blended space concepts of pent-up aggression, Johanna as the object of desire, violence and retribution, and fratricide.

A composite CIN allows mappings between two works related to each other in one or more of their spaces to be further connected by means of extrapolated connections between other, corresponding spaces. The music spaces of both CINs are closely connected, given their hypothesized memetic relationships and their more general textural and tonal alignments (represented by the arrow connecting the two CINs). Given this, we can hypothesize correspondences between the two works' generic spaces and their blended spaces, such that a 'meta-blended space' might be extrapolated (dotted arrows). This identifies the concepts of misogynistic violence, retribution and fratricide as arguably common to the two works and draws on a 'biographical

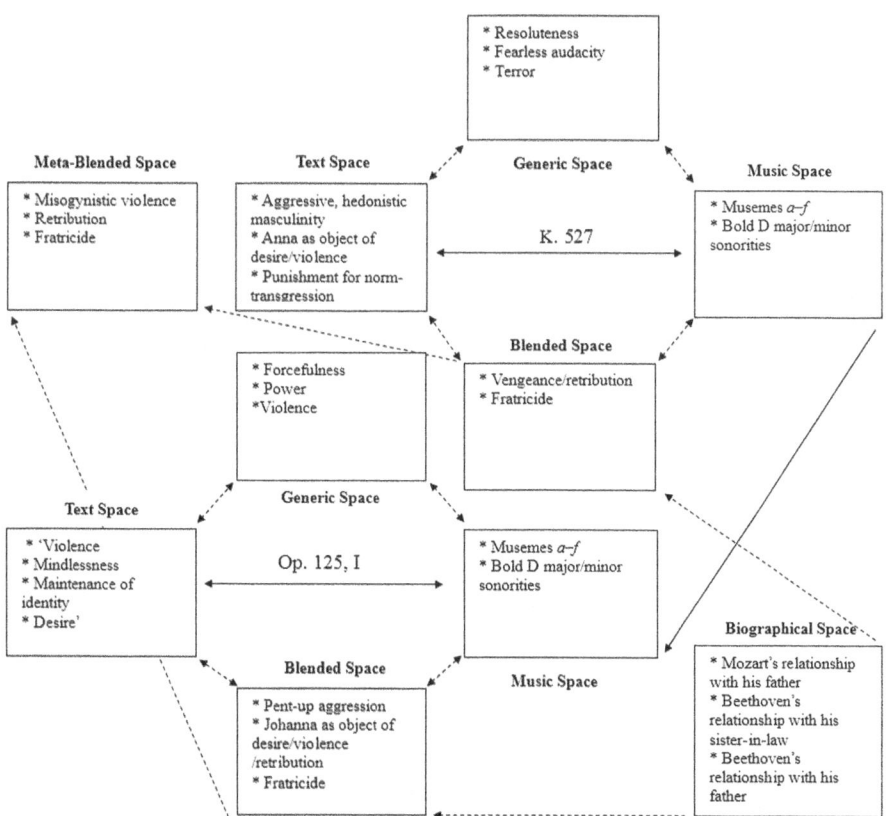

Fig. 1. Composite CIN for *Don Giovanni* and Beethoven's Ninth Symphony, I

space' as supporting evidence for the linkage. The memetics of this linkage, and a possible neurobiological mechanism, are considered below.

Fratricide, an issue not considered in Sect. 3, is a further element which aligns *Don Giovanni* with Op. 125, I. Giovanni kills the father figure of the Commendatore as an unintended consequence of his (attempted?) rape of Anna – a reading which would of course imply a quasi-incestuous relationship between Giovanni and Anna. Drawing upon Freudian psychology, Keller implicates Haydn as a father figure to Mozart, citing the latter's allegedly mocking uses of F minor – a key of similar emotional significance for Haydn as G minor was for Mozart and C minor for Beethoven – in Barbarina's 'L'ho perduta', No. 24 of *Le nozze di Figaro* (1786) and Alfonso's 'Vorrei dir', No. 5 of *Così fan tutte* (1790), both overblown displays of trivial or mock emotion [29]. Keller contends that 'the ionisation of F minor was a subtle means whereby Mozart's unconscious allowed itself to discharge its ambivalence [to Haydn], which would have been absolutely intolerable on the conscious level' [30]. Keller might presumably argue that the death of the Commendatore, in a passage in F minor, is to be understood in this context. But it is not inconceivable that Leopold Mozart was the intended 'victim'. This is certainly not a new reading – the film version (1984) of Peter Schaffer's play *Amadeus* (1979) makes it melodramatically explicit – yet it is perhaps supported by Mozart's apparent ambivalence towards his father.

At the risk of ascribing another cruel and unedifying motive to Beethoven, it might be argued that he too is committing a form of fratricide by these connections, because for a number of years he entertained a Freudian 'family romance' which attempted to

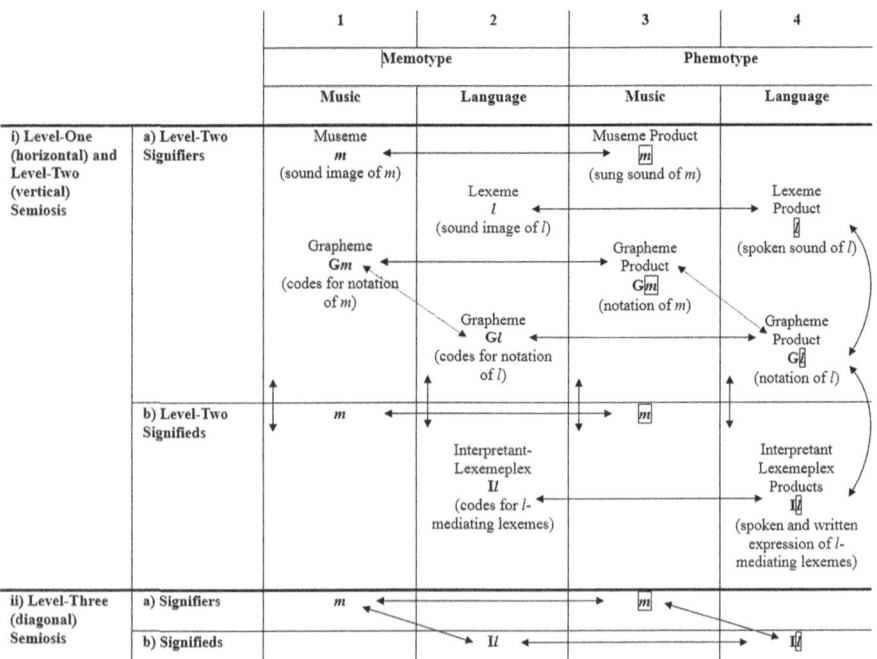

Fig. 2. The Memetic-Semiotic Nexus of an *m-l* Music-Language M(us)emeplex

airbrush his real father – the undistinguished, alcoholic and violent Bonn court tenor Johann van Beethoven – from history and, bizarrely and improbably, replace him by a noble parent. For years, Beethoven did nothing to correct numerous rumours that he was the illegitimate son of either King Frederick II (1712–86) or King Friedrich Wilhelm II (1744–97) of Prussia. It is perhaps not unconnected that the dedicatee of the Ninth Symphony was Friedrich Wilhelm II's son, Friedrich Wilhelm III (1770–1840), on the warped logic of the family romance, Beethoven's own 'half-brother' [31].

The inter-dimensional connections represented by the double-headed arrows in Fig. 1 align with Saussure's definition of the sign. He argued that '[t]he linguistic sign unites ... a concept and a sound image' [32]. These may be formulated memetically as 'memotypes' (brain-located, Calvinian-wired forms of the meme) associating in musico-conceptual memeplexes and giving rise to certain 'phemotypic' (extrasomatic, physical) products [5]. Such associations, although 'stable' [32], are not historically immutable, and so can be seen as the vehicle for the evolution of meanings and socio-cultural immanence in an evolutionary cultural semiotics. Figure 2 (after [33]) generalizes situations in which a museme m is associated (both privately, as in the Mozart-Beethoven connection here, and publically) with an extra-musical concept represented by its sound-image, the word, or 'lexeme', l, forming a complex, m–l.

In Fig. 2 i a, columns 1 and 3, and at the lowest level of referring ('level-one semiosis'), $\boxed{m}$ – the physical sonority, through which m, via the intercession of voices or musical instruments, impinges upon us most directly – is represented, in a 'horizontal' memetic-semiotic relationship, as the phemotypic (coded-for) meme-product of the memotypic (coding-for) m. Thus, $\boxed{m}$ acts as a (somewhat abstract) signifier for m. $m \leftrightarrow \boxed{m}$ is often associated with a 'grapheme' $\mathbf{G}m \leftrightarrow \mathbf{G}\boxed{m}$, which partly governs the arguably superficial matter of notating m and which, while not essential for its existence, is nevertheless (in the case of literate cultures) often significant for its transmission. The same principle is true, of course, in the case of lexemes. By analogy with $m \leftrightarrow \boxed{m}$, columns 2 and 4 of Fig. 2 i a illustrate corresponding relationships for the lexeme l, which codes for the spoken expression $\boxed{l}$. Paralleling $\mathbf{G}m \leftrightarrow \mathbf{G}\boxed{m}$, $\mathbf{G}l$ is a grapheme coding for the written expression $\mathbf{G}\boxed{l}$. As with the music-related memes, the phemotypic forms $\boxed{l}$ and $\mathbf{G}\boxed{l}$ act as signifiers (again somewhat abstractly) for the associated memotypic signified forms l and $\mathbf{G}l$ respectively. Note that a lexeme not only articulates an extra-musical concept, but also the natural-language name of an m (such as 'falling $\hat{1}$–$\hat{5}$–$\hat{1}$ line' (Museme a) or 'vii$^{\#4}_3$–I$^6_3$ progression' (Museme b)).

As represented in Fig. 2 i b, columns 1 and 3, and at an intermediate level of referring ('level-two semiosis'), $\mathbf{G}m$ also exists, now as a *signifier*, in 'vertical' semiotic co-adaptation with m, even though it is essentially independent of it (their relationship is 'arbitrary' [32]). $\boxed{m}$ is similarly associated, as signified, with the corresponding phemotypic signifier meme, $\mathbf{G}\boxed{m}$. Analogously, l and $\mathbf{G}l$ function as signifiers of the signified language 'interpretant-lexemeplex' $\mathbf{I}l$. By this is meant the wider network of cognate lexemes which provide the context for l and which anchor it in a broader web of signification [32]. The components of $\mathbf{I}l$ ultimately devolve to the 'back-end' mental models and images for which l (and $\mathbf{I}l$) are the 'front end'. In this sense, $\mathbf{I}l$ is the essence of the 'conscious propositional thought' tokened by l [34]. As with the m-related memes, $\boxed{l}$ and $\mathbf{G}\boxed{l}$ function as signifiers of the signified $\mathbf{I}\boxed{l}$.

As symbolized in Fig. 2 ii, and at the highest level of referring ('level-three semiosis'), the 'diagonal' association between $m \leftrightarrow \boxed{m}$, as signifier, and $\mathbf{l} \leftrightarrow \boxed{\mathbf{l}}$, as signified, forms a $m-l$ m(us)emeplex, one either confined to a particular individual or shared more widely within a cultural community. In such associations, the presence of the musical element triggers/cues the verbal in consciousness (or vice versa).

The various spaces in Fig. 1 and their equivalents in the form of the cells in Fig. 2 are connected by double-headed arrows, which represent the associations or linkages between phenomena in different dimensions and substrates by which understanding and meaning emerges. While the representation of patterns and their linkages on a two-dimensional page is useful to foster clarity of exposition, it also appears that this mirrors structural localization and interconnection in the brain. The HCT offers a mechanism for such linkages because beyond the localized connections implicated in the regional cloning of hexagons, Calvin hypothesizes the existence of '*faux*-fax links', longer-range connections which associate hexagons in one area of cortex, such as those encoding musemes in the auditory cortex, with hexagons in other areas, such as those encoding verbal-conceptual thought in the pre-frontal cortex [13].

6 Conclusion

This chapter has covered a number of complex, interconnected issues and cannot claim to have offered more than a limited overview of how (to take perhaps the fundamental issue) linkage between sensory-musical and verbal-conceptual thought is implemented. In particular, there is still a considerable gap in our knowledge of how low-level neurobiological functions relate to their high-level psychological correlates. But it has at least suggested that accounts of musical structure and meaning can be built upon a memetic foundation, which is itself supported by established neurobiological and psychological principles; and that this foundation can support fresh insights – many able to be explored and modelled computationally – into particular musical works. In the case of the connections hypothesized between Mozart's *Don Giovanni* and Beethoven's Ninth Symphony, and mindful of the risk of wanton iconoclasm, a number of music-structural, music-historical and music-biographical insights – perhaps even, 'at last', a truer 'understanding', to borrow Rich's words – appear to have emerged.

References

1. Agawu, V.K.: Playing with Signs: A Semiotic Interpretation of Classic Music. Princeton University Press, Princeton (1991)
2. Hopkins, A.: The Nine Symphonies of Beethoven. Heinemann, London (1981)
3. Dawkins, R.: The Selfish Gene. Oxford University Press, Oxford (1989)
4. Rosen, C.: The Classical Style: Haydn, Mozart, Beethoven. Faber, London (1997)
5. Jan, S.B.: The Memetics of Music: A Neo-Darwinian View of Musical Structure and Culture. Ashgate, Aldershot (2007)
6. Blackmore, S.J.: The Memes' Eye View. In: Aunger, R. (ed.) Darwinizing Culture: The Status of Memetics as a Science, pp. 25–42. Oxford University Press, Oxford (2000)

7. Blackmore, S.J.: The Meme Machine. Oxford University Press, Oxford (1999)
8. Abert, H.: Mozart's Don Giovanni. Ernst Eulenburg, London (1976)
9. Meyer, L.B.: Style and Music: Theory, History, and Ideology. University of Chicago Press, Chicago (1996)
10. Rushton, J.G.: W.A. Mozart Don Giovanni. Cambridge University Press, Cambridge (1981)
11. Narmour, E.: The Analysis and Cognition of Basic Melodic Structures: The Implication-Realization Model. University of Chicago Press, Chicago (1990)
12. Gjerdingen, R.O.: Music in the Galant Style. Oxford University Press, New York (2007)
13. Calvin, W.H.: The Cerebral Code: Thinking a Thought in the Mosaics of the Mind. MIT Press, Cambridge MA (1996)
14. Killian, N.J., Jutras, M.J., Buffalo, E.A.: A map of visual space in the primate entorhinal cortex. Nature **491**, 761–764 (2012)
15. Jan, S.B.: Music, memory, and memes in the light of Calvinian neuroscience. Music Theory Online **17** (2011)
16. Jan, S.B.: A memetic analysis of a phrase by Beethoven: Calvinian perspectives on similarity and lexicon-abstraction. Psychol. Music **44**, 443–465 (2016)
17. Fisher, B.D.: Wolfgang Amadeus Mozart Don Giovanni. Opera Journeys, Coral Gables (2002)
18. McClary, S.: Feminine Endings: Music, Gender, and Sexuality. University of Minnesota Press, Minneapolis and London (2002)
19. McClary, S.: Getting down off the Beanstalk: the presence of a woman's voice in Janika Vandervelde's Genesis II. Minnesota Composers' Forum Newsletter (1987)
20. Fink, R.W.: Beethoven antihero: sex, violence, and the aesthetics of failure, or listening to the Ninth Symphony as postmodern sublime. In: Dell'Antonio, A. (ed.) Beyond Structural Listening? Postmodern Modes of Hearing, pp. 109–153. University of California Press, Berkeley (2004)
21. Rich, A.: Poems: Selected and New, 1950–1974. Norton, New York (1975)
22. Kinderman, W.: Beethoven. Oxford University Press, Oxford (1995)
23. Schenker, H.: Beethoven's Ninth Symphony: A Portrayal of Its Musical Content, with Running Commentary on Performance and Literature as Well. Yale University Press, New Haven and London (1992)
24. Chua, D.K.L.: Beethoven's Other Humanism. J. Am. Musicol. Soc. **62**, 571–645 (2009)
25. Cook, N.: Theorizing Musical Meaning. Music Theory Spectr. **23**, 170–195 (2001)
26. Spitzer, M.: The retransition as sign: listener-orientated approaches to tonal closure in Haydn's Sonata-form movements. J. R. Music. Assoc. **121**, 11–45 (1996)
27. Jan, S.B.: Replication, parataxis, and evolution: meme journeys through the first movement of a Mozart sonata. In: Miranda, E.R. (ed.) A-Life for Music: Music and Computer Models of Living Systems, pp. 217–260. A-R Editions, Middleton (2011)
28. Cook, N.: Analysing Musical Multimedia. Clarendon, Oxford (1998)
29. Steptoe, A.: The Mozart-Da Ponte Operas: The Cultural and Musical Background to Le nozze di Figaro, Don Giovanni, and Così fan tutte. Clarendon, Oxford (1988)
30. Keller, H.: Key characteristics. Tempo **40**, 5–10, 13–16 (1956)
31. Solomon, M.: Beethoven. Schirmer, New York (1998)
32. Nattiez, J.-J.: Music and Discourse: Toward a Semiology of Music. Princeton University Press, Princeton (1990)
33. Jan, S.B.: From holism to compositionality: memes and the evolution of segmentation, syntax and signification in music and language. Lang. Cogn. **7**, 1–38 (2015)
34. Carruthers, P.: The cognitive functions of language. Behav. Brain Sci. **25**, 657–726 (2002)

Music and Dementia: Two Case-Studies

Alexis Kirke[1(✉)], Belinda Dixon[2], and Eduardo R. Miranda[1]

[1] Interdisciplinary Centre for Computer Music Research, School of Humanities,
Music and Performing Arts, Faculty of Arts, University of Plymouth,
Drake Circus, Plymouth, UK
{Alexis.Kirke,Eduardo.Miranda}@Plymouth.ac.uk
[2] BBC Radio Devon, Seymour Road, Plymouth, UK
Belinda.Dixon@bbc.co.uk

Abstract. In this paper two current related projects on music and dementia are described. One is a form of design science research. It details the making of a 60 min BBC radio program which was produced in collaboration with people living with dementia and experts and carers. The program consisted of a mixture of tunes and documentary segments. These discussed various topic relating to dementia, radio and music (including an on the above memory jingles research). The structure of the program was designed in such a way as to make it more understandable to people living with dementias. The second project is a project which culminated in a performance made up of memory jingles, some of which were algorithmically generated and developed for an early-stage dementia patient. She provided a list of her ordered daily activities and a description of one of her medication dosages. The daily activity list was rhythmically adjusted, and a tune was written to it, by a composer. However it is not possible for all people with dementia to have a "composer-in-residence". Hence computer music techniques were also investigated towards some form of automation of composition. This algorithm was used to compose a tune for the medication description from the volunteer. A few weeks later she exhibited the ability to recall both tunes and words in multiple informal environments (including high pressure situations).

Keywords: Alzheimer's · Dementia · Jingles · Algorithmic composition · Radio · Broadcast · Memory · Reminiscence

1 Introduction

Music as a means to help those living with dementias has been widely studied. For example the Alzheimer's Society in the UK run Singing for the Brain sessions [1] in which people living with dementia can attend with carers. During these sessions familiar songs are sung, sometimes with synchronized movements. The sessions provide a social venue as well. The film "Alive Inside" [2] attracted much attention, premiering at the Sundance festival, and demonstrating anecdotally the positive effects of music on residents in care homes living with dementia. However there has not been as much attention paid to the use of music to create new memories as opposed to reminiscence on older ones, nor on the use of radio broadcasting in supporting people with dementia. In this paper two projects which are currently addressing these issues are introduced. The first - Project EAR (Environments for Alzheimer's-friendly Radio) – involved working alongside the BBC to investigate ways of making radio broadcasts more dementia-friendly. The project takes the approach of design science research [3] and short survey information was used to structure a fully-produced 60 min broadcast on the BBC Radio Devon "Music, Memory and Making Radio". It is now being used as a case-study to get broader feedback from listeners with dementias, their carers and experts, and those who are not affected by dementia. The second project utilizes music to aid memory, culminating in a performance, made up of memory jingles developed for an early-stage dementia patient. The week before the performance she exhibited the ability to recall both tunes and words in multiple informal environments (including high pressure situations such as radio interviews [4]), with only two cases of forgetting or mistakes.

2 Related Work

The use of non-pharmacological methods such as music in therapies for dementias and Alzheimer's disease has a long history [5]. Music has been widely used in wellbeing therapy. Examples include testing whether individualised or classical relaxing music in the background in a residential home was more effective at calming people with Alzheimer's disease and related disorders [6]. Reminscence therapy is another approach using music from the patient's past. [7] examined the positive effects of reminiscence therapy on depressed elderly persons with dementia. [8] surveyed a number of such approaches, suggesting that reminiscence therapy can improve both mood and some cognitive function.

[9] actually performed a systematic review covering the effects of music therapies on those with Alzheimer's. They suggest that short duration music therapy leads to moderate reduction of anxiety, and small positive effects on behavioural symptoms. Extending the length to three months has a large effect on reducing anxiety.

Aside from as anxiety and social issues, the best known symptoms of dementia and Alzheimer's disease are memory recall and retaining new memories. Music has also been utilized in relation to these symptoms. It has been found that autobiographical recall in patients with dementia improves significantly when music is playing [10]. In terms of creating new memories, people with Alzheimer's exhibit frontal lobe damage and [11] showed using near-infrared spectroscopy that pre-frontal cortex activity is decreased by music in such a way as to help memory encoding. [12] showed that those with mid-term Alzheimer's were able to memorize gesture sequences better with a musical mnemonic than without. [13] suggests that music recognition is spared in dementia and Alzheimer's. [14] later concluded that musical memory including lyrics may be spared in the early and mid-stages of Alzheimer's, and even preserved in some late-stage patients.

It is a short step from these ideas to considering explicitly using music to help memorization of words in patients with Alzheimer's. As far back as [15], it was found that some patients diagnosed with Alzheimer's can, with practice, learn new words for a new song, even when they are not able to remember new spoken words in general. [16] used lyrics of unfamiliar children's songs accompanied by either a sung or spoken audio of the words, and found that those with Alzheimers had higher recognition accuracy for the sung words than the spoken words. Whereas older adults without Alzheimer's showed no significant difference. [17] involved a single Alzheimer's patient and found that they were able to learn new words with music better than words without music. This work was extended to 6 patients successfully [18]. However [19] found mixed results of putting words to music – in that there was not a significant improvement in memorization of specific phrases when music was added to the phrases. Though there was a better memory of the concept behind the words. These final results, although very helpful, are a long way from being conclusive. They depend on the music used and the way words are fitted to the melodies. Some melodies and lyrics are simply more memorable than others. These factors are not specifically addressed or tested in [19]. Their work also raised the issue of what environment should be used for learning: the tests were done in time limited laboratory conditions. Whereas recreational music listening is usually done in a far more relaxed and repetitive way. Clearly more research needs to be done to systemize the composition and presentation of memory songs.

3 Radio Documentary

One way many people listen to music is on broadcast radio. Project EAR (Environments for Alzheimer's-friendly Radio) is a project working alongside BBC Radio Devon which investigates making the mechanics of radio-broadcasting more dementia friendly. As part of the project a 60 min BBC Radio Devon programme was produced and broadcast which utilized some of the initial feedback on radio and dementia. The initial feedback stage was conducted using small sample discussions. There was a one-to-one long informal meeting with a person with dementia, visits to Plymouth Crownhill Alzheimer's Society Memory Café, and Exmouth Carers Support Group. The following were also contacted for feedback and responded: Life Care Radio, Alzheimer's Society Singing for the Brain Leader Plymouth, Alzheimer's Society Singing for the Brain Leader Exmouth, Director Plymouth Music Zone, and Alzheimer's Society Employee. There was no standardized questionnaire used, but the general question of "how can we make radio more dementia friendly" was put to people, including some of the answers already provided to give people a starting point for discussions.

The key points that came from the initial discussions were:

1. Consistency - Avoiding DJ/presenter changes and switch-around when possible, pre-warn. Avoid too many schedule changes. Keep jingles consistent for as long as possible.
2. Content - Chatting preferable to long periods of music. People with dementias may prefer shorter "bitesize" information elements. Hits and headlines shows.

3. Speech - Avoid "gabbling", people speaking over each other, speaking over music with lyrics, or at least giving useful information at that time.
4. Information - Reinforce importance of time checks and including the full time of day and date if possible. Repeat key information.
5. Interaction - Find a simpler route to where to get more information as many people living with dementia are unable to go online. Support for people with dementias wanting to get involved in phone-ins.

This information was used to structure the fully-produced 60 min broadcast on the BBC Radio Devon "Music, Memory and Making Radio" [20, 21]. The programme structure had an unusual mix of music and speaking, multiple repetitions of the presenter's names and the subject of the documentary, mini-features kept as short as possible, and during the recording of interviews, signs were put up asking people to speak clearly. The precise structure of the program is shown in Table 1. It incorporated mini-features on what makes music memorable, how music can be used to help people with dementias (in the memory jingles project), and the initial findings regarding dementia-friendly radio broadcasts. The broadcast is now being used as case-study to get broader feedback from listeners with dementias, their carers and experts, and those who are not affected by dementia. Some of these are shown in Table 2. It is also being used by BBC Radio Devon to promote dementia friendly broadcasting to the BBC nationally.

Table 1. Structure of "Music, Memories and Making Radio" broadcast BBC Radio Devon December 27th 2014.

Time	Type	Topic
00:00	Spoken	Preview of topics and introduction
01:30	Spoken	Ear worms and memory jingles
08:22	Music	Humorous
13:04	Spoken	Repeated introduction
13:28	Spoken	Radio and dementia: cocktail party effect
17:38	Spoken	Repeated introduction and re-cap
18:18	Spoken	Music and reminiscence (including some brief music clips)
27:42	Music	Bridge over troubled water
32:12	Spoken	Musical memory
36:00	Music	My first, my last, my everything
38:25	Spoken	Time checks; music and action (including music clips)
47:15	Music	Toms diner
49:40	Spoken	Repeated introduction and summary
50:15	Spoken	Programmes targeted at people with dementia
55:28	Music	Toms diner opening to fade out
55:44	End	

Table 2. Feedback from listeners

Listener	Structure	Content
Male with vascular dementia (UK)	"It's the first time that I've actually sat for a full hour and listened to a radio station." "Way put together absolutely brilliant."	"Never been enough to interest me. Listened to today, full hour every bit, so interesting, learning for me." "I think it's bloody great."
Female with Alzheimer's (AU)	"Very long" "Somewhat UK specific" "Maybe the music clips are shorter" "The whole show is shorter"	"Good idea about time checks" "Mention alongside this the actual day of the week" "Fascinating, engaging, and has given me much to think about"
Female with lewy body dementia (UK)*	"In a way, the musical breaks take it down to digestible chunks." "Some of it I lost a little bit of the track of it." "In a way it's not directed at people with dementia is it?"	"I did find it interesting I must admit." "Went into quite a lot of interesting bits and pieces." "Tend not to know what documentaries are about. Can't follow them." Found one particular scientist's comments "very confusing".
Male with frontotemporal dementia (UK)		"Whilst I agree that music is a vital part of dementia, but, everybody's taste is different. My taste of music would not suit the next person. The idea of a dedicated dementia radio program is fantastic."
Male with lewy body dementia (UK)		"The piece where "doreen" from plymouth sang different things would not be practical as there are too many things to remember."
Female with dementia (UK) [observation by professional]	"Every time any snippet of music played, [PWD] tended to tap her foot and/or nod in time, sometimes smiling too" "Where there was a lot of similar sounding talk in the radio programme - probably scripted elements rather than chatter of "real" people! - she tended to close her eyes and possibly nod off."	"[PWD] very much enjoyed Rosie and Elsie's story, and like the way it presented the situation in a positive light. " "[PWD] said 'If you live alone you depend on the radio - only if you are lucky you come across a programme that really appeals'."
Carer - lead of carer support group (UK)		"Over all I thought the programme was excellent. I do think there should have

(*Continued*)

Table 2. (*Continued*)

Listener	Structure	Content
		been a little more information on dementia - how it affects sufferers and carers."
Hospital radio production company (UK)	"Were very impressed, we will certainly be seeking to use many of the strategies that you talked about in our shows"	
Carer and Alzheimer's expert (US)	"Very easy to listen too."	"This is absolutely fascinating and very well done"
Male clinical music therapist (UK)	"I wonder if there could be some short spells of silence dispersed into the programme? […] This might help someone re-engage in listening after periods of habituation."	
Clinical music therapist (UK)	"Perhaps more music than talks" "making the talks even shorter".	
Care home services manager (UK)	"The last part of the broadcast was the most enjoyable due to the content and songs used to engage." "I believe items played out to popular themes will engage more but bringing it is to a conversation in a radio play would be good." "The parts containing popular tunes in a more full version were more engaging."	
Care home manager/activities co-ordinator (AC) [joint response]	"We thought it was both excellent and suitable for people living with dementia, and we had no ideas on how it could be improved, it was an hour long but the time went really quickly." "it was a great deal of what [AC] does, phrases, singing, short jingles, funny poems, music quizzes, feeding them words to jog there memory." "It was very engaging programme, with short clips to listen to, and the mixture of music was very good"	"Thought it was excellent" "The programme very enjoyable" "The programme techniques would also help to educate carers of people living with dementia e.g., the Cocktail Party and understanding the difficulties people living with dementia have in communication and others should be more aware of the back ground noises (The cocktail party)." "It was all good and would be something that could be put on the activity programme."

4 Remember a Day and Memory Jingles

The Remember a Day project began with a meeting with a trustee of the Alzheimer's society, who was asked what information might be useful for people living with dementia to have memory support for. He said that their daily plan, phone numbers and medication would be useful. An Alzheimer's Society session of Singing for the Brain was attended and a lady of 83 who was in the early stages of dementia was recruited to collaborate on the project. She had tentative diagnoses of Alzheimer's or Dementia with Lewy bodies, and Parkinson's disease. She provided her regular daily routine reminders, and an example of a medication she took regularly. Her daily plan is: open curtains, check calendar/diary, let the dog out, have breakfast, take medication, feed dog, brush teeth, shower, dress, walk the dog, clean dishes, clean the cooker, and brush the dog. An example of the medication was her Parkinson's disease medication: Cobeneldopa which she takes twice a day, dosage 25/100.

The daily plan was set to music manually written by a composer. The medication description was set to music with the help of an algorithmic composition system. The process for writing the daily plan tune was to firstly re-arrange the words to make them more rhythmic and lyrical: "Wake up, Pull curtains, Do you diary, Let the dog out, Have breakfast, Take tablets, Feed dog. Clean your teeth and take a shower, get dressed and walk the dog, do the dishes, clean the cooker, brush dog". A first draft of the tune was then composed manually by the first author. The process used was to tread a compositional line between direct copying of old tunes, while still keeping the tune pleasant, recognizable and clichéd. This was to aid memory. The resulting tune is shown in Fig. 1.

Fig. 1. Daily plan song

It was interesting that there were repeated questions from people who heard the tune who thought they recognized the music it was based on. This supports the generic nature of the composition – however it was not based on any particular tune. The use of descending phrases for "have breakfast, take tablets, feed dog" and then again for the second half of the tune are particularly clichéd.

The process for the second tune was a result of the recognition that even if "memory jingles" are effective tools for those living with dementia, people cannot have their own personal composers assigned to them throughout the country or world. Hence some level of automation would be desirable. The automation was only partially achieved in preparing for the performance. The method used was to base the timing of notes on the syllable rhythms in the entered text, and the pitches on the vowels in each syllable. The standard model of a syllable is: (i) consonant or consonant cluster; (ii) a vowel or syllabic consonant; (iii) a "coda", often another consonant. In English the most common form of syllable is produced by pairing a vowel and a consonant. There are consonants which syllabic too, such as "y". This model only covers a subset of words but is used as a first approximation in the system described here.

The system is written in Matlab and first takes a text string as input. In this case "cobeneldopa, twice a day, twenty five, one hundred". The system then goes through and converts the text in vowels, consonants and pauses, giving:

"CVCVCVCCVCV-_CCVCV-_V-CVC-_CCVCCV_CVCV-_VCV_CVCCCVC"

Note that because "y" is a syllabic consonant, it is converted to "V" not "C". The "_" represents the shorter pause of a word gap, the "-" the longer space of a comma. Next the system gets rid of consecutive repeats. Thus becoming:

"CVCVCVCVCV-_CVCV-_V-CVC-_CVCV_CVCV-_VCV_CVCVC"

These are then converted to syllables using a VC and CV rule moving forwards through the string:

"SSSSS-_SS-_S-SC-_SS_SS-_SV_SSC"

where each "S" represents a syllable.

The string is then analyzed for any free standing vowels or consonants, which clearly are also syllables. There are none in this case. Finally it removes straggling consonants and vowels, on the assumption (only approximately correct) that they do not make independent syllables:

"SSSSS-_SS-_S-S-_SS_SS-_S_SS"

It can be seen that the final analysis is incorrect. But it does give the approximate syllable structure with pauses. These are then converted to musical pitches based on Table 3. Each syllable is either a vowel, or a consonant-vowel or vowel-consonant pair. So the syllable's vowel is used to define the pitch from Table 3. These pitches were selected initially based on letter frequency mapped on the frequency of desired pitches by the composer (first author). However they were tweaked compositionally to get the final Table 3 values, during multiple informal tests by ear. The rhythms of the notes were defined by placing rests between them, with short rests between "_" and longer rests for "-".

Table 3. Mapping from vowels to pitches

Vowel	Dictionary occurrence frequency	Associated note	MIDI value
A	8.5 %	D	62
E	11.2 %	C	60
I	7.5 %	E	64
O	7.2 %	F	65
U	3.6 %	G	67
Y	1.8 %	A	69

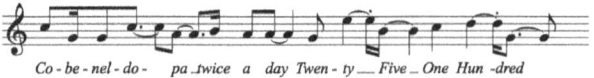

Fig. 2. Memory tune for the medication

After the text "cobeneldopa, twice a day, twenty five, one hundred" was entered into the system, the syllabic analysis was not only inaccurate but the resulting rhythmic effect was found to be unsuitable in terms of emphasis on syllables. The input was therefore adjusted by hand to give the final desired compositional effect. This involved deleting or adding certain letters and punctuation, to remove, shift or add syllables to the tune. The final melody is show in Fig. 2. This approach means that the system is not yet suitable for full automation, but at least begins to address some of the issues and ask some of the questions needed for a more broadly automated approach. It certainly sped up the composition of the memory jingle.

Both tunes and words were sent to the collaborator living with dementia, on her tablet. A few weeks later she exhibited the ability to recall both tunes and words in multiple informal environments (including high pressure situations). This supports some of the other formal and informal testing done on "memory jingles" already discussed, as well as the methods used by one leader of an Alzheimer's Society Singing for the Brain Session. The leader has set the days of the week to a well-known tune, and also encourages attendees' carers to set shopping lists to music as well [22].

The tunes were used to construct a piece of music called Remember a Day, for mezzo soprano, cello and electronics, which was premiered at Peninsula Arts Contemporary Music Festival 2014. A recording is available here [23]. The performance was in fact in the form of a musical 'embedding' session itself. The 3 movements were very repetitive, so as to maximize the embedding of the tunes in the collaborator attending the concert. However the main purpose of the performance was to raise awareness of dementia (it was introduced by the Alzheimer's Society UK) and to encourage the use and investigation of memory jingles. The resulting awareness raising was very successful with interviews about the collaboration appearing on BBC Radio 4 and BBC Radio 2 at peak times. Also there were invitations to speak about memory jingles at a carer-support group.

5 Conclusions and Future Work

In this paper two related projects involving music and dementia have been described. One is a project described was a form of design science research. It detailed the making of a 60 min BBC radio program which was produced in collaboration with people living with dementia and experts and carers. The structure of the program was designed in such a way as to make it more understandable to people living with dementias. Currently in this project we are receiving feedback from listeners living with dementia and their carers as to how understandable and enjoyable they found the programme. This includes direct individual feedback – from those with dementia who listened to the program, and also feedback from listening groups. For example, in one listening group people with dementia and their carers gathered, under the leadership of an enabler from the Alzheimer's Society, to listen to the programme and provide feedback.

The second is a project which culminated in a performance made up of memory jingles developed for an early-stage dementia patient. The patient provided a list of her ordered daily activities and a description of one of her medication dosages. The daily activity list was rhythmically adjusted, and a tune was written to it, by a composer. Computer music techniques were also investigated towards some form of automation of composition. An algorithm was used to compose a tune for the medication description from the volunteer. A few weeks later she exhibited the ability to recall both tunes and words in multiple informal environments (including high pressure situations). This project has now been developed into a 4–5 year project plan and collaboration with an expert music therapy group to fully investigate and automate the memory jingle system. In terms of evaluation plans, there have been attempts to use non-automated music composition to make text more memorable for people living with dementia - and their testing plans included a control. In other words: people with dementia trying to remember text with and without music, and people who did not have dementia were included as well. So we would utilize experience from these previous projects in testing our planned automated system.

References

1. Bannan, N., Montgomery-Smith, C.: Singing for the brain. **128**(2), 73–78 (2008)
2. Downs, M.: Embodiment: the implications for living well with dementia. Dementia **12**(3), 368–374 (2013)
3. Park, Y., El Sawy, O.A.: Towards a design theory for hedonic systems: delivering superior user experience in the digital home entertainment context. In: Proceedings of the Third International Conference on Design Science Research in Information Systems and Technology. Georgia State University, Atlanta (2008)
4. Vine, J., Kirke, A., Abbott, D.: The Jeremy Vine Show, BBC Radio 2, London, UK. https://www.youtube.com/watch?v=qeT-G8w-KbM. Accessed Feb 2015
5. Olazaran, J., et al.: Nonpharmacological therapies in Alzheimer's disease. **30**(2), 161–178 (2010)
6. Gerdner, L.: Effects of individualized versus classical "relaxation" music on the frequency of agitation in elderly persons with Alzheimer's disease and related disorders. Int. Psychogeriatr. **12**(1), 49–65 (2000)
7. Ashida, S.: The effect of reminiscence music therapy sessions on changes in depressive symptoms in elderly persons with dementia. J. Music Ther. **37**(3), 170–182 (2000)
8. Cotelli, M., Manenti, R., Zanetti, O.: Reminiscence therapy in dementia: a review. Maturitas **72**(3), 203–205 (2012)
9. Ueda, T., Suzukamoa, Y., Satoa, M., Izumia, S.: Effects of music therapy on behavioral and psychological symptoms of dementia: a systematic review and meta-analysis. Ageing Res. Rev. **12**(2), 628–641 (2013)
10. Larkin, M.: Music tunes up memory in dementia patients. Lancet **357**(9249), 47 (2001)
11. Ferreri, L., Bigand, E., Perrey, S., Muthalib, M., Bard, P., Bugaiska, A.: Less effort, better results: how does music act on prefrontal cortex in older adults during verbal encoding? An fNIRS study. Front. Hum. Neurosci. **8**, 301 (2014)

12. Moussard, A., Bigand, E., Belleville, S., Peretz, I.: Music as a mnemonic to learn gesture sequences in normal aging and Alzheimer's disease. Front. Hum. Neurosci. **8**, 294 (2014)
13. Cuddy, L., Duffin, J.: Music, memory, and Alzheimer's disease. Med. Hypotheses **64**(2), 229–235 (2005)
14. Cuddy, L., Duffin, J., Gill, S., Brown, C., Sikka, R., Vanstone, A.: Memory for melodies and lyrics in Alzheimer's Disease. Music Percept. **29**(5), 479–491 (2012)
15. Prickett, C., Moore, R.: The use of music to aid memory of Alzheimer's patients. J. Music Ther. **28**(2), 101–110 (1991)
16. Simmons-Stern, N., Budson, A., Ally, B.: Music as a memory enhancer in patients with Alzheimer's disease. Neuropsychologia **48**(10), 3164–3167 (2011)
17. Moussard, A., Bigand, E., Belleville, S., Peretz, I.: Music as an aid to learn new verbal information in Alzheimer's disease. Music Percept. **29**(5), 521–531 (2012)
18. Moussard, A., Bigand, E., Belleville, S., Peretz, I.: Learning sung lyrics aids retention in normal ageing and Alzheimer's disease. Neuropsychol. Rehabil. **24**(6), 894–917 (2014)
19. Simmons-Stern, N., Deason, R., Brandler, B., Frustace, B., O'Connor, M., Ally, B., Budson, A.: Music-based memory enhancement in Alzheimer's disease: promise and limitations. Neuropsychologia **50**(14), 3295–3303 (2012)
20. Kirke, A., Dixon, B.: "Music, Memories and Making Radio", BBC radio devon, Plymouth, UK. http://www.bbc.co.uk/programmes/p02fhkl6. Accessed Feb 2015
21. Kirke, A., Dixon, B.: http://www.alexiskirke.com/2015/01/03/alexis-co-presents-bbc-devon-radio-program/. Accessed Feb 2015
22. Chapman, S.: Personal Communication, January 2014
23. Kirke, A.: Remember a day, Peninsula arts contemporary music festival, Plymouth, UK. http://www.alexiskirke.com/2015/02/25/remember-a-day-movements-1-2-and-3-now-available-online/. Accessed Feb 2015

Strictly Rhythm: Exploring the Effects of Identical Regions and Meter Induction in Rhythmic Similarity Perception

Daniel Gómez-Marín[✉], Sergi Jordà, and Perfecto Herrera

Music Technology Group, UPF, Barcelona, Spain
daniel.gomez@upf.edu
http://mtg.upf.edu/home

Abstract. This paper is inspired in the ideas of rhythmical variation and evolution, which are connected to similarity and contrast. Two experiments on rhythm similarity are presented that examine the possible relations between objective metrics and human similarity ratings. We wanted to test the possible differences in similarity ratings when a beat was induced and when it was not. The experimental design is based on identical regions inserted in the rhythmic stimuli which are progressively shifted. Twentyone subjects participated in 2 experiments devised to calibrate the effect of identical regions and beat induction in similarity ratings. Results show that identical regions can influence similarity ratings more likely when there is not a meter induced. On the other hand, the induction of a pulse is prone to elicit an attention to coincidences between rhythms. It is also observed that coincidences in the first region of a rhythmic pattern have more importance than coincidences on other regions in order to be correlated to human similarity ratings. Practical consequences of these findings are discussed in the context of tools and agents for music creation.

Keywords: Rhythm · Similarity metrics · Syncopation · Edit distance

1 Introduction

Rhythmic similarity is a research topic of rhythm perception, that links the knowledge of cognitive mechanisms with musical practice. Knowing how alike two rhythms will appeal to a human listener is connected with the tasks of rhythmic variation and development, which are fundamental for music composition and performance. To predict how similar two rhythms are requires the comprehension of the processes that a sound undergoes from its acoustical stimulus until it can be described by its rhythmical characteristics. Some authors have used this knowledge of rhythm perception to elaborate theories and define metrics that can somehow answer the question of rhythmic similarity. For being considered relevant, these metrics have to be contrasted with perceptual similarity experiments. The most developed similarity metrics can be divided on two main categories, either in the computation of string dissimilarity (i.e. the edit distance) or in pulse induction and an implied set of temporal hierarchies (i.e. syncopation-based metrics).

The main goal of this paper is to study the relation between current similarity metrics and subjective similarity measures, and the context in which these measures are undertaken. Particularly there is an interest in understanding if the metrics are consistent both in isolated scenarios (such as an experimental settings) as to common music listening, performing and composing scenarios where a pulse is present. Two experiments were carried out, one where similarity ratings were given to a set of pairs of rhythms without any beat induction and a second experiment where the same pairs of rhythms were rated with an artificial beat induction. The difference in similarity ratings between the two experiments is explored and the results show that very often ratings differ when the same pair of patterns is compared with and without an induced beat. The discrepancy in the results suggests that different mechanisms operate in each case, each focusing in different elements of the rhythms. This different rating behaviours are related to the fact that rhythms autonomously induce the pulse by which they are going to be measured afterwards [5].

After a concise state of the art on rhythm perception and similarity metrics (Sect. 2), we present in Sect. 3 the methods and techniques used to test our hypotheses. Sections on results (4 and 5) and its relevance (Sect. 6) complete this paper.

2 State of the Art

2.1 Rhythm Perception

Making sense of a musical rhythm implies the ability to feel a pulse when presented with a sequence of sound events. One theory suggests that different rhythmic patterns have different induction strengths, which is the ease by with which subjects generate an internal clock commonly embodied by tapping or nodding when listening to music [13]. It is found experimentally that when a constant time cue or a rhythmic context is given, subjects are more accurate at reproducing an induced pattern. Further research suggests that this internal clock is dynamic and can adapt to temporal changes in the stimulus [7]. There are several approaches to beat induction modeling using different techniques, methods and results [2].

Lerdhal and Jackendorf propose that the pulse or tactus is used to determine the temporal structure of a musical pattern, based on isochronous subdivisions of the beat that have different salience weights or hierarchies [8]. When a musical phrase is analyzed using these hierarchies, or salience profiles, the notion of syncopation, and particularly the notion of syncopation level emerges [9]. The syncopation level is based on assigning weights to the notes on a musical phrase based on their rhythmic relations with the beat. The syncopation salience of a sound event is related to its challenging or reinforcement of the beat, where a syncopation is determined by presence of an onset anticipating the beat (or an important subdivision of it), filling the expectancy of a beat with a silence or a tie challenging the continuity of the beat [5].

Different authors use and expand the concepts of syncopation and syncopation level. Experiments have suggested a correlation between the syncopation level of a musical phrase and the difficulty for subjects to reproduce a rhythm [3]. The hierarchies established for the subdivisions and repetitions of the pulse are further explored, suggesting the existence of different weight profiles for musicians and non musicians [6]. Syncopation has also been considered when exploring the desire to move and the experience of pleasure in subjects exposed to drum breaks, suggesting that intermediate degrees of syncopation elicit the strongest desire to move and pleasure in music associated with groove. The authors propose extension of the syncopation level from the monophonic version on Longuet-Higgins and Lee to a new polyphonic measure [17]. Syncopation is a concept based on the perceptual phenomena of beat expectancy, caused by measurable features of a rhythmic pattern. This concept is used successfully in different studies associated to rhythm perception and cognition.

2.2 Rhythmic Similarity

What does it mean that two rhythms feel similar? what are the criteria involved in such a judgement? what can we generalize from that claim? Many authors have explored the idea of formally modelling and predicting human subjects' ratings by means of a similarity value computed from rhythm-derived numerical features. The notions of syncopation, rhythmic salience and weight profiles have all played a role in this rhythmic similarity exploration. The simplest syncopation measure, by which two patterns can be compared, is a single number, resulting of accumulating the syncopations encountered in a musical phrase according to one of the weight profiles exposed above. More elaborated values establish how similar is the syncope of two phrases by means of a syncopation histogram (counting the different levels of syncopation found a musical phrase). Some authors [16] have found some correlations between human similarity judgements and syncopation histograms. Others such as Cao et al. [1] propose the grouping of rhythms by families that share a same level of syncope within a given window of analysis. This measure is based on dividing a phrase in isochronous fragments and labeling each fragment depending on its relation with the beat (N if the event reinforces the beat, S if it is syncope, O if it is neither). A rhythmic pattern can then be represented by a sequence of N, S or O. The resulting sequences constitute the different rhythmic families. Although the experiments show that families are a powerful discriminator for distances, the authors also report on another factor that has a higher relation with similarity which is the pattern of onsets. The authors propose that if two patterns share an identical region (IR) their similarity ratings are likely to be high. Although the authors do not explicitly define the concept of IRs on their paper, some inferences can be made from the stimuli they use to test them:

– The size of the identical regions is always longer than a beat and no longer than two and a half beats.

- Each identical region has at least three onsets.
- The identical region is always at the beginning of at least one of the tested rhythms.
- Shifts between identical regions in from pattern to pattern are always one beat or one and a half beats.
- Rhythms that are compared among them have the same amount of onsets. They have 6 or 7 onsets.
- Only in one case there is a repetition of a small fragment of one pattern present in two regions of another pattern.

The edit distance is a metric commonly used for comparing two strings, measuring the amount of transformations that one string must have in order to become the other. For example, "the eight-pulse rhythm [x x . x x . x .] may be obtained from the seven-pulse rhythm [x x . x x . .] by inserting the symbol x between the sixth and seventh pulses in the seven-pulse rhythm. A deletion is the inverse operation of an insertion. A substitution replaces one symbol for another. For instance, the eight-pulse rhythm [x x x x x x . .] may be converted to the six-pulse rhythm [x x x . . .] by changing the sixth symbol in the eight-pulse rhythm from x to . (a substitution) and deleting the first two x symbols. Thus, the edit distance simply permits the comparison of rhythms that have different numbers of pulses as well as onsets, since deletions shorten the duration of a rhythm, and insertions lengthen it" [15].

The edit distance has been used as a tool for establishing similarity ratings between musical phrases [10,11]. Recent experiments show how the edit distance between rhythms fairly correlates with human judgements [4,14,15]. Experiments based on a prototype rhythm, the clave son, and variations of it show that the higher the edit distance, the further the perceived closeness between both patterns [12].

2.3 Precision of Metrics

As presented above, some of the rhythmic similarity metrics correlate with human similarity ratings but none has the ability to distinguish between two closely similar rhythms. The edit distance for example, seems to be a good method for clustering patterns in similarity groups, but fails at establishing further differences among patterns, bringing patterns rhythmically different into the same category. One case could be these three different rhythms,

$$1 0 0 0 1 0 0 1 0 0 1 0 1 0 0 0$$
$$1 0 0 1 0 0 1 0 1 0 0 0 1 0 0 0$$
$$1 0 0 1 0 1 0 0 0 1 0 0 1 0 0 0$$

all located at edit distance 2 from the "clave son"

$$1 0 0 1 0 0 1 0 0 0 1 0 1 0 0 0$$

but to a listener they are clearly different [12].

The shortcoming of the edit distance to establish differences among clearly different rhythms opens the door for new analyses. The question of how can a group of different rhythms that are equidistant to a reference (i.e. at a low edit distance values) be differentiated and ranked by human listeners becomes relevant. The following experiments deal with rhythmic patterns that are located at a same or close edit distance from a source, but that are recognized as different. The experiments will try to reveal relevant aspects for the definition of similarity metrics that allow a more precise and subtle classification.

Two experiments are designed to explore the characteristics of the IRs, specifically to test the relation between their sizes, locations and shift size with experimental rhythmic similarity ratings. Furthermore, we want to understand the implications of IRs when comparing two rhythms in the presence and in absence of a pulse.

3 Method

3.1 Materials

Measures. The algorithms used to measure similarity between pairs of rhythmic phrases are:

The edit distance (ED): it is used only to pre-select the patterns that will be used as stimuli of the experiments. All the pairs, as will be presented on the next section, are sought to have a constant edit distance of 2.

Pattern Coincidence (PC): is measured as the percentage of equal onsets present on both patterns on the same specific region. It can be measured for the complete pattern as a single distance value, or as a set of distance values representing the coincidences found in between beats, named Pattern Coincidence by Beat (PCB).

Family Difference (FD): This measure is based on replacing the letters of the syncopation families by numbers. If there is a syncopation it is quantified as 1, if there is nothing it is marked as 0, if there is a reinforcement of the beat it is quantified as −1. Then, when comparing between two families a difference between values for each beat is computed. It can be summed up as a single value or it can be left as discrete distance values between each intra-beat region, named Family Difference by Beat (FDB).

Family Coincidence (FC): As discussed in the previous section, syncopation families are strings of letters indicating if there is a syncopation, a reinforcement or nothing within each two beats of a musical phrase. Family coincidence is measured as the percentage of syncopation coincidences found between two complete phrases. Family coincidence by beat (FCB) is a group of boolean values representing if there was a coincidence or not in between each two beats of the rhythms being measured.

To compute the PCB, the PC between each beat of the two patterns is measured obtaining a 4 number vector. Then a linear regression between all the similarity ratings and all the 4-number-vectors is computed in order to obtain the best weights for each element of the vector. The same procedure is used to obtain the FDB and the FCB.

Stimuli. We selected 9 patterns as bases to create variations by shifting them. This way we created 4 variations per base pattern, yielding the total of 36 patterns used as stimuli. The variation patterns were created so that a small fragment of the base pattern (Identical Region or IR) was displaced 1 to 4 positions. Performing this shift both base and variation patterns contain the same IR but located at a certain distance from the original position. The original position of the IR was also controlled, each group had an IR selected from position 1,2,3,4 and 6. The size of all the IR is 6 steps measured from the first onset to the last onset. There are 3 or 4 onsets present on each IR. The edit distances of each main pattern to their variations is 2 (17 patterns), 3 (15 patterns), 4 (3 patterns) and 5 (1 pattern). Ideally, a fixed edit distance between main patterns and their variations would have been set; but given the need to shift the IR with precision, edit distance between patterns is 2 or 3 in most pairs. A 37th pair, consisting of two identical patterns, was added for controlling the consistency in the answers. Rhythms are reproduced with a clave sound sampled from the Roland TR-727 with no dynamic changes.

System. The system used to carry out the experiment was implemented in Pure Data Extended. It consists of two play buttons to reproduce each rhythm of the pair. After listening to a pair of patterns subjects rate similarity on a 7-step Likert scale. Levels 0, 2, 4 and 6 of the scale were labeled as "The same", "quite similar", "not very similar", "not similar at all". Levels 1, 3 and 5 were not labeled.

3.2 Subjects

Twenty-one subjects (19 males, 2 females), recruited among the MTG staff and UPF pool of students, participated as subjects in this experiment. All of them with musical experience of more than 5 years at least as amateur performers. Two of the subjects were formed in non western musical traditions. The subjects were invited to participate freely in the experiment and there was no reward for their participation.

4 Experiment 1 - Stimuli Without Rhythmic Context

The 37 rhythm pairs were presented in a subject-specific randomized order and without any possibility to listen to them more than once. On the interface each pattern is played by pressing its corresponding button (labeled as pattern A and pattern B) which is disabled after clicked. Once both rhythms have been played, the 7 step Likert scale is enabled for the subject to rate similarity. Once one pair of rhythms is rated, a button to go to the next pair is enabled. When the next button is pushed a 4-s pause is started and then the next pair is loaded and the play buttons are active again. This procedure is repeated until all the 37 pairs are ranked. After finishing the experiment a questionnaire is presented verbally to the subjects in order to asses particular aspects of the activity. The questions asked are: How difficult do you think the experiment was? Did you use any physical action (nodding, tapping, other) to help you measure similarity? How did you asses the similarity? Did you use any algorithm to define similarity? Do you think any part of the pattern is more important than other in your ratings? The data collected from the experiment is the index of the pair of rhythms, the similarity rating given by the subject and the order in which the pairs were assigned to pair A and pair B.

The analysis of the results is based on the mode of the ratings for every stimuli pair. To get a better picture of the results of experiment 1, pairs with more than 50 % of the results scattered over 2 Likert scale marks were discarded as inconsistent between subjects. Only 16 % of the pairs were removed, namely pairs 1, 3, 4, 19, 23 and 35. The dispersions of all pairs is shown in Fig. 1. Each pair of stimulus, plotted by its similarity ratings and the shift of the IR, is organized by groups from a to i on Fig. 3. There is a trend that suggests that an increase in the shift reduces the similarity rating (Friedman chi-squared = 23.878, df = 4, p-value = 8.45e-05) with significant Spearman rank order correlations (a: −0.97, b: −0.87, c: −0.95, d: −0.87, e: −0.87, f: −0.89, g: −0.46, h: −0.82, i: −0.22. P-Values a: 0.0048, b: 0.0539, c: 0.0138, d: 0.0539, e: 0.0539, f: 0.0405, g: 0.4338, h: 0.0886, i: 0.7177). Low P-values and high negative Spearman rank order correlations suggest a negative correspondence between shift and similarity, the further the IR is shifted the lower the similarity rating. Possible relations

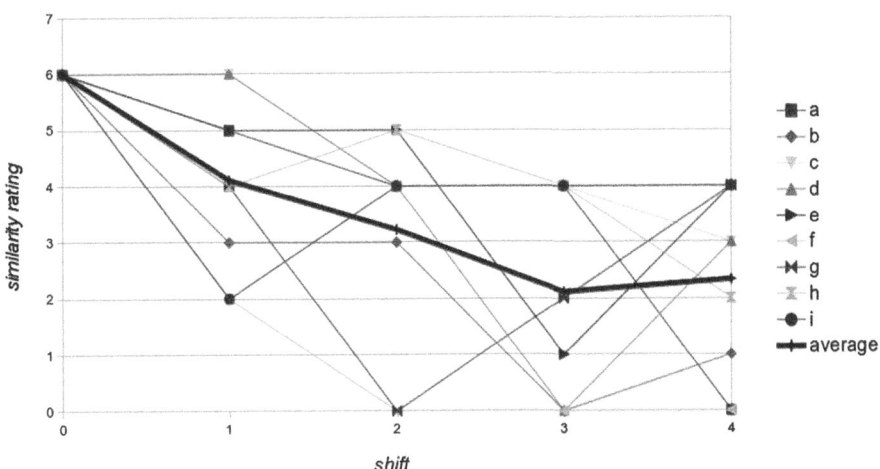

Fig. 1. Similarity rating vs. shift without the presence of a rhythmical context discriminated by groups, from a to i. 6: the same, 0: not similar at all

between objective measures (see Sect. 3.1) and the similarity results obtained in the absence of a rhythmical context are presented on Table 1. All Spearman Correlation values are all below significance, suggesting that similarity ratings are not correspondent to any of the objective measures from the rhythmic patterns.

To calculate the PCB, FCB and FDB the PC, FC and FD are computed between each of the four beats of every pair. Then a linear regression between the four computed values (all patterns are 4 beats long) and the prediction is computed to extract the weights for each beat. These weights will be discussed in Sect. 6.

Table 1. Spearman Rank correlation values for each objective metric and the similarity ratings without a rhythmic context

Objective metric	Spearman correlation
PC	0,114158372
PCB	0,230098172
FCB	0,426401379
FDB	0,316359972
FD	0,093654438

These results suggest a relation between the IR and similarity ratings when the rhythms are presented to the subjects without beat induction. It also gives clues to the features of the IRs such as the size and shift, complementing the results of Cao et al.

5 Experiment 2 - Stimuli with Rhythmic Context

In this experiment we wanted to test if a rhythmic context, given the presence of a metric-inducing sound (i.e. a kick drum), could modify (and in which sense) the similarity ratings given to the same pairs used in experiment 1. In every stimuli of this experiment a kick drum is played four times on the start of every beat at a tempo of 120 beats per minute, then the kick drum and one of the patterns of the pair is played simultaneously, then just the kick drum again four times and finally the kick drum simultaneously with the remaining pattern. Again, the 37 rhythm pairs were presented in a subject-specific randomized order. The same interface was used as in experiment 1, but this time the play button reproduced the whole sequence of kick, kick + rhythm A, kick, kick + rhythm B. Two play buttons were active so this time subjects could listen twice to the whole identical sequence. After finishing the experiment the same questionnaire as in experiment 1 is presented verbally to the subjects in order to asses particular aspects of the activity. The data collected from the experiment is the index of the pair of rhythms, the similarity rating given by the subject and the order in which the pairs were presented during the whole sequence.

As in experiment 1, the analysis of the results is based on the mode of the ratings for every stimuli pair. In order to get a better picture of the results obtained in experiment 2, the stimuli pairs are analyzed in search for the most consistent inter-subject ratings (Fig. 4). Ratings with 50 % of the results spread out three or more perceptual scale values are removed, namely pairs 23, 24, 26, 27, 28, 35, being the 16 % of the original set.

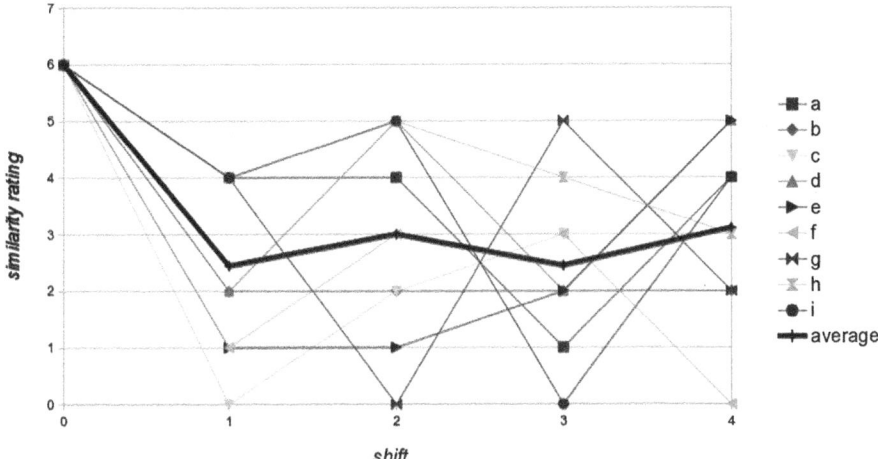

Fig. 2. Similarity rating vs. shift with the presence of a rhythmical context discriminated by groups, from a to i

Every stimulus pair is compared with the shift of the IR from one pattern to the other and with the similarity rating obtained when a rhythmic context was present (Fig. 2). These results show some significant correlation values correlation values (a: −0.67, b: −0.71, c: −0.05, d: −0.32, e: −0.05, f: −0.67, g: −0.50, h: −0.82, i: −0.67) but very high P-values on the Spearman Correlation test (a: 0.2152, b: 0.1817, c: 0.9347, d: 0.6042, e: 0.9347, f: 0.2189, g: 0.3910, h: 0.0886, i: 0.2189). Friedman rank sum test has also an elevated P-value = 0.5834. These values strongly suggest that no aspect of the IR is relevant to asses rhythmic similarity when a pulse is induced.

Possible relations between similarity ratings and the different objective measures extracted from the patterns were also analyzed (Fig. 3). As in experiment 1, the PCB, FDB and FCB are computed after the PC, FC and FD are computed between each of the four beats of every pair. A linear regression between the four computed values (all patterns are 4 beats long) and the prediction is calculated to extract the weights for each beat. These weights will be discussed in the next section.

The PC measure has a Spearman correlation value just above significance with the similarity ratings (0.54365, p-value = 0,001902). Measures in which beats are weighted independently also exhibit just above significance Spearman correlation values: PCB (0.76171, p-value = 1,01E-003), FCB (0.52926,

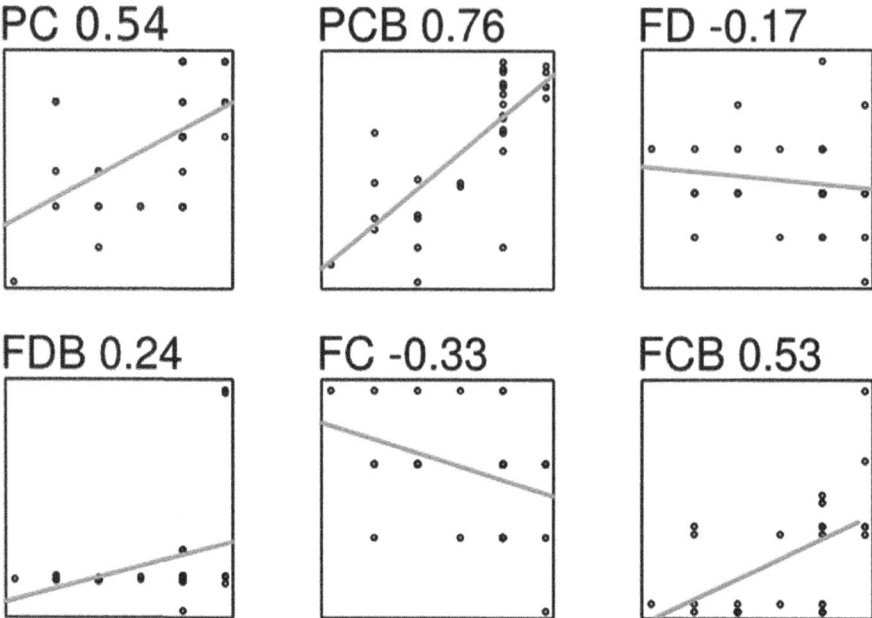

Fig. 3. Objective similarity measures plotted against human similarity ratings of experiment 2. Spearman correlation value on top of each plot. Pattern Coincidence (PC), Pattern Coincidence by beat (PCB) and Family Coincidence by beat (FCB) have an above significant Spearman correlation.

p-value = 0,002635). These values, opposed to the analysis of the IR, evidence how different objective measures respond accordingly to similarity ratings when a pulse is present.

6 Discussion and Conclusions

A general view of the data shows a clear difference between the similarity results obtained for the same pairs of rhythms depending whether they are presented within a rhythmic context or not. This can be seen on Fig. 4, where the between-subject similarity obtained for the 37 pairs in both experiments is not convergent. In some cases it is the same (pairs 2, 12, 24, 25, 26 29, 30, 31, 36) in some cases highly contradictory (pairs 3, 4, 9, 13, 17, 18, 22, 23, 27, 35) but generally in disagreement (75 % of the pairs). The same pairs of rhythms are rated differently depending on the presence or absence of a rhythmic context.

The influence of shift in similarity ratings in experiment 1 and experiment 2 also differ in tendency. While on experiment 1 (no rhythmic context) shift seems to have an inverse correspondence with similarity, for most of the groups on experiment 2 (with rhythmic context) no direct relation with the shift is appreciated. Presumably the emergence of IRs and their shift as a relevant factor for

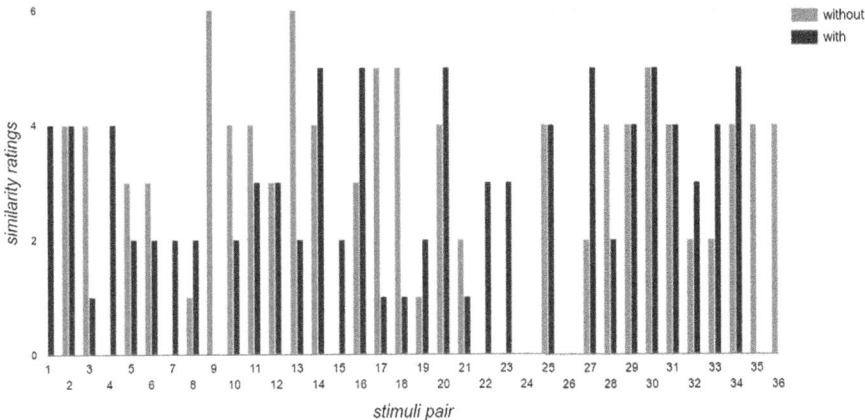

Fig. 4. Similarity ratings for all stimuli pairs. Results with rhythmic context dark gray, without rhythmic context light gray.

rhythmic similarity only in the case where there is no rhythmical context, could be related to an alternative perceptual mechanism triggered when no metrical cues are offered to decypher a musical sequence in terms of its rhythmical properties. This mechanism could be analogous to comparing the similarity between two words by looking at the letters and their order and not by their meaning. It seems to be clear that a shallow similarity computation may happen based on superficial features and no rhythm context whereas a more abstract and layered mechanism operates when a metric context is set.

This previous observation is aligned with the fact that the amount of notes needed for a beat to be induced is from 5 to 10 [2]. This could lead to conclude that in experiment 1 a sense of beat was acquired just as every phrase was ending and therefore no metrical structure was ever induced during this experiment. Nevertheless as 36 pairs of rhythms at 120 BPM were listened during experiment 1, a reminiscent notion of the tempo after each exposition could be accumulated and influenced further comparisons. This observation is out of the analysis and all results of experiment 1 are treated as non beat inducing. Another factor that is left out is the possible use of memory to recall a rhythm that just finished with the late acquired meter, so the rhythm is evoked with a meter although such meter was not originally present.

Groups that have lower correlation between the shift and the similarity ratings are groups in which the IR had an origin closer to the start of the rhythm. The farthest the origin, the least correlation between shift and similarity ratings (see Fig. 5). Spearman correlations for different origins are origin 1: -1.0000, origin 2: -0.8721, origin 3: -0.9000, origin 4: -0.6669. Their respective pairwise two-sided p-values are 0.0001, 0.0539, 0.0374, 0.2189. Although all Spearman correlations are high, their significance decreases progressively as the origin of the IR increases. This decline in significance can be related to a loss of strength in the alternative perceptual mechanism mentioned above. In other words the

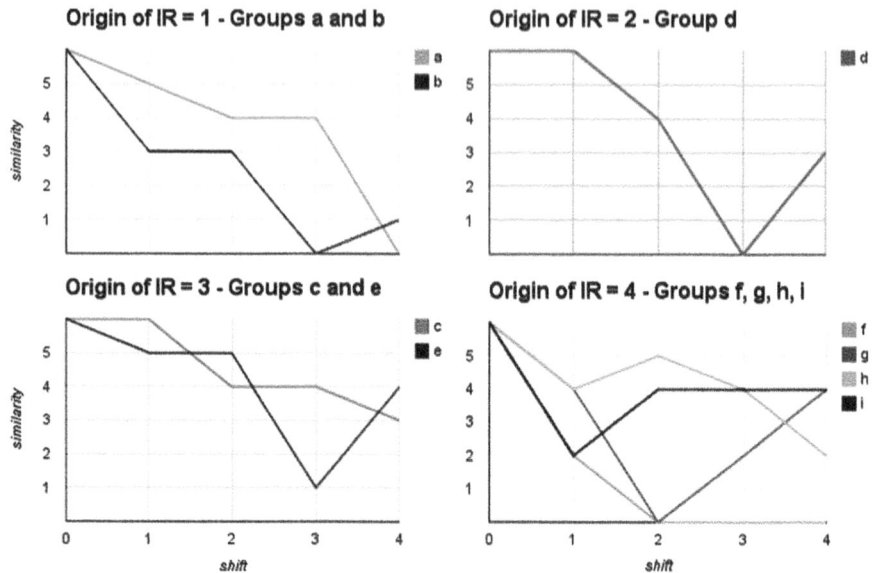

Fig. 5. Relationship between origin and shift for experiment 1.

IR effect is stronger when the IR is on the first steps of a sequence. The matter of what happens when the IR is further than 4 steps was not considered while preparing the stimuli, therefore is out of the range of the experiments.

The same analysis of the influence of the IRs origin and shift with similarity in experiment 2 yields the following Spearman correlation values: origin1: −0.6708204, origin 2: −0.3162278, origin 3: 0.00000001, origin 4: −0.97467943. The corresponding pairwise two-sided p-values are 0.2152, 0.6042, 1.0000, 0.0048 respectively. None of the p-values accounts for significance, again showing a disengagement between inducing a meter and the relevance of having an IR in two patterns. This can lead to the conclusion that a mechanism based on IRs is not relevant when an induced meter is present.

A different phenomena occurs with rhythms assessed in a metrical context. Figure 6 shows that the highest correlations between objective measures and subjective similarity ratings are obtained when subjects were exposed to a rhythmic context. Correlation indexes of the data collected without a rhythmic context, on the other side, are always below significance. Measures with correlations above significance are the pattern coincidence (PC), pattern coincidence by beat (PCB) and family coincidence by beat (FCB). The best Spearman correlation ranks are obtained with measures computed by beat and weighted independently. One way to interpret the weights is to think of them as analogous to importance and could be paired with a notion of awareness in a perceptual sense. These weights could possibly be giving clues of hierarchies imposed on different sections of a pattern when a subject evaluates similarity in a rhythmic context.

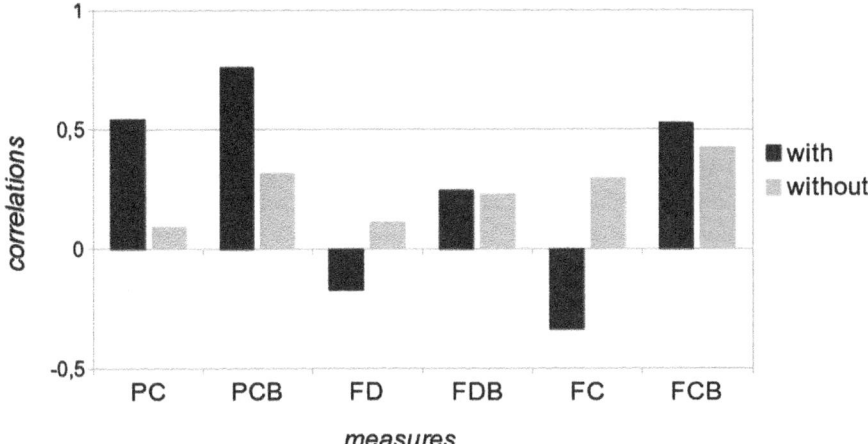

Fig. 6. Spearman correlation between different objective measures extracted from the patterns and the resulting perceptual results of each experiment. Light gray: without beat induction (Experiment 1), dark gray: with beat induction (Experiment 2)

Table 2. Weights for each beat for the different measures correlated above significance in experiment 2

Metric	Beat1	Beat2	Beat3	Beat4
PCB	4.21520	1.15980	0.94951	0.70146
FCB	−1.47619	0.10389	−1.04761	−1.93506

Looking at Table 2, we see that coefficients for beat 1 are very prominent both for the PCB (pattern coincidence by beat) and the FCB (family coincidence by beat) measures. Although the weight curve is different for both of them. A progressive descending curve for PCB, suggests a decline in importance of the beats as time advances. An n-shaped curve for the FCB suggest a higher relevance for the first and last beats of the rhythms.

As a final summary five observations regarding both experiments can be presented.

- Similarity ratings of patterns change depending on the presence or absence of a pulse which metrically coincides with the onsets of the patterns being measured.
- In the absence of a pulse, a mechanism based on searching identical regions (IR) of one pattern into the other one is predominant over coincidences and syncopation for giving a similarity rating.
- Similarity ratings without a rhythmical context are inversely related with the shift in steps of the IR from one pattern to the other.
- In the presence of a pulse, a mechanism based on coincidences and syncopation is more relevant for predicting human similarity ratings.

– Similarity ratings in the presence of a pulse weight particular differently the regions of the rhythms being compared.

Our studies on rhythm similarity, in addition to providing hints on the working of the cognitive musical processes, is leading towards interesting practical applications. These correlated measures and their coefficients can be the source of algorithms used in musical classification and creation scenarios. Further research could use implementations of our results into metrics to analyze melodic data sets. Generative algorithms can also make use of these results as rules to create new rhythms based on a seed pattern controlling the desired similarity level.

Acknowledgements. We would like to thank Julián Burbano for his help in the analysis of the data. This research has been partially supported by the EU funded GiantSteps project (FP7-ICT-2013-10 Grant agreement nr. 610591).

References

1. Cao, E., Lotstein, M., Johnson-Laird, P.N.: Similarity and families of musical rhythms. Music Percept. Interdisc. J. **31**(5), 444–469 (2014)
2. Desain, P., Honing, H.: Computational models of beat induction: the rule-based approach. J. New Music Res. **28**(1), 29–42 (1999)
3. Fitch, W.T., Rosenfeld, A.J.: Perception and production of syncopated rhythms. Music Percept. **25**(1), 43–58 (2007)
4. Guastavino, C., Gomez, F., Toussaint, G., Marandola, F., Gomez, E.: Measuring similarity between flamenco rhythmic patterns. J. New Music Res. **38**(2), 129–138 (2009)
5. Honing, H.: Without it no music: beat induction as a fundamental musical trait. Ann. N.Y. Acad. Sci. **1252**(1), 85–91 (2012)
6. Ladinig, O.: Temporal expectations and their violations. Ph.D. thesis, Institute for Logic, Language and Computation (ILLC), University of Amsterdam (UvA) (2009)
7. Large, E.W., Jones, M.R.: The dynamics of attending: how people track time-varying events. Psychol. Rev. **106**(1), 119 (1999)
8. Lerdahl, F., Jackendoff, R.: A Generative Theory of Tonal Music. MIT Press, Cambridge (1985)
9. Longuet-Higgins, H.C., Lee, C.S.: The rhythmic interpretation of monophonic music. Music Percept. Interdisc. J. **1**(4), 424–441 (1984)
10. Mongeau, M., Sankoff, D.: Comparison of musical sequences. Comput. Humanit. **24**(3), 161–175 (1990)
11. Orpen, K.S., Huron, D.: Measurement of similarity in music: a quantitative approach for non-parametric representations. Comput. Music Res. **4**, 1–44 (1992)
12. Post, O., Toussaint, G.: The edit distance as a measure of perceived rhythmic similarity. Empir. Musicol. Rev. **6**(3), 164–179 (2011)
13. Povel, D.J., Essens, P.: Perception of temporal patterns. Music Percept. Interdisc. J. **2**(4), 411–440 (1985)
14. Thul, E., Toussaint, G.T.: Rhythm complexity measures: a comparison of mathematical models of human perception and performance. In: ISMIR, pp. 663–668, September 2008

15. Toussaint, G.T., Campbell, M., Brown, N.: Computational models of symbolic rhythm similarity: correlation with human judgments. Anal. Approaches World Music **1**(2), 380–430 (2011)
16. Tutzer, F.: Drum rhythm retrieval based on rhythm and sound similarity. Master's thesis, Department of Information and Communication Technologies, Universitat Pompeu Fabra, Barcelona (2011)
17. Witek, M.A., Clarke, E.F., Wallentin, M., Kringelbach, M.L., Vuust, P.: Syncopation, body-movement, pleasure in groove music. PloS One **9**(4), e94446 (2011)

Cross-Cultural Comparisons of Unconstrained Body Responses to Argentinian and Afro-Brazilian Music

Luiz Naveda[1(✉)], Isabel C. Martínez[2], Javier Damesón[2],
Alejandro Pereira Ghiena[2], Romina Herrera[2],
and Manuel Alejandro Ordás[2(✉)]

[1] School of Music - State University of Minas Gerais, Belo Horizonte, Brazil
luiznaveda@gmail.com
[2] Laboratorio para el Estudio de la Experiencia Musical - Facultad de Bellas Artes, Universidad Nacional de La Plata, La Plata, Buenos Aires, Argentina

Abstract. A number of evidences show that musical cultures differ in a number of aspects including cognitive priorities, musical function and relationships between music, movement and dance. From the methodological point of view, it is very difficult to describe the understanding of rhythm structures: tapping methods are limiting, surveys are very subjective and analyses of performances are ambiguous and multivariate. In this study we realize cross-cultural comparisons between unconstrained movement responses of Brazilian and Argentinian acculturated subjects, responding to samba and chacarera music. The analyses were realized by means of methods that track the density of kinematic events in the metrical structure. The results contrast to traditional models of metric structure by revealing an intrinsic diversity, variability and asymmetry of movement responses and metrical models. The results also show morphological characteristics connected to cultural differences.

Keywords: Cross-cultural · Movement · Rhythm · Meter · Embodiment

1 Introduction

The tradition of empirical approaches to music is rooted in the knowledge of naturalistic observation and science, whose principles are guided by formalization, search for "universals", empirical evidence and attempts to produce generalizable results supported by statistical significance [1]. The comparison between different musical cultures offers a formidable opportunity to validate such observations across the large diversity of musical phenomena [2]. Following this opportunity, the application of empirical approaches to cross-cultural research seems to respond to questions posed by ethnomusicological studies, where the search for universals in music is delineated from the comparisons between cultures. However, the disrupting diversity in music making shows that the variability of music engagement defies the very notion (or the hypothesis) of universals in music.

The original version of this chapter was revised: An acknowledgment has been updated. The correction to this chapter is available at https://doi.org/10.1007/978-3-319-46282-0_31

© Springer International Publishing Switzerland 2016
R. Kronland-Martinet et al. (Eds.): CMMR 2015, LNCS 9617, pp. 464–482, 2016.
DOI: 10.1007/978-3-319-46282-0_30

Although the recent access to modern capturing technologies and media has fostered the quest for universals in culture, the actual development of empirical research in music seems to have followed an older precedent. By the end of 19th century, the interest of European scholars for non-Western cultures motivated the idea of making comparisons between Western and non-Western musics. This idea led to the emergence of Comparative Musicology (later evolved onto Ethnomusicology) [3]. At that time, the reaction of musicology was to approach non-Western music by means of analytical tools designed for the analysis of Western classical music. The use of analytical instruments developed to approach Western traditions led to a number of superficial accounts of non-Western music cultures, together with concomitant biased interpretations [e.g.: focus on the analysis of melodies, scales and intervals, as described in [4]. Later, the idea of universals in the traditional musicology was questioned both by arguments of the so called "new musicology", and by the inquiry about music cultures reported in the comparative studies and ethnomusicology [5]. Similarly, by using the modern empirical approaches designed to cope with the priorities and constraints of Western music, we might repeat the same methodological mistake that affected musicology in the past: the use of analytical instruments that shape the results according to culturally specific assumptions.

The bias that analytical views impose to the observation of cultural phenomena and the problems that such a limited epistemological view of knowledge has caused in modern sciences have been discussed under the criticism of post-modern and post-colonial literature. The main argument is that modern sciences discard "epistemological disturbances" and ignores alternative knowledge in order to preserve a single view that is necessary to build representations of certainty, evidence and generalization in modern scientific production [6]. Regardless the criticism, the accumulative set of artificial procedures, tasks and limitations necessary to capture and analyse, for example, a single movement recording, is indeed disturbing. It negatively affects the validity and generalization of findings by corrupting ecological validity. Ultimately, it dissociates the scientific observation and its representations from the phenomenon of musical culture itself. Although the conflicts between the principles of empirical methods and the elements of musical knowledge in different cultures pertain to a larger epistemological discussion, a careful design of experiment and analysis might help to develop better accounts of musicological information and to avoid the repetition of methodological problems that affected the 19th century musicology.

1.1 Empirical Approaches to Rhythm

The study of musical rhythm across different cultures is especially vulnerable to methodological problems. The relationships between musical rhythm and presumably "non-musical" activities such as dance, worship, labour or walking demonstrate that rhythm engagement in societies is not exclusively accessible through the acoustic medium [7–11]. The body and the methods capable of capturing the structure of the rhythm performed by the body may offer a key analytical channel to the structure of performance and perception of rhythm. Additionally, more comprehensive approaches to cultural diversity would require a careful assessment of the scope of the cultural phenomenon (e.g.: internal connections between music and other modalities), the instruments of analysis and their underlying assumptions, which may only be found in interdisciplinary readings.

A review of the literature in ethnography, for example, demonstrates widespread connections between rhythm engagement and the performances of dance and body movement in different cultures. A number of musical traditions and myths attest the presence of sophisticated body responses to music [12, 13]. Ethnographic literature reports that dance and movement perform an active musical role in cultures where metrical models are not isochronous or polymetrical [7, 14] or timing deviations are modulated by participatory displays [15, 16]. Conversely, the vast majority of empirical studies on rhythm are based on information collected from the reduction of the movement of acculturated subjects to a very simplistic account of body movements, often limited to a discrete indication of time events. As such, the methodological demands reduce the window of the analysis into simplistic set of evidences, which methodologically isolates rhythm complexity from the representation. The main obstacle in this tradition of empirical research is to find alternative ways to analyse the phenomenon of metrical engagement without framing the universe of study on the basis of a narrowed (or anthropocentric) assumption of rhythm engagement. The support of the theories of embodiment in music [17, 18] and the possibility of enaction of rhythm models by acculturated subjects may provide theoretical and empirical conditions to access better accounts of rhythm in culture.

1.2 Rhythm and Embodiment

When Bohlman [19] developed his essay on the ontologies of music, he posited an ontology that considered music *in the body and/or beyond the body* (p. 32). The idea that a part of musical meaning is related to its mapping with *the* physical, and also that music is embodied in ritual and dance practice, puts, on the one hand, an emphasis on the consideration of the body at the core of musical fabric, and on the other, discusses the value of Western categories used so far to account for what is the knowledge in the practice of modern scientific music research.

It is precisely due to the recovery of the meaning of the body in music cognition [17, 20, 21], together with the development of the science of evolutionary music [22, 23] and developmental musical neuroscience [24], [25] that embodied meaning in music becomes a relevant topic that is again at the centre of discussions [26]. Music *as text* loses its primacy and music *as act* is actually the force that leads current debates about experience in the multidisciplinary field of biocultural music.

Communicative musicality, that is to say, the human capacity to share and exchange rhythmic, temporal and gestural patterns during communication [27] emerges as a core concept that describes the state of affairs in the cultural practice of music. It is around this basic embodied knowledge that the practice of music and dance can evolve in different cultural contexts. Moreover, different manifestations of musical understanding may arise out of the diversity of temporal organization that characterizes a variety of musical practices.

Concerning temporal music organization, traditional music theory modelled the theory of meter following the temporal constraints of Western academic music [28]. According to many traditional viewpoints, all other music cultural practices (so called "world music") were treated as deviations from the universal rule of time in Western music organization. Cognitive psychology pursued for the last four decades the investigation of the cognitive reality of music theoretical constructs, among them those of musical time and metric structure [29–31]. The beat has been, and it is still considered as the basic unit of analysis. It is thought about as an essential tool in order to organize the study of musical time, and to shape and guide the experimental work. Even the most complex rhythmic organizations of some cultural traditions are forced to enter into the corset of the beat (see for example the analysis of the *agbekor* African tradition in [32]).

Beyond the acknowledgment that time is the unavoidable human dimension that is inherent to the practice and experience of music, the multiplicity of temporal organizations found in musical cultures suggests that time research should be seriously reconsidered in all what concerns to the ways musical time is currently approached. Therefore, experimental design and testing techniques could be reframed by discussing, on the one side, the validity of the ethnocentric model of strict adjustment to the beat, as the rule against which all other events are assessed and, on the other hand, adopting a perspective of cultural diversity that guides music inquiry.

In this study, we discuss alternatives to the study of rhythm in culture by looking at the body and rhythm in culture: acculturated subjects responding to rhythm structures present in musical styles. We describe an experiment that compares metrical responses in two Latin-American cultures by means of the analysis of unconstrained body movements. The complexity encoded in the ecological setting is approached by cross-cultural comparisons supported by an exploratory analysis of body responses to music, captured by means of a motion capture system. The movement responses of acculturated subjects to samba and chacarera music styles are compared using descriptors that reveal the rhythm engagement in a diversity of representations. In our attempt to reduce the methodological bias, the methods did not explicitly assume the existence of beat and/or spatial or temporal instructions for the task, not even the subjects' awareness of metrical components. As such, we might be able to grasp a range of different mental models produced by Argentinian and Brazilian musical cultures, without sacrificing cultural idiosyncrasies in favour of traditional experimental control.

In the following sessions we describe the realization of the experiment and discuss the process of adapting empirical approaches according to the reported concerns about validity, generalization and ecological setting in the context of cross-cultural analysis of musical rhythm.

2 Methodology

The methodology used in this study involves a typical experimental setup where movement data from acculturated subjects from Argentina and Brazil is recorded and analysed using computational approaches. Procedures and analytical approaches used in the process are specifically adapted to cope with a less constrained experimental design, which might help to reduce the bias introduced by other methods. The rationale behind each experimental procedure is discussed in the following sessions while the analytical procedure is proposed and detailed in [33].

2.1 Participants

Twelve subjects participated voluntarily in the study: 6 acculturated Argentinian subjects (3 males and 3 females, mean age = 33.2, SD = 9.9) and 6 acculturated Brazilians subjects (3 males and 3 females, mean age 24.3, SD = 3). The subjects were randomly selected from university music students both at the National University of La Plata (Argentina) and at Federal University of Minas Gerais (Brazil). All participants were informed about the characteristics of the experiment and provided formal consent to participation.

2.2 Apparatus

Participants' movements were recorded using a motion capture system (Optitrack, Natural Point) equipped with 8 infrared cameras and a control system (PC). Before the experiment, 4 rigid-bodies (groups of markers) were placed at the torso (4 markers), head (4 markers), left (4 markers) and right (4 markers) hands of the subjects, totalizing 16 markers. Then, subjects were informed about the experimental setup and recordings involved in the study. Subjects were also oriented to move freely within the perimeter of the recorded area (signalized on the ground). Stimuli (monaural samples) were reproduced through one speaker connected to a sound card in a computer. Stimuli were synchronized with video and mocap recordings by means of synch markers in the audio, mocap and video. Video recordings were also produced for reference purposes.

Pre-processing of mocap files involved synchronization of files, basic filtering and cleaning using the software Motive (Natural Point). Further processing and organization of the dataset were partially realized using algorithms developed by the authors and the Mocap Toolbox [34] for Matlab (Mathworks).

2.3 Procedures

All the subjects performed two tasks, each for both styles of music stimuli: chacarera and samba. In the first task the subjects were asked to try free and spontaneous movement "strategies" in response to music. Strategies were defined and instructed as an unrestricted way to respond to the rhythm of the music being played. No other orientation, limitation or task was given, and subjects were free to move around minding the boundaries of the recording area. In the second task, the subjects were instructed to (i) choose the best movement strategy experimented in the first task; and (ii) continuously perform the chosen movement strategy until the end of the musical sequence (stimulus).

The analysis presented in this study was applied to a 12-bar length segment extracted from the second part, as illustrated in Fig. 1. In our analysis, we only considered the movement of the hands. The first two bars of the recordings were ignored in order to isolate the data from biased adaptation of the subject to the task and stimuli (Fig. 1).

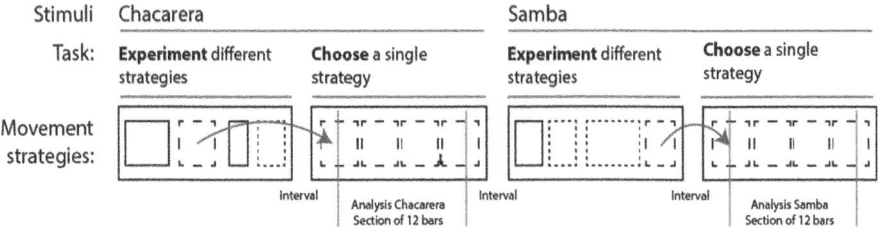

Fig. 1. Schematic representation of the phases of the experiment, tasks, type of stimuli and repetitions of the "strategies" used in the experimental trials.

In order to avoid the effects of timing (fatigue and/or bias due to temporal expectations) in task accomplishment, subjects were not explicitly informed about the duration of the stimulus. Sessions' trials lasted for approximately 60 s. After the experiment the subjects responded to questionnaires containing questions about the interaction with the experimental task, personal experience and personal details. The recordings were realized in Brazil and Argentina using the same setup, conditions and protocols.

2.4 Stimuli

Chacarera music is, along with *zamba, milonga, malambo*, and of course *tango*, one of the most representative rhythms of Argentina. Chacarera music exhibits Western metric features such as a steady beat (tactus) and a metric hierarchy that combines binary and ternary levels; the rhythmic base is organized according to a polyrhythmic structure of crossed binary and ternary meters (6/8–3/4). The rhythmic phrase of the stimulus used in the present study consists on a structure that combines 4 ternary beats-6 binary beats × 12 eighth-notes, that is to say, 12 low level metrical elements organized polyrhythmically in groups of 3 and/or 2 eighth-notes by beat, and played, respectively, at a rate of 158 BPM (6/8) or 105 BPM (3/4).

The history of Brazilian *samba* music is often seen as an outcome of the lundu-maxixe-samba genealogy of styles in Brazil. These styles denote not only a group of music styles but also related dance forms that influenced each other in an intricate cross-fertilization between styles and modalities. Modern samba music is generally described as having a binary meter music form (2/4), with accentuation in the second beat, and a rhythmic texture that is characterized by a variety of syncopated rhythms. The stimulus used in this study contains real rhythm samples of *surdo, caxixi* and *pandeiro* percussions. The rhythmic basis of the stimulus is formed by 4 beats (2 bars) × 16 sixteenth-note structure, that is to say, 16 metrical elements organized polyrhythmically in groups of 4 sixteenth-notes per beat, played at 95 BPM.

2.5 Analysis

Cross-cultural experiments raise a number of limitations that have a direct impact in the development of technical and experimental solutions for the procedures. While the interaction between the methods used to analyse behavioural data and cultural specifics is rarely discussed in the literature, analytical approaches seem to carry assumptions and concepts that often result in misrepresentation of the phenomenon, partly because they reproduce specific cultural and epistemological viewpoints [35]. Methods involved in cross-cultural analyses should ideally support and record not only a range of possible responses, but also an expected variability of individual and cultural expressions in the universe of study. In our specific context, the method should reveal the differences regarding timing, shape, organization and position of the movement actions across different musical stimuli. The challenge is how to provide such a rich and informative description of spontaneous movement responses to music without referring to a complex account of different movement profiles that cannot be compared.

The freedom to perform spontaneous movements depends on the freedom of movement of the limbs, which has a direct impact on the ecological validity and thus, the generalization of the results. It is evident that the psychological and physical state of the subject in the laboratory, the limitation and occupation of the space, and the experimental setup itself impose constraints and obstacles, which make the idea of "free" movement questionable. However, the concept of free movements used in this study reflects the condition of absence of external obstacles, fixed tasks or limits, as in typical cultural musical contexts such as a dance club, party or a private room[1]. The main challenges in the analysis of this sort of movement are (i) the lack of clear temporal demarcation of metrical accents and (ii) the lack of direct access to the subject´s experiential categories of the events. We opted to approach these challenges by (i) defining events as changes of direction and (ii) organizing the density of events across annotated categories of meter, extracted from the stimuli. The method is briefly described below.

2.5.1 Analysis of Directional Changes

The analytical approach applied here (proposed in [33]) uses (i) a sequence of trajectories in the 3D space and (ii) the time based categories extracted from the annotation. In our case, it is assumed that movements respond to the musical categories of musical meter and that both movement and annotation are synchronized. The process involves four procedures, illustrated in the Fig. 2:

---

[1] Environments where spontaneous body movements are performed in culture also impose other sort of limitations such as socio-cultural codes and limitations of physical space.

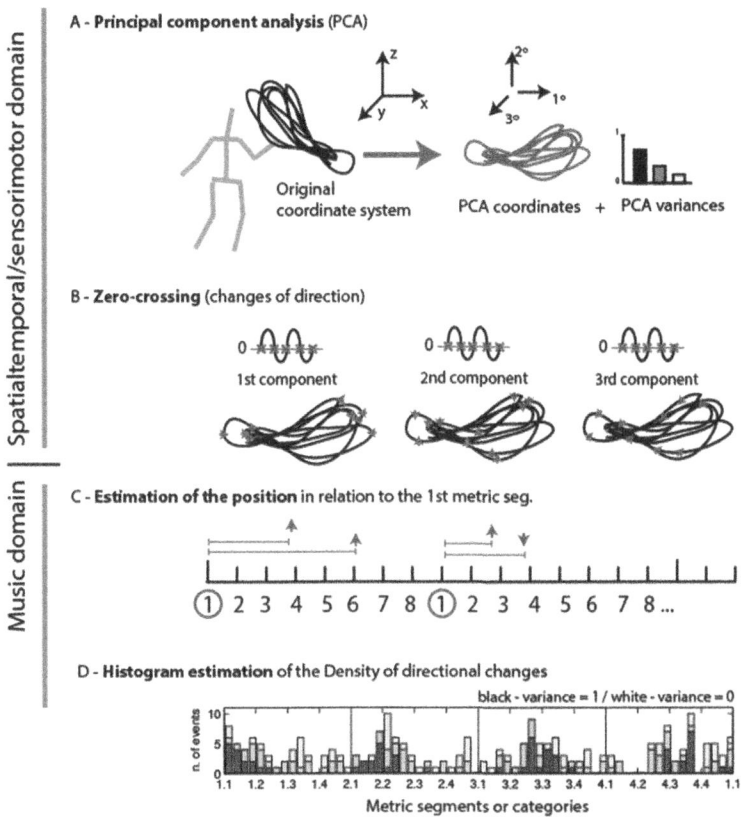

Fig. 2. Schematic representation of the processes involved in the calculation of the density of directional events.

(A) **PCA analysis** - The original trajectories are reconstructed from the components of a Principal Component Analysis (PCA). Practically, the PCA applies a linear transformation of the three-dimensional vectors, that results in a sort of rotation of the coordinates of the original trajectories into an angle that best explains the variance in the data.

(B) **Zero-crossing detection** - For each PCA component (or dimension), the changes of direction are retrieved by detecting zero-crossing positions in the velocity patterns of each component (first order time derivative). Zero-crossing positions in the component's velocity patterns retrieve time positions that indicate when and where an orthogonal change of direction appears in the PCA component.

(C) **Estimation of metric positions** - The time points are subtracted by the time point of the first beat of the model of meter, which results in a time difference in relation to the starting time position, normalized by the length of the metric cycle annotated in the metric model of the musical stimuli. In the metric model of samba music, this cycle is composed of sixteen 16th-note segments distributed across 4 beats (16 metrical segments, 4 beats, 2 bars). For chacarera stimuli we used a metric model of twelve 8th-note segments (12/8) distributed across 4 beats (12 metrical segments, 4 beats, 1 bar).

(D) **Histogram representation of the density of directional changes** - Finally, time differences are normalized and organized in a histogram that displays the density of events across each level of the model of meter used in the annotation.

The directional changes' detection procedure is applied to all three PCA components. Once PCA has been run, zero-crossings indicate orthogonal changes of direction with respect to a coordinates system (the PCA components) that best represents the variance of the data. In other words, the method retrieves changes of direction organized across dimensions that efficiently reflect the organization of the shapes of the overall movement. It provides an elegant way to avoid the imposition of the coordinates system of the mocap recording and to reveal the organization of the gesture shape according to the subject's perspective.

2.5.2 Variances

The variances of the components after PCA are expressed in ratios. They are important cues to evaluate the relevance of events and the morphology of movement's gestures. The concentration of the variance in one component indicates that movement profiles tend to be shaped as a "line" in the space. Variances distributed in two components indicate a "plane" morphology. Evenly distributed variances across the three components indicate "spherical" explorations of space in the trajectory of movement. Changes of direction in the components with higher variances might be more important, perceptible and cognitively relevant because the variance indicates a focus on movements across specific axes. Figure 3 shows the density of directional changes for the left-hand of a subject, and the corresponding trajectories in the 3D Cartesian space.

2.6 Processing and Organization of the Dataset

Before the analysis, the motion capture recordings were pre-processed for better adaptation to the analytical procedures and isolation of possible biases. Part of the basic filtering and cleaning were processed in the motion capture system's software (Motive, Natural Point). In Matlab, the trajectories were subjected to final cleaning and filtering. The positions and orientations of the rigid bodies placed at head, torso and hands were calculated from the set of markers using MocapToolbox [34]. In order to extract the whole-body displacement out of the movement of the hands, trajectories were normalized frame-by-frame in relation to the geometrical centroid of the body. The orientations of the markers were also normalized in relation to the angles of the plane formed by the markers attached to the torso. The last process isolates the movement of the hands from the rotations of the torso.

The data of the histogram displayed in the results (2 hands × 12 subjects × 2 stimuli = 48 sets) was organized according to the analytical scenarios that are presented in the next sections (styles; nationality x styles). Each histogram represents the density of events across 12 (chacarera) or 16 sections (samba) of the model of metric segments. The whole dataset corresponds to events recorded along 2304 musical beats. In order to

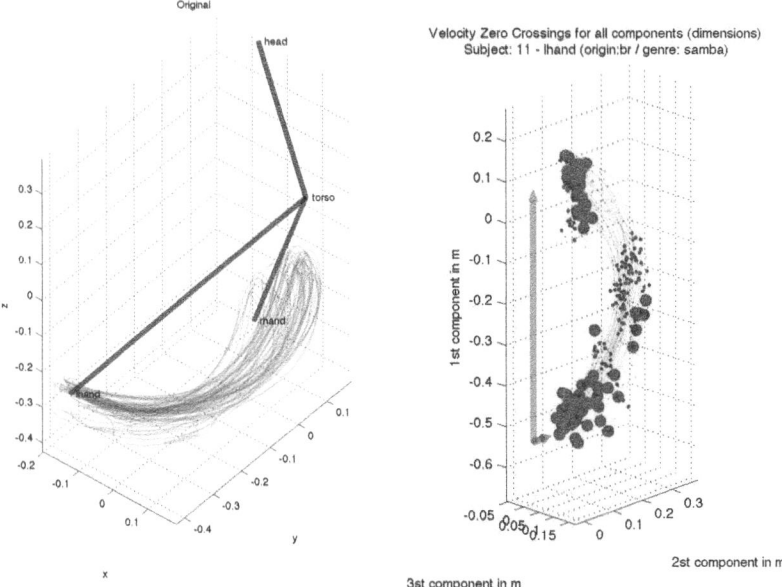

Fig. 3. Original trajectories and stick figure representation of the morphological connections between head, torso and hands. 3b. The same trajectories reoriented in order to reflect the PCA components and the directional events (red markers). The marker's size is proportional to the variance. The length and direction of the arrows indicate, repectively, the proportion of PCA variance and the orientation of the PCA component

avoid excess of bias generated by components with very low variances, events in components with less than 10 % of the total variance were ignored.

3 Results and Discussion

3.1 Variances

The distribution of the variances of PCA components for all subjects, for both hands and styles is displayed in Fig. 4 (expressed in ratios). A high variance in the first PCA component indicates in the morphology of the hand's trajectory that the movement is oriented across one single dimension. This means that most of the hand movements are displayed across a sort of "imaginary line" shape. Trajectories exhibiting less differences between variances in all components (ellipsoid distributions) are not so common in our universe of movements. Figure 5 shows several examples of such trajectories. The first row in Fig. 5 shows examples of trajectories with higher tendency to ellipsoidal distributions. The second row shows trajectories with higher differences between variances, in particular, with variances highly concentrated in the first PCA component. The examples in Fig. 5 demonstrate how the distribution of PCA variances reflect a quality of the shape of the gestures.

474   L. Naveda et al.

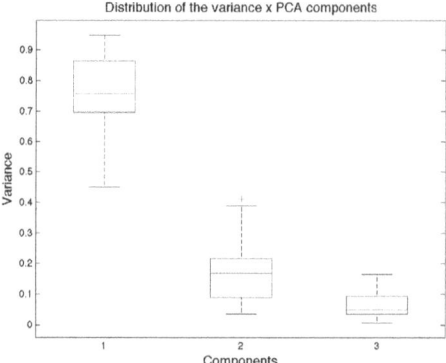

Fig. 4. Distributions of the variances for all trials (N = 48, 12 subjects, 2 hands, 2 music styles), expressed in ratios. The box-plots indicate the distributions of the variances attributed to the 3 components obtained after running PCA (1st component, mean = 0.76, SD = 0.12; 2nd component, mean = 0.17, SD = 0.01; 3rd component, mean = 0.06, SD = 0.03).

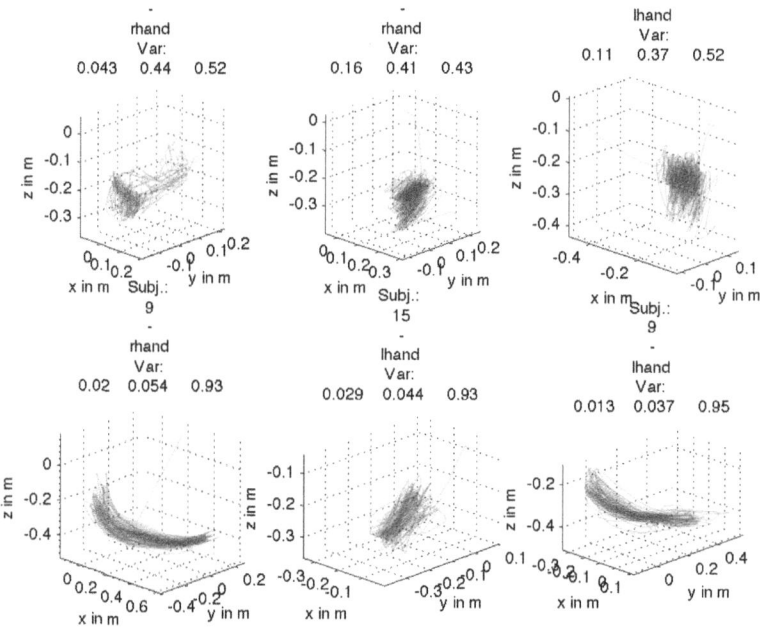

Fig. 5. Six examples of trajectories (after PCA) in the dataset (lhand and rhand indicate left and right hands, respectively. The values after Var: indicate the variances). The first row shows trajectories with lowest differences between variances in each component (indicating a tendency to spherical distributions). The second row shows the trajectories with higher differences between variances, in special gestures with variances concentrated in the first component.

3.2 Differences Between Music Styles (All Subjects)

Figures 6 and 7 show the density of directional changes for chacarera and samba, respectively, for all subjects and for both hands. The graphs display the number of events and their distribution across the model of meter of each music style. The metric events are also discriminated in relation to the respective PCA component (1st, 2nd, and 3rd) using three levels of grey, described in the legend. It is very important to interpret the histograms taking into account the variance distribution shown in Fig. 4. For example, the first component (black bars) should be read as changes of direction across the axis that correspond to almost 80 % of the variance (mean = 0.76, SD = 0.12). Although it is not possible to access the subjective relevance or intentionality of each directional change, the granularity of the information across metrical segments might indicate important trends about the cultural settings studied here.

The information presented in Fig. 6 shows that there are no clear events in the distribution of events across metrical segments for chacarera. Segments 1.2 and 4.1

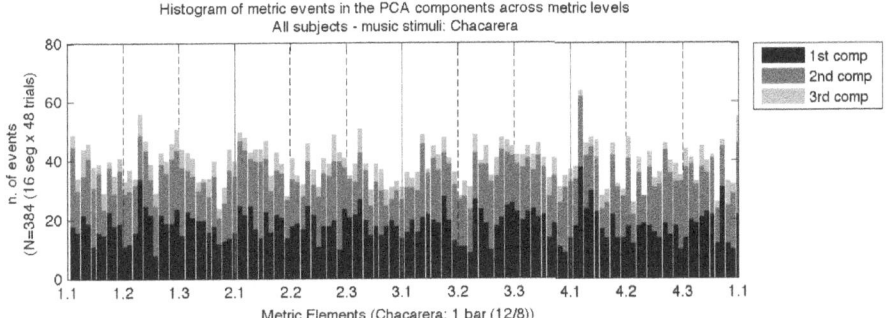

Fig. 6. Density of directional events across 1 bar (12/8), chacarera style, Argentinian and Brazilian subjects collapsed. The shades in grey indicate the quantity of events associated with each PCA component.

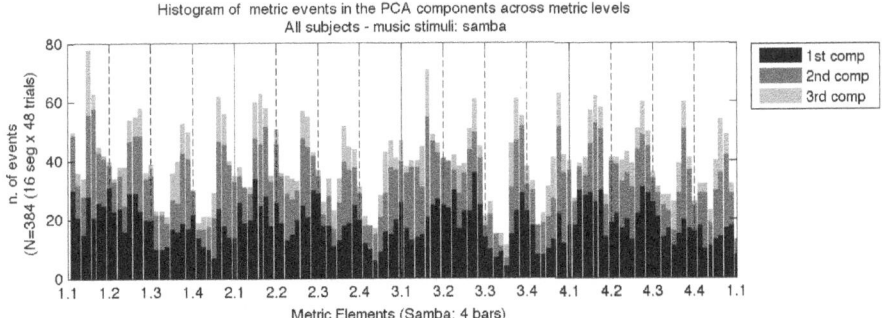

Fig. 7. Density of directional events across 1 bar (12/8), samba, Argentinian and Brazilian subjects. The shades of grey indicate the proportion of events associated with each PCA components (black = 1, white = 0).

show a small peak of activity and segments 1.3, 2.3 and 3.3 show apparent stable densities of activity. Since Argentinians and Brazilians contribute with different quantities of events to the overall result, subtle patterns may be hidden or cancelled by these contributions.

Figure 7 shows the results for samba, for all subjects. The histogram displays peaks that point at every segment of the metrical model (16th-notes), if all contributions of directional changes of all PCA components are taken into account. The 1st PCA component (darker graph), however, seems to be less clear in the signalization of 16th-note patterns. Peaks of event densities are also delayed in relation to the start of metric segments, which suggests several possibilities: (1) a flexible movement-metrical relationship, (2) an intentional delay or a (3) fuzzy contribution resulted from the inherent motor variability. In the first half-beat of every bar in samba music (2/4), at 1.1–1.2 and at 3.1–3.2 segments, the event's density tends to be sustained, suggesting a detachment of metrical engagement. For example, we could hypothesize that subjects use this metrical region to perform improvisations with the hands, or simply that they loose the connection with the metrical model. The activity in response to samba music (the density of events) seems to be larger than what is observed in the responses to chacarera, in all what concerns to the quantity of events accounted for across the metric model.

3.3 Cross-Cultural Differences: Chacarera

The results displayed in Figs. 8 and 9 show direct cross-cultural comparisons, as represented from the methods used in this study.

Figures 8a and b show the concentration of events across the metric segments of chacarera music performed, respectively, by Argentinians and Brazilians. In this case, it was expected that Argentinians, as acculturated "experts", would enact a kind of ground truth for the metrical engagement. Figure 9 shows the difference between Figs. 8a and b, implemented as a simple subtractive operation. In this representation, the results of Argentinian subjects are subtracted from results of Brazilian subjects at each histogram bin. Therefore, positive results at a given metric segment reflect that Argentinians performed more changes of direction than Brazilians. Conversely, negative results indicate that Argentinians performed less changes of direction than Brazilians (or that Brazilians performed more).

The results displayed in Fig. 8 confirm that part of the constant density of events across metric levels verified in Fig. 6 (chacarera, all subjects) is a product of cancellations after subtraction between the results of Argentinians and Brazilians. While Argentinian subjects exhibit a peak of events at the beginning of metric segments, the peak of events for Brazilian subjects lies in the middle of several metric segments (see Fig. 8b). The negative-positive oscillation observed in several metric segments in Fig. 9 seems to confirm this hypothesis (in this case, oscillation results from the interaction between delays and the subtraction). The occurrence of erratic peaks across the metric segments and some relevant peak densities at the second 8th-note of every beat for Brazilian subjects may suggest an attempt to entrain into a binary division across the compound ternary subdivision of chacarera. However, this hypothesis is very

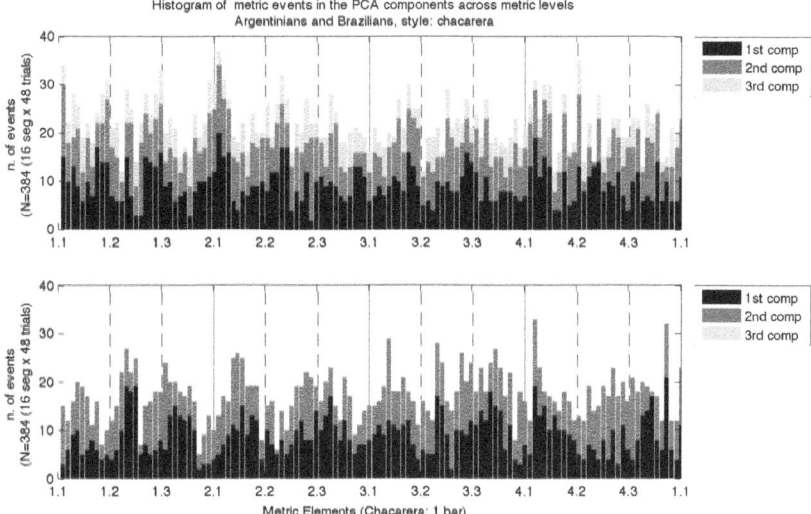

Fig. 8. a. Density of directional events across 1 bar (12/8), music style chacarera, Argentinian **subjects**. b. Density of directional events across 1 bar (12/8), music style chacarera, Brazilian **subjects**. The shades of grey indicate the proportion of events associated with each PCA components.

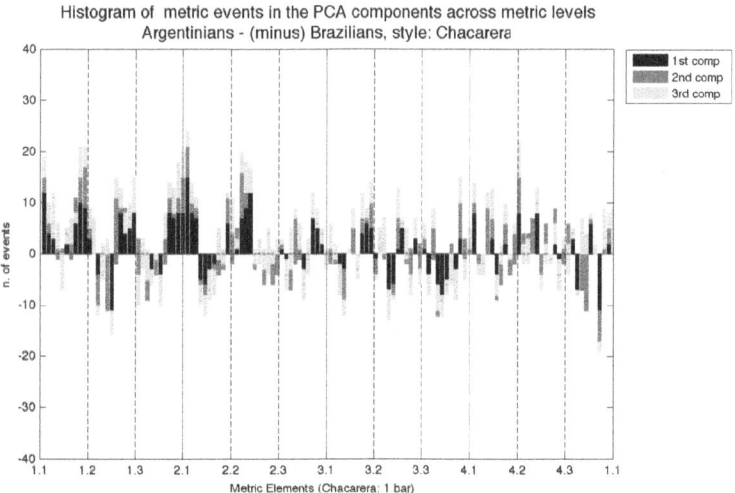

Fig. 9. Differences between densities of directional events across 1 bar (12/8), music style chacarera, results of Argentinian subjects minus the results of Brazilian subjects.

speculative and would require further verification or a different experimental design. In this specific case, a well conducted test of hypothesis could reveal how internalized metric models react to non-acculturated music.

3.4 Cross-Cultural Differences: Samba

The results displayed in Figs. 10 and 11 show the densities of directional changes for samba, as performed by Brazilians and Argentinian subjects, respectively. The main observation is the apparent intense activity that Brazilian subjects apply in response to samba music. The graphs show that the peaks observed in Fig. 7 are indeed a contribution of the activity of Brazilian subjects. However, peaks of the 1st component do not reflect this observation so clearly. This suggests that 16th-note peaks may result from the contribution of two PCA components, or that Brazilian subjects might be using plane-like shapes (e.g. ellipses) as a form to entrain to 16th-notes. Peaks are also not synchronized with the starting point of the metric segments, which suggests that changes of direction occur just after the "head" of the metric segment or at the point of deceleration (since the range of the body is limited, changes of directions are preceded by deceleration). Deceleration, or more specifically the sensation of deceleration, could be perceived by the subjects as a form of embodiment of the metric accent.

Brazilian subjects also show a curious lack of activity on the 4th 16th-note in every beat. Such clear lack of activity may reflect a kind of "bridge" where the hands consistently travel across two points without interruptions (changes of direction). Argentinian subjects show less activity in the first beats of the 2/4 bars (1.1 and 3.1 segments). It must be noted that samba music is characterized by a hidden 1st-beat (marked by a dumped low drum attack) while the second beat is often stressed. This musical aspect may have induced non-acculturated subjects to skip or spread changes of direction across the first beat region. As displayed in Fig. 11, there are differences in the levels of activity between subjects at the first beat positions. Differences of activity between Brazilians and Argentinians may also reflect that Argentinians entrain to

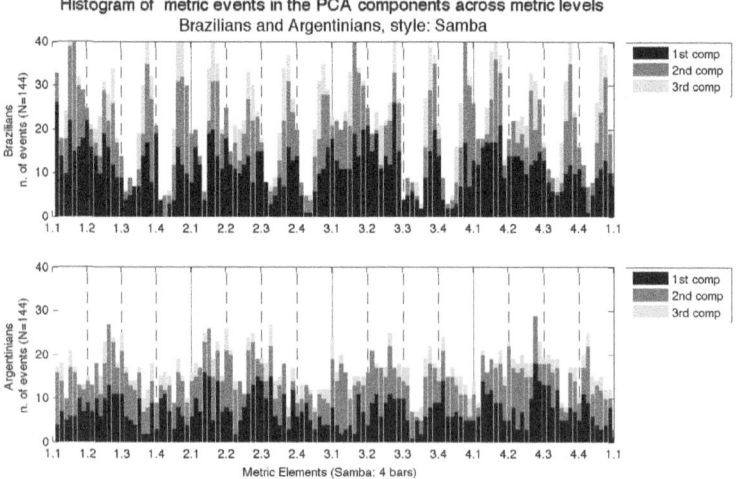

Fig. 10. Density of directional events across 1 bar (12/8), chacarera for Brazilian subjects. **10b.** Density of directional events across 1 bar (12/8), chacarera for Argentinian subjects. The shades of grey indicate the proportion of events associated with each PCA components.

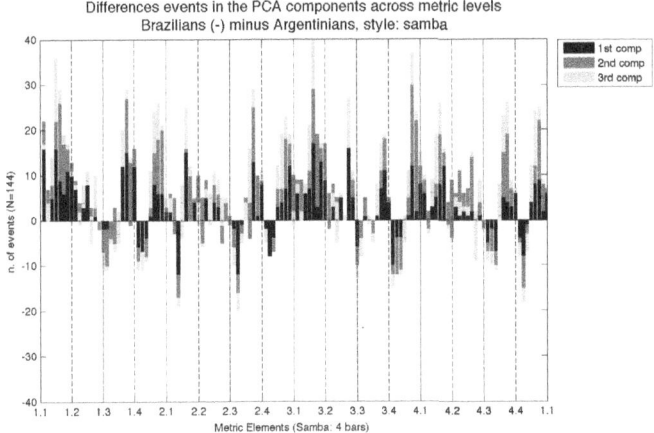

Fig. 11. Differences between densities of directional events across 2 bars (2/4), samba music, for the results of Brazilian subjects minus the results of Argentinian subjects.

musical meter by engaging into a "choreographic" motor program without clearly attuning to sharp movement changes (that generate changes of directions) as Brazilians do. Another possibility is that Argentinians attune to morphological cues such as a shape or region in space. The profile of events for Argentinian subjects also shows the emergence of offbeat accents in every beat.

4 General Discussion

In this chapter, we attempted to explore methods that are less biased by experimental control and more comprehensive to the embodied nature of musical phenomena, such as musical rhythm and dance engagement. The shift to an experimental and analytical design that is less concerned about numerical significance and hypotheses testing and more apt to the limits of ecological validity helped to reveal cultural idiosyncrasies that are less dependent on methodological assumptions and less limited by experimental control. The methods are experimental in the field of study, and, surely, many technical and conceptual issues deserve discussion and consequent improvement. However, the strategies and results might contribute both to the knowledge of cultural representations of meter and to the development of conceptual ideas about metrical models in music and dance. Even if the results encompass a small universe of musically trained individuals, they still exhibit intriguing idiosyncrasies that emerge from the exploratory analysis of the massive quantitative data resulted from the data collection.

Regarding the cross-cultural comparisons, the results show that cultural differences are reflected in the timing, the morphology of the movements and the strategy of signalization of structures of meter. Most of the unconstrained movements seem to be performed as a "line", which involves opposite movement changes (e.g.: forward-backward). Directional changes pertained to the second PCA component may indicate the emergence of movements describing a plane in space, and are present in some tendencies observed in the graphs.

The main contribution of the present study derives from the comparison between the responses of Argentinian and Brazilian participants and the kind of differences found between the musical cultures and musical structure. Brazilian subjects, for example, seem to move in a more active display and tend to delay the changes of direction in relation to metrical rules induced by music. The density of events in the same group suggests subjects' preferences to perform percussive-like gestures in relation to the metrical cues provided by music. In a different way, results of Argentinian subjects express a variable (perhaps choreographic) display of changes, but what is particularly interesting is that subjects entrain to metric segments using more accurate changes of direction in time. To the extent that the experimental settings did not include any particular constraint to shape subjects' movements, it is assumed that the resulting movement's morphology and gestural quality in both groups might be an indication of their engagement with particularities of the cultural practice of rhythm and metric in music. Further investigation, following the detail of the results reported in this study, could involve specific tests of hypothesis in experimental setups well designed for this kind of investigation. Nevertheless, more exploratory studies using robust numerical data are needed in order to provide better hypotheses for testing (for a discussion about the topic see [36]).

The discussion proposed here may also contribute with alternative methods for the assessment of metric engagement in contexts where either traditional tapping or survey techniques are not feasible (e.g.: experiments with infants or cultures that are not familiar with control tasks), or the analysis of free movement responses to music are needed. We must acknowledge that our analysis lies on the assumption that changes of direction denote subjects' enactment or embodiment of metrical accents. Even if the scope of this hypothesis is restricted to account for a full embodied engagement with metric cues in music, the recording of free movement responses simplifies data collection and provides a larger number of observations. It also facilitates the identification of characteristic features in the universe of study, the increase of sampling, and further replications of the study.

Concerning methodology, the analytical technique that was employed here makes use of simple algorithms that are novel in their combination and application, but involve trivial and widely available computer methods. The information is represented almost entirely as data visualization, which helps the evaluation, and avoid measures of centrality which, otherwise, would not be applicable due a range of assumptions necessary to avoid violations of the techniques. In this respect, responses to musical meter involve intricate interdependencies across observations in time and space. Deviations from centrality either in temporal or spatial information also cannot be considered as a result of random disturbances because they may result from culturally specific behaviours or personal intentionality (see for example [15]). Therefore, violations of assumptions about independence and homogeneity of variance would certainly make the application of traditional significance measurements unsuited (see for example the discussion presented in [37, 38], regarding human movement). Moreover, as suggested in many examples of our results, variability should be considered as a relevant form of signalization of meter and should not be underestimated given the influence of improvisation practices in Western and non-Western music.

Acknowledgements. The authors wish to acknowledge the support of SEMPRE in the realization of the research project. This research has also been supported by the ANPyCT (PICT-2013-0368), and realized at the Laboratory for the Study of Musical Experiencia (LEEM/FBA/UNLP, La Plata, Argentina. We also want to thank the Laboratory CEGEME/UFMG, Prof. Mauricio Loureiro and the student Raphael Borges, who helped the realization of the experiments in Belo Horizonte, Brazil. The authors are thankful to the subjects that participated in this study and to the anonymous reviewers.

The author Luiz Naveda gratefully acknowledges FAPEMIG (Research Support Foundation of Minas Gerais) for the financial support (projects CHE - APQ-02689-15 and CHE - BIP-00223-16).

References

1. Honing, H.: On the growing role of observation, formalization and experimental method in musicology. Empir. Musicol. Rev. **1**, 2–6 (2006)
2. Stevens, C.: Cross-cultural studies of musical pitch and time. Acoust. Sci. Technol. **25**, 433–438 (2004)
3. Parncutt, R.: Systematic musicology and the history and future of western musical scholarship. J. Interdisc. Music Stud. **1**, 1–32 (2007)
4. Toner, P.G.: The gestation of cross-cultural music research and the birth of ethnomusicology. Humanit. Res. **14**, 85–110 (2007)
5. Beard, D., Gloag, K.: Musicology: The Key Concepts. Theatre Arts Books, New York (2005)
6. Santos, B.: Toward an epistemology of blindness why the new forms of 'Ceremonial Adequacy' neither regulate nor emancipate. Eur. J. Soc. Theor. **4**, 251–279 (2001)
7. Clayton, M.: The social and personal functions of music in cross-cultural perspective. In: Hallam, S., Cross, I., Thaut, M. (eds.) The Oxford Handbook of Music Psychology, pp. 35–44. Oxford University Press, Oxford (2008)
8. Clayton, M., Sager, R., Will, U.: In time with the music: the concept of entrainment and its significance for ethnomusicology. ESEM CounterPoint **1**, 1–82 (2004)
9. Styns, F., van Noorden, L., Moelants, D., Leman, M.: Walking on music. Hum. Mov. Sci. **26**, 769–785 (2007)
10. Desmond, J.: Embodying difference: issues in dance and cultural studies. Cult. Crit. **26**, 33–63 (1994)
11. Hanna, J.L.: To Dance is Human: A Theory of Nonverbal Communication. University of Chicago Press, Chicago (1987)
12. Sodré, M., Samba, O.: Dono do Corpo. Codecri, Rio de Janeiro (1979)
13. Browning, B.: Samba: Resistance in Motion. Indiana University Press, Bloomington (1995)
14. London, J.: Hearing Rhythmic Gestures: Moving Bodies and Embodied Minds. (2003)
15. Keil, C.: Participatory discrepancies and the power of music. Cult. Anthropol. **2**, 275–283 (1987)
16. Gerischer, C.: Osuingue baiano: rhythmic feeling and microrhythmic phenomena in Brazilian percussion. Ethnomusicology **50**, 99–119 (2006)
17. Leman, M.: Embodied Music Cognition and Mediation Technology. MIT Press, Cambridge (2007)
18. Varela, F.J., Thompson, E., Rosch, E.: The Embodied Mind: Cognitive Science and Human Experience. MIT Press, Cambridge (1991)
19. Bohlman, P.V.: Ontologies of music. In: Rethinking Music, pp. 17–34 (1999)
20. Johnson, M.: The body in the Mind: The Bodily Basis of Meaning, Imagination, and Reason. University of Chicago Press, Chicago (2013)

21. Larson, S.: Musical Forces: Motion, Metaphor, and Meaning in Music. Indiana University Press, Bloomington (2012)
22. Cross, I.: The evolutionary nature of musical meaning. Musicae Sci. **13**, 179–200 (2009)
23. Cross, I.: Music and meaning, ambiguity and evolution. In: Miell, D., Macdonald, R., Hargreaves, D. (eds.) Musical Communication, pp. 27–43 (2005)
24. Gallese, V., Lakoff, G.: The brain's concepts: the role of the sensory-motor system in conceptual knowledge. Cogn. Neuropsychol. **22**, 455–479 (2005)
25. Trevarthen, C.: Musicality and the intrinsic motive pulse: evidence from human psychobiology and infant communication. Musicae Sci. **3**, 155–215 (2000)
26. Cross, I., Morley, I.: The evolution of music: theories, definitions and the nature of the evidence. In: Communicative Musicality, pp. 61–81 (2009)
27. Malloch, S., Trevarthen, C.: Communicative Musicality: Exploring the Basis of Human Companionship. Oxford University Press, Oxford (2009)
28. Christensen, T.: The Cambridge History of Western Music Theory. Cambridge University Press, Cambridge (2002)
29. Deutsch, D.: Psychology of Music. Elsevier, San Diego (2013)
30. Sloboda, J.A.: The Musical Mind: The Cognitive Psychology of Music. Oxford University Press, Oxford (1985)
31. Krumhansl, C.L.: Cognitive Foundations of Musical Pitch. Oxford University Press, New York (1990)
32. Fitch, W.T.: The biology and evolution of rhythm: unraveling a paradox. In: Rebuschat, P., Rohrmeier, M., Hawkins, J.A., Cross, I. (eds.) Language and Music as Cognitive Systems, pp. 73–95 (2012)
33. Naveda, L., Martínez, I., Damesón, J., Pereira Ghiena, A., Herrera, R.: Methods for the analysis of rhythmic and metrical responses to music in free movement trajectories. In: Aramaki, M., Kronland-Martinet, R., Ystad, S. (eds.) Proceedings of the 11th International Symposium on Computer Music Multidisciplinary Research (CMMR), pp. 248–262. The Laboratory of Mechanics and Acoustics, Marseille (2015)
34. Toiviainen, P., Burger, B.: MoCap Toolbox Manual. University of Jyväskylä, Jyväskylä (2011)
35. Santos, B.: A non-occidentalist west? Learned ignorance and ecology of knowledge. Theor. Cult. Soc. **26**, 103–125 (2009)
36. Cumming, G.: The new statistics why and how. Psychol. Sci. **25**, 7–29 (2014)
37. Stergiou, N., Harbourne, R.T., Cavanaugh, J.T.: Optimal movement variability: a new theoretical perspective for neurologic physical therapy. J. Neurol. Phys. Ther. **30**, 120–129 (2006)
38. Stergiou, N.: Innovative Analyses of Human Movement. Human Kinetics Publishers, Champaign (2004)

Correction to: Music, Mind, and Embodiment

Richard Kronland-Martinet, Mitsuko Aramaki, and Sølvi Ystad

**Correction to:
R. Kronland-Martinet et al. (Eds.):**
Music, Mind, and Embodiment, **LNCS 9617,**
https://doi.org/10.1007/978-3-319-46282-0

In the original version of the book, the following belated corrections have been incorporated:

In the chapter "Musical Meter, Rhythm and the Moving Body: Designing Methods for the Analysis of Unconstrained Body Movements", the acknowledgment was missing. This has been added.

In the chapter "Cross-Cultural Comparisons of Unconstrained Body Responses to Argentinian and Afro-Brazilian Music", the acknowledgment has been updated.

The correction book has been now updated with the changes.

The updated versions of the chapters can be found at
https://doi.org/10.1007/978-3-319-46282-0_3
https://doi.org/10.1007/978-3-319-46282-0_30

© Springer International Publishing Switzerland 2018
R. Kronland-Martinet et al. (Eds.): CMMR 2015, LNCS 9617, p. E1, 2016.
https://doi.org/10.1007/978-3-319-46282-0_31

Author Index

Aramaki, Mitsuko 22
Arcos, Josep-Lluis 71
Armitage, Joanne 146

Bernardes, Gilberto 243
Berthaut, Florent 153
Bigo, Louis 213
Black, Dawn A.A. 322
Bourdin, Christophe 22
Braund, Edward 271, 405

Chadefaux, Delphine 22
Cocharro, Diogo 243
Conklin, Darrell 213
Coorevits, Esther 88, 167

Dahl, Luke 3, 153
Damesón, Javier 42, 464
Davies, Matthew E.P. 243
Dixon, Belinda 438
Dufrenne, Marvin 22

Eaton, Joel 132

Gerhard, David 297
Gómez-Marín, Daniel 449
Gorton, David 167
Guedes, Carlos 243

Hamanaka, Masatoshi 387
Haugen, Mari Romarheim 58
Hebert, David G. 283
Herrera, Perfecto 449
Herrera, Romina 42, 464
Hirata, Keiji 387

Jan, Steven 420
Jensen, Kristoffer 283
Jordà, Sergi 449

Kirke, Alexis 438
Kronland-Martinet, Richard 22

Leman, Marc 167
Li, Shengchen 322

Loeckx, Johan 261
Lui, Simon 346

Martínez, Isabel C. 42, 464
Miranda, Eduardo R. 88, 132, 190, 271, 405, 438
Moelants, Dirk 167

Naveda, Luiz 42, 464
Neff, Patrick 111
Ng, Kia 146
Nunes, Helena de Souza 190
Nunes, Leonardo de Assis 190
Nymoen, Kristian 58

Ordás, Manuel Alejandro 42, 464
Östersjö, Stefan 167

Pearce, Marcus 358
Pereira Ghiena, Alejandro 42, 464
Perez-Carrillo, Alfonso 71
Plumbley, Mark D. 322

Rozé, Jocelyn 22

Schacher, Jan C. 111
Schramm, Rodrigo 88, 190
Schubert, Emery 358
Su, Li 309

Tojo, Satoshi 387
Trochidis, Konstantinos 346

Ubbens, Jordan 297

Visi, Federico 88, 190
Voinier, Thierry 22

Walther-Hansen, Mads 228
Wanderley, Marcelo 71

Yang, Yi-Hsuan 309
Ystad, Sølvi 22

Zeiner-Henriksen, Hans T. 373

The manufacturer's authorised representative in the EU is Springer Nature Customer Service Centre GmbH, Europaplatz 3, 69115 Heidelberg, Germany. If you have any concerns regarding our products, please contact ProductSafety@springernature.com

Printed and bound by CPI Group (UK) Ltd, Croydon, CR0 4YY

23/03/2026

02076662-0019